W9-AIL-718

THE

4TH EDITION

POWERS *of the* PRESIDENCY

THE
POWERS
of the
PRESIDENCY

4TH EDITION

CQ PRESS

Los Angeles | London | New Delhi
Singapore | Washington DC

Los Angeles | London | New Delhi
Singapore | Washington DC

FOR INFORMATION:

SAGE Publications, Inc.
2455 Teller Road
Thousand Oaks, California 91320
E-mail: order@sagepub.com

SAGE Publications Ltd.
1 Oliver's Yard
55 City Road
London EC1Y 1SP
United Kingdom

SAGE Publications India Pvt. Ltd.
B 1/I 1 Mohan Cooperative Industrial Area
Mathura Road, New Delhi 110 044
India

SAGE Publications Asia-Pacific Pte. Ltd.
3 Church Street
#10-04 Samsung Hub
Singapore 049483

Publisher: Rolf A. Janke
Acquisitions Editor: Doug Goldenberg-Hart
Assistant to the Publisher: Michele Thompson
Developmental Editor: Andrew Boney
Production Editor: David C. Felts
Reference Systems Manager: Leticia Gutierrez
Reference Systems Coordinator: Laura Notton
Typesetter: C&M Digitals (P) Ltd.
Proofreader: Jennifer Thompson
Indexer: Jennifer Pairan
Cover Designer: Candice Harman
Marketing Manager: Carmel Schrire

Copyright © 2013 by SAGE Publications, Inc.

All rights reserved. No part of this book may be reproduced or utilized in any form or by any means, electronic or mechanical, including photocopying, recording, or by any information storage and retrieval system, without permission in writing from the publisher.

Printed in the United States of America.

Library of Congress Cataloging-in-Publication Data

The powers of the presidency / edited by CQ Press.

p. cm.
Includes bibliographical references and index.

ISBN 978-1-4522-2627-9 (pbk.)

1. Executive power—United States—History. 2. Presidents—United States—History. I. Congressional Quarterly, inc.

JK511.P75 2013
352.23′50973—dc23   2012031498

This book is printed on acid-free paper.

13 14 15 16 17 10 9 8 7 6 5 4 3 2 1

★ TABLE OF CONTENTS

The story of the powers of the presidency begins with James Madison and the Constitutional Convention of 1787, but it does not end there.

Madison was part of the Virginia delegation; other members included George Washington, the general who won the Revolutionary War; George Mason, the chief advocate of a Bill of Rights; and Edmund Randolph, the state governor. At the outset of the convention, Madison persuaded his fellow Virginians to sponsor a plan of government that included separate executive, legislative, and judicial branches. The convention agreed to adopt the Virginia Plan, then raised a crucial question: what powers should each branch have?

The convention resolved this issue by establishing what political scientist Richard Neustadt, in his classic book *Presidential Power* calls "separated institutions sharing powers." In other words, each branch of government is separate from the other two. Although presidents and members of Congress are elected independently, most of the powers the Constitution assigns to the president are shared with Congress, just as the powers given to Congress are shared with the president. Consider these examples:

- Congress is charged to make laws, while the president both proposes laws for Congress to consider and vetoes objectionable bills passed by Congress.
- The president appoints federal judges and high-ranking members of the executive branch, but the Senate may reject those appointments.
- The president is commander in chief of the armed forces, but Congress has the power to declare war and appropriate funding for an army and navy.
- The president can negotiate treaties with other countries, but the Senate must ratify those treaties before they can take effect.
- The president is charged to oversee the myriad departments and agencies of the executive branch, but only Congress can pass the laws that create those organizations and authorize their budgets.

All of the executive's "shared powers" receive full treatment within the pages of *The Powers of the Presidency,* with an emphasis on how the exercise of these powers has evolved—often controversially—through the more than two centuries of U.S. history since the Constitution was written.

In addition, this volume considers unilateral powers of the presidency, which have been brought into sharp relief during the administrations of George W. Bush and his recent predecessors. One of these—the only one explicitly granted in the Constitution—is the pardon power. Most of the others derive from the ambiguous presidential "vesting clause." And in light of the recent financial crisis, the role of the president as "chief economist" has been heavily updated and revised.

Although presidential and congressional powers are both spelled out in vesting clauses, the difference in wording has led to debate over intended meaning. The congressional clause, which begins Article I of the Constitution, states: "All legislative powers *herein granted* shall be vested in a Congress of the United States" (emphasis added). A list of specific powers is included in the article.

The presidential clause begins Article II: "The executive power shall be vested in a president of the United States of America." Because the words "herein granted" do not appear in this clause, some argue that the "executive power" extends beyond the powers of the presidency spelled out in the rest of Article II. Others maintain that the delegates to the Constitutional Convention intended no such thing.

Who is right? There is no way to know; the delegates never debated the vesting clause and, after the Constitution was ratified, they often disagreed with each other about what they had meant. For example, when President George Washington declared in 1793 that the United States would remain neutral in the war between Britain and France, Madison objected, claiming that the president had no authority to make that decision on his own. Alexander Hamilton, a New York delegate at the Constitutional

Convention and Washington's secretary of the Treasury, responded that the vesting clause granted the president that authority.

The debate about the powers of the presidency, both those that are unilateral and those shared between the president and Congress, has never ended and will continue. As Edward S. Corwin writes in *The President: Office and Powers,* the Constitution extends a never-ending "invitation to struggle" about what the powers of the presidency are and where they end.

★ CONTRIBUTORS

Meena Bose, Director, Peter S. Kalikow Center for the Study of the American Presidency and Peter S. Kalikow Chair in Presidential Studies, Hofstra University

Jasmine Farrier, Associate Professor of Political Science, University of Louisville

Thomas S. Langston, Professor of Political Science, Tulane University

Michael Nelson, Fulmer Professor of Political Science at Rhodes College and Senior Fellow, Miller Center of Public Affairs at the University of Virginia

Bruce Nesmith, Joan and Abbott Lipsky Professor in the Department of Political Science, Coe College

Andrew C. Rudalevige, Associate Professor of Political Science; Walter E. Beach Chair in Political Science, Dickinson College

Justin S. Vaughn, Assistant Professor of Political Science, Boise State University

Unilateral Powers of the Presidency

by Andrew C. Rudalevige

The Constitution won ratification in part by being vague. Yet Article II wins out, as Edward Corwin once commented, as its "most loosely drawn chapter."[1] Its very first sentence provides one of the document's least specific but potentially most far-reaching grants of power: that "the executive power shall be vested in a President of the United States of America." By contrast, the parallel language pertaining to Congress in Article I's vesting clause includes a key qualifier, that "all legislative powers *herein granted* shall be vested in a Congress." Does the discrepancy imply that "the executive power" goes beyond the list of powers delineated in the rest of Article II, as claimed by proponents of presidential power as early as the George Washington administration? Even if so, what is that power, exactly? What unilateral actions might it allow the president to take? On this point the document is silent. The answer has been crafted instead by history, worked out in practice and through interbranch contestation.

THE EXECUTIVE POWER

The American government under the Articles of Confederation had no separate executive branch at all. Most of the state constitutions at the time sharply limited executive authority: the Virginia constitution of 1776, for example, required that the governor work within the constraints of an independent Council of State, forbade claims of prerogative, and limited executive powers to those specifically granted by the assembly. Thus perhaps it was no surprise that James Wilson's motion at the Constitutional Convention to create a new executive office "consist[ing] of a single person" was met by an awkward silence.[2]

Still, concerned by the ineffectiveness and potential dangers of legislative dominance, the drafters of the Constitution endorsed Wilson's motion. And they shied away from having Congress dictate the boundaries of presidential action. Instead they left the range of executive powers undefined and ripe for reinterpretation by later presidents.

To be sure, the other executive example fresh in the Framers' minds was that of King George III. Thus the Constitution grants presidents only a limited array of explicit powers. Presidents were given the ability to grant reprieves and pardons, which the Framers believed might be useful in resolving domestic insurrections such as Shays's Rebellion of 1786 (which in many ways had prompted the Constitutional Convention in the first place). Consistent with the fundamental constitutional principle of checked authority, though, many of the other powers in Article II come with an asterisk of sorts. Presidents' treaties must be ratified by two-thirds of the Senate, and their appointments confirmed by a Senate majority. Presidents may suggest laws, but Congress must pass them (and can override presidential vetoes); presidents may conduct wars, but Congress has the power to declare them. Presidents have control of their department heads, but Congress decides what departments exist in the first place, as well as how much the departments have to spend each year. As defenders of the Constitution sparred with antifederalist writers like the pseudonymous "Cato," they did not dispute his contention that "to live by one man's will [becomes] the cause of all men's misery." Instead, they sought to show that presidents' powers were hemmed in by institutional checks ranging from their inability to impose taxes or appointees to Congress's power to impeach and remove them from office.[3]

At the same time, as Alexander Hamilton pointed out in *Federalist* No. 70, only some of the "energy" of the executive branch comes from a president's formal powers and ability to resist legislative encroachment. The crucial choice to create a single executive, rather than the plural presidency favored by some at the convention, gives its occupant a leg up on its rivals for power. The fact that Congress is a divided body run by collective choices gives presidents inherent advantages of "decision, activity, secrecy, and dispatch." Presidents can make decisions quickly and discreetly and can often act on them alone. Even if they do not get the final say, presidents often get to make the first move—which itself

1

may shape the landscape over which subsequent decisions are taken. "The executive, in the exercise of its constitutional powers," as Hamilton noted, "may establish an antecedent state of things, which ought to weigh in the legislative decision."[4]

To these advantages were added powers that Article II was taken to imply. The divergent wording of the vesting clauses that introduced Articles I and II has already been noted; Hamilton called this clear evidence that the subsequent discussion of presidential powers in Article II merely specified limits on various aspects of the "more comprehensive grant contained in the general clause." If so, the president's ability to control what would later be termed the "unitary executive branch" is absolute. Others suggested that inherent powers were also implied by the president's duty to "take care that the laws be faithfully executed" (President Grover Cleveland called this "a grant of all the power necessary to the performance of his duty in the faithful execution of the laws"); in the presidential oath of office to "preserve, protect, and defend the Constitution"; or by the office of commander in chief, even in peacetime.[5]

Are presidents, then, limited to the specific powers affirmatively listed in the Constitution? Or can they take whatever actions they deem in the public interest, so long as those actions are not actually prohibited by the Constitution? President Theodore Roosevelt argued the latter: that "it was not only [the President's] right but his duty to do anything that the needs of the Nation required unless such action was forbidden by the Constitution or by the laws." Here are the seeds of what one scholar has termed "venture constitutionalism."[6]

The argument held special force in times of national emergency. English philosopher John Locke, in his *Second Treatise of Government* (1690), defended "prerogative," defined as the power of the executive "to act according to discretion, for the publick good, without the prescription of the Law, and sometimes even against it." Legislatures were slow, Locke argued, and the law could not foresee all "accidents and necessities" that might arise. Indeed, even where statutes existed, their rigid implementation might sometimes do more harm than good. Thus the executive needed discretion to set a policy course even in normal times, while in dire crisis "it is fit that the laws themselves should give way to the executive power, or rather to this fundamental law of nature and government, [namely] that, as much as may be, all the members of society are to be preserved."[7] Abraham Lincoln would later put the point this way: "often a limb must be amputated to save a life; but a life is never wisely given to save a limb. . . . [M]easures, otherwise unconstitutional, might become lawful, by becoming indispensable to the preservation of the constitution, through the preservation of the nation."[8]

James Madison, however, argued that presidential action, to be "properly executive, must pre-suppose the existence of the laws to be executed"—and that "to see the laws faithfully executed constitutes the essence of the executive authority." From this might be deduced the power to remove subordinate officers responsible for executing the law (itself a question at issue in the first Congress in 1789), but little else. Madison charged Hamilton with arguing for an expansive theory of presidential power not from the Constitution's text but from "*royal prerogatives* in the *British government.*"[9] President William Howard Taft likewise held that "the President can exercise no power which cannot be fairly and reasonably traced to some specific grant of power or justly implied within such express grant as proper and necessary to its exercise. There is no undefined residuum of power which he can exercise because it seems to him to be in the public interest."[10] Even Wilson, the most persuasive advocate of a strong new executive branch at the Constitutional Convention, assured delegates that the only strictly executive powers under the Constitution should be to carry out the laws and choose personnel. Indeed, if presidents were vested with vast executive authority, why bother to point out in Article II that they could require written opinions from their department heads?[11]

This struggle, between presidents claiming the power to act without clear constitutional mandates and critics arguing to the contrary, underlines much of U.S. history. While the evidence from the Framers' debates probably favors the critics, in practice, Hamilton's view has decisively won out.[12]

Congress may be the first branch of government, leaving presidential power as the residual authority left over from other actors in the system. Yet those leavings have hardly been meager: silence (in the constitutional text) has not proven golden (for advocates of a limited executive, at least). The powers it implies, however tacitly, have been given substance by years of continuous reinterpretation by presidents, courts, and even legislators. As such they have served as sources of the president's ability to act alone, even absent specific congressional delegation of power, in ways whose extent and potency have grown beyond anything the Founders could have foreseen. On its face, for example, the "take care" clause directs the president to administer statutes in a manner faithful to legislative language and intent. But in an 1890 case, the Supreme Court ruled that executing the laws could not be "limited to the enforcement of acts of Congress or of treaties . . . according to their *express terms*" but rather included "the rights, duties and obligations growing out of the Constitution itself, our international relations, and all the protection implied by the nature of the government under the Constitution."[13]

By this reasoning, presidents could in theory undertake any action deemed necessary to carry out their constitutional duties, to provide for the nation's defense, or to protect the common good. Is this legitimate? What are those duties, and where do they leave off? What does that defense require? For that matter, who gets to decide the substance of the "common good"? To the extent those answers are the president's to give, the potential of unilateral powers is both awesome and rightly controversial.

The remainder of this chapter traces the growth and tools of executive discretion, as well as its limits. As legislators realized after Watergate, these methods have the potential for abuse. More recently, the renewed claims to unilateral executive authority of the George W. Bush administration, especially after the terrorist attacks of September 11, 2001, led to renewed debate over what presidential powers are necessary and appropriate. President Barack Obama inherited a capacious, but controversial, toolbox.

THE GROWTH OF EXECUTIVE DISCRETION

Federalists such as Hamilton wanted a national government that "left substantial freedom of action to high officials and kept Congress out of most administrative details."[14] And, in fact, Congress generally trusted the revered first president to get the new nation on its feet. However, in 1793 Washington unilaterally declared U.S. neutrality in the war between France and England. Washington argued that his constitutional responsibility to represent the nation implied the power to keep the United States out of war. This rationale did not convince James Madison, who retorted that the proclamation was invalid because only Congress could decide issues of war and peace. "Those who are to conduct a war cannot in the nature of things, be proper or safe judges, whether a war ought to be commenced, continued, or concluded," he argued.[15]

But even Thomas Jefferson, who urged Madison to attack the Neutrality Proclamation, adopted a broad view of the executive powers upon attaining them. He purchased the Louisiana Territory without prior congressional approval, ordered offensive naval action against Mediterranean piracy, and spent unappropriated funds to restock military stores after the U.S. frigate *Chesapeake* was seized by Britain in 1807. In an 1810 letter he argued that "to lose our country by a scrupulous adherence to written law, would be to lose the law itself, with life, liberty, property and all those who are enjoying them with us; thus absurdly sacrificing the end to the means."[16]

That logic took its strongest tangible form during the Civil War, when Abraham Lincoln took an array of unilateral actions beyond his constitutional authority—blockading Southern ports, spending unbudgeted funds on weapons and ships, expanding the armed services, censoring the mail, suspending the right of *habeas corpus* to hold prisoners without charges or trial, and even instituting military tribunals in place of the civilian judiciary. When Supreme Court chief justice Roger Taney ruled that Lincoln had usurped the sole power of Congress to suspend writs of *habeas corpus* during an emergency, Lincoln ignored the decision.[17] Later, by executive proclamation, he ordered that slaves be emancipated without compensation to their owners.

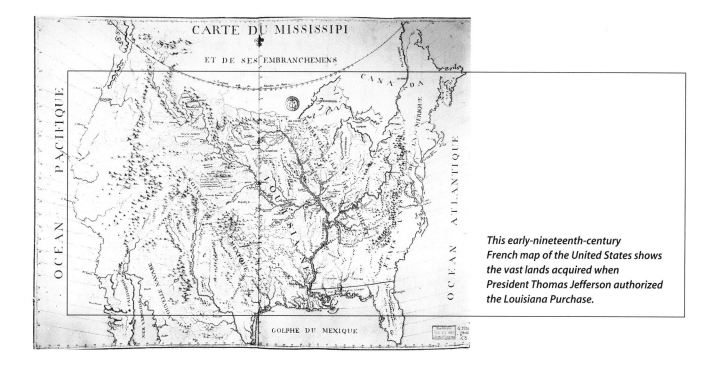

This early-nineteenth-century French map of the United States shows the vast lands acquired when President Thomas Jefferson authorized the Louisiana Purchase.

Lincoln claimed such an extensive array of emergency war powers to preserve the Union that he became, in the words of presidential scholar Clinton Rossiter, a "constitutional dictator." Yet Lincoln did ask Congress for retroactive approval of his actions (for instance, in the Habeas Corpus Act of 1863), and put himself before the voters in 1864.[18] In the end, legal nuances paled before the emergency at hand. In the *Prize Cases* (1863), shipowners whose vessels were seized trying to run the Union lines sued on the grounds that the blockade itself was unconstitutional because Congress had not declared war. This was technically true, but, the Court ruled, war was simply a fact and Lincoln was required to defend the nation.[19]

To be sure, for most of the nineteenth century Congress took an assertive view of the legislative role in governance. Even Jefferson and his allies, notes historian Leonard White, "emphasized the responsibility of the executive branch and the administrative system to Congress." Congress held tight reins over executive branch actions through highly detailed statutes, strict budget controls, and reviews of even the most mundane administrative matters.[20] Though the Supreme Court ruled in 1827 that Madison was right during the War of 1812 to overrule governors and activate state militias—arguing that the president alone defines emergencies when the nation is at war or is faced with imminent hostilities[21]—this was an exception to pre–Civil War claims of presidential emergency powers. In most instances, presidents deployed U.S. forces against pirates abroad or Native American uprisings at home to protect U.S. citizens and their property. Their actions usually were based on a specific congressional grant of authority, such as the power that Congress gave James Monroe to protect American merchant ships against pirates, or the congressional declaration of war on Mexico in 1846. In general, early presidents—even the headstrong Andrew Jackson—exhibited restraint in exercising their commander-in-chief responsibilities. And during Reconstruction, legislative dominance seemed to bounce back from Lincoln's exertions; for a time, as legislator George Hoar wrote, if senators "visited the White House, it was to give, not to receive, advice."[22] The Supreme Court, which had upheld Lincoln's naval blockade and subsequent seizure of foreign merchant ships, decided in 1866 that the president had not possessed the power to bypass civilian courts and institute military trials in Union territory. The idea that the Constitution could be suspended by some "theory of necessity" was "pernicious" and "false," Justice Davis wrote in *Ex parte Milligan*. Indeed, "it could be well said that a country, preserved at the sacrifice of all the cardinal provisions of liberty, is not worth the cost of preservation."[23]

Still, that Supreme Court decision came down safely after the war was over. Even during the late nineteenth century some historians' shorthand convention of presidential torpor is not fully accurate. Presidents Rutherford B. Hayes,

James A. Garfield, Chester A. Arthur, and Grover Cleveland, for example, strongly defended presidential appointment and administrative powers against congressional incursion, to popular acclaim. In *In re Neagle* (1890), the Court agreed with the attorney general's contention that the presidential oath must, "by necessary implication," be read to "invest the President with self-executing powers; that is, powers independent of statute."[24] In like fashion, the Court held in 1895 that the federal government's powers were not limited to legislation punishing interference with governmental functions after the fact. That extra power—the residual between the power utilized by congressional legislation and "the entire strength of the nation"—could be used by the president proactively, in the absence of contrary law, when federal functions were threatened. In 1915 a third decision (*U.S. v. Midwest Oil*) held that when presidential assertions of power in an area had been accepted frequently over time by Congress, such historical acquiescence might set a precedent governing executive-legislative relations as much as constitutional doctrine in "determining the meaning of a statute or the existence of a power."[25]

By the early 1900s Americans expressed a growing acceptance of federal (and presidential) responsibility in the United States and abroad. Theodore Roosevelt, as already described, made clear his belief that as "steward of the people" the president enjoyed a range of residual executive powers implied in the Constitution. Such powers, Roosevelt argued, were neither enumerated in the Constitution nor assigned broadly to a specific branch; instead, they resided in basic concepts such as national sovereignty and the public good. The president was to represent the nation as a whole, distinct from the parochialism of locally elected legislators. Woodrow Wilson turned this into a grand version of popular stewardship, viewing the party system not as a constraining force but as a nearly parliamentary means for translating the president's program into policy change.[26]

But the Constitution says very little about what powers might be available to a stewardship presidency. Political scientist Richard Pious suggests that "like Excalibur's sword, [the president] must wrest his powers from the Constitution before he can wield them."[27] In those terms the image of a truly discretionary presidency did not begin to take shape until World War I.

In part this was because by the twentieth century, "total war" was at hand, blurring the lines between combatants and civilians and involving the entire social, economic, and industrial capacities of nations. It thus required swift, massive, and sustained national organization and mobilization, the capacities for which lay mostly in the executive branch. In 1917 Congress passed a spate of laws granting Wilson broad powers along these lines: he was empowered to nationalize defense-related facilities; to regulate food production, manufacturing, and mining; to fix prices on commodities; to raise an army; to restrict exports; and to regulate and censor external communications. Wilson also was granted broad authority to monitor actions by resident aliens, to regulate or operate transportation and communications facilities, and to reorganize executive branch agencies where necessary. In effect, then, he was granted almost free rein to conduct the war and to direct the domestic economy.[28] Even so, Wilson did not shy away from asserting inherent prerogatives as commander in chief. Issuing two thousand executive orders along the way, he claimed the right to go beyond the scope of congressional authorization in creating wartime agencies, enforcing "voluntary" press censorship, and coordinating private industry. Nor did the powers Wilson asserted in wartime vanish once hostilities ceased—in the postwar 1918–1921 "Palmer Raids," for example, supposed communist subversives were searched, detained, and even deported without warrant. The precedents set would endure for later presidents in a ratchet-like expansion of executive power.

The New Deal and World War II

By the twentieth century, in Wilson's phrase, "the President [was] at liberty both in law and conscience to be as big a man as he can."[29] From Franklin D. Roosevelt's time forward, these tools became expectations rather than possibilities. The Great Depression, World War II, the cold war, the post–September 11, 2001, global war on terror, and the "Great Recession" starting in 2008 dramatically raised Americans' demands on their presidents as well as the size, scope, and reach of the federal government. Richard E. Neustadt, in a play on Wilson's observation, noted that the president could certainly still be big; "but nowadays he cannot be as small as he might like."[30]

Franklin Roosevelt gave permanence to Theodore Roosevelt's stewardship view of the presidency and made it part of the very definition of the "modern presidency."[31] Elected in the depths of economic depression, and given wide latitude by Congress and the American people, Roosevelt relied heavily on executive initiatives to attack the economic crisis and rally the nation. He issued 654 executive orders in 1933 alone. These included his inauguration day proclamation closing all banks for four days to restructure the crumbling banking system (the authority for which was grounded in a law left over from World War I) and the creation of mechanisms for implementing New Deal programs. In most cases, Roosevelt received quick and sometimes retroactive congressional approval. In 1933, for example, legislators approved a law granting Roosevelt emergency powers to alleviate the bank crisis after only eight hours of debate. Congress also uncharacteristically appropriated discretionary funds so that the executive branch could develop programs more quickly and perhaps more effectively than might be possible via normal legislative procedures.[32] The

crisis prompted support for decisive action and enabled Roosevelt to stretch the boundaries of his constitutional powers to the limit. "In the event Congress shall fail to act, and act adequately, I shall accept the responsibility, and I will act," FDR proclaimed in 1942. "The President has the powers, under the Constitution, and under Congressional acts, to take measures necessary to avert a disaster. . . ."[33]

Roosevelt was seeking a law governing wage and price controls, and he got one. But the 1942 speech highlights his willingness to use executive authority, broadly defined, with or without congressional approval. This highly muscular view of presidential discretion was buttressed by the sheer growth in the federal government during the 1930s and 1940s that brought with it an explosion in the size of the executive branch and its responsibilities. Congress found it increasingly difficult to grapple with the scope and complexity of new national programs and began the widespread delegation of authority that marks contemporary government.

After World War I, Congress had reasserted itself in foreign policy, and its powerful isolationist wing resisted Roosevelt's efforts to support the European nations facing Nazi expansionism. Still, even before Pearl Harbor, Roosevelt made broad claims of authority to prosecute the war. The 1936 *Curtiss-Wright* decision—still cherished by presidents, if by few scholars of constitutional law—endorsed a "very delicate, plenary, and exclusive power of the President as the sole organ of the federal government in the field of international relations—a power which does not require as a basis for its exercise an act of Congress."[34] Roosevelt moved unilaterally in many instances, basing his actions on powers that he claimed derived from his constitutional duties as commander in chief and chief executive. Seeking to sidestep congressional declarations of neutrality as Europe fell into war, for instance, in 1939 he declared a "limited" state of emergency, which allowed him to invoke existing but dormant statutes to prepare the nation militarily. After the fall of France, Roosevelt declared an "unlimited national emergency," under which he reorganized the executive branch and prepared to deal with the domestic economy once the United States entered into hostilities, spending more than $15 billion appropriated for military preparedness measures. In neither instance did Roosevelt seek prior congressional authorization for his actions.

As the war approached, Roosevelt also concluded a series of executive agreements, thus evading the Senate ratification needed for treaties, most famously transferring fifty destroyers to Britain in return for eight Caribbean naval bases. Such a transaction violated a 1917 statute prohibiting the transfer of warships to a belligerent nation, and also the 1940 Neutrality Act, since the ships were usable military equipment; however, the attorney general's opinion justifying the agreement grounded it in various principles including the "plenary powers of the President as Commander-in-Chief of the Army and Navy and as head of state in its relations with foreign countries." In January 1941, months before lend-lease legislation finally passed, FDR began to arrange $3 billion in supplies for the Soviet Union. An executive agreement with Denmark in April 1941 allowed U.S. forces to occupy Greenland, followed in July by an agreement to defend Iceland as well; by October the navy was told to provide "neutrality patrols" near merchant ships and sink Axis ships even if they were not near the convoys. Once Congress declared war in December 1941, Roosevelt dropped even the pretense of delegated powers. His seizure of defense plants immediately after Pearl Harbor, for example, was based on claims of authority given to him by the Constitution and "the laws," although he never made clear which ones.[35]

Domestically, FDR worried about sabotage of the war effort. Even though the Supreme Court had sought to limit the use of evidence obtained through wiretapping, and Roosevelt failed to receive legislative authorization overriding that decision, he pressed on, directing Attorney General Robert H. Jackson in 1940 to surveil "persons suspected of subversive activities against the Government of the United States." Had large scale domestic sabotage broken out during World War II, Jackson later wrote, "there is no doubt in my mind that President Roosevelt would have taken most ruthless methods to suppress it. . . . [H]e did not share the extreme position about civil rights that some of his followers have taken."[36]

Executive Order 9066, issued in 1942, made that point clear. The order spurred the detention of 112,000 Japanese Americans on the West Coast in internment camps for the duration of the war, justified by the need to prevent espionage and sabotage. Though endorsed by Congress and (at least tacitly) by the Supreme Court, this decision later came to be viewed as a gross violation of the civil liberties of U.S. citizens. In 1988 Congress appropriated reparations for those interned.[37]

The Permanent Emergency

As noted above and detailed further below, crises empower the executive branch: a menacing world requires the swift decision-making capacity of centralized leadership. And the postwar period, marked by wars cold and hot, ushered in a seemingly perpetual period of crisis. "Emergencies in policy" by prewar standards, Richard Neustadt wrote in 1960, became business as usual, "a way of life."[38] With the threat of nuclear Armageddon as backdrop, national security became the primary justification for unilateral executive action in the years after World War II. The bipolar standoff between the United States and the Soviet Union expanded U.S. commitments around the world, and a consensus on the need for assertive executive leadership prompted Congress to accede to presidential dictates across a wide spectrum of domestic and international policy domains.[39]

Many scholars characterize the period between the late 1940s and early 1970s as one of relative congressional decline in which legislators appeared to surrender many of their traditional prerogatives. On this subject, Allen Schick noted that "when Congress controls, it legislates the particulars; when Congress withdraws, it legislates in general terms."[40] Indeed, statutes in both domestic and foreign policy areas became far less detailed and constraining compared to those passed before Roosevelt.

This development was applauded in many quarters. Scholars began to tout "presidential government," openly supporting the idea that broad executive discretion would lead to more efficient and effective administration. Constitutional constants such as separation of powers and federalism, long defended as essential for safeguarding citizens' rights and liberties, now appeared to be impediments to progressive government. Strong presidential leadership was needed to overcome the parochial fragmentation and delays inherent in the nation's structure of governance. If, as Corwin concluded long before Watergate, "the history of the presidency has been a history of aggrandizement," that aggrandizement got generally good reviews.[41]

The presidency that evolved from the New Deal

Two children and an adult await buses in Hayward, California, that will take them to an internment camp. Japanese-American relocation during World War II was authorized by Franklin Roosevelt's Executive Order 9066, issued February 1942.

through the Vietnam War was thus the presidency at its least constrained—leading to a state of affairs ultimately and enduringly dubbed by historian Arthur Schlesinger Jr. as the "imperial presidency."[42] The tools of that presidency are described in the next section.

TOOLS OF UNILATERALISM: THE MODERN PRESIDENCY

Changes in the presidency starting from the time of the New Deal have "added up to so thorough a transformation that a modifier such as 'modern' is needed to characterize the post-1932 manifestations of the institution that had evolved from the far more circumscribed traditional presidency."[43] Modern presidents have immense visibility and thus agenda-setting powers, and they have creatively used their formal and informal powers to carve out influence over policy formulation and implementation. The tools of contemporary executive unilateralism are tallied briefly below.

Agenda Setting

The rise of radio, and then television, meant that presidents could seize the public's agenda through what John F. Kennedy's aide Ted Sorensen called "direct communication" without "alteration or omission."[44] The mechanics of the industry helped too. It was far easier for the mass media to focus on one person than on the inchoate multitudes in Congress, far easier to follow a personal narrative than an institutional collective. To be sure, television also shaped presidential agendas—Kennedy's civil rights program in 1963, for example, was decisively prompted by the televised brutality against peaceful marchers in Birmingham, Alabama. And the rise of cable television and especially the Internet has at times fragmented audiences as much as it has united them. But generally, the stewardship presidency was reinforced by moving Theodore Roosevelt's "bully pulpit" to the broadcast age.

The power of agenda setting also links closely with the expanded role of the president in the legislative arena. Into the 1920s, the constitutional invitation to provide Congress with measures the president deemed "necessary and expedient" was rarely an open one. But Franklin Roosevelt's famous "hundred days" marked new boundaries. During this time a flood of proposals rolled out of the executive branch and into law, receiving remarkable legislative deference. In the House temporary rules even prevented members from amending administration proposals on the floor. By the time Dwight Eisenhower took office, legislators not only accepted but demanded a presidential agenda. Despite his initial reluctance to do so, Eisenhower complied and even created a White House staff devoted to congressional liaison.

Even as divided government became a regular feature of American governance, the presidential program remained an important part of the legislative agenda. After his party lost control of Congress in the 2006 midterms, for example, George W. Bush denied that he was "out of the policy business"—to the contrary, he said, "the microphone of the president has never been louder. . . . Without presidential involvement, nothing will happen."[45]

Once bills reached the president's desk, they faced a newly aggressive veto pen. The earliest presidents used the veto only on bills they thought unconstitutional; FDR, by contrast, reportedly told his cabinet to "find me something I can veto." Even the supposedly passive Eisenhower vetoed nearly two hundred bills in eight years. But veto bargaining was as important as the act itself. Barack Obama issued some thirty veto threats as "statements of administration policy" in his first thirty months in office—only two had to be made good.[46] And though he did not issue a single veto in his first five years in office, George W. Bush would later comment that "the best tool I have besides persuasion is to veto." After all, the veto made him part of the legislative process. Presidents came to take full advantage of that leverage.[47]

Controlling the Bureaucracy: People and Process

One of the modern presidency's greatest tasks is to control the federal establishment itself. The president may be chief executive, but this does not ensure prompt bureaucratic execution of White House dictates. Close to four million people work for the executive branch, spread across fifteen cabinet departments and nearly sixty independent agencies.[48] They report to the president on paper, but in practice are suspended between the branches, buffeted in the battles between president, Congress, and courts; between interest groups and the national interest; between presidential directives and their own statutory duties and organizational cultures. Presidents may be vexed most by the tenacity of linkages forged between the professional bureaucracy and Congress. The power of Congress over lawmaking and budgets, the tenure offered by civil service rules, and the relatively temporary nature of presidential terms of office make it incredibly hard for presidents to force their preferences upon the permanent government. Presidents have used two major strategies for seeking bureaucratic control: centralization and politicization.[49]

Centralization

Centralization refers to the shift of functions from the wider executive branch to the Executive Office of the President (EOP), which was created in 1939. The most obvious ramification is the growth of the White House staff over time, from a handful of personal aides under Franklin Roosevelt to at least fifteen hundred employees with substantive duties in the early twenty-first century. Presidents have used their White House and EOP staffs as an alternate mechanism for coordinating and formulating policy. The EOP now houses aides, and aides to aides, devoted to policymaking (domestic, economic, and national security), communications (with the public, the bureaucracy, Congress, and interest groups), and its own internal administration. New staff units spring up to reflect salient presidential and societal concerns, from energy (under Richard Nixon) to the drug czar (under Reagan) to an AIDS outreach office (under Bill Clinton) to one (under Barack Obama) coordinating responses to global climate change.[50] In many cases Congress has provided the requisite statutory authority afterward. But there have sometimes been limits to congressional acquiescence. For example, FDR's tendency to use executive orders to create wartime agencies and fund them with funds appropriated for other purposes eventually provoked a backlash. In 1944 Congress barred use of any appropriations for an agency created through executive order unless the funds were authorized specifically for that agency.[51] In 2011 Congress prohibited funding for any staffer with the title "Assistant to the President for Energy and Climate Change"; while mostly symbolic, the action suggested the occasional frustration legislators have with presidential "czars."

One recent work on presidential power calls the president "chief budgeter,"[52] despite the vesting of the power of the purse in Congress, and thus a division of EOP worth special mention is the Office of Management and Budget (OMB). From its position astride the annual budget process, OMB gives the president particular leverage over bureaucratic behavior. Prior to 1921, presidents had little centralized control over agency requests for funding, but the passage of the Budget and Accounting Act that year required a unified executive budget and thus gave presidents a new mechanism for managing their agenda. In 1933 Franklin Roosevelt transferred all executive branch budget-making authority from department heads to the Bureau of the Budget (OMB's forerunner, itself created by the 1921 law). In 1939 Roosevelt moved the bureau from the Treasury Department to the newly created EOP, making it a truly presidential agency rather than simply a departmental coordinator.[53]

Upon arriving in the EOP, the Budget Bureau organized not only the president's budget but the president's legislative program as well. That included efforts to control monies after funds were appropriated, through allotment and impoundment, and the "central clearance" of agency testimony and legislative proposals. In 1970 Richard Nixon sought to enhance the Bureau's ability to influence agency management practices as well, reorganizing it into the Office of Management and Budget. Ronald Reagan added regulatory review functions to the mix. *(See "Rulemaking and Regulatory Review," p. 9.)* Though presidents have never been entirely satisfied with OMB's management reach, the agency continues to be a centerpiece of their efforts to shape bureaucratic outputs and outcomes, housing offices overseeing procurement, financial management, and government technology efforts. President Clinton reorganized OMB in 1994 to merge managerial and budgetary staff into "Resource Management Offices," an arrangement that has survived two changes of administration. George W. Bush's long-term "President's Management Agenda" empowered OMB to develop the Program Assessment Rating Tool (PART) system, intended to grade programmatic effectiveness and ultimately link it to funding decisions.

There are various criticisms of this tendency toward staff growth and the creation of a "presidential branch," though most complaints seem to come from those opposing the policies of particular presidents. Future presidents are unlikely to reverse this trend, because the desire to control the bureaucracy is common to Democratic and Republican presidents alike. Presumably, though, the battle over the bureaucracy will remain a major source of conflict between the branches.[54]

Politicization

Another front of that battle concerns presidential efforts at politicization—their efforts to structure and staff the bureaucracy in ways that make bureaus more responsive to their will. There are some six thousand executive branch political appointments, ranging from the cabinet secretaries down to lower level "Schedule C" posts deep within the bureaucracy. If, as the Reagan administration felt, "Personnel is Policy," presidents pay close attention to those personnel, even where (as in the inspectors general corps) they are ostensibly nonpartisan. Through appointing personal loyalists across the executive branch, presidents have sought, in the words of one George W. Bush aide, to "implant their DNA throughout the government." To be sure that DNA is faithfully replicated, they have developed aggressive personnel recruitment and vetting operations, a process that extends to candidates for the federal judiciary. In 2001 Bush required that the White House Office of Personnel interview and approve every candidate, even for subcabinet appointments often delegated to cabinet officers.[55]

These efforts can be controversial—loyalty that trumps competence, after all, can lead to performance in office that reflects badly on the president, as the aftermath of Hurricane Katrina in the fall of 2005 proved. Late in George W. Bush's second term, the White House and Justice Department were roundly criticized for emphasizing the appointment of "loyal Bushies" (and firing those they thought less loyal) in choosing U.S. attorneys around the country.[56]

Even more contested are efforts to control the personal views or behavior of executive branch employees via oath or test. Woodrow Wilson, for example, sought to dismiss government employees alleged to hold socialist or other "un-American" views in the lead up to World War I by issuing a 1917 executive order giving agency heads the power to fire any employee judged "inimical to the public welfare." Later, as the nation became caught in the grip of the cold war with the Soviet Union, Harry S. Truman's Executive Order 9835 in 1947 instituted loyalty oaths for all federal employees to root out possible communist sympathizers.[57] On another front, Reagan ordered in 1986 all executive branch agencies to establish random drug-testing programs for personnel in "sensitive" positions. Civil libertarians asserted that random tests violated the privacy rights of public employees, but in 1989 the Supreme Court ruled that mandatory drug tests were constitutional under certain conditions.[58]

To be sure, high-level appointees must receive Senate confirmation. However, the Civil Service Reform Act of 1978 gave presidents more leeway over appointments just below those requiring confirmation (in what was now called the Senior Executive Service): Reagan used this tool to remove numerous career officials from key positions and replace them with his own partisans, while using staffing cuts to eliminate entire offices of civil servants.

Presidents also use "recess appointments" to circumvent the confirmation process. Article II, Section 2 of the Constitution, allows presidents to fill vacancies while the Senate is in recess, until the end of the next Senate session. In the 1790s, of course, logistics dictated long breaks from the Capitol. While these days legislators are in near-continuous session, recess appointments remain a way of installing contested nominees without Senate interference. After Reagan failed to abolish the Legal Services Corporation statutorily, for example, he used recess appointments to install an entirely new board hostile to the agency's mandate. In all he made nearly 250 recess appointments in eight years, a figure that dropped off under George H. W. Bush and Bill Clinton, though in late 2000 Clinton made a rare recess appointment to the federal judiciary. George W. Bush embraced this strategy; he made 171 recess appointments, including two federal judges and the ambassador to the United Nations; Barack Obama followed at a similar pace, with thirty-two in his first three years in office.[59] Recess appointments attract dissent and may serve only as a temporary fix for a president seeking responsiveness—such appointees are rarely confirmed by the Senate for full terms. Indeed, starting in 2007 the Democratic Senate held *pro forma* sessions even during breaks in the legislative session, a practice copied by the Republican House starting in 2011. The idea was that since Congress did not formally recess, no recess appointments could be made. Yet in early 2012,

President Obama made several such appointments nonetheless, most notably installing a head of the Consumer Financial Protection Bureau who had been held up by Senate filibuster. Obama argued that since the *pro forma* sessions were held on the basis that they would involve no substantive action, members should still be considered in recess. Senators argued that the Constitution did not give the president the authority to decide the legitimacy of their sessions. As a political matter, Obama won the day, at least in the short run; but legal challenges to the legitimacy of policy decisions made by the appointees seemed inevitable.

POLICY IMPLEMENTATION

Article II of the Constitution requires presidents to "take care that the laws be faithfully executed." It is less clear what constitutes fidelity to this charge when the laws themselves are vaguely drafted or even (to presidents' minds at least) unconstitutional. Thus presidents have sought to increase their influence over policy implementation by mechanisms ranging from control over agency rulemaking to executive command.

Rulemaking and Regulatory Review

Congress frequently finds itself unable or unwilling to respond to complex national problems with highly specific statutory language. Instead, legislative language sets goals, timetables, and standards, delegating to the executive branch the power to hammer out the frequently arcane technical matters that carry out a statute's intent.

Thus the substance of any law is in many ways determined by the regulations issued in its name; rulemaking by executive agencies can serve as a relatively low-salience mechanism for effecting tangible policy change, sometimes in ways not anticipated by a statute's legislative authors.[60] The "No Child Left Behind" education reforms passed in 2001 provide a good example: how increased testing and accountability requirements would actually affect schools and students was not clear until the Department of Education had issued rules governing what kind of tests were required and how state standards for measuring pupil performance could be defined. When Congress failed to reauthorize the law on schedule, the Obama administration effectively amended it in 2011 and early 2012 by announcing new standards for implementation, including waivers to selected states from some of the law's more demanding requirements. Part of the appeal to presidents of the politicization process noted above, therefore, is that it helps ensure that even lower-level appointees are in tune with administration policy preferences. It is no accident, to continue the example above, that the Department of Education is one of the most politicized agencies in the federal government. In recent years, the Environmental Protection Agency and Food and Drug Administration have also been targeted by presidents seeking to modify the regulatory burden on business.

The importance of the rulemaking process rose with the growth of the American federal establishment and the administrative state. By the 1970s, federal regulation reached into most corners of the U.S. economy, from consumer protection to workplace safety. President Nixon thus sought to give OMB the power to approve regulations, and Presidents Gerald R. Ford and Jimmy Carter directed agencies to consider the inflationary impact and cost-benefit ratio of new regulations. However, it was left to Ronald Reagan to move regulatory review into OMB's extant process of central clearance. In February 1981 he issued an executive order stating flatly that "regulatory action shall not be undertaken unless the potential benefits to society for the regulation outweigh the potential costs to society." OMB—in particular, its Office of Information and Regulatory Affairs (OIRA)—had the power to recommend that regulations be withdrawn if they could not "be reformulated to meet its objections." In 1985 another order extended OMB's reach to agency "prerulemaking activities," defined as almost any activity that could lead to consideration of the need for a regulation. This order also required OMB to approve an annual "regulatory program" submitted by each agency and prohibited actions not in that program unless cleared by OMB observers. The process as it developed was largely off-the-record—over the phone or via confidential comments—which served to shield it from legislative or judicial review. Despite congressional grumbling, there was little legislative reaction; regulatory review has remained in place throughout all subsequent presidencies. George W. Bush strengthened OIRA's focus on cost-benefit analysis. His desire for regulatory responsiveness in environmental policy attracted perhaps the most attention, as scientists charged that technical review procedures were being shunted aside in favor of political considerations, usually favoring development over preservation. Obama was accused of the opposite bias, unilaterally imposing new environmental protections in ways that burdened business. For presidents of all parties, then, regulatory review has become a fixture of the administrative presidency, if not one with any statutory basis.[61]

Signing Statements and Item Vetoes

Another means of directing policy implementation is the use of "signing statements" issued upon the signing of a bill into law. These statements provide constitutional commentary on aspects of the new statute to influence its judicial interpretation, guide rulemaking, and announce the mechanisms by which the executive branch will enforce the disputed provisions—if at all. While examples can be found dating to the Monroe administration, and certainly to the constitutional claims of the "imperial" Lyndon B. Johnson and Nixon years, Reagan and his successors were more self-conscious and

systematic about the strategy. Indeed, George W. Bush's use of signing statements was markedly aggressive—by one count, he issued more than all other presidents combined, recording 116 separate objections to the Consolidated Appropriations Act of 2005 alone.[62] President Obama limited his issuance of such claims—especially after receiving a bipartisan scolding from Congress in 2009—but pointedly declined to rule out their use entirely, arguing that "such signing statements serve a legitimate function in our system, at least when based on well-founded constitutional objections."[63]

In this context presidents have argued that Congress cannot interfere with any processes leading to the utilization of Article II powers such as the proposal of legislation or the selection of nominees to office. In 2001, for instance, George W. Bush said that a section of a statute directing the administration to submit a bill addressing bovine disease control would be interpreted instead as a suggestion. In 2009 Obama stated likewise in discussing legislative language conditioning appointments to an advisory committee: "I will construe these provisions to require the Secretary to consider such congressional recommendations, but not to be bound by them. . . ."[64]

Claims about foreign affairs powers have, perhaps, been more notable. For example, after Reagan issued a national security directive with strict enforcement provisions governing the disclosure of information deemed sensitive, Congress passed a bill forbidding the administration from enforcing those provisions. Reagan signed it—but stated that since it "impermissibly interfered with my ability to prevent unauthorized disclosures of our most sensitive diplomatic, military, and intelligence activities. . . , in accordance with my sworn obligation to preserve, protect, and defend the Constitution, [it] will be considered of no force or effect. . . ." Along similar lines, the younger Bush, like other presidents, routinely included language in signing statements rejecting provisions that would in his view "unconstitutionally constrain my authority regarding the conduct of diplomacy and my authority as Commander-in-Chief."[65] In late 2005 that position brought the signing statement into the public eye when he asserted that he would construe the Detainee Treatment Act's ban against the "cruel, inhuman, or degrading treatment or punishment" of prisoners "in a manner consistent with the constitutional authority of the President to supervise the unitary executive branch and as Commander in Chief and consistent with the constitutional limitations on the judicial power." In late 2006 a signing statement to the U.S.-India Peaceful Atomic Energy Cooperation Act claimed Congress could not "purpor[t] to establish U.S. policy with respect to various international affairs matters." Bush would take legislative direction, including a ban on the transfer to India of certain nuclear materials, only as "advisory." In 2009 Obama similarly argued that in requiring "the Executive to take certain positions in negotiations or discussions" Congress had "interfere[d] with my constitutional authority to conduct foreign relations. . . . I will not treat these provisions as limiting my ability to engage in foreign diplomacy or negotiations."[66]

In these cases and others, then, presidents claimed the right to determine how—and whether—the law would be implemented. The formulaic nature of the language used in asserting these executive claims tended to conceal their extraordinarily broad affirmations of presidential power. While their practical impact on policy implementation is unclear, they have been largely unchecked thus far. Though a circuit court once scolded the Reagan administration's effort to avoid parts of a contracting act by saying "this claim of right for the President to declare statutes unconstitutional and to declare his refusal to execute them . . . is dubious at best," courts have usually ignored the practice. At the least, such presidential assertions have proven hard to overturn; and more often than not, Congress has not tried.[67]

Signing statements, if taken literally, constitute a form of line-item veto. The Constitution does of course provide that presidents may disapprove bills passed by Congress, subject to override by two-thirds of each chamber. But unlike more than forty state governors, presidents may not pick out specific provisions in legislation for the veto pen. Despite this, they have long claimed the right to refuse to spend appropriated funds when, as in Ulysses S. Grant's declaration, they were "of purely private or local interest"; at times Congress itself has given presidents discretionary impoundment power in order to limit expenditures. By 1950, in fact, statutory language authorized President Truman to impound funds if spending became unnecessary due to "changes in requirements" or "other developments."[68]

President Nixon upped the ante, arguing that while Congress had the power to appropriate funds, the executive power covered their actual expenditure. "The Constitutional right of the President of the United States to impound funds," he claimed, "is absolutely clear." His impoundments subsequently encompassed as much as a fifth of the federal government's discretionary spending, aimed largely at programs whose passage he had opposed. In 1975 the Supreme Court ruled against such impoundments in *Train v. City of New York*; by then, Congress had already made them illegal in the Budget and Impoundment Control Act of 1974.[69]

However, as the 1980s and early 1990s produced record budget deficits, presidents revived pressure for some form of line-item veto power. "I'll make the cuts, I'll take the heat," Reagan asserted in his 1986 State of the Union address. In 1996 Congress passed the Line Item Veto Act. It provided the president with "enhanced rescission" power that allowed the president's proposed vetoes of specific spending or revenue items to go into effect unless Congress passed a bill that reinstated the spending. That bill would, in turn, be subject to presidential veto. As a result, the president could rescind spending with the support of just one-third plus one member of either the House or the Senate. Senate Appropriations chair Ted Stevens (R-Alaska) called this "the most significant delegation of authority by the Congress to the President since the Constitution was ratified." Clinton used the power to propose cancellation of about forty items in 1997, but the law was struck down by the Supreme Court in 1998. The item veto procedure, the Court held, did not follow the Constitution's presentment clause, which only a constitutional amendment could change. When persistent deficits returned in the mid-2000s, so did proposals for item veto authority. The House passed one version of this in 2006 and another in early 2012 after President Obama endorsed the notion.[70] However, Obama declined to interpret the Fourteenth Amendment in order to unilaterally override the statutory debt limit in 2011, when the United States came close to default.[71]

Executive Orders

A key instrument of presidential power is the executive order. Though defined nowhere in the Constitution, executive orders in various forms—including proclamations, national security directives, presidential decision memoranda, and the like[72]—are generally construed as presidential directives intended to carry out other executive powers. As such, an executive order's legal authority derives either from existing statutes or from the president's constitutional responsibilities, not from any specific congressional approval. Executive orders usually pertain directly to government agencies and officials. They are used most frequently to issue binding directives to members of the executive branch; to shape regulatory action; to reorganize agencies or decision-making procedures; to control the military; or even to make new policy, especially in areas where Congress has not acted or where presidential initiative is generally accepted. The Louisiana Purchase was consummated by proclamation, as was emancipation of the slaves during the Civil War; and presidents have used executive orders to create Native American reservations, grazing areas, military reservations, and millions of acres of conservation land. More recently, presidents have kicked off their administrations by issuing multiple orders designed to set the tone for their administration. One of the first actions by President Clinton in January 1993 was to reverse a "gag rule" that had, under the Reagan and George H. W. Bush administrations, prohibited abortion counseling and referrals at family planning clinics that received federal funding. In his turn, George W. Bush reversed Clinton's order in January 2001—and also put a sixty-day hold on all regulations approved in the last days of his predecessor's

Processing Executive Orders

Proposed executive orders can originate from almost anywhere in the executive branch. A few are drafted directly in the White House, but most originate from the various departments and agencies. Some orders, such as those fulfilling campaign pledges, may be drafted at the express instruction of the president. Most, however, are devised by career personnel in the departments and agencies and aim to implement federal regulations, propose new rules or procedures, or to reorganize presidential advising in some manner. In any case, and because executive orders have the force of law, they are crafted largely by professional legal counsel at the instruction of the president's appointees. Rarely does a president take a direct hand in writing an order.

Each proposed executive order is composed and submitted according to precise procedures, as laid out in 1962's Executive Order 11030 (as amended over time to remove references to carbon paper and the like). It must be prepared in a specific format and style and must contain language explaining its nature, purpose, background, and effects, along with the presidential authority under which it is issued. The proposed order is then sent to the Office of Management and Budget (OMB), where it is examined for adherence to the current administration's overall policy and budgetary goals and cleared with a range of interested agencies across the executive branch. If approved, the order is sent next to the attorney general, whose office scrutinizes it for potential legal problems. Because both the attorney general and the director of OMB typically are among the president's closest advisers, clearance by these offices normally can be assumed to signify presidential approval, though at times White House staff weigh in with new objections late in the process.

Finally, the proposed order is transmitted to the Office of the Federal Register, a part of the National Archives and Records Administration. The order is reviewed once more for stylistic and typographical errors, after which it returns to the president for final approval. If signed by the president, the order and two copies are published in the *Federal Register*, the official publication of the executive branch. It is only upon the moment of publication in the *Federal Register* that an executive order takes force.

Not all executive orders follow these precise steps. Those requiring expedited action—relating to some natural emergency or international crisis, perhaps—may bypass much of the lengthy clearance process and go directly to the president for final approval. Moreover, the text of an order dealing with some aspect of national security may be treated as confidential, in which case only the order's number is published in the *Federal Register*. For most executive orders, however, the process is relatively routine, even if their substance is often internally contentious.

term. And Obama continued this sequential game by reversing a number of Bush's orders, rescinding a 2001 order limiting access to presidential records and setting aside the legal rulings justifying torture of detainees.[73]

As this sequence suggests, executive orders are hardly unfettered. Not only can subsequent administrations change them, Congress or the courts can also overturn them. In late 2006, for example, a district court judge overturned George W. Bush's September 2001 executive order naming various groups and individuals as "specially designated global terrorists," objecting to the president's claim to "unfettered discretion."[74] But outright negation is relatively rare. And in the interim, executive orders can give the president power to model or remodel the policy landscape, often under the political radar—they "hide in plain sight." If nothing else, they have dramatically reshaped the government's organization chart: unilateral orders in various guises have created a majority of the federal administrative agencies catalogued in the *U.S. Government Manual*.[75]

During the nation's first hundred or so years, executive orders were issued without any system of publication or recording. They were not formally tracked until 1895, and their numbering began only in 1907, with numbers assigned retroactively to the time of Abraham Lincoln. A century later, in January 2007, President Bush issued Executive Order 13422. However, haphazard record-keeping throughout much of history—even after 1907—leads scholars to estimate that between 15,000 and 50,000 directives were never recorded. To respond to growing concerns that such lax procedures undermined democratic accountability, Congress in the Administrative Procedures Act (APA) of 1946 mandated that the number and text of all executive orders, executive branch announcements, proposals, and regulations must be published in the *Federal Register*, the official U.S. government record. Exceptions to this rule are the "classified" executive orders pertaining directly to sensitive national security matters, which are entered into the *Federal Register* by number only. Furthermore, in 1994 the Supreme Court held that the development of presidential executive orders was not subject to the APA's requirements for public comment or a balanced research process.

While the average annual number of executive orders issued by presidents has dropped since the early 1940s, the number of significant orders has risen dramatically over time. One exhaustive survey of the executive orders issued between 1936 and 1999 found that after a surge in usage during World War II the proportion of substantively significant orders tripled from the 1950s to the 1990s. Another study similarly concluded that the number and scope of substantive orders has risen impressively since the Reagan administration. In one example, George W. Bush created an

TABLE 1-1 **Executive Orders, by President, 1789–2011**

President	Years in office	Number of orders	Average per year
Washington	8.00	8	1.00
J. Adams	4.00	1	0.25
Jefferson	8.00	4	0.50
Madison	8.00	1	0.13
Monroe	8.00	1	0.13
J.Q. Adams	4.00	4	1.00
Jackson	8.00	11	1.38
Van Buren	4.00	10	2.50
W.H. Harrison	0.08[a]	0	—
Tyler	4.00	17	4.25
Polk	4.00	19	4.75
Taylor	1.25	4	3.20
Fillmore	2.75	13	4.73
Pierce	4.00	35	8.75
Buchanan	4.00	15	3.75
Lincoln	4.00	48	12.00
A. Johnson	4.00	79	19.75
Grant	8.00	223	27.88
Hayes	4.00	92	23.00
Garfield	0.50[b]	9	—
Arthur	3.25	100	30.77
Cleveland	4.00	113	28.25
B. Harrison	4.00	135	33.75
Cleveland (2d term)	4.00	142	35.50
McKinley	4.75	178	37.47
T. Roosevelt	7.25	1139	157.10
Taft	4.00	752	188.00
Wilson	8.00	1841	230.13
Harding	2.60	487	187.31
Coolidge	5.40	1259	233.15
Hoover	4.00	1011	252.75
F. Roosevelt	12.33	3728	302.35
Truman	7.67	896	116.82
Eisenhower	8.00	486	60.75
Kennedy	2.92	214	73.29
L. Johnson	5.08	324	63.78
Nixon	5.60	346	61.79
Ford	2.40	169	70.42
Carter	4.00	320	80.00
Reagan	8.00	381	51.13
G.H.W. Bush	4.00	166	41.50
Clinton	8.00	364	45.50
G.W. Bush	8.00	291	36.38
Obama[c]	2.75	95	34.55

SOURCE: Calculated from Lyn Ragsdale, *Vital Statistics on the Presidency: Washington to Clinton*, rev. ed. (Washington, D.C.: Congressional Quarterly, 1998), 346–352, and the *Federal Register*, www.archives.gov/ federal-register/executive-orders/.

NOTES: Includes both numbered and unnumbered executive orders. a. Harrison died after only one month in office. b. Garfield was assassinated after six months in office, during which he issued nine executive orders. At that rate his average would have been eighteen per year. c. Through Sept. 2011.

Office of Faith-Based and Community Initiatives and department-based centers thereof, then mandated that faith-based organizations receive the "equal protection of the laws" in federal procurement efforts. As Bush told a 2002 gathering of representatives from such organizations,

"I got a little frustrated in Washington because I couldn't get the bill passed out of the Congress. They were arguing process. . . . Congress wouldn't act, so I signed an executive order—that means I did it on my own." Obama, likewise worried about legislative meddling (as he saw it) in the detention and trial of prisoners at Guantanamo Bay, revamped the process on his own as well, by executive order in March 2011.[76]

Such orders are supposed to be grounded in statutory authority. As such they often show the unintended consequences of congressional delegation. Clinton's 1996 proclamation setting aside nearly two million acres in Utah for preservation purposes, for example, rested on a 1906 statute long forgotten by Congress, but not by presidents. The accumulation of a large body of administrative law replaced the need for unilateral presidential action in routine matters, such as personnel administration and regulatory procedures. Of the almost two thousand executive orders issued between 1945 and 1965, more than 80 percent were based on existing statutory authority, indicating in part the breadth of the statutory web woven after World War II.[77] Even congressional efforts to constrain executive authority sometimes legitimated it. A good example is the International Emergency Economic Powers Act (IEEPA). The IEEPA was passed in 1977 to rein in the use of its titular powers. But by providing a statutory process for declaring emergencies as a means of preventing economic transactions with disfavored regimes, Congress formalized a previously shadowy claim to power, and presidents declared thirty "national emergencies" between 1979 and 2000. In some cases, these were vehicles for overriding clear legislative preferences, as when President Reagan applied IEEPA sanctions against Nicaragua in 1985 as a substitute for those Congress had refused to enact. In others, they extended national policy on the president's terms and timetable, as in Obama's series of orders in 2011 dealing with Libya, North Korea, and Syria.[78]

Some scholars argue that it is unwise or illegitimate for Congress to delegate broad discretionary authority to the president, and executive orders can certainly arouse animosity when they are used to bypass or confront Congress. In 1963, for example, John Kennedy used Executive Order 11063 to bar racial discrimination in federally subsidized housing after finding the legislative route blocked by southern conservatives. Lyndon B. Johnson later issued an executive order to create minority hiring guidelines for federal contracts after Congress failed to embody affirmative action in the Civil Rights Act of 1964.

As these examples suggest, safeguarding or promoting civil rights has been a persistent rationale of executive orders, beginning with Franklin Roosevelt, who eased racial segregation of defense plants during World

War II. Many orders were applied to operating procedures and rules within executive branch agencies, while others reshaped the implementation of entire federal programs when Congress proved unable or unwilling to act. For example, in 1948 Harry Truman used Executive Order 9981 to integrate the armed forces, an action that, combined with calls within the Democratic Party for stronger civil rights protection, split Democrats and sparked the creation of a separate "Dixiecrat" party during the 1948 election. Johnson's creation of "affirmative action" noted above was followed, if somewhat redefined, by Nixon's "Philadelphia Plan," a 1969 executive order instituting racial hiring quotas on federal projects. Nixon's action ran contrary to the 1964 Civil Rights Act, which forbade quotas of any kind, but his order was upheld by a federal court of appeals based partly on the implied power of the president to set federal procurement policies.[79]

A telling example of the controversy created when presidents use executive orders to bypass Congress on issues involving discrimination is an order never actually signed: President Clinton's 1993 promise to lift a long-standing ban on homosexuals serving in the military. The proposal, coming early in Clinton's term, erupted into a major political firestorm that threatened to overtake the rest of his nascent domestic agenda. He abandoned the idea of an executive order and sought an unofficial compromise with congressional and military leaders that eventually took the form of a "don't ask, don't tell" directive issued by the military.[80] Clinton's experience highlights the limits of the discretionary presidency, at least in peacetime. But in 2011, having determined the Defense of Marriage Act (DOMA) was unconstitutional, President Obama ordered the Justice Department to stop defending the act in federal court. While this did not remove DOMA from the books, it did raise new barriers to its enforcement.

As with the use of the veto, unilateral strategies are most pronounced among presidents facing a Congress controlled by the other party. Nixon used executive orders to restructure and gain tighter presidential control over the executive branch after Congress turned down his reorganization proposals. Reagan used an executive order to preempt congressional action mandating drug testing for federal employees. George H. W. Bush sidestepped Congress to give a new White House Council on Competitiveness the power to assess the economic consequences of new regulations. Clinton's use of executive orders became more strategic after the Republican Party took over control of Congress in 1995. As Clinton aide Rahm Emanuel explained in 1998, "sometimes we use [an executive order] in reaction to legislative delay or setbacks. Obviously, you'd rather pass legislation that can do X, but you're willing to make whatever progress you can on an agenda item." When Obama's Democratic Party lost its House majority in the 2010 midterms, friends and foes alike suggested an administrative strategy that bypassed Congress was the likely outcome.[81] Indeed, the president subsequently set out a campaign of unilateral action based on the notion that "we can't wait" for legislative gridlock to ease. Dozens of administrative changes were announced over a year-long period leading up to the 2012 election, aimed at showing a presidential desire to take action to revive the economy even if his congressional agenda was stalled. The agenda included initiatives governing a variety of popular programs ranging from mortgage foreclosures to student loans to prescription drug costs to rural job creation.[82]

Executive orders are less controversial when based clearly on existing statutory authority. But they may spark dispute when they rely instead on the happily vague "executive power" of the Constitution or implied powers. Presidents frequently maintain that they have the constitutional authority to act unilaterally because they possess inherent war or emergency powers during periods of apparent crisis. They may also claim implied authority to act in the absence of legislative action in a given area. Federal courts tend to judge each case individually, but usually give presidents the benefit of the doubt when Congress has failed to decide an issue over a prolonged period. Making matters still more complex, Congress often gives presidents retroactive authority for their unilateral actions, particularly during emergencies. In the 1793 dispute, Congress reluctantly approved Washington's proclamation of neutrality a year after he made it, a pattern repeated enough that presidents often proceed on the assumption that Congress will acquiesce eventually.

Checking presidential power requires that the other branches know what power is being exercised, and this has not always been the case. As noted above, federal law mandates the publication of executive orders and proclamations, but it also allows for secret orders to protect the public interest, when they deal with military or intelligence matters. For example, Truman's 1952 executive order creating the National Security Agency, the largest and most secretive of the nation's intelligence organizations, remained officially classified for more than forty years after he issued it. Beyond this presidents also use classified executive directives drafted through the National Security Council staffing process.[83] In the mid-1980s, such national security directives underlaid policies in Iran and Nicaragua that ran afoul of the statutory bans on arms sales to terrorists and aid to the contras, respectively.[84] They provided negotiation instructions to diplomats working on nuclear arms control and shaped the Strategic

EXECUTIVE ORDER 13527 (BARACK OBAMA)

Executive Order 13527
December 30, 2009
Establishing Federal Capability for the Timely Provision of Medical Countermeasures Following a Biological Attack

By the authority vested in me as President by the Constitution and the laws of the United States of America, it is hereby ordered as follows:

Section 1. *Policy.* It is the policy of the United States to plan and prepare for the timely provision of medical countermeasures to the American people in the event of a biological attack in the United States through a rapid Federal response in coordination with State, local, territorial, and tribal governments.

This policy would seek to: (1) mitigate illness and prevent death; (2) sustain critical infrastructure; and (3) complement and supplement State, local, territorial, and tribal government medical countermeasure distribution capacity.

Section 2. *United States Postal Service Delivery of Medical Countermeasures.*

(a) The U.S. Postal Service has the capacity for rapid residential delivery of medical countermeasures for self administration across all communities in the United States. The Federal Government shall pursue a national U.S. Postal Service medical countermeasures dispensing model to respond to a large-scale biological attack.

(b) The Secretaries of Health and Human Services and Homeland Security, in coordination with the U.S. Postal Service, within 180 days of the date of this order, shall establish a national U.S. Postal Service medical countermeasures dispensing model for U.S. cities to respond to a large-scale biological attack, with anthrax as the primary threat consideration.

(c) In support of the national U.S. Postal Service model, the Secretaries of Homeland Security, Health and Human Services, and Defense, and the Attorney General, in coordination with the U.S. Postal Service, and in consultation with State and local public health, emergency management, and law enforcement officials, within 180 days of the date of this order, shall develop an accompanying plan for supplementing local law enforcement personnel, as necessary and appropriate, with local Federal law enforcement, as well as other appropriate personnel, to escort U.S. Postal workers delivering medical countermeasures.

Section 3. *Federal Rapid Response.*

(a) The Federal Government must develop the capacity to anticipate and immediately supplement the capabilities of affected jurisdictions to rapidly distribute medical countermeasures following a biological attack. Implementation of a Federal strategy to rapidly dispense medical countermeasures requires establishment of a Federal rapid response capability.

(b) The Secretaries of Homeland Security and Health and Human Services, in coordination with the Secretary of Defense, within 90 days of the date of this order, shall develop a concept of operations and establish requirements for a Federal rapid response to dispense medical countermeasures to an affected population following a large-scale biological attack.

Section 4. *Continuity of Operations.*

(a) The Federal Government must establish mechanisms for the provision of medical countermeasures to personnel performing mission-essential functions to ensure that mission-essential functions of Federal agencies continue to be performed following a biological attack.

(b) The Secretaries of Health and Human Services and Homeland Security, within 180 days of the date of this order, shall develop a plan for the provision of medical countermeasures to ensure that mission-essential functions of executive branch departments and agencies continue to be performed following a large-scale biological attack.

Section 5. *General Provisions.*

(a) Nothing in this order shall be construed to impair or otherwise affect:

(i) authority granted by law to a department or agency, or the head thereof; or

(ii) functions of the Director of the Office of Management and Budget relating to budgetary, administrative, or legislative proposals.

(b) This order shall be implemented consistent with applicable law and subject to the availability of appropriations.

(c) This order is not intended to, and does not, create any right or benefit, substantive or procedural, enforceable at law or in equity, by any party against the United States, its departments, agencies, or entities, its officers, employees, or agents, or any other person.

Barack Obama
The White House
December 30, 2009

SOURCE: *Federal Register*, 75, No. 3, January 6, 2010, Presidential Documents.

Defense Initiative. They even implemented the "Plan for Economic Warfare against the USSR," which laid out aggressive plans for hindering Soviet commerce. Needless to say, this plan did not receive congressional review or approval. While the penchant for executive secrecy and, particularly, for excluding Congress from foreign policy decision making briefly lessened a bit with the end of the cold war and the dissolution of the former Soviet Union, the September 11, 2001, terrorist attacks reactivated the trend. *(See "The 'New' Imperial Presidency?" p. 22.)*

Secrecy and Executive Privilege

Executive orders may also be used to create secrecy—that is, to create a system for classifying government documents or other information in the name of national security. Governments always have pursued secrecy in sensitive diplomatic or military matters, but the idea that the United States should maintain a formal classification system did not take hold until the eve of World War II, when Franklin Roosevelt authorized in March 1940 the classification of military intelligence information. The test of what constituted secrets worth classifying, Roosevelt said, was "what the Commander in Chief of the Army and Navy thinks would be harmful to the defense of this country to give out."[85]

As the war progressed, subsequent executive orders extended classification beyond its original confines, and the trend did not end once hostilities ceased. Instead, the exigencies of the cold war led presidents to expand the categories of information deemed essential to national security. Truman used two executive orders to extend classification authority to any executive branch agency when secrecy was deemed essential. While Roosevelt extrapolated his 1940 executive order from authority provided by a 1938 statute classifying military charts, Truman's expansion of secrecy was based simply on an assertion that inherent executive powers gave him the responsibility to do whatever was necessary to protect national security.[86] Constitutional scholars debated the legality of Truman's claim but worried even more about the effects of pervasive secrecy on democratic accountability if Congress was kept under- or misinformed.[87] The government could now classify virtually anything, and there were few mechanisms to guard against the tendency toward the overclassification that is inevitable when agencies hoard information as a valuable resource, when they skirt the law in pursuit of other ends, or when they simply wish to hide their mistakes. By the Kennedy administration, the classification system itself was classified. Under President Nixon's 1972 order, "national security" encompassed any information in "the interest of the national defense or foreign relations of the United States," including information about domestic intelligence activities. President Reagan extended the standard classification period for documents and suspended automatic declassification.[88]

Issues of secrecy seemed to change with the end of the cold war and the collapse of the Soviet Union, with greater declassification of documents dating back to World War II. A highly charged twist to this effort concerned documents related to military personnel missing in action or held as prisoners of war during the Vietnam War. In 1992 President George H. W. Bush issued an executive order expediting the declassification of Vietnam-era materials, and President Clinton expanded this effort with his order dated Veterans' Day 1993. A 1995 Clinton executive order streamlined declassification procedures for archival material more than twenty-five years old and reversed extant policy by providing that in unclear cases the government's basic stance should be against classification. However, in March 2003 George W. Bush issued an executive order that removed the default stance toward declassification, exempted additional information (such as that pertaining to "current vulnerabilities" in security) from the automatic declassification process, enhanced the ability of the vice president to classify documents, and gave the Central Intelligence Agency (CIA) new power to resist declassification decisions. (The CIA also worked with the National Archives to reclassify previously public information.) In late 2009 the pendulum swung back toward openness with an Obama executive order intoning that "our democratic principles require that the American people be informed of the activities of their Government."[89] On the flip side, angered by the unauthorized release of information (including the high-profile "WikiLeaks" disclosures of diplomatic cables), the Obama administration was more aggressive than any of its predecessors in prosecuting alleged leakers.

More generally, the exercise of executive privilege to prevent the release of information has been claimed by presidents as part of the broader "executive power," which limits the ability of other branches of government to define the boundaries of that power. Nixon, indeed, argued that "the manner in which the president exercises his assigned executive powers is not subject to questioning by another branch of the government." His attorney general, Richard Kleindienst, told the Senate in 1973 that the president could direct any member of the executive branch to refuse information in response to congressional request: "your power to get what the President knows," he said, "is in the President's hands."[90]

It was Eisenhower's attorney general, William P. Rogers, who came up with the phrase "executive privilege." But the practice it described goes back to the Washington administration, which concluded it had the right to withhold information from Congress concerning military operations and diplomatic negotiations. Over time most presidents claimed the right to determine what, in President James K. Polk's phrase, was "compatible with the public interest to communicate." Largely these claims concerned sensitive issues of foreign relations. Later, as the Executive Office of the President grew, the claim expanded to provide for the confidentiality of advice to presidents from their staffs, using the model of lawyer-client privilege.[91]

Nixon's efforts to withhold incriminating tape recordings from the criminal trial of his subordinates led to a unanimous Supreme Court decision in 1974 overturning his assertion of executive privilege. But if Nixon lost that battle, presidents arguably won the war—since the Court also held that, while inapplicable in this case, some sort of communications "privilege is . . . inextricably rooted in the separation of powers under the Constitution." When "military, diplomatic, or sensitive national security secrets" were at stake, the Court owed the president "great deference."[92] In 1994 a circuit court divided executive privilege into "deliberative process privilege" and "presidential communications privilege." Both could sometimes be valid grounds for denying information to other branches, but the latter, when invoked, made the relevant documents "presumptively privileged."[93]

Thus even after Watergate, whether called by its name or disguised as "deliberative process privilege," "attorney work product" and "attorney-client privilege," "internal departmental deliberations," "secret opinions policy," "deliberations of another agency," and the like, executive privilege was alive and well. Refusing a congressional request for documents concerning the administration's policies in Haiti, for instance, Clinton administration attorney general Janet Reno made the startling claim that Congress had no power to conduct oversight of foreign affairs, due in part to the "sole organ" doctrine of the 1936 *Curtiss-Wright case*; the investigating committee backed down. George W. Bush likewise refused to turn over documents relating to Federal Bureau of Investigation (FBI) investigations into organized crime or allegations of campaign finance violations in the 1996 campaign. He also resisted allowing National Security Adviser Condoleezza Rice to testify before the 9/11 Commission, and he only relented after extracting written assurances from House and Senate leaders that her appearance "does not set, and should not be cited as, a precedent for future requests" for any White House official to testify before a legislative body.[94]

In general, then, as one scholar has noted, "With a nontrivial amount of freedom to craft new kinds of unilateral directives, citing national security concerns and executive privilege as justifications for concealing their actions, presidents have obstructed the efforts of members of Congress to keep pace."[95]

EMERGENCY POWERS

Secrecy is, of course, most critical to foreign affairs. But in times of crisis, whether foreign or domestic, Congress has endorsed or allowed enhanced presidential discretion.

Foreign Affairs

The United States has entered into five declared wars, one civil war, and numerous undeclared hostilities in its history. In each instance presidents have asserted claims to some type of emergency powers to deal with the threat, but the justifications put forth have differed starkly. In some cases presidents assert an aggressively broad view of the president's inherent war powers, based largely on wedding the presidential oath of office with the vesting and commander-in-chief clauses. When President Reagan sent marines to Lebanon in 1982, he said the troops had been deployed under his "constitutional authority with respect to the conduct of foreign relations and as Commander-in-Chief."[96]

That sort of assertion can be justified by the existence of an obvious crisis, as in the Civil War. Ironically, it can also be justified by a situation's relative lack of severity, that is, by its supposed standing as a police action rather than as a "real" use of force that would require a declaration of war.

CATEGORIES AND EXAMPLES OF EMERGENCY POWERS

When emergencies are declared, or during times of crisis, the president has at hand a broad array of potential powers. These emergency powers can be grouped into three categories of actions the president may take:

POWERS OVER INDIVIDUALS

Confine individuals seen to be threats to national security

Restrict travel of Americans to other nations (such as Cuba) or travel of some foreigners to the United States

Restrict movement of citizens within the United States

Require persons, because of their backgrounds, associations with certain groups, or ownership of particular articles (such as weapons), to register with government officials

Restrict certain persons from working in industries critical to national security

Remove federal employees regarded as threats to national security

Suspend writs of *habeas corpus*

Declare martial law

Assign armed forces to conflicts in foreign nations

POWERS OVER PROPERTY

Order stockpiling of strategic materials (such as uranium)

Impose restrictions on exports (such as computer equipment)

Allocate materials in ways necessary to aid national defense

Require industries to give priority to government contracts and seize industries failing to comply with such orders

Fix wages and prices

POWERS OVER COMMUNICATIONS

Withhold information from Congress and the public deemed potentially sensitive to national security

Monitor and censor communications between the United States and other nations

Require foreign representatives to register with U.S. government

SOURCE: U.S. Congress, House of Representatives, Committee on the Judiciary, Subcommittee on Administrative Law and Governmental Relations, *Hearings on H.R. 3884, National Emergencies Act*, 94th Cong., 1st sess., March 6–April 9, 1975, 22–23; Robert E. DiClerico, *The American President* (Englewood Cliffs, N.J.: Prentice-Hall, 1979), chap. 8.

The Civilian Conservation Corps, part of President Franklin D. Roosevelt's New Deal program, not only provided relief for jobless young men during the Great Depression but helped protect and conserve the nation's natural resources. Roosevelt visited one of the camps in Big Meadows, Virginia, in August 1933. Seated with Roosevelt are, from left, Gen. Paul B. Malone, Col. Louis Howe, Secretary of the Interior Harold I. Ickes, Director of the Civilian Conservation Corps Robert Fechner, Secretary of Agriculture Henry A. Wallace, and Assistant Secretary of Agriculture Rexford G. Tugwell.

retaliate against the perpetrators of the September 11, 2001, terrorist attacks, and to renew the fight with Iraqi president Saddam Hussein.

But every president exercises a mix of inherent and delegated war powers simultaneously. Lyndon Johnson asked for discretionary authorization to ramp up hostilities in Vietnam via the Gulf of Tonkin Resolution in 1964, but did not feel bound in turn to draw down forces when Congress soured on the war; Richard Nixon, in fact, simply ignored the resolution's repeal by Congress in 1971. While George H. W. Bush requested approval for armed action against Iraq during the Gulf War, he never claimed to need it—and, indeed, would later assert that "I didn't have to get permission from some old goat in the United States Congress to kick Saddam Hussein out of Kuwait." An interesting twist in the first Gulf War and later in Kosovo and Libya was presidents' reliance on United Nations and NATO obligations, respectively, as a substitute for congressional action in activating presidential war powers.[98]

William McKinley, Theodore Roosevelt, William Howard Taft, Woodrow Wilson, and Calvin Coolidge, for example, used U.S. troops to rule Cuba, Nicaragua, Haiti, and the Dominican Republic, and even to occupy Veracruz, Mexico. The decision by President George H. W. Bush in 1989 to send troops into Panama to capture Gen. Manuel Noriega, Panama's leader and a reputed leader in the international drug trade, also falls into this category. Bill Clinton used force in Haiti, Sudan, Afghanistan, and, most aggressively, in Kosovo, without requesting or receiving legislative sanction. In 2011 Barack Obama did the same in Libya. Most dramatically, Harry Truman never sought legislative approval for his extended "police action" on the Korean peninsula (and later sought to use the fact of conflict to justify his seizure of the nation's steel mills when a strike loomed).[97]

In other cases presidents have received broad congressional grants of executive authority to prosecute a war. Wilson and Franklin Roosevelt, during World Wars I and II, respectively, benefited from this pattern. And, as detailed below, Congress authorized George H. W. Bush to repel Iraqi forces from Kuwait in 1991 and George W. Bush to

Presidents do not always inform legislators about their actions abroad. The use of "executive agreements" with foreign leaders is one mechanism whereby presidents can institute policy change without going through the arduous process of receiving Senate ratification of a formal treaty. President Reagan concluded 3,000 such agreements between 1981 and 1988, compared to only 125 treaties. Agreements likewise outnumbered treaties by more than nine to one under Presidents George H. W. Bush and Clinton.[99]

Other covert operations involve espionage and, frequently, the use of force. The CIA and its cousin organizations over time have long constituted a "secret arm of the executive, with a secret budget."[100] The high-water mark for "black ops" was perhaps in the 1950s when the United States quietly helped guide the overthrow of governments in Iran, Guatemala, and Laos. Still, despite some high-profile failures, as at the 1961 Bay of Pigs invasion of Cuba and with contra operations in 1980s Nicaragua (the high profile being one definition of failure, perhaps), covert operations remain important weapons in the foreign affairs arsenal. In the early 2000s, CIA operatives were among the first in Afghanistan and Iraq; without telling Congress, the agency also put in place an electronic surveillance program that placed small groups of operatives in the mountainous border region between Afghanistan and Pakistan.[101] Espionage has obvious value in the battle against terrorism. A military mission used the fruits of both human and signals intelligence in the raid in Pakistan that killed Osama bin Laden, the head of the terrorist group al Qaeda in May 2011.

Although Congress has sought to require consultation about and notification of intelligence operations (for example, in the 1975 Church Committee hearings and the subsequent Intelligence Oversight Act), presidents have been reluctant to fully comply. In part, they correctly fear the difficulty Congress has in keeping secrets; sometimes, though, secrecy is simply a useful means to fend off legislative interference. It is difficult to balance the need for confidentiality with the need for accountability, as suggested by an extraordinary handwritten 2003 letter from Sen. John D. Rockefeller IV (D-W.Va.), ranking member of the Senate Select Committee on Intelligence, to Vice President Richard B. Cheney. "The activities we discussed [dealing with domestic surveillance] raise profound oversight issues. . . ." Rockefeller wrote. "Given the security restrictions associated with this information, and my inability to consult staff or counsel on my own, I feel unable to fully evaluate, much less endorse these activities."[102]

Even congressionally approved war powers often lead to states of emergency that long outlive the war itself. Recall that FDR closed the banks in 1933 under authority granted Wilson in World War I. As noted above, multiple stand-by powers were available to presidents through the mid-1970s, when a special Senate Committee on National Emergencies and Delegated Powers found 470 statutes on the books that combined to give presidents the right to seize private property and regulate private enterprise, restrict travel, organize and control all means of production and transportation, assign military forces overseas, and institute martial law.[103] But some claims are even more remote. When members of the Senate Foreign Relations Committee asked Nixon's secretary of defense Melvin R. Laird what would happen if Congress cut off all funds for continued U.S. involvement in Indochina, they were informed that the president could bypass Congress entirely and spend unappropriated funds through authority granted in a 1799 "feed and forage" statute. This law, enacted during a time when Congress met only half a year at a time, allowed the secretary of war to obtain advance funding to provide supplies to American soldiers in remote outposts without having to await congressional appropriation. It was still on the books more than 170 years later.[104]

Presidents have also sometimes sought to win domestic political advantage under the cover of national security claims. For example, Nixon's use of intelligence agencies to

PROCEDURES FOR EMERGENCY ORDERS

The National Emergencies Act of 1976 (PL 94–412) terminated all states of emergency legally in effect until that time, including some dating as far back as the 1930s. The act also set in place procedures for declaring and, equally important, terminating future states of emergency. As this brief overview suggests, the provisions of the National Emergencies Act were intended to force Congress and the president, acting singly or together, to ensure that any state of emergency does not outlive the conditions on which it was based.

The president by law cannot declare a state of national emergency without also specifying the provisions of existing law or constitutional provisions under which the proposed action falls. Furthermore, any proclamation of a national emergency must be transmitted immediately to Congress and published in the *Federal Register*.

During a declared national emergency the president and all relevant executive branch agencies or departments must maintain files on all rules, regulations, executive orders, or any other activities carried out to address the emergency. This information must be transmitted promptly to Congress. Matters requiring confidentiality are to be handled in a prescribed manner (they may, for example, be restricted to members of congressional intelligence committees and those staff

members with security clearances). All expenditures made by the executive branch to address the emergency also must be reported to Congress within ninety days after each six month period following the declaration of the emergency.

The law also specifies how states of emergency are to be terminated. No later than six months after an emergency is declared, the two houses of Congress must meet to consider a concurrent resolution to determine whether the emergency should be terminated. The resolution must go through the normal congressional procedures, but is bound to a specific schedule to avoid delays. Should Congress be unable or unwilling to terminate the emergency (perhaps because of some disagreement between the House and the Senate), it must consider another such resolution within the next six-month period.

The president can terminate unilaterally a declared state of emergency when it is deemed that the conditions mandating the emergency have passed. But, to avoid another situation where states of emergency endure legally for decades, the law calls for automatic termination of an emergency upon the anniversary of its declaration, unless the president previously notifies Congress (and publishes in the *Federal Register*) of the need to continue the emergency. One way or another, states of emergency are to be terminated.

investigate Americans and determine whether they were threats to national security entailed domestic surveillance aimed at groups opposed to U.S. action in Vietnam and included secret wiretapping, breaking into offices, and infiltrating groups with government informers. Details of past activities came to light when Congress held investigative hearings in the mid-1970s, and the ensuing controversies forced Ford and Carter to narrow the range of permissible domestic surveillance actions and to impose stricter control over federal agents. In 1981, however, Ronald Reagan issued an executive order loosening considerably extant restrictions. Revelations in 1988 that the FBI had relied on this broad authority to conduct an extensive covert surveillance program against groups opposed to U.S. policy in Central America sparked tremendous controversy. Critics charged that the investigatory and surveillance tools granted law enforcement in the October 2001 USA PATRIOT Act, while necessary in some cases, could likewise be used to persecute political dissidents rather than prosecute terrorists.[105]

Economic Crisis

Presidents also wield emergency powers during periods of serious economic instability. During such times, presidential power appears to emanate exclusively from statutes, although presidents have shown ingenuity in stretching the boundaries of that authority. For example, the Trading with the Enemy Act of 1917 gave the president the authority to impose an array of economic measures in times of war or national emergency. This law was intended as a wartime measure, but it was not repealed at war's end. Subsequent presidents, such as Franklin Roosevelt, delightedly discovered the apparent statutory justification for emergency actions to manage a faltering economy.

Roosevelt's actions had been taken in response to a stark crisis, but Nixon's August 1971 declaration of an emergency in response to a growing imbalance in the U.S. balance of payments struck many observers as overly dramatic. Here, too, however, Nixon had legislative sanction from the Economic Stabilization Act of 1970. The law authorized the president to "issue such orders as he may deem appropriate to stabilize prices, rents, wages and salaries." Nixon announced he was disconnecting the value of the dollar from the gold standard, levying a 10 percent surtax on imports, and freezing domestic prices for ninety days. The overall effect was to devalue the dollar, drive down the prices of U.S. goods overseas, and temporarily halt inflation.[106]

In September 2008 economic crisis returned to center stage as a number of financial institutions faced collapse. Banks, insurers, and mortgage companies were either liquidated or sold for pennies on the dollar—the venerable Lehman Brothers investment firm went bankrupt as the director of the International Monetary Fund warned the world economy was "on the brink of a systemic meltdown."[107]

President George W. Bush urged legislation creating a $700 billion Troubled Asset Relief Program (TARP); the draft bill, only three pages long, gave the administration near-complete discretion to bail out financial institutions (indeed, it read, "decisions by the Secretary pursuant to the authority of this Act are non-reviewable and committed to agency discretion, and may not be reviewed by any court of law or any administrative agency").[108] After much market turmoil a revised version of this legislation was adopted. In 2009 President Obama expanded the spirit if not the letter of TARP by extending it to the automobile companies General Motors and Chrysler, forcing both to restructure their debts and firing the chief executive officer at GM (inevitably now known as "Government Motors").[109] Both auto companies began to repay their government loans, though two years later the United States still owned a quarter of GM. The Obama administration also took unilateral steps to aid homeowners facing foreclosure.

Domestic Unrest and Natural Disaster

Presidential emergency powers include the authority to call out federal troops or to take control of state national guards (descendants of the state militias) to quell domestic unrest or to deter violence. Such authority has been used in the United States to put down illegal labor strikes, ensure delivery of the mail, impose order during natural disasters and urban riots, and prevent volatile situations from exploding.

Before the 1940s, and particularly during the late nineteenth century, presidents became involved in domestic disorders most frequently during labor strikes. Until passage of the Wagner Act of 1935 ensuring the right to collective bargaining and establishing procedures for labor negotiations, strikes usually were considered illegal and often resulted in violence between strikers and company security forces. President Grover Cleveland's use of troops to break the 1894 Pullman strike in Chicago was the most famous example of a practice that had virtually ended by the 1950s. However, in March 1970 President Nixon responded to a postal strike by declaring a state of emergency and calling out federal troops to take over the postal system and keep mail deliveries flowing. Nixon's use of troops to sort and deliver the mail was unusual, but it showed how presidents can react to potential disturbances.

In the 1950s and 1960s presidents relied on federal troops or state national guards to ensure calm during efforts to enforce racial desegregation. The first and perhaps most notable instance was in 1957 when Dwight Eisenhower sent troops into Little Rock, Arkansas, to enforce desegregation of Central High School in the face of resistance from state officials and angry mobs. In 1962 John Kennedy federalized the Mississippi National Guard to ensure the integration of the University of Mississippi, and in 1963 he confronted Alabama governor George Wallace by sending federal troops to enforce the integration of the University of Alabama.

During the late 1960s soldiers were used frequently to quell urban riots or to maintain order during demonstrations against U.S. involvement in Vietnam. For example, the April 1968 assassination of civil rights leader Martin Luther King Jr. sparked widespread rioting throughout more than one hundred cities and forced President Johnson and various governors to call out 55,000 troops. In May 1970 President Nixon directed troops to maintain order on various college campuses after the deaths of some college students during protests against the U.S. incursion into Cambodia. In 1992 George H. W. Bush sent marines to help quell the riots and looting that followed the acquittal of Los Angeles police officers accused in the severe beating of an African American suspect.

Finally, presidential emergency powers are frequently used during natural disasters such as hurricanes, floods, or earthquakes. By declaring a state of emergency in a given locale, the president sets in motion the government machinery that can provide immediate aid, such as food, shelter, and police protection, not to mention longer-term assistance such as federally guaranteed, low-interest home and business loans. This enables the federal government to soften the economic effects of the disaster; not surprisingly, even federalism-minded governors are quick to request such a presidential designation when natural disasters strike. President Clinton made disaster relief a mechanism for building political support after the massive floods along the Mississippi River in 1993 and the Northridge earthquake in southern California the next year. From 2009 to 2011 alone, President Obama issued more than 200 disaster area declarations. However, local reliance on the national government can be a double-edged sword for a president. In 1992 Floridians criticized the tardy response by federal aid agencies to the massive damage caused by Hurricane Andrew that August. In August 2005 Hurricane Katrina devastated the Gulf Coast and especially the city of New Orleans—killing perhaps 2,000, causing $80 billion in damage, and forcing tens of thousands of residents to evacuate their homes. President George W. Bush declared states of emergency in the affected states (covering 90,000 square miles) even before the storm made landfall. But federal officials' slow reaction to, and even apparent denial of, suffering on the ground, all of it broadcast around the clock on television and Internet outlets, prompted widespread anger at the administration's perceived incompetence.[110] In

President Grover Cleveland's suppression of the Pullman Strike of 1894 is an example of presidential enforcement authority. Here, a meat train leaves the Chicago stockyards under escort of U.S. Cavalry.

this area, as in others, expectations for presidential action may be inflated—but they are real.

THE RESURGENCE REGIME

The question of accountability for the unilateral exercise of presidential power emerged with renewed force in the 1970s. The war in Vietnam and Nixon's "incursion" into Cambodia, his excessive use of impoundment, domestic surveillance and other abuses of civil liberties, and, finally, Watergate suggested to many observers an out-of-control "imperial presidency." Congress began to seek ways to limit what was perceived widely as a gradual but systematic aggregation of expansive executive power and its apparent abuses in both the domestic and foreign policy spheres. Throughout the decade legislators erected a "resurgence regime" that aimed to rein in the discretion enjoyed by the chief executive and create a much greater role for congressional advice and consent in interbranch relations.[111] Congress intended to play a key role in authorizing and overseeing America's military deployments and covert adventures, in controlling the nation's finances, and in keeping a close eye on executive corruption.

Even a partial list of enactments gives a sense of the scope of that ambition. For example, the Congressional Budget and Impoundment Control Act of 1974 prohibited unilateral presidential spending decisions and created important centralizing structures (the Budget Committees, the Congressional Budget Office [CBO]) to guide the legislative budget process. In foreign policy, the War Powers Resolution (1973) was enacted to ensure that Congress had a say in the use of U.S. forces. The Case Act of 1972, tightened in 1977, was meant to force the president to reveal the executive agreements with foreign nations negotiated outside of legislative view; the Hughes-Ryan Amendment (1974) and the Intelligence Oversight Act (1980) were passed to keep legislators informed of covert operations. The Non-Detention Act (1971), the Justice Department's own Domestic Intelligence Guidelines (1976), and the 1972 *Keith* decision[112] and 1978 Foreign Intelligence Surveillance Act (FISA) all limited presidents' security powers at home. The National Emergencies Act of 1976 terminated ongoing states of emergency as well as the attendant emergency presidential powers and mandated that future states of emergency would lapse after six months unless renewed.

The executive branch's workings were to be made more transparent through an expanded Freedom of Information Act (1974), various "government in the sunshine" laws, and the timely release of presidential documents mandated by the 1974 Presidential Materials and Presidential Records Act of 1978. In 1974 the Supreme Court ruled in *U.S. v. Nixon* that the president's power to assert "executive privilege" was not absolute and could be reviewed by the courts. The role of money in politics was to be diminished by a new Federal Election Commission established by the Federal Election Campaign Act of 1974; and should all this fail, investigations of executive malfeasance would be conducted under a new independent counsel operation created by the Ethics in Government Act (1978).

Meanwhile, the use of legislative vetoes increased even as federal programs received shorter-term authorizations to ensure more frequent congressional reviews of executive agencies. Congress also dramatically expanded its own institutional capacities for overseeing the executive branch by hiring thousands of additional staff and by creating or expanding congressional support agencies such as the General Accounting Office (renamed the Government Accountability Office in 2004) and CBO.

The "New" Imperial Presidency?

In the late 1970s, Congress appeared to have successfully limited presidential discretion. Ex-president Gerald Ford complained that "We have not an imperial presidency but an imperiled presidency. Under today's rules . . . the presidency does not operate effectively."[113]

But the resurgence regime was itself built on fragile foundations. Even in the decade following Nixon's resignation, the office of the presidency retained a solid base of authority grounded in the powers and strategies traced throughout this chapter. Especially after Ronald Reagan's

election in 1980, presidents aggressively used many of these unilateral tools—from regulatory review to signing statements to recess appointments—to enhance their influence over bureaucratic agencies and avoid legislative dictation.

The statutory side of the resurgence regime also crumbled. In some cases, as in the IEEPA example above, efforts to specify the limits of presidential powers gave statutory status to powers earlier exercised only informally. In other cases, Congress itself backed away from using the processes it had created to challenge the president, or failed to make them work. Most dramatically, the War Powers Resolution did not rein in presidents' use of force, as myriad post-1973 unilateral military deployments, from Grenada to Kosovo, suggest. In the latter example, although 800 U.S. aircraft flew more than 20,000 air sorties against 2,000 Serbian targets, Bill Clinton did not deem that troops had, in the language of the War Powers Resolution, been "introduced into hostilities or into situations where imminent involvement in hostilities is clearly indicated by the circumstances."[114] In 2011 Barack Obama not only discounted the need for legislative approval to commit U.S. forces to a North Atlantic Treaty Organization (NATO) operation in Libya but argued the operation did not count as "hostilities" at all. House Speaker John Boehner (R-Ohio) responded that this claim "defie[d] rational thought." But Congress did not act to restrain presidential action.[115]

The Congressional Budget Act, likewise, failed to bring discipline to federal spending; deficits veered upward in the 1980s, and again, even more sharply, in the 2000s after a brief blip into surplus ended in fiscal 2001. Perhaps more important, the deliberative process laid out in 1974 was often honored in the breach: though thirteen budget bills each year required passage, in the ten fiscal years 2002 through 2011, a *total* of eleven such bills—barely one per year—were passed by the October 1 deadline. The outcome of late budgets and the massive omnibus bills that resulted was to increase the president's veto leverage, especially after Clinton's successful showdown with the Republican Congress in 1995–1996.[116] In fiscal 2008, for instance, the budget finally passed three months into the fiscal year, after Congress failed to override George W. Bush's vetoes aimed at preventing limits on timing or funding for the Iraq War.

To be sure, not every element of the resurgence receded at once, or for all time. Most obviously, Clinton's impeachment and trial in 1998–1999 was the first since 1868 and the first ever of an elected president. Yet while it seems strange to talk about congressional deference in that context, even this period highlighted the potential powers of the president and renewed legislative acquiescence to their use. Clinton himself set the tone after the Democrats lost Congress in 1994: "I think now we have a better balance of both using the Presidency as a bully pulpit and the President's power of the Presidency to do things, actually accomplish things, and . . . not permitting the presidency to be defined only by relations with the Congress."[117] In 1998 cruise missiles were fired at Sudan and Afghanistan at the president's order even as the House debated his fate. The very process of impeachment—in the face of hostile public opinion—helped to discredit it, and to encourage the expiration of the independent counsel statute in 1999.[118]

But it was the George W. Bush administration, beginning in 2001, that expended the most systematic effort in rebuilding, and aggressively justifying, the post-Watergate unilateral infrastructure. "I have an obligation to make sure that the Presidency remains robust. I'm not going to let Congress erode the power of the executive branch," Bush noted in 2002. Vice President Richard Cheney, who got started in political life as a staffer in the Nixon White House, argued that he had "repeatedly seen an erosion of the powers and the ability of the president . . . to do his job," thanks to the resurgence regime.[119]

In some areas, that attitude was translated into action even before the 2001 terrorist attacks. As noted above, the Bush administration cracked down on Freedom of Information Act releases, increased federal executives' ability to withhold information from public view, and issued an executive order to expand past administrations' capacity to delay or bar the opening of historical records. Legislative requests for information were also routinely denied or delayed. The administration went to court, successfully, to defend its ability to withhold—even without formally claiming executive privilege—documents from congressional auditors or others seeking information about the energy task force headed by Vice President Cheney.[120]

The brutal September 11, 2001, attacks on New York and Washington, D.C., however, brought tremendous renewed visibility and leverage to the presidential office. President Bush acted aggressively to move the country onto a war footing, and on a variety of fronts legislators hastened to expand his authority. A $40 billion Emergency Response Fund was immediately appropriated for the president to use as he saw fit in assisting victims of the attack and strengthening national security. And with just one dissenting vote in either chamber—most Senate discussion of the bill actually took place after the vote—Congress passed a resolution three days after the attacks, stating that "the president has authority under the Constitution to take action to deter and prevent acts of international terrorism against the United States" and granting him the power to use "all necessary and appropriate force against those nations, organizations, or persons he determines planned, authorized, committed, or aided the terrorist attacks that occurred on September 11, 2001, or harbored such organizations or persons, in order to prevent any future acts of international terrorism against the United States. . . ."[121] This Authorization for the Use of Military Force (AUMF), used first in the overthrow of the

Taliban regime in Afghanistan, would become critical to justifying far-flung executive action. On the domestic front, the USA PATRIOT Act, which Congress passed rapidly to administration specifications in October 2001, enhanced the executive's prosecutorial tools and power to conduct criminal investigations by relaxing limits on surveillance and softening the barrier between domestic law enforcement and foreign intelligence gathering. The Patriot Act was renewed, largely unchanged, in spring 2006 and again in 2011.[122]

In the fall of 2002, Congress passed another broad delegation of authority to use force against Iraq. This came after the administration's September 2002 *National Security Strategy of the United States* urged preemptive (thus, executive-driven) action against potential threats.[123] Despite the 1991 Gulf War and a decade of sanctions, Saddam Hussein remained in control of Iraq, and most U.S. policymakers believed he retained weapons of mass destruction of some sort. Soon after the 2001 attacks, the president ordered that invasion options be prepared. In early 2002 he signed a secret order giving the CIA authority to assassinate Saddam Hussein. By summer military planning was well under way.[124]

The White House counsel's office advised the president that war with Iraq would not require legislative approval. The argument was (1) that the president's commander-in-chief powers were themselves sufficient; (2) that the AUMF already encompassed it; and (3) that the congressional resolution from the first Gulf War granted any necessary authority, since Iraq had violated the terms of the 1991 cease-fire. However, this was not a question of repelling a sudden attack on the United States or an ally; nor could it be argued there was no time for congressional deliberation. There was little evidence to tie the Iraqi regime to the September 11 attacks, and the 1991 resolution spoke only to the liberation of Kuwait.[125] Thus, given that legislators seemed willing and even eager to authorize war, the Bush administration asked in October 2002 for discretionary power to use force against Iraq. Legislators removed sweeping language from the president's draft that would have allowed him to use "all means" to "restore international peace and security in the region," but the final wording was broad nonetheless: the president was "authorized to use the Armed Forces of the United States as he determines to be necessary and appropriate in order to defend the national security of the United States against the continuing threat posed by Iraq." Though UN weapons inspectors were unsuccessful in locating weapons of mass destruction (WMDs), American air strikes began in March 2003, followed quickly by ground forces. Troops would not end combat operations until 2010; they left Iraq entirely at the end of 2011.

Through fiscal 2011, Congress had approved more than $1.36 trillion in spending, largely in supplemental appropriations bills outside the normal budget process, for military and reconstruction operations in Afghanistan and Iraq (additional spending on intelligence and covert operations was undisclosed, but substantial). WMDs were never found, leading to questions about the efficacy of U.S. intelligence operations and whether the administration had overstated the threat posed by the Iraqi regime and understated the potential costs of the operation.[126]

Despite the legislative deference he received after the attacks on September 11, 2001, President Bush often preferred to act alone rather than ask for congressional sanction. The administration's interpretation of the commander-in-chief power was perhaps broadest, and certainly most controversial. It was grounded in the idea that the executive power is indivisible (and thus that the commander-in-chief power is separable from Congress's overlapping powers to declare war and to provide for the regulation of armed forces and hostilities), a strong version of what is known as "unitary executive" theory. In its mildest iteration, that theory—drawn from Article II's vesting clause—simply holds that all of the executive powers under the Constitution are exercised by the president, but does not dictate what the "executive power" might mean in substance. In more extreme versions, as endorsed by the George W. Bush administration, the theory holds not only that Congress cannot infringe on the executive power but that only the president himself can determine the boundaries of that power.[127]

Such "unitarian" logic underlay a number of the administration's claims. In October 2001, for instance, President Bush issued a secret executive order authorizing the National Security Agency (NSA) to track communications between individuals abroad with suspected terrorist connections and Americans within the United States. This action was contrary to FISA, the 1978 law noted above, which required issuance of a warrant by a special surveillance court in such cases. FISA did allow for wiretapping for fifteen days after the declaration of war, and for emergency wiretaps for up to seventy-two hours (increased from twenty-four hours after September 11) before issuance of a warrant.

When the initiative was revealed by the media in late 2005, the administration dubbed it the "Terrorist Surveillance Program" and argued that the president had both inherent and statutory power to order such wiretaps. "My legal authority is derived from the Constitution, as well as the [September 2001] authorization of force by the United States Congress," President Bush told a news conference.[128] A 2006 Justice Department white paper defending the NSA program argued that far from violating FISA, the president was following its letter, since AUMF should be read as direct statutory approval for the wiretapping program. In this reading, wiretapping was a "fundamental incident" of warfare similar

to the detention of enemy combatants approved by the Supreme Court elsewhere (see the *Hamdi v. Rumsfeld* case, below). In addition, the Justice Department argued,

> the NSA activities are supported by the President's well-recognized inherent constitutional authority as Commander in Chief and sole organ for the Nation in foreign affairs to conduct warrantless surveillance of enemy forces for intelligence purposes to detect and disrupt armed attacks on the United States. The President has the chief responsibility under the Constitution to protect America from attack, and the Constitution gives the President the authority necessary to fulfill that solemn responsibility.[129]

Because neither FISA nor Congress generally could limit the president's "core exercise of Commander in Chief control," the administration argued that any statute that sought to do so was simply unconstitutional and did not need to be enforced.

Similar claims were made about confidentiality, as noted above, in the George W. Bush administration's consistent claim in signing statements that legislatively imposed reporting requirements would be treated as advisory requests. The theory was also prominent in the administration's treatment of prisoners captured during various anti-terror operations after 2001, a policy largely devised via executive order and memo.[130] Some detainees were kept at so-called "black sites" run secretly by the CIA around the world. Hundreds more were imprisoned at the custom-built prison at the U.S. naval base in Guantanamo Bay, Cuba. Those captured in Afghanistan were given a blanket designation by the president not as prisoners-of-war (POW) but rather as "unlawful enemy combatants," without the rights POW status confers.[131] One result, in practice, was that previous army regulations constraining interrogation methods were superseded, setting off an extended controversy over the definition of torture and the relationship of extreme interrogation methods to U.S. law. Techniques employed at Guantanamo Bay were apparently transferred to other military facilities, often in tragically embellished form. The most notorious example was at the Abu Ghraib prison outside Baghdad in 2004. By 2005 CIA personnel had been implicated in the deaths of at least four prisoners in agency custody. Late that year the president conceded the existence of the "black sites"; around the same time, the practice of "extraordinary rendition," which involved sending prisoners abroad for interrogation in countries unencumbered by due process of law, also came to light.[132] The president repeatedly insisted that "we do not torture," but at the same time his Office of Legal Counsel (OLC) issued legal definitions of torture that many observers criticized as overly narrow.[133]

In any case, as a memo constructed by a working group of administration attorneys concluded, "in order to respect the President's inherent constitutional authority to manage a military campaign, [the prohibition against torture] as well as any other potentially applicable statute must be construed as inapplicable to interrogations undertaken pursuant to his Commander-in-Chief authority."[134] Congress could not encroach on the exercise of that authority. Thus, as noted above in the discussion of signing statements, when legislators did overwhelmingly approve limits on interrogation procedures, the president asserted his right to implement those procedures "consistent with the constitutional authority of the President to oversee the unitary executive branch and as Commander in Chief."

José Padilla, center, was designated an "enemy combatant" by the George W. Bush administration in 2002. Because of unilateral action by the president, Padilla was able to be held in prison for three years without ever being officially charged with criminal allegations.

Barack Obama campaigned against some of Bush's strongest claims, and upon taking office in 2009, he set some of them aside. He issued orders "ensuring legal interrogations" (notably rescinding the Justice Department's post–September 11, 2001, opinions regarding torture and the executive authorizations that flowed from them). He revoked Bush's orders regarding regulatory review and reined in the wider diffusion of authority departments had to classify information.[135] He also issued an executive order aiming to close the detention facility at Guantanamo Bay within a year.

However, Congress put in place repeated statutory restrictions that made that closure impossible. Obama complained, but did not seek to unilaterally override the law.

Indeed, the Obama administration claimed its power flowed from statute rather than from some fount of inherent authority. Sometimes this was quite clear: FISA, for example, was amended in 2008 to authorize the previously unilateral surveillance program, and President Obama continued to exercise powers under the new law. More often the administration argued that the AUMF provided statutory authority to underwrite the war powers. This sometimes led to actions quite similar to those utilized by George W. Bush, and sometimes beyond them. In one notable case in 2011, an unmanned drone was used to kill two American citizens in Yemen, one of whom (Anwar Awlaki) had allegedly masterminded several attempted terrorist attacks against the United States. The Obama administration argued this targeted attack, even far from the Afghan or Iraqi fronts, was within the laws of war as they applied to the war on terror. As Obama's White House counsel argued, his boss was "mindful as president of the United States not to do anything that would undermine or weaken the institution of the presidency."[136]

This implied other important continuities across the administrations. For example, "extraordinary renditions" continued. So did the use of the "state secrets" doctrine to keep sensitive issues out of the court system, even as the number of classified documents rose (rather than declining, as the early Obama order had implied). And so did efforts by the administration to bypass the civilian justice system. President Bush had asserted that in time of war he was empowered to detain indefinitely without charge or counsel even American citizens arrested within the United States. The designation of this sort of "enemy combatant" was, according to the president, entirely up to him; judges and legislators had no power even to review that status.[137] Under this principle U.S. citizens Yaser Hamdi, captured on the Afghan battlefield, and José Padilla, arrested at Chicago's O'Hare Airport, were held in isolation in a military brig for as long as three and a half years. In its 2004 decision in *Hamdi v. Rumsfeld,* the Supreme Court rejected the notion that the executive had sole discretion over the designation of combatants and required that they receive at least some procedural safeguards: "A state of war is not a blank check for the President when it comes to the rights of the Nation's citizens," the majority held.[138]

However, a plurality of the court held that the AUMF did constitute affirmative legislative delegation to the president sufficient to name enemy combatants in the first place. The 1971 Non-Detention Act was held inapplicable to Hamdi's case since taking prisoners was so central to armed conflict that "it is of no moment" that the AUMF did not specifically override it. As a result, a circuit court panel upheld José Padilla's detention as well, though in late 2005 the administration formally charged Padilla with criminal conspiracy and moved him to the civilian court system.[139]

Despite the conviction, the Padilla criminal case was marred by controversy over his treatment by military interrogators, raising questions about the utility of the criminal courts in such cases.[140] Questions arose as well over how the other, noncitizen, detainees noted above were to be tried—if at all. President Bush proposed using a system of military tribunals created by presidential "military order" in November 2001. In drafting the order the administration relied heavily on World War II–era precedents stemming from the case of German saboteurs captured within the United States. While the use of tribunals has a long history, critics charged that they were inappropriate in this case, that Congress had the power to regulate the detention regime, and that the president had in any case tailored tribunal procedures in ways that limited the rights of the accused.[141]

Though the order stated that individuals bound over for the tribunals had no right to "seek any remedy" in state or federal court, prisoners did challenge the legality of their detention (asserting *habeas corpus* rights despite their status as noncitizens) and the process by which their status was to be determined. In *Hamdan v. Rumsfeld,* decided in June 2006, the Supreme Court held that the structure and procedures of the tribunal system as established—particularly its rules of evidence—violated both the Geneva Conventions and the Uniform Code of Military Justice (UCMJ). The justices did not address the president's power to detain Hamdan or others for the duration of hostilities. But they held that the AUMF was insufficient grounds for the president to establish tribunals that deviated from standard court-martials and that doing so required legislative sanction.[142] The various enemy combatant cases combined when President Bush responded to the *Hamdan* decision by proposing the Military Commissions Act of 2006. As passed by Congress in October of that year, the act amended the UCMJ to provide legal authority for the tribunals at Guantanamo Bay, allowing for amended evidentiary standards and immunizing U.S. personnel against criminal prosecution for interrogation tactics short of torture occurring before passage of the 2005 Detainee Treatment Act. The act also retroactively stripped detainees of the right to file *habeas corpus* petitions in federal court; this portion of the law, however, was later overturned by yet another Supreme Court decision, *Boumediene v. Bush.*[143] The definition of "unlawful enemy combatant" was put in statute but left wide room for executive discretion: it could include any "person who has engaged in hostilities or who has purposefully and materially supported hostilities against the United States or its co-belligerents who is not a lawful enemy combatant."[144] The Obama administration, after announcing that high-profile detainees would be tried in civilian courts,

backed down under public and legislative pressure and eventually issued a 2011 executive order restarting the military tribunal process, stressing the "executive branch's continued discretionary exercise of existing detention authority."[145] In early 2012 the system was expanded for the first time to include a defendant not accused of being part of the war with al Qaeda.[146]

As this suggests, presidential power may be insisted upon by others as well as claimed by presidents themselves. In the FISA Amendments and Military Commissions Acts legislators followed an old pattern in regularizing many of the powers previously claimed unilaterally by the president. The war on terror swept away what remained of the resurgence regime of the 1970s, which no longer bound, or even guided, legislative-executive interaction. President Bush, given the extraordinary circumstances after the terrorist strikes of 2001, was a particular beneficiary of this practice. Congressional oversight over executive behavior was largely absent, prompting bipartisan accusation that the legislature had become a "broken branch."[147]

Oversight increased during periods of divided government, such as after the 2006 and 2010 midterm elections. But such division also caused legislative dysfunction and made it hard for Congress to unify against presidential unilateralism. The precedents already set suggested that future presidents would rely upon a "normal" balance of presidential-congressional power far more tilted toward the "imperial" end of the spectrum than could have been foreseen by the post-Watergate generation of legislators—or, for that matter, by the Framers of the Constitution.

Unitary Executives in the Constitutional Framework

As noted at the outset of this chapter, the Framers sought to build interlocking institutions that would provide "those who administer each department the necessary constitutional means and personal motives to resist encroachments of the others."[148] The goal was to separate institutions rather than to separate powers; in fact, powers would necessarily overlap to the extent required to give each branch some ability to prevent unilateral action by the others. American government is therefore prone to tremendous inertia, even stalemate. Despite the consistent, and often successful, efforts of presidents over two centuries and more to expand their institutional resources past the sparse grants of Article II, they ultimately remain subject to its constraints.

Unilateral presidential power, then, is a real temptation for presidents, legislators, and the public alike. But as Supreme Court justice Robert Jackson explained in 1952, such power suggests "both practical advantages and grave dangers for the country."[149]

The practical advantages are clear. After all, how can one provide direction to an enormous nation, with an enormous

JUSTICE JACKSON'S TEST OF PRESIDENTIAL EMERGENCY POWERS

Justice Robert Jackson's concurring opinion in *Youngstown Sheet and Tube Co. v. Sawyer* (1952)—dealing with President Harry Truman's order seizing the nation's steel mills to prevent a strike during the Korean War—remains a classic analysis of the conditions under which a president may possess and exercise extraordinary powers.[1] More important, Jackson's dispassionate examination suggests when emergency prerogative powers may not exist.

Mr. Justice Jackson, concurring:

The actual art of governing under our Constitution does not and cannot conform to judicial definitions of the power of any of its branches based on isolated clauses or even single Articles torn from context. While the Constitution diffuses power the better to secure liberty, it also contemplates that practice will integrate the dispersed powers into a workable government. It enjoins upon its branches separateness but interdependence, autonomy but reciprocity. Presidential powers are not fixed but fluctuate, depending upon their disjunction or conjunction with those of Congress....

1. When the President acts pursuant to an express or implied authorization of Congress, his authority is at its maximum, for it includes all that he possesses in his own right plus all that Congress can delegate. In these circumstances, and in these only, may he be said (for what it may be worth) to personify the federal sovereignty. If his act is held unconstitutional under these circumstances, it usually means that the Federal Government as an undivided whole lacks power. A seizure executed by the President pursuant to an Act of Congress would be supported by the strongest of presumptions and the widest latitude of judicial interpretation, and the burden of persuasion would rest heavily upon any who might attack it.

2. When the President acts in absence of either a congressional grant or denial of authority, he can only rely upon his own independent powers, but there is a zone of twilight in which he and Congress may have concurrent authority, or in which its distribution is uncertain. Therefore, congressional inertia, indifference or quiescence may sometimes, at least as a practical matter, enable, if not invite, measures on independent presidential responsibility. In this area, any actual test of power is likely to depend on the imperatives of events and contemporary imponderables rather than on abstract theories of law.

3. When the President takes measures incompatible with the expressed or implied will of Congress, his power is at its lowest ebb, for then he can rely only upon his own constitutional powers minus any constitutional powers of Congress over the matter. Courts can sustain exclusive presidential control in such a case only by disabling the Congress from acting upon the subject. Presidential claim to a power at once so conclusive and preclusive must be scrutinized with caution, for what is at stake is the equilibrium established by our constitutional system.

Into which of these classifications does this executive seizure of the steel industry fit? It is eliminated from the first by admission, for it is conceded that no congressional authorization exists for this seizure....

Can it then be defended under flexible tests available to the second category? It seems clearly eliminated from that class because Congress has not left seizure of private property an open field but has covered it by three statutory policies inconsistent with this seizure.... None of these were invoked. In choosing a different and inconsistent way of his own, the President cannot claim that it is necessitated or invited by failure of Congress to legislate upon the occasions, grounds, and methods for seizure of industrial properties.

This leaves the current seizure to be justified only by the severe tests under the third grouping, where it can be supported only by any remainder of executive power after subtraction of such powers as Congress may have over the subject. In short, we can sustain the President only by holding that seizure of such strike-bound industries is within his domain and beyond control of Congress. Thus, this court's first review of such seizures occurs under circumstances which leave presidential power most vulnerable to attack and in the least favorable of possible constitutional postures....

[N]o doctrine that the Court could promulgate would seem to me more sinister and alarming than that a President whose conduct of foreign affairs is so largely uncontrolled, and often even is unknown, can vastly enlarge his mastery over the internal affairs of the country by his own commitment of the Nation's armed forces to some foreign venture.... No penance would ever expiate the sin against free government of holding that a President can escape control of executive powers by law through assuming his military role....

The essence of our free Government is "leave to live by no man's leave, underneath the law"—to be governed by those impersonal forces which we call law.... With all its defects, delays and inconveniences, men have discovered no technique for long preserving free government except that the Executive be under the law, and that the law be made by parliamentary deliberations.

1. *Youngstown Sheet and Tube Co. v. Sawyer*, 343 U.S. 579 (1952).

---

national executive establishment and enormous public expectations, and still hope to limit the authority necessary to meet those needs? Congress—even a Congress suspicious of executive power—will not abolish the discretionary presidency. During a crisis, especially, quick and forceful response is required; while the structural constraints imposed by "separate institutions sharing powers"[150] might be maddening to participants in normal times, they could be fatal to the republic when crisis or war intrudes. The problems of administration that arose during the Articles of Confederation period in a much smaller country, with a much smaller Congress, in what seemed a much larger world, were sufficient to drive the Framers to submerge their fear of monarchy and empower a single person as president. A globalized, polarized world seems to call out for endowing leadership sufficient to match its powers to the tasks at hand. Abraham Lincoln, in defending his remarkable usurpation of power during the early months of the Civil War, asked simply, "Must a government of necessity be too strong for the liberties of its people, or too weak to maintain its own existence?"[151]

Lincoln's experiences during the Civil War were unique, but history is dotted with other moments when this dilemma emerged powerfully. Yet while few doubt the need for presidents to wield extraordinary powers in times when the crisis is apparent to all, debates rage when claims to emergency powers seem overstated. Indeed, the dangers of unilateral authority are indeed "grave," because once those claims are asserted they logically admit no limits. And a crisis model of presidential leadership may foster in the White House itself a view of the office that should exist only during crises: the quick response to problems with little deliberation or consultation with Congress, the temptation to resort to extraconstitutional (even unconstitutional) means to achieve important ends, and the tendency to function as if the president were above the law. Such attitudes—which some observers saw in Nixon's 1970 decision to invade Cambodia, Reagan's efforts to support rebels in Nicaragua, Clinton's tussle with the independent counsel's office, or George W. Bush's broadest claims of commander-in-chief authority—ultimately may do the institution of the presidency more harm than good, if they invite congressional and public backlash. Even Locke's version of prerogative had crucial checks; it was only legitimate as it reflected the public commonweal, and executive control in the absence of legislative direction was temporary, good only until "the Legislature can be conveniently assembled to provide for it."[152] Laws can be amended; but in a government under the law, they cannot be long ignored. In that very American context the constraints on prerogative are even stronger.

The long struggle between presidential claims to extraordinary powers and the right of Congress to impose its constitutional will probably will never be resolved entirely. Nor is there any one right resolution. In our separated system, legitimating large-scale change requires bridging its divisions by persuasion and coalition. While executive discretion is, in fact, increasingly important, the framework within which that discretion may be exercised—the beating of the bounds between the branches—is not a matter for decree but deliberation. While presidents' arguments have been distinctly unitarian, the Constitution is in turn devoutly trinitarian. Ambition, Americans should hope, will continue to counteract ambition.

NOTES

1 Edward S. Corwin, *The President: Office and Powers,* 5th rev. ed., with Randall W. Bland, Theodore Hinson, and Jack W. Peltason (New York: New York University Press, 1984), 3.

2 Jack N. Rakove, *Original Meanings: Politics and Ideas in the Making of the Constitution* (New York: Vintage, 1997), 249–59; James Madison, *Federalist* No. 48, in Alexander Hamilton, James Madison, and John Jay, *The Federalist Papers,* with an introduction by Clinton L. Rossiter (New York: New American Library, 1961). All citations to *The Federalist Papers* are to this edition.

3 "Cato," Letter V of November 22, 1787, in *The Anti-Federalist Papers and the Constitutional Convention Debates,* ed. Ralph Ketcham (New York: Mentor, 1986), 317; in response, see especially Alexander Hamilton, *Federalist* No. 69.

4 Alexander Hamilton, *Federalist* No. 70; John Jay, *Federalist* No. 64; "The Pacificus-Helvidius Letters," in *The Evolving Presidency,* 2d ed., ed. Michael Nelson (Washington, D.C.: CQ Press, 2004), 39–47.

5 "Pacificus-Helvidius Letters"; Grover Cleveland, *The Independence of the Executive* (Princeton: Princeton University Press, 1913), 14–15.

6 Theodore Roosevelt, *An Autobiography* (New York: Da Capo Press, 1985), 372; Ryan J. Barilleaux, "Venture Constitutionalism and the Enlargement of the Presidency," in *Executing the Constitution: Putting the President Back into the Constitution,* ed. Christopher S. Kelly (Albany: State University of New York Press, 2005).

7 John Locke, *Second Treatise of Government,* ed. C. B. Macpherson (Indianapolis: Hackett, 1980 [1690]), 84. See also Michael A. Genovese, *Presidential Prerogative* (Stanford: Stanford University Press, 2011).

8 Lincoln letter to Albert G. Hodges, April 4, 1864, reprinted in *The President, Congress, and the Constitution: Power and Legitimacy in American Politics,* ed. Christopher H. Pyle and Richard M. Pious (New York: Free Press, 1984), 65; see, too, his Message to Congress, July 4, 1861.

9 "Pacificus-Helvidius Letters," emphases in original. However, see Madison's argument in *Federalist* No. 41 regarding the extra-constitutional demands of national self-preservation.

10 William Howard Taft, "*Our Chief Magistrate and His Powers*" (1916), in Pyle and Pious, *President, Congress, and the Constitution,* 70–71.

11 See, for example, David Gray Adler and Michael A. Genovese, "Introduction," in *The Presidency and the Law: The Clinton Legacy,* ed. David Gray Adler and Michael A. Genovese (Lawrence: University Press of Kansas, 2002).

12 For a detailed recounting, see Andrew Rudalevige, *The New Imperial Presidency: Renewing Presidential Power after Watergate* (Ann Arbor: University of Michigan Press, 2005), which informs much of this chapter.

13 *In re Neagle,* 135 U.S. 1 (1890); see also Corwin, *President: Office and Powers,* 170–171. A dissenting opinion sardonically noted that the presidential oath of office also included fealty to Article I ("the Congress shall have powers . . . to make all laws. . . .").

14 Leonard White, *The Federalists* (New York: Macmillan, 1948), 512.

15 "Pacificus-Helvidius Letters"; Stanley Elkins and Eric McKitrick, *The Age of Federalism: The Early American Republic, 1788–1800* (New York: Oxford University Press, 1993), 336–365.

16 Jefferson to John V. Colvin, September 10, 1810, reprinted in Pyle and Pious, *President, Congress, and the Constitution,* 62.

17 *Ex parte Merryman,* 17 Fed. Cas. 9487 (1861). Note that while the Constitution anticipates the possibility of suspending the

writ in times of "rebellion or invasion," this is enumerated in Article I.

18 Clinton Rossiter, *Constitutional Dictatorship* (Princeton: Princeton University Press, 1948); and see Richard M. Pious, *The American Presidency* (New York: Basic Books, 1979), 55–60.

19 *Prize Cases,* 67 U.S. (2 Black) 635 (1863). However, as Arthur M. Schlesinger Jr. points out, the justices endorsed such executive power only in cases of domestic rebellions or invasions, and not, as some later presidents asserted, for use against other sovereign nations. See Schlesinger, *The Imperial Presidency* (Boston: Houghton Mifflin, 1973), 64–66. For a defense of Lincoln's notion of prerogative power, see Benjamin Kleinerman, *The Discretionary President* (Lawrence: University Press of Kansas, 2009).

20 Leonard White, *The Jeffersonians* (New York: Macmillan, 1951), 552.

21 *Martin v. Mott,* 12 Wheat. 19, 23–33 (1827).

22 Hoar quoted in Wilfred E. Binkley, *President and Congress,* 3d rev. ed. (New York: Vintage, 1962), 185.

23 *Ex parte Milligan,* 71 U.S. (4 Wall.) 2 (1866).

24 Binkley, *President and Congress,* chaps. 8–9; *In re Neagle,* 135 U.S. 1 (1890).

25 *In re Debs,* 158 U.S. 564 (1895); *U.S. v. Midwest Oil Co.,* 236 U.S. 459 (1915).

26 James Ceaser, *Presidential Selection* (Princeton: Princeton University Press, 1979), 170 and chap. 4.

27 Pious, *American Presidency,* 49.

28 Corwin, *President: Office and Powers,* 269–270.

29 From his 1908 book *Constitutional Government in the United States,* quoted in Binkley, *President and Congress,* 215.

30 Richard E. Neustadt, *Presidential Power: The Politics of Leadership* (New York: Wiley, 1960), 5.

31 Fred I. Greenstein, "Toward a Modern Presidency," in Greenstein, ed., *Leadership in the Modern Presidency* (Cambridge, Mass.: Harvard University Press, 1988), 3; William E. Leuchtenburg, *In the Shadow of FDR: From Harry Truman to Ronald Reagan* (Ithaca: Cornell University Press, 1983).

32 Louis Fisher, *Presidential Spending Power* (Princeton: Princeton University Press, 1975), 61–64.

33 Franklin D. Roosevelt, "Message to Congress on Stabilizing the Economy," September 7, 1942; much of the text was repeated in FDR's radio address that evening.

34 *United States v. Curtiss-Wright Export Corp.,* 299 U.S. 304 (1936). But for a critique of the decision and the use presidents have made of it, see Louis Fisher, "Presidential Inherent Power: The 'Sole Organ' Doctrine," *Presidential Studies Quarterly* 37 (March 2007): 139–52.

35 See Ibid.; Pious, *American Presidency;* John Roche, "Executive Power and the Domestic Presidency: The Quest for Prerogative," *Western Political Quarterly* 5 (December 1952); Barton J. Bernstein, "The Road to Watergate and Beyond: The Growth and Abuse of Executive Authority Since 1940," *Law and Contemporary Problems* 40 (spring 1976).

36 Bernstein, "Road to Watergate," 64; Robert H. Jackson, *That Man: An Insider's Portrait of Franklin D. Roosevelt* (New York: Oxford University Press, 2003), 68–73.

37 *Korematsu v. United States,* 323 U.S. 214 (1944); Civil Liberties Act of 1988 (P.L. 100-383).

38 Neustadt, *Presidential Power,* 3.

39 It is worth noting that the postwar crisis was not just de facto but de jure. The United States officially lived under a state of declared national emergency from 1933 to 1975: Roosevelt's bank emergency (1933), Truman's mobilization after North Korea's invasion of South Korea (1950), Nixon's use of troops to maintain mail deliveries (1970), and Nixon's response to international economic conditions (1971), all remained in force until passage of the National Emergencies Act in 1976. On the role of nuclear weaponry in presidential power, see Garry Wills, *Bomb Power: The Modern Presidency and the National Security State* (New York: Penguin Press, 2010).

40 Allen Schick, "Politics Through Law: Congressional Limitations on Executive Discretion," in *Both Ends of the Avenue,* ed. Anthony King (Washington, D.C.: AEI Press, 1983), 161; James Lindsay, "Deference and Defiance: The Shifting Rhythms of Executive-Legislative Relations in Foreign Policy," *Presidential Studies Quarterly* 33 (September 2003): 530–546.

41 Corwin, *President: Office and Powers,* 4. See, for example, James MacGregor Burns, *Presidential Government: The Crucible of Leadership* (Boston: Houghton Mifflin, 1965). A contemporary version of this argument can be found in James Sundquist, *Constitutional Reform and Effective Government* (Washington, D.C.: Brookings, 1986); and, as regards foreign affairs, in John Yoo, *The Powers of War and Peace* (Chicago: University of Chicago Press, 2005).

42 Schlesinger, *Imperial Presidency;* Rudalevige, *New Imperial Presidency,* chap. 2.

43 Greenstein, "Toward a Modern Presidency," 3.

44 Sorensen quoted in Samuel Kernell, *Going Public: New Strategies of Presidential Leadership,* 3d ed. (Washington, D.C.: CQ Press, 1997), 86.

45 Andrew Rudalevige, *Managing the President's Program: Presidential Leadership and Legislative Policy Formulation* (Princeton: Princeton University Press, 2002), chap. 3; "President Bush on Iraq, Immigration, and Elections" (interview transcript), *Washington Post,* December 20, 2006, A16.

46 Statements of Administration Policy may be found on the Office of Management and Budget website, www.whitehouse.gov/omb/legislative_sap_default.html.

47 Charles M. Cameron, *Veto Bargaining: Presidents and the Politics of Negative Power* (New York: Cambridge University Press, 2000); *Weekly Compilation of Presidential Documents* (April 26, 2002), 692.

48 This figure includes approximately 700,000 postal employees and 1.4 million military personnel.

49 Terry Moe, "The Politicized Presidency," in *The New Direction in American Politics,* ed. John E. Chubb and Paul E. Peterson (Washington, D.C.: Brookings, 1985); Scott C. James, "The Evolution of the Presidency: Between the Promise and the Fear," in *The Executive Branch,* ed. Joel D. Aberbach and Mark A. Peterson (New York: Oxford University Press, 2005), 27–30; Bert A. Rockman, ed., "Symposium on the Administrative Presidency," special issue of *Presidential Studies Quarterly* 39 (March 2009).

50 See John Burke, *The Institutional Presidency,* 2d ed. (Baltimore: Johns Hopkins University Press, 2000); Matthew J. Dickinson, *Bitter Harvest: FDR, Presidential Power, and the Growth of the Presidential Branch* (New York: Cambridge University Press, 1997); Karen M. Hult and Charles E. Walcott, *Empowering the White House: Governance under Nixon, Ford, and Carter* (Lawrence: University Press of Kansas, 2003); David E. Lewis, "Staffing Alone: Unilateral Action and the Politicization of the Executive Office of the President," *Presidential Studies Quarterly* 35 (September 2005): 496–514.

51 Fisher, *Presidential Spending Power,* 36.

52 Steven A. Shull, *Policy by Other Means: Alternative Adoption by Presidents* (College Station: Texas A&M Press, 2006), 73.

53 Executive Order 8248.

54 John Hart, *The Presidential Branch,* 2d ed. (Chatham, N.J.: Chatham House, 1995). On the tensions between Congress and the presidency over the direction of public policy, see Charles O. Jones, *The Presidency in a Separated System,* 2d ed. (Washington, D.C.: Brookings, 2005); Joel Aberbach and Mark Peterson, eds., *The Executive Branch* (New York: Oxford University Press, 2005), especially chap. 13; and Jon Bond and Richard Fleisher, eds., *Polarized Politics: Congress and the President in a Polarized Era* (Washington, D.C.: CQ Press, 2000).

55 Thomas J. Weko, *The Politicizing Presidency: The White House Personnel Office, 1948–1994* (Lawrence: University Press of Kansas, 1994), 89; and, generally, Mike Allen, "Bush to Change Economic Team," *Washington Post,* November 29, 2004, A1; David E. Lewis, *The Politics of Presidential Appointments* (Princeton: Princeton University Press, 2008); Richard Nathan, *The Administrative Presidency* (New York: Macmillan, 1983); Alexis Simendinger, "Help Wanted," *National Journal* (December 16, 2006): 26–29; David A. Yalof, *Pursuit of Justices: Presidential Politics and the Selection of Supreme Court Nominees* (Chicago: University of Chicago Press, 1999).

56 Dan Eggen and Paul Kane, "Justice Department Would Have Kept 'Loyal' Prosecutors," *Washington Post,* March 16, 2007, A2.

57 Corwin, *President: Office and Powers,* 115–125.

58 *Skinner v. Railway Labor Executives Association,* 489 U.S. 602 (1989); *National Treasury Employees Union v. Von Raab,* 489 U.S. 656 (1989).

59 Simendinger, "Help Wanted," 29; Henry Hogue, Recess Appointments: Frequently Asked Questions, Report RS21308 (Washington, D.C.: Congressional Research Service, March 29, 2010); updated by author: Obama made additional recess appointments in July and December 2010.

60 Cornelius Kerwin, *Rulemaking: How Government Agencies Write Law and Make Policy,* 3d ed. (Washington, D.C.: CQ Press, 2003).

61 See Executive Orders 12291 (1981), 12498 (1985), and 13422 (2007); Kenneth R. Mayer, *With the Stroke of a Pen: Executive Orders and Presidential Power* (Princeton: Princeton University Press, 2001), 125–134; Cindy Skrzycki, "Tiny OIRA Still Exercises its Real Influence Invisibly," *Washington Post,* November 11, 2003, E1; Philipp Steger, "Bringing Science into Politics: The Debate on Scientific Integrity in U.S. Policymaking," *Bridges* 5 (April 14, 2005), www.ostina.org/content/blogsection/7/149/.

62 *Weekly Compilation of Presidential Documents* (December 8, 2004), 2924; and see Christopher S. Kelley, "To Be (Unitarian) or Not to Be (Unitarian): Presidential Power in the George W. Bush Administration," *White House Studies* 10 (December 2010): 115–38; Kelley and Bryan Marshall, "Going it Alone: The Politics of the Constitutional Signing Statement," *Social Science Quarterly* (March 2010): 168–87.

63 Barack Obama, "Memorandum for the Heads of Departments and Agencies: Presidential Signing Statements," Office of the White House Press Secretary, March 9, 2009.

64 Statement on the Omnibus Public Land Management Act of 2009, *Public Papers of the President, 2009,* March 31.

65 Phillip J. Cooper, *By Order of the President: The Use and Abuse of Executive Direct Action* (Lawrence: University Press of Kansas, 2002), 204–210; the Reagan statement is cited on p. 205. For George W. Bush, see *Public Papers of the Presidents, 2001,* May 24 (p. 575), November 28 (p. 1459), and December 28 (p. 1554). See also Christopher Kelley, "The Unitary Executive and the Presidential Signing Statement," (Ph.D. diss., Miami University of Ohio, 2003); Phillip J. Cooper, "George W. Bush, Edgar Allen Poe, and the Use

and Abuse of the Presidential Signing Statement," *Presidential Studies Quarterly* 35 (September 2005): 515–532.

66 See Section 1003 of the Detainee Treatment Act (P.L. 109-148); "President's Statement on Signing of H.R. 2863," Office of the White House Press Secretary, December 30, 2005; "President's Statement on H.R. 5682," Office of the White House Press Secretary, December 18, 2006; "President's Statement on Signing H.R. 2346," Office of the White House Press Secretary, June 26, 2009.

67 See *Ameron, Inc. v. U.S. Army Corps of Engineers, et al.,* 787 F.2d 875 (3d Cir. 1986); on the difficulty of overturning signing statements, see Cooper, *By Order of the President,* 222; see also 18 *Opinions of the Office of Legal Counsel* 199 (1994), listing Supreme Court decisions that purportedly condoned signing statements, from *Myers v. U.S.* in 1926 to *Freytag v. Commissioner* in 1991.

68 James Sundquist, *The Decline and Resurgence of Congress* (Washington, D.C: Brookings, 1981), 202.

69 Fisher, *Presidential Spending Power,* 165; Schlesinger, *Imperial Presidency,* 239; *Train v. City of New York,* 420 U.S. 35 (1975).

70 Rudalevige, *New Imperial Presidency,* 141–149.

71 Section 4 of the Fourteenth Amendment, adopted to reassure creditors that the post–Civil War United States would pay its (but not the Confederacy's) war debts, reads, "the validity of the public debt of the United States, authorized by law . . . shall not be questioned." But Section 5 reads, "The Congress shall have the power to enforce, by appropriate legislation, the provisions of this article."

72 Proclamations generally encompass such hortatory matters as Thanksgiving Day or National Black History Month, but some—the 1793 Neutrality Proclamation, the 1863 Emancipation Proclamation, etc.—involve substantive issues that carry the force of law. The Supreme Court, in *Wolsey v. Chapman,* 101 U.S. 755 (1879), ruled that there is no material difference between proclamations and executive orders; nor is there much practical difference between executive orders and the other forms of presidential orders described most comprehensively by Cooper, *By Order of the President.* See also Mayer, *With the Stroke of a Pen;* William G. Howell, *Power without Persuasion: The Politics of Direct Presidential Action* (Princeton: Princeton University Press, 2003); Adam Warber, *Executive Orders and the Modern Presidency* (Boulder: Lynne Rienner, 2006).

73 Mayer, *With the Stroke of a Pen,* 66f; Cooper, *By Order of the President.* Obama's executive orders are listed at the National Archives website, www.archives.gov/federal-register/executive-orders/obama.html.

74 Adam Liptak, "Judge Rules 2001 Listing of Terrorists Violated Law," *New York Times,* November 29, 2006, A24.

75 Cooper, *By Order of the President,* 70; David E. Lewis, *Presidents and the Politics of Agency Design* (Stanford, Calif.: Stanford University Press, 2003). For an extended discussion of the "first mover" advantage orders grant, see Howell, *Power without Persuasion.*

76 Mayer, *With the Stroke of a Pen,* 79–87; Howell, *Power without Persuasion,* 83–85; Executive Order 13279; Executive Order 13567.

77 Ruth Morgan, *The President and Civil Rights* (New York: St. Martin's Press, 1970), 5.

78 Harold Hongju Koh, *The National Security Constitution: Sharing Power after the Iran-Contra Affair* (New Haven: Yale University Press, 1990), 46–48; Relyea, "National Emergency Powers"; and see Executive Orders 13566, 13570, 13572, and 13573.

79 Executive Order 11246. See Mayer, *With the Stroke of a Pen,* 203–206.

80 See Elizabeth Drew, *On the Edge* (New York: Touchstone, 1994).

81 Emanuel quoted in Alexis Simendinger, "The Paper Wars," *National Journal,* July 25, 1998, 1737; Eugene Robinson, "Obama's Opportunity to be the Decider," *Washington Post,* November 19, 2010.

82 See, for example, "We Can't Wait: Obama Administration Announces Steps to Boost the Rural Economy, Promote Job Creation," Office of the White House Press Secretary, February 21, 2012. A section of the White House website lists the various "we can't wait" initiatives: www.whitehouse.gov/economy/jobs/we-cant-wait.

83 George H. W. Bush called these National Security Directives, Bill Clinton called them Presidential Decision Directives, and George W. Bush called them National Security Presidential Directives. Legislative efforts in the late 1980s to obtain a list of national security directives failed; Rep. Lee Hamilton (D-Ind.) complained in 1988 that such directives "are revealed to Congress only under irregular, arbitrary, or even accidental circumstances, if at all." See Cooper, *By Order of the President,* 144, 165, 194–195.

84 On the Iran-contra controversy see, among many works, Jane Mayer and Doyle McManus, *Landslide: The Unmaking of the President, 1984–1988* (Boston: Houghton Mifflin, 1988); Lawrence E. Walsh, *Final Report of the Independent Counsel for Iran/contra Matters, Vol. I: Investigations and Prosecutions* (Washington, D.C.: United States Court of Appeals, District of Columbia Circuit, August 4, 1993).

85 Schlesinger, *Imperial Presidency,* 339.

86 Ibid., 340.

87 Pious, *American Presidency,* 348; more broadly, see Daniel Patrick Moynihan, *Secrecy* (New Haven: Yale University Press, 1998).

88 The Nixon and Reagan orders are Executive Order 11652 and 12356, respectively.

89 The Clinton, Bush, and Obama orders are Executive Order 12598, 13292, and 13526, respectively.

90 Nixon, "Statement on Executive Privilege," *Public Papers of the President,* March 12, 1973; Richard Kleindienst, Hearings before the Senate Subcommittee on Intergovernmental Relations, "Executive Privilege, Secrecy in Government, Freedom of Information," 93d Cong., 1st sess., April 10, 1973, Vol. I, 20, 45, 51.

91 Schlesinger, *Imperial Presidency,* 156–159; Mark J. Rozell, *Executive Privilege: Presidential Power, Secrecy, and Accountability,* 3d ed. (Lawrence: University Press of Kansas, 2010); Louis Fisher, *The Politics of Executive Privilege* (Durham, N.C.: Carolina Academic Press, 2004).

92 *U.S. v. Nixon,* 418 U.S. 683 (1974).

93 *In re Sealed Case,* 121 F. 3d 729 (D.C. Cir. 1998).

94 Rozell, *Executive Privilege,* 136–38, 149–53; "Excerpts from White House Letter on Rice's Testimony," *New York Times,* March 31, 2004, A14.

95 William Howell, "Unilateral Powers: A Brief Overview," *Presidential Studies Quarterly* 35 (September 2005): 425.

96 Ronald Reagan, "Letter to the Speaker of the House and the President Pro Tempore of the Senate on the Deployment of United States Forces in Beirut, Lebanon," August 24, 1982.

97 Schlesinger, *Imperial Presidency,* chap. 6; Ryan C. Hendrickson, *The Clinton Wars* (Nashville, Tenn.: Vanderbilt University Press, 2002).

98 Louis Fisher, "War Power," in *The American Congress: The Building of Democracy,* ed. Julian E. Zelizer (Boston: Houghton Mifflin, 2004), 696. Note that the War Powers Resolution specifically prohibits use of treaty obligations as an approval mechanism.

99 Kiki Caruson, "International Agreement-making and the Executive-Legislative Relationship," *Presidency Research Group Report* 25 (fall 2002): 21–28; Shull, *Policy by Other Means,* chap. 6.

100 Bernstein, "Road to Watergate," 81; on the Afghan war, see Bob Woodward, *Bush at War* (New York: Simon and Schuster, 2002). More generally, see John Prados, *Safe for Democracy: The CIA's Secret Wars* (Chicago: Ivan Dee, 2006).

101 This was revealed by new CIA director Leon Panetta in July 2009, as he announced he was terminating the program. See Carrie Johnson and Joby Warrick, "Bush Anti-Terror Policies Get Reluctant Re-Visit," *Washington Post,* July 13, 2009, www.washingtonpost.com/wp-dyn/content/article/2009/07/12/AR2009071202118.html?sid=ST2009071502512.

102 The letter was dated July 17, 2003, and is available at www.talkingpointsmemo.com/docs/rock-cheney1.html.

103 See Harold C. Relyea, National Emergency Powers, CRS Report 98-505 GOV, Congressional Research Service (August 30, 2007).

104 See Fisher, *Presidential Spending Power,* 240.

105 See Rudalevige, *New Imperial Presidency,* 65–74, 109–113, 180–181, 241–248; Geoffrey R. Stone, "The Reagan Amendment, the First Amendment, and FBI Domestic Security Investigations," in *Freedom at Risk,* ed. Richard O. Curry (Philadelphia: Temple University Press, 1988); William C. Banks and M. E. Bowman, "Executive Authority for National Security Surveillance," *American University Law Review* 50 (October 2000): 1–130; Stephen J. Schulhofer, *Rethinking the Patriot Act* (New York: Century Foundation Press, 2005); "Abuse of Authority: The FBI's Gross Misuse of a Counterterrorism Device," *Washington Post,* March 11, 2007, B6.

106 Allen J. Matusow, *Nixon's Economy* (Lawrence: University Press of Kansas, 1998).

107 Jonathan Alter, *The Promise: President Obama, Year One* (New York: Simon and Schuster, 2010), 4.

108 Henry M. Paulson Jr., *On the Brink* (New York: BusinessPlus, 2010); the text of the plan may be found at "Treasury's Bailout Proposal," http://money.cnn.com/2008/09/20/news/economy/treasury_proposal/index.htm.

109 Alter, *The Promise,* prologue and chap. 11; M. Stephen Weatherford, "Economic Crisis and Political Change," in *The Obama Presidency: Appraisals and Prospects,* ed. Bert A. Rockman, Andrew Rudalevige, and Colin Campbell (Washington, DC: CQ Press, 2012), 295–330.

110 Douglas Brinkley, *The Great Deluge: Hurricane Katrina, New Orleans, and the Mississippi Gulf Coast* (New York: William Morrow, 2006); Christopher Cooper and Robert Block, *Disaster: Hurricane Katrina and the Failure of Homeland Security* (New York: Times Books, 2006).

111 Rudalevige, *New Imperial Presidency,* chap. 4.

112 *U.S. v. U.S. District Court,* 407 U.S. 297 (1972).

113 Ford interview in *Time* (November 10, 1980), 30.

114 Louis Fisher and David Gray Adler, "The War Powers Resolution: Time to Say Goodbye," *Political Science Quarterly* 113 (spring 1998): 1–20; Shull, *Policy by Other Means,* chap. 7.

115 Jennifer Steinhauer, "Obama Adviser Defends Libya Policy to Senate," *New York Times,* June 29, 2011, A8.

116 Elizabeth Drew, *Showdown: The Struggle between the Gingrich Congress and the Clinton White House,* paperback ed. (New York: Touchstone, 1997); Victoria Allred, "Versatility with the Veto," *CQ Weekly* (January 20, 2001): 176.

117 *Public Papers of the Presidents, 1995,* 1475.

118 David Gray Adler, "Clinton in Context," in David Gray Adler and Michael A. Genovese, eds., *The Presidency and the Law: The Clinton Legacy* (Lawrence: University Press of Kansas, 2002).

119 *Weekly Compilation of Presidential Documents* (March 13, 2002), 411; Cheney quoted in Dana Milbank, "In Cheney's Shadow,"

Washington Post, October 11, 2004, A21; and see Bob Woodward, "Cheney Upholds Power of the Presidency," *Washington Post,* January 20, 2005, A7.

120 See *In re Cheney* (02-5354), U.S. Circuit Court for the District of Columbia, May 10, 2005; Mitchel Sollenberger and Mark J. Rozell, "The Unitary Executive and Secrecy in the Bush Presidency: The Case of the Energy Task Force Controversy," in *The Unitary Executive and the Modern Presidency,* ed., Ryan J. Barilleaux and Christopher S. Kelley (College Station: Texas A&M Press, 2010).

121 The AUMF is P.L. 107-140.

122 The Patriot Act is P.L. 107-56, as renewed and amended by P.L. 109-177 and P.L. 112-14.

123 See George W. Bush, 2002 State of the Union Address; *National Security Strategy of the United States of America* (September 17, 2002), Part V. The classified version of the document evidently discussed the use of preemptive nuclear strikes to halt the transfer of weapons of mass destruction. See Mike Allen and Barton Gellman, "Preemptive Strikes Part of U.S. Strategic Doctrine," *Washington Post,* December 11, 2002, A1.

124 Ron Suskind, *The Price of Loyalty* (New York: Simon and Schuster, 2004), 70–76; Glenn Kessler, "U.S. Decision on Iraq has Puzzling Past," *Washington Post,* January 12, 2003, A1; Bob Woodward, *Plan of Attack* (New York: Simon and Schuster, 2004); Thomas E. Ricks, *Fiasco* (New York: Penguin Press, 2006).

125 Mike Allen and Juliet Eilperin, "Bush Aides Say Iraq War Needs No Hill Vote," *Washington Post,* August 26, 2002, A1.

126 P.L. 107-243; for a timeline, see Michael R. Gordon and Bernard Trainor, *Cobra II: The Inside Story of the Invasion and Occupation of Iraq* (New York: Random House, 2006). For critical assessments of the use of intelligence, see Ricks, *Fiasco;* Mark Danner, *The Secret Way to War* (New York: New York Review Books, 2006). In June 2011, Brown University's "Costs of War" project estimated spending on the wars, including medical and disability care and interest costs, at nearly $4 trillion: see "The Costs of War Since 2001," Watson Institute for International Studies, Brown University, June 2011, http://costsofwar.org/.

127 See especially John Yoo, *War by Other Means* (New York: Atlantic, 2005) and Steven G. Calabresi and Christopher S. Yoo *The Unitary Executive* (New Haven: Yale University Press, 2008); and Justice Antonin Scalia's dissenting opinion in *Morrison v. Olson* (1988). A useful journalistic treatment is Jess Bravin, "Judge Alito's View of the Presidency: Expansive Powers," *Wall Street Journal,* January 5, 2006, A1. For an academic overview see Barilleaux and Kelley, eds., *The Unitary Executive and the Modern Presidency.*

128 "Press Conference of the President," Office of the White House Press Secretary, December 19, 2005.

129 U.S. Department of Justice, *Legal Authorities Supporting the Activities of the National Security Agency Described by the President,* January 19, 2006, 1–2, 10–11, 17, 30–31.

130 David Johnston, "CIA Tells of Bush's Directive on the Handling of Detainees," *New York Times,* November 15, 2006.

131 Joseph Margulies, *Guantanamo and the Abuse of Presidential Power* (New York: Simon and Schuster, 2005).

132 See, among many others, Jane Mayer, *The Dark Side* (New York: Random House, 2009); Glenn Carle, *The Interrogator* (New York: Nation Books, 2011).

133 The term "torture," the Justice Department argued, was legally limited to acts sufficient to cause pain equivalent to, for example, "organ failure . . . or even death," and then only if inflicting such pain (and not, say, gaining information) was the "precise objective" of the interrogator. In late 2004 the administration ostensibly toned down this definition but continued to argue that any

previously approved techniques did not constitute torture. For contrasting views of this analysis, see Margulies, *Guantanamo* and Yoo, *War by Other Means.* The original documentation may be found in Karen Greenberg and Joshua Dratel, eds., *The Torture Papers* (New York: Cambridge University Press, 2005) as Memo 14, 172–217.

134 See the *Working Group Report on Detainee Interrogations in the Global War on Terrorism: Assessment of Legal, Historical, Policy, and Operational Considerations,* U.S. Department of Defense, April 4, 2003, 21 and Section III generally; reprinted in Greenberg and Dratel as Memo 26; see especially 286, 302–307.

135 See Executive Orders 13491, 13489, 13497, and 13526.

136 Quoted in Charlie Savage, "Obama's War on Terror May Resemble Bush's in Some Areas," *New York Times,* February 18, 2009, A20.

137 Brief for Respondents-Appellants, June 2002, *Hamdi v. Rumsfeld* (Fourth Circuit Court of Appeals, 02-6895); Government's Brief and Motion, August 27, 2002, *Padilla v. Bush* (U.S. Dist. Court, Southern Dist. of New York, 02-4445); Jennifer Elsea, "Presidential Authority to Detain 'Enemy Combatants,'" *Presidential Studies Quarterly* 33 (September 2003): 568–601.

138 *Hamdi v. Rumsfeld,* 542 U.S. 507 (2004).

139 *Padilla v. Hanft,* 05-6396, 4th Circuit Court of Appeals, September 9, 2005. He was convicted in 2008 and sentenced to seventeen years in prison.

140 Dan Eggen, "Padilla Case Raises Questions about Anti-Terror Tactics," *Washington Post,* November 19, 2006, A3.

141 The November 13, 2001, order is printed at 66 *Federal Register* 57833. For a critique and general history of tribunals see Louis Fisher, *Military Tribunals and Presidential Power* (Lawrence: University Press of Kansas, 2005). Key court cases include *Ex parte Quirin,* 317 U.S. 1 (1942) and *Johnson v. Eisentrager,* 339 U.S. 763 (1950).

142 *Hamdan v. Rumsfeld,* 05-184 (June 29, 2006). The Court also held that the charge against Hamdan, conspiracy, could not be tried by military commission since it was not a violation of the laws of war. An earlier question, affirming that U.S. courts' jurisdiction reached to prisoners held in Guantanamo Bay, was settled in *Rasul v. Bush,* 542 U.S. 466 (2004).

143 *Boumediene v. Bush,* 553 U.S. 723 (2008).

144 P.L. 109-366 (October 17, 2006).

145 Executive Order 13567.

146 The defendant, Ali Musa Daqduq, was detained in Iraq by U.S. forces for "serious violations of the laws of war." Charlie Savage, "Iraqi Prisoner Tied to Hezbollah Faces U.S. Military Charges," *New York Times,* February 24, 2012, A12.

147 Thomas Mann and Norman Ornstein, *The Broken Branch* (New York: Oxford University Press, 2006).

148 Madison, *Federalist No. 48* and *No. 51.*

149 Concurring opinion to *Youngstown Sheet and Tube Co. v. Sawyer,* 343 U.S. 579 (1952).

150 Neustadt, *Presidential Power,* 33.

151 Quoted in Schlesinger, *Imperial Presidency,* 59; see also Rossiter, *Constitutional Dictatorship;* and Kleinerman, *Discretionary President.*

152 Locke, *Second Treatise,* 84.

SELECTED BIBLIOGRAPHY

Barilleaux, Ryan J., and Christopher S. Kelley, eds. *The Unitary Executive and the Modern Presidency.* College Station: Texas A&M Press, 2010.

Bessette, Joseph M., and Jeffrey K. Tulis, eds. *The Constitutional Presidency.* Baltimore: Johns Hopkins University Press, 2009.

Cooper, Phillip J. *By Order of the President: The Use and Abuse of Executive Direct Action.* Lawrence: University Press of Kansas, 2002.

Corwin, Edward S. *The President: Office and Powers.* 5th rev. ed., with Randall W. Bland, Theodore Hinson, and Jack W. Peltason. New York: New York University Press, 1984.

Fisher, Louis. *Presidential War Power.* 2d rev. ed. Lawrence: University Press of Kansas, 2004.

Howell, William G. *Power without Persuasion.* Princeton: Princeton University Press, 2003.

Mayer, Kenneth R. *With the Stroke of a Pen: Executive Orders and Presidential Power.* Princeton: Princeton University Press, 2001.

Nelson, Michael, ed. *The Presidency and the Political System.* 9th ed. Washington, D.C.: CQ Press, 2010.

Neustadt, Richard E. *Presidential Power and the Modern Presidents: The Politics of Leadership from Roosevelt to Reagan.* New York: Free Press, 1990.

Posner, Eric A., and Adrian Vermeule. *The Executive Unbound: After the Madisonian Republic.* New York: Oxford University Press, 2010.

Rockman, Bert A., ed., "The Administrative Presidency." special issue of *Presidential Studies Quarterly* 39 (March 2009).

Rozell, Mark J. *Executive Privilege: Presidential Power, Secrecy, and Accountability.* 3d ed. Lawrence: University Press of Kansas, 2010.

Rudalevige, Andrew. *The New Imperial Presidency: Renewing Presidential Power after Watergate.* Ann Arbor: University of Michigan Press, 2005.

Schlesinger, Arthur M., Jr. *The Imperial Presidency.* Boston: Houghton Mifflin, 1973.

Shull, Steven A. *Policy by Other Means: Alternative Adoption by Presidents.* College Station: Texas A&M Press, 2006.

chapter 2

Head of State

by Thomas S. Langston

In every government, there is one or sometimes more than one person whose job it is to embody the nation and preside at ceremonies celebrating a people's unity and spirit. This role, of head of state, responds to a powerful psychological need for symbolic leadership. The duties of a head of state are as various, and their significance as varied, as the times demand. In many countries the function of head of state (sometimes called chief of state) is fulfilled by a monarch with little governmental authority or an official whose post was created to separate symbolic from substantive executive responsibilities. One of the fundamental characteristics of the American form of government is that the Constitution does not separate these duties, making the chief executive simultaneously the head of state.

The role of head of state is not simply another of the "hats" presidents are often said to wear. Rather, being head of state is one half of the two-sided coin of executive responsibility. This inevitably creates tension in what is expected of the American presidents. To fulfill their duties as head of government, presidents are party leaders who have to "wheel and deal" with other elected officials. But as head of state, presidents are supposed to be above the unsavory business of everyday partisanship and politicking. Another source of tension is that although Americans are famously suspicious of power, they want their government to deliver, and their presidents to reach for whatever power they may need to defend them in a crisis. The consequence of such tensions is inescapable paradox; presidents are expected to embody the nation's suspicion of power while making the government work and keeping the people safe from harm. Similarly, presidents are expected to be better than the people but simultaneously one of them.[1]

Sometimes throughout history, presidents have seemed either too fond of their role as head of state or too careless in its performance. The result has been a series of reactions and counterreactions, and a wide array of precedents as to how best to resolve the paradoxes of American political culture as they weigh upon the president. Thomas Jefferson, the third president, was aghast at what he considered the monarchical trappings of the George Washington administration. Fearing that too high a tone in the presidency threatened to set the nation on a path away from its republican roots, President Jefferson went to extremes to downplay the ceremony attendant upon his fulfillment of what were inescapably ceremonial functions. He horrified the European diplomatic corps but struck a blow for the dignity of ordinary American manners when he received the British ambassador to the United States in his house slippers. President Jimmy Carter likewise reacted against the imperial trappings of the Richard Nixon era. To distance himself from his predecessor, who had infamously succumbed to the temptations of power, "Jimmy" (instead of "James Earl") walked from the Capitol to the White House following his inauguration, curtailed the playing of "Hail to the Chief," and carried his own suit bag on and off *Air Force One*. Carter's public humility may have been cleansing to the nation after Watergate, but a combination of economic crisis and setbacks in foreign affairs made him, and the nation, appear weak. His successor, Ronald Reagan, successfully campaigned against Carter's alleged weakness, and his skillful fusing of his dual role as head of state and head of government helped him become the first president since Dwight Eisenhower to serve out two full terms.

A skillful exercise of the head of state role can do more than help a president hold onto power. In a moment of crisis, it can have a profound effect on the confidence of the nation. Many citizens were reassured and inspired by George W. Bush's visit to Ground Zero following the tragic events of September 11, 2001, and by his claim to the gathered firefighters and police officers that "I can hear you, the

---

Previous contributors to this chapter include Mary Stuckey and Daniel C. Diller.

rest of the world can hear you, and the people who knocked these buildings down will hear all of us soon."[2] Bush displayed both his empathy with those who perished in the Twin Towers and the rescue workers who were still there and his resolve to strike back.

As chief of state then, presidents symbolize the people's identity and values. Because the United States is famously a nation "with the soul of a church," the head of state role has inescapably religious overtones. This is so despite the constitutional principle of the separation of church and state, and despite the fact that as president, the head of state seeks to represent *all* the people, including those Americans who are not religious in any conventional sense of the term. As head of state, each president is tasked with leading the unofficial *civil religion* of the American nation, which can be defined as the values and beliefs the people generally hold about the relationship of their nation with God. A chief tenet of the civil religion is that America is an exceptional nation—a chosen land—destined by the deity for greatness. In times of crisis, heads of state have buttressed the confidence of the nation by recalling them to their alleged role in the unfolding of a divine plan. When American presidents have led the nation into war, for a prime example, they have done so typically with soaring rhetoric patterned after that of a preacher consecrating his congregation before sending them to do battle with the forces of evil.

The American position of head of state is laden with heavy expectations. Although presidents can delegate certain ceremonial functions to their representatives, while they are in office they cannot escape their chief of state role. At every moment they represent the United States to the international community and to the American people. Even after they leave office, presidents cannot leave behind their symbolic duties. The most consequential ex-presidents are elevated into the pantheon of American heroes, where they continue to inspire dedication to the ideals with which they were particularly associated. Today, even run-of-the-mill ex-presidents claim a symbolic role in memorializing their time at the nation's "helm" by offering the public an idealized, presidency-centered, version of history at their privately funded presidential museums.

CEREMONIAL DUTIES AND FUNCTIONS

Presidents spend a lot of time in their head of state role, presiding over an endless series of ceremonies that range in tone from the solemnity of the inauguration to the informality of a White House barbecue. They greet foreign ambassadors, dedicate monuments, present medals to war heroes, buy Girl Scout cookies, visit schools, throw out the first ball on opening day of the baseball season, and hold state dinners for foreign chiefs of state. These national ceremonies have much the same purpose for the country as religious rituals have for a church or temple. Ceremonies at which the head of state presides create shared symbols and sentiments that comfort, motivate, unify, and consecrate the people.

Because such events dramatize and personalize the presidency, and evoke an emotional attachment to the nation through the person of the president, they are not moments to be wasted. On ceremonial occasions, then, presidents do more than call for unity and patriotism; they campaign for their reelection, make policy proposals, articulate their political philosophies, and claim the high ground in disputes with an opposing party or branch of government. Presidents who neglect ceremonial duties may have more time to devote to policy development and administration, but they sacrifice a tool of leadership that can be used not only to inspire the nation to greater accomplishments, but also to advance their own agendas.

Constitutional Ceremonial Duties

The Constitution obliges presidents to perform several ceremonial duties. They are required to take an oath of office, periodically inform Congress about the state of the Union, and receive "Ambassadors and other public Ministers." Because these constitutional ceremonial duties firmly designate the president as leader of the whole nation, the nation's first president, George Washington, and his successors could safely assume the role of chief of state. Both the oath of office ceremony and State of the Union address physically place the president out in front of other government officials and focus the nation's attention on the president's opinions and recommendations. The president's duty to receive ambassadors implies that foreign governments are to regard the president as the official representative of the United States. Because the international community sees the president as chief of state, domestic chief of state responsibilities could not be assumed gracefully by anyone but the president.

Oath of Office and Inauguration

Article II, Section 1, Clause 8, of the Constitution requires the president-elect to recite the following thirty-five-word oath before assuming the presidency: "I do solemnly swear (or affirm) that I will faithfully execute the Office of President of the United States, and will to the best of my ability preserve, protect, and defend the Constitution of the United States." The occasion for this oath taking is not described in the Constitution, but the inaugural ceremony at which it is administered has become one of the U.S. government's most important traditions and the president's first chief of state function.

Like a coronation, the inaugural ceremony symbolically invests presidents with the power of their office. At the inauguration the president appears before the people not as the manager of one of the three coequal branches of government but as the preeminent leader of the nation who swears to "preserve, protect, and defend" the Constitution.

The oath of office conjures up heroic images of the nation's heritage. The new president's recitation of the same oath that George Washington, Thomas Jefferson, Abraham Lincoln, Woodrow Wilson, Franklin D. Roosevelt, and every other president has repeated conveys a sense of historic continuity and links the incumbent to the glories of past presidencies.

Washington established the tradition that presidents deliver an inaugural address after taking the oath of office. Inaugurals help presidents articulate their vision of the nation's unfolding story, in which naturally they place themselves at the center, and to relate that vision to their policy and political agendas. Often, there is a strong sense of religious affirmation, as there was in Washington's first inaugural, in which he introduced the theme of the American

nation thriving under divine protection. "No people can be bound to acknowledge and adore the Invisible Hand which conducts the affairs of men more than those of the United States," he instructed his audience, since every "step by which they have advanced to the character of an independent nation seems to have been distinguished by some token of providential 'agency.'" Presidents also routinely use the occasion of their inaugural address to heal the wounds of the election campaign while simultaneously making their first formal plea for unity behind their own agenda. At moments of crisis, presidents have even used the occasion to challenge and chide all who might oppose them. In the midst of the Great Depression, the newly elected president Franklin Roosevelt called upon the people to recall their destiny and their courage, and he called upon Congress to lead, follow, or at the very least get out of the way by granting the president powers normally reserved for times of war. When Barack Obama assumed office near the beginning of what emerged as the worst financial crisis since the 1930s, he

CONSTITUTIONAL BASIS OF PRESIDENTIAL HEAD OF STATE ROLE

The Framers of the Constitution did not specifically designate the president as the nation's head of state, but they created no other office that reasonably could claim the head of state power. Presidents are the logical possessors of the title of head of state under the Constitution because they are chosen by a national electorate, are never out of session, and are recognized as the voice of U.S. foreign policy. Consequently, the president can be said to represent the entire nation, is always available to provide ceremonial leadership, and is positioned to perform both international and domestic ceremonial functions.

The Framers never considered establishing a head of state office separate from the presidency. The creation of a single office that would be filled by one person serving as both the ceremonial and executive leader of the nation, however, was not their only option. The continuing transfer of executive power from the monarch to the prime minister in Great Britain provided the Framers with a model of a political system in which the ceremonial and executive functions were separated.[1] Given the objections of many members of the convention to any pretense of royalty in the presidency and the unanimous concern that no president would have the means to become a despot, it is somewhat surprising that the Framers accepted the fusion of the two roles without debate.

One can imagine the convention designating a member of Congress such as the Speaker of the House or president pro tempore of the Senate as head of state, especially because most of the delegates considered the legislature to be the most important branch of government. Such an arrangement would have augmented Congress's power by making it the ceremonial focus of the government, while diminishing the symbolic resources available to any president who sought dictatorial power.

The Framers also could have created an executive council composed of several persons instead of a unitary presidency. They seriously considered this option, but the focus of their debate was on the safety of lodging enormous executive powers in the hands of one person, not on dividing presidential functions

between executive officials. The original proposal for a single executive, made by James Wilson of Virginia, was strongly opposed by Benjamin Franklin, Edmund Randolph, George Mason, Roger Sherman, and other prominent members of the convention who feared that having a single executive would lead to despotism or the subordination of the country's interests to the interests of the executive's home region. After several days of debate, however, the Framers decided to reject proposals for a plural executive or an executive advisory committee attached to the presidency in favor of a single executive.[2] Presumably, had the convention opted for an executive committee instead of a single president, the head of state power would have resided in the entire committee, not in one specified member.

According to political scientist Rexford G. Tugwell, an executive committee would not have captured the imagination of the American people the way individual presidents have:

> Since he [the president] would not have been alone in the White House in semi-royal state, with relatives and associates of consuming interest to all his fellow citizens, it would not have been a matter of such consequence whether or not he had an invalid wife and irresponsible children, . . . or whether he possessed social graces as well as wisdom and political talent. He would not, in other words, have been the focus of interest and the symbol of Union for the whole American people, watched with avid curiosity and criticized inevitably by those with standards of conduct differing from his own.[3]

By creating a single executive, the Framers guaranteed that public attention and therefore symbolic power would flow to the president.

1. Erwin C. Hargrove and Michael Nelson, *Presidents, Politics, and Policy* (Baltimore: Johns Hopkins University Press, 1984), 20.

2. Donald L. Robinson, *To the Best of My Ability* (New York: Norton, 1987), 69–76.

3. Rexford G. Tugwell, *The Enlargement of the Presidency* (Garden City, N.Y.: Doubleday, 1960), 481.

too sought to reassure the nation of its unquestioned greatness, and—more optimistically—encouraged the unnamed opposition party to put aside as "childish things" such presumably stale debates as "whether our Government is too big or too small" or "whether the market is a force for good or ill."

Just as the inaugural address is the first opportunity for a new president to assume the role of chief of state, the inauguration and the parades and parties that have usually followed it also provide the first glimpse of the new chief of state's ceremonial style. Some presidents (Washington, John Adams, John F. Kennedy) have preferred formal events while

PRESIDENT BARACK OBAMA'S INAUGURATION

The election of an African American to the nation's highest office, just decades after the triumph of the midcentury civil rights movement, and but one hundred and forty three years after the end of the Civil War, was an event of enormous symbolic significance. From the moment Barack Obama entered the contest for president, commentators and ordinary citizens around the world had been captivated by the possibility of his election. By placing Obama in the White House, the United States would be able to claim a form of redemption. Americans of all partisan leanings would be able to answer affirmatively the nagging question that had been asked around the world in 2008, "Is America ready for a black president?"

President Obama had in fact had little to say about race, either his own racial identity or race relations, in his campaign. The one notable exception was a speech the president was goaded into making to lay to rest a controversy stirred by the revelation that the African American pastor of his predominantly black Chicago church had damned the United States from the pulpit.[1] Neither Reverend Jeremiah Wright's outspokenness nor Obama's reticence made any difference, especially after Obama won the general election. The fact of Obama's race was enough to make his inauguration one of the most captivating moments in the nation's history.

The most well-attended, most viewed, most expensive presidential inaugural in American history began with a symbolic reenactment of the final stages of President-elect Abraham Lincoln's journey by train to the nation's capital. Lincoln's 200th birthday was just a few weeks away, and the bipartisan Joint Inaugural Committee had been astute enough to realize the dramatic appeal of linking Obama's coming to office with remembrance of the national martyr. It had been their choice to make "A New Birth of Freedom," a phrase from Lincoln's famed Gettysburg Address, the theme of the Obama inaugural.[2] Along the way from Philadelphia to D.C. on January 17, 2009, the president-elect spoke to crowds from the rear platform and paused to pick up his vice president–elect, Sen. Joseph Biden of Delaware.

Over the next four days, millions of visitors came to the capital city to participate in a variety of events, many of them free and open to the public. On January 18 the D.C. Metro (the subway) set a new ridership record and scores of Hollywood celebrities and entertainers from around the country performed a live show on the National Mall in front of the Lincoln Memorial.[3]

In his inaugural address, which another record-breaking crowd watched live and on television, the president focused on the economic crisis at hand but did so in words that echoed inaugurals of the past. In the process, he continued in the lengthy tradition of such addresses, by recalling the country's greatness and its history of coming together at moments of stress. Near the end, however, he injected a more personal comment about himself and in the process acknowledged the magnitude of the moment in the nation's history of racial conflict and

reconciliation. "This," the president said, "is the meaning of our liberty and our creed; why men and women and children of every race and every faith can join in celebration across this magnificent Mall, and why a man whose father less than 60 years ago might not have been served at a local restaurant can now stand before you to take a most sacred oath."[4]

Following the inauguration and the swearing-in, and the evening's full schedule of balls, the press handed in the reviews. For the most part, they revealed the obvious; the nation, and indeed the world, had been enthralled by the unfolding of the story of what one newspaper termed the "United States of Obama." The usually reserved *International Herald Tribune* declared Obama an "icon for the youth and a sign of deliverance for an older generation. . . ."[5]

Obama's inauguration was a historic moment in the presidential performance of the role of head of state. It was also a disaster-in-the-making, because the enormity of the inauguration seems not merely to have raised public perceptions of the president to unrealistic heights, but the expectations of the president himself. Obama seemed sincerely to have believed that if only he made smart choices and said the right words, he could actually maintain the spirit of unity so evident at his inaugural, and bring a divided Congress together in a spirit of non-ideological, postpartisan harmony. The results included a painfully public smashing of inaugural day illusions, as the president's signature legislative accomplishment, health care reform, was passed without a single Republican vote in Congress, after which Republicans regained control of the House of Representatives in the midterm elections of 2010.[6]

1. "Obama's Speech on Race," *New York Times*, March 18, 2008, www.nytimes.com/interactive/2008/03/18/us/politics/20080318_OBAMA_GRAPHIC.html#. Prior to this speech, Obama had had a great deal to say about race, most memorably in the autobiographical *Dreams from My Father: A Story of Race and Inheritance* (New York: Broadway, 2004).

2. Senator Feinstein Announces 2009 Inaugural Theme, "A New Birth of Freedom," Joint Congressional Committee on Inaugural Ceremonies, press release, November 5, 2008, http://inaugural.senate.gov/media/releases/release-11052008-inauguralwebsite.cfm.

3. Mike McPhate, "Metro Sets Sunday Ridership Record," *Washington Post*, January 19, 2009, http://voices.washingtonpost.com/getthere/2009/01/metro_sets_sunday_ridership_re.html.

4. Barack Obama, Inaugural Address, Washington, D.C., January 20, 2009, American Presidency Project online database, www.presidency.ucsb.edu/ws/index.php?pid=44&st=&st1=#axzz1nE4xKnd8.

5. "Press Review: World Hails 'United States of Obama,'" *Washington Post*, January 21, 2009, http://articles.cnn.com/2009-01-21/politics/obama.international.press.reaction_1_inauguration-newspaper-front-pages-barack-obama?_s=PM:POLITICS.

6. See Joel Aberbach, "'Change We Can Believe in' Meets Reality," and George C. Edwards, "Strategic Assessments: Evaluating Opportunities and Strategies in the Obama Presidency," in Bert A. Rockman, Andrew Rudalevige, and Colin Campbell, eds., *The Obama Presidency: Appraisals and Prospects* (Washington, D.C.: CQ Press, 2012), 11–36, 37–66.

others (Jefferson, Carter) have favored more informality. Increasingly, inaugurals are major political and social events, with balls and receptions in several locations around the nation's capital and in the candidate's home state, many of which are televised. They are an opportunity for the president to share his success with his backers, and to say "thank you" to at least some of those who funded and staffed the increasingly large, privately organized and paid-for campaigns that are required to win office. Reagan's 1981 inaugural festivities—the most expensive in history up to that time—set the tone for those to follow. Reagan's inaugural parade featured eight thousand marchers, eight $100-a-ticket balls, and a nationally televised inaugural "gala" featuring Hollywood entertainers. The cost of the festivities was estimated at $16 million, compared with just $3.5 million spent for the Carter inaugural in 1977.

George H. W. Bush, Bill Clinton, and George W. Bush all hosted elaborate inaugural celebrations. George W. Bush's 2001 inaugural committee raised nearly $40 million to pay for elaborate celebrations that drew tens of thousands of his supporters to Washington, D.C.[3] Obama's inaugural festivities shattered previous records. The election of the first African American to the presidency, and Obama's success in making the most of large numbers of highly motivated small contributors and volunteers in his campaign, inspired large numbers of people to want to take part in the celebration. The cost of the festivities and ceremonies were about the same as in the George W. Bush administration (a little more than $40 million), and the costs of additional security were in proportion to the unprecedented size of the event, generating controversy over the price tag.[4] Ignoring the controversy, the president's private fund-raisers worked closely with the Joint Congressional Committee that oversees the official swearing-in ceremony, along with officials from the District of Columbia, Virginia, and Maryland, and the outgoing White House to prepare for the crush of up to two million inaugural visitors. Outgoing President Bush declared a state of emergency in the District of Columbia to free up emergency funds from the federal government and the National Mall was opened to the public for the ceremony itself for the first

time, where they were able to watch events unfold on over-sized television screens. In the evening, the president and his wife, along with the vice president and his wife, put in appearances at all of the "official" balls, including the low-cost "Neighborhood Ball" held at the D.C. Convention Center, and a Youth Ball televised by MTV.

In sum, a president's choices in planning the inauguration reveal his political principles, his style of governance, and his understanding of the connection between the substance and the ceremony of the new administration.

State of the Union Address

The Constitution also states that the president "shall from time to time give to the Congress information of the State of the Union, and recommend to their Consideration such Measures as he shall judge necessary and expedient." From this clause developed the ritual of the president's annual message, or "State of the Union address," as it has been known since 1945. *(See "The State of the Union Address," p. 175, in Chapter 4.)*

George Washington delivered the first annual message to Congress on January 8, 1790. John Adams, who enjoyed royal formalities, followed Washington's precedent, but Thomas Jefferson objected to having presidents deliver their annual messages in person. Like many of his Democratic-Republican colleagues, he thought the custom, which had derived from the British monarch's speech from the throne at the opening of Parliament, had royal pretensions. As part

INAUGURAL POEMS

Presidents have sometimes attempted to use the celebrity and visibility of their office to promote changes in the lifestyle of the nation. John F. Kennedy intended to use his position to encourage interest in the fine arts and U.S. culture. He and his wife, Jacqueline, set an example for the nation by frequently patronizing the work of artists, musicians, and writers.

Kennedy began his patronage of the arts the day he became president. He asked the venerable poet Robert Frost to recite a poem at his inauguration ceremony on January 20, 1961. The eighty-six-year-old Frost planned to read a short introductory verse he had composed for the occasion followed by his poem "The Gift Outright." The poet began reading his introductory verse, but the bright sunlight magnified by the glare from the snow that had fallen the day before blinded him. Frost read only three lines before stopping. He said, "I'm not having a good light here at all. I can't see in this light." He tried to continue with the help of Vice President–elect Lyndon B. Johnson, who shaded the poet's manuscript with a top hat, but Frost still could not see. He gave up on the introductory verse, saying, "This was to have been a preface to a poem which I do not have to read." He then recited "The Gift Outright" from memory in a clear voice, including a wording change in the last line made at the incoming president's request.

In 1993 Bill Clinton, who cherished his connections to John Kennedy, also included a poem as part of his inaugural. Poet Maya Angelou's "On the Pulse of Morning" testified to the changes the nation had encountered since 1960.

At Barack Obama's inauguration, the incoming president renewed what has become a tradition only among Democratic presidents by inviting the poet Elizabeth Alexander to read a poem she had written for the occasion, "Praise Song for the Day," which captured the hopeful tone Obama hoped to set.

Rutherford B. Hayes was the first president to use an eagle as the official presidential seal. In 1903 Theodore Roosevelt added a circular seal around it, bearing the words "Seal of the President of the United States," and in 1945 Harry Truman changed the eagle's head from one side to the other. The ring of fifty stars represents the fifty states.

of his effort to "put the ship of state back on its republican tack," he submitted his report to Congress in writing.[5] Presidents continued to send, not deliver, the Annual Message, as it was then known, until Woodrow Wilson revived the custom of presenting the message as a speech in 1913.

The Constitution does not mandate the scheduling of the address, but by tradition, it is given in late January or early February. At the president's request, Congress sends an invitation to the White House, which the president accepts, and the speech is then scheduled. It is always given in the House chamber, reflecting its symbolic importance as a message given simultaneously to Congress and to the American people. Besides the vice president (as president of the Senate), most cabinet officials, and members of the Joint Chiefs of Staff, the audience in the chamber includes justices of the U.S. Supreme Court. An international audience now listens in as well. The speech is televised live and receives considerable media attention both before and after it is given. It is considered a major test of the president's political abilities.

Because the State of the Union address is an annual ritual in which presidents are expected to put forward their agenda before Congress for the coming year, it is difficult for presidents to keep the speech brief, and few of these speeches have the same rhetorical grandeur of an inaugural. Despite the limitations of the form, because all three branches of the federal government are represented in the House chamber, the State of the Union address gives presidents an important opportunity to enact their unique role as the sole voice of the nation. In characterizing the state of the union, presidents become, in effect, the national historian, reflecting on the past as a frame for the actions they desire in the future. As rhetoricians Karlyn Kohrs Campbell and Kathleen Hall Jamieson put it, "[T]he annual message has been, from the outset, one symbolic moment in which the head of state has

woven the cloth of common national history, character, and identity."[6]

Reception of Ambassadors

The Constitution gives the president the duty to "receive Ambassadors and other public Ministers." The authors of the Constitution regarded the reception of foreign visitors as a purely ceremonial responsibility. It was to be given to the president, according to Alexander Hamilton, because Congress could not conveniently perform this function. He wrote in the *Federalist* No. 69 that presidential reception of ambassadors "is more a matter of dignity than of authority. It is a circumstance which will be without consequence in the administration of the government; and it was far more convenient that it should be arranged in this manner than that there should be a necessity of convening the legislature, or one of its branches, upon every arrival of a foreign minister."[7] Subsequently, however, the presidential responsibility to receive ambassadors was used by chief executives as a constitutional justification of their authority to recognize or deny recognition to foreign governments. *(See "The Recognition Power," p. 227, in Chapter 5.)*

In the spirit of this constitutional provision, presidents have customarily received the official ambassador of every recognized foreign government. The growth of the Washington diplomatic corps during the twentieth century and the overcrowded presidential schedule have forced presidents to receive most ambassadors, especially those from smaller countries, in groups at the White House to save time.

Customary Ceremonial Functions

Presidents and their representatives also perform numerous chief of state functions that do not have their origins in the Constitution and are not based on a specific legal sanction. Some of these activities have been established as annual events by a succession of presidents. Others are performed by individual presidents for their public relations value. Presidents can choose to de-emphasize their chief of state role by delegating ceremonial functions to the vice president and others, but they cannot escape many events and practices that the American people have come to regard as part of the president's job. A president who claims to be too busy to light the national Christmas tree or to congratulate the World Series champions would waste valuable opportunities to score political points and would risk being perceived as indifferent to American life. Like the three ceremonial functions based on the Constitution, these informal chief of state activities emphasize the president's role as the leader of the nation, but many of them also serve to humanize the president and symbolically bridge the gap between the president and the people.

National Endorser: The Head of State Sheds His Grace on Thee

A presidential proclamation or dedication is a national stamp of approval for cultural events, national monuments, public works projects, charity drives, and special weeks and days. Such proclamations promote national concern and awareness of worthy organizations and causes by indicating that the president thinks the object of the proclamation is important enough to recognize. Often presidents highlight their recognition of a charity, organization, or movement by inviting its leaders to the White House. Such an invitation is a further measure of the group's importance, because time is made in the president's schedule to accommodate the visit.

Presidential recognition of an event, cause, group, or monument can inspire patriotic sentiments. A new hydroelectric dam is said to be not just a source of power for a particular region, but an engineering feat and a symbol of American industrial might and technological ingenuity. The work of a charitable organization such as the American Red Cross is praised as an example of the nation's caring spirit.

Presidential endorsements are constantly in demand by organizations and charities, and the president's staff must choose which will receive presidential time. On occasion, the incumbent president is able to signal support for a minority constituency with a controversial agenda through a proclamation, and to do so without making news outside of the target group, as in President Obama's annual proclamations of June as Lesbian, Gay, Bisexual and Transgender Pride Month. Many more of the causes presidents endorse from year to year are determined by precedent. The United Way, Easter Seals, American Cancer Society, and many others receive annual presidential endorsements. In other instances, the president is called upon by Congress to give his seal of approval to some cause dear at one time to the legislative branch. Such is the case whereby every president since Dwight Eisenhower in 1959 has been required by a law passed the previous year, at the height of the cold war, to proclaim May First to be not Labor Day, but "Loyalty Day."[8]

PRESIDENTIAL MEDAL OF FREEDOM

Created in its modern form by President John F. Kennedy in 1963 as a civilian honor, the Presidential Medal of Freedom remains the nation's highest award for civilian achievement. Only the president can award the lustrous red, white, and blue enameled medal, which recognizes significant contributions to American life, the country's national security, or even to world peace. Only about five hundred people have received the medal as of June 2012. The winners have included scientists, writers, government officials, artists, movie stars, sports legends, corporate leaders, billionaire investors, and celebrity chefs. Among past winners are astronaut Neil Armstrong, comedienne Lucille Ball, civil war historian Bruce Catton, legendary investor Warren Buffett, labor leader Cesar Chavez, former first lady Betty Ford, longtime senator J. William Fulbright, industrialist Edgar Kaiser, civil rights legends including John Lewis, and baseball greats Jackie Robinson and Stan Musial.

Early in 1963 President Kennedy issued the executive order renaming the Medal of Freedom and establishing new, broad-based criteria for awarding the Presidential Medal of Freedom to individuals "who had made especially meritorious contributions to (1) the security or national interests of the United States, or (2) world peace, or (3) cultural or other significant public or private endeavors."

President Lyndon B. Johnson and every president who followed him have awarded additional medals during their terms of office. Presidents have sole discretion to decide who gets the award, or even whether it will be given at all. Presidents have tended to select medal winners who have had long and distinguished careers. However, a few highly publicized specific accomplishments have garnered awards. President Richard Nixon, for example, gave medals to the astronauts of the history-making *Apollo 11* moon mission in 1969 as well as to the astronauts and mission operations team of the near-tragic *Apollo 13* mission in 1970.

Government service is a persistent theme among the recipients. President Johnson made a point of rewarding key figures in his administration with the president's medal, and other presidents followed suit. For example, President Gerald R. Ford named his secretary of state, Henry Kissinger, and president Jimmy Carter his national security assistant, Zbigniew Brzezinski. Six former presidents—John Kennedy (from Johnson), Lyndon Johnson (from Carter), Ronald Reagan (from George W. Bush), Gerald R. Ford (from Clinton), Jimmy Carter (also from Clinton), and George H. W. Bush (from Obama)—and two former vice presidents—Hubert H. Humphrey (from Carter) and Nelson A. Rockefeller (from Ford)—have been given the award. In all, about a third of the president's medals have gone to government officials.

Although Presidential Medal of Freedom winners are usually Americans, presidents also have selected a few foreign recipients over the years. Bill Clinton honored Simon Wiesenthal and George W. Bush honored British prime minister Tony Blair, a stalwart ally in the wars of the Bush years, as well as Pope John Paul II. In his first two years in office, Barack Obama's picks have been particularly international, including Archbishop Desmond Tutu of South Africa, Muhammad Yunus of Bangladesh, British astrophysicist Stephen Hawking, and Angela Merkel, the chancellor of Germany.

SOURCE: Bruce Wetterau, *The Presidential Medal of Freedom: Winners and Their Achievements* (Washington, D.C.: Congressional Quarterly, 1996). A list of recipients from the Clinton Administration forward is available at www .senate.gov/pagelayout/reference/two_column_table/Presidential_Medal _of_Freedom_Recipients.htm.

President Clinton, left, stands with former president Jimmy Carter, right, and former first lady Rosalynn Carter after Clinton awarded the couple the Presidential Medal of Freedom, the nation's highest civilian honor, during a ceremony at the Carter Center in August 1999. Carter is one of six former presidents to receive the award.

Conveyor of Awards and Congratulations

In accordance with their role as national spokesperson, presidents are expected to be the conveyors of national awards and congratulations. Presidents routinely invite citizens to the White House, where they are congratulated on their accomplishments and presented with an award or memento of their visit. Presidents also bestow a variety of official awards, the most prominent of which are the Medal of Honor, the nation's highest military honor, and the Presidential Medal of Freedom, the highest civilian honor bestowed by the government. *(See box, Presidential Medal of Freedom, p. 41.)*

Presidents have used this role as a tool of moral and patriotic leadership. In congratulating American heroes, presidents make a moral statement by holding up those individuals to the nation as examples to emulate. Presidential congratulations encourage citizens to be as dedicated as a spelling bee champion, as brave as a war hero, as creative as a great artist, or as resilient as a person celebrating a hundredth birthday.

President Reagan developed presidential congratulations into a political art. He made a practice of weaving the introduction of carefully selected heroic Americans into his upbeat State of the Union addresses. His heroes included an infantry medic who rescued wounded soldiers in Grenada, a

twelve-year-old prodigy of gospel music, a woman about to graduate from West Point despite having escaped to the United States from Vietnam only ten years before with no possessions or knowledge of English, and a seventy-nine-year-old Harlem woman who cared for infants born of mothers addicted to heroin.

Every president since Reagan has used this device when addressing Congress. George W. Bush opened his historic speech to Congress on September 20, 2001, with the emotionally powerful introduction of Lisa Beamer, the widow of Todd Beamer, who had participated in the effort by passengers of the hijacked United Flight 93 to retake the plane from terrorists on September 11. Apparently because the passengers resisted the hijackers, the plane crashed to the ground in Pennsylvania before it could strike an intended target in Washington, D.C.

Congratulating a hero brings obvious political benefits to presidents. Members of championship sports teams are routinely invited to the White House where they joke with the president and present the chief executive with a jersey, game ball, or other memento of their victory. The president can become identified with their sport, demonstrate good humor, and be photographed with America's current sports idols.[9] Presidents gain similar public relations benefits from congratulating artists, scientists, heroic members of the armed forces, and others who have performed feats of skill, intelligence, or courage. Presidents can bask in the reflected glory of those they honor, and they can also hope to earn support for their policies by associating those policies with heroic or otherwise admirable Americans.

First American

Alexis de Tocqueville, a French aristocrat and author who traveled widely in the United States during the first half of the nineteenth century, observed that "public officers themselves are well aware that the superiority over their fellow

Throwing out the first baseball of the 1910 major league season, President William Howard Taft began a tradition that most succeeding presidents have followed.

citizens which they derive from their authority they enjoy only on condition of putting themselves on a level with the whole community by their manners."[10] Most presidents have understood that although Americans want their president to be an exceptional person who is intelligent, decisive, and inspiring, they also want a leader with common tastes and experiences. Americans want to believe that their president rose to the top through hard work and moral integrity, rather than a tireless drive to stand apart. For their part, presidents strive hard, regardless of their backgrounds, to project an image that connects them with the lives of ordinary Americans.

Presidents who appear aloof, professorial, or urbane or who seem to take an unseemly pleasure in the trappings of their office risk alienating many citizens who are attracted to politicians with folksy images. American heads of state work hard to combine their presidential images with evidence that they share tastes in common with the people. They may eat jelly beans (Reagan) or pork rinds (George H. W. Bush) or watch football (Nixon), basketball (Clinton and Obama), or NASCAR (George W. Bush). They may make their own breakfast (Ford) or carry their own bags (Carter). They may hunt deer (Johnson), chop wood (Reagan), or clear brush (George W. Bush). If they enjoy sports, they are wise to avoid spending too much time engaged in "club" sports such as tennis and golf, and better advised to bowl (Nixon), jog (Clinton), ride a mountain bike (George W. Bush), or play a rough game of pick-up basketball, as Obama was doing on November 26, 2010, when he took an elbow to the face, requiring a dozen stitches to his lip. All this behavior serves the same end: establishing commonality with the American people.

Presidential appearances at cultural events also can reinforce the image of a president as an average person. Presidents attend historical and artistic exhibits, ethnic festivals, and other events where they can display their interest in American life. They have been especially fond of attending sporting contests. Since William Howard Taft threw out the first baseball of the 1910 major league season on April 14 in Washington, most presidents have observed the tradition. Kennedy wanted to make such a good appearance at the yearly event that he secretly practiced his throwing on the White House grounds.[11] George W. Bush traveled to Yankee Stadium in New York City to throw out the first ball in the third game of the 2001 World Series. The appearance was meant to underscore not only Bush's identification with baseball fans, but also his solidarity with New York after the terrorist destruction of the World Trade Center.

Presidents who have "connected" with the American people in their tastes and manners have at times frustrated their opponents, who try in vain to break up the apparent "love affair" between a particularly adept head of state and the mass public. Andrew Jackson was preeminently a president of the average white American adult males who constituted the electorate in his age. In an era when politicians with patrician backgrounds and elite educations still believed they should hold pride of place in the nation's government on account of their superior attainments, Jackson rose to the presidency by virtue of his status as a war hero and man of the people. His inaugural day festivities famously ended in a near riot in the White House as the throngs of ordinary Americans who had descended upon the city to see their champion ascend to the nation's highest office trashed the inaugural reception in the rush for punch and cake. The nation's self-proclaimed elite were aghast, and when the barely schooled president blocked an extension of the charter of the nation's central bank, they thought they had caught their prey. In Jackson's 1832 reelection campaign, his opponents broadcast the president's veto message in which he rallied against the privileged on the part of the simple folk of the countryside and the cities. In this era before polling, the bank's supporters did not realize Jackson's veto message would be a "hit" with the people, who rallied to the defense of their tribune and sustained him in the White House.

Many decades later, Ronald Reagan similarly drove to distraction the nation's better-educated elite with the way that he seemed to charm ordinary voters. Reagan was an unabashed sentimentalist who loved his country and articulated its ideals in inspiring rhetoric. Though his policies were not always popular, and his approval ratings were not exceptional, he established a particularly strong relationship with the American people as head of state, and majorities of Americans stood by this man who so artfully shared their love of country even when a less well-liked president might have been thrown to the congressional wolves. In his second term, Reagan was forced to acknowledge that he had misled the people about his administration's actions in the Iran-contra affair. Reagan's ultimate defense, that whatever he had done wrong, he had done in a righteous cause, diffused the situation. If he had abused power, he had not done so as Richard Nixon had, in pursuing "enemies" at home, but in defense of American ideals abroad. At the very least, he had meant well. To his critics, this was no defense at all and they derided Reagan as the "teflon" president, for it seemed he had a protective cover. Inconvenient facts that might have dethroned a lesser head of state slid off; the people had chosen their symbol and were not anxious to see him go.

Among the more recent presidents, Bill Clinton projected an inconsistent personal image, which damaged his relationship with the mass public. Clinton's biography as a self-made man who rose from a difficult childhood in tiny Hope, Arkansas, provided a solid base on which to build an image as an ordinary American. Clinton skillfully used his small-town origins to his advantage during the 1992 campaign. But after becoming president his early failure to project a likable personal image contributed to his sharp drop in popularity. The initial impression some Americans

PRESIDENT OBAMA'S "BEER SUMMIT"

On July 16, 2009, a distinguished African American professor at Harvard University was arrested on his front porch by a white police sergeant. The cop, Joseph Crowley, had been called to the professor's home to investigate a possible break-in. The two men at the scene turned out to be the professor, Henry Louis Gates Jr., who was locked out of his house, and his driver. Gates's encounter with the police ended with his arrest for disorderly conduct, allegedly for a vociferous tirade against the responding officer. In the immediate aftermath, the professor charged that a "rogue" cop motivated by racial bias had violated his rights, while the officer insisted he had "done nothing wrong," had given Gates ample warning to stop "yelling," and defended his character against the charge that he was a racist.[1]

Formal charges were quickly dropped but the incident received substantial attention in the press at a time when the president, Barack Obama, was struggling to unite the public behind his controversial plan to expand access to health care to uninsured Americans. At a prime time news conference six days after the arrest, Chicago *Sun-Times* reporter Lynn Sweet invited the president to comment on the arrest of his friend, Professor Gates.

President Obama had had little to say about race relations in America before this event, either as president or during his campaign. "He does not inject race into the conversation regularly because it clears the room" commented Donna Brazile, a Democratic strategist.[2] On this occasion, however, the president dove head first into what was already a media frenzy. In his lengthy reply to Sweet's question, the president sought the high ground.[3] The fact of his own election, the president remarked, is "testimony to the progress that's been made" in race relations in America. "And yet the fact of the matter is, is that this still haunts us. And even when there are honest misunderstandings, the fact that blacks and Hispanics are picked up more frequently and often time for no cause casts suspicion even when there is good cause." The president's efforts to preach conciliation and lecture on racial profiling were, however, to no avail, for earlier in his remarks he had committed a serious gaffe by tossing out the observation that "the Cambridge Police acted stupidly in arresting somebody when there was already proof that they were in their own home." The president tried to shift attention away from his own comments in the days after the press conference. Two days following his remarks, he had a phone conversation with Sergeant Crowley and afterward made an unannounced visit to the White House press room in an effort to talk about the story. Admitting that his "choice of words" might have been better "calibrated," the president nevertheless stuck by his belief that the arrest was an "overreaction."[4]

Being head of state can be a burden, and the president reflected on his situation at his impromptu press conference. Admitting that "(n)obody's been paying much attention to health care" since he became part of the story of the arrest, Obama nevertheless defended his decision to speak out on the issue. Because "race is still a troubling aspect of our society," he remarked, "Whether I were black or white, I think that me commenting on this and hopefully contributing to constructive, as opposed to negative, understandings about the issue is part of my portfolio" as president.[5] The president may have been correct that a white president would have felt equally obliged to speak out on Gates's arrest, but the American public by and large did not approve of the way that this president did so; whites disapproved by a margin of two-to-one.[6]

Sergeant Crowley ironically showed the president a way out of his dilemma. In the president's phone conversation with Crowley, the officer jokingly suggested that cooler heads might prevail if all involved could get together for a beer. The White House took the idea and ran with it, quickly assembling what the press dubbed the "Beer Summit." Sitting around a table with the president and the vice

developed of their new president was of a cerebral, but unfocused, Ivy League "policy wonk" with Hollywood pretensions. One damaging incident occurred on May 18, 1993, when it was reported that *Air Force One* was delayed at the Los Angeles airport, keeping two runways closed because of security procedures, so that the president could get a $200 haircut from a Beverly Hills hairdresser. While subsequent investigation suggested that the haircut in fact caused no delays, the damage was done from a public relations standpoint.

Political scientist Fred I. Greenstein wrote that during Clinton's first months in office he tended "to confine himself to impersonal and distinctly noninspirational messages on such themes as the need to 'grow the economy.' He and his associates did little to humanize his presidency: Hillary Clinton became the all-business Hillary Rodham Clinton; daughter Chelsea dropped from sight; and the campaign bus was garaged."[12]

Clinton responded to his sliding poll numbers by bringing David Gergen, a Republican media strategist, into his administration. Among other adjustments, Clinton agreed to allow more news coverage of his family life and scheduled an increasing number of media opportunities that allowed him to display his considerable talent at interacting with ordinary Americans. Clinton particularly excelled at events that called for the expression of sympathy or identification with the downtrodden. He became so adept at personalizing his speeches and projecting concern

Not all presidential summits are formal. In the much touted "Beer Summit," President Obama brought together Professor Henry Louis Gates Jr. (left) and Police Sgt. James Crowley (center) for reconciliation after Crowley arrested Gates in his own home. All three men drank different beers and, reportedly, had a pleasant time.

resolution, the frenzy to an end, and permitted the president to get back to health care reform.[7]

1. For Gates's comment on Crowley, see "Gates Fallout: President vs. Policeman," *Good Morning America*, ABC News, http://abcnews.go.com/video/playerIndex?id=8163272. For Crowley's comments, see the same video plus Beverly Ford and Rich Schapiro, "Sgt. James Crowley, Cop Who Arrested Harvard Professor Henry Louis Gates Jr., Denies He's Racist," *New York Daily News*, July 23, 2009, http://articles.nydailynews.com/2009-07-23/news/17928870_1_gates-cambridge-police-department-james-crowley.

2. Huma Khan, Michele McPhee, and Russell Goldman, "Obama Called Police Officer Who Arrested Gates, Still Sees 'Overreaction' in Arrest," *ABC Nightline*, July 24, 2009, http://abcnews.go.com/Politics/story?id=8163051&page=1&singlePage=true.

3. "The President News Conference," July 22, 2009, American Presidency Project online dababase, www.presidency.ucsb.edu/ws/index.php?pid=86456&st=&st1=#axzz1nE4xKnd8.

4. Khan, McPhee, and Goldman, "Obama Called Police Officer."

5. Ibid.

6. "Obama's Ratings Slide Across the Board: The Economy, Health Care Reform and Gates Grease the Skids," Pew Research Center for the People and the Press, July 30, 2009, http://people-press.org/2009/07/30/obamas-ratings-slide-across-the-board/.

7. Helene Cooper and Abby Goodnough, "Over Beers, No Apologies, but Plans to Have Lunch," *New York Times*, July 30, 2009, www.nytimes.com/2009/07/31/us/politics/31obama.html?_r=1&hp. About a year after the incident, the Cambridge Police Department issued a report from an expert panel that assigned blame to both Gates and Crowley. See Milton James Valencia, "Sergeant, Gates Both to Blame, Report Says, *Boston Globe*, July 1, 2010, www.boston.com/news/local/massachusetts/articles/2010/07/01/sergeant_gates_both_to_blame_report_says/ (accessed August 24, 2011). Gates' attorney, Harvard University Law School professor Charles Ogletree, set his client's story in a broader context in *Presumption of Guilt: The Arrest of Henry Louis Gates Jr. and Race, Class, and Crime in America* (New York: Palgrave MacMillan, 2010).

president just outside the Oval Office, the formerly irate academic and the still-defiant officer were both on their best behavior. Their willingness to agree to disagree, as Crowley said to the press immediately afterward, and the fact that no one at the "summit" departed in any way from the unwritten script of "folks having a drink at the end of the day and hopefully giving people an opportunity to listen to each other" as the president said beforehand, at last brought the narrative to a

that many observers dubbed him "the Great Empathizer," a modification of Ronald Reagan's moniker, the "Great Communicator." Clinton's phrase, "I feel your pain," uttered during the 1992 presidential campaign, was often cited derisively by critics as evidence that his talent for empathy was shallow or manipulative. But Clinton's ability to project compassion was one of his premier political assets. In Clinton's second term, his confession of an affair with a White House intern brought back to the surface his earlier image as a man suffering from an exaggerated sense of entitlement, but the widespread impression that his partisan opponents were not "playing fair" in their zeal to remove him from office gave him an opportunity, which he seized, to reassert his image as a caring man who

understood and would fight for the average citizen, who was presumably more concerned about the economy than the details of the president's relationship with Monica Lewinsky.

Despite his privileged upbringing and his Ivy League degrees, George W. Bush proved adept at connecting with the American people. Voters in 2004, for instance, declared that they preferred Bush to his Democratic opponent, John Kerry, as a potential guest in their homes.[13] Bush's somewhat erratic grammar and lack of facility with words provided late-night comedians with solid material, but they also conveyed the image of Bush as a regular guy. The president's reputation for being abrasive and sharp, perhaps even a bit of a bully, was a distraction at times, but served him well after the terrorist attacks of September 11, 2001, when he reframed himself as first and foremost defender of the nation and its liberties in a dangerous world.

Barack Obama's cool and cerebral personality allowed him to maintain and project calm in the campaign season of 2008, which was concluded against the backdrop of a financial crisis that threatened devastating panic in the markets. But his muted personality has hampered his ability to sustain the passionate commitment of core supporters through the ups and downs of tough partisan fights with Congress. Liberals and progressives soon took to bemoaning the apparent lack of passion emanating from the White House.

Obama's fiercest critics charged that he was not really an American at all. All manner of charges were hurled at the president, including false allegations that he was not in fact a natural born citizen as the Constitution requires all presidents to be, and that he was educated in a jihadist madrassa. The president typically took the high road and was slow to respond. Even the presentation of his official Hawaiian birth certificate did not inhibit those "birthers" who claimed he was born in Kenya. Though his opponents were careful not to mention the president's mixed-race ancestry, there was considerable speculation in the press that sour grapes about the election of the nation's first nonwhite head of state fueled the steady stream of stories that sought to call into question Obama's suitability as president.

Presidents who can position themselves as "regular" in this sense without sacrificing their ability to appear presidential have found the right balance between the formal demands of the office and the need to affirm democracy by displaying the common touch.

First Celebrant

National holidays reduce societal divisions by emphasizing universal patriotic themes and common traditions. Millions of Americans of all races, religions, and regions share the common experience of watching fireworks on the Fourth of July or preparing a banquet on Thanksgiving. On Veterans Day most American citizens will recall someone who served in the military, and on Memorial Day many will remember someone who died in a war. Holidays, therefore, can draw a nation together and enhance citizens' sense of belonging to a single national culture.

As chief of state, presidents lead the nation's observation of annual holidays. They light the national Christmas tree, deliver a patriotic address on the Fourth of July, and lay a wreath at the Tomb of the Unknown Soldier on Memorial Day. Presidents also commemorate milestone holidays of importance to the nation. Gerald Ford addressed many events associated with the U.S. Bicentennial in 1976, and Bill Clinton delivered a nationally televised speech from the Lincoln Memorial to a crowd of millennium revelers just after the clock struck midnight on January 1, 2000.

Presidents traditionally have issued statements celebrating official holidays such as Memorial Day and Thanksgiving and unofficial holidays such as St. Patrick's Day. They cannot, however, proclaim an official federal holiday without an act of Congress. George Washington was the first president to proclaim a national holiday. In response to a congressional recommendation, he declared that a national day of thanksgiving should be observed on Thursday, November 26, 1789.[14] This proclamation contributed to the development of the Thanksgiving holiday now observed in the United States. The most recent holiday established by the government commemorates the birthday of Martin Luther King Jr. After initial opposition, Ronald Reagan signed legislation on November 2, 1983, declaring the third Monday in January beginning in 1986 to be a legal federal holiday honoring the civil rights leader.

Holidays can also prove divisive and alienating, however. The fight to add a holiday in honor of Dr. King was long and difficult. When presidents light the annual Christmas tree, they can also be understood as relegating other religions to second-class status. Some Native Americans object to celebrations of Thanksgiving and Columbus Day.

As with endorsements, presidents have to be aware of the complicated nature of celebrating holidays. When a president selects certain holidays to celebrate, he is also celebrating a specific version of the national identity, one that usually is endorsed by a majority of citizens, but that can also underline the minority status of others.[15]

First Eulogist

When a disaster occurs at home or abroad, or when a prominent American dies, the president is expected to lead the nation in mourning. The president routinely issues statements eulogizing Americans who have died. Presidential statements concerning death come in three main forms: brief statements announcing a death or disaster, more extended statements following the death of a specific person or persons, and still lengthier, formal eulogies given at funerals or memorial services.[16] The president's attendance at funerals, however, generally is reserved for former presidents, high government officials, close presidential friends and relatives, or people who died in national tragedies. In all cases, the president, as chief of state, finds a connection between the decedent and the polity, usually holding up the recently deceased as an exemplar of citizenship and, in the case of foreign leaders, of more generalized democratic values.[17]

When presidents do attend funerals in the United States in their role as chief of state, they usually address the mourners. President Nixon delivered the eulogy at Eisenhower's state funeral at the U.S. Capitol on March 30, 1969. President Clinton delivered a eulogy at Nixon's funeral in California on April 27, 1994. Both President George W. Bush and

Vice President Richard B. Cheney eulogized Ronald Reagan when he died in June 2004.

Presidents also must respond to the deaths of Americans who died while serving their country. Perhaps the most famous of all presidential speeches, Lincoln's Gettysburg Address, was delivered during Lincoln's visit to the site of the great battle where thousands of Union and Confederate troops lost their lives. During a war presidents rarely

President Ronald Reagan and staff grimly watch television reports on the Challenger disaster that killed seven astronauts. Americans often look to the president to lead them in dealing with national tragedy.

have time to memorialize individual members of the armed services. In peacetime, however, presidents often honor Americans whose deaths capture the attention of the nation. For example, President Reagan addressed the nation on January 31, 1986, at the memorial service for the seven astronauts killed in the *Challenger* space shuttle disaster, and President Clinton spoke at the April 23, 1995, memorial service for the victims of the Oklahoma City bombing. President George W. Bush proclaimed September 14, 2001, a national day of "prayer and remembrance" for the victims of the World Trade Center and Pentagon terrorist attacks. He eulogized the dead at a nationally televised, multifaith service held at Washington's National Cathedral on that day.

As head of state, presidents receive invitations to the funerals of foreign leaders. Johnson attended Konrad Adenauer's funeral in Cologne in April 1967, and Nixon traveled to Paris to attend Charles de Gaulle's funeral in November 1970. Presidents rarely go to funerals overseas because of the difficulty of postponing other business and arranging security measures on short notice.

If the president does not go to the funeral, a representative is sent in the president's place. The decision of whom to send to a foreign funeral depends on the importance of the country to the United States, the current state of diplomatic relations between the two nations, and the deceased leader's political relationship with the United States. The vice president or secretary of state usually represents the president and the nation at the funerals of prominent world leaders. Former presidents who worked closely with a fallen

leader also sometimes attend. President Reagan and Vice President Bush did not attend Egyptian president Anwar Sadat's funeral in October 1981 for security reasons, but Reagan asked former presidents Nixon, Ford, and Carter to represent the United States. At the funerals of leaders of countries that have a strained or minimal relationship with the United States, the U.S. ambassador to that country often will represent the president.

The Imperative to See and Be Seen

George Washington adopted the monarchical tradition of the "procession" and thereby established the precedent that presidents should travel widely among the American people. He made two regional tours as president: New England in 1789 and the South in 1791. For Washington, the purpose of these tours of the states was "to become better acquainted with their principle Characters and internal Circumstances, as well as to be more accessible to numbers of well-informed persons"—in other words, to see and be seen.[18] Since then, presidents have been expected to leave the capital occasionally to reacquaint themselves with the nation's problems and listen to the public's needs and complaints. Franklin Roosevelt explained his own need for such travels: "I have always thought it was part of the duty of the Presidency to keep in touch, personal touch, with the Nation. . . . [N]ow I am going to the Coast . . . to have a 'look-see,' to try to tie together in my own mind the problems of the Nation, in order that I may, at first hand, know as much about the questions that affect all the forty-eight states as possible."[19]

Citizens may become apathetic toward politics and government if they perceive that leaders in the capital do not care what happens in the rest of the country. By traveling out to the people in the "provinces," presidents can show their interest in the culture of particular regions. They can reawaken public interest in their administration's programs and in government in general. Presidents consequently now engage in multiple town meetings during their administrations, when they visit small towns and meet with carefully selected members of the public, who are allowed to ask questions (sometimes approved in advance). Such events allow presidents to offer the appearance of keeping in touch with all of their constituents.

Five years after a bomb destroyed the Alfred P. Murrah Federal Building in Oklahoma City, President Bill Clinton helped dedicate the Oklahoma City National Memorial in April 2000. Where the nine-story building once stood, 168 bronze and stone chairs memorialize each victim of the bombing.

Presidents who neglect this aspect of the chief of state role may find themselves in trouble with the public. George H. W. Bush was perceived as neglecting California following riots in Los Angeles in 1992, especially when Democratic presidential candidate Bill Clinton made a point of going to the city. As president, Clinton was equally quick to respond, visit, or speak out on events such as the murder of Matthew Shepard, a gay man, in 1998 and the shooting at Columbine High School in Littleton, Colorado, in 1999.

Simply speaking out or even visiting may not be enough. George W. Bush was heavily criticized for a general lack of concern immediately following Hurricane Katrina, for instance. Critics complained that it took him too long to visit the area, although he appeared within days of the disaster and visited twice more within the month. Failure to appear among the people will make matters worse for a president, but appearing is a necessary, not a sufficient, condition for political success as chief of state.

HEAD OF STATE ROLE AND PRESIDENTIAL POWER

The ceremonial and symbolic aspects of the presidency appear less important than the responsibilities that come with the president's other powers. When presidents veto bills, sign treaties, nominate Supreme Court justices, issue pardons, or order military actions, they obviously have exercised presidential power. As chief of state, however, the president acts neither as a commander nor as an administrator.

The effects of ceremonial leadership are less observable and impossible to quantify. Consequently, the chief of state duties are seldom described as a power and are sometimes denounced as a waste of the president's time.

Although the president's authority to dedicate a monument or congratulate an astronaut may mean little, the symbolism of the chief of state role does constitute a real power, because it enhances presidential authority and legitimizes and magnifies other presidential powers. As political scientist Clinton Rossiter explained, "No President can fail to realize that all his powers are invigorated, indeed are given a new dimension of authority, because he is the symbol of our sovereignty, continuity, and grandeur."[20]

The presidency, therefore, is elevated above other offices and institutions not just by its legal authority, but by its symbolic mystique. This mystique has been built up by two centuries of veneration for an office that has been occupied by many of the nation's greatest heroes. Rossiter also said, "The final greatness of the Presidency lies in the truth that it is not just an office of incredible power but a breeding ground of indestructible myth."[21] Astute chief executives wield that mythic power in the service of their more concrete ones.

Symbolic Leadership

The symbolic power of the chief of state role is both immense and important. Presidents can use ceremonial occasions to underline their other powers (George W. Bush announcing "mission accomplished" on the deck of an aircraft carrier during the war on Iraq), to buttress their political position when those other powers may be faltering

GEORGE WASHINGTON AS THE FIRST HEAD OF STATE

When George Washington became president, it was inevitable that the head of state role would become a prominent aspect of the presidency. His status as a military hero and the leader most identified with the American Revolution both in the United States and abroad made him a national symbol even before he became president. Because he had embodied the higher purposes of the revolution, his acceptance of the presidency brought legitimacy to the Constitution. Presidents since Washington have derived respect and authority from their presidential office and powers. With Washington, however, the flow of benefits was reversed. It was he who brought legitimacy and prominence to an office that had no tradition or established operating procedures and would have been distrusted by the people had he not held it.[1]

Washington believed his primary task as president was to unify the country and establish strong political institutions. In no other presidency were ceremony and symbolism more important to the fulfillment of the president's goals. John Adams saw George Washington as a master of dramatic, symbolic leadership. Many years after Washington's death he commented:

> We may say of him, if he was not the greatest President he was the best Actor of the Presidency we have ever had. His address to The States when he left the Army: His solemn Leave taken of Congress when he resigned his Commission: his Farewell Address to the People when he resigned his Presidency. These were all in a strain of Shakespearean and Garrickal excellence in Dramatic Exhibitions.[2]

Washington understood that everything he did as president would set a precedent for future presidents and that even small matters of ceremony could affect the reputation and success of the new government and his office. He wrote:

> Many things which appear of little importance in themselves and at the beginning, may have great and durable consequences from their having been established at the commencement of a new and general government. It will be much easier to commence the administration, upon a well adjusted system, built on tenable grounds, than to correct errors or alter inconveniences after they shall have been confirmed by habit.[3]

Washington, therefore, carefully performed ceremonial functions so as to strike a balance between the dignity and accessibility of the presidency. He traveled to his New York inauguration in a carriage, acknowledging the cheers of crowds, but gave a highly formal speech at his inauguration and did not participate in the public revelry surrounding the occasion. Early in his presidency he established a system of formal receptions known as "levees," which allowed him to frequently receive members of government and the public but also to maintain a solemnity that preserved his aura of authority. He also accepted the formal title of "President of the United States" granted by Congress but did not endorse or participate in Vice President John Adams's campaign to have Congress establish the ostentatious presidential title "His Highness the President of the United States and Protector of the Rights of the Same."[4]

Washington's attention to the details of his head of state role had significance beyond establishing the proprieties of his office. Washington was also determined to strengthen the common identity of Americans and the primacy of the federal government over the states. The weakness of the federal government and its dependence on the states under the Articles of Confederation had greatly disturbed Washington and had been the motivation behind the establishment of the new government.

Convincing the nation of the primacy of the federal government and inspiring in the American people a sense of common identity were difficult tasks. The Constitution clearly gave the federal government legal preeminence over the states. Nevertheless, most Americans felt a greater allegiance to their state than to the Union, and state officials naturally tended to resist federal authority as an intrusion into their jurisdictions. The fledgling government lacked the tools to implement government policy. In particular, the federal government had no army or navy and only a few federal marshals who could gather information and enforce federal laws. Consequently, Washington had to rely on state governors to provide militia and law enforcement officers to deal with violations of federal statutes.

Washington used his head of state role to counter impressions that the federal government lacked authority and did not deserve the primary loyalties of the people. He traveled to every state to underscore national unity, taking trips to the northern states in 1789 and to the southern states in 1791. He also insisted that foreign governments deal with him, the representative of all the people, instead of with Congress, which was chosen by local constituencies. When Congress voted for a day of thanksgiving in November 1789, Washington issued the proclamation instead of having Congress ask the states to issue it, as had been done with similar declarations under the Articles of Confederation.[5]

Even when seemingly trivial matters of protocol were concerned, Washington was careful to assert the primacy of the presidency and the federal government. During his tour of New England in 1789 he asked to dine with John Hancock, the governor of Massachusetts, but indicated that Hancock should call on him first. When Hancock claimed to be too ill to visit the president, Washington canceled dinner and wrote a stiff note to the governor: "The president of the United States presents his best respects to the Governor, and has the honor to inform him that he shall be at home 'till 2 o'clock. The President of the United States need not express the pleasure it will give him to see the Governor; but at the same time, he most earnestly begs that the Governor will not hazard his health on the occasion."[6] Washington scored an important symbolic victory for the presidency and the Constitution when Hancock relented after a two-day standoff. The governor, who continued to profess an illness, was carried to the president's lodgings by several servants.[7]

1. Glenn Phelps, "George Washington and the Founding of the Presidency," *Presidential Studies Quarterly* 17 (spring 1987): 352.

2. Quoted in Clinton Rossiter, *The American Presidency*, 2d ed. (New York: Harcourt, Brace, and World, 1960), 92.

3. Quoted in James Hart, *The American Presidency in Action, 1789* (New York: Macmillan, 1948), 12.

4. Joseph E. Kallenbach, *The American Chief Executive: The Presidency and the Governorship* (New York: Harper and Row, 1966), 274.

5. Phelps, "George Washington and the Founding of the Presidency," 351.

6. Quoted in Ibid., 351–352.

7. Hart, *American Presidency in Action, 1789*, 20.

(Bill Clinton's triumphant State of the Union Address in the midst of his impeachment scandal), and to gain support that they may have lacked previously (through invitations to the White House, signatures on photographs, and speeches given to select audiences or in specific cities).

Presidents also use their symbolic power when they engage in ceremonies for the people. They can provide uplift in times of crisis (Franklin Roosevelt's jaunty cigarette holder became a symbol of hope during the Great Depression), calm in times of trouble (Reagan's address in the wake of the *Challenger* disaster), strength in time of war (Woodrow Wilson's principled stand in the war "to make the world safe for democracy" and George W. Bush's comments at Ground Zero), and compassion in time of peace (Lyndon Johnson's address following the historic civil rights march in Selma, Alabama). Presidents acting symbolically as chief of state also let citizens know what is important culturally by inviting performers and artists to the White House and by attending events outside of it. They reflect national identity by representing the people at those events.

The chief of state role equips presidents with several symbolic assets through which they can reinforce their executive leadership. Presidents are seen as the symbol of national unity, the symbol of national continuity, and the symbol of the federal government. Although presidents may have varying success at using these assets to further their policies, all presidents possess them by virtue of holding office and exercising presidential powers.

Symbol of National Unity

The Constitution provided for three independent branches of government, but the president, not Congress or the courts, has become the symbol of national unity. The presidency's emergence as a unifying symbol was predictable. George Washington, who was a national symbol even before he became president, saw his presidential role primarily as that of a national unifier who would draw together the citizens of the thirteen states and the followers of various political philosophies into one nation. Although no president since has been able to remain as nonpartisan as Washington, few presidents have been slaves to their parties, and most have worked in some way to reduce national divisions. In addition, presidents are the most identifiable national leaders and the only elected officials (with the exception of vice presidents) who have a national constituency. As such they are seen as the guardian of the interests of the whole nation against the narrow demands of partisan and sectional groups.

The president's status as a symbol of national unity is an especially valuable political asset because much of what the president does as chief executive and party leader divides the nation. Political scientist Thomas E. Cronin has observed that presidents

> necessarily divide when they act as the leaders of their political parties, when they set priorities that advantage certain goals and groups at the expense of others, when they forge and lead political coalitions, when they move out ahead of public opinion and assume the role of

national educators, and when they choose one set of advisers over another. A President, as a creative executive leader, cannot help but offend certain interests.[22]

Being a symbol of national unity allows presidents to heal some of the wounds they open while acting in their other roles and to maintain the public's confidence in them as leader of the entire nation. Eisenhower was particularly adept at projecting an image of an amiable unifier while hiding his political side, thereby maximizing the unifying potential of his chief of state role.[23] George W. Bush claimed that he was "a uniter, not a divider," but he had considerably less success than Eisenhower in fostering that image. Bush presided over one of the most politically polarized periods in recent American history, and many consider him responsible for that polarization.[24] Even making adept use of his chief of state role has not been enough to heal the divisions in the nation, but it has helped to keep those divisions from becoming even more serious. When Americans do not like the president as an individual, they generally continue to respect the office.

The power of the presidency as a unifying symbol is demonstrated by the public's reaction to an international crisis. Even when Americans disagree with the president's policies, they have tended to rally around the president when the nation's interests are threatened by a foreign power. Public opinion polls have shown that presidential approval ratings usually improve when the nation becomes involved in a war or other international crisis. For example, President Kennedy's public approval rating jumped thirteen percentage points in 1962 after the Cuban missile crisis. In 1975 Ford's public approval rating shot up eleven points after he ordered marines to rescue the crew of the merchant ship *Mayaguez,* which had been seized by Cambodian forces. George H. W. Bush's approval rating briefly reached 89 percent after the swift defeat of Iraq by a U.S.-led coalition in the 1991 Persian Gulf War.

But even this record score was topped by George W. Bush, who received the approval of 90 percent of Americans polled ten days after the September 11, 2001, terrorist attacks against the World Trade Center and the Pentagon. That rating represented an amazing jump of thirty-nine percentage points over the rating he held the week before the attack. As the nation continued to fight a war against terrorism in Afghanistan amid the possibility of additional terrorist attacks on the U.S. homeland, Bush's approval rating remained near record levels until plummeting in 2005. The sustained support for President Bush reflected the gravity of the threat to the United States and the public's desire for a unified and vigorous response to the attacks.

Although presidential approval ratings will improve the most when the public perceives that the president has acted skillfully or boldly to meet an international crisis, even clear foreign policy failures can add to a president's popularity. In

May 1960, the Soviets shot down an American U-2 spy plane over Soviet territory. President Eisenhower denied the United States was conducting intelligence flights over the Soviet Union, but when Moscow produced the captured pilot, Eisenhower took responsibility for the missions. Eisenhower's approval rating jumped six percentage points after the incident, despite heightened East-West tensions and the collapse of a summit meeting in Paris later in the month. Similarly, after the U.S.-sponsored Bay of Pigs invasion of Cuba by exiled Cuban nationals in 1961, President Kennedy's approval rating improved eleven points, to 83 percent, even though the invasion was considered a disaster.[25] The public rallied around Eisenhower and Kennedy in these situations not because they achieved anything, but because they were the symbols of the United States during a time of international confrontation.

These effects, however, tend to be short-lived. Extended crises and protracted armed conflicts can severely strain a president's relationship with the public. At the height of the Vietnam War, for example, Lyndon Johnson was so besieged by protestors that he drastically reduced his public speaking. The war in Iraq damaged George W. Bush's standing in the polls. All the major polling organizations listed his public approval numbers as hovering between the high 30 percent approval and low 40 percent approval range for most of the summer of 2006.[26] A president's ability to serve as a symbol of national unity in time of crisis is inversely related to the length of the crisis.

Symbol of Continuity

Presidents also benefit from occupying an office that is identified with the continuity of the United States and the stability of its political institutions. The American people see the president not only as the current national leader but also as the latest in a long line of presidents who have guarded the freedom and laws of the United States. Lincoln, perhaps the most celebrated U.S. president, is remembered primarily for preserving the Union. When political rivals challenge the president, they are in the position of confronting the defender of the Constitution and the heir of Washington, Jefferson, Lincoln, and the Roosevelts.

Presidents work hard to fortify their symbolic power by emphasizing past associations. In particular, they often cite and quote the Framers, Lincoln, and both Roosevelts to justify their policy and political preferences. Contemporary Republicans often add Reagan to that list. George W. Bush did less of this than most of his predecessors, preferring scriptural to political references, although he, too, mentioned the country's shared political past, noting in his first inaugural, for instance, a letter written by John Page to Thomas Jefferson. Such references are usually liberally sprinkled throughout presidential speeches, as they seek to connect themselves to the nation's history. Barack Obama

invited comparisons to Lincoln in the elaborately staged inaugural celebration of 2008. Since taking office, he has found occasion to cite or quote Lincoln about fifty times a year, on average.[27] In his 2012 State of the Union address, he sought to align himself with Lincoln, who in this instance was cited as "Republican Abraham Lincoln," a proponent of limited government.

Yet special links to the past need not be present for a president to take advantage of the inherent continuity symbolized by the office. When Bill Clinton went to Normandy in June 1994 to commemorate the fiftieth anniversary of the Allies' D-Day invasion, he could not claim to have a personal link to the heroics he would honor. He was the first president born after World War II, and he had avoided service in the military during the Vietnam War. As chief of state, however, he was inherently linked to American history, the survival of the nation, and the succession of generations. His speeches on the occasion emphasized the victory of the World War II generation and the obligation of his own generation to build on their sacrifice.

The history of the presidency itself demonstrates the stability of the nation's political institutions. Power has always been transferred peacefully from one president to the next. The unbroken chain of presidents has survived assassinations, civil war, impeachment proceedings, election fraud, and a presidential resignation. Even before the presidency faced any of these trials its continuity impressed Martin Van Buren, president from 1837 to 1841, who wrote: "The President under our system, like the king in a monarchy, never dies."[28]

When presidents leave office they continue to symbolize the United States of a past era and the continuity of the nation's democratic institutions. Although there have been exceptions, retiring presidents customarily attend the inaugural ceremonies of their successors, thereby symbolically demonstrating the strength of the Constitution, which provides for the peaceful and orderly transfer of presidential power.[29] Former presidents also can contribute to an image of stability during crises. At John Kennedy's funeral, Herbert C. Hoover, Harry S. Truman, and Dwight Eisenhower sat with Lyndon Johnson in a show of nonpartisan support. Together they constituted a powerful symbol of continuity that reassured a nation not yet recovered from the shock of Kennedy's assassination.[30]

Similarly, all the living ex-presidents appeared together at ceremonies honoring Richard Nixon and Ronald Reagan upon their deaths. Political differences, political animosities, and even political failures are subsumed by the importance of honoring the presidency as a symbol of service to the nation.

Symbol of Government

As chief of state the president symbolizes not only the nation but also its government. Because the presidency is occupied by a single familiar individual who has broad executive powers, including the prerogative to initiate policy, it is the most dynamic and understandable element of the federal government.

For many Americans, presidential actions become synonymous with governmental action. For example, a president unveiling a tax reform proposal to a national television audience is more easily understood than the bargaining and consultations within the executive branch that produced the proposal or the complex political and procedural battles that will be fought over the tax reform issue in Congress. The proposal is seen as emanating not from the Treasury Department or the executive branch, but from the president. Historians and journalists frequently organize American history according to presidential administrations. Policy programs, military conflicts, and economic conditions all become identified with the president who was serving at the time they came into existence, even if that president was not primarily responsible for them. The presidency, therefore, is used by many Americans as a "cognitive handle" that personalizes and simplifies the detailed processes of governing the nation.[31]

George W. Bush recognized the link between the image he projected after the September 11, 2001, terrorist attacks and public confidence in the U.S. government. The attacks occurred while Bush was making an appearance at a grade school in Florida. Initially, he was transported by *Air Force One* to secure military bases in Louisiana and then Nebraska. Later in the day, he returned to Washington to demonstrate that the government was operating and that he was in charge. That night he delivered a televised address to the American people from the Oval Office in which he declared: "Our country is strong. A great people has been moved to defend a great nation. Terrorist attacks can shake the foundations of our biggest buildings, but they cannot touch the foundation of America. These acts shatter steel, but they cannot dent the steel of American resolve."

Over the next several weeks, Bush made numerous high-profile public appearances to bolster public morale, even though these appearances required extraordinary security arrangements. Like Franklin Roosevelt after Pearl Harbor, Bush recognized that public optimism was essential to fostering the recovery of a shaken nation and affirming its confidence that the government was doing everything possible to prevent further attacks.

Being the most visible symbol of government can work against presidents as well as for them. Public expectations of the president are often unreasonable. Because it is easier to blame an individual for society's problems than to understand all the complicated factors contributing to

In May 1860 President James Buchanan greets Japan's first envoys to the United States.

them, presidents receive much unjust criticism. Public dissatisfaction with federal government policies or local conditions over which the president has little control may be translated into disapproval of the president.

For better or for worse, presidents symbolize the government as a whole. Their status can rise and fall with public perceptions of the performance of that government. Similarly, presidents can, through judicious use of the role of chief of state, influence those perceptions. This is true both at home and abroad.

Tool of Foreign Policy

As chief of state, the president is the ceremonial representative of the United States to the international community. Presidents make ceremonial visits to foreign countries and greet foreign dignitaries who visit the United States. Whether presidents are receiving visitors in the White House or touring the world, they are expected to fulfill both their diplomatic and ceremonial responsibilities. When U.S. presidents visit Great Britain, for example, they usually have a ceremonial meeting with the reigning monarch and a policy meeting with the prime minister.

The international chief of state role, however, cannot be neatly separated from the president's activities as the architect of U.S. foreign relations. State visits and other international ceremonies and spectacles that the president undertakes as chief of state are tools of foreign policy. They are a means of communicating the intentions and attitudes of the administration and improving the relationships of the United States with foreign governments.

Presidents and their representatives also use international ceremonial appearances and events to lobby for the support of foreign peoples and leaders. The foreign public observes U.S. presidents most often in their chief of state role. When presidents admire landmarks, make speeches, and attend state dinners on their foreign trips, they are trying to increase their popularity overseas and establish a reservoir of good will to benefit U.S. interests. International respect for a president will enhance the image of the United States, the confidence of the U.S. public, and the president's ability to exert leadership in the international arena. In these globalized and increasingly interdependent times, even the world's lone superpower is loath to act entirely alone, and the necessity of international coalition building has led to an increased reliance on international good will. Henry A. Kissinger is credited with creating "shuttle diplomacy" between foreign capitals during his service in the Nixon and Ford administrations, but it is now a fact of life for presidents, their secretaries of state, and other high-ranking administration officials.

Greeting Foreign Leaders

Presidents must entertain many visiting chiefs of state, prime ministers, and other foreign dignitaries every year. These visits often include a photo session and a state dinner attended by selected members of Congress, administration officials, and national celebrities.

The manner in which presidents receive a foreign chief of state sends a signal to that leader and other nations about U.S. policy. President Carter's friendly greeting of Chinese vice premier Deng Xiaoping in January 1979 was a ceremonial act with profound diplomatic implications. Before, during, and after Deng's visit to the United States, the vice premier had pointedly attacked the leaders of the Soviet Union for pursuing an aggressive foreign policy. The Carter administration's warm reception of Deng and its refusal to condemn his belligerent rhetoric signaled tolerance for the vice premier's views and a clear tilt toward the Chinese in the trilateral relationship. When George W. Bush received Russian president Vladimir Putin in November 2001, he wanted to emphasize not only the warmer relations developing between the two countries, but also the warmer personal relationship he was developing with the Russian president. Symbolically, the Bush White House achieved this

FOREIGN HEADS OF STATE

The division of the head of state and head of government roles between two or more individuals in most European governments demonstrates that a nation's chief executive does not also need to be its figurehead, as is the case in the United States. In many nations, including Belgium, Denmark, Great Britain, the Netherlands, Norway, and Sweden, a king or queen serves as chief of state even though the monarchy has lost executive powers. In these countries the monarchs have become integrative figures who embody the history and ideals of their nations.

In other countries such as France, Germany, Israel, and Italy, the chief of state role is assigned to an elected official who serves alongside the head of the government.[1] Many democracies in Latin America have followed the model of the United States, lodging both the chief of state and chief executive powers in a single president.

Significantly, no democratic nation has both a monarch and a president, perhaps because the symbol of a nation cannot be divisible.[2] Yet no chief executive can be entirely insulated from ceremonial duties. Even when a chief of state's office is a cherished part of the national culture grounded in centuries of tradition, such as the British monarchy, the person who wields power will be expected to preside at some symbolic functions. In particular, chief executives must greet important foreign visitors who want to meet with the most powerful person in the country, not just the reigning figurehead.

1. Merlin Gustafson, "Our Part-Time Chief of State," *Presidential Studies Quarterly* 9 (spring 1979): 164.
2. David F. Prindle, "Head of State and Head of Government in Comparative Perspective," *Presidential Studies Quarterly* 21 (winter 1991): 57.

goal by scheduling, after the formal meetings in Washington, a two-day visit to Bush's ranch in Crawford, Texas, where Bush treated Putin to a Texas barbecue.

Presidents also can make a statement about their foreign policy priorities through their invitations to visit the United States. In 1977, for example, Carter wished to emphasize the importance of U.S. relations with its North American neighbors. Consequently, the first two foreign leaders he invited to the White House were President José López Portillo of Mexico and Prime Minister Pierre Trudeau of Canada.

Chief of State in Wartime

Presidents want to maintain good relations with foreign leaders because they can become important sources of support. When presidents go to war, for instance, increasingly they do so as part of a multinational force. Presidents prefer, when possible, to have the support of U.S. allies and of the United Nations when committing troops abroad. Such support is facilitated by firm personal relationships and the kind of mutual trust that can come only from knowing a person individually. Winston Churchill and Franklin Roosevelt, for example, had a warm personal relationship, which eased their negotiations during World War II. British prime minister Tony Blair and President George W. Bush shared an equally close relationship, which contributed to their ability to work together during the Iraqi war.

Another important function of the chief of state in wartime is to bolster the morale of the troops themselves. As national symbol, the president can be a powerful reminder of the purpose of an armed conflict, and the presence of the commander in chief can help the troops to remain focused and committed to the tasks at hand. The president can also wield his role as chief of state to help maintain public support for a war. He can present medals, talk with the families of service personnel, bring those who serve to State of the Union addresses as important symbols of the war effort, and he can use his ceremonial function to make implicit arguments justifying the need for war.

In general, the American people defer to the president, especially in times of war. Because his ability to function as commander in chief includes the unilateral exercise of power, it is important that the president act in ways that reaffirm his commitment to democratic values. The chief of state role allows him to do this by giving him a forum in which it is appropriate to discuss such values, and his commitment to them. It also allows him to be seen speaking and interacting with the troops, foreign leaders, and the American public in ways that look democratic and can thus counteract any criticism that he is assuming too much power.

Partisan Politics

When a political system separates the chief of state role from that of the chief executive, the chief of state can transcend partisanship. The British monarch takes no official position in the political struggles between British political parties. Such nonpartisanship is impossible for the U.S. president, who must function as the leader of a political party as well as chief of state.

Virtually everything the president does in public as chief of state has political significance. Political scientist David F. Prindle observed that skillful presidents can take advantage of the ambiguity of their office for partisan purposes:

> A dominant president, that is, one that both functions as a symbol and has pre-eminent policy-making authority, is an ambiguous sort of figure. Ordinary citizens are liable to confuse the two roles, seeing the partisan utterances of the politician as the disinterested pronouncements of the symbol. The Head of State role can thus be used by clever presidents to overawe opposition to the programs they advocate as Head of Government.[32]

Partisanship can provide both an opportunity and a challenge for a president. Presidents Clinton, George W. Bush, and Obama, for instance, faced a nation that was sharply divided along partisan lines, giving them both implacable enemies and fervent supporters. Clinton swung between a strategy of confrontation and conciliation. After the opposition party gained control of Congress in the midterm elections just two years into his first term, Clinton moved to the center on a number of divisive issues, and used the ceremonial stature of his office to his advantage as he competed with Congress for credit over legislative compromises.[33]

Bush used the chief of state role to partisan advantage differently than his predecessor. According to political scientist Peri Arnold, by acting as if he not only won the 2000 election outright but also achieved a popular mandate, Bush used the divided nature of Congress and the public to create the perception of a country unified under his administration. He did not dwell on the differences the election magnified but claimed the fact of his election as a justification of his policy proposals.[34] The terrorist attacks of September 11, 2001, elevated Bush's stature enormously and generated for the president political capital to advance his national security agenda. In the 2002 midterm elections, the White House spent some of this capital to elect Republican candidates to Congress, by communicating the message that failure to support the Bush agenda to fight back against U.S. enemies with tough new laws that critics said infringed on American civil liberties was un-American.

Barack Obama campaigned on a pledge to transcend old-fashioned party politics. Once in office, he found that he had no choice but to work closely with the ideologically united Democratic majority in the House of Representatives if he hoped to achieve significant legislative victories. The passage of a stimulus package in 2009 and an expansion of government-guaranteed health care in 2010 were strictly partisan affairs. In forging a health care bill, the president managed even to alienate core Democratic constituencies, which wanted a "public option," while failing to attract a single Republican vote. If there was a postpartisan or nonpartisan or even bipartisan path that the president might have followed, Obama did not find it. Nor did he find a way to buttress his partisanship by a skillful use of his symbolic powers to unify the public. The electorate responded instead to the partisan pleadings of the opposition party, which regained control of the House in a landslide defeat for the president and his party in November 2010.

The dignity and status conferred on presidents as the nation's ceremonial and symbolic leader can at times increase their popularity with the American public and their bargaining advantages over other government officials. The chief of state role also provides presidents with a justification to preside over events that have obvious public relations appeal. Chief of state activities can be staged to make presidents look patriotic, amiable, concerned, skilled, and noble. Because chief of state activities are built into the president's job description, the role allows presidents to campaign subtly throughout their term without having to appear overly political or self-serving. But the head of state

JIMMY CARTER'S ATTEMPTS TO "DEPOMP" THE PRESIDENCY

During Jimmy Carter's presidential campaign leading up to his 1976 election, he perceived that the American people were still disturbed by the Watergate scandal and wanted the next president to restore their trust in government. Carter's emphasis on establishing an honest and unpretentious administration helped to propel him to the White House past several better-known Democratic candidates and the Republican incumbent, Gerald R. Ford. As president, Carter was determined to eliminate barriers between the presidency and the people.

Carter began his campaign to "depomp" the presidency on his first day as president. After his inauguration ceremony, he and his wife got out of their limousine and walked up Pennsylvania Avenue to the White House. This gesture symbolized his intention to cut back on the privileges surrounding his office. After Carter's term was over, he wrote about his decision to walk back to the White House:

> I began to realize that the symbolism of our leaving the armored car would be much more far-reaching than simply to promote exercise. I remembered the angry demonstrators who had habitually confronted recent Presidents and Vice Presidents, furious over the Vietnam war and later the revelations of Watergate. I wanted to provide a vivid demonstration of my confidence in the people as far as security was concerned, and I felt a simple walk would be a tangible indication of some reduction in the imperial status of the President and his family.[1]

Thereafter Carter continued his efforts to undo the imperial presidency. He sold the presidential yacht, carried his own garment bag, donated blood, and ordered the White House thermostat to be set at sixty-five degrees in the winter.[2] In addition, he stopped the practice of having "Hail to the Chief" played when he entered the scene of an official event, delivered a Franklin D. Roosevelt–style fireside chat, and was often photographed in informal clothing.

Carter also attempted to dispel the imperial atmosphere surrounding the presidency by emphasizing his accessibility. During the first several months of his presidency, he held frequent press conferences and question-and-answer sessions with federal employees. He also attended town meetings in rural communities, conducted a phone-in talk show in which members of the public could ask him direct questions, and, when traveling within the country, lodged in the homes of American families.[3] Carter even invited John B. Shanklin, a Washington, D.C.,

hotel worker, to the White House, just as he had promised during a 1974 encounter with Shanklin at the outset of Carter's campaign for the Democratic nomination.

During his first months in office, Carter's openness appealed to the American people, and he enjoyed high public approval ratings. As time passed, however, Carter and his aides suspected that they had gone too far in eliminating pomp from the presidency. As the president's popularity dropped throughout most of his first year and a half in office, it appeared that Carter's populist style had made him seem less presidential than past chief executives and had muted the patriotic message contained in presidential symbols. For some people, Carter's actions also seemed to be weakening the office of the president.[4] Carter recalled: "I overreacted at first. We began to receive many complaints that I had gone too far in cutting back the pomp and ceremony, so after a few months I authorized the band to play 'Hail to the Chief' on special occasions. I found it to be impressive and enjoyed it."[5] As his term progressed, Carter tried to establish a balance between the regal symbols that contributed to an image of himself as a powerful, decisive president and the populist symbols that had helped him to get elected.

Carter had initially misinterpreted what the public wanted after the Watergate scandal. Undoubtedly, the people desired honesty and openness in the White House, but not at the expense of the symbolism that contributed to the presidency's historic and paternal image. The imperial presidency of Richard Nixon did not end in disgrace because he enjoyed the ceremonial display of his office, but rather because he had broken the law, cut himself off from everyone but a handful of advisers, and betrayed the trust of the American people. Carter learned that the symbols of the presidency contribute to presidential power, and no president can reject them without risking an erosion in popular support. Significantly, since Carter, no president has renewed his effort to move the ceremonial presidency off of center stage.

1. Jimmy Carter, *Keeping Faith* (New York: Bantam Books, 1982), 17–18.
2. Larry Berman, *The New American Presidency* (Boston: Little, Brown, 1987), 314.
3. Harold M. Barger, *The Impossible Presidency: Illusions and Realities of Executive Power* (Glenview, Ill.: Scott, Foresman, 1984), 378.
4. Thomas E. Cronin, *The State of the Presidency*, 2d ed. (Boston: Little, Brown, 1980), 159.
5. Carter, *Keeping Faith*, 27.

role is not magical, and cannot protect all presidents from political disaster.

Presidential Popularity

One of the most important factors affecting presidents' domestic political power is the public support they receive. When a solid majority of Americans backs the president on a particular issue, other political institutions, including Congress, rarely will launch a challenge. The chief of state role can fortify the president's popularity. Some Americans will support the office of the presidency even when they disagree with the incumbent's policies. They believe the office symbolizes the nation and the government. Some Americans will also support the person of the president

even when they disagree with the president's positions, because they have accepted whomever holds the office as their legitimate symbolic leader. In these situations as well, the head of state role fortifies a president's stature. Democratic pollsters in 1984, the year of Reagan's reelection, were frustrated by the president's ability to coast to victory on the theme of American renewal ("It's morning again in America" heralded the Republican campaign), when numerous polls showed that majority opinion was closer to their candidate, Walter Mondale, than the president on a number of highly important policy positions.

Presidents benefit from chief of state activities because such activities make them appear presidential. Formal ceremonies such as the State of the Union address and a state dinner for a foreign head of state feature the president in the role of the nation's leader and guardian and underscore the president's links with the past glories of the office and its revered former occupants. Conversely, chief of state activities also personalize the president. Less formal ceremonies such as a trip to a sporting event or a White House reception for a civic group make the president appear as an average, friendly person who shares the everyday interests and concerns of Americans.

Finally, many Americans will support an incumbent's foreign policies because the president is the representative and symbol of the United States before the world. Few events make a president look more like a world leader than a summit meeting with a prominent head of state or a glittering reception in a foreign country. Presidents attempt to maximize the public relations benefits of their chief of state role by dramatizing their foreign tours and staging them for television. President Nixon timed his historic arrival in Beijing in 1972 to coincide with Sunday night prime-time television viewing hours. The president's return to Washington also was timed to coincide with prime time, even though this required a nine-hour "refueling stop" in Alaska.[35]

Intragovernmental Relations

Although the public often thinks of presidents as leaders who run the country, they are far from omnipotent. Congress can block most presidential initiatives, and the courts can declare a presidential action unconstitutional. Cabinet officers and other members of the executive branch can check presidential power by withholding information, slowing down implementation of presidential directives, leaking details of controversial policies to the media, publicly announcing their opposition to a policy, or resigning to protest a presidential decision. Consequently, presidential power depends on the authority of presidents to issue orders and make proposals as well as on their ability to persuade others that those orders and proposals are correct.

The president's status as chief of state strengthens the president's ability to influence other members of the government. Political scientist Richard E. Neustadt observed:

> Presidential "powers" may be inconclusive when a President commands, but always remain relevant as he persuades. The status and authority inherent in his office reinforce his logic and his charm. . . . [F]ew men—and exceedingly few Cabinet officers—are immune to the impulse to say "yes" to the President of the United States. It grows harder to say "no" when they are seated in his oval office at the White House, or in his office on the second floor, where almost tangibly he partakes of the aura of his physical surroundings.[36]

Such presidential lobbying is hard to resist, especially for members of the president's own party who risk political

isolation if they do not have a good record of supporting the chief executive. Presidents, therefore, can exploit the symbolic power of their office to pressure an official or member of Congress for support.

Presidents also can use the glamour and social prestige of the White House to influence members of Congress and other public leaders by granting or denying them access to White House meetings and social functions. Officials want to be close to the president not just because they benefit from having access to the chief executive's authority, but also because they wish to bask in the glow of presidential celebrity. An invitation to a White House dinner or reception can be one of the most sought after tickets in Washington. It allows the lucky invitee to rub elbows with the most powerful and famous people in the country, and it is a confirmation of that person's importance to the president. Although presidents and their staffs will invite members of the other party to White House events in the name of bipartisanship, political allies of the president receive more invitations than political enemies. Politicians who engage the president in a particularly bitter political battle or become enmeshed in a scandal may be cut off from the president's presence entirely.[37]

Furthermore, when presidents are faced with a stubborn Congress, their status as chief of state bolsters their ability to appeal to the people over the head of the legislative branch. In a strategy known as "going public," presidents have presented their case to the people on an issue and hope that favorable popular opinion and active public pressure on individual legislators will influence Congress to back presidential policy.[38] Franklin Roosevelt had great success with this tactic. His popularity with the American people weakened resistance in Congress to his New Deal programs. Reagan also used this strategy successfully. During his first year in office, he asked the public to pressure Congress to support his efforts to change dramatically the federal government's taxing and spending policies. Despite a solid Democratic majority in the House of Representatives, he was able to pass a large tax cut and bolster spending on defense.

Other presidents have been less successful at using public opinion. In September 1919, President Wilson undertook a cross-country crusade to promote U.S. entry into the League of Nations. After making dozens of speeches in twenty-nine cities across the Midwest and West, he became ill and returned to Washington, D.C., where he suffered a stroke on October 2. Despite Wilson's efforts, the public remained skeptical of an activist foreign policy, and the Republican-controlled Senate refused to ratify the Treaty of Versailles, which established the league.

President Clinton hoped that public pressure would push a skeptical Congress to adopt his comprehensive health care reform bill in 1994. On August 3, he held a news conference to implore action by Congress on the legislation.

He also spoke to pro–health care reform rallies and endorsed a bus caravan touring the nation to drum up support. But opponents of the Clinton plan countered with their own campaign that portrayed Clinton's complex approach as an expensive, overly bureaucratic one that would limit choice of doctors and erode the quality of care. Despite the president's efforts, public support for his plan sank during August and September. The bill died without coming to a final vote in either house of Congress.

Some evidence exists that speeches help the president persuade members of the executive branch and the bureaucracy in general. These speeches serve as signals to those who do not normally interact with the president about what he is thinking and how he understands the priorities of the administration. Thus, the primary audience may not be the mass public at all, but other members of the Washington community of policymakers.[39]

However, some scholars, most notably George C. Edwards III, argue that presidential speech making is largely ineffective as a tool of pressuring Congress and thus is a waste of valuable presidential time. He notes that the public pays little attention to presidential speeches and is generally uninterested in policy. Edwards suggests that presidents are better off "staying private" than "going public," if they want to influence members of Congress.[40]

Presidents continue to try to persuade the public of the merits of their policies even though their success in doing so is decidedly mixed. Even if they are unable to garner public support for specific policies, such speech making is an important part of the institution. If nothing else, it allows the president to play his role as chief of state and connect to the mass public.

Extragovernmental Power

The president is indisputably the nation's first celebrity. One 1969–1970 survey found that 98 percent of adult Americans knew who was president, a much higher percentage of recognition than for any other public figure except the vice president, who was known by 87 percent. In contrast, only 57 percent knew the name of one senator from their state, and only 39 percent could identify their representative in the House. A 1995 national survey found even less recognition of public figures other than the president: only 60 percent could identify the vice president, 46 percent could name one senator from their state, and 33 percent could name their representative.[41] Majorities among Americans polled in 2003 could not name any of the cabinet departments of the executive branch or any of the justices of the Supreme Court.[42] In this political environment, the president has a clear advantage over other members of the federal government.

The president, the first lady, and former occupants of the White House frequently head the list in "most admired person" polls. In 2005, for instance, the three most admired men in America, according to a Gallup poll, were George H. W. Bush, Bill Clinton, and Jimmy Carter. Hillary Rodham Clinton was the most admired woman, followed by Oprah Winfrey, Condoleezza Rice, and Laura Bush.[43] Most national radio and television news broadcasts will discuss the president's major activity of the day, and few adult Americans would not be able to recite some basic details about the president's personal and political background. More than nine million people tried to telephone the White House during President Carter's call-in radio press conference in 1977. In just the first five months of the Clinton administration, the first family received 3.5 million pieces of mail. By 2006 the White House had so much difficulty handling e-mail that people were sent responses explicitly stating that the administration could not hope to answer even a small fraction of the messages received. Constant attention contributes to the president's political power and gives presidents and their families influence over national culture and attitudes.

But it can also constrain the president, whose every move—and every mistake—is magnified, and presidents are often held responsible for the problems of their family members. Richard Nixon, Jimmy Carter, and Bill Clinton had difficulties because of their brothers' various antics. More recently, George W. Bush had to contend with headlines caused by his daughters' underage drinking and by the arrest of one of his nieces on drug-related charges. No presidential relative has caused serious political difficulties for a chief executive, but most presidents have had to worry that they might.

The Digital Head of State

With the advent of the Internet, electronic communication has become increasingly important to politics in general and to the president's ability to communicate with the American public through his role as chief of state. Each president in the Internet age has used the presidential website, at www .whitehouse.gov, to showcase the administration's accomplishments and to educate and mobilize supporters. Visitors can take a virtual tour of the White House and find transcripts of the president's major speeches, press conferences, proclamations, and news releases, as well as satisfy their curiosity about the president and his family, and presidential history. Barack Obama's campaign made extensive use of social media, and his White House website encourages visitors to sign up for e-mail alerts and to "follow" the president on Facebook, Twitter, and similar sites. Such communication can be important in a world that is characterized by fragmentation and diversity. It is difficult for presidents, or for anyone else, to break through the noise of the contemporary world. Stiff competition for people's attention makes it is hard for presidents to be sure of being heard when they speak. Having an electronic presence online allows presidents to reach people they may not be able to get to in any other way.

The Internet allows presidents to broadcast their view of issues and events and to reveal certain aspects of their personalities, but it does so in a way that minimizes the authority of the presidency. On the Internet, a government web page is perhaps more authoritative than a blog, but there is no guarantee that Internet users will find the government site when doing a web search or that they will access it. The days when the president could monopolize conversations by monopolizing air space or time are gone. The Internet allows for more voices to enter any conversation and for voices that do not belong to the administration to be heard.

Presidents are also increasingly sophisticated about using more traditional means of electronic communication, such as radio and television. President Reagan began the practice of reaching his conservative Republican base by broadcasting a weekly Saturday radio address, something that all his successors have continued. By taking the time to offer a brief speech that is geared toward their supporters, presidents can keep them happy, reassure them that the administration is keeping them in mind, and explain their policy preferences in a forum where they have the listeners' attention.

As chief of state, presidents can also use cable and even network television to their advantage. George W. Bush's staff carefully selected and screened audiences for his town hall meetings. He consequently was asked questions such as "How can I help you accomplish your goals?" Such screening and selection was ridiculed by the president's opponents, but it made for better television for the president than the protests that accompanied Lyndon Johnson's public speeches and allowed the chief executive to appear to enjoy consensus support. Barack Obama has not been as artful or fortunate in his use of television. In a showdown with the Republican-controlled House of Representatives in the summer of 2011, over the conditions under which the lawmakers would agree to raise the nation's debt ceiling, the major networks gave the House Speaker the opportunity to rebut the president's remarks, diminishing the president's opportunity to buttress his policy position by appearing singly before the public in a moment of crisis.

Through well-managed use of the electronic media—television, radio, and the Internet—presidents can connect with the American people in ways that are otherwise difficult. They can foster images of themselves as competent leaders, and they can raise money and bolster support for their policies and for themselves. Presidents sometimes encounter difficulties because they cannot control what is said over the Internet or by late-night television hosts, but the electronic chief of state is likely to be among the most important aspects of the role in the twenty-first century.

Spiritual Leadership

The president's role as an unofficial spiritual leader was first exercised by George Washington, who said in his first inaugural address that

> it would be improper to omit in this first official act, my fervent supplications to that Almighty Being who rules over the Universe.... No people can be bound to acknowledge and adore the invisible hand, which conducts the Affairs of men, more than the People of the United States. Every step, by which they have advanced to the character of an independent nation, seems to have been distinguished by some token of providential agency.

Since then, all presidents have mentioned God in their inaugural addresses.[44] Washington also added the words "so help me God" after the oath of office. Every president has followed Washington's example, thereby making an acknowledgment of God part of the president's first official act.

In his famous second inaugural address, Abraham Lincoln turned the conventions of the American civil religion upside down, suggesting that the "mighty scourge of war" was god's punishment to "both North and South . . . as the woe due to those by whom the offence" of slavery had come. The speech, though it is memorialized in Lincoln's monument alongside his better known Gettysburg address, was a political dud. The North was in no mood to be humble in the approach to victory, especially not after Lincoln's assassination shortly after he delivered his inaugural "sermon." Somewhat ironically, the tendency of presidents to make religious and moral references has been even more prevalent in the modern era. Political scientist Barbara Hinckley found that religious and moral references in inaugural addresses occurred with greater frequency during the post–World War II period than before. The inaugural addresses of Presidents Truman through Reagan contained fourteen times as many religious and moral references as partisan political references. Even in the economic addresses of these presidents, moral and religious references were twice as common as partisan political references.[45] This phenomenon was encouraged by the cold war, when American presidents frequently and explicitly pitted the "god-fearing United States" against the "godless communists." For example, at Eisenhower's urging the phrase "Under God" was added to the Pledge of Allegiance in 1954 and in 1956, Congress passed legislation (PL 84–140) declaring "In God We Trust" the national motto.

Although Americans expect their president to speak as head of the civil religion at their inaugurations and at moments of crisis, the people do not want the president to govern the country according to a private conception of God's will or use the presidency to promote a specific religious faith. Even at the height of the cold war, Eisenhower often professed his faith in God and spoke of the importance of religion in American society, but he was careful not to define God narrowly. In a 1959 speech to the National Council of Churches, he stated that the spiritual unity of the West included not only Judeo-Christian traditions but also "the Mohammedans, the Buddhists and the rest; because they[,] too, strongly believe that they achieve a right to human dignity because of their relationship to the Supreme Being."[46] As the first Roman Catholic to become president, Kennedy made a point of scheduling meetings with Protestant and Jewish groups during the first months of his presidency.

The rising influence of Christian evangelicals in American politics has complicated the performance of the head of state role. Presidents are warmly received when they promote religious faith in general and speak in the tradition of Washington of the divine character of the American nation, but they are widely perceived to have crossed the line when they stray into support of a particular religious tradition. Jimmy Carter was a "born again" Christian and was watched carefully during his four years in office for any sign of deviation from the norms that govern a president's public avowals of faith. George W. Bush came to office with the support of a vocal and energized evangelical community,

and in his 2001 inaugural ceremony, two invited clergy caused a controversy by praying during the ceremony in the name of Jesus Christ instead of using broader references to God. In his leadership of what his administration, but not his successors, called the "Global War on Terror," Bush was accused of being motivated by his personal religious convictions, and even of communicating in coded language with his more devout followers. Despite this, the president was carefully ecumenical in memorializing the victims of September 11 and in urging respect for Islam as one of the world's major religions.

Barack Obama's fitness for the role of civil religious leader was called into question early in his campaign for the presidency when a network news program played clips from the sermons of Obama's pastor, the Reverend Jeremiah Wright. In one sermon, Wright denounced the government for its alleged hypocrisy and criminal conduct, concluding with the refrain "God Damn America."[47] Obama was slow to respond, but eventually he disowned Wright and put the issue behind him. It was, however, only one in a series of incidents and allegations through which the president's opponents sought to portray him as unfit for the presidency on account of being unfit to fulfill its symbolic responsibilities.

PUBLIC REACTION TO THE DEATH OF A PRESIDENT

The reaction of Americans to the death of a president provides dramatic evidence of the public's emotional attachment to the presidency. Americans regard the death of an incumbent president not just as the death of their elected leader, but also as the death of the symbol of the government, the guarantor of the nation's security and stability, and a person almost as familiar as a family member.

Although no systematic studies were done of public reactions to the deaths of incumbent presidents before John F. Kennedy, anecdotal evidence suggests that Americans have often experienced a traumatizing grief when an incumbent president has died. Hundreds of thousands of people lined the railways to view the train carrying Abraham Lincoln's body from Washington, D.C., to Albany, New York, and west to the grave site in Springfield, Illinois. The massive outpouring of grief for Franklin D. Roosevelt, who had led the nation through the Great Depression and World War II, demonstrated that an incumbent's death by natural causes also could produce a national spasm of emotion.

Nor was it necessary for the president to have been perceived as a great historical figure. After the shooting of James A. Garfield in 1881, large crowds took to the streets of major cities seeking news of the president's condition. The attack was the main topic of church sermons the next Sunday, and Garfield, who had entered office only four months before as a dark-horse candidate from Ohio, was lionized in the press as a great statesman.[1] Similarly, William McKinley and

Warren G. Harding were mourned deeply by the public despite their relative lack of historical prominence.

After the assassination of President Kennedy on November 22, 1963, social scientists at the National Opinion Research Center at the University of Chicago hastily constructed a survey designed to probe the American people's feelings in the aftermath of the tragedy. The survey showed that the death of President Kennedy produced a response in the American people usually associated with the death of a relative or close friend.

The interviewers asked 1,384 persons a series of questions about their reactions to the assassination. Only 19 percent of the respondents said they were able to continue their day "pretty much as usual" after hearing of the assassination. Sixty-eight percent of the respondents reported that at some time during the four-day period between the assassination and the president's funeral they "felt very nervous and tense." Fifty-seven percent said they "felt sort of dazed and numb." Fifty-three percent said they had cried. Seventy-nine percent said when they first heard about the assassination, they "felt deeply the loss of someone very close and dear." Seventy-three percent felt anger, and 92 percent felt sorry for Kennedy's wife and children.[2]

1. Charles E. Rosenberg, *The Trial of the Assassin Guiteau* (Chicago: University of Chicago Press, 1968), 7.

2. Paul B. Sheatsley and Jacob J. Feldman, "The Assassination of President Kennedy: A Preliminary Report on Public Reactions and Behavior," *Public Opinion Quarterly* (summer 1964): 189–215.

Cultural Leadership

Details about the lives of presidents and their families are sought eagerly by the U.S. media outlets. Just as the British scan their newspapers and magazines for information about the royal family, the American public avidly follows the private lives of the first family, the closest American equivalent to royalty.

Under the national spotlight, presidents and their families are well positioned to influence the lifestyles, habits, and cultural activities of Americans. Presidents will often spark new trends in clothing, foods, hobbies, or athletics even if they do not try to do so. Ronald Reagan's fondness for jelly beans and Clinton's penchant for Big Macs led to increased attention for both products.

First ladies can have an equally dramatic effect on national trends. Uncounted women, fascinated by the glamorous Jacqueline Kennedy, adopted her hairstyle and clothing tastes. Many Americans disapproved of Nancy Reagan's consultations with an astrologer, but popular interest in astrology increased after knowledge of her hobby was made public.

Some presidents have deliberately tried to influence the lifestyle of the nation. Theodore Roosevelt not only urged Americans to live an active life full of outdoor pursuits, but he also set an example for his fellow citizens to emulate. He climbed trees on the White House grounds, swam in the Potomac, played marathon tennis matches, and went for obstacle walks in which he would go over or through anything that stood in his way. Roosevelt also promoted vigorous activity by inviting athletes, explorers, cowboys, and other citizens who led strenuous lives to the White House. In addition, Roosevelt waged a campaign to make simplified phonetic spelling acceptable, but he found such a controversial cultural reform beyond even his powers.[48]

Decades later, the Kennedys, with their patronage of cultural events and recognition of the achievements of writers, artists, and performers, awakened American interest in the fine arts. The president and first lady also promoted interest in science and history. At one famous dinner in 1962 honoring American Nobel Prize winners, the president declared: "This is the most extraordinary collection of talent . . . that has ever been gathered together at the White House—with the possible exception of when Thomas Jefferson dined alone."[49] Mrs. Kennedy, dismayed by the meager White House library, stocked it with 1,780 great works of literature selected by James T. Babb, Yale University's librarian. She also recovered many historical pieces from museums, private collections, and White House storage

Presidents rarely escape the demands of the office. Even on vacation they are briefed and expected to carry out certain duties. Here President Obama signs into law the "James Zadroga 9/11 Health and Compensation Act" in Kailua, Hawaii.

areas and had the executive mansion redecorated in authentic early-nineteenth-century style.

However, not all presidential interests catch on as national trends. George H. W. Bush played horseshoes and ate pork rinds, and neither became popular with the mass public. Nor is there evidence that Clinton's jogging or that of George W. Bush has led to an increase in the number of the nation's runners. Even though they cannot always influence American behavior, presidents remain important national icons. They are treated as national exemplars, their behavior serving as a barometer of the nation's cultural and even moral health.

HEAD OF STATE BURDENS

One of the justifications of the British monarchy offered by its contemporary proponents is that it shelters the prime minister from many ceremonial duties. Prime ministers can devote their time and energies to formulating policy and dealing with Parliament and foreign governments while the royal family presides at ceremonial functions and absorbs media and public attention. Presidents have no shield against ceremonial activities equivalent to that represented by the British monarchy. Although family members, vice presidents, cabinet secretaries, and other presidential associates can lighten the president's ceremonial burden, the president is responsible for innumerable ceremonial functions and never ceases to be chief of state. Between lobbying a member of Congress to support a bill and meeting with the National Security Council to discuss an international hot spot, the president may be scheduled to greet Olympic athletes or Miss America. The president's chief of state duties, therefore, may interrupt or even interfere with the president's duties as chief executive.

Calvin Coolidge, who as president refused to overcrowd his schedule, warned:

> The duties of the Presidency are exceedingly heavy. The responsibilities are overwhelming. But it is my opinion that a man of ordinary strength can carry them if he will confine himself very strictly to a performance of the duties that are imposed upon him by the Constitution and the law. If he permits himself to be engaged in all kinds of outside enterprises, in furnishing entertainment and amusement to great numbers of public gatherings, undertaking to be the source of inspiration for every worthy public movement, for all of which he will be earnestly besought with the inference that unless he responds civilization will break down and the sole responsibility will be on him, he will last in office about 90 days.[50]

Few presidents, however, have been able or have wanted to limit their activities the way Coolidge said he did, and several have driven themselves to exhaustion. Because the chief of state duties increase the presidential workload, one can argue that they are an onerous burden. In addition to the drain on a president's time and energy, the chief of state role can make the president more vulnerable to assassination attempts, reinforce unreasonable public expectations of the president, and contribute to an atmosphere of deference that may warp the president's judgment. In response to these problems, some observers of the presidency have suggested that the office be reformed so that the president, like the British prime minister, is free of ceremonial responsibilities.

Demands on Time

Presidential time is a scarce resource. Presidents are ultimately responsible for everything that the executive branch does. They must have time to preside over policy meetings, review the work of their staff and cabinet, establish working relationships with members of Congress, read intelligence reports, study new policy proposals, hold press conferences, and perform numerous other functions necessary to the operation of the government and their administration. In addition, they must find time for political campaigning, personal relaxation, and ceremonial functions.

No chief executive can begin to satisfy all the requests for presidential attention. Woodrow Wilson and Franklin Roosevelt, two presidents with a hands-on managerial style, complained of the burdens of their office. Wilson called the presidential workload "preposterous," and Roosevelt claimed to work fifteen-hour days.[51] Lyndon Johnson related in his memoirs: "Of all the 1,886 nights I was President, there were

not many when I got to sleep before 1 or 2 a.m., and there were few mornings when I didn't wake up by 6 or 6:30."[52] Even presidents such as Eisenhower and Reagan, who were noted for their willingness to delegate responsibility and authority to their subordinates, faced daily decisions about which activities would have to be sacrificed to the pressures of time.

Although presidential responsibilities expanded greatly in the twentieth century, eighteenth- and nineteenth-century presidents also had more work than time in which to do it. George Washington found himself overwhelmed by the number of visitors he had to receive and civic functions he had to attend. He complained: "From the time I had done breakfast and thence till dinner and afterwards till bedtime I could not get relieved from ceremony of one visit before I had to attend to another."[53] Washington approached the problem in his typical manner—by asking the advice of colleagues he trusted. He solicited the opinions of Alexander Hamilton, John Jay, James Madison, and John Adams. After hearing their recommendations, Washington decided to limit his public entertaining to a dinner every Thursday at four o'clock for government officials and their families, a public levee on Tuesday afternoons for men, and a public tea party on Friday evenings for men and women.[54]

The enormousness of presidential responsibilities received a judicial validation in 1807. Chief Justice John Marshall subpoenaed President Jefferson to appear before the grand jury in Richmond considering former vice president Aaron Burr's indictment for treason. Jefferson refused to appear. He justified his decision in part by explaining that a president's duties as chief executive should not be set aside for an appearance at a trial: "The Constitution enjoins his constant agency in the concerns of six millions of people. Is the law paramount to this, which calls on him on behalf of a single one?"[55] The court accepted Jefferson's refusal to appear and withdrew its request for his testimony. The president cooperated fully with the investigation and offered to give a deposition, but the court never asked him for one.

Of all presidential activities, ceremonial functions are usually regarded as the most expendable and are frequently delegated to other individuals. Each year the White House turns down hundreds of requests for the president's time from groups and organizations seeking to publicize their causes through an appointment with the president. Many ceremonies over which presidents have presided are trivial when compared with the weighty affairs of state. For example, appearing at the annual White House Easter egg roll is a questionable use of the president's time, considering the unending procession of problems that require the president's attention. Yet public expectations, historic traditions, and opportunities for favorable media coverage combine to perpetuate White House ceremonies and events that are unrelated to policymaking or the president's constitutional roles.

Risks to the President's Health

Scholars and presidents have generally agreed that the presidency is a tremendous physical burden.[56] The pressures of the presidency can weaken the health of even the strongest person. Presidents usually work long hours, must occasionally take extended trips that require physical and mental stamina, and must endure enormous emotional stress arising out of the responsibilities of their job. Presidents seldom look as vigorous when they leave office as when they entered it.

One study of presidential longevity has shown that most presidents have failed to reach the age to which they were expected to live at the time of their election. Excluding the four presidents who were assassinated, twenty-one of the thirty-two presidents who died of natural causes failed to reach their individual life expectancy. As the nation and presidential responsibilities have expanded, so has the tendency of presidents to die prematurely. From 1841 to 1991 only five of twenty-eight deceased chief executives reached their individual life expectancies.[57] This occurred despite advances in medicine and the excellent medical care available to presidents.

Illnesses can and have inhibited the execution of presidential duties. Four presidents—William Henry Harrison, Zachary Taylor, Warren G. Harding, and Franklin Roosevelt—died of natural causes before their terms expired. Several other presidents, including Wilson and Eisenhower, were incapacitated by illness during their incumbency.[58] Ronald Reagan temporarily assigned his executive functions to Vice President Bush when he underwent surgery for cancer.

George E. Reedy, who served as press secretary under Lyndon Johnson, has argued that even if ceremonial functions do take up valuable presidential time, the primary source of strain on presidents is not long workdays but the knowledge of the consequences of their actions.[59] From war to welfare reform, presidential policies can have life and death consequences. For presidents who have served during the atomic age, the knowledge of their responsibility as the person who must decide to use nuclear weapons can be particularly stressful. Lyndon Johnson wrote that he felt relief after hearing Richard Nixon complete the oath of office in part because "I would not have to face the decision any more of taking any step, in the Middle East or elsewhere, that might lead to world conflagration—the nightmare of my having to be the man who pressed the button to start World War III was passing."[60]

Reedy maintains, as others have, that chief of state duties can provide presidents with a psychological release from the overwhelming responsibilities of their office.[61] These ceremonial events allow presidents to get away from the strains of decision making, and because ceremonies are an accepted presidential responsibility, presidents are unlikely to feel as if they are neglecting their duties.

The effect of the chief of state role on a president's mental and physical health may depend on that individual's personality. For those presidents who revel in the spotlight of national attention or are stimulated by an affirmation of public affection, such as Theodore Roosevelt, Franklin Roosevelt, Ronald Reagan, Bill Clinton, and George W. Bush, chief of state duties can be the most enjoyable and rejuvenating aspect of the presidency. Those presidents, however, who are uncomfortable with the public attention showered on them, such as William Howard Taft and Herbert Hoover, or who feel that they are wasting time when they divert their attention from policy matters, such as James Polk or George H. W. Bush, will likely regard chief of state duties as a burden, not a release.

Presidential Vacations

Perhaps because of the pressures associated with the office, presidents frequently leave the White House for vacation. While the duties of the presidency travel with the chief executive, presidents take the opportunities afforded by such travel to hike, fish, and otherwise enjoy themselves. Richard Nixon was a frequent visitor to his retreats in Key Biscayne, Florida, and San Clemente, California. Clinton was more peripatetic, visiting almost every state in the nation. George W. Bush set a record for presidential vacation days. By August 2003, he had spent a reported 27 percent of his time on vacation. His father spent a total of 543 days on vacation, while Reagan took 335 vacation days, and Clinton some 152. Jimmy Carter took the fewest number of days off at 79.[62]

So important is presidential relaxation that presidents used to have the services of a yacht, first the *Williamsburg* (decommissioned by Eisenhower) and then the *Sequoia* (sold by Carter), and still have a compound in the Catoctin Mountains of Maryland, Camp David. A favorite retreat for weekends and working vacations, Camp David began as a Works Progress Administration project in 1935, serving as an example of creating parks out of worn-out agricultural land. It was originally designed as a retreat for federal employees and their families but was redesigned for Franklin Roosevelt, who needed a safe place for recreation during the Second World War. He named his compound Shangri-La. It subsequently was renamed Camp David in honor of Eisenhower's grandson.

While presidents often spend weekends at Camp David, much presidential work also goes on there. Winston Churchill is among the British prime ministers who have spent time at Camp David, Nikita Khrushchev visited during the Eisenhower administration, and most, famously, the Camp David Accords between Israel and Egypt were signed there in 1978. Camp David has also been the site of other kinds of ceremonies. For example, Dorothy Bush, daughter of one president and sister of another, was married there in 1992.

Presidential vacations both allow the president to escape some of the pressure of Washington and facilitate his role as chief of state by allowing him to relax in ways that further his identification with the American public, display his diplomatic skills, and enact his role as First American. Presidents are never completely on vacation, but they appear to need—and certainly enjoy—even brief respites from official Washington.

Risks to the President's Safety

The assassination of a president is an even greater national disaster than the death of a president by natural causes. There may be time to prepare for the transfer of power to the vice president when a president dies from an illness, but an assassination usually does not allow for a period of administrative or emotional preparation. Not only can an assassination cause governmental confusion, but it also can send the country into shock, because people perceive an attack on the president, the symbol of the United States, as an attack on the nation itself.

Assassination attempts against presidents have not been uncommon. Lincoln, James A. Garfield, William McKinley, and Kennedy were killed by their assailants. Andrew Jackson, Truman, Ford (twice), and Reagan (who was wounded) survived attempts on their lives. In addition, President-elect Franklin Roosevelt was attacked three weeks before his first inauguration; and three presidential candidates, Theodore Roosevelt, Robert F. Kennedy, and George Wallace, all were shot—with Kennedy being killed. In all, presidents, presidents-elect, and presidential candidates have been attacked thirteen times. All but three of these attacks occurred in the twentieth century.

In 1995 concerns about security led to the closure of Pennsylvania Avenue in front of the White House. Security analysts judged that a truck bomb of the type used in the devastating attack on the Oklahoma City federal building in April of that year posed a threat to the White House. The September 11, 2001, terrorist attacks led to even tighter presidential security. The attacks made clear that the United States and its government were a target for well-organized terrorist groups. So great was the concern for the protection of the White House that public tours were stopped for a while after the attacks. The closing of "America's main street" and the suspension of White House tours symbolized the difficulty of reconciling the need to protect presidents with the tradition that they should be accessible to the people.

The most dangerous presidential activities are those that require the president to appear before a large crowd.[63] Because the chief of state role often involves such appearances, it contributes to the danger of assassination. The symbolic goal of many chief of state events is to bridge the gap between the government and the people. This goal is difficult to accomplish from inside a bullet-proof limousine or behind a wall of Secret Service agents. Consequently, presidents, especially those running for reelection, still seek personal contact with gatherings of voters while nervous Secret Service agents scan the crowd for possible danger. Yet the benefits of a ceremonial event or symbolic gesture in a location where the president's safety cannot be absolutely guaranteed must always be weighed against the risk of an assassination attempt.

The threat of assassination and the cumbersome security measures necessary to ensure the president's safety have forced changes in the way presidents perform their chief of state role. The days when presidents were expected to wade unprotected into a crowd of citizens to shake hands are gone. Just before leaving office Ronald Reagan commented that he would have liked to have gone to see the Army-Navy football game as many other presidents had done, but he did not because "nobody wants to run 75,000 people through a magnetometer." Reagan even justified his lack of church attendance, a traditional activity of the president, on the grounds that the security measures needed to ensure his safety would disrupt the congregation.

In today's extraordinarily security-conscious world, the president, likely for security, as well as political reasons, is largely confined to communicating with the American people via orchestrated events in front of carefully screened groups and televised speeches and press conferences. As a result, presidents are increasingly isolated from their constituents. When presidents place themselves before a crowd, as George W. Bush did when he addressed rescue workers at the World Trade Center site three days after the September 11 attacks, it is often considered a brave and confident gesture.

Excessive Public Expectations

For better or worse, the presidency is an idealized and romanticized office that elicits high expectations from the American people. With each election the public hopes for a president who will combine the best qualities of past presidents and achieve a range of contradictory goals.

Godfrey Hodgson has agreed that the expectations of the American people are not easily reconciled:

> The things "the people" want are mutually inconsistent. They want lower taxes and higher benefits. They want to be sure of the supply of gasoline, *and* they do not want to pay higher prices for it. They want national security and disarmament. They do not want American boys to be sent abroad to be killed, and they want the United States to be respected and feared.[64]

The chief of state role contributes to high public expectations of the presidency by creating the public perception that presidents have more power than they actually do. Political scientist Merlin Gustafson wrote: "When one person exercises both symbolic and political authority his public image tends to become distorted. A substantial portion of the public may be led to identify the presidential person with the governmental process, and assume that he alone determines national policy or 'runs the country.'"[65]

The public tends to blame and praise presidents for virtually everything that occurs during their terms regardless of their actual level of responsibility for conditions. For example, the public holds presidents responsible for economic prosperity even though the natural swings of the business cycle, foreign economic conditions, and economic shocks such as droughts and oil embargoes guarantee that even the best presidential economic policies will not yield economic growth all the time.

When judging presidents, the public often ignores the fact that the Constitution was designed to prevent any one person from completely dominating the government. Presidents must work with a Congress that may be controlled by the opposing party and is always composed of members primarily concerned with serving their home states and districts. Presidents also must avoid unconstitutional actions and must motivate executive branch subordinates who are capable of undermining presidential policies and initiatives. Yet presidents who cannot get their legislative proposals passed into law or their programs implemented often are accused of being weak leaders or poor compromisers. In short, even though presidents are constrained by the Constitution, they are often expected to be as effective as if they were absolute monarchs.

High public expectations and their often negative effect on presidential approval ratings can cause presidents to take actions that are popular but that are not in the public interest. In the worst case, presidents may be tempted to skirt legal constraints in pursuit of effective leadership. Cronin has commented:

> Our expectations of, and demands on, the office are frequently so paradoxical as to invite two-faced behavior by our presidents. We seem to want so much so fast that a president, whose powers are often simply not as great as many of us believe, gets condemned as ineffectual. Or a president often will overreach or resort to unfair play while trying to live up to our demands.[66]

Dangers of Deference

Because presidents are partisan political leaders they are routinely attacked by their political opponents and scrutinized by a combative press. Yet because they are the chief of state, a symbol of the unity and power of the United States, they also are treated with deference.

Presidents are provided with a mansion, guards, aircraft, and custom-made automobiles and have every need attended to by a host of servants. They are addressed as "Mr. President" even by close friends they have known for many years. The strains of "Hail to the Chief" greet them when they enter the scene of an important occasion. An omnipresent contingent of reporters seeks their thoughts on any subject, no matter how mundane or irrelevant to national policy. Despite the democratic origins of the presidency, the president enjoys the luxury and veneration usually reserved for monarchs.

The intoxicating effects of the deference given to presidents are reinforced by the historic significance of the presidency and the White House. Newly elected presidents become members of an elite and celebrated club. They know historians will rate them against Lincoln, Washington, and other "great" presidents. Election to the presidency ensures that many books will be written about their lives. When they have left office, politicians and journalists will continue to seek their opinions as elder statesmen. Presidential libraries will be constructed to hold their official papers, and when they die their graves will become national landmarks. Presidents are reminded daily of their place in history as they live in a house that is one of the nation's most cherished monuments and that was occupied by every president except George Washington. In the White House they are surrounded by the artifacts of past administrations. They can view the portrait of George Washington that was rescued by first lady Dolley Madison in 1814 when the British burned the capital, or they can write at the desk given to President Rutherford B. Hayes by Queen Victoria in 1880 and used by many presidents since.

Outside the White House presidents can take a walk through the gardens past the magnolia tree planted by Andrew Jackson in memory of his wife, Rachel, or the Rose Garden originally planted by Ellen Wilson and redesigned under John Kennedy. George Reedy has observed that an "aura of history" can envelop a president:

> He lives in a museum, a structure dedicated to preserving the greatness of the American past. He walks the same halls paced by Lincoln waiting feverishly for news from Gettysburg or Richmond. He dines with silver used by Woodrow Wilson as he pondered the proper response to the German declaration of unrestricted submarine warfare. He has staring at him constantly portraits of the heroic men who faced the same excruciating problems in the past that he is facing in the present. It is only a matter of time until he feels himself a member of an exclusive community whose inhabitants never finally leave the mansion.[67]

The deference shown presidents because they are chief of state and the mythic atmosphere created by presidential privileges and the regal White House environment may ennoble some presidents by giving them a sense of destiny or historic duty, but the royal trappings of the office also can have damaging effects. During the Nixon administration, the well-being of the president and the presidency became more important than the law. The respect given to Nixon as chief of state and the privileges of the presidency, which he relished, undoubtedly enabled Nixon and his staff to justify more easily to themselves violations of the law and unethical political tactics.

In addition, if the deference shown presidents causes them to believe they are always right and above criticism, meaningful debate on presidential policies may be squelched. Presidents who become overconfident of their own judgment may feel resentment toward staff members who disagree with their opinions. Such an attitude will likely cause subordinates to avoid expressing negative opinions to preserve their own influence with the president. Political scientist Robert DiClerico has written:

> Presidents have a tendency to become intoxicated by the deference and veneration shown to the Office they hold. They begin to see themselves as deserving of praise and come to view challenge and disagreement as an affront. . . . The isolation of presidents from the disquieting advice of staff members was especially pronounced in the Johnson and Nixon administrations. Both men were lacking in a sense of security, and consequently they were especially susceptible to the arrogance generated by the intoxicating atmosphere of the Presidency.[68]

Presidents accustomed to being treated like monarchs inside the White House grounds may also develop a deep resentment of criticism coming from outside the White House. This may cause a president to rely exclusively on a small group of loyal advisers. Even if the president permits disagreement and frank discussion within this group, an isolated decision-making process will deprive the president of valuable sources of insight and information.

Proposals for Change

Given the problems inherent in having a president who is both the nation's chief executive and chief of state, observers of the presidency have occasionally put forward proposals to reform the chief of state role. Change could be accomplished through executive orders or practices that formalize the delegation of most chief of state duties away from the president or through a constitutional amendment that assigns ceremonial duties to a new or existing office. More sweeping reforms of the presidency, such as the creation of a plural executive or the incorporation of parliamentary elements into the American political system, also would affect the chief of state role.

Altering the president's chief of state role has not been a major concern of presidents and their advisers. The most prominent executive branch study of the issue was done by Eisenhower's Advisory Committee on Government Organization, also known as the Rockefeller Committee. The committee, which functioned throughout Eisenhower's tenure in office and studied the organization of the entire executive branch, recommended merely that the vice president perform many ceremonial duties to lighten the president's chief of state burden.[69] Presidents have commonly delegated ceremonial duties to the vice president and other individuals, but no president has set up formal rules about which officials should preside at which events.

Most proposals for changing the president's chief of state power by amending the Constitution have come from scholars and public officials who have speculated on ways to make the presidency more efficient while acknowledging the difficulty of convincing the American people that such reforms are desirable.

One such proposal was a constitutional amendment introduced by Rep. Henry S. Reuss, D-Wis., in 1975. It would have created an office of "Chief of State of the United States" separate from the presidency. The office as conceived by Reuss would be a purely ceremonial position. The president would nominate a candidate for chief of state who would be confirmed by a majority vote of both houses of Congress. To promote the office's nonpartisanship, the chief of state's four-year term would begin two years into the president's term and last two years into the next administration. There would be no limit on the number of terms a chief of state could serve. The amendment designated the chief of state as "the ceremonial head of the United States" and "the sole officer of the United States to receive ambassadors and other public ministers." In addition, the chief of state would carry out ceremonial duties "as recommended by the president." The chief of state was to be paid a salary identical to that of the president and to be subject to the same impeachment provisions.

When introducing the amendment, Reuss acknowledged that tinkering with the Constitution was controversial. He maintained, however, that the demands of the chief of state role on the president's time and the dangers of the "symbolic deification of the president" warranted amending the Constitution.[70] Besides, having a chief of state who lacked both power and tradition would be little more than an empty symbol.

Consequently, neither Congress nor the American people showed much interest in Reuss's amendment. Most Americans are not eager to alter an institution to which they are accustomed and with which they associate many of the nation's foremost heroes. Given that Abraham Lincoln, Franklin Roosevelt, and other great presidents were able to use the power of the presidency to meet the nation's great crises, they reason, the solution to the nation's problems will not be found by changing the presidency but by electing leaders who can make it work.

Political scientist Thomas S. Langston has suggested that even if dramatic constitutional changes in the presidency are unlikely, some reduction in deference for the president might be achieved if presidents were given "competition" for historical honors:

> We celebrate Presidents' Day. Why not celebrate Speakers' Day? How about a Speakers' Memorial in Washington, D.C.? And if Andrew Jackson, the archenemy of paper money, can be made to grace the twenty-dollar bill, surely we should not be timid about proposing that famous Speakers of the House, or senators, also ennoble our currency.[71]

The wives of America's leaders are often some of the most recognized faces internationally, as well as frequent presidential envoys. First Lady Michelle Obama (center) and Dr. Jill Biden (far left) took a leading role in communicating America's support for Haiti after that nation experienced a devastating earthquake in 2010.

At the turn of the millennium, however, neither the American public nor the American political establishment appeared interested in departing from the memorialization of presidents. In 1997 an elaborate federal memorial to Franklin Roosevelt was dedicated near the Mall in Washington, D.C. In 1998 Congress passed bills renaming Washington National Airport and the Central Intelligence Agency complex after Ronald Reagan and George H. W. Bush, respectively. In 1999 it renamed the venerable Old Executive Office Building next to the White House after Dwight Eisenhower. In 2001, motivated by public interest in a popular biography of John Adams, Congress passed a bill authorizing construction of a new monument to the second president on federal land in the District of Columbia.

DELEGATION OF CHIEF OF STATE FUNCTIONS

Starting with George Washington, presidents have sought ways to control the number of ceremonial events over which they must preside. Presidents have delegated ceremonial tasks to family members, vice presidents, cabinet officers, close associates, and staff members. Like representatives sent to negotiate with foreign governments, these substitute chiefs of state have authority because they either occupy an important office within the administration or have a personal relationship with the president. Because they do not possess the power of the presidency, their presence does not have the symbolic force of a presidential appearance, but they are substitutes that most groups readily accept.

First Lady and Family

Presidents have often delegated ceremonial functions to their wives. First ladies are fitting presidential representatives

because they are nearly as well known as the president and are themselves recognized symbols of American history and culture. When a first lady addresses an organization or presides over a ceremonial event, the audience understands that the president is being represented by an intimate confidante and adviser.

Eleanor Roosevelt's ceremonial activism set the standard for modern first ladies. Franklin Roosevelt frequently sent his wife to the scene of strikes, disasters, and centers of poverty as his personal representative. She also traveled to England, South America, and the South Pacific during World War II to encourage U.S. troops and allies. All succeeding first ladies also performed chief of state duties. Jacqueline Kennedy had a powerful symbolic appeal in her own right. In her travels with the president overseas, she routinely received a rapturous reception, causing the president at one stop on his European tour to introduce himself with the famous line, "I am the man who accompanied Jacqueline Kennedy to Paris."[72] Rosalynn Carter made an ambitious goodwill tour of Latin America in 1977 in which she carried out diplomatic as well as ceremonial missions. Nancy Reagan visited several foreign countries as her husband's representative. In two of her early trips, she quite appropriately took the position that by right would have been occupied by an American king or queen, namely the 1981 wedding of Prince Charles and Lady Diana in Great Britain and the 1982 funeral of the American-born Princess Grace, in Monaco. In the summer of 1995 Hillary Clinton and her daughter, Chelsea, made a five-nation tour of South Asia that focused on issues related to women and children. Mrs. Clinton also chaired the U.S. delegation at a United Nations Fourth World Conference on Women, held in China in September 1995. In a major speech at the conference, she proclaimed the administration's position "that it is no longer acceptable to discuss women's rights as separate from human rights."[73] Laura Bush became the first first lady to deliver the weekly presidential radio address on November 17, 2001. She spoke against the repression of women by the Taliban regime in Afghanistan. Michelle Obama made a surprise visit to Haiti in April 2010, to express the president's concern for the nation as it began to rebuild after a devastating earthquake.

The first lady, because she is presumed to have the president's ear, can serve as an important delegate. But because she has no political power in her own right, she is not suited for all occasions. For those events, the president may send another of his political partners, the vice president.

Vice Presidents

The Constitution gives the vice president no formal policy-making or administrative powers other than to preside over the Senate and break tie votes in that body. As a result, few vice presidents of the nineteenth and early twentieth centuries had a significant role in their administrations. Modern vice presidents have become more involved in policymaking, but they continue to perform many ceremonial functions.

Vice presidents are well positioned to act as substitute chiefs of state because their office is associated with the presidency. Vice presidents run on the same ticket as their presidential running mates and are the only officials besides presidents who are elected by the entire nation. In addition, although their office may at times seem trivial, vice presidents are first in line for the presidency. Fourteen vice presidents have become president, including eight who succeeded to the presidency when the incumbent died in office and one when the incumbent resigned. The political and historic link between the two offices makes the vice president an appropriate stand-in for the president at ceremonial functions.

Since the advent of the airplane, presidents have frequently sent their vice presidents on ceremonial missions overseas. Sometimes these missions have included serious negotiations with leaders of important nations, but often their purposes have been more symbolic than substantive. Hubert H. Humphrey, who served as Lyndon Johnson's vice president, explained the vice president's diplomatic role: "He can perform assignments that the President feels would be unwise for him to take on himself, but for which an official lower than Vice President would be unsuitable."[74]

These assignments have included representing the United States and the president at inaugurations, coronations, and funerals of foreign leaders and major world figures. George H. W. Bush, who traveled more than one million miles and visited more than seventy countries as vice president, frequently took President Reagan's place at ceremonial functions overseas. Bush's attendance at the funerals of foreign dignitaries became so common that he joked that his motto should be: "I'm George Bush. You die, I fly."[75]

Presidents can enhance the symbolic effect of a vice presidential trip by demonstrating their interest in it and designating the vice president as their personal envoy. John Kennedy would usually hold a publicized meeting with Lyndon Johnson before the vice president left on a foreign mission. Immediately after entering office, Jimmy Carter sent Vice President Walter F. Mondale on a tour of Europe and Japan to demonstrate the importance of close allied cooperation with the Carter administration. In a South Lawn ceremony, President Carter bolstered his vice president's status by declaring: "Vice President Mondale has my complete confidence. He is a personal representative of mine, and I'm sure that his consultation with the leaders of these nations will make it much easier for our country to deal directly with them on substantive matters in the future."[76]

In the aftermath of the September 11, 2001, terrorist attacks, Vice President Richard B. Cheney facilitated the president's chief of state role in an unusual manner. The attacks had raised grave concerns that assassination plots or further attacks on Washington could result in both Bush and Cheney being killed. To ensure that the Bush-Cheney administration would survive, the vice president was assigned to stay out of harm's way so that he could lead the government if an attack succeeded in killing the president. Thus instead of replacing President George W. Bush at ceremonial functions, Cheney remained in a secure, and often undisclosed, location while the president kept a busy public schedule to reassure the nation. It was vital that the president, not a replacement, bolster the nation's confidence through ceremonial and patriotic appearances. Cheney's role complemented his, and the president's, preference that he operate behind the scenes, where he exercised unusual influence in the actual governing of the nation. Joseph Biden, vice president to Barack Obama, kept busy in the number two spot with both international travel (to some twenty-nine nations in the first three years of his term) and domestic responsibilities.

Cabinet Members and Personal Advisers

Cabinet members often operate as assistant chiefs of state within the area of their department's concern. For example, the education secretary makes ceremonial visits to public schools; the housing and urban development secretary tours inner-city housing projects; the commerce secretary speaks to business groups; the interior secretary addresses environmentalist groups; and the defense secretary inspects military installations and presides at ceremonies honoring war heroes and veterans. In addition, cabinet members often use ceremonial occasions or symbolic settings to make speeches that unveil a new program or announce a policy decision affecting their department.

The secretary of state has a special ceremonial role. After the president and vice president, the secretary of state is the nation's highest diplomatic and ceremonial representative. The secretary meets with foreign ministers who visit the United States and often heads U.S. delegations at funerals, inaugurations, and other special ceremonies overseas that are not attended by the president or vice president. In matters of protocol the secretary of state also is considered to be the highest-ranking cabinet officer. This unofficial rank is reinforced by the Succession Act of 1947, which designates the secretary of state as the first cabinet officer in line for the presidency and the fourth government official after the vice president, Speaker of the House, and president pro tempore of the Senate.

During the Nixon administration, National Security Adviser Henry Kissinger transformed his post from that of a behind-the-scenes presidential aide into a rival of the secretary of state for the diplomatic spotlight. The force of Kissinger's personality, his close relationship to President Nixon, and his celebrated diplomatic missions to the People's Republic of China and the Soviet Union made him the most recognized symbol of Nixon's foreign policy. During Kissinger's second trip to China in October 1971, he participated in ceremonial activities, including visits to the Great Wall of China and other Chinese landmarks. Kissinger also was constantly at the president's side during the historic 1972 summit meetings in Beijing and Moscow. Kissinger's activities resembled those of the secretary of state so much that he was criticized by some defenders of the State Department for having usurped the role of the secretary. After Secretary of State William Rogers resigned, Kissinger assumed the post in September 1973.

In the aftermath of the cold war, in a strategic setting of rising powers and ad hoc coalitions, today's presidents and their surrogates are called upon to deal personally with a great many heads of state, and to show the world that the United States cares about the troubles of a globe with more nations than at any time in the past. George H. W. Bush, who was president when the cold war ended, was best known for

Henry Kissinger became the most recognized symbol of President Richard Nixon's foreign policy. Originally national security adviser, he became secretary of state in 1973.

his effective personal diplomacy with a few other powerful heads of state. When faced with the crisis of Iraq's invasion of Kuwait, the president worked the telephone while James Baker, his secretary of state, hit the pavement in the Middle East and Europe. While Bill Clinton traveled a great deal overseas, George W. Bush relied on his advisers to do most of his traveling for him. As secretary of state, first Colin Powell and then Condoleezza Rice each took between fourteen and eighteen trips abroad a year. Obama's secretary of state, Hillary Clinton, has outdone them all, earning the "most traveled" title for her first two years in office, and maintaining a frenetic international schedule through the latter half of what she insisted would be her one and final term as secretary of state.[77]

CONCLUSION

When the president acts as chief of state, the role both offers strong advantages and imposes important constraints upon him. The most important constraint is on his time. Presidential ceremonial duties require a significant investment of time and energy on the part of the chief executive. But, in exchange, the president receives the benefit of reinforcing the public perception of him as a leader, the person who represents the nation at all of its most important ceremonial occasions, who speaks for the nation, and who in a sense embodies the nation. That can be a powerful resource for him in times of political trouble.

Because the role of chief of state allows the president to rely on the public's respect for the institution, and to conflate that respect with public attitudes toward the individual, it reflects the president's public image, not his private one. When acting as chief of state, presidents are expected to be "presidential" and behavior that strikes the public as being unsuitable for a president can undermine their faith in his ability to perform the other roles required by the office. Success as chief of state, however, can lead the public to have more faith in the president's capacity in his other roles. On balance, then, the president gains much more than he loses when acting as the nation's symbolic and ceremonial leader.

NOTES

1 Thomas E. Cronin and Michael A. Genovese, *The Paradoxes of the American Presidency* (New York: Oxford University Press, 2003).

2 George W. Bush, remarks at Ground Zero, September 14, 2001, www.americanrhetoric.com/speeches/gwbush911groundzero-bullhorn.htm.

3 Joseph Curl, "Inaugural Price Tag in Line with History," *Washington Times,* January 20, 2005, http://washingtontimes.com/national/20050119-103531-1062r.htm.

4 Eric Boehlert, "The Media Myth about the Cost of Obama's Inauguration," Media Matters, January 17, 2009, http://mediamatters.org/columns/200901170003.

5 Arthur M. Schlesinger Jr., "Annual Messages of the Presidents: Major Themes of American History," in *The State of the Union Messages of the Presidents 1790–1966,* vol. 1 (New York: Chelsea House, 1966), xiv.

6 Karlyn Kohrs Campbell and Kathleen Hall Jamieson, *Deeds Done in Words: Presidential Rhetoric and the Genres of Governance* (Chicago: University of Chicago Press, 1990), 55.

7 Alexander Hamilton, *Federalist* No. 69, in Alexander Hamilton, James Madison, and John Jay, *The Federalist Papers* (New York: New American Library, 1961), 420.

8 For details on presidential proclamations, see American Presidency Project, "Proclamations," www.presidency.ucsb.edu/proclamations.php.

9 For more discussion of this point, see Michael Hester, "America's #1 Fan: A Rhetorical Analysis of Presidential Sports Encomia and the Symbolic Power of Sports in the Articulation of Civil Religion in the United States," dissertation, Georgia State University, Department of Communication, 2005.

10 Quoted in Richard Pious, *The American Presidency* (New York: Basic Books, 1979), 5.

11 Theodore C. Sorensen, *Kennedy* (New York: Harper and Row, 1965), 368.

12 Fred I. Greenstein, "The Presidential Leadership Style of Bill Clinton: An Early Appraisal," *Political Science Quarterly* 108, no. 4 (1993–1994): 598.

13 See the poll published in July 2004, www.casa-chia.org/Strategems/Archived/July04.html.

14 James Hart, *The American Presidency in Action, 1789* (New York: Macmillan, 1948), 24–25.

15 For a further discussion of this point, see Vanessa Beasley, *You the People: American National Identity in Presidential Rhetoric* (College Station: Texas A&M University Press, 2004); and Mary E. Stuckey, *Defining Americans: The Presidency and National Identity* (Lawrence: University Press of Kansas, 2004).

16 In 2005, for instance, the president announced some fifty disasters (not counting Hurricane Katrina), the deaths of fifteen individuals, and gave two eulogies. See *Weekly Compilation of Presidential Documents,* www.gpo.gov/nara/nara003.html.

17 For a more extended discussion, see Mary E. Stuckey, *Slipping the Surly Bonds: Reagan's Challenger Address* (College Station: Texas A&M University Press, 2006).

18 Ibid., 17.

19 *Public Papers of the Presidents of the United States, Franklin Roosevelt, Containing the Public Messages, Speeches, and Statements of the President, 1937* (Washington, D.C.: Government Printing Office, 1938), 379.

20 Clinton Rossiter, *The American Presidency,* 2d ed. (New York: Harcourt, Brace and World, 1960), 18.

21 Ibid., 102–103. See also David K. Nichols, *The Myth of the Modern Presidency* (University Park: Pennsylvania State University Press, 1994), 22–23.

22 Thomas E. Cronin, "The Presidency and Its Paradoxes," in *The Presidency Reappraised,* 2d ed., ed. Thomas E. Cronin and Rexford G. Tugwell (New York: Praeger, 1977), 79; and David F. Prindle, "Head of State and Head of Government in Comparative Perspective," *Presidential Studies Quarterly* 21 (winter 1991): 56–57.

23 Fred I. Greenstein, *The Hidden-Hand Presidency: Eisenhower as Leader* (New York: Basic Books, 1982), 5.

24 See, for example, Alan I. Abramowitz and Walter J. Stone, "The Bush Effect: Polarization, Turnout, and Activism in the 2004 Presidential Election," *Presidential Studies Quarterly* 36 (2006): 141–155; Carl M. Cannon, "A New Era of Partisan War," *National Journal,* 2006, 43–44; Juan Enriquez, *The United States of America: Polarization, Fracturing, and Our Future* (New York: Crown, 2005); and Gary C. Jacobsen, "Polarized Politics and the 2004 Congressional and Presidential Elections," *Political Science Quarterly* 120 (2005): 199–218. See especially Philip A. Klinkner, "Mr. Bush's War: Foreign Policy in the 2004 Election," *Presidential Studies Quarterly* 36 (2006): 281–296.

25 Erwin C. Hargrove and Michael Nelson, *Presidents, Politics, and Policy* (Baltimore: Johns Hopkins University Press, 1984), 23.

26 Polling data on President Bush's overall job rating can be found at www.pollingreport.com/BushJob.htm.

27 Tabulated from the American Presidency Project database, www.presidency.ucsb.edu/ws/index.php#axzz1mIv4g8K3.

28 Quoted in Arthur Bernon Tourtellot, *The Presidents on the Presidency* (Garden City, N.Y.: Doubleday, 1964), 36.

29 Four presidents who finished their terms chose not to attend the inaugural ceremonies of their successors: John Adams, John Quincy Adams, Martin Van Buren, and Andrew Johnson.

30 Pious, *American Presidency,* 7.

31 Dale Vinyard, *The Presidency* (New York: Scribner's, 1971), 5.

32 Prindle, "Head of State and Head of Government in Comparative Perspective," 58–59.

33 "The Emperor's New Polls," Editor's Note, *Mother Jones* (September/October 1995), September 10, 2006, www.motherjones.com/commentary/ednote/1995/09/klein.html.

34 Peri Arnold, "One President, Two Presidencies: George W. Bush in Peace and War," in *High Stakes and Big Ambition: The Presidency of George W. Bush,* ed. Steven E. Schier (Pittsburgh: University of Pittsburgh Press, 2004), 147.

35 Robert E. DiClerico, *The American President,* 4th ed. (Englewood Cliffs, N.J.: Prentice Hall, 1995), 135–136.

36 Richard E. Neustadt, *Presidential Power and the Modern Presidents: The Politics of Leadership from Roosevelt to Reagan,* 3d ed. (New York: Free Press, 1990), 30.

37 Herman Finer, *The Presidency: Crisis and Regeneration, an Essay in Possibilities* (Chicago: University of Chicago Press, 1960), 103.

38 Samuel Kernell, *Going Public: New Strategies of Presidential Leadership* 3d ed. (Washington, D.C.: CQ Press, 1997).

39 Matthew Eshbaugh-Soha, *The President's Speeches: Beyond Going Public* (New York: Lynne Reinner, 2006).

40 George C. Edwards, III, *On Deaf Ears: The Limits of the Bully Pulpit* (New Haven: Yale University Press, 2003), and *The Strategic President: Persuasion and Opportunity in Presidential Leadership* (Princeton: Princeton University Press, 2009).

41 Fred Greenstein, "What the President Means to Americans," in *Choosing the President,* ed. James David Barber (Englewood Cliffs, N.J.: Prentice Hall, 1974), 125; and Richard Morin, "Who's in Control? Many Don't Know or Care," *Washington Post,* January 29, 1996, A6.

42 See www.informationclearinghouse.info/article5158.htm.

43 Polling data can be found at http://pollingreport.com/news.htm.

44 James David Fairbanks, "The Priestly Functions of the Presidency: A Discussion of the Literature on Civil Religion and Its Implications for the Study of Presidential Leadership," *Presidential Studies Quarterly* 11 (spring 1981): 225.

45 Barbara Hinckley, *The Symbolic Presidency: How Presidents Portray Themselves* (New York: Routledge, 1990), 73–79.

46 Quoted in James David Fairbanks, "Religious Dimensions of Presidential Leadership: The Case of Dwight Eisenhower," *Presidential Studies Quarterly* 12 (spring 1982): 264.

47 Brian Ross and Rehab El-Buri, "Obama's Pastor: God Damn America, U.S. to Blame for 9/11," ABC News: The Blotter, March 13, 2008, http://abcnews.go.com/Blotter/DemocraticDebate/story?id=4443788&page=1.

48 Joseph E. Kallenbach, *The American Chief Executive: The Presidency and the Governorship* (New York: Harper and Row, 1966), 280.

49 Sorensen, *Kennedy,* 384.

50 Quoted in Tourtellot, *Presidents on the Presidency,* 366.

51 Ibid., 365 and 369.

52 Lyndon B. Johnson, *The Vantage Point* (New York: Holt, Rinehart, and Winston, 1971), 425.

53 Michael P. Riccards, *A Republic, If You Can Keep It: The Foundation of the American Presidency, 1700–1800* (New York: Greenwood Press, 1987), 87.

54 Ibid., 88.

55 Hart, *American Presidency in Action, 1789,* 46.

56 Robert E. Gilbert, *The Mortal Presidency: Illness and Anguish in the White House,* 2d ed. (New York: Fordham University Press, 1998), 1–18.

57 Ibid., 2–6.

58 Louis W. Koenig, *The Chief Executive,* 6th ed. (New York: Harcourt Brace, 1996), 80–85.

59 George E. Reedy, *The Twilight of the Presidency: From Johnson to Reagan,* rev. ed. (New York: New American Library, 1987), 45.

60 Johnson, *Vantage Point,* 566.

61 Reedy, *Twilight of the Presidency,* 46. See also Gustafson, "Our Part-Time Chief of State," 167; and Thomas E. Cronin, *The State of the Presidency,* 2d ed. (Boston: Little, Brown, 1980), 158.

62 For information, on presidential vacations, see http://ask.yahoo.com/20031001.html.

63 In seven of the nine attacks on incumbent presidents, the assailants assaulted the chief executive with a handgun while he was near a crowd. The exceptions were the 1950 attack by two men with automatic weapons on the Blair House in Washington, D.C., where Harry Truman was staying while the White House was being renovated, and the 1963 fatal shooting of John Kennedy by Lee Harvey Oswald, who used a high-powered rifle to kill the president as he traveled through Dallas in a motorcade.

64 Godfrey Hodgson, *All Things to All Men: The False Promise of the Modern American Presidency* (New York: Simon and Schuster, 1980), 241.

65 Gustafson, "Our Part-Time Chief of State," 169.

66 Cronin, "Presidency and Its Paradoxes," 69.

67 Reedy, *Twilight of the Presidency,* 21.

68 DiClerico, *American President,* 225.

69 Gustafson, "Our Part-Time Chief of State," 164.

70 U.S. Congress, House, *Congressional Record,* daily ed., 94th Cong., 1st sess., July 21, 1975, 23716–23719.

71 Thomas S. Langston, *With Reverence and Contempt: How Americans Think about Their President* (Baltimore: Johns Hopkins University Press, 1995), 143.

72 "Nation: La Presidente," *Time,* June 9, 1961, www.time.com/time/magazine/article/0,9171,938093,00.html.

73 "Jacqueline Kennedy, Laura Bush, and More: A Look at First Ladies Abroad," *Washington Post,* www.washingtonpost.com/wp-dyn/content/gallery/2010/04/13/GA2010041302971.html?sid=ST2010041304954.

74 Cited in Joel K. Goldstein, *The Modern American Vice Presidency* (Princeton: Princeton University Press, 1982), 160.

75 David S. Cloud, "Loyal Lieutenant Bush Seeks Job at the Top," *Congressional Quarterly Weekly Report,* August 6, 1988, 2176.

76 *Public Papers of the Presidents of the United States, Jimmy Carter, Containing the Public Messages, Speeches, and Statements of the President, 1977,* Book 1 (Washington, D.C.: Government Printing Office, 1978), 11.

77 Howard LaFranchi, "Hillary Clinton, Obama's Road Warrior, Snags 'Most Traveled' Title," *Christian Science Monitor,* February 7, 2011, www.csmonitor.com/USA/Foreign-Policy/2011/0207/Hillary-Clinton-Obama-s-road-warrior-snags-most-traveled-title.

SELECTED BIBLIOGRAPHY

Barger, Harold M. *The Impossible Presidency: Illusions and Realities of Executive Power.* Glenview, Ill.: Scott, Foresman, 1984.

Bunch, Lonnie G., Spencer R. Crew, and Mark G. Hirsch. *The American Presidency: A Glorious Burden.* New York: HarperCollins, 2000.

Campbell, Karlyn Kohrs, and Kathleen Hall Jamieson. *Deeds Done in Words: Presidential Rhetoric and the Genres of Governance.* Chicago: University of Chicago Press, 1990.

Cronin, Thomas E., and Rexford G. Tugwell, eds. *The Presidency Reappraised.* 2d ed. New York: Praeger, 1977.

Dallek, Robert. *Hail to the Chief: The Making and Unmaking of American Presidents.* New York: Oxford University Press, 2001.

Edwards, Erica R. "The Black President Hokum." *American Quarterly* 63 (March 2011): 33–55.

Edwards, George C., III. *On Deaf Ears: The Limits of the Bully Pulpit.* New Haven: Yale University Press, 2003.

Eshbaugh-Soha, Matthew. *The President's Speeches: Beyond Going Public.* New York: Lynne Reinner, 2006.

Finer, Herman, *The Presidency: Crisis and Regeneration: An Essay in Possibilities.* Chicago: University of Chicago Press, 1960.

Gilbert, Robert E. *The Mortal Presidency: Illness and Anguish in the White House.* 2d ed. New York: Fordham University Press, 1998.

Gustafson, Merlin. "Our Part-Time Chief of State." *Presidential Studies Quarterly* 9 (spring 1979): 163–171.

Han, Lori Cox. *Governing from Center Stage: White House Communication Strategies in the Television Age of Politics.* Cresskill, N.J.: Hampton Press, 2001.

Hargrove, Erwin C. *The President as Leader: Appealing to the Better Angels of Our Nature.* Lawrence: University Press of Kansas, 1999.

Hart, James. *The American Presidency in Action, 1789.* New York: Macmillan, 1948.

Hinckley, Barbara. *The Symbolic Presidency: How Presidents Portray Themselves.* New York: Routledge, 1990.

Langston, Thomas S. *With Reverence and Contempt: How Americans Think About Their President.* Baltimore: Johns Hopkins University Press, 1995.

Lapham, Lewis H. *The Wish for Kings: Democracy at Bay.* New York: Grove Press, 1993.

Lowi, Theodore J. *The Personal President: Power Invested, Promise Unfulfilled.* Ithaca: Cornell University Press, 1986.

Medhurst, Martin J., ed. *Beyond the Rhetorical Presidency.* College Station: Texas A&M University Press, 1996.

Neustadt, Richard. *Presidential Power and the Modern Presidents: The Politics of Leadership from Roosevelt to Reagan* New York: Free Press, 1991.

Nichols, David K. *The Myth of the Modern Presidency.* University Park: Pennsylvania State University Press, 1994.

Novak, Michael. *Choosing Presidents: Symbols of Political Leadership.* 2d ed. New Brunswick: Transaction Publishers, 1992.

Phelps, Glenn. "George Washington and the Founding of the Presidency." *Presidential Studies Quarterly* 17 (spring 1987): 345–363.

Pious, Richard. *The American Presidency.* New York: Basic Books, 1979.

Prindle, David F. "Head of State and Head of Government in Comparative Perspective." *Presidential Studies Quarterly* 21 (winter 1991): 55–71.

Reedy, George E. *The Twilight of the Presidency: From Johnson to Reagan.* New York: New American Library, 1987.

Riccards, Michael P. *A Republic, If You Can Keep It: The Foundation of the American Presidency, 1700–1800.* New York: Greenwood Press, 1987.

Rossiter, Clinton. *The American Presidency.* 2d ed. New York: Harcourt, Brace and World, 1960.

Rubenstein, Diane. *This Is Not a President: Sense, Nonsense, and the American Political Imaginary.* New York: New York University Press, 2008.

Ryfe, Donald. *Presidents in Culture: The Meaning of Presidential Communication.* New York: Peter Lang, 2005.

Shogun, Colleen. *The Moral Rhetoric of American Presidents.* College Station: Texas A&M Press, 2005.

Smith, Jeffrey. *The Presidents We Imagine: Two Centuries of White House Fiction on the Page, on the Stage, Onscreen, and Online.* Madison: University of Wisconsin Press, 2009.

chapter 3

Chief Administrator

by Justin S. Vaughn

Article II of the Constitution lists the president's powers. Section 1 of the article clearly grants executive power to the president: "the executive Power shall be vested in a President." Section 3 makes the president responsible for the execution of federal laws: the president "shall take Care that the Laws be faithfully executed."

In theory, these directives make the president responsible for carrying out or executing the laws of the federal government. In practice, however, the ambiguity of this mandate often has increased the power of the presidency. For example, by broadly interpreting the authority to execute the law, Grover Cleveland used federal troops to break a labor strike in the 1890s and Dwight D. Eisenhower sent troops to help integrate a public school in Little Rock, Arkansas, in 1957.

At the beginning of the Constitutional Convention, the Framers expressed uncertainty about the exact nature of the executive. They derived many of their political ideals from seventeenth- and eighteenth-century European writers such as John Locke, Jean Jacques Rousseau, and Baron de Montesquieu, whose theories emphasized both popular sovereignty and individual liberty. If the Framers had fully adopted the political beliefs of these writers, the chief executive would be a directly elected public official responsible only to the people and representing the popular will.

Still, the Framers feared the effects of an unrestrained democracy. They were afraid that the chief executive might be too inclined to accede to popular demands in ways harmful to minority rights. Consequently, they attempted to insulate the office of president by having the public participate in presidential selection only indirectly through the electoral college.

The debate over the strength of the executive spilled over into the effort to define the exact nature of the president's administrative duties. Influenced by classical liberal writers, such as Montesquieu, the Framers dispersed power by structuring an executive branch separate and independent from the legislature. In doing so, they gave the presidency sweeping administrative responsibilities to "faithfully execute" the laws. But to keep the presidency from becoming too powerful, they subjected it to certain constraints by giving Congress immense powers of its own. The president has the power to appoint officials of the executive branch, but the Senate must confirm many of the appointments. And the president is in charge of administering the federal laws and programs, but Congress creates them, and it may change them at any time. Specifically, Congress can create and destroy agencies, and it determines whether they are going to be located in the executive branch or outside it. In other words, if it chooses, Congress can make an agency completely independent of the president.

The legislature also has the power of appropriation, which gives it ultimate control over federal agencies. Congress can define exactly what an agency has the power to do and not do. Consequently, as political scientist Peter Woll has observed, "Congress has virtually complete authority to structure the administrative branch and determine where formal lines of accountability shall be placed. It may or may not decide to let the President exercise various types of control."[1]

In *The Federalist Papers,* Alexander Hamilton defined the president's administrative activities as "mere execution" of "executive details." His was a narrow interpretation, for he in no way understood what would develop later. Hamilton, however, saw the president as the person solely responsible for administrative action. In *Federalist* No. 72 he wrote,

> The persons, therefore to whose immediate management these different [administrative] matters are committed, ought to be considered as the assistants or deputies of the chief magistrate, and on this account they ought to derive

---

Previous contributors to this chapter include Shirley Anne Warshaw, W. Craig Bledsoe, James Brian Watts, and Mark J. Rozell.

their offices from his appointment, at least from his nomination, and ought to be subject to his superintendence. This view of the subject will at once suggest to us the intimate connection between the duration of the executive magistrate in office and the stability of the system of administration.[2]

Since the 1930s Congress has delegated to the president the broad authority to achieve several general goals. Congress will often pass laws, leaving to the president and the executive branch the discretion to define the regulations and programs to be put into effect. This practice has come into being through political events, not by design. Americans increasingly look to the president for leadership in times of crisis and in everyday affairs, making the chief executive responsible for a growing portion of the nation's successes and failures. Consequently, the administrative responsibilities of the presidency have grown tremendously. As the presidency evolved, presidents found themselves serving as chief administrators, chief personnel officers, chief financial officers, and chief law enforcers—all part of the job of "chief executive."

The executive power shall be vested in a president of the United States of America.

—from Article II, Section 1

Political scientist Clinton Rossiter was so impressed with the demands on the presidency that he introduced his classic book, *The American Presidency,* with a quotation from Shakespeare's *Macbeth:* "Methought I heard a voice cry 'Sleep no more!'"[3] A few days before he was assassinated on November 22, 1963, President John F. Kennedy wrote Rossiter to comment on the use of the quote from *Macbeth.* Kennedy believed the quote to be apt but thought an even more appropriate one could be found in Shakespeare's *King Henry IV, Part I,* in which Glendower boasts, "I can call spirits from the vasty deep," and Hotspur replies, "Why so can I, or so can any man; but will they come when you do call for them?" Kennedy pointed to the difference between presidents' calling for action and actually accomplishing their desired goals. After almost three years in office, he understood the paradoxical nature of presidential power and its limitations.

THE PRESIDENT AS CHIEF ADMINISTRATOR

Although the Founders placed a high priority on the presidency's executive duties, the Constitution provides very few instructions about the president's tasks as head of the executive branch. Specific presidential administrative powers have evolved as the presidency has matured.

The Constitution does not make direct provisions for the vast administrative structure that the president must oversee. It does, however, authorize the president to demand written reports from the "principal Officer in each of the executive Departments, upon any Subject, relating to the Duties of their respective Offices" (Article II, Section 2). This clause implies a division of labor within the executive branch and clearly establishes an administrative hierarchy with the president as the chief administrative officer.

Similar to chief executives in private corporations, the chief executive in the White House tries to persuade subordinates in government to conform to presidential objectives. In other words, the chief executive tries to give direction to the administration. Presidents do not have time to follow through on every action taken by the bureaucratic departments and agencies directly under their control. After all, they sit atop a federal executive structure that has approximately three million civilian employees. They must, then, develop techniques that give them control over this vast administrative organization. Because this organization has grown tremendously since the early days of the Republic, analysis of the president's power as chief executive entails discussion of the structure of the executive branch.

Structure of the Executive Branch

Often the term *bureaucracy* is considered pejorative, because to many it suggests red tape, inflexibility, and confusion. Opposition to "big government" has become almost synonymous with opposition to bureaucracy. Political candidates from both major political parties usually decry the evils of the burgeoning U.S. bureaucracy, denouncing it for removing Americans from the decision-making process of their federal government.

Those who work in the federal bureaucratic structure—"bureaucrats"—are often criticized for being unproductive and obstinate. Political scientist Charles T. Goodsell has written that

the employee of bureaucracy, that 'lowly bureaucrat,' is seen as lazy or snarling, or both. The office occupied by this pariah is viewed as bungling or inhuman, or both. The overall edifice of bureaucracy is pictured as overstaffed, inflexible, unresponsive, and power-hungry, all at once.[4]

Bureaucracy, however, has a technical meaning. The German sociologist Max Weber saw the bureaucratic model of organization as one distinguished by its large size, its formulation of rules and procedures, the presence of a clear hierarchy, the systematic maintenance of records, and the employment of a full-time appointed staff who perform specific duties using technical knowledge.[5]

By this definition, a large corporation or university is a bureaucracy, and so is the federal government. The

President George W. Bush, right, meets with the Homeland Security Council, Vice President Dick Cheney, and members of his cabinet, Friday, June 1, 2007, to discuss the federal government's preparedness for the year's hurricane season in the White House Situation Room.

departments, agencies, bureaus, commissions, and offices of the executive branch make up most of the federal bureaucracy. Although not as large and usually not as visible as the executive branch, Congress and the courts have their own bureaucracies.

Despite the negative connotations of the term, a *bureaucrat* is simply an administrator who carries out the policies of the elected officials of government. The structure of the federal bureaucracy under the president's control can be broken down into the Executive Office of the President (EOP), the cabinet departments, the executive agencies, and the regulatory commissions.

Executive Office of the President

In 1939 Executive Order 8248 created the Executive Office of the President to advise the president and to help manage the growing bureaucracy. The EOP includes a variety of offices, including the White House Office, the Council of Economic Advisers, the National Security Council (NSC), and the Office of Management and Budget (OMB)—agencies conceived to help the president control the expanding executive branch.

Since then the EOP has grown tremendously, with a budget of $434 million in 2010. Its most important components are the White House Office, the NSC, and OMB.

The White House Office consists of the president's closest assistants. Their roles and titles vary from one administration to another, but under each new president it is this group that oversees the political and policy interests of the administration. Serving as a direct extension of the president, these people do not require Senate confirmation. The creation of the White House Office has allowed the president to centralize executive power within the White House at the expense of the cabinet secretaries.

In 1947, early in the cold war, Congress passed the National Security Act, which created the NSC to help coordinate military and foreign policies. Responsible for coordinating activities between the State Department and the Defense Department, the NSC has four statutory members: the president, the vice president (added in 1949), the secretary of state, and the secretary of defense. The act further names the chair of the Joint Chiefs of Staff and the director of the Central Intelligence Agency (CIA) as advisers to the NSC. In addition to the NSC but distinct from its formal membership is the NSC staff. Made up of foreign policy advisers and headed by the national security adviser, the NSC staff has evolved into an apparatus used by many presidents to implement their own foreign policy goals. Because the role of the NSC and its staff is purely advisory, presidents have used it to varying degrees. President Kennedy, preferring his own close advisers, used the NSC infrequently. President Richard M. Nixon, however, gave the NSC formal authority in formulating and executing foreign policy. *(See "National Security Council," p. 238, in Chapter 5.)*

The role of the NSC as an advisory structure is largely dependent on the influence of the national security adviser (NSA), who is both assistant to the president for national security affairs and staff director of the National Security Council. Zbigniew Brzezinski, President Jimmy Carter's NSA, often was the dominant player in advising the president on foreign policy issues, as the Iranian hostage crisis showed. In contrast, Ronald Reagan's six national security advisers were less influential with the president, eclipsed by his secretaries of defense and state. Presidents Bill Clinton and

George W. Bush had a strong relationship with their national security advisers, who were integrated into their national security and foreign policy advisory teams. In the early years of the Obama administration, however, the position has been characterized by turnover and competitive squabbling. Obama's initial NSA, Gen. James Jones, resigned after a tenure described as "unhappy" in the White House, one where he unsuccessfully battled against key individuals such as Secretary of Defense Robert M. Gates and Chairman of the Joint Chiefs of Staff Admiral Mike Mullen over the size and scope of the administration's surge in Afghanistan.[6] Jones was replaced by Tom Donilon, a longtime political operative and government employee close to Vice President Joseph Biden's family who had previously served as Jones's deputy.

In 1970 President Nixon created the Office of Management and Budget to replace the Bureau of the Budget (BOB), established in 1927. Its staff members help presidents achieve their policy objectives by formulating and administering the federal budget. Departments and agencies of the executive branch must submit annual budget requests to OMB. Besides preparing the budget, OMB serves as an important managerial tool of the president by reviewing the organizational structure and management procedures of the executive branch, assessing program objectives, and developing reform proposals. In the early 1980s, President Ronald Reagan relied heavily on OMB director David Stockman for the technical expertise necessary to implement his political objectives concerning the budget.

Recent presidents have considered the director of OMB among their closest advisers. Both Presidents Clinton and George W. Bush gave their OMB directors cabinet status and both eventually moved their OMB directors into the White House as chief of staff. Leon Panetta, Clinton's OMB director, replaced Thomas "Mack" McLarty as chief of staff in 1994, and Joshua Bolten replaced Andrew Card as chief of staff in 2006. Similarly, when Barack Obama's OMB director, Peter Orszag, left the administration for a position in the private sector, the administration and pundits alike viewed it as a great loss. Subsequently, Orszag's successor, Jacob Lew, became first a close adviser to President Obama and later his third chief of staff in January 2012.

Cabinet Departments

The cabinet is made up of the heads, or "secretaries," of the major departments of the government. Originally, there were only three cabinet departments—State, War, and Treasury. By 2002 the number had grown to fifteen with the creation of the Department of Homeland Security. Lacking any constitutional or statutory base, the cabinet is primarily an advisory group. Although presidents may work closely with individual cabinet officers, they rarely use the collective cabinet for advice. Once President Abraham Lincoln,

opposed by his entire cabinet on an issue, remarked, "Seven nays, one aye; the ayes have it." President Eisenhower, who held regular cabinet meetings and listened to opinions of others, came closer than any other modern president to making the cabinet a truly deliberative body.

Each cabinet secretary is appointed to head a specific department with a specific constituency. Although presidents make the appointments, with Senate confirmation, the power they have over a specific department is limited. One reason is that the president can appoint only a limited number of a department's employees. When President Bill Clinton came into office in 1993, for example, he could appoint only about one hundred people to positions in the Department of Transportation—less than 1 percent of its employees.

Executive Agencies

Executive agencies are agencies or commissions that are not considered to be a part of the cabinet and that often have quasi-independent status by law. Examples of these executive agencies include the National Aeronautics and Space Administration (NASA), the Small Business Administration (SBA), and the Environmental Protection Agency (EPA).

The difference between a "presidential" agency and an "independent" agency often is vague. Generally, heads of presidential agencies and commissioners serve at the discretion of, and may be removed by, the president. Independent agency heads and commissioners are appointed for fixed terms of office and have some independence from the president in their operations.

Government corporations, such as the Tennessee Valley Authority (TVA), also fall into the category of executive agencies. Similar to private corporations, these organizations perform business activities such as operating a transportation system (Amtrak) or selling electricity (TVA). Government corporations are generally controlled by boards of directors and are run like businesses. Because the president appoints these boards and their chairs, they have come increasingly under the control of the presidency.

Regulatory Commissions

Regulatory commissions are responsible for regulating certain segments of the economy. Many of them, such as the Food and Drug Administration (FDA) and the Occupational Safety and Health Administration (OSHA), are located within cabinet departments. FDA is a part of the Department of Health and Human Services, and OSHA is in the Labor Department. Other regulatory agencies, such as the Consumer Product Safety Commission and the Federal Trade Commission, are independent in their relationship to the executive branch and so are insulated from regular presidential control and policy direction.

By statutory law each independent regulatory agency is governed by a bipartisan board of commissioners, who serve overlapping terms of five years or more. Although presidents have the power to appoint board members, they do not have the power to remove these appointees from office unless they can prove incompetence. This ensures a certain amount of independence from executive control— that is, presidents cannot fire commission members simply because they do not like the policy direction of the agency, and they cannot veto agency actions.

Still, presidents influence regulatory commission policies by choosing the commissioners and the chairs. Bipartisanship rarely means much in the composition of these boards, for presidents always have been able to name board members who share their views regardless of political party affiliation. Many conservative Democrats share the same policy beliefs as Republicans, and many liberal Republicans share the same policy beliefs as Democrats. Although commissioners serve long, overlapping terms, presidents still have the opportunity to place a majority of their appointees in any given agency.

Bureaucratic Growth and Reform

In 1789 President George Washington's administration consisted primarily of the three cabinet departments (State, Treasury, and War) and employed only a few hundred people. By 1816 the number of federal civilian employees had grown to a little more than 4,800. Only about 500 of these worked in Washington, D.C. Most of the rest were scattered throughout the country providing mail service as employees of the Post Office Department. By 1931, however, the number of federal civilian employees had reached slightly more than 600,000, and by 1953 the number had expanded to about 2.5 million. By 2010, however, the number of federal civilian employees was only 2.1 million, after topping out at 3.2 million in 2000.[7]

Although the number of federal employees has remained relatively constant since the 1950s, federal expenditures have continued to increase. Between 1965 and 2001, annual federal expenditures jumped from $118 billion to more than $1.8 trillion. This period also saw an increase in the number of people working for the federal government as either contractors or consultants or through grant-in-aid programs administered by state or local governments. Federal employment figures usually overlook the large and growing number of people who work indirectly for the federal government as employees of private firms and state and local governments that are largely, or entirely, funded by U.S. taxpayers. In 1978 Secretary of Health, Education and Welfare Joseph A. Califano observed that although his department employed almost 144,000 people, it indirectly paid the salaries of about 980,000 more in state and local governments through numerous grant-in-aid programs.[8]

Every president, eventually frustrated by the large and often unresponsive bureaucracy, talks of bureaucratic reform. Reform-minded presidents must move carefully, however. They must convince key members of the bureaucracy that proposed changes are worth making for the country as a whole and that they will not hurt individual bureaucrats. In addition, and far more important, presidents are subject to the same private interest pressures that afflict an individual agency. By the time they reach office, presidents have become indebted to people who have contributed to their campaigns and helped them achieve their political stature. Presidents therefore are reluctant to undermine an agency that might serve one of their clientele groups.

As a result of these factors, few presidents are successful in achieving the reforms they seek. When President Jimmy Carter came into office, he vowed to make a wholesale overhaul of the ninety-five-year-old civil service system, but the Civil Service Reform Act (1978) that finally passed Congress in Carter's second year in office had little effect. Campaigning for office, Carter had promised to reduce the nineteen hundred existing federal agencies to two hundred. After he took office, however, the campaign promise was quickly forgotten and never appeared in the civil service reform law. In fact, in attempting to win their support for the reform measure, Carter promised civil service employees, "No one will be demoted, have their salaries decreased, or be fired as a result of reorganization. You need not fear that."[9]

President Reagan entered office after pledging during the 1980 election campaign to dismantle the newly created Department of Education. Although Reagan and his White House staff urged the secretary of education, first Terrel H. Bell (1981–1984) and then William J. Bennett (1985–1988), to dismantle the department, each sought to protect the department.[10]

Some presidential reforms have been more successful. In 1993 President Clinton promised to reduce the number of federal employees, cut bureaucratic waste, and, in the process, improve the efficiency and effectiveness of the workforce by "reinventing government." After a six-month study, the National Performance Review, under the direction of Vice President Al Gore, offered several recommendations to save $108 billion and cut 252,000 jobs, mostly managerial, from the 2.9 million-person federal workforce. The final annual report of Gore's commission noted that the reforms resulted in a reduction of the federal workforce by 426,000 and savings of $136 billion. Thirteen of the fourteen departments were reduced in size; only the Department of Justice grew larger. Commission recommendations also resulted in the elimination of 640,000 pages of internal agency rules and of some 250 programs and agencies, including the Tea-Tasters Board and the Bureau of Mines. The Clinton initiative enjoyed widespread support from the public and from both Republicans and Democrats in

Congress. Because the initial cuts were achieved through attrition, early retirements, and buyouts, and by cutting paperwork, the National Performance Review proposals also had widespread support among government employees' unions.

George W. Bush brought into office a distinctly business-minded approach to bureaucracy. His administration focused on how well individual agencies and organizations performed their functions and devised a plan to base future funding levels on, in part, each bureaucratic entity's performance score. In 2001, through the Office of Management and Budget, the administration developed the Program Assessment Rating Tool (PART) to help provide a standard model of assessing program effectiveness. Although there were skeptics and critics of the administration's approach, and although implementation took longer than initially expected, the administration also received accolades for organizational ingenuity. The program also helped facilitate privatization of a large bulk of the government's workload. Upon taking office, Barack Obama left in place a large part of Bush's performance management system, seeking to revise some aspects of the PART system and reverse privatization trends. Although Obama did not rescind Bush's executive order that initially established the position in government responsible for performance oversight, he did make some changes in the use of performance information. For example, Obama's "Accountable Government Initiative" focused less on grading program success and more on requiring organizational elites to identify priorities, demonstrate progress, and explain relevant trends.[11]

Carter's and Clinton's efforts are typical—in fact, the evolution of the federal bureaucracy has been largely a history of presidential attempts at reform. Although these efforts were aimed at reducing the power of the bureaucracy, instead they gradually increased it. In examining these recurring efforts, presidential scholar Michael Nelson has pointed out the irony in bureaucratic reform: the disparity between what reforms have intended and the actual results has led to increases instead of reductions in the power and scope of bureaucracy.[12]

The Founders were ambivalent about the exact nature of the government's administrative structure and about who was to control it. And because the subject was not mentioned in convention debates, it was not mentioned in the Constitution. Nelson argues that this ambivalence helped to create the rapid growth that later characterized the American bureaucracy. By not spelling out the exact nature of the government's administrative structure, the Founders created a situation that allowed the bureaucracy to come under the simultaneous control of both the president and Congress in the nineteenth century. The system of dual control allowed administrators to increase their own independence by playing one institution off the other. Nelson observed:

The Constitutional Convention, in loosing the agencies from their old legislative moorings (politically necessary if the support of executive power adherents was to be won) without tying them securely to the presidency (equally politic if anti-federalist support was to be kept), forced agencies to find and exercise relatively independent power. Agencies began to learn to play one branch off of another; if neither president nor Congress was supreme, then law was, and the agencies interpreted and implemented the law.[13]

Nelson concludes that the power of bureaucracy has grown in part because of the attempts to control it. For example, early reformers, intent on controlling the bureaucracy by making it less susceptible to corruption, actually made it less efficient and responsible. To make it harder for public employees to defraud the government, agencies developed elaborate systems of internal checks and balances. These checks and balances took time to operate. Efficiency, responsiveness, or some other value often was sacrificed for the sake of preventing official cheating.

Nelson's historical account of bureaucratic reform points out that bureaucratic power usually endures even throughout the most challenging of reforms. Although the historical record indicates that reformers have unintentionally increased the power and scope of bureaucracy, attempts at reform will undoubtedly continue. Future presidents, like their predecessors, will become frustrated with the sluggishness and unresponsiveness of their administrations. Efforts at deregulation, civil service reform, and cutbacks in government expenditures that aim at removing the financial support for various bureaucratic agencies therefore will continue. Political scientist Robert Sherrill has outlined the problem: "Because so many portions of the bureaucracy are no longer responsive to the needs of the general public, and because they do their narrowly selfish work without fear of reprisal from the public, it may seem useless to talk of reform. But it isn't useless to talk of reform; it is only naive to expect much."[14]

Control of the Bureaucracy

Presidents often complain that they lack sufficient control over the executive branch bureaucracy. They are quick to blame the bureaucracy for the many problems that hinder the implementation of presidential programs. Franklin D. Roosevelt, in one of the best-known illustrations of a president's lack of control over the bureaucracy, reportedly had the following exchange with one of his aides:

"When I woke up this morning, the first thing I saw was a headline in the *New York Times* to the effect that our Navy was going to spend two billion dollars on a shipbuilding program. Here I am, the Commander in Chief of the Navy having to read about that for the first time in the press. Do you know what I said to that?"

"No, Mr. President."

"I said: 'Jesus Chr-rist!'"[15]

Other presidents faced similar frustrations later. Contemplating what it would be like for Eisenhower to be president instead of a general, Harry S. Truman once said, "He will sit here and he will say, 'Do this! Do that!' And nothing will happen. Poor Ike—it won't be at all like the Army! He'll find it very frustrating."[16] In office nineteen months, Clinton was surprised to find that a $310 million spy complex was being built without his administration's knowledge. The budget for the National Reconnaissance Office was buried in the budget for intelligence discretionary funds, known as the "black budget." Cost overruns brought the building to the attention of the Senate Intelligence Committee, which eventually disclosed the project to the Clinton administration.

Chief executives expect to have their orders obeyed and their programs set in motion. Yet upon assuming office, they often find that their programs rarely are implemented as promptly or as efficiently as they would like. They must face, and learn how to manage, an obstinate and unruly bureaucracy. Controlling the bureaucracy has become a major priority for most presidents. All presidents after Franklin Roosevelt, whether liberal or conservative, have shared the desire to make the bureaucracy more responsive to their program objectives. Historian Arthur M. Schlesinger Jr. commented: "As any sensible person should have known, the permanent government has turned out to be, at least against innovating presidents, a conservatizing rather than a liberalizing force."[17]

Presidents face a tremendous task when they try to manage the bureaucracy and make it work for them. To control a specific agency, the chief executive must know what the agency does now and did in the past, the preferences and inclinations of its members, and the pressures being put on the agency by clientele groups. In addition, the president must anticipate the political implications of the agency's actions. Ideally, the chief executive should be able to do this for the hundreds of departments, bureaus, boards, commissions, independent commissions, and public corporations under White House supervision. But even with the help of the Executive Office of the President, it is an almost impossible task. Presidential scholar Richard M. Pious wrote: "It takes a few weeks for a new administration to learn how to intervene in the affairs of a bureau; it may take a few years for the president to know enough to stay out of them."[18] Instead of being intimately involved in every little detail of an agency's affairs, a president must learn to delegate—that is, the president must be a manager. According to presidential scholar Thomas E. Cronin:

> He must constantly delegate, he must be most precise about what he is delegating, and he must know whether and for what reasons the agencies to which he is delegating

share his general outlook. He must be sensitive to bureaucratic politics, to the incentives that motivate bureaucrats, and to the intricacies of their standard operating procedures. He must have some assurance (and hence an adequate intelligence system) that what he is delegating will be carried out properly.[19]

Unfortunately, most presidents have not done well in this respect. They often have misunderstood the bureaucracy and have concentrated on the goals instead of the implementation of policy. Political scientist Richard Rose has argued that "once in office, a president is much more concerned with choosing what to do than he is with how these decisions are implemented (that is, how choices are turned into routine government activities) or the conduct of program activities on a continuing basis."[20]

In addition to the problems of understanding the exact nature of the bureaucracy, presidents must face problems inherent in the political process itself that make it difficult to control their administrations. Upon entering office, presidents find that most bureaucratic institutions are already fixed. If they want to reorganize, as did Nixon, they run the risk of a confrontation with Congress. Few presidents want to risk an outcry of disapproval from a Congress that tries to protect the interests of its constituencies, who are often the clients of the existing bureaucratic agencies. Instead, newly elected presidents attempt to do the best they can with the bureaucratic structures already at their disposal. Constitutional inhibitions also make it difficult for the chief executive to fashion the bureaucracy into a more responsive institution. Presidential programs require legislative approval and appropriations, and they are subject to review, and possible nullification, by the courts. Even with statutory and constitutional authority, the president often faces untold difficulty in making the bureaucracy more responsive. Although the Constitution charges presidents with the execution of the laws, the formal authority to take that action is often statutorily vested in a cabinet secretary or the head of a specific agency. In theory, such presidential appointees will carry out the president's objectives. In practice, however, heads of departments and agencies often operate independently of the president and are more attuned to their clientele groups than to the administration's goals.

Instruments of Presidential Control

Although the obstacles to effective management of the bureaucracy are great, presidents do have two tools that afford them at least a small measure of influence: their authority to appoint top officials and their own centralized management staff—the Executive Office of the President.

Appointments. Presidents appoint fifteen cabinet heads and some six thousand other executive officials, including all members of the independent and regulatory agencies. In other words, presidents may hire or fire almost all of their top officials at will, except the board members of independent regulatory commissions. This authority gives them great control over their immediate aides and department and agency heads, but not over the vast majority of the executive branch. David Lewis has shown that presidents consider their ability to use political appointees to be so powerful, they do so even when it hurts performance, in order to increase agency responsiveness to presidential direction.[21]

In addition to the power of removal, presidents may also attempt to make appointments that are ideologically compatible with their policies. President Reagan attempted to transform departments and agencies by appointing officials who shared his desire to curb the size and influence of the federal establishment. For example, Reagan appointed Thorne Auchter, an opponent of "unnecessary" federal rules, to head the Occupational Safety and Health Administration and Robert F. Burford, who helped to lead a movement to return greater control of federal lands to the states, as director of the Interior Department's Bureau of Land Management. Similarly, President Clinton attempted to place his stamp on the bureaucracy by keeping control of appointments firmly within the White House. Both George W. Bush and Barack Obama continued this practice and kept all subcabinet appointments largely under the control of the White House, ensuring ideological consistency throughout their administrations.[22]

Centralized Executive Power. In 1933 Franklin Roosevelt found himself facing a bureaucracy staffed by holdovers from preceding conservative Republican administrations. He feared that his New Deal programs, if left to the discretion of these bureaucrats, would never be put into effect, at least not in the way they were intended. To ensure compliance with the intent of the New Deal legislation, he established numerous new agencies, such as the short-lived National Emergency Council, to coordinate directives through new and old agencies committed to his liberal programs. By adding on to the existing bureaucracy, Roosevelt created an organizational monster.

Roosevelt also found it difficult to get the information he needed to implement his policies. Frustrated by the bureaucratic mess of his administration, he asked Congress to expand his supervisory staff. Congress agreed, and on September 8, 1939, Roosevelt issued Executive Order 8248, which, as noted earlier, established the Executive Office of the President. In so doing, Roosevelt created a miniature bureaucracy to help him control the vast executive apparatus and thus expanded the modern presidency. Clinton Rossiter described the creation of the EOP as a "nearly unnoticed but nonetheless epoch-making event in the history of American institutions."[23]

Roosevelt maintained that only a strong, well-staffed presidency could provide unity and direction to the federal government. Later presidents agreed and continued trying to centralize power within the White House to control the bureaucracy. More often than not, however, such attempts overloaded the White House staff and undermined the effectiveness of the presidency. By the early 1970s, the presidency was attempting to centralize all policy at the White House by using White House staff to oversee programs of high presidential priority.[24] In attempting to centralize power within the White House, Nixon structured his staff in a way that limited his associates to those over whom he had the most control. This attempt at centralization isolated him and put him out of touch with the rest of the government.

However interested these presidents might have been in centralizing power, it did not work. The White House staff was simply not large enough to control the massive executive branch, which in the early 1970s was made up of nearly five million military and civilian employees and spent more than $300 billion annually. This observation points to the reality that no presidential mechanism has ever been large enough or powerful enough to control the bureaucracy. Some scholars maintain that presidents should not be in complete control of the bureaucracy.[25] They contend that the president's role in overseeing the success or failure of federal programs should be relinquished to the executive departments. Most federal laws, they argue, deliberately provide for discretion to be given to top departmental and agency officials. Richard Rose has pointed out that the work of the executive branch is carried out by operating departments granted specific powers and responsibilities by acts of Congress, and not by presidential delegation.[26] Therefore, both appointed and career executives should have the liberty to apply standards, revise regulations, and interpret legislative intent to fit specific situations, and the president and the EOP should not be involved in most situations. These scholars hold the view that Congress is as much in charge of administration as the president, for it is Congress that creates the laws, funds the programs, and confirms the executive branch appointments.

Most presidents oppose this view. They argue that only the president can provide the coordination necessary to master the complexity of the federal bureaucracy. Cronin summarized the presidential perspective: "Only the president should have discretion over budget choices and the administration of federal policies. He is the one charged with faithfully executing the laws. . . . [A] strong presidency makes a major difference in the way government works, and . . . this difference will be in the direction of a more constructive (desirable) set of policy outcomes."[27]

This is the position that Alexander Hamilton advocated in *Federalist* No. 70: "A feeble Executive implies a feeble execution of the government. A feeble execution is but another phrase for a bad execution; and a government ill-executed, whatever it may be in theory, must be, in practice, bad government."[28]

At the heart of this argument is the idea that the government bureaucracy has become so large and diverse that the White House itself spends more time reacting to the whims of the bureaucracy than controlling it. Former presidential adviser McGeorge Bundy maintained that the executive branch often "more nearly resembles a collection of badly separated principalities than a single instrument of executive action."[29] The answer, according to this logic, is more hierarchy. An accountable president must be able to control the bureaucracy. However, research by Andrew Rudalevige has cast doubt on the phenomenon and its effectiveness.[30] Rudalevige shows that presidential centralization attempts have not been as pervasive or as linear as rhetoric surrounding the trend would otherwise suggest. Further, Rudalevige finds that centralization does not universally improve the likelihood of president's successfully getting their preferred policy initiatives through Congress.

Lt. Col. Oliver North testifies, in July 1987, before the joint House-Senate panels investigating the Iran-contra affair. North said that he and President Ronald Reagan never discussed the diversion of Iranian arms sales profits to the contra rebels.

Information Management

Part of the problem of management is the control of information. The maxim "Knowledge is power" is never truer than in the executive branch. Presidents must deal with a highly specialized and expert bureaucracy.

Obtaining Information. How does a president gather the information necessary to make informed decisions? One way is to rely on information supplied by bureaucratic agencies themselves. But if this is the chief executive's only source of information, then the presidency runs the risk of being dominated by, or dependent on, the bureaucracy. To a large extent this dependence on the bureaucracy is unavoidable. Compared with the rest of the executive branch, the president's management staff—the Executive Office of the President—is small, usually about sixteen hundred employees. Thus the president and the EOP must make decisions on the facts and opinions supplied by the agencies themselves. But even if the EOP were enlarged to give the presidency greater information-gathering capability, it could never become large enough to provide the president with relevant information for all policy decisions for every agency. As Peter Woll has written, "The scope and technical complexity of administrative legislation and adjudication alone precludes this, even if there were no legal and political obstacles to presidential control. What is of greater importance is the fact that the president alone cannot personally comprehend these areas."[31]

Those who insist on expansion of the EOP argue that presidents need larger staffs to channel information from the multitude of agencies for which they are responsible. Because the offices within the EOP, such as the Office of

Management and Budget, are not dependent on any clientele or constituency group but serve as the president's staff, they are viewed as being independent of the political pressures that other agencies endure. But the EOP suffers from political tensions just like any other executive bureaucracy. In examining the effects of information within the EOP, Woll described the need for presidents to be sensitive also to other major departments and agencies, such as the Department of Agriculture, which have powerful support from Congress. According to Woll, "Such political support has a way of showing up in the White House sooner or later, and if OMB were continually at odds with the agencies it supposedly supervises, its job would be made impossible both politically and practically."[32] Not only do agencies outside the EOP constantly seek to channel their points of view to the White House, but EOP offices also inevitably become advocates of particular viewpoints of their own. Such advocacy within the president's own management staff poses a serious problem for chief executives who attempt to remain detached from many of their top advisers in the EOP. This detachment allows key EOP staffers to make decisions based on their own particular interests and without presidential supervision. Thus it becomes increasingly difficult for presidents to maintain the type of information surveillance necessary to remain knowledgeable and up-to-date. According to the *Tower Commission Report,* the involvement of Reagan aides Lt. Col. Oliver L. North and John M. Poindexter in the Iran-contra scandal was the result of a lack of presidential control of key advisers. Their strong advocacy of support for the Nicaraguan contras coupled with the president's lack of direction in the activities of his aides resulted in a policy disaster for the Reagan administration.[33]

Transmitting Information. Not only the gathering of information but also its transmission can be a big obstacle for presidents. The transmission of information from one level of the administrative hierarchy to another provides those who receive it with the opportunity to screen out a portion of the information before sending it on. Screening out information may be deliberate on the part of those who wish to frustrate the efforts of a president, or it may be unintentional. Economist Anthony Downs estimated that as much as 98 percent of information can be lost or distorted in this way.[34] With as large a bureaucratic structure as the president must attempt to control, the task of disseminating information is particularly formidable. Presidents cannot simply assume that their instructions, statements of policy, or program directives are traveling down the bureaucratic hierarchy as they intended. To ensure that presidential communications from the EOP have been received and accurately understood, presidents must do follow-up—that is, they must check for agency compliance and require regular feedback. Because administrative agencies resist supplying feedback in the same way that they resist sending information through regular channels, presidents must conscientiously monitor bureaucratic activity to maintain control at the top of the bureaucracy. This monitoring requires extra personnel; it is one reason that most presidents have called for a larger Executive Office of the President.

Building on the experience of previous administrations, President George W. Bush sought to centralize information management in the Office of Management and Budget. In mid-2001 the Bush administration established the President's Management Agenda, which was developed to ensure that the president's policy goals were transmitted throughout the administrative hierarchy of each department. Political appointees were rewarded for successfully meeting the goals of the President's Management Agenda, which often focused on budgeting issues such as privatization and outsourcing.[35] The President's Management Agenda became one of the prime vehicles that the Bush administration used in an effort to reduce federal spending, which had been a stated goal of the 2000 campaign. By fiscal year 2002, however, the Bush administration began running a budget deficit.[36] Agencies were scored on color-coded scorecards for how well the administration's management and budgeting goals had been addressed. Political executives and members of the senior executive service (SES) were rewarded personally for moving their agencies' scorecard from a red, which meant unsatisfactory, to a green, which meant satisfactory.

Permanent versus Presidential Government

Beneath this desire to manage the transmission of information throughout the federal bureaucracy more deliberately is an equally important motivation for greater presidential control of the bureaucracy—an antipathy toward, and a contempt for, the bureaucracy because of its ability to frustrate presidential policy. Most presidents never completely trust civil servants and are not completely at ease with their own political appointees. They fear that bureaucrats and department appointees develop loyalties that may obstruct presidential policy objectives. With this view comes a widely accepted belief among presidential scholars that an administration's failures result from ineffective management of the bureaucracy. Or, more specifically, an administration's failures result from the attempts of careerists (career civil servants who have made their careers in a particular department or agency) to supplant the policies of the president with those of their own.

Arthur Schlesinger Jr., a former Kennedy staffer, said of the Kennedy administration:

> Our real trouble was that we had capitulated too much to the existing bureaucracy. Wherever we have gone wrong . . . has been because we have not had sufficient confidence in the New Frontier approach to impose it on the government. Every important mistake has been the consequence of excessive deference to the permanent government. . . . The problem of moving forward seemed in great part the problem of making the permanent government responsive to the policies of the presidential government.[37]

Consequently, many presidents have sought to reform the executive branch to make the bureaucracy more responsive to their policy initiatives. They want to provide the EOP with a larger staff and greater resources for coordination of the various departments and agencies and their programs. According to Cronin, these presidents see themselves as "the recipients of endless special-interest pleas and narrow-minded agitation, even from many of their own cabinet members. In its crudest form, their goal is to presidentialize the executive branch."[38] To gain control over what they perceive to be hostile environments, they push for strong bureaucratic reform measures.

Presidential scholar Louis W. Koenig has argued for reforms that would give presidents powerful administrative control over the bureaucracy:

> The strong presidency will depend on the chief executive's capacity to control and direct the vast bureaucracy of national administration. Ideally, the president should possess administrative powers comparable to those of business executives. What the president needs most can be simply formulated: a power over personnel policy, planning, accounting, and the administration of the executive branch that approaches his power over the executive budget.[39]

Nixon stands out among recent presidents for the depth of his animosity toward the bureaucracy and his suspicion that it was seeking to sabotage his administration. In line with his view of a hostile bureaucracy, Nixon attempted to adopt strategies of governance designed to decrease the

Chief of Staff H. R. Haldeman, left, was called the "Berlin Wall" because he jealously guarded the entrance to the Oval Office. He is shown here meeting with President Nixon and aide C. Stanley Blair.

role of bureaucracy and increase the power of the White House staff. After abandoning a legislative strategy to put his stamp on domestic policy, Nixon turned to an administrative strategy that called for taking over the bureaucracy and concentrating on achieving policy objectives through administrative action.

Public administration scholar Richard P. Nathan referred to the Nixon administration as the "anti-bureaucracy administration." He noted that over the course of Nixon's tenure in office "there was no reduction in mistrust of the bureaucracy. On the contrary, these attitudes hardened to the point where unprecedented reorganizational steps were planned for the second term to take control of the machinery of domestic government."[40] Hostility toward the bureaucracy could be found in several statements of Nixon's aides. One staff member referred to the "White House surrounded"— apparently by a bureaucracy more attuned to the policies of interest groups than to those of the president. In June 1972 another Nixon aide, former White House staff assistant Michael P. Balzano, described the federal bureaucracy in the following terms: "President Nixon doesn't run the bureaucracy; the civil service and the unions do. It took him three years to find out what was going on in the bureaucracy. And God forbid if any president is defeated after the first term, because then the bureaucracy has another three years to play games with the next president."[41] This view of a hostile bureaucracy probably contributed greatly to some of Nixon's later difficulties in the Watergate affair.

Nathan also pointed out that Nixon's 1973 decision to develop an administrative strategy for his second term brought up an important question. What should be the role of the elected chief executive in influencing the career professionals of the executive branch agencies? Should Congress, the courts, interest groups, the press, and the public be as powerful as the president in controlling the executive branch, or even more so? Nathan argued that the president "should have the most important role in this area of modern government. Purely as a practical matter, the chief executive is in a much better position than a large

group of people in a legislative body or the courts to give cohesive policy direction and guidance to the work of large public bureaucracies."[42]

The President's Administrative Style

How the chief executive organizes the EOP affects the success of any administration. Eisenhower, pointing to the need for a president to give considerable thought to administrative organization, wrote: "Organization cannot make a genius out of an incompetent. On the other hand, disorganization can scarcely fail to result in inefficiency and can easily lead to disaster."[43]

Presidents have used different styles in running their administrations. Some are comfortable with a system that is tidy and neat; others prefer a chaotic system that allows them to be innovative. In choosing their administrative styles, they determine how much advice and information they want to receive from within government and how much they want to receive from outside. Their decisions on administrative style determine whether they will give competing assignments and have overlapping jurisdictions or rely on aides with specific and narrowly defined responsibilities. Presidential scholars have traditionally divided these patterns of presidential organization and management into two systems: circular and hierarchical.

The Circular System

Some presidents, such as Franklin Roosevelt and John Kennedy, did not adopt a system with rigid lines of responsibility. They gave staffers different jobs over time and nurtured a competitive spirit. In this way they hoped to find the best person for any given task. Political scientist Stephen Hess described this style of staff organization as "circular," with the president at the hub of the wheel.[44] With no chief of staff to filter out less important information or decide who can and cannot see the president, this system permits large numbers of people—staffers, cabinet secretaries, members of Congress—to have relatively easy access to the Oval Office. Top staffers report directly to the chief executive.

Roosevelt is the clearest example of a hub-of-the-wheel president. Choosing a wide-open, free-wheeling, conflict-loaded system, Roosevelt delighted in encouraging and cultivating chaos in his staff. Although it was seldom clear either to outsiders or insiders where the lines of authority ran, there was never the slightest doubt that Roosevelt was in charge. It was not unusual for Roosevelt to assign two of his top assistants to work on the same problem without informing either of them that the other had the same task. For example, Roosevelt pitted Secretary of State Cordell Hull against Assistant Secretary of State Raymond Moley at the International Monetary and Economic Conference held in London in 1933. The two men, both assigned the responsibility of working out a policy on protective tariffs, had widely differing views. Hull considered protective tariffs a terrible mistake, and Moley was convinced that they were indispensable to industrial recovery at home during the New Deal. Hull, who was chairing the U.S. delegation at the conference, was surprised when Roosevelt sent Moley as his personal liaison when the conference stalled. Who had more authority? Which view was closer to Roosevelt's? No one knew until Roosevelt sided with Hull. Infuriated by the whole episode, Moley resigned.

At whatever cost, Roosevelt had no intention of being isolated in the White House. He was determined to get as much information from as many people as he could, even if doing so meant duplicating assignments or bruising egos. Political scientist Frank Kessler described the Roosevelt system:

> One hundred or so persons could get to him directly by telephone without being diverted by a secretary. He employed no chief of staff and permitted few of his staffers to become subject matter specialists. Except for Harry Hopkins, to whom he turned almost exclusively for foreign policy assignments, staffers were assigned problems in a variety of areas. He wanted to be sure that no staffer would become so steeped in an issue area that he would be forced to lean on that person for advice. Everyone but FDR had to be expendable.[45]

The Hierarchical System

Other presidents, such as Dwight Eisenhower and Richard Nixon, valued formal, hierarchical relationships. They felt more comfortable with an arrangement that placed greater coordinating and integrating responsibilities on a chief of staff. According to Hess, these presidents designed a highly structured pyramid system with themselves at the pinnacle.[46]

Leaning heavily on his experience in the army, Eisenhower delegated as much responsibility to his staff as possible. The key to Eisenhower's pyramid operation was Chief of Staff Sherman Adams, who served, in effect, as a deputy president. As a former member of Congress and governor of New Hampshire, Adams came to the Eisenhower administration with a great deal of government experience.

Eisenhower placed much confidence in Adams and would not read memos or reports coming across his desk unless his chief of staff had seen them first. Adams wrote: "Eisenhower simply expected me to man a staff that would boil down, simplify and expedite the urgent business that had to be brought to his attention and keep . . . work of secondary importance off of his desk."[47]

The Nixon administration epitomized the pyramid staffing pattern. Similar to the Eisenhower system, Nixon constructed a highly stratified organization with himself at the top and a chief of staff standing between him and the rest of the executive branch. Because he preferred to make decisions from option papers rather than through face-to-face communications, Nixon allowed papers to get through to him more easily than people. Nixon's chief of staff (before the Watergate scandal forced his resignation), H. R. Haldeman, became known as the "Berlin Wall" because he jealously guarded the entrance to the Oval Office—even from passage by other high-level staff members. According to Kessler, "Once Federal Reserve Board Chairman Arthur Burns met Nixon for his allotted ten minutes but, on his way out, he remembered something else he wanted to tell the president. Haldeman reportedly thrust his arm across the doorway telling Burns to make another appointment."[48]

Although Nixon's operation was successful in freeing the president to think out broad policy initiatives, Haldeman often was criticized for controlling access to the president too tightly. Critics also argued that Haldeman took too much responsibility upon himself. But two other chief Nixon aides, speechwriter William Safire and National Security Adviser Henry A. Kissinger, contended that Haldeman was performing the very role that the president assigned him. Nixon wanted to be protected from the "unnecessary" intrusions of his lower staff.[49] Haldeman himself reportedly once insisted, "Every president needs an S.O.B., and I'm Nixon's."

Patterns of Organizational Change

Not all presidential organizational styles fit neatly into the circular or hierarchical systems exemplified by Roosevelt and Nixon, respectively. Political scientist Charles O. Jones, in *The Presidency in a Separated System,* reports that neither the circular nor the hierarchical system adequately reflects how presidents do their work.[50] Relying on these systems to explain the ways in which presidents organize their administrations may oversimplify the vast differences in presidential organization and management. Presidents face different concerns and obstacles when it comes to organizing their administrations. Jones writes: "The process of designing a presidency at the top is allowed to be quite personal, suited to the perception of needs and responsibilities of the occupant. As a consequence, there is an astonishing lack of accepted wisdom as to how it should be done."[51]

Consequently, presidents often resort to trial and error when organizing and staffing their administrations.

Instead of relying on the circular or hierarchical system to describe presidential organization and management, Jones looks at organizational changes that take place within individual administrations. These changing patterns of management better portray how presidents go about their work. Jones identifies four organizational patterns of change that describe presidential administrative styles: stable, adjustable, renewable, and transitional. A stable pattern reflects a high degree of continuity in the organizational structure of a president and a high degree of continuity in the personnel serving throughout a president's term. An adjustable pattern reflects ordinary organizational adaptation and ordinary personnel changes through a president's term. A renewable pattern reflects major organizational restructuring and substantial personnel changes during a presidency. A transitional pattern occurs when one president succeeds another.

Presidents reflect more than one organizational pattern throughout their tenure in office. For example, the administrative styles of Jimmy Carter, Ronald Reagan, George H. W. Bush, Bill Clinton, and George W. Bush do not fit neatly into the hub-of-the-wheel or the pyramid administrative system. Instead, their administrations reflect changing patterns of management. Similarly, in his 2011 State of the Union address, Barack Obama promised to send to Congress a plan to reorganize the federal government. The ensuing plans, however, were light on specific details, and by late summer that year had gone nowhere.

The Carter Administration

The first two and one-half years of the Carter administration were stable, but shortly after midterm the Carter presidency undertook a renewal. This renewal reflected a change in Carter's administrative philosophy. When Carter entered office, he put in place a cabinet government and a decentralized system of administration, one in which substantial authority was to be delegated to the department secretaries. He proclaimed: "I believe in cabinet administration. There will never be an instance while I am president where members of the White House staff dominate or act in a superior position to the Cabinet."[52]

Carter originally organized his staff along functional lines instead of strict lines of command. He devised three administrative levels: the president at the top, nine key aides on the next level, and the rest of the staff below. He envisioned no pecking order. All of his aides, especially those on the level right below him, would have equal access to the president. As Carter's term progressed, the role of the White House staff increased at the expense of the various departments and agencies in the executive branch.

Part of the reason Carter's commitment to cabinet government did not last can be found in a personal work style that proved cumbersome in the White House. Carter had a passion for details that often obscured larger policy goals. Kessler wrote: "Often he overlooked the big picture because he was bogged down in particulars. Memos that crossed his desk in the Oval Office were often returned to the sender with Carter's comments penciled in the margin. He went so far as to correct his young staffer's grammar."[53] Because of his predilection for immersing himself in detail, Carter spent much of his time consuming large amounts of factual information. Early in his administration, senior career civil servants from OMB were astounded to learn that they were to brief Carter personally instead of his top aides on the defense budget. Once, in a meeting that lasted from three o'clock in the afternoon to eleven o'clock at night, the president devoured every piece of information that OMB could feed him. This commitment to detail pushed the administration away from a hub-of-the-wheel approach to a more structured pattern. Political scientist Colin Campbell has suggested that "every fiber of Carter's personal makeup had actually been conspiring all along to run a highly centralized administration. Here the president's tendency to engross himself in details served as the fifth column."[54]

In 1979, after thirty months in office, Carter, in an unusual Camp David retreat with some of his most trusted political advisers, restructured his senior staff and cabinet as his public approval ratings plummeted. The recommended personnel changes led to the resignation of six cabinet secretaries and to the appointment of Hamilton Jordan as chief of staff.

Under Jordan's direction, the White House began to solidify its control over bureaucratic operations. In the first few months of the Carter administration, cabinet secretaries and the heads of many other agencies had enjoyed great latitude in appointing people to fill vacancies. Personnel officers in each of the departments eventually were told, however, that the White House wanted to be consulted on all appointments to high government positions. This announcement was a major blow to the departments, because they had been promised great flexibility and control over their own affairs.

The Reagan and George H. W. Bush Administrations

The twelve years of the Reagan and Bush administrations represent a "transitional" presidency, moving through periods of adjustment, renewal, and, finally, transition. The Reagan administration itself moved from an early period of normal adjustment with several changes in cabinet secretaries to a period of renewal as political events unfolded during Reagan's eight years in office. As a vice president elected to follow his own party's immensely popular president, Bush faced some special problems in setting up his administration during the transition period.

Reagan cared little for the details of the presidency. Throughout his administration, he conveyed almost a nonchalance about the specifics of presidential organization and management. Preferring one-page mini-memos that boiled down even the most complex issues to the bare essentials, Reagan operated largely through massive delegation of duties. He maintained a "nine-to-five" schedule characteristic of pyramid presidents who prefer delegation to detail.

Although Reagan had certain broad policy goals he wanted accomplished, he left it to others to organize his administration to achieve these goals. The responsibility for organizing the Reagan presidency fell to James A. Baker III, Michael K. Deaver, and Edwin Meese III, all key Reagan political advisers in the 1980 presidential campaign. The result was a modified pyramid form of staffing in which authority was divided between Baker, who served as chief of staff, and Meese, who served as counselor to the president. Baker was charged with handling political matters and selling the president's programs to the public, the press, Congress, and interest groups. Meese was charged with policy formulation. Deaver's responsibilities included scheduling, appointments, and travel.

Dividing power among Baker, Meese, and Deaver, Reagan gave these three aides almost unlimited access to him in his first term. This arrangement kept Reagan from becoming completely isolated, as Nixon had become by having only a single chief of staff in Haldeman. Meese served as Reagan's political conscience, keeping him true to his conservative policy goals in domestic policy. Baker focused on legislative issues and foreign policy, and Deaver managed the day-to-day operations of the White House. It was a system that suited Reagan's personality and one with which he was comfortable.

Once in office, Reagan exercised great control over the appointment process in the departments and agencies, thereby imposing exceptional discipline on his administration. By ensuring the ideological compatibility of his nominees, Reagan could delegate and not worry about subordinates sabotaging his programs. Reagan's most effective source of discipline early in his administration, however, was OMB under the direction of David Stockman (1981–1985). By mastering the intricacies of the budget process and controlling the budgets of the various departments and agencies, Stockman was able to impose a stringent regimen on the departments and agencies and bring them under the policy directions of the Reagan administration.

The Reagan administration's pattern of renewal roughly corresponded with a changing White House staff and cabinet and events relating to the Iran-contra affair. Although Reagan had one chief of staff during his first administration, he had three during his second: Donald T. Regan, Howard H. Baker Jr., and Kenneth Duberstein. In addition, after the 1984 election Reagan's cabinet underwent five changes. There were no mass firings, but the changes

after the election represented a natural point for renewal. The initial Reagan appointments drew heavily from those outside the Washington circles of power. At the point of renewal, Reagan's new appointees often reflected more experience in federal government.

Reagan attempted to maintain a modified pyramid with a tight system of discipline in formulating and implementing presidential initiatives throughout most of his administration. The success of this kind of system depends on a president knowing when to become involved in details and which issues merit concentrated attention. Many who served in the Reagan administration give the president credit for involving himself energetically in important issues such as tax reform and contra funding. One aide stated: "He [Reagan] has a ruthless sense of priorities. He really knows that he can accomplish a few things. He's going to pick some good people and let them handle the rest."[55]

Yet the success of the type of system Reagan used requires that the president have some knowledge of all issues to eliminate those issues that will not receive priority. In several instances, Reagan lacked the depth of knowledge in a specific policy area to make this determination. Political scientist Paul Quirk argues that presidents, such as Reagan, who adopt a "minimalist" approach that relies heavily on the advice of subordinates often have difficulties making intelligent decisions. He writes: "By never paying attention to the complexities of careful policy arguments, one never comes to understand the importance of thorough analysis."[56] In 1987 the *Tower Commission Report* charged that President Reagan relied too much on a bottom-up administrative system. The report noted that Reagan, by delegating too much responsibility to the NSC, did not give enough attention to important details of security policy. His inattention resulted in the secret sale of military equipment to Iran and the diversion of funds to assist U.S.-backed forces in Nicaragua during 1985 and 1986. This ill-fated undertaking became the subject of much public attention and embarrassment to the Reagan administration. The *Tower Commission Report* concluded that Reagan's management style put too much responsibility for policy review and implementation on the shoulders of his advisers: "The president should have ensured that the NSC system did not fail him. He did not force his policy to undergo the most critical review of which the NSC participants and the process were capable. . . . Had the president chosen to drive the NSC system, the outcome could well have been different."[57]

The George H. W. Bush presidency reflected a period of transition from one administration to another within the same political party. Although Bush had to live up to expectations arising from the legacy of the popular Reagan administration, he attempted to put his own stamp on his administration by appointing staffers and cabinet members who embodied his priorities. Some of those appointees,

Here George H. W. Bush meets in the Oval Office with (from left to right) Deputy National Security Adviser Robert Gates, Secretary of Defense Dick Cheney, Chairman of the Joint Chiefs of Staff Colin Powell, Chief of Staff John H. Sununu, and National Security Adviser Brent Scowcroft. Gates, Cheney, Powell, and Scowcroft would all go on to serve under President George W. Bush as well.

however, were holdovers from the Reagan administration. Several cabinet appointments made in the waning months of the Reagan administration appeared to be transitional appointments. Bush called on three members of the last Reagan cabinet and two others who had served in earlier Reagan cabinets to serve in his administration.

Many of those appointed to the administration were longtime political associates and friends of George H. W. Bush. One of those longtime political friends proved to be an embarrassment in the early days of the Bush presidency. Former senator John G. Tower, R-Tex., was not confirmed by the Senate as secretary of defense because of problems with alcohol and women. Most Bush appointees, however, were highly regarded. Their competence allowed the president a certain amount of confidence to grant his staff and cabinet the freedom to provide direction to and control over his administration.

There was never any question about the type of management system Bush would use. He chose a chief-of-staff system similar to Reagan's. His years of service in the Reagan administration and his close association with James Baker, Reagan's former chief of staff, contributed to Bush's understanding of presidential management and the ways in which he desired to organize his presidency.

Bush modified the pyramid system, however. Unlike Reagan, Bush wanted to be somewhat involved in the day-to-day operations of his staff. With many friends and close associates on his cabinet and staff, Bush had no desire to be isolated. Although his personality and close friendships among his appointees might point to an administration organized along a hub-of-the-wheel model, Bush saw the need for a chief of staff who would keep the administration

in line. For that position, he chose John H. Sununu, a former governor of New Hampshire and a Washington outsider who was not afraid to offend those who disagreed with him. Although vigorous in his pursuit of Bush's objectives, Sununu was not able to stand between Bush and his close associates within the administration. Too many staffers retained access to the president.

After the transition period, most of the Bush presidency was stable, with few adjustments and no wholesale firing of cabinet members that had characterized other administrations. Sununu met a premature demise as chief of staff—partly because of accusations that he had used air force jets for personal reasons at taxpayers' expense. Otherwise, many staffers and cabinet members remained in their positions until the end of the administration. Six of Bush's fourteen cabinet secretaries served until the next administration. Four of those who left took other jobs in the administration. The Bush presidency was one of few traumas in personnel and organization. In particular, the foreign policy team, which included National Security Adviser Brent Scowcroft, Secretary of Defense Richard B. Cheney, Secretary of State James Baker, and Chairman of the Joint Chiefs of Staff Colin L. Powell, brought new cohesion to the White House–cabinet relationship and added overall stability to the Bush administration.

The Clinton Administration

The way in which President Clinton set up his administration exemplified another organizational pattern not found within traditional geometric models. As is the case with all presidents, the organization of the Clinton administration directly reflects the president's personality. Clinton had run a "hands-on" campaign and wanted to extend that approach to the organization and governing of his presidency. Thus the staffing and organizing of the Clinton presidency took place in Little Rock, Arkansas, the headquarters of the Clinton campaign, under the watchful eye of the president-elect and his wife, Hillary Rodham Clinton. The result of their efforts was a loosely structured and accessible presidency, staffed largely with inexperienced Washington outsiders.

Initially, the Clinton White House was largely unstructured. Elizabeth Drew, in *On the Edge: The Clinton Presidency,* describes Clinton's governing style in the early months of his administration:

> The unhierarchical structure and the collegial style of the Clinton White House seemed, at first, wonderful. Clinton himself contributed to the informality, often wandering the halls and dropping in on aides or on the Vice President. Aides felt fairly free to drop in on him. In March, Bruce Lindsay said, "More people tend to walk in on him than probably any of his predecessors." A peephole in the door leading from the back corridor to his office enabled an aide to see if he was on the phone, or talking with people, before going in.[58]

Clinton enjoyed the informal structure. He encouraged a large number of meetings with a large number of people attending. His desire was to get as much information from as many people as possible. This allowed him to place himself in the middle of his administration, participating directly in the formulation of policy.

Clinton initially had no desire for either a strong chief of staff, such as Sununu, or the highly structured White House organization that a strong chief of staff would necessitate. During the transition, Clinton chose Thomas F. "Mack" McLarty III as his chief of staff. McLarty, a business executive and Clinton boyhood friend, had limited Washington experience. He was to serve as an "honest broker" instead of a strong chief of staff who had unchallenged control over access to the president. The honest broker structure was designed by both McLarty and Clinton during the transition period after they had carefully studied the organizational structures of previous administrations.[59] Because McLarty did not impose a specific view or try to take charge, Clinton had the freedom he wanted to circulate among his staff in search of different views.

This nonhierarchical system with a weak chief of staff was complicated by the informal policy role assigned to Hillary Clinton. She participated in many of President Clinton's policy decisions, although her influence waned during the second term. She was heavily involved in the staffing and organization of the Clinton administration, and she continued her involvement through key policymaking roles in the administration. Drew reports that, for some Clinton aides, Mrs. Clinton appeared to serve in the first term as a de facto chief of staff, because White House staffers had to make their policy arguments to the president through her. One White House aide reportedly said: "[Mrs. Clinton] concerns herself with the overall management of the White House and what she feels is a failure to integrate the president's politics into the workings of the White House. She expresses frustration about the loose management of the White House and the inability to hold some people accountable."[60] The strong influence of Mrs. Clinton, coupled with the weak chief of staff system under McLarty, proved to be troublesome for the administration.

The Clinton White House made its first significant adjustment five months after the inauguration. In an effort to improve the management of the White House, and thus Clinton's approval rating, which had fallen steadily since he had taken office, McLarty was vested with more authority. McLarty in turn brought David Gergen into the administration as director of communications to give the Clinton presidency a more mature and moderate image. Gergen, who had served in the Nixon and Reagan White Houses, was experienced in Washington and was generally known as a political centrist. In addition, McLarty attempted to shore up lines of responsibility and to limit access to the president. The purpose was to structure the president's time better, freeing him to work more on larger policies instead of the details of policy. Despite McLarty's attempts to tighten control within the administration, it was not apparent that any real organizational change took place. There was little coordination of policymaking among various groups within the White House and little clear responsibility. One Clinton aide said, "It's a floating crap game about who runs what around here. The last person who has an idea can often get it done, whether it's part of the strategy or not. The situation hasn't improved."[61]

By mid-1994 the public approval rating of Clinton's presidency and his ability to govern reached another low. Realizing that his presidency was in serious trouble, Clinton once again made significant changes in his White House staff. Acquiescing to advice from his closest advisers, Mrs. Clinton, and Vice President Gore, Clinton replaced his long-time friend McLarty as chief of staff with Leon Panetta, the budget director. Panetta was given great latitude to rearrange the White House staff. He attempted to tighten the White House organization. He controlled access to Clinton much more closely by reducing the number of meetings staffers had with the president and drastically reducing walk-in privileges to the Oval Office. He also tightened lines of authority and generally attempted to return management of the White House to a more traditional, strong chief-of-staff model. McLarty stayed on the White House staff as a counselor to the president. Because his main ally no longer held a position of significant power, Gergen was sent to the State Department. Both men eventually left the administration. Panetta, too, later left the administration and was replaced by Erskine Bowles.

President Bush and Chief of Staff Andrew Card leave the White House, Feb. 10, 2006, to speak to the House Republican Conference in Cambridge, Md.

With few exceptions, the Clinton cabinet was chosen for its diversity, not for experience or loyalty to Clinton. Most cabinet members had little Washington experience. One of the ways Clinton attempted to ensure loyalty, and thus control, over his cabinet was to have the White House approve subcabinet appointments. His transition team concluded that the Carter administration made a fatal organizational mistake in not ensuring the loyalty of those holding subcabinet positions. For Clinton, not ensuring loyalty from his cabinet secretaries may have been a mistake. A few cabinet members, such as Attorney General Janet Reno, often took public positions that differed from Clinton's. This created a public perception of lack of respect for the president among some of his cabinet members.

The George W. Bush Administration

Although George W. Bush spoke disparagingly about Washington politics in his presidential campaign, once elected he set about appointing an administration of experienced Washington insiders. Many of Bush's key appointments were people who had substantial experience in past Republican administrations. Early assessments of Bush's appointments marveled at the return of the Ford administration, because of the large number of key appointees who had served President Gerald R. Ford, including most prominently Donald H. Rumsfeld. But in fact Bush also drew heavily from the ranks of those who had served in his father's administration and in the Reagan administration.

As did Clinton, Bush favored a close family associate for the position of chief of staff. But unlike Clinton's first appointee, Andrew Card came to the Bush administration with vast Washington experience. He first served in the Reagan White House and then in the George H. W. Bush administration as deputy to the chief of staff and as secretary of transportation. In the early months of the George W. Bush presidency, Card received high marks from observers for running a tightly focused and efficient staff system that enabled Bush to maintain discipline in the White House. And he did so in large part by avoiding the kind of heavy-handed leadership approach of his former boss, Bush senior's chief of staff, John Sununu.

Bush gave substantial independent authority to his vice president, Dick Cheney. Cheney was an experienced Washington politician. He had served in the Nixon, Ford, and George H. W. Bush administrations, as well as in Congress. A former White House chief of staff and defense secretary, Cheney had substantial executive branch and departmental leadership experience. Two other key Bush confidants were political strategist Karl Rove and White House counselor Karen Hughes. Rove had served as Bush's lead strategist during his 2000 campaign. Rove also informally served the role as the administration's key link to conservative constituency groups. Karen Hughes was Bush's closest adviser during his tenure as governor of Texas. Bush included Hughes in all major policy discussions in the White House and placed her in charge of the White House communications operation, including the Press Office. Another major White House appointment was Condoleezza Rice as national security adviser. Rice had served as a chief adviser to the senior Bush's national security adviser, Brent Scowcroft, and then as chief national security adviser to George W. Bush's 2000 presidential campaign.

On the cabinet side, Bush appointed experienced Washington insider Donald Rumsfeld as secretary of defense. Rumsfeld, the oldest defense secretary in history, had held the same post in the Ford administration when he was the youngest. Another familiar face, Colin L. Powell, was tapped to be secretary of state. Powell had served in both the Reagan and George H. W. Bush administrations, most prominently as chair of the Joint Chiefs of Staff during the 1991 Persian Gulf War.

Although Bush drew heavily from past GOP administrations for his top staff, he assembled a diverse group. After the first year of the Bush presidency, a Brookings Institution study found that Bush had appointed the highest percentage of minorities of any president to the Executive Office of the President (11 percent) and the second highest percentage of women (28 percent, just below Clinton's 29 percent). Another distinctive feature of Bush's appointments was the large proportion (29 percent) from the president's home state of Texas.[62]

Early in his term the president established two new White House units: the Office of Strategic Initiatives (OSI) and the Office of Faith-Based and Community Initiatives.[63] The OSI, headed by Karl Rove, was intended to develop long-term administration policy. The Office of Faith-Based and Community Initiatives was first headed by a Democrat and university professor, John J. DiIulio Jr. after Bush created the latter office by means of executive order, the role of the office immediately attracted criticism from constituencies concerned about the effort to develop policies that would provide government funding for religious organizations involved in charitable and other public services. DiIulio left the office in late 2001 after political battles within the White House.

In the aftermath of the September 11, 2001, terrorist attacks on the United States, the Bush administration made some important staffing decisions. Most important was the creation of a White House office, the Office of Homeland Security (OHS), headed by former Pennsylvania governor Tom Ridge. The OHS coordinated the activities of more than forty federal agencies and departments aimed at protecting the nation from terrorist activities. The OHS was led by a new Homeland Security Council composed of the OHS director, the attorney general, the directors of the Federal Bureau of Investigation (FBI), CIA, OMB, and the Federal Emergency Management Agency (FEMA); the secretaries of defense, Treasury, agriculture, transportation, and health and human services; and the president's and vice president's chiefs of staff. However, when the Department of Homeland Security was created by Congress in 2002, the White House Office of Homeland Security lost its preeminent role.

During the second term, Bush continued to maintain a strong chief of staff system. In 2006 first-term chief of staff Andrew Card was replaced by Joshua Bolten, who had been appointed OMB director in 2003. Bolten was viewed as having even firmer control over White House and cabinet personnel than Card had. Soon after becoming chief of staff, Bolten suggested that there would be staff changes at all levels of the administration. Within months of Bolten's statement, Secretary of the Treasury John Snow was replaced by Henry Paulson, a former partner of Bolten's at the Goldman Sachs investment firm. Paulson played a major role in the administration's response to the September 2008 near-collapse of the nation's financial system. For example, rather than infuse federal mortgage agencies Fannie Mae and Freddie Mac with needed cash, Paulson instead ushered them toward government conservatorship. Paulson also ultimately became manager of the newly created (in 2008) Emergency Economic Stabilization fund, and he was perhaps most noteworthy for his position that the government inject funds into all major American banks, regardless of need, in order to protect weaker banks from market forces.

Another key second term staff member for the George W. Bush administration was Stephen Hadley, who replaced Condoleezza Rice as national security adviser when Rice became secretary of state. Hadley has been credited as one of the key individuals who helped convince President Bush the ongoing war in Iraq was not going well and that changes needed to be made. Also notable, though for more onerous reasons, were staffers such as Lewis "Scooter" Libby, Vice President Cheney's chief of staff who was convicted of obstructing justice in the Valerie Plame scandal, and Attorney General Alberto Gonzales, who misled Congress regarding the political nature of the U.S. attorneys firings scandal in 2006–2007.[64]

The Barack Obama Administration

Although Barack Obama spoke of hope and change on the campaign trail, his administration, similar to George W. Bush's, was largely populated by well-known figures from the Washington political class. In addition to selecting long-time senator Joseph Biden as his vice presidential running mate, Obama turned to individuals such as influential Rep. Rahm Emanuel (D-Ill.) as his chief of staff, Rep. Ray LaHood (R-Ill.) as transportation secretary, and former first lady and Sen. Hillary Clinton (D-N.Y.) as secretary of state, as well as former secretary of energy and New Mexico governor Bill Richardson and Republican senator Judd Gregg as early but ultimately failed nominees for other cabinet slots. (Richardson withdrew his own name as controversy grew over a federal grand jury investigation, and Gregg demurred over ideological differences with the president after having initially indicated a desire to put partisanship aside.)

Obama recruited numerous others out of the private and academic sectors, including high-profile figures like Secretary of the Treasury Timothy Geithner and National Economic Council director Lawrence Summers. As the nation faced economic turmoil in the face of bank crises,

At the 2009 G-20 Summit President Obama confers with Timothy Geithner, secretary of the Treasury and one of Obama's recruits from the private sector. Geithner was previously the CEO of the Federal Reserve Bank of New York.

mortgage defaults, and a weak dollar, the pressure on Obama's economic team was immense. While many analysts suggested the actions of the team helped keep the nation from sinking further into recession, the recovery remained weak as the Obama administration entered the reelection campaign season. Whether this sluggishness was a consequence or a cause for the relative organizational dysfunction that the president's economic team demonstrated remained an open question. Shirley Warshaw has noted that the economic policymaking team proved to be a thorny one, as key leaders like Summers and Christina Romer, chair of Obama's Council of Economic Advisers, were unable to collaborate well and ultimately resigned.[65] The president's foreign policy team has not been quite as organizationally flawed, in large part due to the formidable nature of the individuals and institutions involved, including secretaries Clinton and Gates, Vice President Biden, and the upper echelon of the military leadership. Nevertheless, high-profile departures occurred, including National Security Adviser General Jim Jones, who clashed with his eventual replacement Tom Donilon, and Gen. Stanley McChrystal, who was fired by the president from his command in Afghanistan after making controversial comments to media outlets. McChrystal was replaced by Gen. David Petraeus, who would later be nominated as the director of the Central Intelligence Agency, replacing longtime government leader Leon Panetta, who went over to serve as secretary of defense to replace the retiring Gates.

Congressional Oversight

Article I, Section 1, of the Constitution states that "all legislative powers herein granted shall be vested in a Congress of the United States, which shall consist of a Senate and a House of Representatives." Section 8 lists specific congressional powers and gives Congress all powers "necessary and proper" to implement them. Over the years these provisions have been used to establish administrative agencies such as the General Accounting Office to implement congressional policies. The constitutional grants of authority have given Congress the power of life and death over these administrative agencies.

Because Congress has the power to enact laws and create and abolish executive branch agencies without presidential consent, members of Congress have significant opportunities to tell the bureaucracy what to do and how to do it. Most programs enacted into law by Congress are technical and complex, however. In an ideal world, statutes are precise and the legislature's intent is clear. But Congress, starting especially in the 1920s, began to use broader statutory language that, in the process, often delegated substantial discretionary authority to executive branch departments and agencies. Congress did so for several reasons: it did not possess the technical capacity for greater precision, it could not reach consensus on the minutiae of increasingly complex policy questions, or it concluded that the fluidity of circumstances required a degree of executive flexibility in policy implementation. As a result, Congress usually states general goals to be achieved by programs administered through bureaucratic agencies.

The Economic Opportunity Act of 1964, for example, states that the poor should have "maximum feasible participation" in the administration of the programs of the Office of Economic Opportunity (OEO). The interpretation of the act was left entirely to OEO and its local branches. Occasionally, Congress specifies precise standards that eliminate bureaucratic discretionary power, as it did in the Securities Act of 1933, which requires that investors receive financial and other significant information about securities being offered for public sale.

The very size of the *Federal Register,* a journal published each weekday in which agencies announce and publicize all the new rules and regulations used in administering programs, indicates the amount of freedom agencies have in interpreting congressional intent. Delegating this authority to the bureaucracy allows Congress to keep its workload manageable. Otherwise the volume and complexity of its work would allow Congress to accomplish little.

By giving agencies considerable leeway in realizing their objectives, however, Congress abrogates a certain amount of control over the bureaucracy. Thus a great deal of public policy is made by the bureaucracy, without any specific direction from Congress. Because administrative agencies have wide latitude in promulgating regulations and establishing policies, the burden of reconciling conflicts among competing interest groups often falls on the bureaucracy instead of on Congress. Peter Woll has written: "Theoretically, Congress still retains the primary legislative power, and is merely appointing an agent to act for it; in fact, however, virtually complete legislative discretion is given to the designated agency or to the President."[66]

Although Congress delegates to executive branch agencies much of its authority to make and implement policy, it retains considerable influence through a variety of activities known collectively as *congressional oversight.* Through laws and precedents, Congress has developed procedures that allow it to monitor the way the bureaucracy exercises its delegated authority.

The Legislative Reorganization Act of 1946 requires congressional committees to oversee those agencies that they create or that fall under their jurisdiction. For many years after passage of this act, members of Congress were more interested in creating new laws than in monitoring ones they had already made. Oversight, therefore, was not a major concern of the committees. With the growth in the 1960s and 1970s of grant-in-aid programs, which gave state and local governments federal funds to administer specific programs in areas such as highways, hospitals, and welfare services, interest groups and state and local officials encouraged legislative oversight of agencies providing goods and services to constituents.

The Legislative Reorganization Act of 1970 increased the capability of Congress to oversee federal programs by giving committees additional staffing and funds to retain outside experts. In addition, the 1970 legislation increased the resources of the General Accounting Office (GAO)—created by Congress in 1921 to oversee the expenditures of the executive branch—and gave it power to review and analyze government programs whenever a congressional committee ordered it to do so. As a consequence, the GAO hired economists, systems analysts, engineers, and management consultants to help monitor and analyze programs as requested by Congress. Despite the Pentagon's objections, during the 1970s about twelve hundred of the GAO's twenty-seven hundred professional staff audited and evaluated Department of Defense programs.[67]

Because legislation often gives an agency considerable latitude in interpreting congressional intent, the tools provided by the GAO improve committees' capacities to monitor agency actions. Committees also can hold either regular hearings or special investigations on specific aspects of a program. And they can monitor an agency's actions through informal means, such as phone calls and visits with bureaucrats, lobbyists, and constituents. Program evaluations, conducted by either the committee's staff or the GAO, often provide ways in which the agency's actions can be changed to bring it into line with what Congress intended.

Legislative oversight has become increasingly important in recent decades. According to Joel D. Aberbach, the number of days of oversight hearings conducted by House and Senate committees increased almost fourfold from 1961 to 1983.[68] One reason for the increase in oversight hearings is the tension arising from divided party control of Congress and the presidency. As divided government has tended to dominate the political landscape since the early 1950s, Congress has become more assertive in its oversight function. In 1987 a Democratic Congress formed a joint committee to investigate the Reagan administration's secret sales of military equipment to Iran and its policy of using the proceeds from these sales to aid the rebel forces in Nicaragua. In the mid-1990s, a Republican Congress exerted its oversight power to investigate the investment activities of the Clintons, known as the Whitewater affair.

Significant congressional oversight by the president's own party is, not surprisingly, far less likely, but it does occur. During the George W. Bush presidency, the Republican-controlled House of Representatives held hearings and investigated the administration's expansive use of executive privilege to conceal certain Department of Justice deliberative materials. Similarly, the Republican-controlled Senate held hearings on the president's use of signing statements as a way of changing the meaning of bills without vetoing them. The hearings led to no significant action, but Democrats obtained full control of Congress in the 2006 midterm election, raising the possibility of more aggressive congressional oversight during the remainder of the Bush administration. Similarly, when Democrats controlled both chambers of Congress during the first two years of the Obama administration, the president's fellow partisans held hearings into his practice of using policy czars to help manage and coordinate leadership efforts on numerous key policy issues.

The Legislative Veto

Fearing that federal bureaucrats—or the president—might abuse the authority delegated by Congress, congressional committees frequently attach to new statutes provisions that allow the committees to pass preemptive judgment on new regulations or other bureaucratic actions. Such provisions are known as *legislative vetoes.* These provisions typically require that no regulatory action can go into effect for a prescribed length of time (such as ninety days), during which Congress can vote to disallow the regulation or action through a simple resolution of both houses, one house singly, or even one congressional committee, depending on the provision in question. These requirements give committees both a formal veto over executive actions and the authority to approve or disapprove the specific actions of an agency.

The legislative veto was first written into legislation used by President Herbert C. Hoover in his attempt to reorganize the executive branch. In 1932 Congress passed a joint resolution that allowed Hoover to reorganize executive agencies but specified that his changes could not take effect for ninety days. During this time either house of Congress by a simple resolution could veto his reorganizations, but neither did.

Perhaps the best example of the use of a legislative veto involved Congress's Joint Committee on Atomic Energy (JCAE) in the 1950s. In setting up the Atomic Energy Commission, Congress required that agency to keep the JCAE informed on the development of its nuclear reactor programs. As Richard M. Pious concluded, "In effect that provision made the committee a 'board of directors' that supervised the peaceful development of atomic energy. The committee determined what technology would be advanced, the location of experimental facilities, and policies relating to the private development of commercial power plants."[69]

The controversy over legislative vetoes grew through the 1970s as use of the device mushroomed. Notable congressional attempts to rein in the executive branch by use of the legislative veto include provisions of the War Powers Resolution of 1973, which restricted the president's power to deploy troops without a formal declaration of war, and the Budget and Impoundment Control Act of 1974, which allowed the president to rescind expenditures only if both houses of Congress approved. Congress resorted increasingly to legislative veto provisions at that time in no small part because of the partisan, ideological, and political conflicts between Richard Nixon and a Congress dominated by Democrats. Simply put, Congress and the executive were locked in a state of mutual distrust, with Congress particularly loath to allow the president more discretion than necessary in carrying out the legislature's will. Describing the effects of legislative control over the bureaucracy, political scientist Allen Schick noted that by 1983 "Congress had adopted more than 250 veto provisions; of these, more than half were enacted during the 1970s."[70]

If Congress saw the legislative veto as the most effective tool possible to ensure that the president and the bureaucracy conformed to the intent of legislation, many presidents viewed the legislative veto as a violation of the doctrine of the separation of powers and as an unconstitutional encroachment on the powers of the presidency. Worse, at least from a presidential perspective, there was no formal way for a president to respond to legislative vetoes because simple resolutions do not go to the president for approval. Legislative vetoes could not themselves be vetoed.

Although the legislative veto has been challenged by various presidents and their attorneys general, not until June 1983 did the Supreme Court rule on this congressional power. In *Immigration and Naturalization Service v. Chadha,* the Supreme Court held the legislative veto to be unconstitutional. It found that the Constitution requires in Article I that "every order, resolution, or vote to which the concurrence of the Senate and House of Representatives may be necessary . . . shall be presented to the president of the United States" who must either approve it or veto it.[71] In other words, the president must concur in any action that Congress takes that has the force of law, including the legislative veto. If Congress wishes to prevent the executive branch from undertaking some action, the Court's majority ruled, Congress must either legislate in greater detail to begin with or pass a regular bill—subject to presidential review—to redress an action it deems unacceptable.

The decision in *Chadha* left unanswered the question of whether the laws to which the veto provisions were attached also were unconstitutional. To date, the Court has been reluctant to go that far. Congress for its part has adapted to life after *Chadha* in two ways. On the one hand, Congress has gone back to using more explicit statutory language, which raises complaints about congressional micromanagement. On the other hand, Congress has resorted to adding even more language in appropriations bills forbidding funding for some specific bureaucratic or presidential actions. This language provides the functional equivalent of a legislative veto if the president accepts the appropriations bill as a whole. The Court has yet to rule on this strategy. Critics of congressional oversight and the legislative veto argue that instead of allowing committees to oversee agencies effectively, the legislative veto gives too much influence to interest groups. They contend that alliances between an agency, its constituent group, and its congressional committee compromise the ability of the committee to monitor agency activities objectively. According to this theory, because the congressional committee is "captured" by the interest groups it serves, its oversight of agencies and programs will be biased to benefit the constituent groups.

Since the *Chadha* decision, Congress has passed numerous laws containing legislative vetoes. Thus presidential expert Louis Fisher argues that the legislative veto continues to survive "by open defiance and subtle evasions" of *Chadha.*[72] For example, in 1989 President George H. W. Bush entered into an informal agreement with Congress, known as the Baker Accord, that restricted the executive branch in its efforts to aid the contras in Nicaragua by requiring that four congressional committees agree to the aid.

Problems of Presidential Control

Congressional oversight and the legislative veto make it much more difficult for the president to control the bureaucracy. Through a variety of oversight techniques, Congress has made significant gains in controlling both foreign and domestic bureaucratic agencies. For example, congressional oversight helped thwart the efforts of the executive branch in its bombing of Cambodia in 1973 and inhibited various other covert intelligence activities during the Nixon years. Political scientists Thomas Franck and Edward Weisband argued that executive dominance in foreign policy has been replaced by a system of policy codetermination in which power is shared by the president and Congress.[73]

As a result, presidents have learned to live with congressional efforts at bureaucratic control, often signing bills that include oversight and veto provisions not completely to their liking. Franklin Roosevelt signed the Lend-Lease Act, under which he lent American destroyers to Great Britain before the United States officially entered World War II, and other wartime measures that gave him extensive war powers, despite the constraints that Congress put on him. Nixon signed the 1974 Impoundment Control Act granting him authority to defer the spending of funds already appropriated by Congress, although either house could veto his actions. Almost any statute that delegates congressional authority to the executive branch will contain provisions for legislative review.

Presidential control of the bureaucracy, however, has not been replaced by congressional control. Congress is much too large and much too overworked to provide effective control of the bureaucracy. According to Pious, "Although Congress' oversight role has increased in recent years, it should not be exaggerated. It is still intermittent, especially in the Senate, where members are spread too thin, serving on too many committees and subcommittees to develop expertise in agency operations."[74]

Reorganization Power

Because the president and Congress often find themselves opposing each other for control of the bureaucracy, presidents frequently look to reorganization as a means of gaining the upper hand and increasing their ability to manage their administrations. In pursuing their reorganization plans, however, presidents find that the affected agencies are strongly protected by their sponsoring congressional committees. Without the cooperation of Congress, it is extremely difficult for presidents to effect any reorganization plan for making the bureaucracy more efficient.

Every president wants to coordinate policymaking efforts as much as possible, but because the number of federal programs has increased rapidly, coordination of the many agencies and departments is difficult. In the area of transportation policy alone, the president must work not only with the Department of Transportation but also with the National Transportation Safety Board and the Federal Maritime Administration, as well as other agencies. This overlap among the agencies means that the executive branch often wastes time and effort trying to manage the development and implementation of public policy.

Brownlow Committee

The first real effort at administrative reorganization recognized these problems of inefficiency in the executive branch. Franklin Roosevelt wanted to establish a line of command that ran directly from the White House through the department secretaries to their subordinates. In March 1936 he created the Committee on Administrative Management and gave it the task of planning the overhaul of the executive branch. With Louis D. Brownlow as its chair and political scientists Charles E. Merriam and Luther Gulick as the other members, the Brownlow Committee concluded in 1937 that the executive branch under Roosevelt had become so complex that "the president needs help."[75]

The Brownlow Committee specifically recommended that the president receive increased administrative support. It proposed the creation of six new presidential assistants, "possessed of high competence, great physical vigor, and a passion for anonymity," who would be assigned at the president's discretion. In addition, it recommended that discretionary funds be put at the president's disposal to allow him to acquire more help as needed. Finally, the committee proposed a major organizational addition to the presidency, consisting of the Executive Office of the President, with the Bureau of the Budget as its centerpiece.[76]

Roosevelt won approval from Congress in 1939 for some of the Brownlow Committee's recommendations, including placing the Civil Service Commission under the control of the White House. He was given reorganization authority for a two-year period. In addition, Roosevelt was permitted to hire the six assistants that the Brownlow Committee recommended.

In Reorganization Plan No. 1, the president moved three EOP offices—the Bureau of the Budget, the Central Statistical Board, and the National Resources Planning Committee—into the State, War, and Navy Building next door to the White House. Soon after Reorganization Plan No. 1, Roosevelt issued an executive order that delineated the organization and responsibilities of the newly expanded presidency. This order detailed the formal relationships in the EOP among the White House Office, the BOB, and the remaining agencies of the executive branch.

Although Roosevelt got much of what the Brownlow Committee had recommended, the reorganization bill that finally passed Congress in 1939 was less than what he had hoped. The original bill was introduced in 1937 and became embroiled in Roosevelt's attempt to modify the composition of the Supreme Court. The final bill was a compromise and lacked most of Roosevelt's initial proposals. According to Peri E. Arnold, "It [the Reorganization Act of 1939] was on its face a congressional product, drafted under the guidance of Representative Lindsay Warren (D-N.C.) as a way of short-circuiting the intense, negative connection between presidential strength and the reorganization program."[77] Even so, the main thrust of the Brownlow Committee's recommendations was preserved, with regard to both structural changes and the intent to strengthen the president's control over the administration. Although Congress has been reluctant to go along completely with presidential recommendations to extend top-level management, it has allowed presidents to gradually centralize control over the bureaucracy in the EOP.

First Hoover Commission

The next major effort at centralizing presidential control occurred during the Truman administration. After large gains in the congressional elections of 1946, Republicans anticipated the end of the Truman presidency in 1948. The Republican-controlled Congress approved legislation to help a new president grapple with the problems of executive branch organization by setting up the Commission on the Organization of the Executive Branch of the Government. In 1947 Truman appointed former president Herbert Hoover as chair.

Hoover set about the task of evaluating the effectiveness of executive branch organization with much enthusiasm. Truman, who could have viewed the commission as a means of criticizing his administration, also was enthusiastic about the project and gave it his full cooperation. It is one of the ironies of the U.S. presidency that Truman was the one to benefit from the Hoover Commission's efforts when the Republicans failed to capture the presidency in 1948.

The Hoover Commission report recommended 277 specific measures that would institute "a clear line of control from the president to these departments and agency heads and from them to their subordinates . . . cutting through the barriers that have in many cases made bureaus and agencies practically independent of the chief executive."[78] The commission's report charged that the executive branch was unmanageable; its lines of communication and authority were confusing; and too few tools existed at the top for the development of effective policy.

The commission suggested three major areas of reform. First, department heads should assume the major authority within their departments instead of allowing it to reside in the bureau chiefs. This recommendation was aimed at overcoming the congressional practice of vesting statutory powers directly in agency chiefs. With department heads more easily held responsible to the president, the lines of authority and responsibility would be more distinct. Second, the commission wanted to achieve greater clarity of direction and greater control by grouping the executive branch agencies into departments "as nearly as possible by major purposes in order to give a coherent mission to each department."[79] Third, the commission recommended that the EOP be strengthened by giving the president a stronger staff, including a staff secretariat in the White House. The president should have absolute freedom in dealing with this staff, giving it shape, and appointing its members.

Truman enthusiastically supported the commission's recommendations, and both Congress and the public gave their support to most of the report's proposals. Eventually, the most important recommendations were realized. The recommendations calling for a larger presidential staff and discretion in the use and organization of the EOP were implemented. And, after the commission's proposals, the Post Office and the Departments of Interior, Commerce, and Labor were reorganized. The NSC and some independent agencies, including the Civil Service Commission and the Federal Trade Commission, also were reorganized.

By and large, the success of the reforms reflected the nonpolitical nature of the report. Hoover and his commission approached the presidency solely in managerial terms without engaging in political ideology. Arnold has observed, "At one and the same time, reorganization planning aimed at strengthening the presidency while presenting the issue of enhanced presidential capacity as merely managerial and irrelevant to politics. Herbert Hoover and his commission of 1947–1948 present perhaps the most successful application of that logic within reorganization planning's history."[80]

Second Hoover Commission

When Dwight Eisenhower came to office in 1953, he faced a bureaucracy that had grown tremendously since Hoover, the last Republican president, had left office in 1933. After twenty years of Democratic control of the presidency, few Republicans had experience in running the federal government. In fact, after years of opposing big government and big spending, Republicans now found themselves in charge of the same government they had criticized. Further complicating things for Eisenhower was a bureaucracy composed mostly of Democrats appointed under Democratic presidents. Searching for a way to make the executive branch more responsive to his leadership, Eisenhower in 1953 called once more on Hoover—at that time seventy-nine years old—to head the Commission on the Organization of the Executive Branch of Government (the Second Hoover Commission).

The First Hoover Commission had been interested primarily in improving the administrative management of the executive branch; the Second Hoover Commission focused on issues of policy and function. At the heart of its recommendations was the idea that the executive branch should reduce its scope—saving money, reducing taxes, and eliminating competition with the private sector. The Second Hoover Commission had a specific conservative ideological agenda that aimed at reducing the growth of the government since the New Deal. It argued that many of the Roosevelt-era programs and agencies had become counterproductive.[81] The commission was more concerned with prescribing what government should do rather than how it should be organized and managed.

Most of the commission's recommendations were of only indirect value to the Eisenhower administration as it wrestled with the problems of a massive executive bureaucracy. Yet for the first time a major reorganization report dealt with the relations between political appointees and career public servants. Among its specific recommendations was the creation of a Senior Civil Service made up of approximately three thousand upper-level career executives serving in administrative positions. The commission proposed that these senior civil servants be able to transfer from one agency to another if their particular skills and competencies suited those agencies. These senior civil servants would constitute a personnel pool that would be rotated regularly to improve management quality. The idea finally became incorporated into general personnel practices in the executive branch with the establishment of the Senior Executive Service in 1978.

Ash Council

In April 1969 Richard Nixon sought to simplify the domestic side of policymaking in the executive branch by creating the Advisory Council on Executive Organization. Intending to use private sector strategies in reorganization planning for his administration, Nixon appointed industrialist Roy Ash, president of Litton Industries, as chair and named four other private citizens to the council. Known as the Ash Council, the reorganization group set out to address three problems: the executive branch's response to increasing demands on the federal government; the organizational problems of the more than 150 executive branch departments, offices, and agencies; and the organizational complications arising from intergovernmental relations.[82]

The Ash Council recommended that the executive branch's domestic programs be directed by a small number of major-purpose superdepartments. The council believed that this reorganization not only would save the government money but also would increase the effectiveness of executive branch management. Specifically, the council proposed that the secretaries of the superdepartments would be assisted by a small number of secretarial officers who would hold

department-wide responsibilities. Secretarial officers would include a deputy secretary who would serve as an alter ego and department manager for the secretary, two undersecretaries, several assistant secretaries, and a general counsel. The recommendations pointed to a desire to "facilitate decentralized management while simultaneously providing for effective secretarial control and department cohesion."[83]

President Nixon sent four departmental reorganization proposals to Congress on March 25, 1971. These proposals would have abolished seven existing departments and replaced them with four new superdepartments. The new Department of Natural Resources would have merged the Interior Department with parts of Agriculture, Defense, and Commerce. The Department of Health, Education, and Welfare would have become the Department of Human Resources. The Department of Community Development would have combined Housing and Urban Development with some of the remaining parts of Agriculture. And the Department of Economic Affairs would have combined Labor with parts of Commerce. But none of the departmental bills ever got out of their congressional committees, and Nixon eventually lost interest in the superdepartments.

Some of the Ash Council's recommendations did become important to executive branch reorganization, however. In its recommendations on the EOP, the council proposed the creation of a Domestic Council and the conversion of the Bureau of the Budget into the Office of Management and Budget. Nixon incorporated these proposals into his Reorganization Plan No. 2, which he submitted to Congress on March 12, 1970.

The Ash Council intended for the Domestic Council to serve as a domestic counterpart to the NSC. It would be a cabinet-level advisory group composed of the president, the vice president, the attorney general, and the secretaries of the Treasury, interior, agriculture, commerce, labor, transportation, housing and urban development, and health, education, and welfare. The important changes to the Bureau of the Budget included expanding its managerial, policy coordination, and program information functions in its reincarnation in the OMB. Both President Nixon's reorganization efforts and the Ash Council's recommendations sought through reorganization to centralize executive branch policy formation in the EOP.

Under the authority granted by Congress through the periodic extension of the Reorganization Act of 1949, presidents could reorganize executive branch entities as they pleased. Congress retained oversight of such reorganizations through a legislative veto provision in the reorganization act.

President Carter used this method several times while in office. In 1978, for example, he ordered four thousand workers involved in border inspection to move their operations from the Justice Department to the Treasury Department. He also shifted thirty-five hundred people from the firearms and explosives division of the Treasury Department to the Justice Department. In 1977 Carter exerted his reorganization powers to their fullest when he established a whole new Energy Department, absorbing two independent agencies—the Federal Power Commission and the Atomic Energy Commission. In 1979 he divided the Department of Health, Education, and Welfare into two new departments, the Department of Education and the Department of Health and Human Services. Congress, however, refused to renew the reorganization act after the Supreme Court declared legislative vetoes unconstitutional in 1983. As a result, executive branch reorganizations must now be achieved through normal legislative procedures. As part of Vice President Gore's National Performance Review to "reinvent government" by making it more efficient, President Clinton reorganized the Department of Agriculture by legislation. In 1994 Congress passed his proposal to merge or eliminate a number of the department's forty-three agencies and reduce staff and personnel.

In 2005 the Bush administration sent Congress the proposed Government and Program Performance Improvement Act of 2005, which would grant the president wide-ranging powers to reorganize the federal government. The key provision in the bill was to provide fast-track authority for specific reorganization proposals. Congress would not be allowed to amend the president's reorganization requests, only vote them up or down. The legislation never reached a floor vote as the 2006 midterm elections neared and the president's approval ratings dipped low, into the mid-30 percent range.

THE APPOINTMENT POWER

As the size of the federal government has grown, presidents have been forced to delegate more and more of their administrative responsibilities to an increasing number of political executives. No single chief executive can make all the important policy and administrative decisions necessary to carry out the functions of the U.S. government. Consequently, one of the most important administrative powers that presidents have is their ability to recruit and appoint people to fill high-level positions in their administrations.[84]

Article II, Section 2, of the Constitution gives the president the power to appoint top political executives. The language of the Constitution separates the appointment process of major executive officers into a two-step procedure shared by the president and the Senate. The president recruits and nominates potential appointees, and the Senate either confirms or rejects the president's appointments. The Constitution also gives Congress the ability to place other appointments within the prerogative of the president (such as the White House staff) or of the department heads without Senate confirmation.

Although the Constitution gives the chief executive the responsibility for selecting the approximately 2.1 million civilian employees (as of 2010) of the executive branch, over the years the chief executive has given up much direct participation in the process to the federal civil service system. Until the 1880s most executive branch jobs were apportioned through *patronage,* the system of granting favors and filling jobs as political rewards. Under such a system, nineteenth-century presidents were able to place their friends and allies in federal government positions. Since 1883 and passage of the Pendleton Act, which created the Civil Service Commission, most agencies must now choose their employees according to their qualifications and ability to do the job.

Because more than 90 percent of executive branch positions are covered by the civil service, only the most senior executive positions are filled by presidential appointees. For example, the Clinton administration could appoint only 222 (less than 1 percent) of the 37,485 employees of the Department of Commerce. By choosing personnel for these positions, presidents articulate their political goals to the bureaucracy.

[H]e shall nominate, and by and with the Advice and Consent of the Senate shall appoint Ambassadors, other public Ministers and Consuls, Judges of the supreme Court, and all other Officers of the United States, whose Appointments are not herein otherwise provided for and which shall be established by Law; but the Congress may by Law vest the Appointment of such inferior Officers as they think proper in the President alone, in the Courts of Law, or in the Heads of Departments.

—from Article II, Section 2

At the beginning of a new administration, Congress publishes *Policy and Supporting Positions*—known as the "plum book"—which lists the top executive branch positions available for direct presidential appointment, many of which require Senate confirmation. Each new presidential administration must appoint approximately 200 members of the White House staff, 15 department heads, 400 to 500 members of the subcabinet, 93 U.S. attorneys, and approximately 150 ambassadors. In addition, agency and department heads appoint 600 to 800 members of the Senior Executive Service and about 1,800 special aides in Schedule C positions, which are exempted from the testing and qualification requirements of the civil service merit system. Altogether, presidents and their subordinates must appoint about 5,200 people to the executive branch.[85] Of these, political scientist Hugh Heclo estimates that presidents are most interested in approximately 300 top political executive posts—cabinet secretaries, undersecretaries, assistant secretaries, and bureau chiefs.[86]

Because executive appointees link the president to the vast organizational components of the executive branch, the right to make such appointments is extremely important to the chief executive's ability to control the disparate components of the federal government. To ensure effective leadership, presidents look for competence and loyalty in their appointees.

The sixteenth-century political theorist Niccolo Machiavelli observed, "The first opinion that is formed of a ruler's intelligence is based on the quality of men he has around him."[87] This observation suggests that an administration is only as good as the people the president appoints to fill it. The immense size of the executive branch makes it impossible, however, for presidents to know most of the people they appoint, much less to make personal assessments of their quality. Upon winning the presidency after several months of campaigning, John Kennedy complained about trying to fill many of his top positions: "People, people, people! I don't know any people. All I know is voters! How am I going to fill these 1,200 jobs?"[88] Kennedy knew fewer than half of his final cabinet appointments.

Some new appointees come to their positions well qualified, but others do not. What occupational and educational characteristics do presidential appointees have? Between 1982 and 1985 a National Academy of Public Administration survey found that 40 percent of federal appointees are transferred or promoted from other positions in the government. Sixty percent, however, come from occupations outside the federal government: 24 percent from business, 16 percent from academic and research communities, 12 percent from the legal profession, 7 percent from state and local governments, and 1 percent from other organizations. The educational level of presidential appointees is relatively high: 19 percent hold bachelor's degrees, 21 percent hold master's degrees, 17 percent hold Ph.D.s, and 34 percent hold law degrees.[89]

In addition to competence and loyalty, presidents consider other factors when making their selections. Most presidents have accumulated many political debts, including money and votes, on their way to the White House, and so they look for ways to reward their chief supporters with major political appointments. Although these selections usually do not constitute the majority of a president's appointments, they are an important consideration. President Truman, for example, appointed banker John Snyder and Democratic National Committee chair Robert Hannegan, both old friends from Missouri, to the positions of Treasury secretary and postmaster general, respectively. Early in his administration, President Clinton appointed Thomas F. "Mack" McLarty III as chief of staff and Mickey Kantor as U.S. trade representative. Both were friends and longtime supporters.

Presidents also make many appointments for purely political reasons. The first presidential personnel selections are the most important politically—they set the tone and priorities of a presidency and so are subject to close public scrutiny. In his study of presidential cabinets, political scientist Richard F. Fenno Jr. commented:

> The presidential decisions leading to the composition of a new 'official family' are taken during the peak period of public interest which attends the national election campaign. As executive decisions go, they are pre-eminently concrete and visible. Among the earliest of presidential moves, they are treated as symbolic acts of considerable significance.[90]

In addition, presidents consider in what ways future political relationships will be affected by their early choices. An administration's success often depends on the ability of the president to forge political alliances and broaden the presidency's base of support. The president's circle of political allies frequently can be expanded through the appointment process. Finally, presidents often use appointments to get on the good side of members of their own political party, interest groups whose support they seek, and, often, members of Congress.

This strategy can backfire, however. William Howard Taft, quoting Thomas Jefferson, used to lament, "Every time I make an appointment I create nine enemies and one ingrate." As political scientist Calvin Mackenzie wrote: "The selection process, particularly in the early stages of a new administration is governed by scarce resources and multiple, competing demands. Opportunities exist for gaining some political advantage from these early personnel choices, but, if used unwisely, those opportunities are easily squandered."[91]

Although many presidents desperately seek better management, rarely are appointments made on the basis of objective consideration such as management ability. Most jobs are filled immediately after the presidential election, when presidents have the largest number of appointments to make and the least amount of time to consider them. Ironically, at this point in their administrations, when they are best able to lure potential appointees, presidents often are unable to take full advantage of one of their greatest administrative powers. The ability to manage may be one of the last considerations applied to a potential appointee, both because the administration is unable to judge its management needs and because political considerations outweigh managerial skill. Characteristics such as an appointee's geographic or ethnic background are often much more obvious and easy to consider than administrative ability.

No matter how well intentioned they may be in trying to fill their appointments, most presidents do not fully succeed in accomplishing their objectives in the appointment process. For example, President Clinton started the staffing process during his campaign. Wishing to instill loyalty and new ideas in his administration, he developed an appointment strategy that emphasized centralizing power in the White House by appointing loyal but qualified individuals. This philosophy of controlling all appointments from the White House, which reflected Clinton's tendency to micromanage, resulted in serious problems for his administration. For one thing, the White House transition team was slow filling positions below the secretary rank. Because subcabinet positions had to be either filled or approved by the White House to ensure loyalty, the process was cumbersome. Clinton would sometimes question a cabinet member's entire slate of nominations because it was not diverse enough or because a single nominee's credentials looked suspect. This had the effect of sending the entire slate back to the secretary. As a result, secretaries often complained that they were understaffed and overworked in the first year or so of the administration. In addition, the emphasis on personal loyalty to Clinton meant that few appointees had any Washington experience. In fact, many appointees felt hostile to Washington and were determined to keep the Clintons out from under its spell.[92]

As a result of the contested results of the 2000 presidential election, President George W. Bush had an unprecedented short election transition period to make his appointments. Given this truncated period, Bush set about making his key appointments at a quicker pace than that of his predecessors. As a result of that effort and a somewhat quickened pace of Senate confirmations, in the first year of the Bush administration confirmation of presidential appointees required an average 7.9 months, compared with 8.3 months during the first year of the George H. W. Bush and Clinton administrations.

George W. Bush's appointees in both his first and second terms tended to be experienced in political Washington and were drawn heavily from his home state of Texas. Consequently, early in Bush's tenure the staff worked together in a collegial fashion and were able to avoid the kind of infighting that has characterized some recent presidential staffs. In addition to experience, Bush placed enormous priority on a history of loyalty to the president as a criterion for choosing staff members. Later, as the country declared a "war on terrorism," the experience and compatibility of Bush's staff appeared to pay off for the administration. As former presidential adviser and scholar Bradley H. Patterson Jr. writes: "No one, but no one, will have to remind Dick Cheney, Colin Powell, Don Rumsfeld, Condoleezza Rice, Paul O'Neill, Andy Card, or Nick Calio who is president, or will need to remonstrate them about not fighting their policy differences in public and not undermining their colleagues by leaking [stories] to their favorite columnists."[93]

Like previous presidents, Obama's nominations primarily related to issue areas that were known to be important to his agenda (that is, the economy, the ongoing wars in Afghanistan and Iraq), and many of the individuals appointed had ties to either his presidential campaign or the previous Democratic administration (that is, Bill Clinton's). Shirley Warshaw has also pointed out the pains the administration took to balance appointments across groups and constituencies.[94] For example, Obama's cabinet hailed from all corners of the nation, though states that had supported him in the 2008 election were favored. Warshaw notes that only two of Obama's appointees here came from states that went for his rival John McCain—Secretary of Defense Robert Gates from Texas and Secretary of Homeland Security Janet Napolitano of Arizona—and Gates was a holdover from the Bush administration, applauded by Democrats as much as Republicans, and only actually lived in Texas for less than a decade, when he served in leadership roles (including as president) at Texas A&M University after his retirement from the Central Intelligence Agency. Obama's cabinet nominees also achieved significant gender and ethnic diversity, with four women, one African American, one Latino, three Asians, and one Arab member.

Barack Obama's larger concern, however, was with the noncabinet appointments he would make. Continuing an ongoing trend away from cabinet-based leadership, Obama focused more on policymakers within his own White House. Indeed, according to Warshaw, it was three full months before Obama called his first cabinet meeting. At the same time, Obama's White House included nearly 470 staff members and a budget of almost $40 million.[95]

Constraints on the Appointment Process

The postelection rush to fill vacancies in the new administration places constraints on the appointment process. Between the election and the inauguration, the president works to establish the policy objectives of the administration. While still forming their policy objectives, presidents or their subordinates must make the vast majority of their most important appointments. Cronin has noted: "Too frequently appointees are not carefully related to policy. Many subcabinet appointments, for example, are made by subordinates, with the president hardly aware of whether the appointee is matched with the position."[96] Once in office many appointees adopt new attitudes as a result of their new institutional responsibilities, or some, perhaps ill-suited for institutional management, may become rigidly wedded to the views of the interest groups with which they most frequently interact.

Presidents often find it difficult to persuade their potential nominees to give up high-paying positions in the private sector and move to Washington, D.C. Since the early 1970s, the gap between the salaries paid to private executives and the salaries paid to those in the federal government who perform equivalent work has grown wider. In 1980 the

Commission on Executive, Legislative, and Judicial Salaries concluded: "There is growing evidence that low salaries are a major reason for highly talented people declining appointment to key positions in the federal government."[97]

The question of whether salary was a significant obstacle in recruiting staff for senior administration positions was raised again by a 2002 Brookings Institution study. The study concluded that the gap between private sector and public sector salaries was growing. While the private sector may provide greater financial incentives than the public sector, the study concluded that "no one can be sure whether these trends in pay inside and outside the government have affected the caliber of people who serve in top federal positions."[98] Although salary may influence the decision of some candidates for senior positions, it does not seem to be a major factor for many others. Some view public service as an important civic contribution, and others view their government connections as a stepping-stone to future earning power when they return to the private sector.

Sometimes presidents have found it difficult to persuade potential nominees to disclose their financial background and income. Because the American public expects executive branch officials to perform their duties without undue regard for special interests, Congress passed strict financial disclosure laws in 1965. Certain top executive branch employees were required to report information about their personal finances to the head of the Civil Service Commission, who could report this information to the president if there seemed to be a conflict of interest. Title II of the Ethics in Government Act of 1978 broadened disclosure provisions by requiring all presidential appointees to complete the Executive Personal Financial Disclosure Report, which publicly discloses their personal financial information. These provisions have been a source of great concern for many potential appointees. E. Pendleton James, President Reagan's assistant for personnel, stated that "literally hundreds" of potential presidential nominees lost interest as a result of demanding disclosure provisions.[99]

Similarly, presidents must sometimes pass up potential nominees because of the person's involvement with a past administration, a scandal, or even the appearance of wrongdoing. For example, in 1989 former senator John Tower was nominated by George H. W. Bush as secretary of defense but was forced to withdraw under opposition from Congress over charges of womanizing and excessive drinking. In *The Confirmation Mess,* law professor Stephen L. Carter argues that the current system for approving presidential nominations demands that more attention be paid to the "disqualifications" than to the qualifications of a nominee. He writes: "We presume the nominees to be entitled to confirmation absent smoking guns, and then we look for the smoke in order to disqualify them."[100] In short, presidents face enormous difficulties in finding appropriate candidates in a shrinking pool of potential nominees who are willing to go to Washington. The difficulties in finding those willing to serve are exacerbated by the fact that appointees must face intense, and often excessive, public scrutiny.

The Role of the Senate

The Senate is an integral part of the appointment process and serves as one of the most important limits to the presidential appointment privilege. The Constitution bestows on the Senate the power to confirm most of the president's major appointments. As a result, the Senate views the appointment procedure as a process in which its members should have a considerable say. As Calvin Mackenzie has observed, "For Senators and Senate committees, the confirmation process is both a responsibility and an opportunity."[101] It is both a constitutional responsibility and a political opportunity. Senators view the appointment process as a way to influence government policy. Cronin has noted that senators even try to influence presidential policy by getting the president to nominate their choices: "They . . . often have candidates of their own. This is especially the case in recent years, for as the staffs of Congress have expanded . . . there are more and more aides to Congress who seek top executive branch appointments."[102]

The number of presidential nominations sent to the Senate for confirmation is staggering. The Senate must process between 90,000 and 170,000 nominations during each Congress (two-year period). Usually, the vast majority of these nominations are routine military commissions and promotions that require little of the Senate's time. Although the number of civilian appointments is much lower, the Senate must still spend a great deal of time and energy processing them. In 1989, the first year of the George H. W. Bush administration, the Senate received more than forty-eight thousand nominations, forty-five thousand of which were routine military commissions and promotions. Most of the rest were routine nominations to such civilian organizations as the Foreign Service, the Public Health Service, and the National Oceanic and Atmospheric Administration. Nominations to top-level policymaking positions in the executive branch—which average only about six hundred a session—require far more attention from the Senate than the routine appointments.

Like most other matters before Congress, the nomination process is handled almost entirely by standing (ongoing) committees. Although each committee has different sets of procedures for managing the appointments referred to them, most committees have developed their own standard procedures. Usually, these procedures require additional background checks and financial disclosures, other than those already required by the president's personnel director and the Ethics in Government Act of 1978, and extensive hearings. The result of this rigorous and lengthy investigative process has been an increase in demands on potential appointees. In his study of the Senate's role in the presidential appointment process, political scientist Christopher J. Deering pointed out that this demanding investigatory process has made the Senate's role in the nomination process not only more thorough but also more demanding: "Unfortunately, the process has . . . become more tedious, time-consuming, and intrusive for the nominees. For some the price is too high."[103] The process is made all the more tedious by the fact that from 1981 to 2001 Congress added more than a hundred new and reclassified positions in the cabinet departments that require Senate confirmation.[104]

The Founders intended the Senate's constitutional role in the presidential appointment process to serve as a check on executive power. But to what extent has the Senate checked presidential power through its confirmation power? All presidents have been successful in getting the majority of their nominees confirmed. For example, more than 92 percent of all civilian presidential nominations were confirmed by the Ninety-eighth Congress (1983–1985). Most nominations that are defeated are defeated in committees. Since 1960 only six nominees have been defeated on the floor of the Senate.

Many presidents have had a few of their potential appointees rejected. The Senate regularly thwarted the efforts of James Madison and Ulysses S. Grant to nominate their choices for executive branch positions freely. John Tyler perhaps had the most difficulty with the Senate in attempting to fill vacancies. His appointees were frequently rejected by the Senate, including four cabinet and four Supreme Court appointees. In one day in 1843, the Senate rejected Tyler's nomination of Caleb Cushing as secretary of the Treasury three times. In 1984 President Reagan's nominee for associate attorney general, William Bradford Reynolds, was turned down by the Senate Judiciary Committee. His opponents argued that Reynolds had been negligent in enforcing antidiscrimination laws during his tenure as chief of the Justice Department's Civil Rights Division.

Nominations are often withdrawn it if becomes apparent that the Senate opposes a particular candidate. For example, in the early months of the Clinton administration two nominations to the Justice Department were withdrawn when it became obvious that the Senate would not confirm the president's nominees. Although the Senate does not often reject a presidential nominee, the thoroughness of its investigations of those who are confirmed and its occasional threats of rejection indicate that the Senate does exert some control over the president's prerogative to appoint key members of the administration. George W. Bush often resorted to recess appointments when the Senate failed to confirm his nominees. John Bolton, nominated as ambassador to the United Nations, was given a recess appointment

in January 2005 after strong Senate opposition emerged among Democrats and some Republicans. A recess appointee, however, may remain in office only until the last recess of the two-year session of Congress.

Sometimes the Senate uses its confirmation power more as a political bargaining chip than anything else. It will often hold the nominee in limbo until the president agrees to support a particular political position. For example, President Reagan's nomination of Edwin Meese as attorney general was used by the majority leader as leverage to exact a promise to support farm aid legislation. During the periods in which the Republicans controlled the Senate in the 1980s and 1990s, Sen. Jesse Helms, R-N.C., repeatedly held up nominations because he found them politically unacceptable or because he wished to force political opponents to compromise on policy issues. Deering has written: "On numerous occasions in recent years, members of the Senate of both parties have placed holds on particular individuals. In some cases, the nominee is the target, in other cases merely a pawn, but in either case the use of nominees as, in effect, hostages has undermined the integrity of the system."[105] By the end of the George W. Bush era, the controversy surrounding these practices had grown to the point that reforms were suggested and, eventually, in 2011, passed. A 2007 Congressional Research Service report documented the various initiatives over the previous three decades to reform the practice of Senate holds and identified several areas of potential concern.[106] In early 2011 a deal was made between Democratic Majority Leader Harry Reid and Republican Minority Leader Mitch McConnell that, among other changes, repealed the use of secret holds, did away with the requirements of reading amendments on the floor (when they are otherwise a matter of the public record), and reduced the number of federal agency nominees that would require Senate confirmation.[107]

The Presidential Personnel System

The process by which presidents select their top political appointees remained relatively unchanged throughout the first 150 years of U.S. history. Presidents had little, if any, staff to help them make their appointments; political parties usually controlled personnel selection for the president. Even when chief executives did become actively involved in the selection process, they often used the existing political party structure. Other nominees were usually suggested to the president by party leaders or members of Congress from the president's party. Too often this dependence on the party resulted in administrations filled with top-level appointees with little loyalty to presidential objectives.

Roosevelt and Truman Administrations

Since Franklin Roosevelt entered the White House, newly elected presidents have needed significant staff support and a centralized procedure for choosing personnel because of the vast number of appointments that must be made in a short period of time. Perhaps more important, a centralized appointment process under the president's control ensures faithfulness to White House policies and objectives.

Until the 1940s, the selection of presidential appointees was haphazard and unfocused. Presidential personnel operations relied heavily on chance to place the right people in the right positions. During the 1940s, however, President Roosevelt attempted to alleviate much of the problem by introducing governmental reforms that removed presidential patronage from the national political parties. For example, he appointed an assistant to handle personnel matters in an effort to improve presidential control over the appointment process. In the decades that followed the presidency's administrative powers increased, allowing it more discretion in personnel selection.

Dom Bonafede attributed the growth of a more centralized selection procedure within the White House after 1940 to three factors. First, political reforms that increased the number of state primaries and emphasized grassroots politics "hastened the decline of the national parties and minimized their brokerage role as conduit and clearinghouse for appointments." Presidents were no longer obligated to party leaders for their election and therefore had less need to reward them with government jobs. Second, the movement toward a strong administrative presidency, which centralized power in the White House, further strengthened the president's hand vis-à-vis Congress and the bureaucracy. Third, "the complexity of domestic and foreign issues, such as arms control, tax reform, federal deficits, and trade imbalances, necessitated elaborate institutional support, placing a premium on substantive knowledge and managerial competence."[108]

Specific recommendations by the Committee on Administrative Management, headed by Louis D. Brownlow, and the two Hoover Commissions helped centralize more power in the presidency. *(See "Reorganization Power," p. 94.)* In 1939, acting on Brownlow Committee recommendations, Congress created the Executive Office of

Dan Fenn, President John F. Kennedy's personnel aide, created a White House appointment process that gave the president recruiting ability independent of the political parties.

the President and brought the Bureau of the Budget under the control of the president within the EOP. These measures began what has become known as the "institutional presidency."[109] The first and second Hoover Commissions further increased the administrative power of the presidency by giving it more control over the vast federal bureaucracy and substantial authority over the appointment process.

President Truman appointed the first full-time staff member responsible only for personnel matters. Although this aide, Donald Dawson, addressed mostly routine concerns and spent a good deal of time in contact with the Democratic National Committee, the new position signaled the growing importance of staffing issues.

Eisenhower Administration

Dwight Eisenhower came to office in 1953 with a strong desire to improve the management of the executive branch but with a dislike for personnel matters. He frequently wrote in his diary that patronage was one of the great banes of his administration and one of the things most likely to cause him to lose his temper. Consequently, he delegated personnel concerns to members of his staff, primarily to Sherman Adams, his chief of staff. Adams, however, soon found the job of personnel director too demanding when added to his other responsibilities. The president then approved the position of special assistant for executive appointments, which several people held during the eight years Eisenhower was in office. These special assistants did not choose the president's appointees. Instead, they managed the appointment process by narrowing the president's choices to candidates with the best qualifications and the fewest political liabilities. More than anything else, Eisenhower sought appointees who were loyal to his political philosophy and his programs.

Kennedy and Johnson Administrations

Shortly after his election, President-elect Kennedy put together a personnel selection staff called "Talent Hunt." Composed of some of the best people from the campaign, Talent Hunt was a loosely organized operation with two objectives. First, it tried to determine the president-elect's political obligations—supporters who helped him win the election—and find appropriate jobs to pay off those debts. Second, it attempted to identify the most important jobs the president would have to fill and to find the best people for those positions. After the inauguration, Talent Hunt broke up, and its members went to their own jobs in the administration.

In mid-1961 Kennedy appointed Dan Fenn of the Harvard Business School faculty to take over the day-to-day personnel responsibilities of the White House. Asked to recommend changes in the traditional method of filling executive positions, Fenn concluded that the procedure was too limited. The most important jobs in the federal government were being filled by an unsophisticated "Whom do you know?" system—a process he called "BOGSAT," or a "bunch of guys sitting around a table."

Fenn attempted to correct this problem by creating a systematic White House appointment operation with three major stages. First, he and his staff developed reliable job descriptions that allowed them to match candidates with positions, something most administrations had not been able to do. Second, Fenn offered the president a wider selection of candidates from whom to choose. He believed that the range of people with whom presidents normally came into contact was too narrow to provide the talent necessary for a successful administration. Third, because he could offer a wider range of choices only by reaching beyond traditional political sources for appointments, Fenn established a network of well-positioned people throughout the country whose opinions the president trusted and who could provide Kennedy with candid information about potential nominees. Although prevailing partisan considerations kept the system Fenn established from working as well as it might have, Fenn's efforts nonetheless marked the first time a president had significant independent recruiting ability, separate from the influence of the political parties.

During Lyndon B. Johnson's administration, the centralization of presidential personnel selection took a giant leap forward. Although Kennedy had put together a significant staff for selecting nominees, he would often bypass the process by selecting appointees without using the system Fenn had established. Johnson, too, would sometimes circumvent his

Frederic V. Malek, President Richard Nixon's personnel director, established the White House Personnel Office in 1971.

personnel staff, but he always maintained the appearance that the selection had been made through the White House personnel system. The authors of one study of the presidential selection process concluded:

> Those who wanted to influence Johnson's appointment decisions quickly got the message that their contact point for this was the personnel staff and that efforts to evade the established personnel selection procedures would be difficult to pull off. This focused more attention on the White House and significantly strengthened its role at the hub of the appointment process.[110]

The Kennedy and Johnson presidencies therefore brought about three important long-term changes in presidential personnel management. First, a full-time personnel staff became a regular component of the White House Office. Second, presidents began to attempt to maintain their independence from traditional political party pressures by recruiting their own candidates. Third, succeeding administrations have developed and followed routine procedures for scrutinizing the background, competence, integrity, and political loyalty of each potential appointee.

Nixon Administration

When Richard Nixon took office in 1969, he at first failed to incorporate in his presidency many of the advances made in personnel selection in preceding administrations. He had little interest in personnel matters and delegated most of the responsibility for filling offices to his staff. His initial appointment process was slow and cumbersome, and too many times the White House appointed people who had little loyalty to the president's programs. As a result, in 1970 Nixon appointed Frederic V. Malek to study the personnel selection process and recommend improvements. Malek called for a personnel system similar to those of Nixon's predecessors: centralization of the recruiting process in the White House, recruitment outreach beyond traditional political party sources of potential nominees, and a more rigorous clearance process.

In 1971 Nixon appointed Malek director of his personnel operation. Malek, acting on his own recommendations, set up the White House Personnel Office (WHPO). Following the examples of the organizations set up by Fenn and John W. Macy, personnel assistant to President Johnson, Malek made the WHPO a tightly organized operation that employed a highly professional staff. The WHPO employed professional headhunters whose sole responsibility was to find the right person for the right job in the administration. In addition, the WHPO developed a much more sophisticated evaluation system than had ever been used in the White House. Thus after two years of haphazard personnel selection the Nixon White House emerged with a firm commitment to centralized personnel decision making for almost all noncareer positions in the federal government. Yet eventually the WHPO lost much of its professionalism, and some of its members went beyond the limits of propriety in attempting to control the appointment process. The WHPO began to manipulate the civil service to benefit the administration. One way was to write job descriptions to fit specific applicants loyal to Nixon. Those unsympathetic were to be transferred to undesirable locations or assignments requiring a great deal of travel. The press and Congress finally intervened, forcing the WHPO to retreat from its continued efforts at centralization.

Ford and Carter Administrations

Gerald Ford's personnel staff spent much of its time trying to clean up the image of the aggressive WHPO under Nixon. The first thing that Ford changed was the name. The WHPO became the Presidential Personnel Office. In addition, Ford reduced the size of the personnel operation and narrowed the focus of its activities to positions traditionally viewed as presidential appointments instead of most noncareer appointments.

Jimmy Carter was the first president to begin planning for his presidency while still running for election. In summer 1976 he set up a small staff in Atlanta to begin working on the staffing of his administration. Carter chose Jack Watson to head the operation, which became known as the Talent Inventory Program (TIP). After Carter won the election, Watson moved his operation to Washington. Once there he became locked in a power struggle with Carter's campaign manager, Hamilton Jordan, over who would control the appointment process. As a result of this struggle, the Presidential Personnel Office floundered for almost two years, and the appointment process was hampered. In fact, throughout the Carter administration there was no central coordination of appointments in the White House, and much of the early work of TIP was ignored.

Carter contributed to the disorder in the appointment process by insisting that cabinet heads be given almost total discretion in choosing their subordinates. As part of his commitment to "cabinet government," Carter had proclaimed during the campaign: "There will never be an instance while I am president where members of the White House staff dominate or act in a superior position to the members of our Cabinet."[111] This promise made good campaign rhetoric, but, by decentralizing the decision-making process outside of the White House, it diminished Carter's ability to control his administration. Some departments made appointments after a rigorous search procedure. Others resorted to "politics as usual" and used political networks to select potential nominees whose main qualifications were friendship and loyalty to department secretaries. As Dom Bonafede described the results, "In an unseemly brief period it became clear to the president's top lieutenants—and only later to Carter himself— that he had made a major mistake in giving secretaries carte blanche authority to hand-pick their assistants."[112]

Reagan and George H. W. Bush Administrations

Reagan viewed the appointment process as an integral part of his plans for changing the direction of the federal government. Determined to avoid the mistakes of the Carter administration, he centralized the appointment process within the White House.

Reagan also made a determined effort to appoint only persons who shared his political philosophy. E. Pendleton James, Reagan's postelection talent search manager and eventual assistant to the president for personnel, declared, "You can't separate personnel from policy."[113] This outlook pervaded the administration's appointment efforts. From the "kitchen cabinet" made up of Reagan's elite, conservative California advisers who chose politically acceptable potential nominees before his election, to the personnel office, which managed appointments during the administration, the strategy was to choose nominees whose political philosophy matched the president's.

The Reagan appointment process benefited from some of Carter's mistakes. James gave the process a consistency it lacked under Carter. During the transition and throughout the first eighteen months of the Reagan administration, James, working with Lyn Nofziger, presided over the day-to-day operation of the administration's personnel selection. As a result, little confusion arose about the process itself or who was in charge. Also, Reagan visibly involved himself in the appointment process. He made the final decision on all of the important appointments during the transition and the first year. The authors of one study noted:

> This proved to be an effective deterrent to those in the departments and agencies and in Congress who might try and wrest control of appointment decisions away from the White House. It is one thing to attempt that when low-level White House staff members are making appointment decisions; it is quite another when those decisions are being made in the Oval Office.[114]

Like Carter, Vice President George H. W. Bush began planning for staffing his administration while running for the presidency. Early in his 1988 campaign, Bush named Charles Untermeyer to begin organizing his personnel operation. But because Bush wished to avoid appearing overconfident, Untermeyer was not allowed to establish a formal office or recruit any nominees until after the election. When Bush won the presidential election, his personnel management team moved rapidly into action. Although Bush anticipated no major policy shifts from his Republican predecessor, he did insist that his administration have his stamp on it, promising to replace 90 percent of Reagan's political appointees.

Bush played a much less visible role than Reagan in selecting appointees for his administration. Those charged with making most of the staffing decisions were given two major criteria by the president-elect: loyalty and experience. Where Reagan had sought ideological loyalty, Bush sought personal loyalty in his appointments. Personal friends of the president and those who had played a major role in Bush's campaign were given priority in the new administration. As one who had been around Washington a long time, Bush also sought experience. The resulting appointments made his administration one of the most experienced and thus one of the most competent in recent history.

Clinton, George W. Bush, and Obama Administrations

During the 1992 fall presidential campaign, Mickey Kantor, Bill Clinton's campaign chair, set up a formal organization—the Clinton-Gore Presidential Transition Planning Foundation—for staffing the hoped-for administration. This early attempt at centralization promised a disciplined staffing process. After the election, however, Kantor ran afoul of other campaign officials and was blocked from heading the transition. The formal responsibility for finding personnel for the new administration fell largely to Harold Ickes, a New York attorney and close friend of Hillary Clinton.

President-elect Clinton, however, abandoned a highly centralized transition operation. Instead, he opted for a kitchen table approach to staffing his administration. Ickes, Mrs. Clinton, Susan Thomases, an attorney and close friend of Mrs. Clinton, and Bruce Lindsey, an attorney and a long-time Clinton loyalist, made most of the actual decisions about staffing the new presidency around a six-foot table at Clinton headquarters in Little Rock, Arkansas. Operating under the dictum that they had been voted to go to Washington to change things, the personnel team chose executive branch staffers who were largely inexperienced in Washington politics. In addition, appointees were young and geographically, ethnically, and racially diverse, as compared with those of previous administrations.

Although Clinton abandoned his early attempt at a centralized transition, he clearly wanted to keep personnel functions within the White House. Clinton based his personnel appointment system on a memo, "Transition Workplan for Reviewing the Staffing and Organization of the White House and Executive Office of the President," written at the direction of Harrison Wellford, a former Carter budget official. The memo urged that appointments to the White House, the Executive Office of the President, the cabinet, and the subcabinet be controlled squarely by the president. This approach contrasted with the Carter system, in which the absence of central coordination of appointments reduced Carter's ability to effectively control his administration.

One of the most distinctive features of the Clinton personnel system was the slowness with which it filled positions in the new administration, stemming in part from his desire for diversity and in part from his system that required White House approval for executive branch appointments. After eight months in office, Clinton still had not nominated political appointees for more than 40 percent of policy-making positions, and about one-third of the posts in independent agencies, on regulatory boards, and on commissions remained unfilled. Clinton was well behind the pace of nominations set by both Carter and Reagan. He was ahead of George H. W. Bush, but as a Republican succeeding another Republican, Bush was in no real hurry to replace personnel.

President George W. Bush was somewhat more successful than his predecessors in getting personnel appointments made in a timely fashion. Even so, by the end of his first year in office one-third of the senior-level posts in the administration had not been filled, either because the president had not named nominees or because those already named had not been approved by the Senate. George W. Bush did appoint more minorities to senior-level posts than former presidents Clinton, George H. W. Bush, and Reagan. And he appointed more women to these high-level posts than either George H. W. Bush or Reagan, and nearly as many as Clinton.

Like his immediate predecessor, Barack Obama also came into office in the midst of a crisis and with the need to assemble his leadership team quickly. Unlike George W. Bush, who had to deal with a truncated transition period due to the 2000 Florida recount, Obama had to handle immediate major policy problems, particularly the declining economy, which had been in extreme jeopardy since fall 2008. The Obama administration's staffing experience reflected that of the previous administration's in multiple ways. In an early assessment, David E. Lewis noted that only 75 percent of the key policymaking positions in the administration had been filled by the eighteen-month mark, a sluggish pace due in large part to delays in the Senate.[115] This marks a slowdown from the administration's initial quick start, where his nominations made and confirmed about doubled those of Bush's at the 100-day milestone.[116]

Since Franklin Roosevelt's administration, presidents have relied on increasingly sophisticated methods of centralizing the appointment power in the White House in their attempts to strengthen control over their administrations. The personnel office is now a permanent part of the White House organizational structure. Succeeding presidents have significantly increased the number of staff assigned to find loyal political executives. Most recent presidents have considered the director of the White House Personnel Office a senior staff member with the title "assistant to the president."

The Removal Power

The ability of presidents to control their administrations often depends on their authority to remove subordinates from office. This issue lies at the very heart of the chief executive's power over the bureaucracy. The power of presidents to remove officials who are not doing their jobs properly or who disagree with presidential goals and programs is, however, controversial and has been significantly limited by the Supreme Court. Because the Constitution does not explicitly grant presidents power to remove officials from office, the legitimacy of the power often has rested on court interpretations of specific presidential removal actions.

The Tenure of Office Act of 1867 provided much debate about whether a president could remove executive branch officials. On the suspicion that President Andrew Johnson intended to fire Secretary of War Edwin M. Stanton, Congress passed the act that made it a high misdemeanor to remove without the Senate's approval any government official whose nomination had been confirmed by the Senate. Congress's intention was to protect incumbent Republican officeholders from retaliation if they did not support Johnson. President Johnson vetoed the bill on the grounds that it was unconstitutional to restrict the president's power of removal, but Congress overrode the veto. When Johnson immediately tested the Tenure of Office Act by attempting to remove Stanton, the House voted 126–47 to impeach him. Tried by the Senate, Johnson was acquitted by one vote. The Tenure of Office Act was virtually repealed early in the Grant administration, once Republicans regained control of the appointment power. It was entirely repealed in 1887 when public opinion forced Congress to introduce legislation to repeal it.

Preferring to avoid the issue as long as possible, the Supreme Court refused to make a definitive ruling on the issue of presidential removal of public officeholders until 1926. In *Myers v. United States* the Court ruled that an 1876 law that limited the president's removal power over postmasters was unconstitutional. In 1917 President Woodrow Wilson had appointed Frank S. Myers to be a postmaster in Portland, Oregon, for a term of four years. Attempting to make his administration responsive to his policy goals, Wilson removed Myers from office in 1920 without the consent of the Senate, although the 1876 statute provided that

postmasters should be appointed and removed by the president by and with the advice and consent of the Senate. Myers sued for his salary in the U.S. Court of Claims. When he received an adverse judgment, he took his case to the Supreme Court.

In delivering the opinion of the Court, Chief Justice William Howard Taft, a former president, strongly argued that presidents cannot effectively administer the executive branch unless they can control their subordinates with the threat of removal for political and other reasons. He stated that the power of removal was implied in Article II of the Constitution, which gives the president the responsibility to see that the laws are faithfully executed. Furthermore, Congress could not constitutionally restrain or limit that power. Taft, referring to the Tenure of Office Act and declaring it had been unconstitutional, contended that presidents cannot carry out their constitutional responsibilities if Congress interferes with their ability to control the executive branch.[117]

The *Myers* case gave presidents sweeping authority to remove not only immediate executive subordinates but also members of independent regulatory commissions, such as the Interstate Commerce Commission and the Federal Trade Commission. Independent regulatory commissioners are appointed under the provisions of statutes that confer upon them a certain amount of independence and freedom from the political control of the president. In creating these agencies, Congress had carefully outlined the provisions by which a commissioner could be removed in an attempt to free these executives from political control. If the *Myers* case applied to all political executives, then the regulatory commissions would lose their political independence. Sooner or later the question of unlimited presidential power of removal would be challenged.

The question of the president's ability to remove independent regulatory commissioners arose early in Franklin Roosevelt's first term in office and was settled in 1935 by the Supreme Court in *Humphrey's Executor v. United States.* President Herbert Hoover had nominated William E. Humphrey to the Federal Trade Commission (FTC) in 1931. Under the terms outlined by Congress in the Federal Trade Commission Act of 1914, FTC commissioners were supposed to serve a term of seven years. The act stated that commissioners could be removed by the president only for "inefficiency, neglect of duty, or malfeasance in office." After his election to office in 1933, Roosevelt wrote Humphrey and requested his resignation from the FTC so that "the aims and purposes of the administration with respect to the work of the Commission can be carried out most effectively with personnel of my own selection." After Humphrey's initial reluctance to resign, Roosevelt again wrote him, this time stating: "You will, I know, realize that I do not feel that your mind and my mind go along together on either the policies or the administering of the Federal Trade Commission, and frankly, I think it is best for the people of the country that I should have full confidence."[118] When Humphrey refused to resign, Roosevelt notified him that he had been removed. Humphrey died in 1934, never having agreed to his removal. The executor of Humphrey's estate decided to sue for salary he believed was due Humphrey but never paid him.

The court of claims asked the Supreme Court to answer two questions before it could render a judgment. First, did the Federal Trade Commission Act limit the president's power to remove commissioners except for reasons stated in the act? Second, if the act did indeed limit the president's power to remove commissioners, was it constitutional?

Roosevelt had made clear that the removal of Humphrey was for political reasons. Justice George Sutherland delivered the Court's opinion that the *Myers* case did not apply to Humphrey because the FTC was "an administrative body created by Congress to carry into effect legislative policies." Therefore, it could not "in any sense be characterized as an arm or an eye of the Executive." Sutherland continued:

> Whether the power of the president to remove an officer shall prevail over the authority of Congress to condition the power by fixing a definite term and precluding the removal except for cause will depend upon the character of the office; the Myers decision, affirming the power of the president alone to make the removal, is confined to purely executive officers.[119]

The *Humphrey* decision not only invalidated Roosevelt's removal of Humphrey but also generally limited presidential removal power to officials who could be classified as "purely executive officers." Except for appointees immediately responsible to the president and those exercising nondiscretionary or ministerial functions, such as White House aides, the president's power of removal could be limited by Congress.

The Supreme Court attempted to make a distinction between "executive" and "administrative" functions within the federal bureaucracy. Presidents have complete control over executive functions, or those that deal with the execution of the policy of the administration and are under the direction of the president, such as the functions of the EOP staff and cabinet members. The Court ruled that presidents do not, however, have complete control over administrative functions or those that have quasi-judicial or quasi-legislative roles, such as the functions of the independent regulatory commissions. Only when Congress chooses specifically to give presidents control over these agencies can they remove officials for merely political reasons.

In 1958 the Supreme Court further clarified the removal power of presidents. In *Wiener v. United States* the Court held that if officials are engaged in adjudicative functions presidents may not remove them for political reasons. In 1950 President Truman had appointed Myron Wiener to serve on the War Claims Commission. When Eisenhower assumed office, he requested Wiener's resignation. When Wiener refused, Eisenhower removed him from office. Similar to Roosevelt's removal of Humphrey, Eisenhower's removal of Wiener was based on purely political reasons. Congress had created the War Claims Commission to adjudicate damage claims arising from World War II, and it had made no provisions for removing commissioners. Wiener sued for his lost salary.

Noting the similarity between the *Wiener* and *Humphrey* cases, the Supreme Court ruled in favor of Wiener. The Court argued that in both cases presidents had removed persons from quasi-judicial agencies for political purposes. Calling the War Claims Commission a clearly adjudicative body, Justice Felix Frankfurter concluded for the Court:

> Judging the matter in all the nakedness in which it is presented, namely, the claim that the President could remove a member of an adjudicative body like the War Claims Commission merely because he wanted his own appointees on such a Commission, we are compelled to conclude that no such power is given to the President directly by the Constitution, and none is impliedly conferred upon him by statute simply because Congress said nothing about it. The philosophy of Humphrey's Executor, in its explicit language as well as its implications, precludes such a claim.[120]

In 1988 the Supreme Court further limited the president's removal power in *Morrison v. Olson* by upholding the independent counsel provisions of the Ethics in Government Act of 1978. In the aftermath of the Watergate scandal, Congress created the independent counsel system to investigate and possibly prosecute high-level executive officers accused of serious crimes. Arguing for the majority, Chief Justice William H. Rehnquist defended the creation of an independent counsel within the executive branch who would not be responsible to the president. Rehnquist asserted that the president's inability to remove an independent counsel in no way damaged the president's ability to govern.[121] Justice Antonin Scalia offered a stinging dissent and argued that the position of independent counsel would lead to political vendettas being fought through legal means.[122] A decade later, many considered this lone dissent prescient when President Bill Clinton was the target of a probe by independent counsel Kenneth W. Starr that many Americans believed to be partisan-motivated. After the completion of this unpopular investigation, which led to Clinton's impeachment, there was little public support for the independent counsel law. On June 30, 1999, Congress allowed the statute that authorized the independent counsel position to expire.

Generally, presidents may remove all heads of cabinet departments and all political executives in the Executive Office of the President. In addition, they may remove at any time the directors of the following agencies: the Arms Control and Disarmament Agency, the Commission on Civil Rights, the Environmental Protection Agency, the Federal Mediation and Conciliation Service, the General Services Administration, the National Aeronautics and Space Administration, the Postal Service, and the Small Business Administration.

THE BUDGETING POWER

The power to control the budget process is one of the most important administrative prerogatives of the presidency. The chief executive is an important participant in the budget process, for often it is the president who decides how and on what money is spent. As presidential scholar Richard Pious has noted, "To budget is to govern. In a system of separated institutions that share power, the question is which institution, and by what authority, determines spending levels for the departments?"[123] In the last part of the twentieth century, the presidency assumed an increasingly important role in determining federal spending and thus more responsibility in governing. Although Congress constitutionally controls the purse strings, the president oversees the formulation and development of the budget.

The Constitution does not clearly establish a budgetary process or spell out the president's role in such a process. Because of this ambiguity, presidents have been able to bring much of the process under their control. Article I of the Constitution gives Congress the powers to tax and spend. Article II, Section 3, gives presidents the power to recommend to Congress such measures as they deem appropriate. ("He shall from time to time give to the Congress Information of the State of the Union, and recommend to their Consideration such Measures as he shall judge necessary and expedient.") Implicit in this power is the idea that presidents may present to Congress a financial program.

Historically, presidents have not taken part in budget planning. Even in modern times, presidential involvement in the process has varied from one administration to another. For many presidents, preparing a budget is a tedious and time-consuming job. President Lyndon Johnson once wrote: "The federal budget is a dry, unfathomable maze of figures and statistics—thicker than a Sears-Roebuck catalogue and duller than a telephone directory."[124] Some presidents have been able to maintain consistent interest in the budget's complexities throughout their terms in office; others have not. Political scientist Lance T. LeLoup examined the roles that past presidents played in the budget process and found that shortly after the first year in office, Dwight Eisenhower and Richard Nixon tired of the tedious budget process. Harry

Truman and Gerald Ford, however, were able to maintain their enthusiasm throughout their administrations.[125]

Budgeting gives the presidency a tremendous amount of administrative power, and most presidents have recognized the importance of the budget in controlling their administrations. They usually approach their first budget optimistically, excited about the potential power to eliminate or cut back programs that they feel have outlived their usefulness. Describing his involvement in his first budget, Lyndon Johnson wrote: "I worked as hard on that budget as I have ever worked on anything.... Day after day I went over that budget with the Cabinet officers, my economic advisers, and the Budget Director. I studied almost every line, nearly every page, until I was dreaming about the budget at night."[126]

Although their enthusiasm may fade, presidents continue to seek to control the budget process. They see their participation in the process as a way of doing things that can benefit the national economy and their own political fortunes. In the words of President Ford, "The budget is the president's blueprint for the operation of government in the year ahead."[127] According to Dennis S. Ippolito in his study of the budget process, presidents become involved in the budget process to achieve a means of administrative management and control: "By affecting the resources available for agencies and programs, the president can seek to promote better planning of what is done, more effective supervision of how it is done, and more systematic evaluation of how well various objectives are accomplished." In addition, Ippolito has pointed out that budget decisions can affect political support: "By emphasizing particular programs or criticizing others, by challenging Congress' spending preferences, by trumpeting the need for fiscal responsibility, or by reiterating commitments to greater economy and efficiency, a president can attempt to dramatize his leadership role and to generate public support for his economic policies and program preferences."[128]

Attempts to control the budget process often force presidents to play a public relations game. Most presidents want to be considered fiscal conservatives. The overwhelming majority of Americans want a balanced budget and want the president to curtail the growth of federal expenditures. Yet presidents must continue to fund existing programs for various groups and for the American public in general. In addition, presidents are expected to present new initiatives, some of which benefit groups to whom presidents have political obligations. The dilemma is one of holding down public expenditures while trying to solve public problems. It is not an easy task, and it makes presidential participation in the budget process much more demanding and important. For example, the 1995 budget battle between President Clinton and a Republican Congress proved to be more than a public relations game. It became a marathon discussion about the size and role of government in American life. The stalemate that resulted came about from fundamental disagreements about overhauling such programs as health and welfare entitlements. Similar battles took place during the 112th Congress between President Barack Obama and especially the House Republicans after Tea Party conservatives led the party to renewed control of the chamber following the 2010 midterm elections. The nation narrowly averted a government shutdown in the spring of 2011 and defaulting on national debt payments in late summer of that year as Obama and Speaker of the House John Boehner struggled to negotiate mutually acceptable deals on spending, deficits, and federal borrowing. That fall, a newly created congressional super-committee began work to scale back the deficit, while Obama gave a speech before Congress concerning his new job creation proposal and promised to unveil a larger deficit-cutting program.

The President's Role in the Budget Process

Presidents had little influence in managing executive branch funds before passage of the Budget and Accounting Act of 1921. Previously, budget requests went directly from each department to the House of Representatives without much interference from the White House. Congress believed it could handle the budget without much help from the president or the White House staff. By the end of World War I, however, both the executive and legislative branches had realized that the massive growth of the federal government needed better fiscal management.

The Budget and Accounting Act of 1921

The Budget and Accounting Act of 1921 gave presidents important managerial controls over the budgeting process and made them the dominant participants in budgetary politics. Ironically, Congress passed this act in an attempt to bring order into its own chaotic budget process. An earlier House committee had pointed to the haphazard nature of a budget process that lacked a coherent review of the executive branch's budget request. But in attempting to alleviate the problem, the act placed the presidency squarely in the budgetary process by requiring presidents to submit to Congress annual estimates of how much money it would take to run the federal government during the next fiscal year. (A fiscal year is the twelve-month span over which financial accounting is conducted. The federal government's fiscal year runs from October 1 to September 30.)

The annual budget message delivered by the president each February recommends how much money should be appropriated by Congress for each department of the federal government. The White House first evaluates all agency budget requests and decides which to accept or alter before submitting the annual budget message. Consequently, presidents become very much involved in the process. They receive more information about the budget than most members of Congress, allowing them to initiate budget discussions on their own terms.

In addition, the Budget and Accounting Act created the Bureau of the Budget (BOB) and placed it under the control of the Treasury Department. Its role was to "assemble, correlate, revise, reduce, or increase the estimates of the several departments or establishments."[129] In 1939, in response to the growing need to coordinate New Deal programs and recommendations from the Committee on Administrative Management (the Brownlow Committee), President Roosevelt moved BOB into the Executive Office of the President.

BOB began instituting a form of "budget clearance" so that the departments could not bypass its budget review process either for statutory authorizations or for annual appropriations. No longer were the departments on their own in requesting funds from Congress. Bureaus and agencies made requests for funds to their departments, and the departments sent their budgets through BOB for consideration by the president. From 1939 to 1969, BOB evolved into a highly influential component of the EOP.

Office of Management and Budget

In 1970 President Richard Nixon changed the name and modified the function of BOB. Emphasizing the management roles of the budget agency, Nixon renamed it the Office of Management and Budget (OMB). As the word *management* implies, new emphasis was placed on providing departments with advice on ways to improve their efficiency to reduce the costs of their operations.

Nixon specifically assigned four major roles to OMB. First, it was to continue many of BOB's functions, especially writing the federal budget. Second, it was to serve as a clearinghouse for new programs and legislation. Third, Nixon wanted some part of the Executive Office of the President to have the ability to track legislation as it moved through Congress. OMB was vested with this capacity. Fourth, OMB was given the specific authority to provide management advice to the various departments and agencies. Since its inception, OMB has served as the centerpiece of presidential budgeting.

Although the president's budget is not submitted to Congress until the February before the first day of the new fiscal year (October 1), the presidential budget process begins at least nineteen months before submission of the finished budget proposal. *(See Table 3-1, p. 111.)* The budget cycle begins in early spring with OMB informing the departments of the fiscal outlook and the spending priorities of the president. During the summer, the OMB director issues specific revenue projections and imposes specific guidelines for departmental spending. On September 1, agencies submit their initial budget requests to OMB. OMB then holds formal hearings on these requests at which departmental officials justify their proposed budgets before OMB examiners.

OMB's director examines the entire budget from November 1 to December 1. Often the director will invite the National Security Council, the Council of Economic Advisers, and several White House aides to participate in the review. The OMB director makes final decisions subject to the economic forecast for the coming fiscal year and communicates these decisions to the departments. The departments may appeal the decisions directly to the president. Usually, however, each department will revise its formal budget to coincide with the budget director's wishes, for presidents rarely reverse their budget directors' decisions.

Congress receives the first official hint of what the president wants in the State of the Union address at the end of January, and specifics are then spelled out in the president's budget message in February. Pending approval by Congress, the budget goes into effect with the new fiscal year, October 1.

Not all agency requests are treated equally. Until the Nixon administration, the Defense Department's budget requests were exempt from control by the president's budgeting organization. During the Kennedy and Johnson administrations, the Pentagon submitted its budget directly to the president without review by the Bureau of the Budget. If BOB believed budget items to be too high, it could appeal to the president. This practice, a reversal of the traditional procedure, placed the burden of proof on the budget office instead of on the department. President Nixon changed the procedure for the Pentagon by leaving final decisions with the NSC and OMB and giving the Defense Department the right of appeal. Since then, presidents have continued to use OMB as a counterbalance to the Pentagon's budget requests.

Current Services Budget

Under the provisions of the 1974 Congressional Budget and Impoundment Control Act (PL 93–344), presidents must submit two budget proposals. When they submit their budget for the upcoming fiscal year, they must also submit, through the supervision of OMB, a *current services budget.* The current services budget provides Congress with an indication of the cost of existing budget obligations and a guide for evaluating additional budget proposals. Specifically, the current services budget includes the "proposed budget authority and estimated outlays that would be included in the budget for the ensuing fiscal year . . . if all programs were carried on at the same level as the fiscal year in progress . . . without policy changes."[130]

Although this procedure was intended to provide Congress with a basis for determining the overall size and direction of existing budget commitments and for assessing and evaluating the president's budget proposals, it has never lived up to its potential. Political scientist Howard E. Shuman has noted that the current services budget has little significance or meaning: "Only budget buffs and perennial budget watchers pay much attention to it. It is, however, a useful document in assessing whether any or how much fundamental change has been made in the old budget to produce the new one."[131]

Uncontrollable Spending

In any given year, much of OMB's current service estimates can be classified as *uncontrollable spending*—that is, expenditures mandated by current law or some previous obligation. Any changes to the spending on these mandated programs require congressional action. By 1995, 64 percent of the federal budget could be classified as uncontrollable spending. These expenditures can be broken down into three major categories.

The first category, fixed costs, consists of legal commitments made by the federal government in previous years. These commitments require the government to spend whatever is necessary to meet these expenses. The largest and most important component of this category is interest on the national debt. Another fixed-cost expenditure is public housing loans. Fixed costs are "uncontrollable" because they can be eliminated only by extreme measures such as default.

The second category is large-scale government projects that require long-term financing. These multiyear contracts and obligations include the building of dams, weapons systems, aircraft, and the space shuttle. Many of these projects are reviewed annually, and expenditure levels are occasionally modified. For example, in 1994 funding was curtailed for the space program and eliminated for the supercollider. Historically, however, most are not.

The third category of expenditures officially designated as uncontrollable is the largest. These programs, called "entitlements," commit the federal government to pay benefits to all eligible individuals. Any attempt to control these expenditures would require changing the laws that created them. Entitlements include Social Security, Medicare, Medicaid, Supplemental Security Income, food stamps, public assistance, and federal retirement. *(See Table 3-2, p. 112.)* In some cases, the federal government pays individuals directly; in other cases, the states determine eligibility and administer the programs. Most of these programs have no limit on the amount of spending they may entail. As more people become eligible for benefits, expenditures increase.

As entitlement spending has pushed federal budget deficits higher, presidents have tried to reduce such expenditures. Nixon and Ford, for example, attempted to decrease entitlement expenditures by restricting eligibility and establishing a limit on benefit increases for several programs. In

TABLE 3-1 **Budget Timetable in the Executive Branch and Congress**

Executive branch	Timing	Congress
Agencies subject to executive branch review submit initial budget request materials.	September 1	
Fiscal year begins.	October 1	Fiscal year begins.
President's initial appropriation order takes effect (amounts are withheld from obligation pending issuance of final order).	October 1	
	October 10	Congressional Budget Office (CBO) issues revised report to Office of Management and Budget (OMB) and Congress.
OMB reports on changes in initial estimates and determinations resulting from legislation enacted and regulations promulgated after its initial report to Congress.	October 15	
President issues final sequester order, which is effective immediately, and transmits message to Congress within fifteen days of final order.	October 15	
Agencies not subject to executive branch review submit budget request materials.	October 15	
	November 15	Comptroller general issues compliance report.
Legislative branch and the judiciary submit budget request materials.	November–December	
President transmits the budget to Congress.	1st Monday in February	Congress receives the president's budget.
OMB sends allowance letters to agencies.	January–February	
	February 15	CBO reports to the budget committees on the president's budget.
	February 25	Committees submit views and estimates to budget committees.
OMB and the president conduct reviews to establish presidential policy to guide agencies in developing the next budget.	April–June	
	April 1	Senate Budget Committee reports concurrent resolution on the budget.
	April 15	Congress completes action on concurrent resolution.
	May 15	House may consider appropriations bills in the absence of a concurrent resolution on the budget.
	June 10	House Appropriations Committee reports last appropriations bill.
	June 15	Congress completes action on reconciliation legislation.
	June 30	House completes action on annual appropriations bills.
President transmits the midsession review, updating the budget estimates.	July 15	Congress receives midsession review of the budget.
OMB provides agencies with policy guidance for the upcoming budget.	July–August	
Date of "snapshot" of projected deficits for the upcoming fiscal year for initial OMB and CBO reports.	August 15	
	August 20	CBO issues its initial report to OMB and Congress.
OMB issues its initial report providing estimates and determinations to the president and Congress.	August 25	
President issues initial sequester order and sends message to Congress within fifteen days.	August 25	

SOURCE: Office of Management and Budget, Circular No. A-11 (1988).

his first full budget year, Reagan proposed an entitlement cut of $11.7 billion. His budget proposal reflected the frustration that many presidents have felt in attempting to deal with uncontrollable expenditures. It said in part, "The explosion of entitlement expenditures has forced a careful reexamination of the entitlement or automatic spending programs. . . . When one looks behind the good intentions of these programs, one finds tremendous problems of fraud, waste, and mismanagement. Worse than this, the truly needy have not been well served."[132]

In 1996 Congress reduced entitlement expenditures for public assistance programs by enacting welfare reform legislation that imposed certain work-related rules on beneficiaries. However, Congress usually finds it difficult to change entitlement programs because of the enormous resistance offered by the groups who would be affected. When President George W. Bush urged Congress to change the Social Security laws in 2005 to allow for personal accounts, he faced insurmountable opposition from interest groups such as the AARP. Similarly, when he suggested willingness to compromise on select reforms to Social Security payouts as part of a deal to raise the nation's debt limit in 2011, President Barack Obama faced an immediate—and powerful—backlash from his constituents within the Democratic Party.

Controllable Spending

The president does have some control over several categories of expenditures. Expenditures that can be classified as controllable are used for salaries and fringe benefits for both civilian and military personnel. Although these expenses technically fit the category of controllable expenditures, the practical problems surrounding spending on salaries and fringe benefits make it difficult for a president to control them completely. Seniority and civil service rules protect so many federal employees that it is futile to attempt real cutbacks in expenditures going to salaries.

A second category of controllable federal expenditures is the general operating expenses of the various departments and agencies. Although conservation measures can be applied to such things as heating, cooling, electricity, transportation, and supplies, expenses will always continue if operations continue. And operating expenses usually increase as inflation increases.

The third category of controllable expenditures is research and development. Medical research, weapons research, and grants to state and local governments make up a large proportion of this category. Again, budget cuts can be made in this category, but only within limits. As a result, even the controllable categories of the federal budget give the president little latitude in budget decisions.

Congressional Response to the President's Budget

Because the presidency traditionally has controlled the compilation of the budget, Congress became dependent on OMB and the presidency for all its budgetary information and complained frequently that it lacked the professional staff it needed to evaluate independently the details, proposals, and estimates of the president's budget. In recent years, however, Congress has become increasingly aggressive in its desire to function equally with the executive branch in its budgetary role.

Congressional Budget Office

To improve its ability to evaluate the budget after constant battles with the Nixon administration, Congress passed in 1974 the Congressional Budget and Impoundment Control Act. The act created the Congressional Budget Office (CBO) and congressional budget committees. CBO was a major innovation for Congress and a major challenge for the presidency. Designed to provide congressional budget committees with a variety of budget and policy information, CBO incorporates several functions performed in the executive branch by OMB.

TABLE 3-2 **Entitlement Spending, 1975–2012 (billions of dollars)**

Category	1975	1985	1995	2000	2004	2008	2012[a]
Social Security and railroad retirement	67.3	190.3	337.0	410.5	496.4	671.4	755.9
Federal employees' retirement and insurance	18.4	49.8	82.2	100.3	117.4	148.0	172.5
Unemployment assistance	12.8	16.2	21.9	21.1	43.1	43.4	58.4
Medical care, including Medicare and Medicaid	26.2	104.2	289.7	363.0	515.4	715.1	958.0
Assistance to students	6.2	9.2	14.8	13.8	25.7	31.1	47.1
Housing assistance	2.1	11.2	25.5	23.9	30.6	33.3	48.7
Food and nutrition assistance	6.6	18.5	37.5	32.4	45.9	60.5	93.0
Public assistance and related programs	12.2	24.6	61.8	85.3	111.5	168.6	177.0
All other payments for individuals	2.0	3.3	4.2	7.2	11.5	8.1	5.5
TOTAL PAYMENTS FOR INDIVIDUALS	153.8	427.3	874.6	1,057.5	1,397.6	1,825.7	2,316.0

SOURCE: *Budget of the United States Government: Fiscal Year 2006, Historical Tables*, www.gpoaccess.gov/usbudget/fy10/sheets/hist11z3.xls (accessed July 28, 2011).

NOTE: a. Estimate.

CBO activities fall into five categories. First, it prepares an annual report on budget alternatives, including fiscal policy options, levels of tax revenues, and budget priorities. Second, it issues five-year budget projections for spending and taxation. Third, CBO projects the long-term costs of bills approved by House and Senate committees and sent to the full Congress for consideration. Fourth, CBO performs a "scorekeeping" function by comparing pending and enacted legislation with targets and ceilings specified by Congress. Fifth, CBO provides Congress with special reports on economic and budgetary issues.

CBO's independent database allows Congress to evaluate presidential budget proposals more effectively. In measuring the success of CBO after its first five years of operation, political scientist Aaron Wildavsky wrote: "The Congressional Budget Office has improved the accuracy of budget numbers by providing a competitive source of expertise, and it has made competent analysis more widely available to those that want it."[133] CBO has allowed Congress to become more independent from the executive branch in its budget-making powers. In his book *The Power Game* political journalist Hedrick Smith wrote: "CBO represents

BUDGETING THEORIES

One of the most important functions served by the budget is to increase presidential administrative control and management of federal agencies and programs. However, the budget process has always been the subject of criticism aimed at improving the efficiency of government management. Over the years, critics, both within the presidency and outside it, have complained about the lack of coordination and centralization in the executive branch's efforts to control the federal administration. Consequently, since the early 1960s various presidents have introduced reforms aimed at making budgeting more efficient, rational, and comprehensive. Rarely, however, have they been as successful as they have hoped.

PLANNING-PROGRAMMING-BUDGETING

In 1961 Secretary of Defense Robert S. McNamara introduced a planning-programming-budgeting (PPB) system into the Pentagon. McNamara brought PPB from the private sector and used it to improve the quality of decision making and budget planning for national security policy. In 1965 President Lyndon B. Johnson announced that PPB also would be applied to domestic operations.

PPB was designed to allow budget decisions to be made by focusing on program goals and on quantitative comparisons of costs and benefits. Once budget officials established priorities among their objectives, they then determined the best expenditure mix in the annual budget to achieve the largest future benefits.

By 1971 PPB had fallen into disfavor with executive budget makers. Although many people had looked to PPB to reform budgeting in the executive branch by making it more rational and less political, PPB failed to gain a permanent place in the budget process for a variety of reasons. It never achieved any great degree of popularity within the departments and agencies in part because it required a formal structure.

In addition, PPB suffered major resistance from Congress. Advocates of PPB apparently forgot that Congress had an important and jealously guarded role in the budget process. Members of Congress who had spent years building up their contacts and knowledge of agency budgets resented a new budget system that disrupted their channels of influence and information in an effort to make budgeting more rational and less political.

MANAGEMENT BY OBJECTIVE

In the late 1950s, economist Peter Drucker developed a management technique for business called management by objective (MBO). In the early 1970s, OMB adopted the system. Similar to PPB, it was an attempt to make budget decisions

more rational. Not as ambitious in its comprehensiveness as PPB, MBO simply stated that agencies should specify goals and alternative means of achieving those goals. It was a system much less centralized than PPB, with less emphasis on long-range planning, but it still was based on agencies making rational choices about their policy goals.

Despite its simplification, MBO also had a short life in the federal government. By the beginning of Jimmy Carter's administration, it had passed from use. Lance T. LeLoup pointed out that many of the problems with PPB remained with MBO. He wrote: "It was difficult to specify and agree on objectives, and to quantify benefits. MBO was not supported at middle and lower levels of agency management because it was still perceived as a system that increased control at the upper levels."[1]

ZERO-BASE BUDGETING

An attempt at presidential control over the national budgeting process was zero-base budgeting (ZBB). Developed in the private sector (like PPB and MBO) by Peter Pyhrr of Texas Instruments Inc., ZBB was first applied to state governments.

Under Pyhrr's direction, Jimmy Carter first implemented it in Georgia while he was governor. In 1977, several months after he became president, Carter instructed OMB to implement ZBB. Carter promised that "by working together under a ZBB system, we can reduce costs and make the federal government more efficient and effective."[2] ZBB was primarily designed to avoid incremental budgeting in which some arbitrary percentage is more or less blindly added to the preceding year's budget. Instead, ZBB aims to force agencies to identify and analyze goals and objectives, making them an integral part of the budget process.[3]

Like PPB and MBO, the appeal of a comprehensive budgeting program such as ZBB is tremendous, but its success has been limited. Budget scholar Allen Schick concluded that the effect of ZBB on the budgeting activities of the executive branch had been almost negligible. Under ZBB, most budget items have been funded at or slightly above past current services levels.[4]

1. Lance T. LeLoup, *Budgetary Politics*, 2d ed. (Brunswick, Ohio: King's Court, 1980), 271.
2. Quoted in Joel Haveman, "Zero-Base Budgeting," *National Journal*, April 2, 1977, 514.
3. Peter A. Pyhrr, *Zero-Base Budgeting: A Practical Management Tool for Evaluating Expenses* (New York: Wiley, 1973), 10.
4. Allen Schick, "The Road from ZBB," in *Contemporary Approaches to Public Budgeting*, ed. Fred A. Kramer (Cambridge: Winthrop, 1979), 216.

the most important shift of power on domestic issues between the executive branch and Congress in several decades."[134]

This competition in the budget process, however, has irritated more than one president. CBO's economic forecasts usually counter OMB's optimistic and more moderate projections, leading to numerous congressional-presidential confrontations over budget proposals. Shuman notes that in the past CBO "angered President Carter because it disputed his energy program savings and angered President Reagan by saying that his economic assumptions about inflation, interest rates, and unemployment were unrealistic, overly optimistic, and wrong."[135] President George H. W. Bush disagreed with various CBO projections on his administration's budget proposals, including the affordability of proposed weapon systems and estimates of the likely effect on economic growth of capital gains tax reductions. Part of the 1995 budget battle between President Clinton and Congress centered around different economic forecasting data produced by OMB and CBO. OMB's numbers were more optimistic than CBO's. After several weeks of negotiations, the White House and Congress agreed that CBO's economic forecast (after consultation with OMB) would serve as a basis for fiscal projections for any budget agreement. CBO then revised its figures slightly upward, but Congress and the White House still remained apart on other budget issues.

Gramm-Rudman-Hollings

With budget deficits growing throughout the 1980s and President Reagan's refusal to support tax increases, Congress believed that additional budget reform was necessary to control spending. In 1985 Congress passed the Balanced Budget and Emergency Deficit Control Act of 1985, also known as Gramm-Rudman-Hollings for its primary sponsors: Sens. Phil Gramm, R-Tex., Warren B. Rudman, R-N.H., and Ernest F. Hollings, D-S.C. Although several budget control measures were discussed, including a line-item veto for the president and a constitutional amendment to balance the budget, a strategy of mandatory spending cuts was the alternative chosen by Congress.

Gramm-Rudman-Hollings represented a major revision in the budgetary process by providing for deficit-reduction targets over six years. By imposing declining deficit ceilings, it would bring the budget into balance by 1991. If the budget process exceeded these guidelines, the president could order across-the-board spending cuts, or sequestration. (Some programs, such as Social Security and veterans' benefits, were exempt from these mandatory cuts.) The act failed to live up to its billing, however. In the 1986 budget process, Gramm-Rudman-Hollings achieved some modest success. In early 1987, when the CBO announced that the deficit for fiscal 1988 would be well above the target for that year, Congress changed the targets. It moved back the budget deficit targets two years so that the federal budget would be balanced in 1993.

In 1987 President Reagan invoked a $23 billion sequestration under Gramm-Rudman-Hollings. On October 19, one day before Reagan was to begin the procedure for automatic spending cuts, the stock market suffered its worst single-day loss ever. In a deal reached between Congress and the president, the sequestration order was repealed and a budget agreement was reached that was supposed to save $75 billion during the next two years. This agreement included spending cuts and some tax increases to ensure compliance with Gramm-Rudman-Hollings targets. But the actual deficit reduction was less than the proposed targets, and by 1990 deficits stood at record levels. Facing a widening deficit gap, President George H. W. Bush and Congress made a budget control agreement for fiscal years 1991 through 1995 that abandoned the Gramm-Rudman-Hollings deficit-reduction timetable. In doing so, Bush broke his 1988 campaign promise of "Read my lips, no new taxes" by agreeing to some tax increases to help bring down the budget deficit.

The 1990 budget agreement, known as the Budget Enforcement Act (BEA), was amended in 1993 to run through 1998. The BEA sought to lower budget deficits by imposing limits on annual appropriations for discretionary spending in three broad areas: defense, domestic programs, and foreign aid. Under the BEA, OMB determines whether the annual caps have been exceeded and, if so, by how much. It then reports those amounts to the president, who may issue sequestration orders that prevent agencies from spending in excess of the limits set by Congress. In addition, the BEA requires Congress to either raise taxes or reduce other entitlements if it creates any new entitlement programs.

Early in his administration President Clinton had to deal with the accumulated deficits of the Reagan and Bush administrations and the new caps on spending imposed by the BEA. The promise to cut the budget deficit was an important part of Clinton's presidential campaign. As a result of governmental fiscal discipline and the huge economic growth of the mid-late 1990s, the budget was brought into balance and eventually achieved annual surpluses in fiscal years 1998 through 2001. Both President Clinton and the Republican Congress elected in 1994 took credit for this achievement. By fiscal year 2002, with the economy slowing down dramatically and the Bush administration having enacted tax cuts, the federal government once again was running annual budget deficits. After the war in Iraq was launched in March 2003, the federal deficit dramatically climbed to meet the costs of the war. By fiscal year 2005, the federal deficit had reached over $300 billion before dropping to $248 billion in fiscal year 2006.[136] The drop would prove short-lived, however, as more than a trillion dollars would be added to the federal budget deficit over the next five years.[137] By the end of August 2011, the deficit reached $1.23 trillion, growing by $134.2 billion in the previous month alone.[138]

Congress and Presidential Lobbying

Because an almost adversarial relationship exists between Congress and the president over development of the budget, presidents must actively lobby Congress for their budget recommendations to become public policy. This difficult task is complicated by the dispersal of congressional budget authority among the House and Senate Appropriations Committees and the various standing committees. After the president submits the budget plan, Congress gives different committees jurisdiction over different aspects of it. The House Ways and Means and Senate Finance Committees consider revenue proposals. The various standing committees consider proposals for changes in laws that affect the uncontrollable expenses. The Joint Economic Committee studies the fiscal implications of the president's proposals. The House and Senate Budget Committees obtain budget information and prepare the budget resolution. The House and Senate Appropriations Committees consider expenditure requests. Presidents must exert influence on these different committees if their proposals are to become grants of spending authority for their departments and agencies.

Probably the most important committees with which presidents have to deal are the Appropriations Committees. These are also the most difficult for presidents to influence, because they are among the most powerful and the most isolated from White House control. The Appropriations Committees work with several independent sources of information when they consider presidential budget requests. They have the figures prepared by OMB, estimates from the substantive committees of possible expenditures of programs under their jurisdiction, program estimates and options prepared by CBO, and tentative spending guidelines prepared by the various budget committees.

In addition to their many sources of information outside OMB, the Appropriations Committees are free from the political control of the president. Their members enjoy tremendous electoral stability, especially those in the House. Since the 1980s, more than 90 percent of House incumbents have been reelected at each election cycle. Although the percentages are not as large in the Senate, the number of Senate incumbents reelected has been well above the 80 percent mark in recent years. According to Richard Pious, "Each committee member can maintain his position in his district through delivery of goods and services and patronage, from agencies eager to please him. The president cannot oust these members from his party, the committee, or the House by purging them if they cross him."[139]

Still, the initiative usually remains with the president. A determined president, who exerts the full force of the presidency, can overcome many congressional objections. The momentum in the budget proceedings belongs to the president, whose administration usually speaks with unanimity. By contrast, Congress often speaks with many confused and chaotic partisan voices and so finds it difficult to defeat presidential budget initiatives. As Shuman has pointed out, because of the consensus it represents the White House can control the debate: the president's "budget and . . . views are the subjects of the lead paragraphs in the early budget stories. Congressional criticism trails as an afterthought at the end of the article."[140] For example, after introducing his first budget in Congress, President Reagan went on the offensive by explaining his budget to friendly audiences. Before a joint session of the Iowa legislature he said, "The budget we have proposed is a line drawn in the dirt. Those who are concerned about the deficits will cross it and work with us on our proposals or their alternatives. Those who are not . . . will stay on the other side and simply continue their theatrics."[141]

In 1995 Congress seized the initiative from President Clinton in attempting to balance the budget. Under the energized leadership of newly elected House Speaker Newt Gingrich, R-Ga., the Republican-controlled Congress tried to deliver on its 1994 campaign promise of a balanced budget. In the early stages of the budget negotiations, Republicans were united behind plans to force President Clinton to side with their proposals to downsize the federal government. But as government shutdowns occurred and public opinion turned toward the White House, Congress became less unified in its budget strategy and goals, and President Clinton remained firm in his refusal to capitulate to congressional demands for sharper cuts in programs such as Medicare and Medicaid. As a result, by early 1996 the budgeting initiative had returned to the president. For the next several years the Republicans proved reluctant to challenge the president's budget leadership. Consequently, when the budget achieved balance and then surpluses by 1998, the White House received most of the political credit. In late 2000 the economy began to slow down dramatically, and in 2001 President George W. Bush responded by convincing Congress to pass a substantial tax cut. Budget deficits returned in fiscal year 2002 and were projected once again to begin growing at a fast rate. By January 2011, the Congressional Budget Office released a report that estimated the government's annual deficit at a record $1.5 trillion.[142] After Republicans took over the House of Representatives following the 2010 midterm elections, a series of deficit and budget-related battles pitted the president against and emboldened conservatives driven especially by members of the new Tea Party caucus. The battle came to a head in late summer 2011 as negotiations to raise the nation's debt ceiling lasted until the eleventh hour; ultimately, the White House was able to strike a deal with the leaders of both chambers, but not before agreeing to massive spending cuts and giving up calls for increased tax revenues.

Sometimes presidents can use the advantages of their office to pressure recalcitrant members of Congress to go along with their budget proposals. And often these tactics are not so subtle. When Vice President Gore telephoned Sen. Richard Shelby, then a conservative Democrat from Alabama, to urge his support of the Clinton administration's first budget, Shelby had television cameras present and publicly challenged the Clinton budget as being too high on taxes and too low on spending cuts. The Clinton White House did not think this rebuff to the vice president and the president's budget should go unchallenged. Clinton promptly retaliated by moving a NASA project worth $380 million a year and ninety jobs from Huntsville, Alabama, to Houston, Texas. The administration then leaked the story to the media to send a message to other Democrats who might be thinking of abandoning Clinton's budget proposal.[143] The president's strategy, however, eventually backfired. A year later, Shelby became a Republican.

Presidential Spending

Although Congress has power over the appropriations process, presidents always have a certain amount of *discretionary power* over spending—that is, they may spend certain funds as they please within broad areas of responsibility. Often Congress delegates discretionary power to the president. In a crisis, for example, especially during wartime, Congress may give the president "lump sum" (that is, very broadly defined) appropriations so that the president and executive branch officials who represent presidential wishes may devote funds as they deem appropriate within the congressional limit. Although the discretionary power does not give presidents unlimited spending authority, it does give them some budget flexibility and some latitude in the actual spending of funds as well as a final opportunity to make policy. As political scientist Louis Fisher has observed, "What is done by legislators at the appropriations stage can be undone by administrators during budget execution."[144]

Sometimes presidents exercise discretionary spending power that Congress has not delegated specifically by interpreting spending authorizations and appropriations as permissive instead of mandatory. In 1959, for example, President Eisenhower simply did not establish a food stamp program that Congress had passed into law. Presidents also can delay setting up appropriated programs in their efforts to frustrate congressional initiatives. In 1975, after Congress had developed a summer employment program, the Ford administration successfully stymied the program by setting it up so slowly that the appropriated funds could not be spent during the fiscal year. Similarly, OMB can delay funding from the Treasury to an agency in an attempt to eliminate the agency or its programs. In 1975 the Ford administration undermined the Community Services Administration by delaying the agency's funds until after the agency's authority expired.[145]

Confidential Funding

Occasionally, Congress grants the president confidential funding for urgent, highly sensitive, or secretive matters. Presidents have complete discretion over such annually funded budget items. For example, during his 1974 visit to Egypt, President Nixon used a presidential contingency fund to give Egyptian president Anwar Sadat a $3 million helicopter as a gift.

Fisher has reported that several confidential accounts are noted in the public record but are not audited by Congress, including four in the White House, six for diplomatic agencies, and one each for atomic energy, space, the Federal Bureau of Investigation, and the Central Intelligence Agency.[146] One of the most notorious confidential funds was President Nixon's Special Projects Fund, which was used to finance a massive spying and sabotage campaign against Nixon's "political enemies."

Secret Funding

In addition to the various confidential funds, presidents may ask Congress for a general appropriation for secret projects. Secret funds do not require either the appropriation (the amount of money granted by Congress) or the expenditure (the amount of money spent by the executive branch) to be a matter of public record.

Secret funding was used for the Manhattan Project during World War II. The development of the atomic bomb required more than $2 billion, which Congress approved with little scrutiny of the purpose of the appropriation.

Secret funding also is used for intelligence organizations such as the CIA. The CIA's expenditures are drawn on requests from the agency's director and are not made public or audited by Congress. CIA activities are financed by secret transfers of funds from the appropriations accounts of other agencies, primarily the Defense Department. This process keeps the CIA budget hidden not only from the public, but also from many members of Congress.

In recent years Congress has attempted to restrict the use of confidential and secret funds and bring existing funds under greater congressional scrutiny. In 1974, after revelations of covert operations overseas, Congress prohibited the CIA from funding operations other than activities intended solely for obtaining necessary intelligence.[147] More recently, there has been a move to make the funding of the CIA and other intelligence agencies a matter of public record. Congress has the power either to control or to limit this type of discretionary power, but so far it has chosen to impose only moderate limitations.

Transfers

Another method of bypassing the congressional appropriations process is to transfer funds. Such transfers occur when Congress permits the executive to shift funds from one appropriation account to another and therefore use appropriated funds for purposes different from those originally intended. In 1970 the Nixon administration used transfer authority to finance the Cambodian intervention with a $108.9 million transfer from military aid accounts for Greece, the Philippines, South Vietnam, Taiwan, and Turkey. In 1972 Congress prohibited transfers of military aid from one nation to another unless the president gave Congress notice. Yet, despite the Nixon administration's agreements to submit transfers to Congress for approval, the war in Cambodia in 1972 and 1973 was financed by more than $750 million in transfer authority already given the president.

Reprogramming

Presidents also may reprogram funds—that is, move funds within an appropriation account from one budget item to another. By shifting funds for projects that had been approved to projects that had not been approved, some presidents have used reprogramming to frustrate congressional intent.

Presidents most frequently reprogram funds within the defense budget. For example, the Pentagon may reprogram funds in an attempt to develop new weapons systems after the House and Senate Appropriations Committees have cut the defense budget. In the 1960s, as many as one hundred reprogramming actions moved several billion dollars in a single year. And between 1956 and 1972, average annual reprogramming in the Pentagon totaled $2.6 billion. Congressional committees once allowed departments to reprogram first and inform them afterward, but because some departments maneuvered around the intent of appropriations measures, Congress now requires at least semiannual notification and, in some instances, prior clearance with the committees.

Impoundment Powers

Until 1974, one tool presidents would occasionally, if sparingly, use in order to overcome the congressional funding prerogative was the power of impoundment—the president's refusal to spend funds that Congress had appropriated for a particular purpose. Historically, presidents have claimed both constitutional and statutory authority to impound funds either by treating the funding as permissive (optional) instead of mandatory and then rescinding spending authority or by deferring spending to future years. The impoundment power is similar to the veto power in that both are attempts to block or thwart congressional actions.

One of the most famous early examples of a president's use of the impoundment power was Thomas Jefferson's refusal in 1803 to spend a $50,000 appropriation for gunboats on the Mississippi River to protect the western frontier. Jefferson carefully informed Congress that the money should be used for the purchase of more advanced boats the next year. Similarly, President Ulysses S. Grant refused to spend funds that Congress had appropriated for

public works projects, arguing that they could be completed for less money than had been appropriated. In both cases, Congress eventually accepted the president's power to refuse to spend congressionally appropriated money.

Congress eventually gave impoundment authority a statutory basis by passing the Anti-Deficiency Acts of 1905 and 1906. These laws allowed presidents to withhold funds for a period of time to prevent deficiencies or overspending in an agency. In 1921 the Bureau of the Budget established impoundment authority when its director, Charles G. Dawes, announced that "the president does not assume . . . that the minimum of government expenditures is the amount fixed by Congress in its appropriations."[148]

Under the New Deal, President Roosevelt occasionally used impoundments for budgetary or policy purposes. In some cases, the president acted with at least the implied consent of Congress. During the Great Depression, for example, spending bills were sometimes treated as ceilings, allowing Roosevelt to refuse to spend money that he believed to be unnecessary. During World War II, Roosevelt argued that his war powers gave him the power to cut spending that was not essential to national security. Presidents Truman, Eisenhower, and Kennedy all used impoundments to cut military spending.

President Johnson, however, used impoundments to curtail domestic spending during the Vietnam War. As the war progressed and inflation rose, Johnson impounded funds designated for agriculture, conservation, education, housing, and transportation. These impoundments were usually temporary, and the funds eventually were released. Although Johnson did not use the power of impoundment to cripple congressionally appropriated programs (many of them were his own), his actions did set an example of impoundment power being used to combat inflation—a power later adopted and expanded by Nixon.

Both Johnson and Nixon used impoundment to control spending, but Nixon's use was unprecedented in its scope and effects. Whereas Johnson relied on temporary deferrals instead of permanent cuts and worked personally with Congress to soothe tempers, the Nixon administration's impoundments seemed designed to eliminate or to curtail particular programs favored by the Democratic Congress. Between 1969 and 1974, the administration made a determined effort to redistribute the emphasis of government services. When Congress overrode Nixon's veto of the Federal Water Pollution Control Act Amendments of 1972, for example, the Nixon administration impounded half of the $18 billion that had been allotted for fiscal years 1973 through 1975, thereby handicapping the program. In addition, the Nixon administration undertook major impoundment reductions in low-rent housing construction, mass transit, food stamps, and medical research programs.

By 1973 Nixon had impounded more than $20 billion, and his budget for fiscal 1974 contained a list of 109 reductions he wanted to make, 101 of which he said would require no congressional approval. Ippolito concluded, "While administration spokesmen advanced a variety of justifications in support of these impoundments—including precedent, statutory responsibilities, and general executive authority—it was apparent that impoundment was being used to enforce the president's policy preferences and budgetary priorities."[149] More than thirty lower-court cases overturned Nixon impoundments. The Supreme Court eventually tackled Nixon's impoundment of funds for water pollution control. In *Train v. City of New York,* the Court ruled that once water pollution control funds had been appropriated by an act of Congress, funds could not be withheld at a later stage by impoundment.[150]

Eventually, public pressure began to build for Congress to do something about Nixon's use of the impoundment power. At first, individual members attempted to intervene personally with the president in an effort to restore funds to certain projects. By 1972 many subcommittees had become concerned about the impoundment pattern that was beginning to emerge—a pattern that threatened their control of the policymaking process. In 1973 the House and Senate Appropriations Committees began holding hearings on the impoundment of funds for low-income housing, and Congress began inserting mandatory language in certain spending bills to eliminate the discretionary authority that had allowed presidential impoundment.

In 1974 Congress adopted the Congressional Budget and Impoundment Control Act. Besides setting up the Congressional Budget Office to improve congressional monitoring of, and deliberation on, the budget, the act sought to control presidential impoundment. It stipulated two new procedures, *rescissions* and *deferrals,* by which presidents could temporarily override or delay congressional appropriations decisions. If presidents wish to rescind (that is, cancel) all or part of the appropriated funds, they must inform Congress. Unless Congress passes a rescission bill within forty-five days permitting the cancellation of funding, presidents must spend the funds. As the Congressional Budget and Impoundment Control Act was originally written, either house of Congress could block a deferral (that is, delay) of spending. But in 1983 the Supreme Court, in *Immigration and Naturalization Service v. Chadha,* ruled the one-house legislative veto unconstitutional.[151] The effect of *Chadha* was to require a resolution by a majority vote of both houses directing that appropriated funds be spent immediately.

Because Nixon resigned in 1974, a few months before the implementation of the impoundment control provisions of the budget act, he never felt the force of the act. The first administration to be confronted with these statutory impoundment limitations was the Ford administration. Of the $9 billion in rescissions requested by President Ford during his term in office, 86 percent were denied by Congress. Only 24 percent of his deferral requests were rejected, however. This pattern has been followed fairly consistently since the Ford administration. Congress usually grants deferrals; in most years, it allows 90 percent of them. But rescissions are a different matter. In recent years, congressional approvals have ranged from 80 percent in 1979 to none in 1990. Usually, Congress approves fewer than half of presidential rescissions.[152] Both the Reagan and Bush administrations called for increased rescission authority in their efforts to reduce the deficit. In March 1996 the Republican-controlled Congress ended months of negotiation to grant to the president "enhanced rescission" authority—a type of line-item veto. *(See "Line-item Veto," p. 160, in Chapter 4.)* President Clinton signed the bill on April 9, 1996. The law gave the president (beginning in 1997) the power to "cancel" individual items in spending and tax bills unless overturned by a two-thirds vote of both houses of Congress. But the president did not possess this authority for long, because the Supreme Court struck down the line-item veto as an unconstitutional violation of separation of powers in 1998 in *Clinton v. City of New York,* 524 U.S. 417.

The line-item veto was revisited when President George W. Bush, in his 2006 State of the Union address, asked Congress to provide him such authority. No action was taken on his request. President Bush had frequently used signing statements as a form of de facto veto of objectionable provisions of authorization bills but sought line-item veto authority for appropriations bills to control rapidly escalating federal spending. Similarly, in 2010, Obama asked Congress for a variation on the line-item veto that would allow presidents to tackle pork-barrel spending projects in budget legislation by identifying specific problematic programs and sending them back to Congress for an up-or-down vote to include or exclude them.[153] Ultimately, Obama did not receive this authority. Further, when Bush's use of signing statements became a campaign issue in 2008, Obama was largely critical of the practice. Although Obama's position on the signing statement was nuanced—he agreed the use of signing statements was legitimate, but felt the way Bush had used them to undermine the intent of legislation was inappropriate—he was generally viewed as being anti-signing statement. This view led to a minor controversy in April 2011 when Obama used a signing statement to express his belief that Congress was exceeding its authority by defunding the positions of key White House staff who had been classified by some in the media as czars.

THE PRESIDENT AS CHIEF LAW ENFORCEMENT OFFICER

"All is gloom in the eastern states," wrote John Marshall in January 1787.[154] Farmers, many of them veterans of the

American Revolution, sought and were denied legislative or judicial relief from their debts. Under the leadership of Daniel Shays, a former officer of George Washington's army, farmers had revolted in Massachusetts. Would, as Marshall plainly worried, the American experiment in democracy survive?

It did survive. Shays's Rebellion was suppressed by Massachusetts militia, though not without considerable effort. The national government, such as it existed at the time, was powerless to assist. The debtors, however, remained resentful, and property owners had become apprehensive. The political leadership of the United States sought a more durable remedy, and a more durable remedy was found.

In February 1787, the thirteen states of the United States were invited by Congress to send delegates to a May convention in Philadelphia for the purpose of amending the Articles of Confederation. But at the urging of leaders such as James Madison and Alexander Hamilton, the convention ended up summarily rejecting the Articles as a basis for continued political union among the thirteen states. The convention's new formula for government was proposed by Congress on September 17, 1787, and ratified by the requisite nine states the next year. On June 21, 1788, the U.S. Constitution became the supreme law of the land.

It would be excessive to say that Shays's Rebellion was the single or even the most significant event leading to the adoption of the Constitution. Serious defects in the Articles had been generally known well before the Massachusetts farmers revolted. The contribution of Shays to the Constitution, rather, was to force the political leadership of the various states to do what they already knew had to be done. Shays aroused "an emotional surge" in favor of a new constitution.[155]

"We the People of the United States" sought in the Constitution to, among other things, "form a more perfect Union, establish Justice, [and] insure domestic Tranquility" (Preamble). They would not repeat the mistake of the Confederation. Americans would not render the national government powerless to promote domestic tranquility and justice.

The Constitution instructed the president to "take Care that the Laws be faithfully executed" and to preside as chief executive over what would become a vast law enforcement apparatus. The president could invoke the authority of "commander in chief" and deploy the armed forces, including units of state militia, to enforce the law. And, because mercy may be a more effective means of promoting domestic tranquility than the sword, the president would be given extensive clemency authority—the power to grant pardons and reprieves. In other words, the president was to be the chief law enforcement officer of the United States.[156]

The president's law enforcement power has grown in rough proportion to the expansion of the responsibilities and power of the national government itself. In 1789, the year Washington was inaugurated as the nation's first president, the national government generally restricted itself to activities such as collecting customs duties, suppressing domestic insurrections, enforcing federal court orders, and regulating American Indian tribes, the mails, and the army and navy. The law enforcement responsibility and power of the national government was potentially great, but actually weak.

Throughout most of the nineteenth century, direct federal enforcement of the law remained limited in scope. Congress generally left enforcement to state and local authorities. As a result, the states had great discretion in deciding whether to enforce a federal statute. The move toward greater federal enforcement of the law picked up speed in the final two decades of the nineteenth century and during the presidential administrations of Theodore Roosevelt, William Howard Taft, and Woodrow Wilson. Later, increased federal regulatory power was a fundamental element of Franklin Roosevelt's New Deal. And with the post–World War II era came novel and renewed demands for national regulation, demands that have been largely met.

As Congress added to the "police power" of the national government—that is, the power to regulate the health, safety, morals, and general welfare of the nation—it also increased the enforcement power of the executive branch. It supplemented the authority already vested directly in the president by the Constitution, or prior congressional act, and it gave the president additional resources to exercise these grants more effectively and with more power.

Yet Congress has not relinquished its own considerable power over law enforcement. To the contrary, it has insisted that power in law enforcement be shared between the president and Congress. The role of each actor, and the relationship of each to the other, must be understood. So must the unique contribution of the judicial branch to the power of the president in law enforcement.

Law Enforcement by the U.S. Government

The Constitution delegates limited power to the national government, which means, essentially, that the national government possesses only those powers that are specifically granted to it by the Constitution, or those that can be fairly implied from specific grants and that are not limited by any other constitutional provision.

The Constitution does not give any branch of the national government explicit authority to regulate the health, safety, morals, or general welfare of the community.[157] Nonetheless, that result has been obtained. Although the Constitution does not make a grant of general police power to the national government, it does grant or enumerate a variety of powers that have been shaped, constitutionally and politically, into what now resembles a general national police power.

Article I, Section 8, of the Constitution enumerates a variety of powers that may be exercised by Congress. For example, Congress may impose and collect taxes, regulate immigration, print currency and punish counterfeiters, provide postal service, and regulate the armed forces and military bases of the United States. Congress may also regulate commerce "among the several States" (the "commerce clause" of the Constitution). These powers constitute just a portion of the significant law enforcement authority of the national government. The basis for an expansive federal law enforcement power is found in the final clause of Article I, Section 8, known as the "necessary and proper clause" of the Constitution: "The Congress shall have Power . . . To make all Laws which shall be necessary and proper for carrying into Execution the foregoing Powers, and all other Powers vested by this Constitution in the Government of the United States, or in any Department or Officer thereof." The Supreme Court has interpreted the "necessary and proper clause" of the Constitution to enlarge the enumerated powers of Congress so that it can exercise expansive police or regulatory powers.

In the 1819 case of *McCulloch v. Maryland*, the Court was asked to determine whether the Constitution gave Congress authority to charter a national bank when such a power was not among those specifically granted the legislative branch.[158] If the national government was to be a government of limited, enumerated powers, the state of Maryland argued, then the Court must find that Congress had exceeded its authority.

Writing on behalf of a unanimous Court, Chief Justice John Marshall agreed completely with Maryland's contention that Congress is granted only limited regulatory power by the Constitution. He also conceded that chartering a national bank is not listed in Article I, Section 8. Marshall was too clever a legal logician, however, and too ardent a supporter of national power to allow congressional regulatory authority to be curbed by such a restrictive interpretation of the Constitution.

The constitutional authority of Congress, Marshall wrote, consists of those powers that are expressly granted by the Constitution, plus (here is where he tied the "necessary and proper clause" to the enumerated powers of Congress) those powers that are necessary and proper to the exercise of its expressly granted powers. If the end (for example, collecting taxes or supporting an army) is legitimate (that is, authorized by an enumerated power), then the means chosen by Congress to promote that end (chartering a national bank) will be upheld judicially, so long as those means are not prohibited by some other constitutional provision.

The attention of the Court then shifted to giving meaning to the enumerated powers. Granted, Congress is authorized to enact any law that helps it, for example, to promote the regulation of interstate commerce, but what exactly does "commerce among the several States" mean? Is the Constitution referring to the actual transportation of goods between two or more states? Or does the commerce clause imply more?

On these questions, once again the antecedents of modern constitutional doctrine were established during the tenure of Marshall.[159] But more than a century of judicial review was required before the modern rule became established: Congress has constitutional authority to regulate anything that *affects* interstate commerce, no matter how slight the effect.[160] Little imagination is required to find an affecting relationship between a specified activity and interstate commerce.[161]

The Supreme Court's expansive interpretation of the Constitution did not mandate a particular national role in law enforcement, and it did not in any sense require Congress to exercise its police power to the fullest lawful extent. Instead, the Court conferred constitutional legitimacy on an expansive national police power. It was up to Congress to exercise that power.

Periodically responding to the perceived need and popular demand for national regulation, Congress has added incrementally to the police power of the federal government. The Interstate Commerce Commission Act of 1887 provided for federal regulation of the railroads. This was followed by the Sherman Antitrust Act of 1890, Pure Food and Drug Act of 1906, Federal Reserve Act of 1913, and Federal Trade Commission Act of 1914. The basis for an extensive federal police power was firmly in place by the time Franklin Roosevelt was inaugurated as president in 1933.

The Great Depression was the singular fact faced by Roosevelt and Congress. Congress deferred to the president, and Roosevelt responded with the New Deal, a collection of programs adding directly to the regulatory authority of the federal government. The banking industry became more thoroughly regulated with the enactment of the Banking Act of 1933. Enactment of the Securities Acts of 1933 and 1934 placed the sale of stocks under direct federal supervision. The National Labor Relations Act of 1935 did the same for labor-management relations; and the Civil Aeronautics Act of 1938, for civilian aviation. Wages and hours of employment became the subject of extensive federal regulation with the passage of the Fair Labor Standards Act of 1938.

Roosevelt and Congress had inherited the rudiments of a federal police power in 1933. By the time the New Deal ended, upon the entry in 1941 of the United States into World War II, the regulatory jurisdiction and power of the federal government had become even more inclusive, intensive, and extensive. Regulating the health, safety, morals, and general welfare of the nation had become a major preoccupation of the federal government.

This role expanded in the post–World War II years. The Federal Housing Act of 1949, and multiple amendments, made Washington the principal source of money for financing inner-city public housing construction and urban renewal. Money received from the federal government, whether in the form of loans, grants, or payments for goods and services, is accompanied by a plethora of regulations and contractual obligations. Various pieces of legislation—the most important being the employment, housing, and public accommodations provisions of the Civil Rights Act of 1964—banned discrimination based on race, color, religion, sex, and national origin. In response to nine Supreme Court decisions from 1986 to 1991 that had made it difficult for workers charging discrimination to win lawsuits, Congress enacted, and President George H. W. Bush signed, the Civil Rights Act of 1991.[162] The law reaffirmed and strengthened the antidiscrimination provisions of the 1964 Civil Rights Act and also amended Title VII to allow for monetary damages for victims of discrimination.

Examples of other federal measures enacted during this period are the Federal Aviation Act of 1958, Consumer Credit Policy Act of 1968, National Environmental Protection Act of 1969, Occupational Safety and Health Act of 1970, Consumer Product Safety Act of 1972, Endangered Species Act of 1973, Americans with Disabilities Act of 1990, and Freedom of Access to Clinic Entrances Act of 1993.

Critics of federal law enforcement often charge that the implementation standards enacted by Congress are too vague, leading to abuses. A frequently cited example is the 1970 Racketeer Influenced and Corrupt Organizations Act (RICO). Congress intended this law to be used as a tool against the activities of organized crime. But its provision for triple damage awards—intended as a deterrent to organized crime and an incentive to plaintiffs—gave private businesses an incentive to sue competitors using RICO. The law is broad enough to allow them to do so. The broad language of the law also has resulted in charges against nonviolent demonstrators—for example, antiabortion groups—for engaging in "racketeering activity." The Supreme Court has refused to narrow the scope of RICO, maintaining that only Congress can rewrite the law. Several efforts to do so have not succeeded.

This summary reveals that the police power of the national government has expanded greatly in the past century. Still, only some of the ways in which power has grown are described here. Not mentioned, for example, are the many and frequent amendments to the Internal Revenue Code (annual amendments that are sometimes mockingly called "Lawyers and Accountants Relief Acts") or to the criminal code. Nor have the more "traditional" exercises of federal police power been noted, such as those dealing with immigration, national security, regulation of Native American tribes, imposition of ethical standards on government employees, import restrictions and taxes, and operation of the postal system.

A policy of selective business "deregulation" initiated by President Jimmy Carter and supported and furthered by his successors—Ronald Reagan, George H. W. Bush, and to a lesser extent Bill Clinton—deserves special mention. Supporters of deregulation argued that it would reduce consumer costs by fostering competition among businesses and by reducing the costs of regulation (that is, the costs of record keeping, administrative monitoring, and legal advice) borne by businesses and passed on to consumers.

Congress has directed deregulation efforts at a limited number of industries—primarily transportation, communications, and commercial credit—and only at selected business practices. Deregulation has thus reduced but not eliminated the national police power over economic activity. American businesses remain thoroughly regulated by the national government.

After enacting laws, members of Congress do not pin badges on their chests and act as enforcement officers. Instead, Congress makes the laws of the United States and then delegates enforcement jurisdiction and power to agencies and personnel of the executive branch. These agencies are also the creation of Congress.

Development of the federal civilian bureaucracy, and its power, has almost paralleled these diverse bursts of congressional energy. Civilian personnel employed by the federal government in nondefense capacities numbered 4,279 in 1816. Almost 80 percent of these were postal workers. By 1901 the number of such employees had increased to 186,532. In 1993 civilian personnel of the national government employed by nondefense agencies totaled 2.09 million.[163] By 2010, the civilian employment of the federal government had grown to nearly 2.8 million.[164]

Not all of these increases can be attributed to the growth of the police power of the national government. The workforce has grown in areas that have little to do with law enforcement, such as space exploration, agricultural advice, and maintenance of national parks. Nonetheless, most of the expansion of the federal civilian workforce is associated with the increased law enforcement role of the national government.

As chief executive and chief law enforcement officer of the United States, the president has been the most direct and most frequent beneficiary of this expansion of the national government.

Presidential Law Enforcement Authority and Power

John Kennedy exercised the legal power of the president when, in September 1962, he deployed first U.S. marshals (and various other federal civilian law enforcement officers) and then regular army troops to Oxford, Mississippi. Kennedy was acting as chief law enforcement officer of the United States. He was, as Article II, Section 3, of the U.S. Constitution requires, "tak[ing] Care that the Laws be faithfully executed."

Enforcing the law, in this case, meant backing a federal court order. In 1961 James Meredith applied for admission to the University of Mississippi ("Ole Miss"). Meredith was a Mississippi citizen, a veteran of the air force, and an African American. Ole Miss did not admit blacks at the time.

Denied admission by the university, Meredith appealed to the federal courts for assistance. His complaint was initially dismissed by a federal district court, but this decision was reversed by the U.S. Court of Appeals for the Fifth Circuit. A panel of Fifth Circuit judges found that Meredith had been denied admission to the university solely because of his race, and they ordered his enrollment.

Prolonged negotiations between Ross Barnett, the governor of Mississippi, and Kennedy and his lieutenants, principally Attorney General Robert F. Kennedy, failed to produce an agreement for the orderly admission of Meredith. Mississippi, it became clear, would not use its own force to protect Meredith and maintain order on the campus. Protection and the maintenance of law and order, if they were to be supplied at all, would have to come from Washington.

Federal protection was provided initially by a contingent of U.S. marshals. A mob formed, however, and the original federal force had to be reinforced. Additional marshals were sent to Oxford, as were almost any federal law enforcement officers who could be spared—game wardens, border patrol personnel, and prison guards. Even this augmented force was threatened by persistent and violent mob attacks.

On September 30, 1962, President Kennedy ordered the mob to disperse. He backed his order (and the original court order) with the deployment of regular army troops to the Ole Miss campus. Meredith was registered.[165] *(See box, John F. Kennedy, the Law, and the "Ole Miss" Campaign, p. 124.)*

Kennedy enforced the laws of the United States when he ordered U.S. marshals and troops onto the Ole Miss campus. In doing so, however, he—as the president of the United States—was also acting according to law. In other words, he was acting according to and within the limitations set by the U.S. Constitution and Congress.

Presidential law enforcement power may be defined by either or both sources. Article II, Section 1, of the Constitution vests in the president the "executive Power" of the United States. Section 2 of Article II designates the president as commander in chief of the armed forces, including, when ordered into national service, the National Guard of the various states. It also gives the president authority to appoint the principal officers of the executive and judicial branches, with Senate confirmation. Finally, Section 3 lays responsibility on the president to "take Care that the Laws be faithfully executed."

The Constitution also confers on Congress authority to delegate to the president and executive branch officers extensive enforcement powers. Article I, Section 8, of the Constitution gives Congress authority to make all laws "necessary and proper" to execute its own enumerated authority as well as any other authority conferred by the Constitution on the government or any branch of the government of the United States.

Consequently, Congress has the authority "necessary and proper" to "provide for the Punishment of counterfeiting" the currency of the United States. Congress has used this authority to make counterfeiting a crime, to create the Secret Service of the Treasury Department, and to give the Secret Service authority to arrest suspected violators.

Although the Constitution and Congress vest considerable law enforcement authority in the president, both also limit that authority. The Constitution provides generally for shared decision making in many aspects of law enforcement. For example, presidential appointees with major law enforcement responsibilities—such as the U.S. attorney general, the deputy and various assistant attorneys general, the director of the FBI, and the U.S. attorney for each judicial district—are subject to Senate approval. Moreover, Article I, Section 9, of the Constitution prohibits the president from spending money for law enforcement unless Congress first authorizes an appropriation for that expenditure. Congress has limited the authority of the president to use military force for law enforcement.

Generally, presidential power falls into two categories: *discretionary* authority and *ministerial* authority. Discretionary authority involves the exercise of judgment and choice (such as that required to fill a vacancy on the Supreme Court). Ministerial authority involves the faithful implementation of decisions made by others (such as that required to pay the salary of the person eventually appointed).

Much of the law enforcement authority of the president is discretionary—setting law enforcement priorities and appointing senior law enforcement officials of the executive branch to implement those priorities. These officials, in turn, are delegated considerable discretion by Congress and the president to set additional law enforcement policies—what types of offenses merit the greatest attention, what resources will be allocated, and what cases will be prosecuted.

In exercising their discretionary authority, presidents are often subjected to external political pressures. A sufficiently aroused public can force the president to be more or less aggressive in enforcing a particular law, as can a sufficiently aroused Congress. Congressional and public dissatisfaction with enforcement of the nation's environmental laws in the early years of the Reagan administration, for example, led eventually to the almost wholesale replacement of the top management of the Environmental Protection Agency and therefore to more aggressive enforcement efforts.

The Constitution reveals four general categories of presidential authority in law enforcement. The first category stems from the "take care clause" of the Constitution. The other three categories are the executive, military, and clemency powers of the president.

The "Take Care" Power of the President

The U.S. Constitution provides in Article II, Section 3, that the president "shall take Care that the Laws be faithfully executed." Two principal interpretations of that clause often are asserted.

One interpretation holds that the "take care clause" imposes an obligation on the president. The text itself is imperative in mood. It is a command to the president to obey and enforce the law. No separate and independent grant of authority to the president is stated, and none can be implied.

Supreme Court Justice Oliver Wendell Holmes Jr. urged this interpretation in his dissent in *Myers v. United States:* "The duty of the President to see that the laws be executed is a duty that does not go beyond the law or require him to achieve more than Congress sees fit to leave within his power."[166]

No one disputes that presidents are obligated to obey the law and to enforce the law with the authority they are granted. Such a view certainly has been supported by the Supreme Court.[167] The Court, however, has gone further. It has fashioned a power-granting interpretation of the "take care clause," one that does not conform to Holmes's more restrictive interpretation.

The primary ruling resulted from an appeal to the Supreme Court in the case of *In re Neagle.*[168] A deputy U.S. marshal was assigned by the attorney general to guard an associate justice of the Supreme Court, Stephen J. Field. The marshal shot and killed an assailant and was prosecuted for murder by the state of California. The marshal argued that inasmuch as he was performing official law enforcement duties as an officer of the United States at the time the assailant was shot, he was cloaked with immunity from state prosecution.

California did not dispute that U.S. marshals generally are not answerable in state courts for their official actions. It contended, however, that the marshal could not have been acting officially when he was guarding Field, because Congress had not expressly given marshals that authority. Without congressional authorization, the marshal was acting merely in the capacity of a private citizen. He was, therefore, subject to the jurisdiction of the California courts.

The Court rejected California's argument and rendered an expansive interpretation of the "take care clause" in the process. The president's power to enforce the law, wrote Justice Samuel Miller, is not limited to enforcing specific acts of Congress. It also involves enforcing the Constitution and the general peace of the land. The Court ordered California to release its prisoner.

Another notable Supreme Court interpretation of presidential enforcement authority arose in response to President Grover Cleveland's suppression of the Pullman strike of 1894.[169] Arguing that the strike, which spread to twenty-seven states and territories, was interfering with interstate commerce and delivery of the mails, two activities assigned by the Constitution to the national government, the president sought and obtained a federal court injunction ordering the strikers to desist. Cleveland then dispatched federal troops to Chicago to enforce the injunction, and anyone resisting was prosecuted for contempt of court.

The defendants challenged both the injunction and the use of military force to enforce the court order. Congress, they argued, had not given the federal court the authority to issue the injunction, and it had not authorized the use of military force by the president to enforce the injunction. The Court rebuffed both challenges.[170]

Neither Supreme Court decision should be read as giving the president power to override or ignore Congress. Instead, the Court invoked the "take care clause" in both instances when Congress had been silent.

Executive Powers of the President

Presidents are elected by the people, presumably to make policy and supervise its implementation. They are not expected to involve themselves in the details of implementation—and, with a few exceptions, they do not.

The same might be said of the attorney general, the Treasury secretary, or even the director of the Federal Bureau of Investigation or the commissioner of the Internal Revenue Service (IRS). Considerable discretion to act is and must be delegated to the men and women who enforce the law: special agents of the FBI who witness a violation of federal law, IRS auditors who discover irregularities in tax filings, and assistant U.S. attorneys who uncover evidence of criminal activity in the files of investigative reports.

The law enforcement power of the president, therefore, depends substantially on the president's ability to affect the behavior of subordinates within the executive branch. And the ability of the president to affect the behavior of these subordinates depends in part on the president's legal authority.

The Constitution says little about presidential authority over officers of the executive branch. The first sentence of Article II, Section 1, states that the "executive Power shall be vested in a President of the United States of America." This appears to give the president great power. However, the Constitution does not define "executive Power." A narrow reading of this provision means that the Constitution merely confers on the president those powers contained in Article II. A more liberal interpretation is that Article II

JOHN F. KENNEDY, THE LAW, AND THE "OLE MISS" CAMPAIGN

U.S. CONSTITUTION

The 1962 confrontation between President John F. Kennedy and Mississippi governor Ross Barnett is remembered today as an instance in which federal power overwhelmed state resistance to a judicial order. Because Kennedy faithfully executed the laws of the United States, James Meredith enrolled as a freshman at the University of Mississippi.

But the judicial branch did not just order Meredith's admission to "Ole Miss," and the president did not just enforce that order. The courts and the president acted according to the laws of the United States. Certain of these laws are reproduced here to illustrate how law is connected with the exercise of presidential power.

Various constitutional provisions also were involved in the Ole Miss controversy. These pertained to individual rights, the powers of the president, the powers of Congress, and the power of the national government in general.

Individual Rights. The Fourteenth Amendment, Section 1, of the Constitution provides that no state may "deny to any person within its jurisdiction the equal protection of the laws." In 1954 the Supreme Court interpreted this passage to mean that segregated public educational facilities were constitutionally impermissible.[1] The U.S. Court of Appeals for the Fifth Circuit applied this rule when it ordered the University of Mississippi to admit James Meredith.[2]

Presidential Power. Article II, Section 1, of the Constitution vests the "executive Power" of the United States in the president. Section 2 of this article designates the president "Commander in Chief" of the armed forces of the United States and, when called into federal service, of the several state militias. Finally, Section 3 of Article II says that the president "shall take Care that the Laws be faithfully executed."

Congressional Power. Congress, under Article I, Section 8, of the Constitution, is given the power to "make all Laws which shall be necessary and proper for carrying into Execution" its own enumerated constitutional powers "and all other Powers vested by this Constitution in the Government of the United States, or in any Department or Officer thereof." Among the enumerated powers of Congress are the power "[t]o raise and support Armies," "[t]o make Rules for the Government and Regulation of the land and naval Forces," "[t]o provide for calling forth the Militia to execute the Laws of the Union, suppress Insurrection[,]" and "[t]o

provide for organizing, arming, and disciplining the Militia, and for governing such Part of them as may be employed in the Service of the United States."

National Power. The "supremacy clause" of the Constitution provides that the "Constitution, and the Laws of the United States which shall be made in Pursuance thereof . . . shall be the supreme Law of the Land." State and local officials are bound by interpretations of the Constitution made by federal courts.[3]

CONGRESSIONALLY ENACTED LEGISLATION

According to its constitutional authority to make all laws "necessary and proper" to carry out the powers of Congress and of the president that are enumerated above, Congress enacted the following laws.

Section 332. Use of Militia and Armed Forces to Enforce Federal Authority. "Whenever the President considers that unlawful obstructions, combinations, or assemblages, or rebellion against the authority of the United States, make it impracticable to enforce the laws of the United States in any State or Territory by the ordinary course of judicial proceedings, he may call into Federal service such of the militia of any State, and use such of the armed forces, as he considers necessary to enforce those laws or to suppress the rebellion."[4]

Section 333. Interference with State and Federal Law. "The President, by using the militia, the armed forces, or both, or by any other means, shall take such measures as he considers necessary to suppress, in a State, any insurrection, domestic violence, unlawful combination, or conspiracy, if it—(1) so hinders the execution of the laws of that State, and of the United States within the State, that any part or class of its people is deprived of a right, privilege, immunity, or protection named in the Constitution and secured by law, and the constituted authorities of that State are unable, fail, or refuse to protect that right, privilege, or immunity or to give that protection; or (2) opposes or obstructs the execution of the laws of the United States or impedes the course of justice under those laws. In any situation covered by clause (1), the State shall be considered to have denied the equal protection of the laws secured by the Constitution."[5]

Section 334. Proclamation to Disperse. "Whenever the President considers it necessary to use the militia, or the armed forces under this chapter, he shall, by proclamation, immediately order the insurgents to disperse and retire peaceably to their abodes within a limited time."[6]

confers authority on the president that is not explicitly defined in the Constitution.

Appointment and Removal of Law Enforcement Officers. The executive power of the president embraces the authority to appoint senior law enforcement officers of the executive branch and judges of the federal judiciary. *(See also "The Appointment Power," p. 97.)* That authority is conferred by the "appointments clause" of Article II, Section 2, of the Constitution. *(See "Instruments of Presidential Control," p. 79.)*

The appointment power of the president applies generally to the senior officers of the executive branch charged with law enforcement responsibility. All cabinet members

serve by virtue of presidential appointment, as do agency heads and members of the subcabinet—that is, policymaking officers immediately subordinate to a cabinet officer and at the level of undersecretary, deputy secretary, and assistant secretary. The president, then, appoints not only the attorney general and the principal officers of the Department of Justice, for example, but also the principal political officers of all federal departments and agencies involved in law enforcement.

These appointees generally serve at the pleasure of the president, which means simply that they may be fired by the president—for good reason, bad reason, or no reason at all. Such a move may be costly politically, but it lies within the

PRESIDENTIAL PROCLAMATION AND EXECUTIVE ORDER

Acting on his constitutional and congressionally delegated authority, President Kennedy ordered federal enforcement of the court desegregation order. First, a force of U.S. marshals and other federal law enforcement personnel were dispatched to the Ole Miss campus. Next, when a mob threatened to overwhelm this force, and when it became apparent that state law enforcement personnel would not assist the beleaguered federal force, the president commanded the secretary of defense to deploy regular army troops to the campus. The following excerpts are from Kennedy's September 30, 1962, proclamation ordering the mob to disperse and from his executive order of the same day, mobilizing the army to enforce the law:

Proclamation 3497
Obstructions of Justice in the State of Mississippi
By the President of the United States of America
A Proclamation

WHEREAS, the Governor of the State of Mississippi and certain law enforcement officers and other officials of that State, and other persons, individually and in unlawful assemblies, combinations and conspiracies, have been and are willfully opposing and obstructing the enforcement of orders entered by the United States District Court for the Southern District of Mississippi and the United States Court of Appeals for the Fifth Circuit; and

WHEREAS, such unlawful assemblies, combinations and conspiracies oppose and obstruct the execution of the laws of the United States, impede the course of justice under those laws and make it impracticable to enforce those laws in the State of Mississippi by the ordinary course of judicial proceedings; and

WHEREAS, I have expressly called attention of the Governor of Mississippi to the perilous situation that exists and to his duties in the premises, and have requested but have not received from him adequate assurances that the orders of the courts of the United States will be obeyed and that law and order will be maintained:

NOW, THEREFORE, I, JOHN F. KENNEDY, President of the United States, under and by virtue of the authority vested in me by the Constitution and laws of the United States, . . . do command all persons engaged in such obstructions of justice to cease and desist therefrom and to disperse and retire peacefully forthwith.[7]

Executive Order 11053
Providing Assistance for the Removal of Unlawful Obstructions
of Justice in the State of Mississippi

WHEREAS, on September 30, 1962, I issued Proclamation No. 3497 reading in part as follows:

and

WHEREAS, the commands contained in that proclamation have not been obeyed and obstruction of enforcement of those court orders still exists and threatens to continue:

NOW, THEREFORE, by virtue of the authority vested in me by the Constitution and laws of the United States, . . . it is hereby ordered as follows:

SECTION 1. The Secretary of Defense is authorized and directed to take all appropriate steps to enforce all orders of the United States District Court for the Southern District of Mississippi and the United States Court of Appeals for the Fifth Circuit and to remove all obstructions of justice in the State of Mississippi.

SECTION 2. In furtherance of the enforcement of the aforementioned orders of the [specified courts], the Secretary of Defense is authorized to use such of the armed forces of the United States as he may deem necessary.

SECTION 3. I hereby authorize the Secretary of Defense to call into the active military service of the United States, as he may deem appropriate to carry out the purposes of this order, any or all units of the [National Guard] of the State of Mississippi to serve in the active military service of the United States for an indefinite period and until relieved by appropriate orders. In carrying out the provisions of Section 1, the Secretary of Defense is authorized to use the units, and members thereof, ordered into the active military service of the United States pursuant to this section.[8]

1. *Brown v. Board of Education*, 347 U.S. 483 (1954).
2. *Meredith v. Fair*, 306 F.2d 374 (5th Cir. 1962).
3. *Cooper v. Aaron*, 358 U.S. 1 (1958).
4. *U.S. Code*, vol. 10 sec. 332.
5. *U.S. Code*, vol. 10 sec. 333.
6. *U.S. Code*, vol. 10 sec. 334.
7. Proclamation 3497, *Code of Federal Regulations*, vol. 3, 225–226 (1959–1963 compilation).
8. Executive Order 11053, *Code of Federal Regulations*, vol. 3, 645–646 (1959–1963 compilation).

legal discretion (authority) of the president, and this discretion may not be curbed by Congress.[171]

Some less senior but still high-ranking law enforcement officers also are subject to presidential appointment. The director of the FBI, the commissioner of the IRS, and the administrator of the Drug Enforcement Administration (DEA) are examples. Other examples are the U.S. attorney for each judicial district of the United States, the chief U.S. marshal, and the commissioner of the U.S. Customs and Border Protection.

Presidential authority to fire these officers varies. U.S. attorneys may be removed at the will of the president. Since 1973 the director of the FBI has been appointed to a ten-year term and may not be fired without cause. In July 1993 President Clinton removed FBI director William S. Sessions because of revelations in a Justice Department investigation of improper use of office. Sessions was the first FBI director in the department's history to be fired by the president.

Two other classes of presidential appointees deserve special note: board members and other high-ranking officers of independent regulatory boards and commissions, and federal judges.

Independent regulatory boards and commissions are largely the product of the "good government" movement of the late nineteenth and early twentieth centuries and the belief that certain aspects of policy implementation could and should be separated from ordinary partisan politics. If the organization implementing policy is legally separated from politics, then the decision makers in that organization will faithfully implement policy created by Congress and will not act to promote the partisan advantage of the incumbent president.

Congress created the Interstate Commerce Commission (ICC) in 1887 to regulate the nation's growing railroad industry and later assigned it jurisdiction over trucking as well. (Congress eliminated the ICC in 1996 but transferred some of its regulatory authority to the Department of Transportation.) After establishment of the ICC, Congress created other independent boards and commissions to regulate business trade practices (Federal Trade Commission, or FTC), labor-management relations (National Labor Relations Board, or NLRB), television and radio broadcasting (Federal Communications Commission, or FCC), sales of stocks and bonds (Securities and Exchange Commission, or SEC), banking (Federal Reserve Board, or FRB), and the nuclear power industry (Nuclear Regulatory Commission, or NRC).

The exact authority of these agencies varies. They generally possess power to make law through what is called "rule making" and to adjudicate disputes about the application of the law through quasi-judicial methods. They also have the authority to investigate unlawful conduct and, in some cases, to prosecute civil violations. (Criminal violations are prosecuted only by the Justice Department.) Their authority may extend to rate setting and licensing of businesses and individuals.

Congress has given the president the authority to appoint the principal officers of these agencies. The president's authority to fire them, however, has been limited to reasons specified by law, and these limitations have been upheld by the Supreme Court.[172] *(See "The Removal Power," p. 106.)* Federal judges, including justices of the Supreme Court, also are appointed by the president, but the president's formal authority over the judicial branch ends there. By explicit constitutional provision (Article III, Section 1), federal judges have life tenure and may not be removed from office except by the impeachment process.

Presidential Authority to Command. In addition to the appointment and removal authority, the president possesses the authority to control the official behavior of certain officers of the government who are charged with law enforcement duties.

Federal judges are an exception in that they enjoy independent status from the chief executive. Similarly, presidents lack command authority in most instances over officers of independent regulatory boards and commissions. *(See "Regulatory Commissions," p. 76.)* The president's command authority over officers of the executive branch who do not enjoy independent status is greater, although still not absolute. If the presidential command is lawful, then failure of a subordinate to obey could constitute neglect or insubordination. The president could remove such an officer and justify the decision to do so. Presidents themselves, however, must obey the law, and they have no authority to command their subordinates to commit a violation.

Occasionally disagreement arises over what the law requires or prohibits. Laws are often stated ambiguously and are subject to different interpretations. The president may fire a subordinate for insubordination when such a disagreement arises.

The great majority of federal law enforcement personnel are not appointed by the president. Instead, they are career civil servants, who obtain their positions through a competitive and nonpartisan selection process. These personnel may be fired only for causes specified by statute or administrative regulation and only after a neutral and procedurally rigorous judicial-type hearing.

Special agents of the FBI, Secret Service, and Bureau of Alcohol, Tobacco, Firearms, and Explosives belong in this category. So do deputy U.S. marshals, assistant U.S. attorneys, IRS auditors, and customs inspectors. In fact, just about all investigating and enforcement officers, supporting staff, and many policymaking officers of the executive branch belong to the civil service.

Civil servants are not obliged to share the same law enforcement goals and priorities with the president. Their goals and priorities are shaped by their personal values and perceptions of what will promote their own interests. The official behavior of civil servants, therefore, should not be expected to conform in all cases with the goals and priorities of the president.

That said, civil servants are obliged to obey all lawful commands of the president and of their own bureaucratic superiors. Willful failure to comply will normally constitute legal cause for discipline, including dismissal. Any bureaucratic resistance to the president must, therefore, be displayed in a less direct, more subtle way to prove successful. More than a century of accumulated experience has provided civil servants with a variety of such methods.

Seasoned bureaucrats know well, for example, the difference between complying with lawful orders and going through the motions of complying. Suppose a president directs federal law enforcement agents to be especially aggressive in investigating members of Congress for corruption. Such an order lies within the discretionary power of the president and is entirely lawful. Most federal agents would comply; that is their job. Other agents, however, may not share the president's enthusiasm for such an investigation. An angry Congress would slice their agency's budget, or particularly powerful members of Congress might retaliate in the future by blocking their appointments to high-level agency positions. In such a case, agents may examine documents (but not too thoroughly) and follow leads (but not too many). They will then document their efforts and pronounce the absence of evidence justifying further investigations, thereby "complying" with the president's order.

The executive power of the president in law enforcement therefore depends substantially on the president's ability to choose trusted appointees who are able to influence the behavior of subordinates. Ideally, subordinates will share the president's values pertaining to law enforcement. Experience shows, however, that at least a degree of bureaucratic resistance may be expected.

Military Power

The Constitution states in Article II, Section 2, that the "President shall be Commander in Chief of the Army and the Navy of the United States, and of the Militia of the several States, when called into the actual Service of the United States." Article IV, Section 4, provides that the United States, "on Application of the [state] Legislature, or of the Executive [governor] (when the Legislature cannot be convened)," shall guarantee "against domestic Violence."

The president's authority to command the armed forces is, however, itself shaped by law. The president and Congress share authority over the armed forces of the United States.

Congress, according to its authority to enact laws "necessary and proper" to "make Rules for . . . Regulation of the land and naval Forces" and "[t]o provide for calling forth the Militia to execute the Laws of the Union, suppress Insurrections and repel Invasions" (Article I, Section 8), has enacted legislation that both authorizes and places limitations on presidential use of the military to enforce the law. *(See box, John F. Kennedy, the Law, and the "Ole Miss" Campaign, p. 124, for a reprinting of these laws.)*

The Constitution does not seriously impede the ability of the president to use military force to assist civil authorities in enforcing the law. To the contrary, wrote Justice David Brewer in 1895: "There is no such impotency in the national government. . . . If the emergency arises, the army of the nation, and all its militia, are at the service of the nation to compel obedience to the laws."[173]

The President shall be Commander in Chief of the Army and the Navy of the United States, and of the Militia of the several States, when called into the actual Service of the United States.

—from Article II, Section 2

Nor does Congress impede the president in law enforcement. Although Congress has specified the conditions in which such force may be deployed, it leaves to the president considerable discretion in deciding if those conditions have been met.

A different situation arises, however, should the president attempt to declare martial law and supplant civil with military authority within the boundaries of the United States. The Supreme Court has ruled that for such an action to be maintained constitutionally, the situation must be so desperate that the civil courts are closed.[174] The military might of the United States must support, not supplant, the law.

Presidents have used military power to enforce the law in several notable instances. George Washington used military force to quell the Whiskey Rebellion. His precedent was followed by Abraham Lincoln, who used a more powerful military force to suppress the Southern rebellion. Both presidents were, legally speaking, enforcing the law.

Defiance of court injunctions against labor strikes in the nineteenth century prompted both Rutherford B. Hayes and Grover Cleveland to deploy troops to enforce the law. In the twentieth century, Dwight Eisenhower and John Kennedy used force when court desegregation orders were met by local resistance. Lyndon Johnson used his military power in 1968 to put down rioting in Detroit. In December 1989 George H. W. Bush ordered the deployment of U.S. forces abroad to enforce federal drug laws. The U.S. military invaded Panama, ousted its drug-trafficking president, Manuel Noriega, and brought him to Florida to stand trial, where he eventually was convicted on drug and racketeering counts. During his second term, George W. Bush used the National Guard to patrol the U.S.–Mexican border to enforce the immigration laws.

Throughout the Bush administration, strenuous legal efforts were made, many spearheaded by legal advisers John Yoo and Alberto Gonzales, to expand presidential powers in this area to include denial of habeas corpus, authorization of harsh interrogation techniques, and secret National Security Agency (NSA) surveillance. Further, since the passage of the USA PATRIOT Act in 2001 and its subsequent partial reauthorizations under both Presidents George W. Bush and Barack Obama, the scope and significance of presidential authority in these areas has been expanded tremendously. These efforts met with mixed success in the realm of the federal judiciary, however. In 2004 the Supreme Court issued three rulings that limited the president's unilateral initiatives, including *Rumsfeld v. Padilla, Hamdi v. Rumsfeld,* and *Rasul v. Bush.*[175] Later, in 2006, the Court sided with Salim Ahmed Hamdan in his case against then-Secretary of Defense Donald Rumsfeld, finding that the Bush administration's military tribunals "lacked the power to proceed" because they violated both the Uniform Code of Military Justice and the Geneva Convention.[176]

Clemency Power

Article II, Section 2, of the Constitution delegates to the president the "[p]ower to grant Reprieves and Pardons for Offenses against the United States, except in Cases of

Impeachment." In other words, it gives the president the ability to be merciful as well as vengeful.

But mercy was not necessarily what the Framers had in mind when they included clemency in the enumerated powers of the president. Alexander Hamilton explained in *Federalist* No. 74: "But the principal argument for reposing the power of pardoning . . . in the Chief Magistrate [president] is this: in seasons of insurrection or rebellion, there are often critical moments when a well-timed offer of pardon to the insurgents or rebels may restore the tranquility of the commonwealth."[177] Hamilton urged that the president—"a single man of prudence and good sense"—alone be given the authority to exercise this power, because the legislature was not well suited to both weighing the national interest against other considerations and acting quickly.[178]

The pardon power was first used in 1792 when President George Washington "most earnestly admonish[ed] and exhort[ed]" the whiskey manufacturers of western Pennsylvania to cease their disobedience and obstruction of the law. They were, the president's proclamation continued, not only refusing to pay taxes on the whiskey produced, but also resisting enforcement of the tax law with violence.[179]

Washington tried issuing demands to end the "Whiskey Rebellion," and he tried applying force. Law and order in the western counties of Pennsylvania, however, were not restored until the president promised and granted the offenders a full and absolute pardon.[180]

A reprieve reduces a sentence already imposed by a tribunal. A person sentenced to death by a U.S. district court or military court martial, for example, may have his or her sentence reduced to a long term of imprisonment by presidential reprieve. The guilt is not wiped out, but the severity of the punishment inflicted on the guilty person is reduced.

Presidential pardons wipe out both guilt and punishment. They restore the person pardoned to his or her full civil rights, as if the offense had never been committed. President Gerald Ford, for example, granted a full and unconditional pardon to his predecessor, Richard Nixon, and relieved the former president of the possibility of being prosecuted for any involvement he may have had in the crimes associated with Watergate. In late December 1992 President George H. W. Bush issued controversial pardons to several key figures who had been implicated in the Iran-contra scandal during the Reagan administration. *(See box, Presidential Pardons, p. 129.)*

Reprieves and pardons may be granted to individuals or to classes of people in the form of "amnesties." For example, Presidents Abraham Lincoln and Andrew Johnson signed amnesties for Confederate soldiers and political leaders, as did Presidents Gerald Ford and Jimmy Carter for draft evaders during the Vietnam War.

The president may attach conditions to either form of clemency. President Nixon, for example, pardoned labor leader Jimmy Hoffa on the condition that Hoffa never again become involved in union activities.

The clemency authority of the president is extensive. It applies to any federal process or offender except, by express constitutional language, those persons tried (or being tried) and convicted through congressional impeachment. Moreover, it is one of the few constitutional powers of the president that does not require legislative assent. Congress, in fact, may not interfere with presidential clemency authority in any manner, including, the Supreme Court has held, the imposition of restrictions on those pardoned.[181]

Hamilton's argument in favor of extensive presidential clemency authority received its strongest validation in the aftermath of the Civil War. The successful reintegration of Southerners into the American political process, by means of clemency, nourished the healing process. Not only did white Southerners regain the right to vote, but they also ascended to high political office. And although no former Confederate soldier or political officer was ever elected president, many later served in the legislative, executive, and judicial branches of the United States.

The pardon process today is handled by the Office of the Pardon Attorney, created by Congress in 1891.[182] The pardon attorney reviews petitions for clemency and makes a recommendation to the attorney general, who then considers the petition and advises the president. Many presidents have not been reluctant to use this authority. Truman pardoned more than 1,500 people who had violated the Selective Service Act during World War II; Gerald Ford issued 404 pardons in just under two and a half years in office; Jimmy Carter issued 563 pardons and commutations in four years; and Ronald Reagan issued 406 pardons during his two terms in office.[183] George H. W. Bush issued only 77 pardons in his one term, but his postelection defeat pardons of six Iran-contra scandal figures, including Secretary of Defense Caspar Weinberger, were controversial. Bill Clinton issued 457 pardons over his two terms in office. Like his father, George W. Bush made relatively few pardons, pardoning only about 200 people during his two terms. Barack Obama's use of the pardon power has been even more limited, using it less than two dozen times in the first three years of his administration. This number was in stark contrast to Franklin D. Roosevelt, who, during his tenure, granted 3,687 pardons.

Perhaps the most controversial gestures of clemency in the modern era were some of the 140 pardons and 36 commutations that Bill Clinton issued on January 20, 2001, his last day in office. Among those, none was more questioned than the pardon of fugitive financier Marc Rich, whose former wife had made appeals for the pardon after she contributed generously to the Democratic Party, the Clinton reelection campaign, and the Clinton presidential library. That Clinton ignored the normal pardon process in the Office of the Pardon Attorney in the Department of Justice angered many of his political foes who believed that the president had acted improperly. The timing of the pardon, in the last moments of Clinton's presidency, added to the sense of suspicion about Clinton's motives. Calls for a congressional inquiry and legal challenge to the pardon were heard, but the fact remained that Clinton had the right under the presidential pardon power to do what he did, and his angry critics had no recourse other than to complain.

The Law Enforcement Bureaucracy

The president commands a vast law enforcement bureaucracy, made up of scores of departments and agencies. Perhaps the most familiar element of this bureaucracy is the Federal Bureau of Investigation. But the FBI is not the national police force of the United States, because, in fact, the country has no such force. Instead, the law enforcement power of the United States is distributed throughout the executive branch.

The FBI is part of the Department of Justice, itself the repository of several other important law enforcement agencies, including the Bureau of U.S. Citizenship and Immigration Services (INS), the U.S. Marshals Service, the Drug Enforcement Administration, and the Criminal Division.

The Justice Department is the lead law enforcement agency at the disposal of the president. The attorney general is the statutory head of the department. Initially, the attorney general served as a part-time legal adviser to the president and the department heads. For example, from 1817 to 1829 William Wirt served in that capacity while maintaining a private law practice. Wirt represented the U.S. government to trial courts as a private counselor and charged a fee for his services, as he would for private clients. The enforcement activities of the federal government were then not extensive enough to require a full-time attorney general.[184]

Today the attorney general commands a variety of important investigatory and enforcement agencies, of which the FBI is only one. The attorney general also commands the principal prosecutorial agencies of the national government, the various U.S. attorneys across the United States, and the centralized prosecutorial divisions in Washington. Finally, the attorney general traditionally serves as the principal legal adviser to the president and supervises for the president clemency and the selection of nominees for federal judicial posts. The attorney general often works closely with the White House counsel in making these decisions, particularly in the selection of judicial nominees. (See box,

PRESIDENTIAL PARDONS

The presidential power to pardon is an absolute one granted by the Constitution. When President Gerald R. Ford granted a full and unconditional pardon to his predecessor, Richard Nixon, controversy arose not over Ford's authority but his timing. Was it wise to circumvent the judicial processes already at work by pardoning someone before he had been charged with a crime? Ford was never able to shake criticism of the Nixon pardon, which contributed to his electoral defeat to Jimmy Carter in 1976. The following is an excerpt from Ford's pardon on September 8, 1974:

It is believed that a trial of Richard Nixon, if it became necessary, could not fairly begin until a year or more has elapsed. In the meantime, the tranquility to which this nation has been restored by the events of recent weeks could be irreparably lost by the prospects of bringing to trial a former President of the United States. The prospects of such trial will cause prolonged and divisive debate over the propriety of exposing to further punishment and degradation a man who has already paid the unprecedented penalty of relinquishing the highest elective office in the United States.

Now, therefore, I, Gerald R. Ford, President of the United States, pursuant to the pardon power conferred upon me by Article II, Section 2, of the Constitution, have granted and by these presents do grant a full, free and absolute pardon unto Richard Nixon for all offenses against the United States which he, Richard Nixon, has committed or may have committed or taken part in during the period from January 20, 1969 through August 9, 1974.

Attorneys General of the United States, p. 130.) Law enforcement responsibility and power are further allocated among the Treasury Department, the Department of Homeland Security, and the Department of Defense.

In one respect, it is misleading to apply the term "chief law enforcement officer of the United States" to the president. Beginning with the Interstate Commerce Commission in 1887, and continuing with the creation of agencies such as the Federal Trade Commission, the National Labor Relations Board, and the Securities and Exchange Commission, Congress has periodically allocated various law enforcement powers to independent boards and commissions within the executive branch but outside the supervisory authority of the president. The power of the president over these agencies generally is limited to appointing board members and other important agency officers when vacancies occur. These officials may not be fired by the president except for cause, which is defined by Congress.[185]

Categories of Federal Law Enforcement

Agencies of the executive branch undertake law enforcement activities that fall into at least eight categories. These categories overlap in many instances and oversimplify a highly complex regulatory scheme, but they do provide an overview of the law enforcement activities of the executive branch.

Economic. Agencies of the executive branch implement a variety of laws seeking to foster economic growth, stability, and competition. Also included in this category are laws designed to advance fairness in business practices and harmonious labor-management relations. The Antitrust

ATTORNEYS GENERAL OF THE UNITED STATES

The attorney general of the United States is the chief legal adviser to the president and is the head of the Department of Justice. Because virtually every official decision made by the president is governed by law, and such a large percentage of the work of the federal government is devoted to enforcing the law, the nature of the attorney general's job almost ensures influence with the president. The attorney general usually is considered one of the inside members of the president's cabinet. The position is one of considerable power.

President George Washington turned to a fellow Virginian, Edmund Jennings Randolph, as his (and the nation's) first attorney general. Randolph had two qualities that have often characterized the individuals who have held that office ever since: talent and controversy.

Before serving with Thomas Jefferson, Alexander Hamilton, and Henry Knox in Washington's first cabinet, Randolph had distinguished himself through his service as a military aide to General Washington, as an attorney general and governor of Virginia, as a delegate to the Virginia constitutional convention of 1776, as a delegate from Virginia to the Continental Congress, and as a delegate to the Constitutional Convention of 1787. Although Randolph refused to sign the convention's final product, the U.S. Constitution, because, among other reasons, he opposed vesting the executive power in a single president, he did urge its ratification by Virginia.

When Thomas Jefferson resigned in 1794 as Washington's first secretary of state, Washington picked Randolph to succeed him. Randolph resigned the following year, however, amid false charges of soliciting bribes and giving secret information to the French government. Although stripped of his public standing by the charges, the capable Randolph led the successful legal defense in the treason trial of Aaron Burr.

Talent and controversy have followed the successors of Randolph. Roger B. Taney, attorney general to President Andrew Jackson, and Harlan Fiske Stone, attorney general to President Calvin Coolidge, became chief justices of the United States (in Stone's case, after serving sixteen years as an associate justice). Other former attorneys general who became Supreme Court justices were Nathan Clifford, Joseph McKenna, James C. McReynolds, Francis W. Murphy, Robert H. Jackson, and Thomas C. Clark.

Harry M. Daugherty was attorney general to President Warren G. Harding and was implicated in the Teapot Dome Scandal. Many people thought that Ramsey Clark, the last attorney general to President Lyndon B. Johnson, should have been indicted for treason, but he was not. Clark remains controversial for visiting Hanoi during the Vietnam War after he left office. Two of President Richard Nixon's attorneys general, John N. Mitchell and Richard G. Kleindienst, went to prison after leaving office and being convicted of crimes. President Reagan's controversial attorney general, Edwin Meese, spent much of his tenure fighting ethics charges stemming from inconsistencies and omissions in his financial disclosure forms.

One attorney general, Charles Joseph Bonaparte, had an unusual family history for an American leader. Bonaparte was the grandson of Jerome Bonaparte, king of Westphalia and marshal of France. Jerome, in turn, was the younger brother of Napoleon I, emperor of France. The American Bonaparte first distinguished himself as a leader of the good-government movement of the late nineteenth and early twentieth centuries, serving consecutively as president of the National Civil Service Reform League in 1904 and as president of the National Municipal League in 1905. This commitment appealed to President Theodore Roosevelt, who rewarded Bonaparte with appointments first as secretary of the navy and then as attorney general.

In 1993 President Bill Clinton wanted to appoint the nation's first woman attorney general. His first two choices for the position, Zöe Baird and Kimba Wood, had to withdraw from consideration because of revelations that they had employed illegal immigrants as nannies. Clinton's next choice for the job, Florida prosecutor Janet Reno, was confirmed by the Senate in March 1993. The selection

Division of the Justice Department enforces laws promoting fair trade practices and proscribing monopolies. Financial institutions are subjected to regulation by the comptroller of currency and by the Internal Revenue Service in the Treasury Department. Employment is subject to enforcement actions by the Occupational Safety and Health Administration and by the Employment Standards Administration of the Department of Labor. Despite deregulation, substantial regulation of the transportation industry is still administered by the Federal Aviation Administration of the Department of Transportation. Energy, a relative newcomer to the federal regulatory scheme, is under the jurisdiction of the Departments of Energy and Interior.

Social. Congress has enacted laws that promote a mélange of social goals: equality, fairness, and material comfort. Antidiscrimination laws, such as the equal employment and fair housing provisions of the Civil Rights Act of 1964, the Age Discrimination in Employment Act, the Civil Rights Restoration Act of 1988, the Americans with Disabilities Act of 1990, the Civil Rights Law of 1991, and the Family and Medical Leave Act of 1993, belong in this category. Their enforcement generally is accomplished by the combined efforts of the Civil Rights Division of the Justice Department, the Equal Employment Opportunity Commission, and the Department of Education. Each agency of the federal government also has an office charged with enforcing internal compliance with these laws, as well as compliance by firms contracting with the agency. A multitude of retirement, medical care, and educational assistance acts are administered by the Social Security Administration of the Department of Health and Human Services, the Department of Veterans Affairs, and the Department of Education.

of Reno was symbolically important and enormously popular. Her reputation for integrity was untarnished, and she was known as a straight-speaking, law-and-order prosecutor.

Although she initially was the most celebrated and highly regarded Clinton appointee, Reno soon became mired in controversy. After a lengthy standoff between federal law enforcement officials and members of a religious cult, who had refused to surrender to the authorities, Reno authorized the FBI to inject nonlethal tear gas into the cult's Waco, Texas, compound. The effort failed to drive out the cult members, and a fire erupted at the compound leading to the deaths of eighty-five people, many of whom were children. Reno testified to Congress that she was responsible for the disaster. Reno's candor earned her immediate praise, but many continued to question her handling of the situation.

Reno continued to serve through Clinton's second term and continued to draw controversy to herself and the Justice Department. But the criticism came from both the left and right wings of American politics and involved many high-profile social issues in the 1990s, including gun control, campaign financing, the return of the young Cuban refugee Elián González to his father in Cuba, and even an investigation of alleged wrongdoing by President Clinton himself. Her eight-year term in office was one of the most tumultuous of any recent attorney general.

In 2001 President George W. Bush turned to former U.S. senator John Ashcroft, R-Mo., for attorney general. (Ashcroft had lost a reelection bid in 2000.) Because of his strong ties to the religious conservative movement, Ashcroft was a controversial choice. Civil liberties and other liberal interest groups mounted a vigorous campaign against his confirmation, yet Bush had the advantage of a Republican majority in the Senate where Ashcroft had been well regarded among his former colleagues. In the most contentious debates of all of the Bush nominees, Ashcroft was eventually confirmed by a 58–42 vote.

During his four years as attorney general, Ashcroft remained a staunch supporter of an expansive interpretation of presidential powers in the war on terrorism. Ashcroft resigned at the end of the first term and was replaced by Alberto Gonzales, the White House counsel and former Texas judge. Gonzales continued to support sweeping interpretations of presidential authority for the president as commander in chief in the war on terrorism. As White House counsel, Gonzales had authored memos giving President Bush constitutional justification as commander in chief for determining who was an enemy combatant and how an enemy combatant could be detained. These memos became a focus of Gonzales's contentious confirmation hearings. Although ultimately confirmed as attorney general, when a vacancy opened on the U.S. Supreme Court during the second term of the Bush administration, his memos on enemy combatants sidelined his nomination to the Court.

On the day of his historic inauguration, Barack Obama nominated Eric Holder to be the first African American attorney general. Prior to the Senate's confirmation, Holder was perhaps best known for his controversial involvement with Bill Clinton's pardon of fugitive financier Marc Rich. Since confirmation, Holder's tenure featured numerous additional controversies, including his characterizing interrogation techniques during the George W. Bush era as torture, his decision to drop a voter intimidation suit against the Black Panthers concerning alleged 2008 election-related actions, his announcement that the Department of Justice would no longer enforce certain provisions of the Defense of Marriage Act, and a 2009 public reference to the United States as a "nation of cowards" when it comes to race relations. Perhaps the most notable—and controversial—decision made by Holder during the first few years of the Obama administration was his decision to try several suspects—including alleged mastermind Khalid Shaikh Mohammed, held in relation to the September 11, 2001, terror attacks—in federal court in New York. This decision was ultimately reversed, however, after yielding significant political pushback from the public and Congress.

Political. Political decisions are made according to a complex system of procedural laws. The often-stated purpose of these laws is to promote fairness and integrity in government. The Voting Rights Act of 1965, for example, forbids racial discrimination in voting and is enforced by the FBI and the Civil Rights Division of the Department of Justice. Bribery of and extortion by federal government officials of all branches also fall under the jurisdiction of the FBI. Violations that the FBI uncovers are prosecuted by the Criminal Division of the Justice Department.

Judicial. Most judicial orders are complied with voluntarily. Judgment is entered against the defendant, and the defendant complies—that is, the defendant makes payment, stops the unlawful activity, or turns himself or herself over to authorities for completion of a jail sentence. Behind every instance of voluntary compliance, however, is at least the implicit backing of armed force. Armed force also may be necessary on occasion to enforce judicial orders and to protect judges, jurors, witnesses, and other participants in a trial. The U.S. Marshals Service of the Justice Department is the agency that usually enforces the authority of the judicial branch. Its power may, in extreme circumstances, be backed by the armed forces of the United States, principally by the army and by Army National Guard units nationalized by presidential order.

Public Health and Safety. The national government oversees many issues of public health and safety. They include transportation safety, a concern of the Federal Aviation Administration (FAA) of the Department of Transportation; occupational safety and health, consigned by Congress to the aptly named Occupational Safety and Health Administration of the Department of Labor; and food purity, which falls under the jurisdiction of the Food and Drug Administration of the Department of Health and Human Services, the Environmental Protection Agency, and the Food Safety and Inspection Service of the Department of Agriculture.

The public health and safety activities of the executive branch also entail enforcement of more commonly known criminal laws, such as those prohibiting interstate kidnapping, prostitution, and transportation of stolen property. Finally, federal laws attempting to stem drug and alcohol abuse in the United States are enforced by the FBI, DEA, FDA, Coast Guard, U.S. Customs and Border Protection, and Bureau of Alcohol, Tobacco, Firearms, and Explosives. Prosecutions are the responsibility of the Criminal Division of the Justice Department and local U.S. attorneys.

In 1984 Congress passed an anticrime bill that revamped federal sentencing procedures to reduce disparities in the sentencing of criminals. The law reduced judicial discretion by creating a ranking system for crimes and requiring judges to follow sentencing guidelines adopted by a presidential commission. The law also eliminated parole for certain federal offenses, increased penalties for drug trafficking, provided expanded government authority to seize the assets of drug traffickers, and made it more difficult to use the insanity defense.

National Security. Treason and espionage are crimes, as are assorted other activities that jeopardize the military and diplomatic interests of the United States. Protection of national security is associated most often with the FBI, but the efforts of the FBI constitute only a part of the whole. Agencies of the Department of Defense—such as the Defense Investigative Service, the Naval Investigative Service, the Office of Special Investigations (air force), and the Intelligence and Security Command (army)—have law enforcement duties to protect national security, as do the Coast Guard, U.S. Customs and Border Protection, and Bureau of U.S. Citizenship and Immigration Services of the Department of Homeland Security and the Office of Security within the Department of State. The Central Intelligence Agency is not given domestic law enforcement authority by Congress, but it may pass to the FBI intelligence it gathers abroad about American national security breaches.

Public Resources. The public resources of the national government consist of money, property, and people. Almost every law enforcement agency of the national government is involved in protecting one or all of these resources. The better known of these agencies are the FBI and the Secret Service. Others include the Postal Inspection Service, Park Police of the Department of the Interior, U.S. Marshals Service, and Federal Protective Service of the General Services Administration. Each department and agency of the executive branch investigates theft, fraud, and personal security through an office of the inspector general.

Public Revenue. Enforcing the nation's tax laws falls primarily under the jurisdiction of the Department of the Treasury. The Tax Division of the Justice Department prosecutes violations of the various tax laws. The 1994 anticrime bill gave the Customs Service authority to stop and search, without warrant, anyone entering or leaving the United States who appears to be violating a currency transaction law. The Customs Service became part of the Department of Homeland Security in 2002 and was renamed U.S. Customs and Border Protection.

Law Enforcement Functions of the Bureaucracy

The bureaucracy performs four general law enforcement functions: investigation, enforcement, prosecution, and custody.

Investigation. Investigation entails fact finding—that is, searching for facts that may help an agency discharge its assigned law enforcement responsibilities. The search for facts may be directed toward enactment of new laws or the enforcement of existing laws with more effective strategies, policies, and priorities. Most agencies of the executive branch conduct fact-finding activities.

For an assortment of reasons—the need for impartiality, prestige, or outside expertise—the president may prefer on occasion that a particular issue in law enforcement be investigated by persons not affiliated with existing agencies. In such instances, the president may appoint a presidential investigatory commission.

The presidential commission normally is a bipartisan panel of Americans who may or may not be employed by the federal government but who have distinguished themselves publicly. The commission receives a presidential mandate to answer a question, or a series of questions, and is supported by a professional staff paid for by the president.

The National Advisory Commission on Civil Disorders, better known as the "Kerner Commission," is a good example. In July 1967 Detroit, Michigan, was torn by urban rioting. Unable to control the rioting with state and local forces, including the Michigan National Guard, George W. Romney, the governor of Michigan, requested the assistance of the president.

President Lyndon Johnson responded by sending troops, and order soon was restored. But the president wanted to know the causes of the rioting and he wanted to know what could be done to prevent similar disturbances.

To answer these questions, Johnson established on July 29, 1967, the Kerner Commission.[186] He appointed Otto Kerner, then governor of Illinois, to chair a panel composed of four members of Congress, one mayor, a state official, a local police chief, and one representative each from labor, business, and civil rights.[187] Two advisory panels, a large investigative staff, and outside consultants and witnesses assisted the panel.

The commission's findings followed months of public hearings, statistical analyses, and review of programs, policies, and procedures.[188] Some of the recommendations found their way into national policy; others were considered but never implemented. The timing of the Detroit riot, and the timing of the resulting report, was not good because President Johnson devoted much of his remaining and limited time in the White House to managing the Vietnam War. Richard Nixon, his successor in 1969, was not receptive to the proposals contained in the report.

More routinely, a law enforcement investigation is directed at enforcing, not changing, policy. The fact finding is aimed at determining whether an unlawful act has been committed, identifying the perpetrators, and gathering evidence that is both admissible in court and sufficient to obtain a favorable verdict.

Most enforcement agencies of the executive branch are involved in this kind of law enforcement. Other investigations take more time, more effort, and considerably more resources. Investigation by the FBI of a national security breach, for example, may require months of investigative work, including surveillance of potential suspects, installation and monitoring of wiretaps, and rigorous background checks.

Certain investigations involve crimes so complex that the resources of multiple agencies from different departments may be mobilized into single task forces. Organized crime falls in this category; agents from the FBI, IRS, and DEA often join with their counterparts from state and local police forces and with federal and state prosecutors to deal with this persistent problem.

Enforcement. Law enforcement involves more than the arrest and conviction of criminal suspects. It also involves the protection of federal resources and execution of judicial orders. Among the many federal agencies participating in enforcement (most often the same ones that conduct investigations), some of the most prominent are the following:

- *Food Safety and Inspection Service (Agriculture Department).* President Theodore Roosevelt is reputed to have been reading Upton Sinclair's *The Jungle* while eating breakfast one morning in the White House. Disturbed by Sinclair's description of the meat-packing industry in Chicago, the president threw his sausage out of the White House window and began working toward enactment of the Pure Food and Drug Act of 1906. Conditions have improved considerably since Roosevelt's day. Meat-packing and other food production and processing industries are now subjected to standards adopted and enforced by the Department of Agriculture. The job of the Food Safety and Inspection Service is to enforce these standards.
- *U.S. Department of Defense.* By order of the president, units of the armed forces of the United States may be used to suppress domestic violence and to remove obstructions to the enforcement of the law. National Guard units of the states may be nationalized for this purpose by presidential order. When they are, they are placed under the operational command of the secretary of defense. The Defense Department and its component Departments of the Army, Navy, and Air Force include internal agencies that have law enforcement responsibilities and authority, such as the Defense Criminal Investigative Service. These agencies, staffed by both civilian and military personnel, provide protective services to the property and personnel of the department. They also enforce laws pertaining to fraud, corruption, and national security. For example, in 1988 investigations conducted by the Naval Investigative Service uncovered a Pentagon procurement scandal. The Naval Investigative Service was renamed in 1992 as the Naval Criminal Investigative Service and staffed by primarily civilian personnel.
- *Federal Bureau of Investigation (Justice Department).* In almost fifty years of leadership, J. Edgar Hoover, the consummate bureaucratic chief, shaped the FBI into a modern, professional, and semiautonomous law enforcement agency. The bureau gained notoriety in the 1930s by apprehending or killing marauding and overly romanticized criminals, such as John Dillinger. The favorable image Hoover and his agents enjoyed was only enhanced by the agency's successful apprehension of enemy spies during World War II and the ensuing cold war. Always sensitive to public opinion, Hoover insisted that his agents conform to rigid dress and behavioral standards. He also initiated programs cultivating the bureau's reputation for effectiveness—the FBI's "ten most wanted list" is one example.

The mystique surrounding and protecting the FBI began to decay somewhat in the 1960s. Critics charged that Hoover was insensitive to civil rights issues and had refused to commit sufficient resources to the investigation of organized crime. Additional blows to the agency came in the wake of Watergate, when its acting director, L. Patrick Gray, admitted to destroying documents important to the initial investigation and when high bureau officers were convicted and imprisoned for illegal activities. In 2001 it was revealed that in the 1960s the FBI, with the full knowledge and consent of Hoover, had fabricated a legal case against an innocent man for alleged organized crime activity. Reacting to criticism that the agency had been lax to combat such activities, the FBI was overly zealous in its quest to land a high-profile conviction in an organized crime investigation. A congressional investigation of this scandal led to widespread criticism of the agency, and one prominent member of Congress, Rep. Dan Burton, R-Ind., called for the removal of Hoover's name from the FBI building in Washington, D.C.

The FBI is the closest thing the United States has to a general police agency in the national government. Its jurisdiction includes investigation and enforcement of laws pertaining to national security, fraud, corruption, civil rights, elections, kidnapping, and robbery of federally insured banks. In 2010 the FBI employed more than 30,000 persons and had a budget of $7.75 billion.

- *Drug Enforcement Administration (Justice Department).* Agents of the DEA have perhaps the most dangerous law enforcement job in the federal government: they enforce national drug laws. Most of the work of the DEA is conducted within the boundaries of the United States. Yet agents may and often do extend their investigations to the drug production, refinement, and transportation centers in Latin America, Europe, Asia, and the Middle East. Here they may advise and exchange intelligence information with their foreign counterparts and, depending on arrangements with the host countries, conduct their own investigations. The $2.1 billion budget authorized by Congress for the DEA for 2010 reflects the agency's importance to federal law enforcement policy.
- *U.S. Customs and Border Protection (Homeland Security Department).* The Border Patrol, which had been part of the Justice Department, and the Customs Service, which had been part of the Treasury Department, were collapsed into a single agency in the Department of Homeland Security in 2002. By 2010, it had more than forty thousand employees and a $10.1 billion budget.
- *U.S. Marshals Service (Justice Department).* U.S. marshals have been a law enforcement resource of the president since the administration of George Washington. In the nineteenth century, marshals acted as the general police force for much of the American West. Large sections of the West had not yet achieved statehood and were organized by Congress as territories of the United States. Television and films have depicted U.S. marshals of this period, of whom Wyatt Earp and Matt Dillon were only two, single-handedly standing between the ordinary law-abiding citizen and a host of predators—gunslingers, horse thieves, and the local cattle baron, all aided, apparently, by corrupt local sheriffs, mayors, and judges.

  The job of the marshal in contemporary American society is less romantic but still important. Marshals enforce court orders, serve court papers, maintain security and order in courtrooms, protect witnesses, escort federal prisoners, and suppress domestic disturbances. Marshals possess general law enforcement power and are an all-purpose force at the disposal of the president and attorney general. In 2010 the budget for the U.S. Marshals Service was comparatively small—$1.15 billion.

- *Secret Service (Treasury Department).* The men and women wearing business suits, sunglasses, and earpieces who surround the president on every occasion are the best-known component of the Secret Service. But guarding the president is just one of the duties of this agency of the Treasury Department. It also provides security for the vice president, former presidents, immediate family members of current and former presidents, the president- and vice president-elect, presidential and vice presidential candidates, and visiting heads of state. A uniformed branch of the Secret Service guards foreign embassies and missions and assists in guarding the White House. The Secret Service also has primary jurisdiction in enforcing laws pertaining to counterfeiting, credit card fraud, and defrauding of federally insured banks with 125 offices in the United States and abroad. Congress appropriated $1.49 billion for the Secret Service in fiscal year 2010, a large portion of which was used to pay the salaries of the estimated five thousand men and women it employs.
- *Internal Revenue Service (Treasury Department).* The IRS not only collects the taxes owed the federal government from individuals and corporations but also processes tax returns from almost every American adult, corporation, partnership, and nonprofit organization. Certain of these returns are selected for audit (usually by computer), a process designed to detect tax fraud and to deter intentional understatement of future tax liabilities. The IRS includes a criminal investigative division, whose agents are authorized to carry firearms, investigate possible criminal violations of the tax code, make arrests, and serve search warrants. In fiscal year 2010, the IRS employed more than 101,000 people and was appropriated a budget of $12.1 billion for operating expenses.
- *Bureau of Alcohol, Tobacco, Firearms, and Explosives (Homeland Security Department).* The bureau has authority to combat illegal firearms use as well as illegal trade practices involving alcoholic beverages and tobacco products. A spate of controversy and bad publicity attended the bureau's disastrous February 1993 raid on the compound of a religious cult in Waco, Texas. Critics charged that the bureau had acted improperly in the raid, which resulted in the deaths of four bureau officers and several cult members. The FBI was called in and the resulting standoff ended two months later in a fire that killed many of the remaining cult members and their children. Later that year, President Clinton proposed that

the bureau be merged into the Justice Department. Congress opposed the idea and the Clinton administration dropped it. In 2002, however, the former Bureau of Alcohol, Tobacco, and Firearms was moved from the Treasury Department to the Department of Homeland Security and renamed adding "and Explosives" to its title to reflect homeland security issues. In fiscal year 2010, the bureau had an estimated budget of $1.12 billion.

Secret Service agents surround President Gerald R. Ford as he works the crowd on a 1976 campaign swing through Louisiana. The Secret Service provides security for the president and the first family as well as for the vice president, presidential candidates, and past presidents and their families.

- *Occupational Safety and Health Administration (Labor Department).* Health and safety in the workplace are the concerns of OSHA. In accordance with legislation passed by Congress, OSHA has put into effect detailed regulations governing matters such as protective clothing for workers, the handling of hazardous substances, and the protective shields on industrial equipment. Inspectors from local OSHA offices inspect work sites and have authority to cite employers who violate or permit violations of the regulations. OSHA administered a budget of $559 million.
- *Federal Aviation Administration (Transportation Department).* The FAA administers and enforces laws pertaining to commercial air travel. Its jurisdiction includes pilot licensing, airport safety and security (with the exception of baggage and passenger screening, which is handled by the Transportation Security Administration of the Department of Homeland Security), air traffic control, and airplane safety. It administered a budget of nearly $12.5 billion in 2010.
- *Coast Guard (Homeland Security Department).* The Coast Guard traces its origins to the nation's first secretary of the Treasury, Alexander Hamilton, who created a service of revenue cutters (small armed ships) to help prevent smuggling and the resulting evasion of customs taxes. The Coast Guard still performs this function. It also enforces regulations pertaining to maritime safety,

licenses boat captains, patrols waterways for hazards (such as icebergs), and rescues people from sunken or disabled vessels. The Coast Guard has an important role in efforts to suppress drug smuggling and to intercept persons attempting to enter the United States illegally by sea. The Coast Guard was transferred from the Transportation Department to the Department of Homeland Security in 2002 and refocused many of its resources to combating terrorism. In fiscal year 2010, Congress gave the Coast Guard a budget of nearly $8.6 billion.

Prosecution. The U.S. attorney is the workhorse of the federal prosecutorial system. Appointed by the president and located within the Department of Justice, the U.S. attorney assumes the lead responsibility for representing the government in court. One U.S. attorney is appointed for each of the ninety-four judicial districts in the United States. Each is supported by a professional legal staff. U.S. attorneys filed nearly 150,000 civil and criminal actions during fiscal year 2009.[189]

Although the U.S. attorney represents the government in most cases, other prosecutorial resources are found in the executive branch. The Department of Justice itself has divisions that may, at times, be involved in litigation. Each division is headed by an assistant attorney general. The jurisdiction of these officials is indicated by their division title: Antitrust Division, Civil Division, Civil Rights Division, Criminal Division, Environment and Natural Resources Division, and Tax Division.

One other component of the Justice Department involved in the prosecution phase of law enforcement is the Office of the Solicitor General. The solicitor general determines which federal or state appellate court decisions will be appealed by the United States to the Supreme Court and then represents the government in the appeal. Because of the considerable influence the Supreme Court has in interpreting the law, including laws allocating power to the president and presidential agencies, this function is particularly critical to the president.

Occasionally Congress gives limited prosecutorial authority and resources to departments and agencies outside of the Justice Department. The solicitor of labor, for example, has authority to initiate civil actions in federal court to enforce wage-and-hour and occupational health and safety laws.

Custody. Conviction of a crime in federal court may lead to a sentence of imprisonment. When it does, the prisoner is usually remanded to the custody of the Bureau of Prisons for punishment. The Bureau of Prisons, which is an agency of the Department of Justice, has responsibility for administering the federal prison system. This responsibility includes guarding the inmates (often from one another) and supplying them with housing, food, recreation, medical care, and rehabilitation services such as education and counseling. The Bureau of Prisons employed an estimated thirty-eight thousand people in fiscal year 2010 with a budget of $6.2 billion.

Law Enforcement within the U.S. Political System

Law enforcement responsibility and power are shared in the U.S. political system, by the national government and the fifty states and their units of local government. They also are shared by the three branches of the national government. With the notable exception of the president's constitutional authority to grant reprieves and pardons, all incidents of presidential law enforcement power may be checked by at least one of the two other branches.

Sharing within the Federal System

Federalism refers to a form of constitutional structure whereby at least two levels of government exercise sovereign power over geographically defined and overlapping jurisdictions. The two levels of sovereign government in the United States are the national government and the fifty independent state governments.

Allocation of law enforcement responsibility and power within the U.S. federal system has evolved significantly since George Washington and members of the First Congress took office in 1789. This evolution generally has increased the power and responsibility of the national government at the expense of state power and independence.

National law enforcement responsibility and power were slight in 1789 and remained so until the Civil War. The states, however, had significant law enforcement responsibility and power during this period. Legislating to promote the public's health, safety, morals, and general welfare was the business of the state legislatures, and it was the business of the local sheriffs, state militia, and state judges to enforce those laws.

This balance gradually shifted, however, in favor of the national government. Led by Chief Justice John Marshall, the Supreme Court handed down rulings in the first decades of the nineteenth century that interpreted expansively the constitutional grants of power to the national government. Congress, the Court ruled, has ample constitutional power to enact any law necessary and proper to carry out its enumerated powers, so long as that law is not proscribed by the Constitution itself.[190] Contrary provisions of state law must yield to laws enacted by Congress in accordance with its constitutional power.[191] State court interpretations of federal law are susceptible to review and possible reversal by federal courts.[192]

Although Marshall and the Supreme Court legitimized an extensive and pervasive national role in law enforcement, a workable consensus among the American people and their elected representatives in Congress that such a role ought to be exercised was not achieved until the latter part of the nineteenth century. Business in the early decades of the American Republic was largely a local activity that was regulated primarily by state and local governments. By the late nineteenth century, however, it had become apparent that many business activities either could not or would not be regulated effectively by state and local governments. The public eventually pressured Washington to assume the burden. Interstate rail transportation came under federal regulatory jurisdiction with enactment of the Interstate Commerce Act of 1887. Today, virtually no business activity is untouched by federal regulation.

The current relationship between the national government and the fifty state governments in law enforcement is complex. Some activities are regulated extensively and simultaneously by both levels of government. Retail sales, occupational health and safety, and banking, for example, are subject to a host of national and state laws and regulations.

Other activities tend to be regulated predominantly by either one or the other level of government. The national government regulates interstate and international airline travel, radio and television broadcasting, and nuclear power production. Most automobile speed limits, assault and battery, marriage and divorce, and medical licensing are principally matters for state regulation.

The current breakdown of state-national law enforcement responsibility reflects the will of Congress. Although Congress is empowered to exert a far-ranging regulatory reach, it leaves the regulation of most activities and the definition and enforcement of most crimes to state governments. Yet Congress may exercise its enforcement authority directly when a special federal connection exists, such as when the crime is committed by a member of the armed forces and on the premises of a military base. Or it may exercise its authority indirectly by mandating that the states adopt national enforcement standards.

When Congress enters a new regulatory field, the reason for such a move can usually be traced to the support of politically powerful interest groups or to the American public, or both. Conversely, lack of congressional interest in a regulatory field is understandable when such a move is supported neither by powerful interest groups nor by a significant segment of the American public. This is especially true when a contemplated law is actively opposed.

Substantial public interest in enacting handgun control led to congressional passage in 1993 of the Brady Bill (named for Reagan press secretary James Brady, who was seriously wounded in the 1981 assassination attempt on President Reagan). President Bill Clinton had strongly backed the measure, which was the most significant gun control law enacted in the United States since 1968. The Brady Bill instituted a five-day waiting period for the purchase of handguns, raised licensing fees for gun dealers, and stipulated that the police be informed of multiple gun purchases.

Little public interest is aroused by the notion of professional licensing by the national government. But the idea arouses strong opposition from well-organized and assertive interest groups such as national and state bar and medical associations. Attorneys and physicians are licensed by state government.

One way in which Congress has sought to ensure that states adopt certain regulatory and enforcement actions has been through the use of unfunded mandates. The 1994 anticrime bill, for example, requires states to take certain law enforcement actions, although the federal government provides no money.

The use of unfunded mandates became pervasive in the late 1980s and early 1990s when the federal government, in response to budgetary restraints, sought to pass on to the states the costs of enforcement activities. State governments protested these federal impositions, and in 1995 the Republican-controlled Congress passed restrictions on the use of unfunded mandates. In so doing, Congress sought to reduce the federal government's regulatory role and to give more autonomy to states and localities.

The relationship between the national law enforcement agencies of the executive branch and their counterparts in state and local governments can be characterized most aptly as competitive but cooperative. Federal law enforcement agencies may request, and often receive, investigatory and enforcement assistance from state and local police forces. Such assistance, for example, may be given to locate and arrest a military deserter, an armed robber of a post office, or a counterfeiter, or it may be given in the form of security for a visiting president or foreign dignitary.

The president and the principal law enforcement officers of the national government are reluctant to deny a reasonable request from a state governor for law enforcement assistance. The request may be for troops to put down a riot, as occurred when President Lyndon Johnson sent troops to Detroit in the summer of 1967. More commonly, though, it will involve special federal attention to local problems that either are beyond the competence of state and local resources to resolve or can be resolved more effectively and efficiently with federal assistance.

In April 1995, after the bombing of a federal office building in Oklahoma City, the FBI coordinated a massive effort involving other government departments as well as state and local authorities to identify and apprehend those responsible for the disaster. The FBI received assistance from the Secret Service; Department of Defense; Drug Enforcement Administration; Bureau of Alcohol, Tobacco, and Firearms; Oklahoma National Guard; Oklahoma Department of Public Safety; and Oklahoma City Police Department.[193] Following the 2001 terrorist attacks, the responsibility for coordinating the federal government's response to terrorism was placed in the Department of Homeland Security, created in 2002.

State and local agencies also receive routine assistance from federal law enforcement agencies. Federal agencies distribute law enforcement assistance grants to state and local governments, offer training in modern law enforcement techniques and technology to state and local enforcement officials, and provide intelligence about local criminal activity.

The federal government also may provide assistance to states and localities to carry out extensive crime-fighting programs. The landmark 1994 anticrime bill, signed into law by President Clinton, provided $30.2 billion in federal assistance to states and localities to hire new police officers, build prisons and boot camps, and initiate crime prevention programs, among other measures. *(See box, Presidential Response to Crime, p. 138.)*

In 2001–2002, the federal government provided substantial assistance to states and localities to assist with efforts to combat the threat of terrorism. President George W. Bush proposed increasing such spending by more than tenfold for fiscal year 2003. Among the plans were grants of $2 billion to states and localities to purchase the equipment needed to respond to any terrorist attack, such as chemical and biological detection systems and protective equipment for citizens; $105 million to enable states and localities to develop terrorist attack response plans; and $245 million to support training exercises for providing aid to victims and responding to

PRESIDENTIAL RESPONSE TO CRIME

The president occasionally sets about to bolster the federal government's law enforcement activities in response to public pressures—usually resulting from highly publicized events or persisting problems with crime. For example, in the 1980s public opinion polls frequently identified the drug scourge as one of the nation's leading problems. First Lady Nancy Reagan led a national campaign to stigmatize drug use among the youth. In 1988, with the national elections looming, Congress authorized $2.7 billion for antidrug law enforcement. President Ronald Reagan signed the 1988 antidrug bill on November 18, 1988. Among the law's provisions were:

- Creation of a cabinet-level position for coordinating a national antidrug strategy
- Harsher penalties for drug dealers
- Federal death penalty for major drug traffickers
- Increased funding for drug interdiction
- Denial of federal benefits to repeat drug-use offenders
- Increased funding for drug treatment, prevention, and education.

In the 1990s, numerous highly publicized incidents of violence outside abortion clinics, some resulting in the murders of abortion providers, emboldened pro-choice activists to pressure a sympathetic Democratic Congress and President Bill Clinton to enact the Freedom of Access to Clinic Entrances (FACE) Act of 1993. This law made it a federal crime to block access to an abortion clinic; it prohibited intimidation of either women seeking abortions or clinic employees; and it gave similar protections to pregnancy counseling centers and places of worship. Violators became subject to both criminal and civil penalties.

Supporters of the measure framed the issue as one of law and order. They maintained that local authorities were unable to provide adequate protection, thereby requiring a federal response. Abortion protesters objected that the law constituted an infringement on their freedom of speech rights. In *Madsen v. Women's Health Center, Inc.*, a Supreme Court majority came down in favor of FACE, ruling that the government's interest in preserving order and protecting the constitutional right of abortion permits restrictions on protest activities outside of abortion clinics.

With the reported increase in all types of crime in the 1990s, especially the most violent type, opinion polls continually identified crime as one of the nation's leading problems. In his 1994 State of the Union address, President Clinton brought the issue to the national forefront as he endorsed a substantial increase in the reach of the federal law enforcement authority. This presidential attention to the issue helped to mobilize public support and prod Congress to pass a far-reaching anticrime bill that established a $30.2 billion trust fund to pay for various anticrime programs. Among the initiatives the 1994 crime bill funded were:

- Hiring 100,000 new police officers
- Constructing new prisons and boot camps
- Providing formula grants for local crime reduction programs
- Banning manufacture and possession of nineteen assault weapons
- Authorizing the death penalty for federal crimes that result in death or murder of federal law enforcement officials
- Allowing juveniles thirteen and older accused of certain crimes to be tried as adults in federal court
- Mandating life imprisonment for conviction of a third violent felony (popularly referred to as "three strikes and you're out").

With terrorism having become the focus of the United States in 2001, President George W. Bush proposed a tenfold increase in spending on domestic efforts to combat that threat. Among the initiatives that Bush proposed were:

- Funding to train firefighters, police, and medical personnel to respond to biological and chemical attacks
- Funding for a program to train personnel to respond to attacks and provide aid and assistance to civilians
- Funding for states and localities to develop their own comprehensive plans to respond to terrorist attacks
- Substantial funding for equipment to enable states and localities to respond to terrorist attacks (protective equipment, chemical and biological detection systems).

attacks. By the end of the Bush administration and start of Barack Obama's presidency, however, these figures had declined considerably.

Sharing within the National Government

High school students learn in civics classes that laws are made by Congress, enforced by the president, and applied by the courts. It is by this means that tyranny in the United States is averted: political power in the national government is divided and allocated to separate and independent branches. Each branch, therefore, has some check on the goings-on (and possible abuses) of the others.

Article I, Section 1, of the Constitution assigns the legislative power to Congress. And Article II vests the executive power of the United States in the president and

imposes on the president the obligation to "take Care that the Laws be faithfully executed." Finally, Article III, Section 1, delegates the judicial power of the United States to the Supreme Court and to such other courts as Congress chooses to create.

Still, there is more to this arrangement than the division and allocation of power to separate and independent branches. Power is also shared. Congress, the legislative arm of the national government, makes law according to its constitutional grant of power, but it does so subject to presidential approval or veto, and often at the president's urging. Congress also delegates practical lawmaking power—the authority to promulgate binding administrative rules and regulations—to the president and officers of the executive branch who may or may not report to the president.

Furthermore, although presidents have the authority to enter into treaties with other countries, they share veto power with the Senate, which must ratify the agreements. The president similarly possesses the authority to appoint federal judges and high executive branch officers, but only with the advice and consent of the Senate.

Congress and the President's Law Enforcement Power

Article I, Section 1, of the Constitution states that "[a]ll legislative Powers" of the United States belong to Congress. This power bears directly, extensively, and frequently on the law enforcement obligations and powers of the president. Four categories of power are available to Congress, which, when exercised, may either increase or restrict the law enforcement power of the president. These are lawmaking, investigation, review of presidential appointments, and impeachment.

Lawmaking. Under its lawmaking power, Congress decided that railroads, airlines, and television ought to be regulated by the national government, and Congress determined that national standards ought to apply to the production of food and drugs. The expansion of the national police power is the product of congressional action.

The legislative work of Congress does not end with asserting the regulatory power of the national government. A system and a process must be set in place for enforcing the law. Agencies must be created and empowered. Then they must employ men and women to enforce the law. Finally, law enforcement officers of the executive branch must be granted specific law enforcement authority.

Congress provides the people necessary to staff the president's law enforcement agencies through authorizing legislation, and it provides for payment of their salaries through separate appropriations bills. Through a similar process, it provides enforcement officers with the personnel and material support necessary to do a satisfactory job.

Federal law enforcement agencies and personnel receive two principal forms of authority from Congress: jurisdictional and enforcement. Jurisdictional authority determines the types of laws a given agency is supposed to enforce; enforcement authority provides enforcement officers with the specific powers to make their enforcement effective.

One agency's jurisdiction occasionally overlaps with another's. For example, the Drug Enforcement Administration has primary jurisdiction over enforcement of the nation's narcotics laws. But that jurisdiction overlaps considerably with the jurisdiction given the FBI, the U.S. Customs and Border Protection, the Coast Guard, and the Food and Drug Administration. In an effort to coordinate a federal antidrug strategy, the Office of National Drug Control Policy (ONDCP) was established by Congress as part of the Anti-Drug Control Act of 1988. Congress also created a cabinet-level position to coordinate the nation's antidrug effort. The Office of National Drug Control Policy

is required by law to submit a national drug control strategy to Congress annually. The ONDCP is part of the Executive Office of the President. *(See box, Presidential Response to Crime, p. 138.)*

As for enforcement authority, special agents and other FBI personnel have congressional authority to "carry firearms [and] serve warrants and subpoenas issued under the authority of the United States." Congress has also given them authority to "make arrests without warrant for any offense against the United States committed in their presence, or for any felony cognizable under the laws of the United States if they have reasonable grounds to believe that the person to be arrested has committed or is committing such felony."[194]

Congress has made similar grants of authority to U.S. marshals, agents of the Secret Service and Drug Enforcement Administration, and a host of other federal law enforcement personnel.[195]

Congress also may limit the authority that it confers on federal law enforcement agencies and personnel. Postal inspectors, for example, have authority to "make arrests without warrant for offenses against the United States committed in their presence."[196] However, they can do this only if the offense is related to the property or use of the Postal Service.[197]

Investigations. Congress may affect the law enforcement power of the president through the exercise of its inherent authority to investigate. Investigations may be conducted for the purpose of determining whether new laws are needed or to determine whether existing laws are being properly enforced.

Congressional investigations frequently are conducted by means of committee hearings. Witnesses give their views on the issue before the committee and subject themselves to questions from committee members and counsel. The testimony may be given voluntarily or under compulsion (subpoena). In most instances, a witness will be placed under oath, which allows prosecution of anyone giving false testimony intentionally.

Impressive resources are available to Congress to assist in these investigations. These may include personal and committee staff, researchers of the Library of Congress, economists of the Congressional Budget Office, auditors of the Government Accountability Office, and analysts of the Office of Technology Assessment. The staffs of each of these congressional agencies have established reputations for objective and competent work.

Television has enhanced the significance of congressional investigations. The specter of organized crime in the United States was revealed starkly in the televised investigations of the Kefauver Committee (Special Committee to Investigate Organized Crime in Interstate Commerce) in the 1950s. The American people heard, for the first time, mention of the "mafia" and "la cosa nostra" from witnesses who testified to the power and pervasiveness of these organizations in American society.

RISE OF THE CZARS

Beginning as early as the presidency of Calvin Coolidge, presidents have sought out talented administrators to help them coordinate White House efforts to manage important policy problems. Labeled with a moniker commonly used in the nineteen and early twentieth centuries to indicate a person powerful in a particular area, usually a certain sector of industry, and borrowed from the now-deposed Russian royalty, by the time the federal government began its incredible growth during the Franklin D. Roosevelt administration, the usage of "czars" became a way presidents attempted to improve their policy leadership efforts. As the government continued to grow and—more important—as public expectations for increased presidential leadership grew along with it, the number of czars presidents used also expanded. However, it was only in the early 1970s, during the Richard Nixon administration, when czars became a conventional aspect of presidential management. With the creation of the White House drug czar, a position later given an institutional home as director of the Office of National Drug Control Policy during the George H. W. Bush administration, the idea of having a single powerful White House employee who enjoyed both the trust and the ear of the president became commonplace.

Over the decades, as presidents began to turn to increasing numbers of czars, there were some grumbles of concern about separation of powers and congressional prerogative, but it was not until the early days of Barack Obama's presidency that the practice of using policy czars became cause for wider controversy. Obama, like his immediate predecessors George W. Bush and (to a somewhat lesser extent) Bill Clinton, had structured his bureaucratic operation in such a way that relied on an unprecedented number of czars, a reflection of both the growing complexity of the Executive Office of the President and the need to signal high-profile policy commitments to constituents concerned with particular issues. Obama's nearly three dozen czars prompted congressional hearings and legislative efforts to legally define and statutorily prohibit the practice of employing czars. Although this legislation proved unsuccessful, Obama did reorganize his administration in a manner that reduced the number of czars and, perhaps more symbolically, his staff began actively avoiding any usage of the czar moniker. Whether the practice of using trusted, high-ranking staffers to manage specific problems that span multiple bureaucratic organizations and agencies is over remains an open question, but it seems likely that the rhetorical usage of the czar label, if nothing else, is on its way to becoming an historical oddity.

held hearings on the extraordinary profits being made by oil companies, compelling the chief executive officers of the major oil companies to explain why windfall profit taxes should not be imposed. The hearings, which were closely followed in the news media, appeared to be primarily a public relations tool instead of an in-depth investigation. Members of Congress were eager to show that they were sensitive to the public's outcries about high energy prices. Windfall profit taxes were not imposed on the oil companies.

Review of Presidential Appointments. The president's appointment authority is important to the president's law enforcement power. Congress exercises a considerable restraint on the president's law enforcement power by saying (within constitutional limitations) which offices are subject to presidential appointment and what limitations are imposed on the presidential authority to remove commissioned appointees.

Congress also influences the president's appointment authority by specifying the appointments that must receive Senate confirmation before the appointees may take office. Although most presidential appointees to law enforcement and judicial positions are approved by the Senate, there is less deference to the president in this area today than there used to be. Refusal to confirm is usually based on judgments about the candidate's professional or ethical fitness. Nonetheless, partisan and ideological considerations often play an important role in considering whether to confirm presidential appointees. As the partisan climate in Washington, D.C., has become increasingly polarized, and as more and more of presidential policy and bureaucratic management efforts are included, recent presidents have increasingly turned to the policy czars to help them navigate the policy process, coordinate the enlarging Executive Office of the President, and avoid the costly delays and blockage incurred in the Senate nominations process. *(See box, Rise of the Czars, this page.)*

The effect of Senate approval on the presidential appointment power, however, cannot be measured solely by reference to the number of times the Senate refuses to confirm. Knowing that appointees must be examined and

Separate Senate and House committees investigated alleged criminal activities committed during the Nixon administration, after burglars traced to the White House were arrested during a break-in of the Democratic National Committee headquarters at the Watergate complex in Washington, D.C. In 1987 a joint committee of Congress investigated the circumstances surrounding the Iran-contra affair. In 1998 the House Judiciary Committee investigated allegations that President Bill Clinton had committed perjury and obstruction of justice in the course of a sexual harassment lawsuit brought against him. After extremely contentious hearings, the committee, voting along party lines, recommended articles of impeachment against the president.

Most congressional investigations are not nearly so spectacular, but they are important nevertheless. For example, in 1987 a subcommittee of the House Committee on Interior and Insular Affairs conducted an investigation into the enforcement of federal law by the Nuclear Regulatory Commission. Its findings were critical, as is indicated by the title of its report: *NRC Coziness with Industry: Nuclear Regulatory Commission Fails to Maintain Arms' Length Relationship with the Nuclear Industry.*[198] In 2005 the Senate

Andrew Johnson was the first of only two U.S. presidents to be impeached. In 1868 Congress failed by one vote to remove Johnson from office. In December 1998 President Bill Clinton was impeached by the House of Representatives, but the Senate vote fell far short of the two-thirds majority needed to convict him.

Representatives determines whether probable cause exists to believe that misconduct warranting removal has occurred and that the accused is culpable.[199] Acting much like a grand jury in a criminal case, the House considers charges of misconduct, hears evidence about the alleged acts of misconduct, and makes a preliminary determination of whether the alleged misconduct, if true, warrants removal, and whether the evidence supports the charges. If the House, by a majority vote, considers the allegations of misconduct sufficiently serious to warrant removal and they are supported by the evidence, it reports one or more articles of impeachment to the Senate for trial.

In its proceedings, the Senate acts much like a trial jury in a criminal case. With the chief justice of the United States presiding, its function is to convict or acquit for each article of impeachment, based on evidence heard in a trial conducted in the Senate chambers. Guilt or innocence is determined by a two-thirds vote of the senators present.[200]

No consensus exists on the meaning of "Treason, Bribery, or other high Crimes and Misdemeanors," the constitutionally stated grounds for removal by impeachment. Alexander Hamilton described the impeachment power as political, for it would be applied to persons committing "injuries done immediately to society itself."[201] Such injuries would include not only treason and bribery, but also such criminal acts as murder, rape, and mayhem. It is not clear that "high Crimes and Misdemeanors" include a violation of the Constitution, a statute not providing criminal penalties, or a failure to enforce the law.

Only two presidents have been impeached (that is, charged) to date. In 1868 the House charged President Andrew Johnson with violating the Tenure of Office Act of 1867.[202] Specifically, the House charged the president with violating his constitutional obligation to take care that the laws are executed faithfully by firing Edwin M. Stanton, his secretary of war, without cause and without prior Senate consent. The Senate, however, failed by one vote to muster the two-thirds majority necessary to convict Johnson.

The precedent furnished by Johnson's ordeal is primarily negative. A narrow interpretation of the precedent would hold that the Senate merely confirmed that violation of the Tenure of Office Act, a legislative measure of dubious constitutional validity, did not constitute a sufficient basis for removal of the president.[203] A broader reading of the Senate's action would find significant the failure of the

confirmed by the Senate may well cause presidents to make their selections carefully. Moreover, knowing that nominees will be subjected to Senate scrutiny should cause the president to insist that backgrounds be subjected to searching investigation before names are announced and submitted.

Impeachment. The ultimate congressional check on executive law enforcement power is removal from office through the impeachment process. Article II, Section 4, of the Constitution gives Congress the power to remove from office the president, vice president, "and all civil Officers of the United States," upon impeachment for and conviction of "Treason, Bribery, or other high Crimes and Misdemeanors."

The removal process is conducted in two stages: impeachment and trial. In the first stage, the House of

Senate to remove a president for what was really political incompatibility.

In 1998 the House of Representatives impeached President Bill Clinton on charges that he had committed perjury and obstructed justice in a lawsuit brought against him by Paula Jones for sexual harassment while he was governor of Arkansas. Clinton thus became the first elected president in history to be impeached. After a Senate trial, the upper chamber voted not to remove Clinton from office.

The Clinton impeachment was highly controversial because of the circumstances surrounding the charges of perjury and obstruction of justice. Clinton had lied in a legal deposition in the sexual harassment suit when he claimed that he had never had a sexual relationship with White House intern Monica Lewinsky. The president's defenders asserted that his indiscretion was merely a personal one and did not deserve the ultimate constitutional punishment of an impeachment. Advocates of impeachment argued that the president was the nation's top law enforcement official and that the crimes of perjury and obstruction of justice were therefore serious enough to merit impeachment, regardless of the circumstances that led to the president's actions.

Another contemporary example of the impeachment power being used against a president is furnished by the events leading to the resignation of President Nixon in 1974. In 1972 employees of the Committee to Re-elect the President, Nixon's personal campaign organization, were arrested by District of Columbia police during a burglary of the Democratic Party headquarters in Washington's Watergate complex.

Investigations by local and federal law enforcement agencies, a federal grand jury, a Senate investigative committee, and a special prosecutor, as well as newspaper and broadcast journalists, revealed evidence not only of involvement by high- and mid-level members and former members of the Nixon administration in the burglary but also of various other allegedly unlawful activities. An impeachment bill was introduced on the House floor and referred to the House Committee on the Judiciary.

After televised hearings, the committee voted to recommend three articles of impeachment to the House. Each one of the three articles charged the president with violating his oath of office and his constitutional obligation to take care that the laws be faithfully executed. The three articles then enumerated specific allegations of misconduct, which, a majority of the committee believed, warranted Nixon's removal: obstruction of justice, abuse of power, abuse of individual rights, misprision (concealment) of a felony, and failure to comply with congressional subpoenas. The House never voted on the three articles because of Nixon's resignation.

Instead of facing certain impeachment, Nixon resigned from office on August 9, 1974. Still, the committee action remains a powerful reminder that the removal power of Congress is not entirely dormant. The circumstances warranting its use must be serious, and the charges must be backed by compelling evidence—a "smoking gun" was the phrase often used by some committee members.

The Judiciary and the President. The judiciary arbitrates and resolves legal disputes according to the law. In doing so, it both supports and checks presidential law enforcement authority. It also creates law enforcement opportunities and burdens for the president and makes law through the process of interpreting law.

The judiciary supports the president's law enforcement power by holding that presidential claims of authority are in accord with the Constitution and laws of the United States. Such pronouncements usually settle any immediate disputes between the president and Congress or the states over the existence and extent of specific presidential law enforcement powers, and they offer reassurance to the American people that their president acted within the law.

The judiciary also supports the president's law enforcement power by invalidating efforts by other political actors, usually Congress and the states, to restrict the president's authority unduly.

Americans witnessed the first type of support for presidential power when the Supreme Court upheld in 1863 assertions of presidential power to deploy military forces to suppress a domestic insurrection (the Civil War) and in 1895 assertions of presidential power to quell strikes inhibiting interstate movement of railroads and delivery of the U.S. mail.[204] Similarly, the Supreme Court upheld in 1890 presidential discretion to use U.S. marshals to maintain peace in situations neither contemplated nor prohibited by legislation.[205] The Court also has protected the president from congressional interference with the power to grant pardons, reprieves, and amnesties.[206]

American judges, however, are an independent lot, constitutionally and in fact. They are not appointed to be mere supporters of the president, and they do not define their own roles in that manner. They have authority to check presidential claims of law enforcement power, and they have the power to make their own authority felt.

The judiciary most often checks the president's law enforcement authority when judges rule against the government in civil or criminal cases. The ruling may be on an important interpretation of law, on the admissibility in a trial of a critical piece of evidence, or on the facts of the case.

When the rulings involve an interpretation of constitutionally or legislatively delegated authority of the president, then the effect may limit the executive law enforcement capability in future cases as well as in the immediate case. Federal law enforcement agents know, for example, that a confession obtained through coercion cannot be used as evidence in a trial.

NOTES

1 Peter Woll, *American Bureaucracy,* 2d ed. (New York: Norton, 1977), 63.

2 Alexander Hamilton, *Federalist* No. 72, in Alexander Hamilton, James Madison, and John Jay, *The Federalist Papers* (New York: Tudor, 1937), 64.

3 Clinton Rossiter, *The American Presidency,* 3d ed. (New York: Harcourt Brace Jovanovich, 1963).

4 Charles T. Goodsell, *The Case for Bureaucracy* (Chatham, N.J.: Chatham House, 1983), 2.

5 H. H. Gerth and C. Wright Mills, *From Max Weber* (New York: Oxford University Press, 1946), 196–199.

6 David Wood, "James Jones, Obama's National Security Adviser, Resigns," *Politics Daily,* October 8, 2010. See also Bob Woodward, *Obama's Wars* (New York: Simon and Schuster, 2010).

7 Data taken from the *President's Budget for FY 2012,* Historical Table 17.1.

8 George J. Gordon, *Public Administration in America,* 2d ed. (New York: St. Martin's Press, 1982), 297.

9 Quoted in Robert Sherrill, *Why They Call It Politics,* 4th ed. (New York: Harcourt Brace Jovanovich, 1984), 260.

10 Kenneth Dodge et al., "Coming of Age: The Department of Education," *Phi Delta Kappan,* Papers from the Duke University Education Leadership Summit, May 2002.

11 Robert Brodsky, "Obama's Performance Agenda a Mix of Old and New," *Government Executive,* May 29, 2009, www.govexec.com/oversight/2009/05/obamas-performance-agenda-a-mix-of-old-and-new/29268/.

12 Michael Nelson, "The Irony of American Bureaucracy," in *Bureaucratic Power in National Policy Making,* 4th ed., ed. Francis E. Rourke (Boston: Little, Brown, 1986), 163–187.

13 Ibid., 169.

14 Sherrill, *Why They Call It Politics,* 259.

15 Quoted in Ibid.

16 Quoted in Richard E. Neustadt, *Presidential Power* (New York: Wiley, 1960), 22.

17 Arthur M. Schlesinger Jr., *The Crisis of Confidence* (Boston: Houghton Mifflin, 1969), 291.

18 Richard M. Pious, *The American Presidency* (New York: Basic Books, 1979), 212.

19 Thomas E. Cronin, *The State of the Presidency,* 2d ed. (Boston: Little, Brown, 1980), 333.

20 Richard Rose, *Managing Presidential Objectives* (New York: Free Press, 1976), 23.

21 David E. Lewis, *The Politics of Presidential Appointments: Political Control and Bureaucratic Performance* (Princeton: Princeton University Press, 2008).

22 Shirley Anne Warshaw, "Ideological Conflict in the President's Cabinet," in *Transforming the American Polity: The Presidency of George W. Bush and the War on Terrorism,* ed. Richard S. Conley. (Indianapolis, Ind.: Prentice Hall, 2005).

23 Rossiter, *American Presidency,* 129.

24 Stephen Hess, *Organizing the Presidency* (Washington, D.C.: Brookings, 1988), 6.

25 David Truman, *The Governmental Process* (New York: Knopf, 1951); Hess, *Organizing the Presidency;* and George Reedy, *The Twilight of the Presidency* (New York: World, 1970).

26 Rose, *Managing Presidential Objectives,* 147.

27 Cronin, *State of the Presidency,* 225.

28 Alexander Hamilton, *Federalist* No. 70, in Alexander Hamilton, James Madison, and John Jay, *The Federalist Papers* (New York: Tudor, 1937), 49–50.

29 McGeorge Bundy, *The Strength of Government* (Cambridge: Harvard University Press, 1968), 37.

30 Andrew Rudalevige, *Managing the President's Program: Presidential Leadership and Legislative Policy Formulation* (Princeton: Princeton University Press, 2002).

31 Woll, *American Bureaucracy,* 241.

32 Ibid., 240.

33 Executive Office of the President, President's Special Review Board 1987, *Report of the President's Special Review Board (Tower Commission Report)* (Washington, D.C.: Government Printing Office, 1987).

34 Anthony Downs, *Inside Bureaucracy* (Boston: Little, Brown, 1967), 116–118.

35 Office of Management and Budget, *President's Management Agenda, FY 2002* (Washington, D.C.: Government Printing Office, 2001).

36 *Mandate for Leadership* (Washington, D.C.: Heritage Foundation, 2000).

37 Arthur M. Schlesinger Jr., *A Thousand Days: John F. Kennedy in the White House* (Boston: Houghton Mifflin, 1965), 683.

38 Cronin, *State of the Presidency,* 226.

39 Louis W. Koenig, *The Chief Executive* (New York: Harcourt Brace and World, 1968), 417.

40 Richard P. Nathan, *The Plot That Failed: Nixon and the Administrative Presidency* (New York: Wiley, 1975), 82.

41 "President Nixon Finds a Real Garbageman to Woo Garbagemen," *Wall Street Journal,* June 21, 1972, 1, 25.

42 Richard P. Nathan, "The Administrative Presidency," in *Bureaucratic Power in National Policy Making,* 4th ed., ed. Francis E. Rourke (Boston: Little, Brown, 1986), 216. See also Richard P. Nathan, *The Administrative Presidency* (New York: Macmillan, 1986).

43 Dwight D. Eisenhower, *The White House Years: Mandate for Change, 1953–1956* (Garden City, N.Y.: Doubleday, 1963), 114.

44 Hess, *Organizing the Presidency,* 2.

45 Frank Kessler, *The Dilemmas of Presidential Leadership: Of Caretakers and Kings* (Englewood Cliffs, N.J.: Prentice Hall, 1982), 60.

46 Hess, *Organizing the Presidency,* 3–4.

47 Quoted in Koenig, *Chief Executive,* 193.

48 Kessler, *Dilemmas of Presidential Leadership,* 72.

49 William Safire, *Before the Fall* (Garden City, N.Y.: Doubleday, 1975); and Henry Kissinger, *The White House Years* (Boston: Little, Brown, 1979).

50 Charles O. Jones, *The Presidency in a Separated System* (Washington, D.C.: Brookings, 1994).

51 Ibid., 103.

52 *Congressional Quarterly Weekly Report,* July 21, 1979, 1432.

53 Kessler, *Dilemmas of Presidential Leadership,* 68.

54 Colin Campbell, *Managing the Presidency: Carter, Reagan, and the Search for Executive Harmony* (Pittsburgh: University of Pittsburgh Press, 1986), 61.

55 Quoted in Ibid., 71.

56 Paul Quirk, "Presidential Competence," in *The Presidency and the Political System,* 2d ed., ed. Michael Nelson (Washington, D.C.: CQ Press, 1988).

57 *Tower Commission Report,* IV–10.

58 Elizabeth Drew, *On the Edge: The Clinton Presidency* (New York: Simon and Schuster, 1994), 98.

59 Shirley Anne Warshaw, "Clashing Ideologies in the Clinton White House," paper presented at the Clinton Presidential Conference, Hofstra University, November 2005.

60 Ibid., 102.

61   Ibid., 241.

62   See Kathryn Dunn Tenpas and Stephen Hess, "The Bush White House: First Appraisals," background paper, Brookings, Washington, D.C., January 30, 2002.

63   Ibid.

64   Philip H. Gordon, "Bush's Second Term Blues," Brookings, Washington, D.C., May-June 2007, www.brookings.edu/articles/2007/05politics_gordon.aspx.

65   See Shirley Anne Warshaw, "The Obama Cabinet: A Team of Rivals or Pragmatic Governance?" in *The Obama Presidency: Change and Continuity*, ed. Andrew J. Dowdle, Dirk C. Van Raemdonck, and Robert Maranto (New York: Routledge, 2011).

66   Woll, *American Bureaucracy*, 11.

67   Pious, *American Presidency*, 222.

68   Joel D. Aberbach, *Keeping a Watchful Eye: The Politics of Congressional Oversight* (Washington, D.C.: Brookings, 1990), 35.

69   Pious, *American Presidency*, 224.

70   Allen Schick, "Politics through Law: Congressional Limitations on Executive Discretion," in *Both Ends of the Avenue: The Presidency, the Executive Branch, and the Congress in the 1980s*, ed. Anthony King (Washington, D.C.: American Enterprise Institute, 1983), 176.

71   *Immigration and Naturalization Service v. Chadha*, 462 U.S. 919 (1983).

72   Quoted in Martin Tolchin, "The Legislative Veto: An Accommodation That Goes on and on," *New York Times*, March 31, 1989, 8.

73   Thomas Franck and Edward Weisband, *Foreign Policy by Congress* (New York: Oxford University Press, 1979).

74   Pious, *American Presidency*, 229.

75   Executive Office of the President, President's Committee on Administrative Management, *Brownlow Commission Report* (Washington, D.C.: Government Printing Office, 1937), 5.

76   Ibid., 6–7.

77   Peri E. Arnold, *Making the Managerial President: Comprehensive Reorganization Planning, 1905–1980* (Princeton: Princeton University Press, 1986), 114–115.

78   Commission on the Organization of the Executive Branch of Government, *General Management of the Executive Branch* (Washington, D.C.: Government Printing Office, 1949).

79   Ibid., 34.

80   Arnold, *Making the Managerial President*, 159.

81   Ibid., 177–193.

82   Ibid., 277.

83   Tyrus G. Fain, ed., *Federal Reorganization: The Executive Branch*, Public Document Series (New York: Bowker, 1977), xxxi.

84   See, for example, Koenig, *Chief Executive*, chap. 8.

85   James P. Pfiffner, "Strangers in a Strange Land: Orienting New Presidential Appointees," in *The In-and-Outers: Presidential Appointees and Transient Government in Washington*, ed. G. Calvin Mackenzie (Baltimore: Johns Hopkins University Press, 1987), 141. The total number of appointees is based on data from the Center for Excellence in Government, February 1989.

86   Hugh Heclo, *A Government of Strangers: Executive Politics in Washington* (Washington, D.C.: Brookings, 1977), 94.

87   Niccolo Machiavelli, *The Prince* (Harmonsworth, Middlesex, England: Penguin, 1961), 124.

88   Quoted in Schlesinger, *Thousand Days*, 127.

89   Pfiffner, "Strangers in a Strange Land," 142.

90   Richard F. Fenno Jr., *The President's Cabinet* (New York: Vintage, 1958), 51.

91   G. Calvin Mackenzie, *The Politics of Presidential Appointments* (New York: Free Press, 1981), 6.

92   Drew, *On the Edge*, 33–34, 99–101.

93   Bradley H. Patterson Jr., "The New Bush White House Staff: Choices Being Made," *White House Studies* 1, no. 2 (2001): 235.

94   Warshaw, "The Obama Cabinet," 51–64.

95   2010 Annual Report to Congress on White House Staff, www.whitehouse.gov/briefing-room/disclosures/annual-records/2010.

96   Cronin, *State of the Presidency*, 164.

97   U.S. Commission on Executive, Legislative, and Judicial Salaries, *Report of the Commission on Executive, Legislative, and Judicial Salaries* (Washington, D.C.: Government Printing Office, 1980), ix, 1.

98   Gary Burtless, *How Much Is Enough?: Setting Pay for Presidential Appointees*, report commissioned by Brookings, Presidential Appointee Initiative, Washington, D.C., March 22, 2002.

99   Quoted in Dick Kirschten, "Why Not the Best?" *National Journal*, June 12, 1982, 1064.

100   Stephen L. Carter, *The Confirmation Mess* (New York: Basic Books, 1994), 7.

101   Mackenzie, *Politics of Presidential Appointments*, 95.

102   Cronin, *State of the Presidency*, 165.

103   Christopher J. Deering, "Damned If You Do and Damned If You Don't: The Senate's Role in the Appointments Process," in *The In-and-Outers: Presidential Appointees and Transient Government in Washington*, ed. G. Calvin Mackenzie (Baltimore: Johns Hopkins University Press, 1987), 119.

104   "Critical Posts in the Bush Administration Remain Vacant as Congressional Session Nears End," *Brookings Institution Report*, December 18, 2001.

105   Deering, "Damned If You Do," 117.

106   Walter J. Oleszek, "Proposals to Reform 'Holds' in the Senate." Congressional Research Service, 2007.

107   Paul Kane, "Senate Leaders Agree on Changes in Filibuster, Confirmation Process," *Washington Post*, January 28, 2011.

108   Dom Bonafede, "The White House Personnel Office from Roosevelt to Reagan," in *The In-and-Outers: Presidential Appointees and Transient Government in Washington*, ed. G. Calvin Mackenzie (Baltimore: Johns Hopkins University Press, 1987), 32.

109   See John P. Burke, *The Institutional Presidency* (Baltimore: Johns Hopkins University Press, 1992), chap. 4.

110   John W. Macy, Bruce Adams, and J. Jackson Walter, *America's Unelected Government: Appointing the President's Team* (Cambridge: Ballinger, 1983), 32.

111   Quoted in Edward D. Feigenbaum, "Staffing, Organization, and Decision-Making in the Ford and Carter White Houses," *Presidential Studies Quarterly* (summer 1980): 371.

112   Bonafede, "White House Personnel Office."

113   Quoted in Ibid., 48.

114   Macy, Adams, and Walter, *America's Unelected Government*, 39.

115   David E. Lewis, "Presidential Appointments in the Obama Administration: An Early Evaluation," in *The Obama Presidency: Change and Continuity*, ed. Andrew J. Dowdle, Dirk C. Van Raemdonck, and Robert Maranto (New York: Routledge, 2011), 5.

116   Ibid.

117   *Myers v. United States*, 272 U.S. 52 (1926).

118   Quoted in Woll, *American Bureaucracy*, 224.

119   *Humphrey's Executor v. United States*, 295 U.S. 602 (1935).

120   *Wiener v. United States*, 357 U.S. 349 (1958).

121   *Morrison v. Olson*, 487 U.S. 654 (1988).

122   Ibid.

123   Pious, *American Presidency*, 256.

124   Lyndon Baines Johnson, *The Vantage Point* (New York: Holt, Rinehart, and Winston, 1971), 34.

125   Lance T. LeLoup, "Fiscal Chief: Presidents and the Budget," in *The Presidency: Studies in Policy Making,* ed. Stephen A. Shull and Lance T. LeLoup (Brunswick, Ohio: King's Court, 1979), 211.

126   Johnson, *Vantage Point,* 36.

127   Gerald Ford, "Budget Message of the President," *The Budget of the United States Government, Fiscal Year 1978* (Washington, D.C.: Government Printing Office, 1977), M–3.

128   Dennis S. Ippolito, *The Budget and National Politics* (San Francisco: Freeman, 1978), 40.

129   *U.S. Statutes at Large* 42 (1921): 20, sec. 206.

130   Office of Management and Budget, *Preparation and Submission of 1977 "Current Services" Budget Estimates,* Bulletin No. 76–4 (Washington, D.C.: Government Printing Office, 1975), 1.

131   Howard E. Shuman, *Politics and the Budget: The Struggle between the President and the Congress* (Englewood Cliffs, N.J.: Prentice Hall, 1984), 225.

132   *Budget of the United States, Fiscal Year 1983: Major Themes and Additional Budget Details* (Washington, D.C.: Government Printing Office, 1982), 37.

133   Aaron Wildavsky, "Constitutional Expenditure Limitation and Congressional Budget Reform," in *The Congressional Budget Process after Five Years,* ed. Rudolph G. Penner (Washington, D.C.: American Enterprise Institute, 1981), 99.

134   Hedrick Smith, *The Power Game* (New York: Random House, 1988), 290.

135   Shuman, *Politics and the Budget,* 287.

136   Richard Wolf, "Federal Deficit Estimate Down to $296B," *USA TODAY,* July 11, 2006; Andrew Taylor, "Budget Deficit Estimates See Contraction," *Associated Press,* January 24, 2007.

137   Congressional Budget Office, "The Budget and Economic Outlook: Fiscal Years 2011 to 2021," January 2011, www.cbo.gov/publication/21999.

138   Martin Crutsinger, "Federal Deficit Totaled $1.23T through August," Associated Press, September 13, 2011.

139   Pious, *American Presidency,* 272.

140   Shuman, *Politics and the Budget,* 60.

141   *New York Times,* February 10, 1982, A1.

142   Congressional Budget Office, "The Budget and Economic Outlook: Fiscal Years 2011 to 2021."

143   Drew, *On the Edge,* 109.

144   Louis Fisher, *Presidential Spending Power* (Princeton: Princeton University Press, 1975), 7.

145   Pious, *American Presidency,* 278.

146   Fisher, *Presidential Spending Power,* 207.

147   *U.S. Statutes at Large* 88 (1974): 1804, sec. 32.

148   Quoted in Pious, *American Presidency,* 278.

149   Ippolito, *Budget and National Politics,* 138–139.

150   *Train v. City of New York,* 420 U.S. 35 (1975).

151   *Immigration and Naturalization Service v. Chadha,* 462 U.S. 919 (1983).

152   John Ellwood and James Thurber, "The Congressional Budget Process Re-examined," in *Congress Reconsidered,* 2d ed., ed. Lawrence C. Dodd and Bruce I. Oppenheimer (Washington, D.C.: CQ Press, 1981), 266.

153   Lori Montgomery, "President Obama Seeks New Version of Line-Item Veto," *Washington Post,* Mary 25, 2010.

154   Letter of John Marshall to James Wilkinson, January 5, 1787, reprinted in *The Papers of John Marshall, 1775–1788,* vol. 1, ed. Herbert A. Johnson (Chapel Hill: University of North Carolina Press, 1974), 200.

155   Samuel Eliot Morison, Henry Steele Commager, and William E. Leuchtenburg, *The Growth of the American Republic,* vol. 1 (New York: Oxford University Press, 1969), 242. Pages 227–261 of this volume describe the events immediately preceding and during the Constitutional Convention.

156   Article II of the Constitution enumerates presidential powers.

157   Article I, Section 8, of the Constitution gives Congress authority to "pay the Debts and provide for . . . the general Welfare of the United States." This is interpreted as a grant of authority for Congress to spend money to promote the general welfare of the nation. It is not interpreted as a grant of authority to enact any regulatory scheme that Congress believes will promote the general welfare.

158   *McCulloch v. Maryland,* 17 U.S. (4 Wheat.) 316 (1819).

159   *Gibbons v. Ogden,* 22 U.S. (9 Wheat.) 1 (1824).

160   *Wickard v. Filburn,* 317 U.S. 111 (1942).

161   What, for example, is the relationship between home-grown food for purely household consumption and interstate commerce? The Supreme Court gave its answer in *Wickard v. Filburn:* If a household grows and harvests food on its own land, and for its own use, then it will be less likely to purchase food products on the commercial market. The effects of this isolated instance of self-sufficiency will eventually be felt across state lines.

162   The most controversial of the nine cases was *Wards Cove Packing Co. v. Antonio,* 109 S.Ct. (1989).

163   U.S. Department of Commerce, Bureau of the Census, *Historical Statistics of the United States: Colonial Times to 1970,* vol. 2 (Washington, D.C.: Government Printing Office, 1975), table Y 308–317, 1102–1103; and U.S. Department of Commerce, Bureau of the Census, *Statistical Abstract of the United States,* 115th ed. (Washington, D.C.: Government Printing Office, 1995), table 527, "Federal Civilian Employment by Branch, Agency, and Area."

164   Office of Personnel Management, Historical Federal Workforce Tables, Total Government Employment Since 1962, www.opm.gov/feddata/HistoricalTables/TotalGovernmentSince1962.asp.

165   Accounts of the Ole Miss incident may be found in Schlesinger, *Thousand Days,* and in Theodore C. Sorensen, *Kennedy* (New York: Harper and Row, 1965).

166   *Myers v. United States,* 272 U.S. 52, 177 (1926).

167   See, for example, *Kendall v. United States,* 37 U.S. (12 Pet.) 524 (1838); *Youngstown Sheet and Tube Co. v. Sawyer,* 343 U.S. 579 (1952) (also known as the *Steel Seizure Case*); and *United States v. Nixon,* 418 U.S. 683 (1974).

168   *In re Neagle,* 135 U.S. 1 (1890).

169   The strike began when the Pullman Palace Car Company cut the wages of its workers and the company refused an offer of arbitration by the American Railway Union.

170   *In re Debs,* 158 U.S. 564 (1895).

171   *Myers v. United States.*

172   *Wiener v. United States;* and *Humphrey's Executor v. United States.*

173   *In re Debs.*

174   *Ex parte Milligan.*

175   David E. Graham, "The US Judicial Response to Post-9/11 Executive Temerity and Congressional Acquiescence," Foundation for Law, Justice, and Society website, www.fljs.org.

176   Jonathan Mahler, *The Challenge: Hamdan v. Rumsfeld and the Fight over Presidential Power* (New York: Farrar, Straus, and Giroux, 2008).

177   Alexander Hamilton, *Federalist* No. 74, in Alexander Hamilton, James Madison, and John Jay, *The Federalist Papers* (New York: Mentor, 1961), 449.

178   Ibid., 448.

179   Proclamation of September 15, 1792, George Washington, *Messages and Papers of the Presidents, 1789–1897,* vol. I, ed. James D. Richardson (Washington, D.C.: Government Printing Office, 1897), 124–125.

180   See Proclamation of July 10, 1795, George Washington, *Messages and Papers of the Presidents, 1789–1897,* vol. I, ed. James D. Richardson (Washington, D.C.: Government Printing Office, 1897), 181.

181   *Ex parte Garland,* 71 U.S. (4 Wall.) 333 (1866). See generally *Schick v. Reed,* 419 U.S. 256 (1974).

182   *U.S. Statutes at Large* 26 (1891): 946.

183   David G. Adler, "The President's Pardon Power," in *Inventing the American Presidency,* ed. Thomas E. Cronin (Lawrence: University Press of Kansas, 1989), 212, 218–219.

184   Forrest McDonald, *The American Presidency* (Lawrence: University Press of Kansas, 1994), 282.

185   *Wiener v. United States; Humphrey's Executor v. United States.*

186   Executive Order 11365, July 29, 1967.

187   Kerner was later rewarded by the president with appointment to the U.S. Court of Appeals for the Seventh Circuit, but he eventually resigned after being indicted and convicted of a felony.

188   Office of the President, National Advisory Commission on Civil Disorders, *Report of the National Advisory Commission on Civil Disorders* (Washington, D.C.: Government Printing Office, 1968).

189   U.S. Department of Justice, "FY 2011 Performance Budget Congressional Submission."

190   *McCulloch v. Maryland* 17 U.S. (4 Wheat.) 316 (1819).

191   *Gibbons v. Ogden.*

192   *Martin v. Hunter's Lessee,* 14 U.S. (1 Wheat.) 304 (1816); and *Cohens v. Virginia,* 19 U.S. (6 Wheat.) 264 (1821).

193   David Johnston, "Just Before He Was to Be Freed, Prime Bombing Suspect Is Identified in Jail," *New York Times,* April 22, 1995, 10.

194   *U.S. Code,* vol. 18, sec. 3052.

195   See *U.S. Code,* vol. 18, secs. 3053 (U.S. marshals) and 3056 (Secret Service); and *U.S. Code,* vol. 21, sec. 878 (Drug Enforcement Administration).

196   *U.S. Code,* vol. 18, sec. 3061 (a) (2).

197   *U.S. Code,* vol. 18, sec. 3061 (b).

198   U.S. Congress, House, Committee on Interior and Insular Affairs, Subcommittee on General Oversight and Investigations, *NRC Coziness with Industry: Nuclear Regulatory Commission Fails to Maintain Arms' Length Relationship with the Nuclear Industry,* Committee Print No. 5, 100th Cong., 1st sess., 1987.

199   U.S. Constitution, Article I, Section 2.

200   U.S. Constitution, Article I, Section 3.

201   Alexander Hamilton, *Federalist* No. 65, in Alexander Hamilton, James Madison, and John Jay, *The Federalist Papers* (New York: Mentor, 1961), 396.

202   *U.S. Statutes at Large* 14 (1867): 430.

203   Compare *Myers v. United States.*

204   *Prize Cases*; and *In re Debs.*

205   *In re Neagle.*

206   *Ex parte Garland.*

SELECTED BIBLIOGRAPHY

Aberbach, Joel D. *Keeping a Watchful Eye: The Politics of Congressional Oversight.* Washington, D.C.: Brookings, 1990.

Aberbach, Joel D., and Mark A. Peterson, eds. *The Executive Branch.* Oxford: Oxford University Press, 2005.

Aberbach, Joel D., and Bert A. Rockman. *In the Web of Politics: Three Decades of the U.S. Federal Executive.* Washington, D.C.: Brookings, 2000.

Arnold, Peri E. *Making the Managerial President: Comprehensive Reorganization Planning, 1905–1980.* Princeton: Princeton University Press, 1986.

Baker, Nancy V. *Conflicting Loyalties: Law and Politics in the Attorney General's Office, 1789–1990.* Lawrence: University Press of Kansas, 1992.

Bundy, McGeorge. *The Strength of Government.* Cambridge: Harvard University Press, 1968.

Burke, John P. *The Institutional Presidency.* Baltimore: Johns Hopkins University Press, 1992.

Campbell, Colin. *Managing the Presidency: Carter, Reagan, and the Search for Executive Harmony.* Pittsburgh: University of Pittsburgh Press, 1986.

Carpenter, Daniel P. *The Forging of Bureaucratic Autonomy: Reputations, Networks, and Policy Innovation in Executive Agencies, 1862–1928.* Princeton: Princeton University Press, 2001.

Carter, Stephen L. *The Confirmation Mess: Cleaning Up the Federal Appointments Process.* New York: Basic Books, 1994.

Dodd, Lawrence C., and Richard L. Schott. *Congress and the Administrative State.* New York: Macmillan, 1986.

Edwards, George C., III. "Why Not the Best: The Loyalty-Competence Trade-off in Presidential Appointments." *Brookings Review* 19 (spring 2001): 12–16.

Fain, Tyrus G., ed. *Federal Reorganization: The Executive Branch.* Public Document Series. New York: Bowker, 1977.

Fenno, Richard F., Jr. *The President's Cabinet.* New York: Vintage, 1958.

Fisher, Louis. *The Politics of Shared Power: Congress and the Executive.* 4th ed. College Station: Texas A&M Press, 2000.

Golden, Marissa Martino. *What Motivates Bureaucrats? Politics and Administration During the Reagan Years.* New York: Columbia University Press, 2000.

Heclo, Hugh. *A Government of Strangers: Executive Politics in Washington.* Washington, D.C.: Brookings, 1977.

Hess, Stephen. *Organizing the Presidency,* 3d ed. Washington, D.C.: Brookings, 2002.

Ippolito, Dennis S. *The Budget and National Politics.* San Francisco: Freeman, 1978.

Jones, Charles O. *The Presidency in a Separated System.* Washington, D.C.: Brookings, 1994.

Kramer, Fred A. *Contemporary Approaches to Public Budgeting.* Cambridge: Winthrop, 1979.

LeLoup, Lance T. *Budgetary Politics.* 2d ed. Brunswick, Ohio: King's Court, 1980.

Lewis, David E. *Presidents and the Policy of Agency Design: Political Insulation in the United States Government Bureaucracy, 1946–1997.* Stanford: Stanford University Press, 2003.

———. "Testing Pendleton's Premise: Do Political Appointees Make Worse Bureaucrats? *Journal of Politics* 69 (November 2007): 1073–88.

———. *The Politics of Presidential Appointments: Political Control and Bureaucratic Performance.* Princeton: Princeton University Press, 2008.

Mackenzie, G. Calvin. *The Politics of Presidential Appointments.* New York: Free Press, 1981.

———, ed. *The In-and-Outers: Presidential Appointees and Transient Government in Washington.* Baltimore: Johns Hopkins University Press, 1987.

Macy, John W., Bruce Adams, and J. Jackson Walter. *America's Unelected Government: Appointing the President's Team.* Cambridge: Ballinger, 1983.

McDonald, Forrest. *The American Presidency: An Intellectual History.* Lawrence: University Press of Kansas, 1994.

Nathan, Richard P. *The Administrative Presidency.* New York: Macmillan, 1986.

Nelson, Michael. *The Presidency and the Political System.* 9th ed. Washington, D.C.: CQ Press, 2009.

Nichols, David K. *The Myth of the Modern Presidency.* University Park: Pennsylvania State University Press, 1994.

Rossiter, Clinton L. *The American Presidency.* 3d ed. New York: Harcourt Brace Jovanovich, 1963.

Rourke, Francis E., ed. *Bureaucratic Power in National Policy Making.* 4th ed. Boston: Little, Brown, 1986.

Rozell, Mark J. *Executive Privilege: Presidential Power, Secrecy, and Accountability.* 2d ed. Lawrence: University Press of Kansas, 2002.

Rudalevige, Andrew. *Managing the President's Program: Presidential Leadership and Legislative Policy Formulation.* Princeton: Princeton University Press, 2003.

Shull, Steven A. *Policy by Other Means: Alternative Adoption by Presidents.* College Station: Texas A&M University Press, 2006.

Smith, Hedrick. *The Power Game: How Washington Works.* New York: Random House, 1988.

Spitzer, Robert J. *President and Congress: Executive Hegemony at the Crossroads of American Government.* New York: McGraw-Hill, 1993.

Warshaw, Shirley Anne. *The Keys to Power: Managing the Presidency.* 2d ed. New York: Longman, 2005.

chapter 4

Legislative Leader

by Jasmine Farrier

The U.S. Constitution, political scientist Richard Neustadt reminds us, did not establish a government marked by "separation of powers"; it created a system of "separated institutions sharing powers."[1] Perhaps nowhere is this more evident than in the constitutional provisions describing the lawmaking process. Article I of the Constitution includes a long list of expressed national powers Congress can initiate, but Article II, Section 3 authorizes the president to recommend to Congress measures deemed "necessary and expedient," and Article I, Section 7 gives the president the power to sign or veto legislation passed by Congress. In addition, the president has the authority "with the Advice and Consent of the Senate" to negotiate treaties with other nations, although treaties gain the force of law only when "two-thirds of the Senators present concur" (Article II, Section 2). The president also has the power to convene "emergency" sessions of Congress (Article II, Section 3). But it is the veto power, and the invitation to recommend legislation to Congress, that together provide the most significant constitutional basis for the president to participate in the legislative process.

Although these formal provisions have remained unchanged since the Constitution was ratified in 1789, the president's informal legislative roles, and a permanent expectation of strong leadership, have changed the balance of power between the branches over the last century. This reflects changing economic and social conditions that have compelled the national government, including the president, to embrace new responsibilities. In addition, technological innovations, particularly radio and television, helped elevate the president's policy agenda–setting role. New international responsibilities during the cold war and in the fight against terrorism in the wake of the attacks on New York City and Washington, D.C., on September 11, 2001, also contributed to an expansion in presidential responsibilities. The brevity and static nature of the constitutional clauses dealing with the lawmaking process, then, mask a considerable increase in the president's ability to influence the legislative agenda and the direction of public policy.

Even so, the constitutionally mandated sharing of powers between the branches, the possibility of partisan congressional turnover during off-year elections, and perennial House-Senate conflicts all continue to constrain the president's legislative influence. All of these dynamics of contemporary political life are rooted in the structures of the Constitution and almost guarantee that the president's relationship with Congress remains fluid, ambiguous, and frequently frustrating. Much of what presidents desire or need, especially in the domestic sphere, still demands congressional cooperation, whether to enact new laws, appropriate funds, or, in the case of the Senate, approve treaties and executive and judicial branch appointments. Congress, however, usually approaches lawmaking from its own unique perspective, due to its members' different electoral constituencies, mixed partisan makeup, staggered terms of office, and a wide variety of approaches to legislative, representative, and oversight duties. In addition, although legislative "gridlock" is usually attributed to divided government (when the Congress is held by one party and the White House another) the House and Senate operate under very different rules and culture that compound the hands-on work needed to pass the president's preferred policies. The result is that the president rarely can take Congress's support for granted, even when Congress is controlled by the president's political party.[2] In the modern era, then, presidents loom much larger in the lawmaking process, but the elevated vantage point is no guarantee that Congress will do their legislative bidding.

THE VETO

The veto is the primary formal tool presidents use to influence congressional lawmaking. All other means of shaping and directing the legislative process must be

Previous contributors to this chapter include Matthew J. Dickinson and Christopher J. Bosso.

understood with reference to this formal power, because only the president's legal capacity to stop legislation gives the other instruments for influencing public policy their teeth.

Constitutional Foundations

The president's authority to block acts passed by Congress has its origins in the 1787 debate over the Constitution, in particular the Framers' efforts to prevent any single branch—and, by extension, any individual or group—from gaining tyrannical political power. These concerns go back to the very roots of the colonial rebellion against strong executives, such as King George III. Yet often overlooked is their equal dread of unchecked legislative power. Thomas Jefferson's second villain in the Declaration of Independence was the English Parliament, a legislature unobstructed by written constitutional limits and loathed widely in the colonies for its apparent disregard for due process of law. These general fears about an overly strong national government were reflected in the Articles of Confederation, the Republic's first constitution. The Articles, which went into effect in 1781, essentially created a league of friendship among the thirteen newly independent states that made the national government a creature of the states and dependent on them for its powers and funds.

Ultimately, however, the national government under the Articles proved unable to promote either national unity or effective government. One problem, at least for those who had agitated for major changes in the Articles, was the absence of any independent national executive authority to administer the laws and resist legislative tyranny.[3] Not only had Congress under the Articles proven unable to govern by itself, but the political and fiscal excesses of state legislatures during the 1780s led to the perception that such bodies were as dangerous to liberty as an unrestrained monarch. Jefferson, reflecting on his experiences as governor of Virginia, wrote, "All the powers of government . . . result to the legislative body. The concentrating of these in the same hands is precisely the definition of despotic government."[4] These sentiments were shared by many of the delegates to the Constitutional Convention, even those who otherwise feared an overly strong national government.

The separation of powers system, then, was designed to rein in the executive and legislative branches by letting them overlap just enough to stimulate peaceful conflict. Ideally, organically different ideological and regional outlooks, combined with different constituencies and election timetables, would force political factions to slow down the pace of action and give incentives toward deliberation and compromise. In *Federalist* No. 48, James Madison rejects bright lines between the branches, or "parchment barriers," as being inadequate to the balance necessary to keep the new legislative body from overreaching its authority, as past

experience showed: "The legislative department is everywhere extending the sphere of its activity, and drawing all power into its impetuous vortex." In *Federalist* No. 51, Madison goes further to explain that the division of the House and Senate, the ambitions of the states, and enhanced executive power are all needed to balance Congress's ambitions. But an "absolute negative" (unilateral executive veto) was considered too far.[5]

The concept of a *veto* (Latin for "I forbid") was well known to the Framers. Indeed, in ancient Rome the veto was used by the plebeians to protect the common people from the excesses of a senate dominated by aristocrats. It later surfaced in medieval Europe as a royal check on newly developing legislatures. In England before the seventeenth century, the monarch had the *absolute* power to deny acts by Parliament, a weapon that Queen Elizabeth I for one used quite frequently.[6] Closer to home, by 1787 a few state constitutions (such as that of Massachusetts) contained a form of executive veto.[7]

Every Bill which shall have passed the House of Representatives and the Senate, shall, before it become a Law, be presented to the President of the United States; If he approve he shall sign it, but if not he shall return it, with his Objections to that House in which it shall have originated, who shall . . . proceed to reconsider it.

—*from Article I, Section 7*

Not surprisingly, then, virtually every plan put forth for revisions in the Articles included some form of an executive check on laws passed by Congress. The Virginia Plan called for a "council of revision" of members from both the executive and the judicial branches. But critics of this idea argued that such a "plural" veto would be too weak, because disputes within the council would undermine decisive executive action. Furthermore, as George Mason of Virginia argued, the veto should be more than a check against legislative intrusion; it also was needed to discourage demagogy and prevent "unjust and pernicious" laws.[8] Other delegates expressed discomfort with having judges act on bills before they came up as legal cases, so the convention eventually granted the veto to the president alone.

Some proponents of a strong executive initially supported an absolute veto, giving Congress no opportunity to respond, but this idea found no support among delegates who were concerned about unresponsive and capricious executives. After some debate, the Framers gave the new executive a "partial negative." The president could reject bills or joint resolutions passed by Congress, but Congress in response could *override* a veto by extraordinary majorities of two-thirds of the members present in each chamber.

Presidents could not veto constitutional amendments, concurrent resolutions, or resolutions passed by only one chamber.[9]

The veto would emerge as the constitutional core of executive independence. "The primary inducement to conferring this power in question upon the executive," wrote Alexander Hamilton in *Federalist* No. 73, "is to enable him to defend himself; the second one is to increase the chances in favor of the community against the passing of bad laws, through haste, inadvertence, or design."[10] The legislature is not infallible, Hamilton argued, and, unless checked, its love of power would ultimately betray both it and the ability of government to function effectively

Opponents of the veto, even those worried about unrestrained legislative power, argued that Congress alone represented the people. The veto might undermine democratic values by allowing the president to block "good" laws or simply to thwart majority rule. But, Hamilton retorted in *Federalist* No. 73, unrestrained majorities are just as dangerous as an unchecked elite, and "the injury which might possibly be done by defeating a few good laws will be amply compensated by the advantage of preventing a number of bad ones."[11] Moreover, allowing the executive to threaten a veto might induce legislative moderation, making actual use of the veto unnecessary.

The Constitution gives the president three choices after being formally presented with a bill passed by Congress: sign the bill into law; veto the bill and return it to the chamber where it originated within ten legislative days after presentation (Sundays excluded); or, finally, do nothing.[12] If the president does nothing, the bill becomes law automatically after ten legislative days. This provision prevents presidents from thwarting the majority will of Congress through simple inaction. The exception to this rule occurs when Congress passes a bill and then adjourns before ten legislative days have elapsed. Any bill not signed by the president when Congress so adjourns dies automatically—that is, it cannot become law. This condition is called a *pocket veto*, which is discussed later in this section.

Several things can happen once a president vetoes a bill and returns it to Congress. If the legislature fails to act at all, the bill dies. If two-thirds of the members present in each chamber pass the bill once again, it becomes law automatically despite presidential disapproval.[13] Such "supermajorities" in each chamber combine to produce a veto *override*. Overrides are rare—only 110 of 2,564 presidential vetoes issued between 1789 and 2011 were overridden—because to sustain a veto the president needs to gain only one-third plus one of the votes of those present in one chamber. (*See Table 4-1, this page.*) Barring an override, Congress can either rewrite the legislation to meet the president's demands (as Hamilton foresaw) or try again months or even years later under new political circumstances.[14]

TABLE 4-1 **Vetoes and Vetoes Overridden, All Bills, 1789–2011**

President	All bills vetoed	Regular vetoes	Pocket vetoes	Vetoes overridden
Washington	2	2	0	0
J. Adams	0	0	0	0
Jefferson	0	0	0	0
Madison	7	5	2	0
Monroe	1	1	0	0
J.Q. Adams	0	0	0	0
Jackson	12	5	7	0
Van Buren	1	0	1	0
W. H. Harrison	0	0	0	0
Tyler	10	6	4	1
Polk	3	2	1	0
Taylor	0	0	0	0
Fillmore	0	0	0	0
Pierce	9	9	0	5
Buchanan	7	4	3	0
Lincoln	7	2	5	0
A. Johnson	29	21	8	15
Grant	93[a]	45	48[a]	4
Hayes	13	12	1	1
Garfield	0	0	0	0
Arthur	12	4	8	1
Cleveland (1st term)	414	304	110	2
B. Harrison	44	19	25	1
Cleveland (2d term)	170	42	128	5
McKinley	42	6	36	0
T. Roosevelt	82	42	40	1
Taft	39	30	9	1
Wilson	44	33	11	6
Harding	6	5	1	0
Coolidge	50	20	30	4
Hoover	37	21	16	3
F. Roosevelt	635	372	263	9
Truman	250	180	70	12
Eisenhower	181	73	108	2
Kennedy	21	12	9	0
L. Johnson	30	16	14	0
Nixon	43	26[b]	17	7
Ford	66	48	18	12
Carter	31	13	18	2
Reagan	78	39	39	9
G.H.W. Bush[c]	44	29	15	1
Clinton	37	36	1	2
G.W. Bush[d]	12	1	1	4
Obama[e]	2	2	0	0
TOTAL	**2,564**	**1,497**	**1,067**	**110**

SOURCE: John Woolley and Gerhard Peters, The American Presidency Project, presidency.ucsb.edu.

NOTES: a. Veto total listed for Grant does not include a pocket veto of a bill that apparently never was placed before him for his signature. b. Two pocket vetoes, later overturned in court, are counted as regular vetoes. c. Two pocket vetoes, attempted by Bush during intrasession periods, are not counted since Congress considered the two bills enacted into law because of Bush's failure to return them to legislation. d. Bush characterized his veto of H.R. 1585 as a pocket veto; however, the 110th Congress treated it as a normal veto. It is counted as a pocket veto here. e. Through December 31, 2011.

Bills vetoed by the president normally are returned to Congress accompanied by a message that states reasons for the president's opposition. (*See box, Veto Messages, p. 156.*) Sometimes the president will cite constitutional concerns, at other times political or policy disagreements, but veto messages are always aimed at advancing the president's views on the bill in question. Whatever their other purposes, veto messages ultimately are political statements directed not only at Congress but also at the public at large. In this sense, the veto message is an additional resource presidents can use in their efforts to influence public policy.

Historical Development

Early presidents, whatever their other political beliefs, conformed to the view that regardless of the policy or partisan intent behind a veto, the message should be couched in terms of constitutionality. The idea that a president should veto a bill simply because it was "bad" politics or policy was not yet widely accepted, and so the relatively few vetoes issued between 1790 and 1830 were confined to bills deemed "unconstitutional."[15]

This narrow interpretation of the president's right (and perhaps duty) to use the veto was expanded significantly during the presidency of Andrew Jackson (1829–1837) of Tennessee—hero of the War of 1812, foe of eastern business and banking interests, and self-styled "Tribune of the People." Jackson actively engaged in intense partisan warfare with Congress and, as political scientist Clinton Rossiter suggests, "revived the veto and purified it of the niceties that had grown up around it" by making it an overtly political instrument.[16] Indeed, in eight years Jackson issued twelve vetoes, more than all previous presidents combined. None of his vetoes was overridden, despite the controversies they created. Perhaps most controversial of all was Jackson's rejection of an 1832 bill to recharter the Bank of the United States, an institution bitterly despised by Jackson's supporters among the frontier settlers and farmers because of its high interest rates and reputation for unseemly political entanglements.

Jackson's veto message of more than 8,000 words explained not only his detailed objections to the specifics in the new charter legislation, but also his constitutional analysis of the famous Supreme Court case that upheld earlier charter legislation (*McCulloch v. Maryland*, 1819), a discussion of state banking capacities, and much more. In this way, Jackson's use of rhetoric showed a commonality with "modern" presidents by throwing himself into the policy fray by engaging Congress, the Court, and public opinion simultaneously.[17]

Although Jackson's immediate successors professed renewed allegiance to the traditional doctrine of restrained veto use, they too proved surprisingly resolute when challenged by the legislature. John Tyler (1841–1845) vetoed two major bank bills supported by his party, and his 1842 veto of a controversial tariff measure sparked the first formal attempt in Congress to impeach a president. The effort failed, and Tyler's successors continued to display the independence pioneered by Jackson. Indeed, of the fifty-nine bills vetoed between 1789 and 1865, more than half were by Jackson, Tyler, and Franklin Pierce (1853–1857).

Post–Civil War Era

The period between the Civil War and the late 1890s saw some of history's most acrid partisan battles, which often spilled over into conflict between the branches of government. Presidents routinely clashed with Congress within a national political arena rife with sharp regional and partisan antagonisms, deep social and economic changes, and sharp disputes over the fundamental role of government. This era, although marked generally by congressional dominance, nonetheless saw surges in the use of the veto as successive presidents attempted to grapple with massive numbers of bills spawned by an often antagonistic Congress.

Andrew Johnson (1865–1869), who succeeded the assassinated Abraham Lincoln (1861–1865), suffered the most, in no small part because he was a former Democrat from Tennessee confronting a Congress controlled by "Radical Republicans" seeking to punish the states of the defeated Confederacy. Johnson was the first president to have Congress override a veto of an important bill, and, among all presidents, he had the greatest percentage of regular vetoes overridden (fifteen out of twenty-one, or 71 percent). Furthermore, Johnson's refusal to abide by the Tenure of Office Act, a law passed over his veto that prohibited presidents from firing political appointees without congressional approval, led directly to his impeachment by the House. Johnson was acquitted in the Senate by one vote. Congress repealed the Tenure of Office Act, which most scholars viewed as unconstitutional, in 1887.[18]

The visibility of and drama surrounding Johnson's veto battles were more the exception than the rule. Most vetoes issued during the late nineteenth century were directed at "private" bills, legislation that benefited specific individuals, companies, or municipalities. (*See Table 4-2, p. 153.*) Private bills in the late 1800s usually provided pensions for Civil War veterans, but many of them were fraudulent or excessive claims and often rushed through late in the congressional session. Grover Cleveland (1885–1889, 1893–1897) vetoed 482 private bills during his eight years in office—43 during one three-day period in 1886 alone.[19] Many of these were pocket vetoes, and only three of Cleveland's vetoes of private bills were overridden.

The Veto in the Contemporary Presidency

Franklin D. Roosevelt (1933–1945) used the veto more vigorously and strategically than all presidents to that time, and probably thereafter. He was the first to veto major tax legislation and openly used the threat of the veto in his legislative strategy, even though his own party controlled both houses of Congress throughout his presidency. "Give me something to veto," he reportedly told his aides, so that he could remind

TABLE 4-2 **Private Bills Vetoed, 1789–2011**

President	Regular vetoes	Pocket vetoes	Vetoes overridden
Washington	0	0	0
J. Adams	0	0	0
Jefferson	0	0	0
Madison	2	0	0
Monroe	0	0	0
J.Q. Adams	0	0	0
Jackson	0	0	0
Van Buren	0	1	0
W. H. Harrison	0	0	0
Tyler	0	0	0
Polk	0	0	0
Taylor	0	0	0
Fillmore	0	0	0
Pierce	0	0	0
Buchanan	2	0	0
Lincoln	0	1	0
A. Johnson	0	2	0
Grant	29	37	3
Hayes	1	0	0
Garfield	0	0	0
Arthur	1	8	0
Cleveland (1st term)	271	82	1
B. Harrison	5	23	0
Cleveland (2d term)	30	99	2
McKinley	4	32	0
T. Roosevelt	27	31	0
Taft	10	7	0
Wilson	7	2	0
Harding	3	0	0
Coolidge	3	17	0
Hoover	4	6	0
F. Roosevelt	317	180	0
Truman	137	38	1
Eisenhower	43	64	0
Kennedy	8	4	0
L. Johnson	12	4	0
Nixon	0	3	0
Ford	3	2	0
Carter	0	2	0
Reagan	2	6	0
G.H.W. Bush	0	1	0
Clinton	0	0	0
G.W. Bush	0	0	0
Obama[a]	0	0	0
TOTAL	**921**	**652**	**7**

SOURCE: *Guide to Congress*, 6th ed. (Washington, D.C.: CQ Press, 2007); *CQ Weekly*, various issues.

NOTES: The official distinction between public and private bills was rather hazy through the 1930s, although private bills generally were classified as those benefiting a single individual rather than a large segment of society (for example, a private pension bill). Beginning in 1936, however, a Library of Congress publication has listed all private bills. a. Through December 31, 2011.

members of Congress that he was part of the lawmaking process.[20] Roosevelt's veto strategy helped establish the modern presidency, with the veto becoming but one instrument of executive influence within an environment of expansive federal government action and power.

Contemporary presidents have adopted Roosevelt's strategic use of the veto to shape legislation, particularly because they so frequently find themselves facing a Congress in which the other major political party controls one or both chambers. Indeed, vetoes are used most frequently when such partisan splits occur. Since the end of World War II, 282 of 485 regular vetoes (58 percent) occurred under divided government. Half of all years between 1945 and 2011 were marked by a president of one party and a Congress of another. Veto rates are higher during these moments of divided government, and the clashes can become more meaningful in elections. A classic example of this strategy took place in 1947, when Harry S. Truman (1945–1953) vetoed the controversial Taft-Hartley Labor-Management Relations Act, a bill passed by a Republican-controlled House and Senate that limited the political activity of federal workers and labor unions.[21] Although the Republican-led Congress overruled Truman's veto, he capitalized on their action to great political effect by rallying labor voters to the Democrats in the 1948 election. At the same time, it is important to note that Truman had 180 regular vetoes while in office and just 42 of those took place during the two years of divided government. The 168 vetoes under unified government during the other six years of his term show that internal party divisions within the New Deal coalition were beginning to put a new strain on presidential-congressional relations. Of course, vetoes are still less likely when the same party controls both branches.

Republican Dwight D. Eisenhower (1953–1961) worked with a Congress dominated by Democrats during all but two of his eight years in office, yet he could rely on a "conservative coalition" of Republicans and southern Democrats to support his agenda and prevent overrides of his vetoes. One notable illustration of this dynamic came in 1959, after liberal northern Democrats had made large gains in the 1958 congressional elections. These Democrats ignored Eisenhower's warnings and tried to push a vigorous domestic agenda, leading Eisenhower to veto a succession of bills authorizing new spending for urban housing, rural electrification, and other domestic programs. These vetoes were upheld by the conservative coalition, and threats of additional vetoes persuaded Democrats to cut back on their efforts.[22]

Democrats John F. Kennedy (1961–1963) and Lyndon B. Johnson (1963–1969), blessed with friendlier partisan majorities in Congress, seldom used the veto, but Republicans Richard Nixon (1969–1974) and Gerald R. Ford (1974–1977) fared differently. Both Nixon and Ford faced off against a Congress dominated by Democrats, so the veto became central to their legislative strategies. Nixon vetoed several major bills he deemed inflationary, and once even appeared on national television to sign a veto of a major appropriations bill. As with Eisenhower, a bipartisan conservative coalition in Congress often proved large enough to sustain Nixon's vetoes.

However, the ultimate success of the veto as a tool for shaping legislation is tied inextricably to a president's overall political "strength." Nixon's deepening legal and political troubles eventually weakened his popular support and, by extension, his influence in Congress. In 1973 Congress soundly overrode his veto of the War Powers Resolution, which aimed at limiting a president's ability to commit U.S. armed forces abroad without congressional approval. Congress also overrode Nixon's veto of the 1974 Budget Impoundment and Control Act, which Nixon opposed because it limited the president's ability to avoid spending funds appropriated by Congress. *(See "Line-item Veto," p. 160.)*

Gerald Ford became president upon Nixon's resignation in August 1974 and, faced with a Congress dominated even more by liberal Democrats after the midterm congressional elections, used the veto frequently and to great effect. Ford was sustained on all but four of the seventeen vetoes he issued in 1975 alone, and used the threat of a veto to stop a popular consumer protection bill from ever passing. Ford's short tenure in office showed how the veto could be used to compensate partially for the severe political handicaps that came with being an unelected chief executive succeeding a disgraced president.

Jimmy Carter (1977–1981), like Kennedy and Johnson, relied on the veto less frequently than his Republican predecessors because fellow Democrats controlled Congress. A notable exception was his veto of a 1977 energy bill that included funds for a nuclear reactor he thought dangerous and expensive.[23] Congress chose not to challenge Carter on that veto, because many in his party also opposed the reactor. On the other hand, in 1980 Carter became the first president since Truman to suffer a veto override at the hands of a Congress controlled by his party after he vetoed a bill limiting the national debt because it contained a provision eliminating import fees on foreign oil.[24] Congress overrode this veto in part because the fees were unpopular with many Democrats and in part because of an apparent weakening in Carter's general public support as the Iran hostage situation dragged on.

The role of the veto during the presidency of Ronald Reagan (1981–1989) was even more telling, since during Reagan's first term Congress was split between a Republican Senate and a Democratic House. Such partisan divisions made it unlikely that Congress would override a veto, which enabled Reagan to veto spending bills contrary to his priorities. So crucial was the veto to Reagan's strategy that he often warned, "My veto pen is inked up and ready to go," when Congress was about to pass legislation he opposed.[25] His veto of a 1981 appropriations bill was so politically effective that Congress reworked the measure to his satisfaction. However, Reagan found it harder to make veto threats work to his advantage in the later years of his presidency, especially after Democrats regained full control over both chambers of Congress following the 1986 midterm elections. Indeed, in 1987 bipartisan majorities in Congress easily overrode Reagan's vetoes of major water pollution and highway bills, signaling a palpable shift in the president's influence with Congress as his presidency entered its final stages.

The two presidents to follow Reagan offered an especially useful contrast in the use of the veto as a means for influencing legislation. George H. W. Bush (1989–1993) issued forty-four vetoes but had only one overridden by the Democrat-controlled Congress. His successor, Bill Clinton (1993–2001), passed his first two years in office without issuing a veto, relying instead on Democratic leaders in Congress to forestall legislative challenges. But in 1994 Republicans gained control over both chambers of Congress for the first time in forty years. It thus seemed only a matter of time before Clinton, faced with a particularly assertive Republican congressional leadership, finally made use of the veto power. Clinton's first veto came on June 7, 1995, twenty-nine months after taking office, when he returned to Congress with his disapproval of a major bill that cut spending of funds already appropriated for that fiscal year. This veto, which was not overridden, foreshadowed a struggle between Clinton and congressional Republicans for control over the direction of federal policy. Indeed, Clinton was to use the veto another thirty-five times during the remainder of his presidency, with only two overrides, thus repeating a veto pattern characteristic of presidents facing a Congress dominated by the other party.

President George W. Bush's (2001–2009) veto strategy represented a return to the pattern of Clinton's first two years in office. Except for a twenty-month period from May 2001 through January 2003 when Democrats narrowly controlled the Senate, Bush enjoyed majority-party support in both chambers of Congress during his first six years as president. In this period Bush vetoed only one bill—a controversial initiative passed by Congress in 2006 to loosen restrictions on federal funding for embryonic stem cell research. His veto was sustained. Bush's lack of vetoes partly reflected the effectiveness of his legislative strategy, particularly on tax and spending bills, which capitalized on the cohesive Republican majority in the House. Bush used this majority to stake out a relatively extreme initial legislative position, and then moderated his stance as necessary to accommodate the more centrist Senate, where the opposition Democratic Party, although in the minority, exercised greater influence. By splitting the difference between the conservative wing of the Republican Party in the House and the more moderate Senate, Bush was able to achieve acceptable legislative outcomes without exercising a veto.

As was predicted by past experiences with divided government, when the Democrats took the House and Senate majorities after the 2006 off-year election, heightened policy divisions between the branches meant additional vetoes. George W. Bush vetoed eleven bills in his last two years in office. Four were overridden by the House and Senate to become law, one in 2007 and the other three in 2008.[26] The first veto came in May 2007: "U.S. Troop Readiness, Veterans' Care, Katrina Recovery, and Iraq Accountability Appropriations Act." Bush's primary objection was to withdrawal language in the Iraq portion of the appropriations bill and he explained in this excerpt of the policy and constitutional components of his veto message.

The veto override bar is set purposefully high at two-thirds of both the House and Senate so political circumstances and the type of legislation shape the success or failure of the attempt. The Iraq veto mentioned above was sustained, as were two other vetoes that touched on national defense and security (a defense authorization bill in 2007 and an intelligence authorization bill in 2008). However, of the remaining eight bills vetoed during the 110th Congress that concerned exclusively domestic policy, four were overridden. The first bill Congress passed over Bush's veto was the Water Resources Development Act of 2007, which authorized dozens of popular water projects. Bush vetoed the bill on November 2, 2007. The House voted to override the veto on November 6 and it passed by more than the necessary amount, 361–54. The Senate did the same on November 8 by 79–14. In both chambers, Republicans joined Democrats to support the bill's infrastructure projects often derided as "pork barrel spending." Two Republican senators from areas still recovering from Hurricanes Katrina and Rita in 2005, David Vitter (R-La.) and Trent Lott (R-Miss.), who normally voted with President Bush, were quoted in the New York Times defending the bill from a local representation perspective. Taking another view, Senate Majority Leader Harry Reid (D-Nev.) said the override "sends an unmistakable message that Democrats both will continue to strengthen our environment and economy and will refuse to allow President Bush to block America's real priorities for partisan reasons."[27]

Despite several dramatic legislative showdowns between President Barack Obama and Congress under a tense political atmosphere, his use of the veto has been spare and noncontroversial. Between January 2009 and December 2011 he vetoed two minor bills, both in the 111th Congress when the Democratic Party held a majority in both chambers. The first veto was against a short-term continuing resolution that Obama said was rendered irrelevant by a normal appropriations bill. The House voted to sustain the veto by a margin of 143–245. The second veto, also sustained by the

House (185–235), struck down a low salience bill designed to enhance legal recognition of out-of-state notarizations.[28] (See box, Veto Messages, p. 156.)

An Instrument of Presidential Power

James Bryce, the nineteenth-century English observer of American government, argued that the veto "conveys the impression of firmness."[29] Given the rarity of vetoes, one is tempted to conclude that the impression is fleeting. Between 1945 and 1992, Congress presented more than 17,000 public bills for the president's signature. Presidents vetoed only 434 of these bills, a veto rate of 2.5 percent.[30] Moreover, on the rare occasions when presidents did veto bills, they often did so from positions of political weakness; the veto was a last-ditch effort to prevent legislation the president opposed from becoming law.[31] From this perspective, the veto does not appear to suggest firmness so much as political impotence.

In this regard, consider the experience of Gerald Ford, who may have been dealt the weakest political hand of any contemporary president. After succeeding the disgraced Nixon, Ford faced a fiercely independent Congress dominated by liberal Democrats in a post-Vietnam atmosphere infused with hostility to presidential power. Such political circumstances gave Ford little option but to rely heavily on the veto, which he issued more frequently against public bills than any other president during the twentieth century. The fact that most of Ford's vetoes were sustained underscores the veto's utility as a blunt instrument for stopping legislation. Nonetheless, his need to rely on the veto indicates his overall lack of influence during the legislative process.

That weakness is telegraphed even more strongly if the veto is overridden, something that historically has occurred to about 4 percent of presidential vetoes. Truman's crafty use of the veto against congressional Republicans should not obscure the fact that his vetoes were overridden twelve times. Reagan's defeat on successive overrides in early 1987 resulted from his weakened political leverage in light of renewed Democratic dominance in Congress, his own troubles concerning secret arms sales to Iran, and the reality that Reagan was in the "lame duck" phase of his second term of office. For that matter, the only override battle that George H. W. Bush (1989–1993) lost came in the last months of his presidency on a bill regulating the cable television industry that was popular with both Democrats and Republicans. Congressional Republicans in this case were more concerned with their reelection prospects than with upholding a veto issued by a president on the verge of suffering a defeat in his bid for reelection.[32]

But if the exercise of the veto often reflects presidential weakness, a veto threat can be a potent bargaining tool. Viewed from this perspective, the rarity with which the veto has been used masks its actual utility to presidents as a means for shaping legislative outcomes. Thus although

VETO MESSAGES

A bill passed by Congress is formally vetoed when the president returns it to Capitol Hill unsigned and accompanied by a message stating the reasons for disapproval. Presidents today rarely write their own veto messages. Instead, the messages typically are composed by professional staff in the Executive Office of the President with input from experts in the Office of Management and Budget (OMB) and other executive branch agencies. The president may scan the final draft and on occasion may pen major parts of controversial veto messages, but the overall process of opposing Congress on a piece of legislation largely is a collective one.

Whether the reasons given for a veto are constitutional, fiscal, substantive, or "merely" political—or a combination of reasons—a veto message is designed with more than Congress in mind. In today's media-saturated political atmosphere any message from the White House to Congress is scrutinized closely for its potential political ramifications. Veto messages thus are crafted carefully, designed above all to sell the president's views on a bill to national opinion makers and to the public, not simply to Congress.

Most veto messages are signed in the relative privacy of the Oval Office and sent by courier to Capitol Hill. They then are delivered to the chamber from whence the bills in question originated, which normally takes the lead in any efforts to override the veto. On vetoes of major bills, however, a president may use the opportunity to convene a public ceremony, complete with supporters and members of the national press, to attack the bill and to generate public sentiment against Congress.

A veto message can be explanatory and detailed, which is useful for the public and the media as well as Congress, especially if the issue is salient, well-known, and likely to merit addition debate. For example, President Andrew Jackson explained his objection to the national bank on policy and constitutional grounds, whereas before only the latter was considered to be a proper basis for presidential objection. The following is an excerpt from the 8,000 word veto message:

> A bank of the United States is in many respects convenient for the Government and useful to the people. Entertaining this opinion, and deeply impressed with the belief that some of the powers and privileges possessed by the existing bank are unauthorized by the Constitution, subversive of the rights of the States, and dangerous to the liberties of the people, I felt it my duty at an early period of my Administration to call the attention of Congress to the practicability of organizing an institution combining all its advantages and obviating these objections. I sincerely regret that in the act before me I can perceive none of those modifications of the bank charter which are necessary, in my opinion, to make it compatible with justice, with sound policy, or with the Constitution of our country.

In 2007 President George W. Bush added an institutional perspective to his veto of a defense appropriations bill that included support for a firm withdrawal deadline from Iraq.

TO THE HOUSE OF REPRESENTATIVES:

. . . This legislation is objectionable because it would set an arbitrary date for beginning the withdrawal of American troops without regard to conditions on the ground; it would micromanage the commanders in the field by restricting their ability to direct the fight in Iraq; and it contains billions of dollars of spending and other provisions completely unrelated to the war. . . this legislation is unconstitutional because it purports to direct the conduct of the operations of the war in a way that infringes upon the powers vested in the Presidency by the Constitution, including as Commander in Chief of the Armed Forces. For these reasons, I must veto this bill.

> GEORGE W. BUSH.
> THE WHITE HOUSE, May 1, 2007

Sometimes, however, a veto message may go completely under the political radar. For example, President Barack Obama vetoed a bill that attempted to expand interstate recognition of notarized documents and electronic legal records. The low-profile 2010 bill was prompted by notary public complaints that state courts did not always accept legitimate notarizations, especially when done electronically. At the same time, the multiyear mortgage crisis in the United States exposed incidents of banking and legal fraud surrounding so-called "robo signings" that quickly moved toxic mortgages from one financial institution to another. The bill at issue was not particularly partisan as previous versions had passed the House but not the Senate in 2006 under the Republican majority and in 2007 when Democrats were in control. The vetoed bill, H.R. 3808, passed the House and Senate during the 111th Congress and President Obama refused to sign during a recess and also returned the bill to the House so it did not count as a "pocket veto." The House voted to overturn the veto on November 17, 2010, 185–235 but failed to gain the necessary two-thirds. Obama explained that the bill could inadvertently contribute to greater fraud:

PRESIDENTIAL MEMORANDUM OF DISAPPROVAL—H.R. 3808

It is necessary to have further deliberations about the possible unintended impact of H.R. 3808, the "Interstate Recognition of Notarizations Act of 2010," on consumer protections, including those for mortgages, before the bill can be finalized. Accordingly, I am withholding my approval of this bill. (*The Pocket Veto Case*, 279 U.S. 655 (1929)).

The authors of this bill no doubt had the best intentions in mind when trying to remove impediments to interstate commerce. My Administration will work with them and other leaders in Congress to explore the best ways to achieve this goal going forward.

To leave no doubt that the bill is being vetoed, in addition to withholding my signature, I am returning H.R. 3808 to the Clerk of the House of Representatives, along with this Memorandum of Disapproval.

> BARACK OBAMA
> THE WHITE HOUSE,
> October 8, 2010

George W. Bush vetoed only one bill during his first six years as president, he issued by one count more than 140 veto threats during that period.[33] By threatening to veto, presidents signal to Congress what is and is not acceptable legislation. Such threats often are effective at moving legislation closer to the president's preferred outcome. Moreover, political scientist

Charles Cameron's research shows that the production of "landmark" legislation is comparatively lower under divided than unified party government, suggesting that the presidential veto threats—which are more likely under divided government—do alter congressional behavior.[34]

Two distinct eras in the Clinton presidency offer particularly good insights into this dynamic. Clinton issued no vetoes in his first two years in office, the longest such stretch since 1850, largely because his party controlled both chambers of Congress.[35] Clinton worked closely with congressional Democrats on legislative compromises that avoided the need for vetoes, yet by late 1994 he was widely seen as having failed to deliver on some of his major campaign promises. Clinton's troubles came about in no small part because his party's majorities in Congress were not large enough to overcome sharp internal partisan and ideological divisions as well as unified opposition by Republicans. Particularly telling was the fate of Clinton's plan for major reform of the nation's health care system, the only piece of legislation in 1993–1994 that he publicly threatened to veto if it did not contain key elements of his own plan. But Clinton's threat was to no avail: congressional Democrats were unable to satisfy enough members of their own party, much less get past almost unanimous Republican opposition. The failure on health care reform contributed to massive losses by Democrats in the 1994 midterm elections, and Republicans took control of both chambers for the first time in forty years.

Clinton now faced a particularly assertive Republican congressional leadership, spearheaded by House Speaker Newt Gingrich, R-Ga., and the veto quickly became the cornerstone of his legislative strategy. This was never more true than in 1995–1996, when Republicans dared him to veto omnibus appropriations bills that made major cuts in his programs and, in the process, risk shutting down most federal government operations. Clinton essentially called their bluff, and congressional Republicans—who apparently had forgotten how Ronald Reagan had outmaneuvered Democrats when the shoe was on the other foot in the 1980s—found that they, not Clinton, were being blamed for the subsequent government shutdowns. Faced with strong public blame for the shutdowns, congressional Republicans backed down each time, and Clinton's political strength grew accordingly. Indeed, thereafter Clinton used the veto as the linchpin of a defensive strategy to force Republicans to accede to his spending and policy priorities at the risk of even more public disapproval. So effective was Clinton in this regard—even when he was entangled in impeachment proceedings related to his sexual relationship with a White House intern—that scholar George Edwards called his use of the veto "nearly unprecedented" in its strategic role and effectiveness.[36]

Even though Clinton succeeded in his veto strategy, Congress still finds ways to dilute the potency of a veto or veto threat. Members often load up major spending bills with "riders," legislative instructions that may change specific policies, or with pet spending programs that the president may be obliged to swallow to ensure passage of the bill. Clinton, for one, had to decide which of many Republican budget riders he could live with and those he would oppose each time he considered spending bills. Congress also tends to wait until late in each session to pass critical spending bills and to rely increasingly on massive omnibus (or "catch-all") bills to pass the budget, appropriate funds, and levy new taxes simultaneously, all in an effort to narrow the president's range of possible responses. Reagan, for example, had to swallow the Boland Amendment restricting U.S. aid to rebels opposing the Nicaraguan government because it was tacked onto a 1984 appropriations bill. The administration's subsequent efforts to get around the Boland Amendment got it into deep political and legal trouble. George H. W. Bush, to gain passage of the 1990 budget act, accepted new taxes, a compromise that angered many in his party and contributed to his defeat in 1992.

Finally, no president can assume automatic support from fellow party members in Congress on veto threats, or even during override battles. Most members of Congress resist being seen by constituents as mere rubber stamps for the president's wishes, especially when the bill in question benefits a member's district or state. This reality was well illustrated in 1987 when Congress overrode Reagan's vetoes of water treatment and highway bills and in 1992 when it overrode Bush's veto of a bill that promised to lower cable television rates. In each case, Republicans abandoned their own president in droves, sacrificing a presidential agenda for their constituents' interests. For their part, fellow Democrats deserted Clinton in two instances, most tellingly in 1997 when Congress overrode Clinton's initial (and only) use of the "line-item veto" provision it created in 1996. *(See "Line-item Veto," p. 160.)*

The threat of a veto can be a positive tool for shaping policy. Its efficacy depends in part on a president's overall popularity, whether and to what extent the president's party controls Congress, the nature of the issue at hand, broad external political conditions, timing, and even luck. But as FDR understood, it also depends on the president's prior record in carrying through on those threats—hence his charge to aides to find something he could veto. Viewed in this way, the power of the veto is gauged not only by its immediate effect on pending legislation, but also on how it affects a president's reputation for using the veto in subsequent legislative bargaining sessions. Sometimes, a veto threat can be taken so seriously that legislators cite it in their decision to change course on an issue. The Republican House of Representatives banned "earmarks" in appropriations legislation soon after winning the majority in 2010. The Senate remained in Democrats' hands and the chair of the Appropriations Committee, Daniel Inouye (D-Hawaii) was in favor of protecting congressional earmark prerogatives, which allow members to direct federal spending toward their districts. However, in January 2011 the president said in his State of the Union address that he would veto spending bills that contained earmarks. In February Senator Inouye issued a press release saying he would issue a moratorium ban on the practice.[37]

However, it is hard to count veto threats with complete precision because they vary in specificity and style, even within a single administration. For example, during the extraordinary conflicts over the debt ceiling increase in the summer of 2011, President Obama issued two different types of veto threats in July via the Executive Office of the President. In the first statement, Obama issued a straightforward veto threat after going into his objections to the pending bill in detail.[38] In the second statement, he gave himself some "wiggle room."[39] (*See box, Veto Threats, this page.*)

Pocket Veto

The Constitution specifically mentions the veto, as well as the method to be used for congressional override. But, like much of the Framers' handiwork, minor provisions have evolved over time into major constitutional battles between Congress and the presidency. One of the most heated of these battles has been over what is now known as the *pocket veto*.

Constitutional Provision

The Constitution gives the president ten legislative days (excluding Sundays) to sign a bill into law or return it to Congress with a veto message. A bill not approved or vetoed by the president becomes law after ten days "unless the Congress by their Adjournment prevent its Return, in which Case it shall not be a Law" (Article I, Section 7). This provision apparently was meant to make it possible to ward off last-minute actions by Congress that might prove dangerous or foolhardy. The president cannot possibly veto and return bills to Congress as prescribed in the Constitution if Congress already has left for home after adjournment, so the Framers determined that under such circumstances it was better that any bill left unapproved at adjournment simply die.

A pocket veto results from executive inaction, not anything the president does actively, and the term reflects the notion that the president "pocketed" a bill rather than acted on it.[40] A president technically cannot "issue" a pocket veto: the entire situation occurs simply because Congress has

Veto Threats

Presidential veto threats are wielded to shape legislative action as well as signal to the public the president's policy stance. These threats can be especially powerful on both fronts if it is done in a widely watched forum, such as a State of the Union address. As veto threats take a variety of formal and informal forms, it is hard to count them with complete precision. Written veto threats also vary in specificity and style, even within a single administration. For example, during the extraordinary conflicts over the debt ceiling increase in the summer of 2011, President Barack Obama issued two different types of veto threats in July via the Executive Office of the President, which issued the following statements to the House Rules Committee. In the first one, excerpted here, Obama issued a straightforward veto threat after going into his objections to the pending bill in detail. In the second example, included here in its entirety, he gave himself some "wiggle room."

FIRST VETO THREAT

July 18, 2011
(House Rules)
STATEMENT OF ADMINISTRATION POLICY
H. R. 2560 – Cut, Cap and Balance Act of 2011
The Administration strongly opposes H.R. 2560, the "Cut, Cap and Balance Act of 2011." Neither setting arbitrary spending levels nor amending the Constitution is necessary to restore fiscal responsibility. Increasing the Federal debt limit, which is needed to avoid a Federal government default on its obligations and a severe blow to the economy, should not be conditioned on taking these actions. Instead of pursuing an empty political statement and unrealistic policy goals, it is necessary to move beyond politics as usual and find bipartisan common ground....

The President has proposed a comprehensive and balanced framework that ensures we live within our means and reduces the deficit by $4 trillion, while supporting economic growth and long-term job creation, protecting critical investments, and meeting the commitments made to provide economic security to Americans no matter their circumstances. H.R. 2560 is inconsistent with this responsible framework to restore fiscal responsibility and is not an appropriate method of reducing the Nation's deficits and debt. The Administration is committed to working with the Congress on a bipartisan basis to achieve real solutions.

If the President were presented this bill for signature, he would veto it.

SECOND VETO THREAT

July 26, 2011
(House Rules)
STATEMENT OF ADMINISTRATION POLICY
S. 627 – Budget Control Act of 2011
The Administration strongly opposes House passage of the amendment in the nature of a substitute to S. 627. If S. 627 is presented to the President, the President's senior advisors would recommend that he veto this bill.

SOURCE: www.whitehouse.gov/sites/default/files/omb/legislative/sap/112/saphr2560r_20110718.pdf; www.whitehouse.gov/sites/default/files/omb/legislative/sap/112/saps627r_20110726.pdf.

adjourned and the bill cannot be returned with a regular veto message. Even so, many presidents have asserted a "right" to use the pocket veto as if it were an active power of the office.

The first president to rely on a pocket veto was James Madison, in 1812, and only twice more before 1830 did a president pocket a bill. The incidence of pocket vetoes increased thereafter, especially against the many private pension bills passed by Congress in the second half of the nineteenth century. The champion of the pocket veto in absolute numbers is Franklin Roosevelt (263), but Grover Cleveland used the device more frequently (averaging 30 a year in office, compared with Roosevelt's 22), largely against the private pension bills for Civil War veterans. All told, presidents through 2006 issued 1,066 pocket vetoes, as opposed to 1,484 "regular" vetoes.[41]

Constitutional Issues

The pocket veto is controversial because Congress and the president often disagree over what constitutes congressional adjournment. The Constitution, as so often is the case, is not clear on this point except for adjournment *sine die* (Latin for "without a day," meaning "without a day being set for meeting again"). Adjournment *sine die* marks the end of a two-year Congress, which itself runs the course of the two-year term of the House of Representatives.

If any Bill shall not be returned by the President within ten Days (Sundays excepted) after it shall have been presented to him, the Same shall be a Law, in like Manner as if he had signed it, unless the Congress by their Adjournment prevent its Return, in which Case it shall not be a Law.

—*from Article I, Section 7*

That the pocket veto is constitutional upon adjournment *sine die* is undisputed; the controversy concerns whether its use is constitutional with other types of recesses or adjournments. Any interpretation narrowing its use to adjournment *sine die* alone tends to benefit Congress. A more expansive definition magnifies executive power over legislation, because presidents might be able to defeat bills through inaction whenever Congress takes a recess, such as between sessions of the same Congress or during holidays occurring within any single session.

This question was not an issue during the nineteenth century, because Congress sat in session, on average, only half a year, and calling members back to Washington to override vetoes could take weeks of travel. But as Congress began to stay in session almost full time and as new technology made communications to and recall of Congress far easier than the Framers ever envisioned, the issue of when the president can legally use the pocket veto grew in importance.

The first real shot in this battle came with the 1929 *Pocket Veto Case,* in which the Supreme Court ruled that President Calvin Coolidge could pocket veto an Indian claims bill passed just before a four-month congressional recess.[42] The justices ruled that the term *adjournment* applied to any break in the congressional calendar that prevented the return of a bill within the required ten-day period, in this case adjournment between sessions. The ruling, as historian Arthur M. Schlesinger Jr. noted, "was based in part on the idea that, if Congress was in adjournment, no officer or agent was authorized to receive on behalf of Congress a bill rejected by the President."[43] To close this apparent loophole both chambers began to appoint "agents"—usually the clerk of the House and secretary of the Senate—to receive presidential veto messages while members were away, thus theoretically negating a president's rationale for a pocket veto. After all, once Congress returned it could deliberate and perhaps override a presidential veto at any time before adjournment *sine die.*

Franklin Roosevelt asserted that this strategy was unconstitutional when he declared a pocket veto of a bill passed before Congress went on a three-day recess, but the Supreme Court ruled in 1938 that pocket vetoes could not occur during such brief recesses if the appropriate agents had been so named.[44] Regular veto procedures, the justices argued, gave the president enough time to consider a bill *and* gave Congress the opportunity to respond, so the use of agents to receive veto messages was deemed constitutional. Congress, not surprisingly, made this practice commonplace thereafter.

The issue lay dormant until the early 1970s, when Richard Nixon's application of the pocket veto again sparked controversy about what kind of congressional adjournment "prevents" regular veto procedures. Despite the 1938 ruling, Nixon declared in 1970 that he would use a six-day holiday recess to pocket the Family Practice of Medicine Act, which provided funds for medical training. Congress had passed the bill unanimously, had appointed agents to receive presidential messages, and arguably would have overridden a regular veto, but Nixon did not give Congress the chance to respond. Nixon created a furor when he asserted that the short recess was analogous to adjournment *sine die.* Members of Congress countered that the bill had indeed become law because Nixon could not pocket a bill during the recess, and Sen. Edward M. Kennedy, D-Mass., subsequently brought suit against the administration.[45] Kennedy's case was upheld by a U.S. court of appeals, which essentially reaffirmed the 1938 Supreme Court decision.[46] The Nixon administration chose not to appeal this ruling to the Supreme Court.

Senator Kennedy figured in a similar lawsuit after President Ford declared a pocket veto against a bill passed just before the intersession break of the Ninety-third Congress. Once again, a federal court of appeals overturned a lower court decision and ruled that the pocket veto cannot be used except after adjournment *sine die* so long as both chambers appoint agents.[47] The Ford administration announced that it would abide by the ruling.[48]

Despite these precedents, in 1983 Ronald Reagan reasserted a more expansive view when he declared a pocket veto of a bill barring U.S. aid to El Salvador. The legislation had been passed just before the end of the first session of the Ninety-eighth Congress. Like Nixon and Ford, Reagan administration officials argued that the pocket veto applied to any congressional recess longer than three days. And, just as before, many in Congress declared that the device applied only to adjournment *sine die.* Thirty-three House Democrats sued the administration, and a U.S. court of appeals in 1984 again reversed a lower-court decision and reaffirmed the standard set in 1976.[49] The administration appealed the decision to the Supreme Court, which in January 1987 declared the particulars of the case moot (since the dispute over aid to El Salvador had long passed) and upheld the decision of the court of appeals.[50] Both sides voiced disappointment that the high court had not settled the matter conclusively.

President George H. W. Bush confused the issue further. In August 1989, with Congress out on a summer recess, Bush declared a pocket veto of a minor bill that would have expedited the signing of legislation to bail out the nation's failing savings and loan industry. In doing so, Bush became the first president since Nixon to pocket a bill during a legislative session. In November 1989 Bush declared a pocket veto of a bill to allow dissident Chinese students to remain in the United States, but nonetheless returned the bill with a "memorandum of disapproval" outlining his objections. The Senate failed to override this "veto."

The Bush administration defended its actions on the basis of the *Pocket Veto Case* of 1929, which had upheld the use of the pocket veto during short congressional recesses. However, many in Congress—especially Democrats— looked instead to the series of more recent federal appeals court cases that had limited the pocket veto to adjournment *sine die,* and in 1990 they responded to Bush's actions with legislation that would codify these rulings. This bill (HR 849) was approved along party line votes by the House Judiciary Committee and the House Rules Committee, but the legislation failed to get to the floor of either chamber because of sharp partisan disagreements over "codifying" rules governing the pocket veto's use.[51]

To add to this legal confusion, in 1991 Bush declared a pocket veto of a bill passed prior to a holiday recess. The legislation honored retiring House member Morris K. Udall,

D-Ariz., by setting up a foundation to promote environmental education. Although Bush said that he supported the thrust of the legislation, he disagreed about how members of the foundation board were to be appointed. This bill was not returned to Congress, but it was not formally vetoed, so legal scholars argued that the bill should be considered a law. However, the Bush administration did nothing to publish or otherwise implement the law, so its legal status was in dispute. Congress, meanwhile, passed another version of the same bill that revised the appointment procedures, which Bush signed into law, leaving the issue of the pocket veto unsettled.[52]

What constitutes constitutional application of the pocket veto thus remains a point of contention between a Congress eager to protect legislative prerogatives and presidents equally keen to find ways to kill unwanted legislation. The issue of the pocket veto may not be settled until the Supreme Court acts. In the meantime, presidents must make their type of veto clear. When President Obama decided to veto the only two bills of his presidency through 2011, Congress happened to be out of session, so he cited the pocket veto case but also returned both bills to the House for the explicit purpose of leaving "no doubt that the bill is being vetoed." Neither veto therefore "counts" as a pocket veto. *(See box, Veto Messages, p. 156.)*

Line-item Veto

Under the Constitution, the veto is an all or nothing bargaining tool; presidents may not, for example, excise items deemed wasteful from an otherwise acceptable spending bill. Those who have supported greater presidential control over federal spending have considered this a major flaw in the veto process, particularly during the era of large federal budget deficits in the late 1980s through early 1990s, and again after 2001. Proposals to give presidents the capacity to pick and choose among specific appropriations, called a *line-item veto* (or *item veto*), have emerged periodically throughout history—to combat allegations of wastefulness in legislative add-ons to larger budget bills that are designed to benefit certain districts, often called "pork barrel" spending. Presidents have long been in favor of budget reforms that expand their institutional purview, but Congress has long been divided on the "line-item veto" because it takes away legislative power to make decisions on how to allocate funds.

Two points are often lost in this debate. First, both Congress and the president share the power of rescission, which means using a version of the legislative process to cancel funding for a project previously approved. Along these lines, for over a century presidents have had the power of impoundment, which is the temporary withholding of funds already appropriated. Although impoundment and rescission have been controversial at times, especially under

When Republicans gained control over both chambers of Congress in 1994 for the first time in forty years, Democratic president Bill Clinton was forced to rely on the veto power as a means of influencing legislation. Here Clinton talks with Nevada legislators after vetoing a bill on the storage of nuclear waste in Nevada.

Richard Nixon, they have been allowed for a variety of administrative and budgetary reasons. Technically, most "line-item veto" proposals are actually versions of rescission that expedite consideration and/or enhance presidential power in the process. Second, the line-item veto is more a symbolic gesture than a budgetary knife. Various studies of its likely effects show only about 10 percent of the budget could be considered appropriate for such a veto and the likely items would be less than 1 percent of all appropriations. Therefore, the real power of the line-item veto, and the point of the debates over it, is not deficit reduction but the deeply held perception that Congress abuses its constitutional authority to help local districts. Thus the line-item veto is part of a longer history of shifting greater budget power and fiscal responsibility toward the White House, which can be equally vulnerable to charges of wasteful spending, but in different ways.[53]

In addition, those opposing the line-item veto argue that it would not materially affect federal spending, because it could not be applied to the massive "entitlement" programs such as Social Security and Medicare that make up the bulk of federal spending and that can be reduced only by changing the laws that mandate these programs.[54] Critics also contend that presidents are no less responsible than Congress for the federal budget deficit, because they can use the regular veto to force legislative compliance if they have the political will to do so, as Clinton proved. Still others point out that any reference to line-item veto provisions in state constitutions ignores fundamental differences between federal and state government responsibilities and authority.[55] Above all, however, the debate over the line-item veto is but one part of the ongoing struggle between the president and Congress over how to share the legislative power in practice.

The Framers appear to have given no attention to a line-item veto during the drafting or ratification of the Constitution, which may reflect the fact that in economic policy debates at the time, federal revenue sources (tariff policy) and regulation (interstate commerce) were more controversial than spending. Moreover, the Framers granted to Congress expressed power over appropriations and revenues but also required presidents to approve or veto all law. However, the idea that the president should be able to veto parts of spending bills has enjoyed some popularity throughout American history. Presidents Madison and Jackson vetoed the direct and indirect funding of road building that the presidents alleged stretched too far the enumerated power of "interstate commerce" for narrow district gains (the 1817 Bonus Bill and 1830 Maysville Road Bill, respectively). The states of the Confederacy included in their constitution a clause that enabled its president to "approve any appropriation and disapprove any other appropriation in the same bill" (Article 1, Section 7, Clause 2). Efforts to pass a constitutional amendment granting such executive power have popped up since the 1870s, but without success. Yet by the 1990s governors in forty-three states had some form of line-item veto. Most of these provisions pertain primarily to spending bills, but others also allow governors to modify substantive laws. At least ten states allow their governors to actually amend spending bills and send them back to the legislature for reconsideration.[56]

Some mid-twentieth-century presidents expressed strong support for a line-item veto, most notably Franklin

Roosevelt and Eisenhower. Roosevelt came closest to realizing his wish when the House voted in 1938 to give the president that power: the effort died in the Senate, however.[57] The issue was set aside through the 1970s, but arose again in the 1980s as the federal budget deficit became a major problem. Like the budget, however, the line-item veto quickly became enmeshed in partisan politics, with Republican presidents Reagan and George H. W. Bush in favor and congressional Democrats generally opposed. Supporters argued that the line-item veto would give presidents greater control over federal spending, especially on programs and projects for which Congress may lack the political will to make cuts. Opponents expressed fears that a line-item veto would give the president excessive power over an area in which Congress traditionally—and constitutionally—took the lead.

This clash of partisan and institutional perspectives prevented proposals for the line-item veto from getting very far during the 1980s. In 1985 Reagan and congressional Republicans pushed for a two-year trial run, but the proposal was rebuffed both then and a year later. Even if the Senate had approved the line-item veto in 1986, it was unlikely that the House, which jealously guards its constitutional power of the purse, would have gone along. President George H. W. Bush also pushed publicly for a line-item veto, but he too had little success.

By the mid-1990s, however, the political dynamics surrounding the line-item veto had changed dramatically. President Clinton, who had possessed a line-item veto as governor of Arkansas, openly supported one for the president. Yet key congressional Democrats continued to fight any action that might infringe on Congress's control over the budget. As it turned out, Clinton found an ally on this issue in congressional Republicans, who in 1994 gained control of both chambers of Congress for the first time since 1952. The line-item veto was included in the Republicans' "Contract with America," in part because they anticipated the election of a Republican president in 1996, and thus the prospects for passing some kind of line-item veto improved dramatically. However, efforts to pass a constitutional amendment creating a line-item veto soon fell victim to resistance in the Senate—where even some Republicans opposed it—so proponents took another tack. After months of negotiations, a bipartisan majority voted to grant to the president "enhanced rescission" authority, the power to "cancel" automatically individual items in spending and tax bills unless overturned by a two-thirds vote of both houses of Congress. President Clinton signed this bill into law on April 9, 1996.[58]

Clinton used this new statutory authority for the first—and only—time in 1997, when he cut items in eleven spending bills, ranging from $15,000 allocated for a police training center in Alabama to $30 million for a military program to intercept asteroids in space. Members of Congress who supported the new authority suddenly were faced with actual cuts in pet projects, and Clinton suffered one of his only two veto overrides when Congress restored funding he had struck out in a military construction spending bill. Officials of both parties in New York, upset over some of Clinton's cuts, supported a lawsuit against the president over the new authority. A six-member majority of the Supreme Court, in *City of New York v. Clinton* (1998), struck down the Line Item Veto Act as unconstitutional, ruling that, as constituted, the line-item veto violated the "presentment clause" in Article I, Section 7 of the Constitution.[59]

Immediate reaction to the Supreme Court's decision was muted in part because soon after the decision, three decades of deficits suddenly turned to surpluses—temporarily. In his first term, George W. Bush's war on terror program abroad and at home, increased domestic expenditures, a series of tax cuts that reduced revenue, and an economic recession all added up to new deficits and fights over how to reduce them. President Bush once again called for the authority to exercise a line-item veto. Its proponents continued to suggest that such an instrument will help presidents to limit federal spending, excise "wasteful" congressional appropriations, and promote their budget priorities. Opponents disagreed with enhancing presidential power in this way as the line-item veto allows presidents to shift spending rather than simply count the money toward deficit reduction. Along these lines, political commentator George Will once described the line-item veto as an "effective instrument of allocation" that helps presidents carry out their electoral "mandates" to shape the overall direction of the federal government.[60]

President Bush proposed legislation in 2006 that would give the president a modified form of the rescission authority exercised by Clinton. Bush's proposal came in the wake of a growing budget deficit and increased public scrutiny of the practice of legislative "earmarks"—provisions members of Congress insert into legislation in order to fund programs that often benefit their constituents, campaign contributors, or pet projects. Under Bush's proposal, the president could eliminate portions of spending bills, as well as tax cuts targeting fewer than one hundred people, and return the excised items to Congress, which would then have ten days to decide whether to repass them by a simple majority vote in each house. Bush argued that this legislation would pass constitutional muster because it was not, constitutionally speaking, a true veto since Congress did not need a two-thirds vote to override the president's action. This last line-item veto effort died in the Senate but various earmark reforms, which accomplish a similar purpose but preserve institutional power, gained momentum under both party majorities since the 2006 elections. The Republican majority largely banned this type of spending in the House in the 112th Congress and the Senate

Sen. Patrick Toomey, R-Pa., (left) Chief Justice John Roberts, Secretary of State Hillary Clinton, and Transportation Secretary Ray LaHood (right) stand along the aisle as President Obama enters the House chamber to deliver his State of the Union address on January 25, 2011. Vice President Biden and House Speaker John Boehner (R-Ohio) stand in front of the flag.

Appropriations Committee followed suit even though it was under Democratic control, as mentioned earlier. As has been the case in previous administrations seeking the line-item veto, those in Congress who support this idea in theory have to reconcile the reality that they may or may not trust the occupant of the White House to use the power in a fiscally responsible way rather than as a permanent tool of threat and negotiation with members.

"Quasi-item Vetoes"

Presidents have compensated for the lack of formal line-item veto power through other means. For one thing, they have "impounded"—or *not* spent—money appropriated by Congress for fiscal or administrative reasons. The concept of impoundment has not been controversial when presidents could show that the expenditure was no longer needed—such as when Thomas Jefferson impounded funds earmarked for new naval ships because the hostilities that had prompted the appropriation had halted—or when unforeseen circumstances delayed spending. But when presidents try to use impoundment to thwart the intent of Congress for fiscal or policy reasons, a sharp conflict is guaranteed.

Presidents rarely resorted to impoundment until the 1970s, largely because they sought to avoid major fights with Congress over control of the purse.[61] In 1973–1974, however, Richard Nixon—concerned about the amount of government spending against the backdrop of rising inflation—impounded nearly $12 billion of congressional appropriations, or more than 4 percent of the money appropriated for the coming fiscal year. Nixon's attempt proved so controversial that the Democrat-controlled Congress passed in 1974 (over Nixon's veto) the Budget and Impoundment

Control Act. This legislation restricted the president's impoundment authority by dividing impoundments into two categories: rescissions, or permanent cancellations of budget authority that required congressional approval, and temporary deferrals of expenditures, which remained in force unless rejected by Congress. Jurisdiction over both categories was assigned to the Appropriations Committees of the House and Senate.

Since then, presidents have continued to "defer" or "rescind" funds under the auspices of the law, although the actions deemed the most controversial have encountered congressional resistance. In 1986, for example, President Reagan attempted to defer $5 billion for housing and urban development programs because Congress had appropriated more money than he had requested, but a federal appeals court ruled that his actions violated the intent of the 1974 law.[62] As mentioned earlier, most "line-item veto" proposals, including the 1996 statute, are misnamed because they are not "true" line-item vetoes but rather elaborate mechanisms to enhance and/or expedite the effects of existing presidential rescission powers.

Presidents also on occasion refuse to abide by specific provisions in laws they sign, or they issue their own interpretations of the law when they think Congress has acted unconstitutionally. In 1959, for example, President Eisenhower announced that he would disregard a provision for congressional access to secret documents because it would violate the president's need to protect national security. In 1971 Nixon insisted that he was not bound by a provision requiring the president to state a specific time period for withdrawal from Vietnam.[63] In both cases, the president effectively undermined the force of the provision in question, yet the constitutionality of these actions has not been tested in court.[64] President George H. W. Bush likewise objected to provisions in appropriations bills that he nevertheless signed into law. In particular, Bush complained about what he saw as unconstitutional congressional interference in executive branch prerogatives, and he expressed his desire for a line-item veto.[65]

Bush's son, President George W. Bush, however, made the most significant use of these presidential "signing statements" as a means of signaling his dissatisfaction with the details of bills even as he signed them into law. According to James P. Pfiffner, through signing statements President Bush implied he would not execute more than 1,000 statutory provisions over the course of his two terms in office. Pfiffner argues that President Bush's use of these statements differed fundamentally from his predecessors.

> For most of U.S. history, presidents have issued signing statements to comment on bills being signed into law. These statements often are hortatory and comment on the merits of the new law. In recent decades, presidents also have used signing statements to indicate portions of laws that they consider unconstitutional. Pointing out such parts of new statutes is not a problem, but indicating that the president may not execute part of the law is problematic . . . this practice undermines the rule of law and threatens the separation of powers system.[66]

In defending this practice, Bush's advisers argued that his actions were consistent with those of previous presidents, and that he had an obligation not to enforce laws that he believed encroached on presidential authority or that were otherwise unconstitutional. Moreover, they assert that just because he reserved the right to disobey a law did not necessarily mean he would not enforce it. Many signing statements, supporters say, are designed to give direction to those responsible for implementing the measure by clarifying the law's intent. But critics suggest that Bush's strategy was tantamount to selectively vetoing portions of a bill without giving Congress the opportunity to override his objections. They point out that many of these bills passed Congress after Bush agreed to compromise on legislative details, only to see Bush then unilaterally assert the right to ignore those compromises.[67] This helps explain Bush's lack of vetoes, they claim; rather than give Congress the opportunity to override his veto, Bush preferred to sign legislation into law even as he announced his intent to ignore those portions he opposed.

Bush's expansive use of signing statements, especially on national security issues, was but one part of a concerted effort by members of his administration to reclaim presidential powers that they believed began slipping away as far back as Nixon's presidency. Critics responded that Bush's effort to aggrandize power in the executive branch raises the specter of a new imperialist presidency. In truth, however, the struggle between the president and Congress to stake out and defend their respective roles in the legislative process is ongoing, its origins dating back to the writing of the Constitution. Whether the issue is pocket vetoes, impoundments, or signing statements, the Constitution is open to different interpretations on these matters. This ambiguity invites "ambition to counteract ambition," as members of both branches assert their institutional prerogatives. In other words, muscular interpretations of vague constitutional boundaries are important tools for any president seeking strategic substitutes to engaging in prolonged legislative conflicts with Congress.[68] The courts may step in to temporarily quell the dispute, but they rarely end it; the institutional clash regarding legislative roles merely erupts at a later date, and often in another form.

At the same time, it is important to remember that checks and balances, combined with the frequency of partisan turnover in recent decades, provide opportunity for other political actors to fight back against, or reverse, presidential aggressiveness. If the public, courts, members of Congress, and the media fail to stop extraordinary and/or prolonged episodes of presidential aggrandizement, the White House does not have any incentive to dilute its expansive view of power. For example, from the first iteration of the USA PATRIOT Act (or, the Patriot Act) in 2001 to a major intelligence overhaul in 2007, President Bush and executive branch officials said repeatedly that the administration would not obey certain reporting requirements to Congress. But Congress was compliant on the issue and did little more than complain. One of these moments came in 2008, which was a low point in Bush's public approval and a potential time for congressional reassertion of power through a new Democratic majority. In response to another instance where the administration said it would not comply with an intelligence reporting provision related to a 2007 law, Sen. Arlen Specter (R-Pa.) said, "this is a dictatorial, after-the-fact pronouncement by him in line with a lot of other cherry-picking he's done on the signing statements. To put it differently, I don't like it worth a damn."[69] Just a few months later, soon after his inauguration, President Barack Obama ordered a review of Bush's signing statements, which he had criticized as a senator and on the campaign trail.

However, Obama's promise was to curtail "abuse" of signing statements, not curtail the practice altogether. In early 2009 he explained his criteria in a memorandum to the agency and department heads of his branch, saying "[i]n exercising my responsibility to determine whether a provision of an enrolled bill is unconstitutional, I will act with caution and restraint, based only on interpretations of the Constitution that are well-founded."[70] Soon after, Obama was embroiled in a war of words with two leading Democrats in the House, Reps. David Obey (D-Wis.) and Barney Frank

(D-Mass.) over a signing statement in which the president said he could ignore a facet of a law concerning international banking aid that provided negotiation instructions. Although Obama pledged to fulfill the mandate as Congress intended, he said as a point of principle that such types of restrictions were open to presidential interpretation of his foreign policy prerogatives. The House took the next step by voting 429–2 to deny federal funds for any activity related to ignoring congressional direction. Obey and Frank went further in a letter to Obama threatening to withhold all money to the International Monetary Fund and the World Bank if Obama went through with such disobedience. According to Phillip Cooper, a scholar who studies signing statements, Obama "has not pushed the envelope as far as the Bush administration in making the kind of claims that Bush made. But he is still using it in ways that were controversial before George W. Bush came to office."[71]

THE PRESIDENT'S PROGRAM

The president's second express constitutional duty in the legislative process is to "from time to time give to the Congress Information of the State of the Union, and recommend to their Consideration such Measures as he shall judge necessary and expedient" (Article II, Section 3). At first blush, this authority to "recommend . . . Measures" seems rather minor, but over time it has become the primary mechanism used by presidents to shape the nation's political agenda, particularly when the nation is not in crisis. To shape the agenda of government—to decide what is or is not a priority—is to decide what government will or will not do.[72] As the political scientist E. E. Schattschneider concluded: "He who determines what politics is all about runs the country, because the definition of the alternatives is the choice of conflicts, and the choice of conflicts allocates power."[73]

Presidents naturally would love to have complete control over the agenda of government, especially at the very start of their terms in office. But in reality a president's control over the agenda is tenuous. At times it is overwhelmed by unforeseen crises such as natural disasters, war, or sudden shifts in the economy. When a crisis occurs, the existing agenda is thrown aside, and a president's "success" is judged solely by the pace and suitability of the response. In the short run, such crises typically magnify a president's agenda-setting power. Franklin Roosevelt's reaction to the virtual collapse of the banking system on the eve of his inauguration in 1933 often is cited as an example of strong presidential leadership. Within days of taking office, Roosevelt called the Democrat-controlled Congress into special session to pass legislation reorganizing the entire federal banking system. Even more important, he went on national radio to persuade citizens to return their savings to the banks, instilling renewed faith in the financial system

and taking the first steps toward economic recovery. This marked the start of the celebrated "First Hundred Days" during which Roosevelt worked with Congress to produce fifteen major bills that collectively reshaped every aspect of the economy, from banking and industry to agriculture and social welfare.[74]

The effect of a crisis on a president's agenda-setting power, however, is typically short-lived and can even backfire if exploited too far. George W. Bush's presidency was fundamentally transformed by the need to respond to the terrorist attacks of September 11, 2001. Prior to the attacks, Bush experienced some legislative success on tax cuts and education reform. But on other issues, including his energy plan and grants of federal aid to religious charities, his legislative initiatives seemed stalled. After the attacks, however, Bush refocused his legislative priorities on war-related issues both at home and abroad. His efforts to do so, at least initially, found strong support within Congress and among the public from domestic initiatives (the Patriot Act) to congressional resolutions supporting war against Afghanistan and Iraq. But as the Iraq war in particular proved longer and more expensive than predicted by the administration, support for his entire antiterror foreign policy agenda began to ebb. As an unexpected civil war continued unabated in Iraq, and U.S. military casualties on both fronts eclipsed the total killed on September 11, 2001, Democrats capitalized on the growing opposition to U.S. involvement to regain control of Congress in the 2006 midterm elections.

Despite such possible political fallout, the next crisis proved equally tempting to the next president. In light of the economic meltdown framing the last months of the 2008 presidential campaign, President-elect Barack Obama's designated chief of staff, Rahm Emanuel, discussed openly the presidential strategy of crisis leadership. In a *Wall Street Journal*–sponsored forum for corporate executives in mid-November 2008, Emanuel elaborated on several examples of successes and failures in presidential use of crises to gain legislative victories. One example of failure, he said, was the international oil crisis of the early 1970s, which provided a moment, ultimately squandered he said, to create new energy policy and reduce U.S. dependency on foreign oil. Likewise, he said, the 2008 economic crisis provided a similar opportunity for the new president.

> You never want a serious crisis to go to waste. Things that we had postponed for too long, that were long-term, are now immediate and must be dealt with. This crisis provides the opportunity for us to do things that you could not do before. . . . The good news, I suppose, if you want to see a silver lining, is that the problems are big enough that they lend themselves to ideas from both parties for the solution.[75]

Crises aside, the presidency has always had a singularly unique *institutional* capacity to shape the nation's agenda of debate and action. As the only political office (along with the vice presidency) with a national majority constituency, the presidency serves as a public focal point, uniquely suited to address issues of national priority. But this unique vantage point assumed greater importance in the second half of the twentieth century, due to the growth in scope and influence of the federal government, the emergence of the United States as a superpower—which amplifies the president's role as commander in chief—and the emergence of modern telecommunications.

Today the president, political scientist Bruce Miroff suggests, commands the most area within the "public space" of U.S. politics, largely forcing other participants in the political process to respond to issues as the president defines them.[76] That reality powerfully influences success or failure on policy initiatives, particularly in issue areas in which Americans have no direct experience. For example, most Americans, including members of Congress, had little means for independently evaluating the Bush administration claims that Saddam Hussein's Iraqi government possessed weapons of mass destruction, or that it was actively involved in supporting terrorist actions against the United States. This made it difficult to oppose Bush's decision to invade Iraq in 2003.

Yet the president's institutional capacity to define the national agenda is a largely modern phenomenon; it proved less potent throughout most of the nineteenth century. The federal government was small, and responsible for few national issues, including territorial expansion, tariffs, and foreign policy. Congress, often led by leaders of national reputation, dominated policy debate. Presidents, on the other hand, were not expected to formulate legislative agendas, prepare and present executive budgets, or do much else except oversee the rather modest executive branch, conduct foreign policy (such as it was when the United States was relatively isolated), and keep a check on Congress whenever necessary and possible. Nor did the dominant public view of government hold that presidents should actively initiate or influence public policy, something that would be difficult in any case without technologies of mass communication. While a handful of presidents in the "premodern" age were known for major legislative accomplishments, not until Franklin Roosevelt did the presidency become a permanently strong institution, one that remained potent in the national eye regardless of the person sitting in the Oval Office. In fact, the presumption of a muscular and ambitious executive branch became so ingrained in the national psyche that by the late twentieth century, if presidents were not immediately successful in getting their programs through Congress, they were often branded as weak leaders by the media.[77] Of course, this stereotype neglects the enduring constitutional complications of a separation of powers system.

Congress and the Presidency: Separate Branches

Any discussion of the president's influence over legislation must first recognize the essential differences between the branches. Above all, the Constitution grants to Congress the preponderance of power over national policy. Only Congress has the enumerated power to make the law, generate revenues, and appropriate funds, but as these measures are laws they would need presidential approval. The Constitution also establishes governing roles and creates policymaking dynamics that set Congress fundamentally far apart from the presidency. In addition, presidential agendas and promises are constantly threatened (or potentially enhanced) by the constant possibility of majority party turnover in the House and Senate every two years. These structural factors have remained remarkably constant throughout history and are important to understanding why presidents succeed or fail in achieving their legislative goals.[78]

Presidents and members of Congress reach office through entirely separate and distinct paths. The national electorate ideally gives the president a broader perspective on issues. In reality, presidents are elected by majorities that are attached disproportionately to one party and certain regions of the country. Presidents can certainly claim policy mandates upon victory, but would be wise to remember that millions of people voted against their ticket and campaign agenda. Members of Congress, by contrast, come to national government out of much smaller, localized constituencies, whether House districts or states. For members of Congress, "all politics is local," as Speaker of the House Thomas P. "Tip" O'Neill was fond of saying.[79] Members of Congress can and do think broadly about policy questions, but their constitutionally assigned roles as representatives of a specific set of citizens require that they tend to their constituents' needs first to gain a majority for their own next contest.

Presidents and members of Congress also serve for different terms of office. A president serves for four years, but members of the House must run for election every two years, which, as the Framers intended, maintains their sensitivity to the momentary needs and opinions of the people. House members' tendency to focus more on short-term concerns can cause problems for a president's agenda. And, because all House members (and one-third of all senators, who serve six-year terms) are up for reelection in the second year of the president's term, midterm elections frequently are construed as public judgments on presidential performance. The president's party almost invariably loses House and Senate seats in midterm elections, and members of Congress from the president's party are keenly aware that public disenchantment with their leader may cause them serious electoral problems. The opposition party, for its part, naturally tries to use these contests to its advantage.

The 2006 and 2010 midterm elections are cases in point. In 2006 Democrats picked up six Senate and thirty-one

House seats to sweep up control of Congress for the first time since 1994. Pundits proclaimed it an especially stinging defeat for the president's party. Judged by the number of Republican seats lost, however, the outcome was not atypical for a midterm election. Since the end of World War II, the average loss for the party of a second-term presidency in its sixth year has been twenty-nine House seats and six Senate seats, almost exactly what took place in 2006. However, the 2006 results took on greater significance in light of more recent midterm elections, especially 1998 and 2002, which exhibited much smaller shifts in party seats, and because they led to the loss of Republican control in Congress. Exit polls suggested that much of the blame for the Republicans' setback could be traced to voter discontent with the Bush administration's handling of the Iraq war, as well as their dissatisfaction with the ethics of the Republican-controlled Congress. In 2010 the partisan results were more mixed. The House turned to a Republican majority with a gain of sixty-three seats. The Senate remained in Democratic hands by a slim margin.[80]

Similarly, the 1994 midterm election results are viewed as a rebuke to President Clinton. His party lost fifty-four House and eight Senate seats, and the opposition Republicans gained control of both chambers of Congress for the first time since 1952. From 1993 to 1994, President Clinton had been able to count on Democratic control of the House and Senate to help him pass much of his legislative program, but Republican control of Congress in 1995 altered the political equation for both Congress and the president by temporarily shifting control over the legislative agenda from the White House to the new and assertive congressional majority.

As time went on, however, House Republicans encountered the reality that an institution made up of 435 semiautonomous individuals is hard-pressed to maintain control over the agenda in the face of the presidency's institutional capacity to dominate the nation's attention. Clinton, as noted earlier, used his institutional powers and his overall political skills to great effect in forcing House Republicans onto the defensive throughout the rest of his presidency, even during the period surrounding his impeachment and trial. Indeed, that Republicans actually *lost* House seats in the 1998 midterm elections, a nearly unprecedented occurrence for the party not in the White House, attested to the degree to which they no longer controlled the terms of debate. In addition, although the Senate majority also went to the GOP in the 1994 elections, Republicans in that chamber had not signed the "Contract with America," which was organized by then-House Republican Whip Newt Gingrich. The House was pleased to make good on nine out of ten specific legislative promises, but even as the parties were more polarized in both chambers, the Senate's supermajority hurdles and slightly more moderate Republican leadership posed numerous challenges—even before the legislation could reach President Clinton's desk for signature or veto. In the fall of 1996, Sarah Binder of the Brookings Institution summed up the chamber differences.

> Unlike the House, where simple partisan majorities can prevail over minority opposition, bipartisan agreement is all but essential in the Senate. Unless the majority in the Senate has a filibuster-proof roster of 60 senators consistently willing to cut off debate, it will continually be stymied by minority opposition. Much of the legislation that grew out of the House Republican Contract with America in 1995 languished and died in the Senate despite the support of the majority, a fate that illustrates well the effects of ideologically distant parties in the Senate.[81]

For these reasons and more, the Senate can provide even more challenges for the president than it does for the House. Members of the Senate serve for six years, with only one-third of the body up for reelection every two years. Thus most senators are not affected directly by a presidential election, and they have much greater freedom to oppose presidential initiatives without as much concern about short-term constituent pressures. The Senate also retains constitutional leverage over the executive through its power to approve presidential nominees to the federal judiciary and to high-level executive branch positions, and through its power to approve or reject treaties with other nations. Moreover, as mentioned above by Binder, the supermajority decision-making procedures in the Senate are designed to protect the minority party to a far greater degree than in the House, which is typically dominated by the majority party.

These characteristics of the Senate guarantee problems for presidents, even with senators of the same party. Jimmy Carter failed to obtain Senate approval for the 1978 Strategic Arms Limitation Treaty despite Democratic dominance of the chamber, and Ronald Reagan faced the greatest opposition on the 1987 Intermediate Nuclear Forces Treaty from conservative Republicans. In June 2001 the decision by Sen. James Jeffords of Vermont to become an independent cost Republicans control of the then evenly divided Senate and forced the George W. Bush administration to alter its legislative strategy accordingly. Even after Republicans regained control of the Senate in 2002, Bush was forced to moderate many of his policies, such as reducing the size of his second round of tax cuts, in order to ensure Senate support.

The two branches also have distinct decision-making cultures and processes that emerge from their fundamentally different governing responsibilities. The president, whose primary constitutional responsibilities are to implement the laws and act as commander in chief of the armed forces, is ultimately responsible for all law he signs, even though the legislative responsibility is shared with Congress. But it goes too far to say that the executive branch speaks with one voice; even within the president's White House staff, aides are quite adept at courting Congress and enlisting the media as allies in their effort to persuade the president to adopt their policy preferences. Officials working in the outlying departments and agencies, moreover, are at least as responsive to congressional preferences as they are to the president's. Nonetheless, final policy decisions emanating from the executive branch do usually reflect the president's overall ideology and political agenda. Loyalty to the president's program is a paramount virtue among all executive branch appointees, particularly those working closely with the president; those who openly dissent find access to the president severely limited, if not cut off completely.[82]

Congress, by contrast, speaks with many voices simultaneously, one for each of the 535 members of the House and Senate—not to mention party leaders, committee chairs, the territorial delegates, staff members, and professionals in the congressional agencies. Congress as an institution rarely (if ever) projects a coherent sense of direction. Members both represent their constituents and make national policy—that is, they play often conflicting roles, because what is good for any member's constituents (such as new services or public facilities) may bode ill for the nation as a whole (in the form of budget deficits, for example). Each member wields one vote, regardless of seniority or party position, and no member can be expelled from the legislature simply because of voting behavior or personal opinion. Only constituents have the right to "fire" their representatives.

This constitutionally generated egalitarianism forces Congress as an institution to adhere to relatively nonhierarchical decision-making processes. To do otherwise would appear antidemocratic. Decisions, whether in the form of new pieces of legislation or agreements on appropriations bills, among other things, are achieved only by building coalitions of members large enough to win a succession of committee and floor votes. Successful legislating depends on knitting together enough diverse interests and demands to overcome opposition, even among members of the same party, using whatever tactics seem reasonable or necessary. This is especially true in the even less hierarchical Senate, where traditional voting rules allow a single member to obstruct the majority—or the president—until agreement surfaces. Even as studies of both chambers of Congress show that party power and cohesion has increased greatly in the past two decades, thus giving party leaders greater leeway in gaining and enforcing party discipline, Congress can never truly rival the hierarchy and unity of the executive branch.[83]

This clash of cultures powerfully shapes the way in which the branches interact. Presidents always want to move quickly to make the most of their limited opportunities through comprehensive and often dramatic policy initiatives. This is true particularly in the first year, as every president knows that the personal popularity so critical to overcoming the normal inertia of the political system inevitably fades. But, assuming the absence of acknowledged crisis, Congress generally prefers a more cautious weighing of the consequences. Each member's constituency must be treated fairly, and coalitions of support must be constructed. Such considerations usually are more important to Congress, particularly to the Senate, than speed or ideological purity. Many a president has chastised Congress for its glacial pace of deliberation, but the legislature by design marches to its own drummer.

These fundamental differences invariably produce clashes between presidents, who must act on behalf of a national constituency, and members of Congress, who promote their more local constituents' needs. Presidents routinely accuse Congress of waste or inertia, but they also find that cumulative local and state interests often overcome any supposed national good. For example, in 1987 Reagan vetoed a popular reauthorization of the Clean Water Act because he argued that its $20 billion appropriation for water and sewage treatment projects was wasteful, but Congress overrode his veto by overwhelming bipartisan margins. Clinton's effort to push a comprehensive overhaul of the nation's health care system ultimately fell prey in part to the tug of special interests, with members of his party unable—and often unwilling—to push the president's plan through determined Republican opposition. George W. Bush's effort to rein in Social Security costs, in part by allowing taxpayers to reduce their Social Security contributions and instead invest that money in individual investment accounts, met with considerable skepticism, even from members of his own party, who feared a political backlash from voters opposed to tinkering with such a sacrosanct program.[84]

Compared to the aggressive style of his predecessor, Barack Obama has thus far showed more patience with the legislative process, prefers not to get personally involved in every detail, and is less combative with Congress. Under both parties' majority rule in Congress, Obama was relatively deferential to the needs of leaders as well as new rank-and-file members as he gave time and policy room to Congress to fill in key details. While Obama racked up many bold legislative successes from economic stimulus, to health care reform, to financial regulation overhaul, his pragmatic style of leadership perplexed the Beltway from the beginning of his term. In light of the debt ceiling debates of summer 2011, analysts pondered whether his interest in compromise, bipartisanship, and hovering above the fray undermined his leadership moments.[85]

Compare these dynamics with those of a parliamentary system, where the prime minister is selected by the majority party (or party coalition) in the legislature. There is no separation of institutions in the American sense, and strong party cohesion is essential to maintaining control over government. In Great Britain, it is usually the case that a strong party majority allows the prime minister to push through major legislation far more easily and quickly than any American president could imagine—at least so long as she or he maintained his party's majority. In the United States, by contrast, members of Congress can openly go against their party and president when constituent interests are on the line. What the Constitution splits apart, party loyalty cannot easily bind together.[86]

While these fundamental differences between the separated powers U.S. system and the parliamentary system are clear, sometimes the U.S. can mimic the qualities of the latter through agreement between the branches. The policy legacies of Franklin Roosevelt, Lyndon Johnson, and George W. Bush show that under certain partisan and policy moments, the president can rack up win after win. Even though Obama has been criticized by both parties for his seemingly passive leadership style, his measurable successes rival these predecessors. In 2009, despite high levels of rancor about his first major policy in office (more than $800 billion economic stimulus), a *CQ* study proclaimed Obama's first year an extraordinarily effective one, as measured by legislative successes. With solid Democratic majorities in both chambers, he won votes in Congress 96.7 percent of the time on issues on which he had staked out a public position.[87]

In 2010 controversy over Obama's health care proposal dominated political news the entire year, but he achieved something that had eluded Democratic presidents for decades. In March, after months of negotiation and compromise and without a single Republican vote in either chamber, Congress passed the health care overhaul. Republicans campaigned to "repeal and replace" in 2010. In early 2011 the House voted to repeal the plan, but the measure died in the Democratic Senate. As the issue bubbled up in the federal court system, where parts of the reform received mixed judicial outcomes, and the 2012 presidential election gained momentum, Obama's long-term health policy legacy looked to be in flux for years.[88]

The relationship between the president and Congress is shaped powerfully by the Constitution. The Framers were far more concerned with checking the potential abuses of power than with speedy or easy legislating. They wanted Congress and the president to compete for power and to protect their own institutional prerogatives, and they endowed Congress with the capacity to withstand executive pressure and to dictate policy if it so willed. Even when dominated by the president's party, Congress as an institution insists on playing its independent constitutional role according to its own needs and internal dynamics. No president can forget those realities. The dynamics of president-Congress relations changes many times, even during a single term. Legislative successes depend on navigating the obstacles set up by the Constitution as well as the latest partisan shifts and the constant scrutiny of the media.

Historical Development

"Whether legislator, opinion-maker, commander, or administrator," noted presidential scholar Clinton Rossiter, "the President molds lasting policy in every sector of American life."[89] Presidents recognize as much; early in his presidential term George W. Bush promised to propose "creative ways to tackle some of the toughest problems in our society."[90] Implicitly criticizing the outcomes of Bush's tenure, early in his presidency Obama said he would take the country in a dramatically different direction than his predecessor:

> Throughout America's history, there have been some years that appeared to roll into the next without much notice or fanfare. Budgets are proposed that offer some new programs or eliminate an initiative, but by and large continuity reigns.
>
> Then there are the years that come along once in a generation, when we look at where the country has been and recognize that we need a break from a troubled past, that the problems we face demand that we begin charting a new path. This is one of those years.[91]

Indeed, as political scientist Bertram Gross wrote in 1953: "Except in wartime, Presidents are now judged more by the quality of the legislation they propose or succeed in getting enacted than by their records as executive."[92] Today the presidency appears to be almost another house of Congress, with presidents involved deeply in all aspects of the legislative process and judged by how well they mobilize support for their programs.

The contrast between these contemporary analyses and the experiences of early presidents is noteworthy. Rather than expecting the president to formulate a legislative program and lobby for its enactment, Congress through the 1800s usually resisted presidential involvement in lawmaking as an unwarranted intrusion.[93] Textbook notions that Congress alone makes law, which the president then simply administers, were taken seriously, and presidents who forgot this constitutional nicety were quickly reminded of it by members of Congress always on guard against such presumptuousness.

Whether the Framers meant the president to play so passive a role is hotly debated. Certainly they viewed the presidency chiefly as a bulwark against congressional mischief or tyranny. Yet Alexander Hamilton argued in *Federalist* No. 70 that "energy in the executive is a leading character of good government."[94] The Framers rejected the more monarchical schemes for the executive proposed early on by Hamilton and others, but they also rejected making the president entirely subordinate to or separate from Congress. The legislature makes the law, but the Framers did give the president a limited number of instruments for influencing legislation. How effectively the president could bring those resources to bear, however, would be another question.

Early Presidents

George Washington discovered rather quickly how difficult it would be for a president to influence legislation when he became the first—and the last—president ever to sit with Congress during actual floor debate. Washington believed that oral communications were essential to fruitful relations between the branches, so on August 22, 1789, he personally presented to the Senate the particulars of an Indian treaty—the very first to be considered under the procedures prescribed by the Constitution—and requested the Senate's immediate advice and consent. But, to his surprise, the Senate did not automatically approve the treaty. Its main points were read aloud—twice, because some senators could not hear for the noise coming in off the street—after which time an awkward silence descended on the chamber. Sen. William Maclay of Pennsylvania then called for a reading of the treaty itself, and of its accompanying papers, and supported a move to refer the entire matter to a committee for further study. Maclay, as he later wrote in his journal, "saw no chance of fair investigation of subjects if the President of the United States sat there, with his Secretary of War, to support his opinions and over-awe the timid and neutral part of the Senate." Washington, wrote Maclay, "started up in a violent fret" at the proposal to refer the matter to committee, exclaiming, "This defeats every purpose of my coming here." The president eventually calmed down and agreed to a two-day delay, but on his return he found many senators still uneasy about his presence. After completing the business at hand, Washington vowed that he would not repeat the experience.[95]

Washington nonetheless actively sought more indirect influence over legislation. He used cabinet members to lobby members of Congress, a task taken up with particular enthusiasm by Secretary of the Treasury Hamilton, whose ardent belief in an energetic presidency and tireless use of his department to initiate and lobby for legislation soon sparked a backlash—and not just in Congress. In a letter to the president, Secretary of State Thomas Jefferson, despite his overall support for Washington, objected strenuously that Hamilton's "system flowed from principles adverse to liberty, and was calculated to undermine and demolish the republic, by creating an influence of his department over the members of the legislature."[96]

Jefferson, whose Democratic-Republican Party in principle glorified the concept of congressional supremacy, also eschewed personal lobbying when he became president. He went so far as to suspend the fledgling tradition of personally delivering an annual State of the Union message. *(See box, The State of the Union Address as Political Theater, p. 179.)* But Jefferson was no passive chief executive. He carefully maintained the forms of separated branches and congressional supremacy but relied heavily on cabinet members and the strong congressional caucus of his party, which held the majority in Congress, to initiate and dominate legislative activity. Secretary of the Treasury Albert Gallatin acted as his primary liaison to the party caucus, but Jefferson personally picked the party's floor leaders, who then became known as the president's chief congressional representatives. The strength of the party caucus, held together in many ways by Jefferson's own political skills (and his widely acclaimed dinner parties), produced a style of governing that in many ways paralleled parliamentary systems.

After Jefferson, however, "King Caucus" gave way to congressional supremacy. Jefferson's model of party government decayed as regional and ideological splits within the Democratic-Republican Party eroded its usefulness as a mechanism for executive leverage. Power flowed back to Congress as an institution, and strong congressional leaders such as Henry Clay and John C. Calhoun actively set the agenda of government through the 1820s. House Speaker Clay in particular dominated tariff and public works matters and with his allies even forced a reluctant James Madison to confront the British in the War of 1812. Congress also began to develop its own institutional expertise in policymaking, in particular through the standing committees, which during the mid-1800s evolved into power centers in their own right as presidents came and went.[97]

In the 1830s, Andrew Jackson momentarily reinvigorated the role of the (now) Democratic Party and its national convention as a means of setting the national agenda. More notably, the breadth and strength of his party organization allowed Jackson to become the first president to appeal directly to the public over the heads of Congress on issues such as the National Bank and the tariff.[98] However, Jackson's overall legislative strategy was largely reactive, and he relied heavily on his veto power to check hostile congressional initiatives. The idea that the president should actively propose and shepherd legislation through Congress was still controversial, and the increasing power of the congressional standing committees limited Jackson's capacity to dominate Congress through the party.[99]

Aside from these few relatively active presidents, and not including Lincoln's emergency actions during the Civil War, nineteenth-century legislating generally was a congressional affair. The president's constitutional responsibilities over foreign policy and the armed forces did not matter much, since the United States during most of this century kept resolutely out of international politics and maintained a minimal peacetime defense and foreign policy apparatus. On the domestic side, the federal government concerned itself largely with matters like post offices, setting tariff rates, and other public works projects. Except in times of crisis, then, the national government did relatively little through the 1800s, and the presidency played a secondary role in policy formation. Congress never shied away from reminding presidents of their "proper" role, and even Abraham Lincoln, toward the end of the Civil War, was admonished by House leaders that the president "must confine himself to executive duties—to obey and execute, not make the laws."[100]

Shift toward Presidential Leadership

The legislative role of the presidency began to change toward the end of the nineteenth century as powerful economic, technological, and social forces reshaped the American landscape, and as the United States began to play a greater role in the world. The industrial revolution brought about a transition from a self-sufficient farm economy to an urban manufacturing economy, from largely localized business concerns to huge national corporations, and, as a result, a shift from a minimalist view of federal government action to calls for it to do more. Issues such as interstate commerce, corporate monopoly, child labor, food and drug purity, monetary policy, agricultural research, and rail transportation became more national in scope and often overlapped with the international trade and diplomacy issues that were growing in importance as the United States became more active in the world.

These trends altered prevailing views about the role of the national government and, by extension, of the presidency. Calls for more active executive leadership on legislation began to be heard as Congress found itself institutionally ill-equipped to handle broad national questions. The legislature by nature is better able to deal with issues that can be broken down by congressional districts or state lines, such as allocation of funds for post offices, than with issues having no clear constituency boundaries. Moreover, popular perceptions that Congress was not attentive to emerging national and international problems legitimized the notion of an energetic president. As the nation entered the new era, the constitutional forms of the two branches in most respects stayed the same, but their dynamics were to change subtly.

Theodore Roosevelt signaled the development of the legislatively active "modern" president.[101] Keenly aware that he possessed the only purely national voice, Roosevelt saw the presidency as a "bully pulpit" for shaping public opinion and pushing legislation through Congress. "In theory the Executive has nothing to do with legislation," Roosevelt wrote in his *Autobiography.*

> In practice, as things are now, the Executive is or ought to be peculiarly representative as a whole. As often as not the action of the Executive offers the only means by which the people can get the legislation they demand and ought to have. Therefore a good executive under the present conditions of American political life must take a

President Theodore Roosevelt was an energetic legislative leader, but his cousin Franklin D. Roosevelt went still further. FDR redefined the role of the national government through his New Deal legislation and vastly expanded the size of the executive branch.

> very active interest in getting the right kind of legislation, in addition to performing his executive duties with an eye single to the public welfare.[102]

Theodore Roosevelt practiced what he preached. The Pure Food and Drug Act of 1906, a landmark consumer law that established the Food and Drug Administration, was pushed through a Congress dominated by agriculture and business interests largely on the strength of the president's advocacy, aided by widespread newspaper coverage. Roosevelt also established the national park system, attacked monopolies, and negotiated the end to a war between Japan and Russia, for which he was awarded the Nobel Peace Prize. Even more instructive was Roosevelt's decision to send an American naval squadron on a global tour in a show of strength intended mainly to impress other naval powers. A Congress suffused with isolationism refused to appropriate money simply to "show the flag," but Roosevelt scraped together funds from other navy accounts to send the fleet, with a few newspaper reporters conveniently aboard, halfway around the world. He then challenged Congress to provide enough money to bring the ships home. Public opinion so strongly supported Roosevelt that Congress did as requested. Theodore Roosevelt was unique in many ways—boundless in energy, aggressively intellectual, eager for public acclaim—but his legacy did not disappear. The nation and Congress had been given a taste of energetic presidential leadership, and succeeding chief executives found both the public and Congress more receptive to their initiatives.

Such an expansive view of presidential power was controversial, even by presidents themselves. William Howard Taft, Roosevelt's immediate successor, advocated a far less grandiose view of the office. Nonetheless, as political scientist James Sundquist points out, Taft went against the tradition of official presidential noninterference in the legislative process by being the first president since Washington to formally present draft legislation to Congress.[103] William H. Taft even went so far as to rebuke his predecessor for misunderstanding the office.

> The true view of the Executive function is, as I conceive it, that the President can exercise no power which cannot be fairly and reasonably traced to some specific grant of power or justly implied and included within such express grant as proper and necessary to its exercise. Such specific grant must be either in the Federal Constitution or in an act of Congress passed in pursuance thereof. There is no undefined residuum of power which he can exercise because it seems to him to be in the public interest. . . .[104]

Woodow Wilson then remade the constitutional order and the "rhetorical presidency" was born.[105] In 1913 Wilson became the first president since John Adams to deliver his State of the Union message personally to a joint session of Congress. He thereafter used the address as a statement of his legislative agenda and to put into practice his belief that the president should lead government more actively.[106] Wilson also asserted his right to guide legislation and in a special address to Congress argued, "I have come to you as the head of the government and the responsible leader of the party in power to urge action now, while there is time to serve the country deliberately, and as we should, in a clear air of common counsel."[107] The legislation that Wilson wanted Congress to pass, the Federal Reserve Act of 1913, was drafted largely in conferences at the White House, with Wilson personally in charge.

The Franklin Roosevelt Model

Despite these gradual changes in the presidency during the first third of the twentieth century, the office of the presidency remained, legislatively speaking, a largely reactive force against a dominant Congress, not the source of initiative and leadership that Americans expect today. Although Theodore Roosevelt and Woodrow Wilson in selected instances had taken the lead with legislation, particularly when conditions for presidential initiative were most favorable, the office had only rudimentary institutional mechanisms for sustained legislative influence.

In the 1930s, however, the presidency underwent a major expansion and took on new responsibilities, entering what scholars call its modern era. The architect of these changes was Franklin Roosevelt, who stepped into the presidency in 1933 during the Great Depression that saw one quarter of the workforce unemployed, public faith in government diminished, and the nation's economic and social fabric threatening to unravel. Roosevelt's predecessor, Herbert C. Hoover (1929–1933), had relied largely on the market system to resolve the crisis, but the voters, who thought Hoover's confidence was misplaced, had blamed him for the country's hardships and subjected him to a humiliating defeat in the 1932 presidential election. The emergency worsened dramatically in early 1933, just prior to Roosevelt's inauguration, giving Roosevelt an unparalleled peacetime opportunity to lead the country. Congress, unable to resolve the crisis on its own, awaited strong direction.

Franklin Roosevelt's immediate attack on the depression was the beginning of a sweeping and sustained rearrangement of national domestic policies, a legacy that

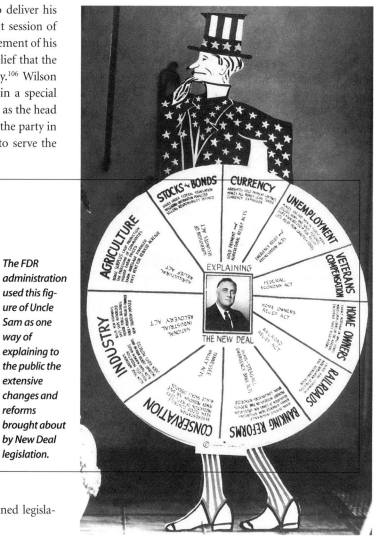

The FDR administration used this figure of Uncle Sam as one way of explaining to the public the extensive changes and reforms brought about by New Deal legislation.

dominated national politics through the mid-1960s, and whose aftereffects endure to some degree to this day. The famous and archetypal "First Hundred Days" of Roosevelt's first term saw Congress, convened in special session, give the new president a blank check to remold the federal government, introduce new programs, and do almost anything necessary to turn the economy around. Roosevelt and his battalions of energetic "New Dealers" took on the task with joyful gusto, pushing major legislation through a willing Congress with unprecedented speed. *(See box, The First Hundred Days of Franklin D. Roosevelt, this page.)* As presidential scholar Clinton Rossiter said of Roosevelt, "In the first Hundred Days he gave Congress a kind of leadership it had not known before and still does not care to have repeated."[108]

Central to Roosevelt's strategy in 1933 was strengthening the direct link between the presidency and the American people, in large part by capitalizing on his ability to communicate directly to citizens via radio. "This nation asks for action, and action now," he said simply in his first inaugural address, which sparked nearly half a million letters of support. "We must act, and act quickly."[109] Roosevelt's speeches, radio "fireside chats," and twice-weekly meetings with reporters all spoke directly to the American people and indirectly to Congress about his dreams and priorities. In the process, Roosevelt focused sustained public attention on the presidency.

Franklin Roosevelt's actions during the New Deal era and World War II combined to redefine the role of national government and the presidency as an institution. By the time FDR died in office in 1945, the executive branch had exploded in size and in the scope of its responsibilities, and the presidency itself had gained a wider array of resources for influencing legislation, making budgets, and implementing programs. The presidency no longer was a single person but an institution, one growing in size and potency as Congress gave the president more staff and more resources to manage the federal bureaucracy, initiate public policy, and lead the nation's defense. Congress delegated these responsibilities to the presidency because legislators realized that the president was better situated to lead during times of perceived crisis and, more important, because Americans demanded an energetic presidency.

THE FIRST HUNDRED DAYS OF FRANKLIN D. ROOSEVELT

Franklin D. Roosevelt, sworn into office on March 4, 1933, convened the Seventy-third Congress into special session on March 9 to consider the Emergency Banking Act, which it passed after eight hours of debate. Roosevelt at first considered sending Congress back home after passage of the act, but the window of opportunity for even more action presented by the crisis seemed too valuable to waste. As historian Arthur M. Schlesinger Jr. later wrote, "In the three months after Roosevelt's inauguration, Congress and the country were subjected to a presidential barrage of ideas and programs unlike anything known to American history."

Below are the major accomplishments of the now legendary "First Hundred Days":

March 9   Emergency Banking Act: reformed the national banking system

March 20   Economy Act: authorized cuts in federal spending

March 22   Beer and Wine Revenue Act: legalized sale of beer and wine

March 31   Civilian Conservation Corps: created employment for youths in a wide range of conservation efforts

April 19   Abandonment of gold standard: detached value of currency from gold

May 12   Federal Emergency Relief Act: created a national relief system

May 12   Agricultural Adjustment Act: established a national agricultural policy

May 12   Emergency Farm Mortgage Act: refinanced farm mortgages

May 18   Tennessee Valley Authority Act: provided for the unified development of the Tennessee Valley

May 27   Truth in Securities Act: required full disclosure of a firm's financial shape when it issued new securities

June 13   Home Owners' Loan Act: refinanced home mortgages

June 16   National Industrial Recovery Act: created a system of federally supervised industrial self-regulation and a $3.3 billion public works program

June 16   Glass-Steagall Banking Act: separated commercial and investment banking; guaranteed bank deposits

June 16   Farm Credit Act: reorganized federal farm credit programs

June 16   Emergency Railroad Transportation Act: created greater coordination in national railroad system

SOURCE: Arthur M. Schlesinger Jr., *The Age of Roosevelt: The Coming of the New Deal* (Boston: Houghton Mifflin, 1959), 20.

When Harry Truman took up Roosevelt's mantle in April 1945, he sat at the center of an office much transformed during the course of FDR's twelve years in office. By capitalizing on developments in mass-communications technology Roosevelt had greatly expanded the president's traditional role as a symbol of national sovereignty, one that would be further magnified during the next several decades with the growth of television. At the same time, the burgeoning number and complexity of government programs and agencies elevated the president's role as policy coordinator and agenda-setter, while also greatly complicating the president's responsibility as chief executive officer charged with managing the federal bureaucracy. Perhaps most important for his legislative role, the United States' movement from isolationism to front and center on the world stage gave new significance to the president's commander in chief and head diplomat responsibilities. Collectively, these developments heightened expectations for presidential leadership. The president, Wilson had once boasted, possessed the freedom "to be as big a man as he can." After FDR, however, it was no longer possible to be as small as one might like.[110]

The Roosevelt Legacy

In important respects, Roosevelt's successors have stood in his historical shadow. The office has grown in power and prestige, but perhaps not proportionately with expectations about what presidents must deliver. This is in large part because the relative distribution of power between Congress and the presidency has not fundamentally shifted, despite the acquisition of new presidential responsibilities. Since the emergence of the United States as a world power after World War II, presidents have had to more fully exercise their roles as commander in chief and chief diplomat, but the foreign responsibilities frequently clash with public demands that domestic matters be given top priority. Moreover, the world is smaller—television and the Internet have brought the world more intimately into every home—and the pace of events has quickened demonstrably. But coalitions of support also seem more fleeting, governing seems all the more difficult, and public expectations about government are greater, creating for the presidency a burden of leadership that may prove too much to bear.[111] And developments that have augmented presidential power, including new communications technology, larger staffs, and heightened visibility, have also benefited Congress.

This is not to argue that presidents have no control over their own destinies, but the extent of their control seems at times to depend less on personal intellect or social skills than on the social, economic, and political contexts within which they govern. Their control also depends on the willingness of other governing institutions, particularly Congress, to cooperate, which is by no means guaranteed. Lyndon Johnson, for example, was a master of the legislative process, having had a long career in Congress as House member, senator, and Senate majority leader. Even so, Johnson's achievement in enacting the Great Society—the most sweeping social agenda since Roosevelt's Hundred Days—depended at least as much on the trauma of John Kennedy's assassination, a national mood supporting broad social change, and an unusually cooperative congressional majority after his landslide 1964 election victory. Johnson's successes in 1965, when Congress approved some 69 percent of his legislative requests, were tempered by the knowledge that times would soon change.[112] "I have watched the Congress from either the inside or the outside, man and boy, for more than 40 years," Johnson commented early in 1965, "and I've never seen a Congress that didn't eventually take the measure of the president it was dealing with."[113]

Jimmy Carter discovered that harsh reality very early in his administration when a Congress dominated by his party proved skeptical of his comprehensive energy plan.

Carter's problems in 1977 and later stemmed not only from his lack of experience in and distaste for Washington politics, but also from the changes in Congress, and in American politics generally, during the preceding decade. Congress had become more open, more fragmented, and more independent, thereby forcing presidents to devise new ways of influencing the legislature. Johnson was able to push through his Great Society programs largely because of his ability to rally a few key committee chairs and other congressional leaders, but Carter found it necessary to lobby virtually every member, a more difficult and frustrating task. In addition, these presidents had very different contexts in "political time" as Johnson's leadership of the Democrats kept the increasing tensions within the diverse Franklin Roosevelt coalition together, but ten years later, Carter's less potent leadership skills could not staunch ideological and regional defections to the Republican Party.[114]

Even Reagan, whose rhetorical skills helped him to translate his 1980 election victory into early legislative success, found his later efforts frustrated by his inability to induce Congress to follow his lead. By the end of his presidency, moreover, the constituencies of the two major parties in Congress had been substantially altered due to the transformation of the once Democratic South into an increasingly Republican voting bloc. This trend led to a growing ideological rift between the two parties, due to a decrease in the number of southern conservative Democrats and northeastern moderate Republicans who once formed the basis of cross-party coalitions. Within the more polarized Congress, an increasing number of votes broke along nearly straight party lines, and partisan affiliation became an increasingly important predictor of roll call voting by legislators.[115] The development of more ideologically cohesive parties in Congress did not necessarily help presidents' legislative prospects, particularly during periods of divided government, as George Bush and Clinton discovered. But even under unified government, as experienced by George W. Bush, a president's legislative agenda was often stymied, particularly in the Senate, due to opposition from a cohesive minority party.

The question of context thus is essential to analyzing a president's ability to set the agenda of government and to persuade Congress to enact those priorities. According to presidential scholar Louis Koenig, Congress most consistently follows presidential leadership in three situations.[116] The first is during perceived crises, when Congress and the nation invariably turn to the president for leadership. Roosevelt and the First Hundred Days is the most-cited example, for it is almost impossible to conceive that the New Deal could have been passed under "normal" political conditions. Likewise, it is hard to imagine that the substantial new "antiterrorism" powers that Congress granted to federal authorities shortly after the September 11, 2001, attacks on the Pentagon and New York City's World Trade Center would ever have been approved in the absence of such a crisis.[117]

Second, in matters of national security and foreign affairs, an area in which the Constitution gives the presidency primacy, Congress is generally more amenable to presidential initiatives. This was particularly true between World War II and the end of the Vietnam War, when a general view that partisan "politics ended at the water's edge" gave postwar presidents an unparalleled range of flexibility. Even with the end of the cold war, and as liberals and conservatives disagreed strongly over the U.S. role in the world, Congress continued to give presidents the benefit of the doubt on issues of national defense. For example, in 1990 President George Bush committed U.S. troops to the Persian Gulf soon after Iraqi forces invaded neighboring Kuwait, and he declared that he was prepared to proceed militarily against Iraq even in the absence of congressional support. Shortly thereafter, Congress, after some debate, passed a joint resolution in support of ousting Iraq from Kuwait. Legislators leery about the use of U.S. combat soldiers in the Gulf wanted to avoid being seen as not supporting troops who were already in harm's way.[118] Although some scholars argue that Congress retains, and uses, its considerable reserve of power to shape media, public opinion and legislative support before military action begins, the Obama presidency showed that Congress is ambivalent at best about using such power.[119] President Obama unilaterally ordered troops to assist in a NATO military operation to oust Muammar Qaddafi from his decades-long dictatorship in Libya in 2011 without seeking explicit congressional authorization. After the War Powers Resolution "clock" of sixty days passed, in a bipartisan reaction, Congress was critical of the administration's actions and constitutional claims of unilateral authority. However, in unusually public displays of institutional ambivalence about undermining presidential action abroad, on two occasions in June 2011 the House failed to authorize the military effort but also failed to order withdrawal or cut funding from the operation.[120]

The tendency for Congress to accede to presidential demands in national security and foreign policy issues had led more than one president to cloak purely domestic programs in the mantle of national security to obtain easier passage. During the cold war, successive presidents defined the interstate highway system, federal education programs, and the space program as essential to national security or pride—highways for easier movement of defense forces, greater education spending to "catch up" to the Soviets after the launch of *Sputnik,* and the Mercury, Gemini, and Apollo programs to win the "space race." These programs thus gained far greater national support than they might have otherwise.

Third, presidents reap benefits from "abnormal" contexts—the combined effects of skilled political leaders, superior partisan dominance in Congress, changing societal values, and, especially, historical timing. Virtually every new president enjoys a postelection "honeymoon" with Congress, a period during which the new occupant of the White House can push priorities within an atmosphere of general cooperation. Presidents usually have their greatest legislative successes during their first six months in office. But as Stephen Skowronek points out, some presidents take office when the existing political "regime" is ripe for reconstruction due to prevailing dissatisfaction with existing policies and political commitments. Historically, these windows of opportunity to change policy direction come on the heels of realigning elections characterized by deep and enduring shifts in voters' partisan allegiances. It is these moments in "political time," Skowronek suggests, that help explain the legislative effectiveness of the nation's greatest presidents, including Jefferson, Jackson, Lincoln, FDR, and Reagan. Conversely, presidents unfortunate enough to take office when their party regime is weakening are dealt a much poorer hand. Such was the case with Pierce, Hoover, and Carter, among others.[121]

Within these broader historical sweeps, a president's legislative success will vary, depending on the general political context and particular events, the strength of congressional majorities, and of course, the president's personal abilities. However, the ability of any president to dominate the agenda of government, to plan and propose new initiatives, and to lobby successfully for these initiatives depends on more than personal skills or intellect. The character of the U.S. political system, the nature of the times, and the types of issues under debate all affect the extent to which any president can influence the national agenda and the legislative process. Regardless of the powers and prestige of the office, presidents are not entirely in control of their own destinies.

The State of the Union Address

Today, the annual State of the Union address plays an essential and potent role in presidents' efforts to influence the national agenda; they use the address to review their accomplishments and outline their goals. Yet the constitutional requirement that presidents give Congress information on the state of the Union has not always played so central a role in presidential strategies. Although both George Washington and John Adams appeared personally before Congress to deliver their annual messages, Jefferson submitted his report in writing in 1801, because he felt a personal appearance aped the practice whereby the king personally opened each new session of the British Parliament. By eliminating a quasi-monarchical rite, notes Arthur M. Schlesinger Jr., Jefferson hoped to instill stronger values of republicanism (that is, representative government) in the young American system.[122]

TABLE 4-3 **Presidential Appearances before Congress, 1789–2011**

President	Number of appearances	Occasions
Washington	10	8 annual messages (1789–1796); 2 inaugural addresses (1789, 1793—second inaugural before Senate only)
J. Adams	6	4 annual messages (1797–1800); inaugural address (1797); relations with France (1797)
Wilson	26	6 annual messages (1913–1918); tariff reform, bank reform, relations with Mexico (1913); antitrust laws; Panama Canal tolls; relations with Mexico; new tax revenue (1914); impending rail strike (1916); "Peace without Victory" (Senate only); breaking relations with Germany; arming of merchant ships; request for war declaration against Germany (1917); federal takeover of railroads; "14 points" for peace; peace outlook; need for new revenue; request for ratification of women's suffrage amendment (Senate only); armistice (1918); request for approval of Versailles treaty (Senate only); high cost of living (1919)
Harding	7	2 annual messages (1921–1922); federal problems (1921); 2 on the Merchant Marine (1922); coal and railroads (1922); debt (1923)
Coolidge	2	1 annual message (1923); George Washington's birthday (1927)
F. Roosevelt	16	10 annual messages (1934–1943); 100th anniversary of Lafayette's death (1934); 150th anniversary of First Congress (1939); neutrality address (1939); national defense (1940); declaration of war (1941); Yalta conference report (1945)
Truman	17	6 State of the Union messages (1947–1952); prosecution of the war (1945); submission of UN charter (Senate only, 1945); Congressional Medal of Honor ceremony (1945); universal military training (1945); railroad strike (1946); Greek-Turkish aid policy (1947); aid to Europe (1947); national security and conditions in Europe (1948); fiftieth anniversary of the liberation of Cuba (1948); inflation, housing, and civil rights (1948); steel industry dispute (1952)
Eisenhower	7	6 State of the Union messages (1953–1954; 1957–1960); Middle East (1957)
Kennedy	3	3 State of the Union messages (1961–1963)
L. Johnson	8	6 State of the Union messages (1964–1969); assumption of office (1963); Voting Rights Act (1965)
Nixon	7	4 State of the Union messages (1970–1972, 1974); Vietnam policy (1969—separate addresses to House and Senate); economic policy (1971); Soviet Union trip (1972)
Ford[a]	6	3 State of the Union messages (1975–1977); assumption of office (1974); inflation (1974); state of the world (1975)
Carter	6	3 State of the Union messages (1978–1980); energy program (1977); Middle East talks at Camp David (1978); SALT II arms control treaty (1979)
Reagan	11	7 State of the Union messages (1982–1988); 2 budget addresses (1981); Central America (1983); U.S.-Soviet summit (1985)
G.H.W. Bush	5	3 State of the Union messages (1990–1992); budget address (1989); Persian Gulf crisis (1991)
Clinton	9	7 State of the Union messages (1994–2000); budget address (1993); health policy reform (1993)
G.W. Bush	9	7 State of the Union messages (2002–2008); budget address (2001); September 11 terrorist attacks (2001)
Obama[b]	5	Job growth address (2011); 2 State of the Union messages (2010–2011); budget address (2009); health policy reform (2009)

SOURCE: *Guide to Congress*, 6th ed. (Washington, D.C.: CQ Press, 2007); *CQ Weekly*, various issues; John Woolley and Gerhard Peters, The American Presidency Project, presidency.ucsb.edu; U.S. House of Representatives, Office of the House Clerk, House History, Joint Meetings, Joint Sessions, and Inaugurations, http://artandhistory.house.gov/house_history/Joint_Meetings/100tocur.aspx.

NOTES: a. On October 17, 1974, President Gerald R. Ford testified before the Subcommittee on Criminal Justice of the House Judiciary Committee on his pardon of former president Richard Nixon for crimes possibly committed during the Watergate affair. b. Through October 2011. Note also that beginning with Ronald Reagan, incoming presidents now give a televised "budget speech" to a joint session of Congress within weeks of the inauguration. This speech, while not technically a State of the Union address, serves to outline the new president's overall legislative agenda.

Jefferson's precedent lasted more than a century. Not until Woodrow Wilson in 1913 did a president appear again before Congress to deliver the address. Wilson revived the earlier tradition set by Washington because he believed that presidents should make personal appeals to the nation and to Congress. Wilson expressed his view in his first personal appearance before Congress for a special message on finance:

> I am very glad indeed to have the opportunity to address the two houses directly, and to verify for myself the impression that the president of the United States is a person, not a mere department of the government hailing Congress from some isolated island of jealous power, sending messages, and not speaking naturally and with his own voice, that he is a human being trying to cooperate with other human beings in a common service. After this experience I shall feel quite normal in all our dealings with one another.[123]

Wilson also changed the content of the annual message. Before his time the State of the Union message usually was a laborious recitation of department and agency activities; it seldom contained substantive legislative proposals. This orientation reflected the view that Congress made law, and suggestions made by presidents were to be given no greater weight than those offered by average citizens. The single nineteenth-century exception to this informal but ironclad rule only underscored prevailing views. Grover Cleveland deviated from tradition and devoted his entire 1887 message to ideas about tariff reform, but his temerity at openly suggesting ideas to Congress sparked a tremendous debate in the press, divided his Democratic Party, and apparently contributed to his defeat in 1888.[124]

Since Wilson, the State of the Union address has become the major vehicle for expounding the president's legislative agenda and priorities, a tendency magnified by the onset of television. Today the president's annual appearance before a joint session of Congress is a major national event. Indeed, it is the kind of quasi-monarchical rite that Jefferson would have abhorred. It is a moment of high ceremony, a pageant duly attended by the members of Congress, the cabinet, the joint chiefs of staff of the armed forces, justices of the Supreme Court, foreign dignitaries, and invited guests. Television cameras pan the House chamber as the president speaks, recording the reactions of particular members of the audience to specific presidential statements or proposals. Media commentators and other political experts routinely begin to judge the presidential "performance" before the president's limousine even leaves the Capitol. The issues raised by the president receive serious consideration in the press, if not always in Congress, and the opposition party usually feels compelled to ask for equal time to state its views. *(See Table 4-3, p. 176.)*

Despite, or perhaps because of, its symbolism, the power of the annual address to shape public opinion and spur on Congress should not be underestimated. Kennedy, for example, used it to launch a national effort to land American astronauts on the moon before the end of the 1960s. Johnson passionately promoted his civil rights and Great Society social programs, and Nixon used the opportunity to propose a sweeping reorganization of the federal establishment and to defend U.S. actions in Vietnam. Reagan, a master of television, used the annual address to spark national and congressional debate on tax reform, on aid to the rebels in Nicaragua, and on his Strategic Defense Initiative weapons program. Bill Clinton, even when dogged by his self-inflicted sex scandal, effectively used the address to stake out the rhetorical high ground on issues such as Social Security and overall federal spending priorities. George W. Bush's singling out Iraq, Iran, and Korea as an "axis of evil" in his first State of the Union address after 9/11 left an indelible mark on the public psyche by effectively linking them with the war on terror, and helped lay the groundwork for the subsequent invasion of Iraq. The nation discusses whatever presidents discuss, if only for a while.

The State of the Union address is an important part of the "conversation" between presidents and Congress, an ongoing dialogue that may be as formal as the address or as informal as the daily contact among presidents, presidential aides, members of Congress, and Capitol Hill staff.[125] The subjects of this dialogue are revealed in part by the major themes expressed in the State of the Union messages of Presidents Kennedy through Barack Obama. *(See Table 4-4, p. 178.)* During the 1970s, for example, the emphasis shifted from foreign to domestic policy concerns, particularly the economy. As political scientist Charles O. Jones notes, "Many

of the domestic requests by Nixon, Ford, and Carter were reform measures seeking to reshape the structure and substance of programs enacted in the 1960s—a shift from issues requiring expansion of government to those demanding consolidation or even contraction of government."[126] The emphasis shifted back somewhat to foreign policy in the 1980s, reflecting the focus of the Reagan administration, and then returned largely to domestic concerns during the 1990s. Since September 11, 2001, however, the focus has again been on foreign affairs, particularly the war on terror and the ongoing conflicts in Afghanistan and Iraq.

The address also is a moment for presidents to proclaim successes, express their grand desires for the future, and engage in a little political theater. Reagan was particularly adept at using his time to praise American "heroes" and to chastise Congress for the way it prepares budgets. *(See box, The State of the Union Address as Political Theater, p. 179.)* In addition to the theater and symbolism, however, the speech also serves as a vehicle by which to itemize the president's legislative priorities. This can often take the form of what political scientist Andrew Rudalevige describes as a "rhetorical logroll," as presidents seek to reward or appease various factions within their administration by publicly recognizing their policy goals and proposals.[127]

The highly visible nature of the address also has its dangers, however, particularly when events cast doubt on or seem to contradict the president's words. In his January 2003 State of the Union address, President George W. Bush asserted that Iraq had tried to acquire "yellowcake" uranium from Niger, a precursor to developing a nuclear weapon. This became one justification for the subsequent invasion of Iraq. Administration officials later retracted the yellowcake claim, citing insufficient proof and contradictory evidence. But the damage had been done, particularly after it was revealed that Joseph Wilson, a former U.S. ambassador, had been sent to investigate whether Iraq had actually tried to acquire the uranium, only to report that the charge was unequivocally wrong. Later, officials in the Bush administration sought to discredit Wilson, allegedly even going so far as to "out" his wife's status as a covert CIA employee. Vice presidential aide I. Lewis "Scooter" Libby resigned his position in the Bush administration after he was indicted in relation to the case in 2005. In March 2007 he was found guilty of perjury, obstruction of justice, and making false statements.

While this example shows that sometimes specific portions of an address (even just a sentence or two) can get outsized attention at the time or years down the road, it is more often the case that the speech is accused of being a relatively generic (and therefore forgettable) laundry list of administrative accomplishments and national challenges. To keep the "Win the Future" theme and legislative ideas of his 2011 address alive throughout the year, Barack Obama's

TABLE 4-4 **Major Themes in State of the Union Addresses, 1961–2011**

President	Year	Major themes
Kennedy	1961	Economy; social programs
	1962	Getting America moving; economy; military strength
	1963	Cuba; economy; tax reduction
L. Johnson	1964	JFK legacy; budget
	1965	Great Society domestic programs
	1966	Vietnam, foreign and defense policy
	1967	Maintaining previous momentum
	1968	Vietnam, foreign and defense policy
	1969	Review of achievements
Nixon	1970	Vietnam, foreign and defense policy
	1971	Vietnam; economic and social policy
	1972	Foreign and defense policy; plea for action on previous requests
	1973[a]	Natural resources; economy; social policy
	1974	Energy; economic issues
Ford	1975	Economy; taxes; energy
	1976	Economic and energy issues
	1977	Energy; achievements
Carter	1978	Economic and energy issues
	1979	Inflation; SALT II
	1980	Foreign and defense policy
	1981[a]	Record of progress; budget priorities
Reagan	1982	Economic and budget issues
	1983	Economic and budget issues
	1984	Federal deficit; foreign policy
	1985	Tax reform; government spending
	1986	Foreign policy; welfare reform
	1987	Foreign policy
	1988	Economic and budget issues
G.H.W. Bush	1990	Broad domestic and foreign policy issues
	1991	Support for Persian Gulf mission
	1992	Economic and budget issues
Clinton	1994	Domestic policy; jobs; crime; health reform
	1995	"Reinventing government"; domestic policy issues
	1996	Broad domestic policy issues
	1997	Balancing the federal budget; building communities; education
	1998	Spending future surpluses wisely; Social Security
	1999	Education; Social Security; health care; racial divisions
	2000	Social Security; health care; education; minimum wage
G.W. Bush	2002	War on terror; homeland defense; tax cuts; economic growth
	2003	Iraq; war on terror; tax cuts; Medicare reform
	2004	Iraq; homeland security; economic growth; tax cuts
	2005	Iraq; Social Security reform; homeland security; war on terror
	2006	Iraq; homeland security; entitlement program reform
	2007	War on terror; Iraq; energy; economic growth; health insurance
	2008	Economic growth; health care; education; energy; war on terror
Obama	2010	Economic growth; health care; innovation; war on terror
	2011	Economic growth; education; balancing the federal budget; war on terror

SOURCE: Charles O. Jones, "Presidential Negotiation with Congress," in *Both Ends of the Avenue: The Presidency, the Executive Branch, and Congress in the 1980s,* ed. Anthony King (Washington, D.C.: American Enterprise Institute, 1983), 103; *CQ Weekly,* various issues; Deborah Kalb, Gerhard Peters, and John Woolley, *State of the Union: Presidential Rhetoric from Woodrow Wilson to George W. Bush* (Washington, D.C.: CQ Press, 2007); John Woolley and Gerhard Peters, The American Presidency Project, presidency.ucsb.edu. See also Colleen J. Shogan and Thomas H. Neale, "The President's State of the Union Address: Traditions, Functions, and Policy Implications," Library of Congress, Congressional Research Service, CRS Report for Congress, 2010.

NOTE: a. Written message to Congress.

media and technology team created a web page dedicated to the speech. It includes a video and transcript of the address as well as follow-up interviews with the president (carried on YouTube.com) and vice president. For those wanting more information on policy and administrative details, there were links to top advisers on different subjects, and a postspeech policy panel video. There was also a link to download a "White House App" for smartphones.[128]

With its high profile and constitutional underpinnings, the State of the Union message is the most visible means by which presidents seek to set their legislative agenda. But it is not the only means. Congress through statute has required the president to make other annual reports. The Budget Act of 1921 requires the president to submit an annual budget message, and the Employment Act of 1946 mandates an annual report on the economy. Hundreds of other reports, messages, and legislative proposals are submitted to Congress annually, all bearing the president's imprint and expressing White House views on important policy matters. Presidents also use public speeches in other contexts to influence the policy agenda. In his examination of the public papers of the presidents during 1949 to 1996, a period spanning ten presidential administrations, Rudalevige counted 2,769 presidential messages containing 6,296 policy proposals.[129] This total ranged from an average high of almost 300 policy proposals per year by Lyndon Johnson to an average low of 81 per year by Reagan. Of course these proposals varied in scope, significance, and level of presidential commitment, but each one had potential political influence.

Preparing Legislation

A president's priorities generally require formal congressional approval. Setting the national agenda is only the first stage in successful presidential leadership, if *leadership* is defined simply as getting proposals approved by Congress. In this process, presidents throughout history have relied on a wide array of personnel and resources.

Drafting legislation is the first *formal* phase of the process. Although members of Congress have often resisted presidential participation in drafting bills, arguing that it violates the constitutional blueprint for separated institutions, presidents always have done so. Early presidents were circumspect about their roles and usually tried to avoid any appearance of interposing their views in a realm zealously guarded by Congress. George Washington, for example, quietly discussed ideas for new measures with cabinet officials and members of Congress. He even secretly helped to compose the odd bill, but he studiously avoided open and direct roles in forming legislation. Instead he assigned cabinet members to consult formally with Congress, an activity deemed more legitimate because department heads appeared regularly before congressional committees on routine business.

THE STATE OF THE UNION ADDRESS AS POLITICAL THEATER

There are at least four ways of looking at the development of the State of the Union address. First, on an institutional level, its evolution reflects dramatic increases in public expectations for presidential legislative leadership and rhetorical skill. On an individual level, from the very beginning of the polity, choices surrounding the delivery of the address, which was not detailed in Article II, expose a president's comfort level with public communication. Third, in addition to the method of delivery, the substance of the address explains presidents' orientation toward the office, approach to current policy exigencies, and their political strategies to overcome the current political landscape. Fourth, the address shows the continuity of constitutional tensions between presidents' dual roles. On the one hand, it showcases their unique place as the ceremonial and symbolic head of state—the personification of the United States for ourselves and the world. On the other hand, the address also spotlights the presidents' role as head of government with a partisan legislative agenda as they sell their ideas to those who can support or block their program: Congress and the American people. So the visual image of presidents being warmly received by members of both chambers and commanding the nation's attention with their address belies the constitutional, institutional, and political obstacles that so often thwart their objectives.

Presidents George Washington and John Adams delivered their "Annual Message" to Congress personally. Thomas Jefferson dispensed with this action, deeming it "monarchical" and a waste of Congress's time, but he may have had an ulterior motive for dispensing with the short-lived tradition as Jefferson was not well-known to be a rousing and comfortable speaker. A century later, Woodrow Wilson revived the Washington precedent on December 2, 1913, but the personal delivery was not a firm tradition for another two decades.

Radio news coverage of the address (when it was delivered personally) began in 1923. Ten years later, widespread public access to radio allowed Franklin D. Roosevelt, for example, to speak directly to the American people and rally the nation out of the depression of the 1930s. But beginning in 1947, television coverage of the event, with its particular capacity to convey complex information through visual images, has elevated the State of the Union address to true political theater. The speech's visual and audio narrative now includes the president's dramatic entry into the chamber (accepting well wishes and surrounded by a large executive branch entourage), star billing (the sergeant-at-arms' booming introduction), and a live, reactive audience during the address (members of Congress assembled) and immediately following it (critics, network commentators, and the opposition party's response after the address is finished).

Televised annual addresses often balance a litany of dry statistics with a panorama of past accomplishments, current endeavors, and future visions (sometimes articulated as catch phrases, such as President Obama's "win the future" theme in 2011). Increasingly, the State of the Union address has become the primary vehicle in setting the nation's annual agenda, with presidents judged on how well they crafted and delivered their messages. In the contemporary television age audience, multiple cameras allow for quick cuts to the audience, including newsworthy guests of honor (usually seated next to the first lady) as well as congressional reactions that show one side of the aisle standing and applauding to certain policy announcements and evaluations and the other side reacting with less enthusiasm. The camera shot of the president speaking often includes the Speaker of the House and the vice president (as president of the Senate), who sit directly behind the president on the dais. During periods of divided government (when the White House and Congress are held by different parties) the Speaker and the vice president are of different parties and can have different physical reactions to the president's words, captured in the same camera frame as the president and thus reminding the audience of the complex outcomes of recent elections.

At the same time as these partisan and policy story lines are writing the next day's news coverage, the *presidency* as the symbol of American strength is celebrated, separating the person from the office temporarily. For example, in January 1998, just days after the Monica Lewinsky scandal broke, Bill Clinton took to the podium. Although the allegations of the affair had flooded the news, he made no mention of it and received the usual unanimous standing ovations and loud, hearty warm welcome all presidents (and audiences) have grown to expect, at least upon their arrival in the chamber. The medium and the message have indeed coalesced as the address has evolved from Washington's speech of barely more than 1,000 words to more than 30,000 under Ronald Reagan. More recent addresses are in the 5,000 to 10,000 word range, but choice phrases and promises can hang in the political air for the rest of the year.

John F. Kennedy, Ronald Reagan, Bill Clinton, and Barack Obama honed their communication skills throughout their careers and brought an element of stagecraft into their State of the Union addresses. But all modern presidents share the same difficult balancing act in this speech, regardless of whether they are known as vibrant orators or not. They often begin and end the address with unifying symbolism, but in between include divisive policy wish lists. Uniformly optimistic rhetoric under even challenging circumstances ("the state of the union is strong") is usually followed by a recitation of the day's daunting policy challenges. General calls for bipartisanship are often interspersed with gentle scolding of Congress on the frequently gridlocked legislative process, or an implicit criticism of past policy decisions. Presidents also acknowledge recent electoral shifts and tragic events. Of course, showing grace to the opposition and including a few jokes always lightens the mood and showcases the confidence of the person at the podium.

SOURCE: Jeffrey K. Tulis, *The Rhetorical Presidency* (Princeton: Princeton University Press, 1987); Deborah Kalb, Gerhard Peters, and John T. Woolley, *State of the Union: Presidential Rhetoric from Woodrow Wilson to George W. Bush* (Washington, D.C.: CQ Press, 2007); Colleen J. Shogan and Thomas H. Neale, "The President's State of the Union Address: Traditions, Functions, and Policy Implications," Library of Congress, Congressional Research Service, CRS Report for Congress, 2010; www.whitehouse.gov/the-press-office/2011/01/25/remarks-president-state-union-address.

Congress itself validated this strategy by directing Secretary of the Treasury Hamilton to draft and submit recommendations for a new national bank, a resolution of state debts, and the promotion of manufacturing—tasks Hamilton took on with such relish that he sparked severe criticism of his dominance over the legislative process.[130]

Hamilton's chief critic, Secretary of State Thomas Jefferson, proved no less energetic once he became president. Although his party stressed congressional supremacy, Jefferson secretly composed bills, which he transmitted through his department secretaries to party loyalists in the legislature, and used his cabinet secretaries for maximum influence on legislating. Jefferson's party caucus enjoyed a solid congressional majority, enabling him to maintain the fiction of his complete separateness from lawmaking even as he wielded a strong hand behind the scenes.

Other nineteenth-century presidents continued this pattern of using cabinet officials to lobby for legislation. They had few alternatives. Presidents had few personal staff members, and Congress did not appropriate funds for even clerical assistance until 1857. Nor did they have extensive networks of personal advisers and assistants.[131] Cabinet officials gave presidents valuable access to congressional committees, acted as the president's eyes and ears, and, as political scientist James Young noted, "allowed Presidents to maintain, for what it was worth, the outward appearance of conformity to community norms which decreed social distance between the President and Congress."[132]

But this system had its disadvantages, chief among them the reality that department heads frequently were selected to pay off political favors or to accommodate rival factions within the president's party. Presidents never were entirely sure of their own cabinet's primary loyalties and had to guard against the tendency of strong cabinet officials to cultivate their own power bases in Congress. Lincoln, for example, had to maneuver continually around such formidable political figures as Secretary of State William H. Seward and Secretary of the Treasury Salmon P. Chase, who led their factions within the Republican Party and regularly clashed with Lincoln over Civil War policies.

The Institutional Presidency

The image of the nineteenth-century presidency is one of a lone figure with little reliable assistance. Contemporary presidents, by contrast, reside at the heart of an immense executive institution, aided in their tasks by about seventeen hundred special assistants, personal aides, policy experts, and clerical staffers distributed among several specialized agencies that collectively comprise the Executive Office of the President (EOP). (See Table 4-5, this page.) The EOP is, in theory, the president's personal bureaucracy, created expressly to help the chief executive oversee cabinet department and agency activities, formulate budgets and monitor spending, craft legislation, lobby Congress, and, above all, promote the president's priorities.

Although the EOP was not formally established until 1939, the presidential bureaucracy dates from 1921, when Congress, recognizing the need for a more centralized

TABLE 4-5 **Employees of the Executive Office of the President, Various Offices, 1941–2011**

Year	White House Office	Office of Management and Budget[a]	National Security Council
1941	53	305	—
1945	61	565	—
1950	295	520	17
1955	290	444	28
1960	446	434	65
1965	292	506	39
1970	491	636	82
1975	525	664	85
1980	426	631	74
1985	362	569	61
1990	391	568	60
1995[b]	400	553	57
2000	398	510	45
2005	406	477	63
2010[c]	469	529	86

SOURCE: Bureau of the Census, Statistical Abstract of the United States (Washington, D.C.: Government Printing Office, various editions); U.S. Office of Personnel Management, Federal Manpower Statistics, Federal Civilian Workforce Statistics, bimonthly; 2010 Annual Report to Congress on White House Staff, www.whitehouse.gov/briefing-room/disclosures/annual-records/2010; Executive Office of the President, Office of Management and Budget, Fiscal Year 2011 Budget, www.whitehouse.gov/sites/default/files/omb/assets/organization/fy2011_omb_budget.pdf.

NOTES: a. Known until 1970 as the Bureau of the Budget. b. Estimate. c. National Security Council and National and Homeland Security Council are listed together as one office in 2010 for personnel and budget purposes. See Executive Office of the President, Fiscal Year 2012, Congressional Budget Submission, www.whitehouse.gov/sites/default/files/2012-eop-budget.pdf.

budgeting process, passed the Budget and Accounting Act. This legislation required the president to coordinate all executive branch spending proposals and present a unified annual budget. To assist presidents in this task, the law also created the Bureau of the Budget (BOB). Thus arose the notion of "central clearance," the use of the BOB to monitor all executive branch spending, to judge new funding requests before they went to Capitol Hill, and, especially, to quash budget proposals not in line with the president's agenda. The president for the first time had a mechanism to coordinate and perhaps control executive branch activities.[133]

Franklin Roosevelt's New Deal spawned a staggering growth in executive branch responsibilities, which in turn strained the capacity of the presidency to coordinate and control government expenditures and actions. At the same time, the outpouring of new policy proposals during the New Deal compelled Roosevelt to expand the BOB's clearance functions to include screening nonbudgetary legislative proposals and enrolled bills passed by Congress and sent to him for his signature. In 1939, in recognition of its expanding functions, the Bureau of the Budget was moved from the Treasury Department to the newly formed EOP.

The EOP, comprised initially of the White House Office, the BOB, and three other staff agencies, was created to help the president bring greater unity of purpose and consistency of action to the executive branch.

Today the EOP includes about a dozen agencies. The most important are the White House Office and related domestic, economic, and homeland security policy staffs; the Office of Management and Budget (formerly the BOB); the National Security Council staff; and the Council of Economic Advisers. Roosevelt intended the EOP agencies (except for the White House Office) to consist primarily of career-based, "neutrally competent" aides who could provide continuity and historical memory. Through time, however, the most important EOP agencies have tended to adopt a more political orientation in which their activities are conducted primarily to serve the interests of the incumbent president. The BOB is a case in point; in 1970 Congress, acting at Richard Nixon's behest, transformed the agency into the Office of Management and Budget (OMB) and later made its director subject to Senate confirmation in recognition of his politicized status. Under Nixon, the OMB became more nearly an instrument of domestic and budgetary policy advocacy, a role that continues to this day. Reagan extended the OMB's clearance power to include regulatory review, and more than any of his predecessors used the agency to ensure that the budgeting process reflected the president's policy objectives. From its origins as a small and even neutral accounting department, the OMB today is a powerful, partisan, and often controversial defender of the president's agenda.[134]

Similarly, the National Security Council (NSC), consisting of the president, vice president, secretaries of defense and state, and others the president may appoint, was established by Congress during the Truman administration to ensure that presidents consulted with the relevant military and diplomatic experts when making foreign policy. The NSC staff, however, has gradually eclipsed the statutory council as the primary source of foreign policy advice to the president. Headed by a special assistant working in the White House, this staff, typically numbering more than fifty specialists, provides information and advice geared to the president's interests and perspective rather than the various foreign policy bureaucracies sitting on the full NSC.

At the apex of the EOP sits the White House Office (WHO), home to the president's closest personal aides and special assistants. Now numbering more than four hundred aides, it was formally established by FDR to house the president's personal staff who handled the president's daily administrative activities: appointments, correspondence, and scheduling. Through the years, however, it has taken on a greater role in policy development and political outreach. Today it works closely with the president in putting together

a legislative program, lobbying Congress for its passage, and overseeing policy implementation.

Other EOP agencies come and go, depending on the president's policy interests and desire to use EOP status to showcase their commitment to a particular policy goal. Thus Lyndon Johnson established the Office of Economic Opportunity within the EOP to dramatize his antipoverty efforts. President George W. Bush appointed a White House aide to oversee an Office of Faith-based Initiatives. President Obama maintained the office but revamped its mission. However, the office remained controversial, as it had from its inception.[135]

As this overview demonstrates, the contemporary presidency is an *institution* with resources and powers that remain potent regardless of the personal traits of individual chief executives. Ironically, the institutional capacity to carry out all these tasks furnishes presidents with a different dilemma: how to ensure that the Executive Office of the President itself responds to the president's needs and wishes. Presidents cannot be involved personally in every action that occurs below them. They must rely on subordinates to monitor and guide the behavior of an institution that is itself designed to monitor and guide the behavior of the executive branch as a whole. Nineteenth-century presidents bemoaned their lack of staff resources; presidents today wonder how they can make their own vast organization run loyally and well.[136]

The President's Agenda

Much of the legislation Congress ponders originates within the executive branch. No longer do presidents maintain a fiction of separation from the legislative process. Indeed, contemporary presidents more often than not are judged by the quality and timing of their annual policy agendas. Congress and the public alike demand that presidents initiate legislation and criticize severely those who do not. Eisenhower, for example, did not propose a formal legislative agenda in his first year in office, only to receive sharp rebukes from members of both parties. "Don't expect us to start from scratch on what you people want," said one angry House member to an administration official. "That's not the way we do things here. You draft the bills and we work them over."[137]

A multiplicity of sources provides the ideas that form the intellectual foundation of the president's program. Before Franklin Roosevelt's administration, presidents were able to base their agendas on their personal views and experiences, because the role of the executive branch was limited and the problems requiring presidential attention relatively few. Theodore Roosevelt's aggressive national park and wildlife conservation policies stemmed at least in part from his background as a western rancher and big-game hunter. Herbert Hoover's experiences as secretary of commerce

How a Bill Becomes a Law

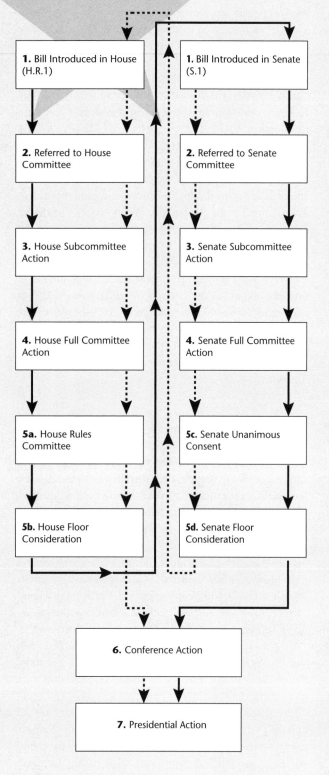

1. Bill Introduced in House (H.R.1)

1. Bill Introduced in Senate (S.1)

2. Referred to House Committee

2. Referred to Senate Committee

3. House Subcommittee Action

3. Senate Subcommittee Action

4. House Full Committee Action

4. Senate Full Committee Action

5a. House Rules Committee

5c. Senate Unanimous Consent

5b. House Floor Consideration

5d. Senate Floor Consideration

6. Conference Action

7. Presidential Action

1. INTRODUCTION OF A BILL IN HOUSE OR SENATE

A proposal that will eventually become law must be introduced by a member of Congress. Often when a member introduces a bill, he or she will find someone in the other chamber to introduce a "companion bill." Each bill is given a number as it is introduced, and numbering is sequential. House bill numbers start with HR, Senate bill numbers start with S.

A bill written in the executive branch and proposed as an administration measure usually is introduced "by request" by the chair of the congressional committee that has jurisdiction.

The following guideline is sometimes referred to as the "textbook" or "orthodox" legislative process. In recent decades, it has been common for major pieces of legislation to skip or alter some of these time-consuming steps. Omnibus bills, committee bypasses, complex and excessive amendments and filibuster threats, House and Senate floor rule innovations, congressional-executive summits, and party leadership "task forces" are all examples of ways that determined lawmakers and party leaders attempt to control the obstacle course of the contemporary legislative process. Some of these "unorthodox" methods result in greater gridlock and some of them result in quicker and more predictable legislative outcomes.[1]

2. REFERRAL TO COMMITTEE

After a bill is introduced it is referred by the parliamentarian to a standing committee. A complex bill (such as health care reform) may be referred to several committees because of overlapping policy jurisdictions. The committee chair(s) then decides which subcommittee will consider the measure. The most common result of committee referral, however, is that the bill is ignored. Of the ten thousand-plus bills proposed each session, on average fewer than 10 percent make it past the committee as laid out next.

3. SUBCOMMITTEE ACTION

The subcommittee holds hearings on the bill. Testimony may be taken from invited witnesses only, or the committee may issue an open call and hear from anyone who wishes to speak. At this point administration representatives have a chance to urge support for a bill. Subcommittee hearings also provide an opportunity for them to oppose a bill they do not like.

When hearings are completed, the bill is "marked up," that is, rewritten to incorporate the subcommittee's changes. These changes may be designed to strengthen (or weaken) the provisions or they may be politically inspired to improve (or reduce) a bill's chance of passage. If the president has objections, it is at this point that friendly committee members and White House lobbyists attempt to amend the bill to meet presidential approval. When the subcommittee has finished its work, the bill is sent to the full committee.

4. FULL COMMITTEE ACTION

The full committee may ratify the subcommittee's actions, or it may repeat the subcommittee's steps by holding more hearings and marking up the bill a second time. This second markup gives the administration another chance to alter the bill if its effort to make changes at the subcommittee level failed. Whether or not the subcommittee steps are repeated, only the full committee formally reports the bill back to the chamber for floor action; a subcommittee cannot report a measure directly.

5A. HOUSE RULES COMMITTEE

After the full committee reports the bill, it is placed on a "calendar" and is ready for floor consideration. In the House, controversial or complicated bills are referred to the Rules Committee, which determines the framework for debate and amendment. A special rule written by the Rules Committee specifies how long debate will last, who will control the time, and how many and what type of amendments may be offered.

After the Rules Committee has recommended a rule, the full House votes on whether to accept it. If the rule does not allow amendments that the president favors, or if the legislation contains provisions the president would like to see deleted, the White House may lobby House members to defeat the rule. The White House is seldom successful in defeating a rule; but when it is, that success is a major victory for the president.

5B. HOUSE FLOOR CONSIDERATION

If, as usually happens, the House accepts the rule, the next step is debate on the bill. Normal House rules limit each member to one hour during general debate, but often the rule imposes more rigid time limits. Roll call votes may be requested if a certain number of members agree to the request. Roll call votes are taken electronically in the House and usually last fifteen minutes.

If the bill originated in the House, it is referred to the Senate for action after passage (see solid line). If the House is completing consideration of a measure referred from the Senate and the bill has not been amended, it is cleared for presidential action. If the bill is a referral from the Senate and has been substantially amended, it may be referred to a conference committee (see No. 6).

5C. SENATE UNANIMOUS CONSENT

To expedite floor consideration, the Senate has developed a procedure, known as the "unanimous consent agreement," similar to the special rules written by the House Rules Committee. A unanimous consent agreement is worked out informally by the majority and minority leaders and by any senator with an interest in the bill under consideration. The agreement specifies how much time will be allotted for debate, what amendments will be considered, and how the time will be divided. Unlike a House rule, however, which needs a simple majority to pass, a unanimous consent agreement must be accepted by all senators on the floor at the time it is proposed. A single objection defeats the agreement.

5D. SENATE FLOOR CONSIDERATION

Floor consideration under a unanimous consent agreement in the Senate is similar to action under a rule in the House. If a unanimous consent agreement cannot be worked out, however, the Senate operates under its normal rules, which are much less restrictive than House rules. There is no time limit on debate. Members opposed to a bill under consideration sometimes "filibuster"—that is, hold the floor by speaking for an extended period of time—to delay or kill a bill. A filibuster can be ended only if sixty senators agree to a "cloture" petition to limit debate. As a result, floor proceedings in the Senate usually take much longer than in the House. Voting in the Senate is not electronic. The roll is called by a clerk who records each senator's vote.

If the bill under consideration originated in the Senate, it is then referred to the House for action after passage (see broken line). If the Senate is completing consideration of a measure referred from the House and the bill has not been amended, it is cleared for presidential action. If the bill is a referral from the House

and has been substantially amended, it may be referred to a conference committee (see No. 6).

6. CONFERENCE ACTION

A bill must be approved by both chambers in identical form before it can be sent to the president. If there are major differences between the versions passed by the House and the Senate, the bill may go to a conference committee, which works out a compromise. The committee usually consists of senior members of the committees that reported the bill. If the president has reservations or objections or prefers the bill passed by one chamber to the version passed by the other, it is in the conference that the White House attempts to influence members to adopt a final version that is acceptable to the administration.

When the conference is completed, the committee files a conference report to which both the House and the Senate must agree. If either rejects the conference agreement, the bill dies. If both agree to the conference report, the measure then goes to the president for final action. Conference committees are more common for reconciling House and Senate differences on high-profile and complex bills.

A conference often can be avoided, however. Even if one chamber has amended a bill substantially, it can refer the measure back to the originating chamber, which may accept all the amendments (clearing the bill for the president), accept some and reject others, or even add some amendments of its own (in which case the bill then bounces back to the other chamber a second time). This back-and-forth process can continue until both chambers have agreed to the measure in identical form, thus clearing it for presidential action. In reality, most bills are cleared in this manner, avoiding an official conference.

7. PRESIDENTIAL ACTION

The president has several options once a bill is received from Congress. To approve the bill, the president signs it, dates it, and usually writes the word "approved" on the document. To disprove or veto the bill, the president refuses to sign it and returns it to Congress within ten legislative days of its presentation (Sundays excluded) with a message stating the president's reasons. The message is sent to the chamber that originated the bill. If no action is taken on the message, the bill dies. Congress, however, may vote to overturn a veto. Debate can precede this vote, with motions permitted to lay the message on the table, postpone action on it, or refer it to committee. If both chambers vote by a two-thirds majority (of those present and voting) to "override" the veto, the bill becomes law. Otherwise the bill is dead.

Normally if the president does not sign the bill within the ten-day period and Congress is in session, the bill becomes law without the president's signature. However, should Congress adjourn before the ten days expire and the president has failed to sign the measure, it does not become law. This procedure is called the pocket veto.

When bills are passed finally and signed, or passed over a veto, they are given law numbers in numerical order as they become law. There are two series of numbers, one for public and one for private laws, starting at the number "1" for each two-year term of Congress. They are then identified by law number and by Congress—for example, Private Law 2, 111th Congress; Public Law 25, 112th Congress (or PL 112–25).

1. See Barbara Sinclair, *Unorthodox Lawmaking: New Legislative Processes in the U.S. Congress*, 3d ed. (Washington, D.C.: CQ Press, 2007).

under Calvin Coolidge (1923–1929) guided his priorities, at least until the Great Depression overtook his presidency.

Recently, however, a surprising proportion of a chief executive's domestic program may come from "outside" sources—Congress, national and international events, the departments and agencies of the executive branch, and public opinion. Congress, with its hundreds of members and thousands of staff, is fertile ground for legislative ideas. Many of the formal legislative proposals that come officially from the White House actually stem from ideas and proposals that have bounced around Capitol Hill for years, waiting to be adopted as political circumstances permit.[138] One such example of policy adoption was Kennedy's domestic program, a large portion of which was based on ideas and options promoted to no avail by liberal congressional Democrats during the Eisenhower years. What Kennedy could not get through Congress, Lyndon Johnson later incorporated into his Great Society program. Reagan's vaunted tax reduction bill of 1981 was the "offspring" of a Republican tax plan pushed by New York representative Jack Kemp and Delaware senator William Roth beginning in the late 1970s. Likewise, Clinton's signature national service initiative, known as AmeriCorps, in many ways grew out of a proposal developed by Northwestern University sociologist Charles Moskos over a decade earlier.[139] George W. Bush's "No Child Left Behind" educational act draws heavily on the findings of several high-powered commissions dating back to the Reagan administration charged with reforming America's educational system. Hundreds of proposed policies float about at all times, each awaiting the power of a president to lift it out of the mass of proposals and give it life.[140]

Crises or other major events also structure the domestic agenda, probably more than presidents desire or care to admit. In fact, Americans now expect government to respond forcefully to new or sudden problems. There is no question, for example, that Hoover's inability to rein in the depression led to his defeat in 1932 and that Franklin Roosevelt attained mythical status for his innovative ("try anything") attack on the economic crisis.[141] The 1957 Soviet launch of *Sputnik* startled Eisenhower into major spending for science education and the space program. The energy crisis of the 1970s, sparked largely by huge hikes in oil prices from producing nations, dominated the fiscal and budgetary agendas of both Ford and Carter. National concern about the AIDS (acquired immune deficiency syndrome) epidemic forced the Reagan administration to increase research funding to combat the disease, while the ominous signs of global warming combined with rising energy costs compelled the George W. Bush administration to fund research into alternative energy sources.[142] The demand that presidents respond to issues or events beyond their control probably will intensify as global economic and political conditions become increasingly intertwined with domestic politics.[143]

Executive branch bureaucrats are another wellspring of policy ideas or options, despite the propensity of presidential candidates to attack the bureaucracy during their election campaigns. In his analysis of the sources of presidential legislative initiatives, Rudalevige calculated that more than a fifth of them originated in the executive branch departments and agencies.[144] Career civil servants are deeply dedicated to particular policy areas and possess the technical expertise and perspectives that come from long tenure. A new president wishing to initiate policies or simply avoid repeating the mistakes of the past may find their experience helpful.

The degree to which any president adopts ideas generated from within the professional bureaucracy depends in part on personal ideology and style. The White House staffs of Republicans Nixon and Reagan, for example, were highly suspicious of the motives and political leanings of career civil servants and tried whenever possible to draw policymaking directly into the White House.[145] Democrats Jimmy Carter and Bill Clinton, by contrast, tended to share civil servants' fundamental beliefs in the positive role of government and thus showed a greater willingness to tap bureaucratic ideas. Nonetheless, Rudalevige's data show that regardless of ideology or partisan background, presidents dating back to Truman on average do not vary considerably in where they find legislative ideas. More than 50 percent of presidents' legislative initiatives have "mixed" parentage, reflecting the combined influence of the executive branch and the president's own EOP or White House staff. Only about 22 percent, in contrast, are "purely presidential" initiatives originating in the White House or EOP.[146]

Whatever the source of any agenda item, presidents must test its technical, economic, and especially, political soundness before sending it off to Congress. Proposals that fail to take politics into account are ripe for disaster. The degree to which this is true is probably proportionate to the degree of change intended. Incremental changes do not as a rule generate massive political resistance, but plans that seek comprehensive change almost guarantee strong reactions from a wide array of affected interests.[147] Carter's massive effort to reform national energy policy, for example, was hammered out by a panel of experts but suffered embarrassing political defeats once it was sent to Congress. The same fate befell Clinton's plan for health care reform, despite the administration's efforts to include as many perspectives as possible before sending it to Congress. The sheer size of the intended plan may have sparked the flames of its own demise.[148] Similarly, George W. Bush was singularly unsuccessful in convincing Congress to support Social Security reform that involved allowing taxpayers to place some of their retirement money into individual investment accounts.

Presidents seek out a wide range of expertise in an effort to avoid such fates, but, as they find out, no source is perfect. For example, the professionals who staff the EOP are valuable sources of technical expertise or economic analysis, but they may not be attuned to the political climate or understand well the vagaries of Capitol Hill. Every president has aides and close friends who are valued for their political acumen and who can offer frank advice to the president in ways that others would not dare, be they Franklin Roosevelt's "brain trust," Carter's "Georgia Mafia," or the Californians making up Reagan's "kitchen cabinet." But such people also may be new to Washington or blinded to political reality by their loyalty to the president when controversial decisions must be made. The failure of Clinton's health care reform effort has been attributed in part to the relative inexperience of his White House staff, particularly those placed in charge of developing the policy.[149]

Cabinet secretaries, in contrast to the days when they were the president's primary advisers (and sometimes competitors), today play a secondary role in judging policy proposals unless they also have close personal ties to the president or preside over a department particularly important to presidential priorities. Presidents frequently fill the position of attorney general, for example, with a close friend or political ally who then enjoys ready access to the Oval Office. Kennedy appointed his brother Robert; Nixon looked to his friend and former law partner John Mitchell; and Reagan appointed his longtime aide Edwin Meese. Each of these was more than a department head; they also were close friends.

By contrast, some cabinet members rarely see the president in private, even on issues central to their departments, and complain that their phone calls are routed to presidential aides whom they technically outrank. Samuel Pierce, for example, was secretary of housing and urban development throughout the Reagan presidency, yet he rarely played a central role in policy development because his department was peripheral to the president's agenda. (In fact, as one famous story goes, Reagan even failed to recognize Pierce at a reception for city mayors.) Clinton's labor secretary, Robert Reich, entitled his memoirs of the Clinton years *Locked in the Cabinet*, a reflection of his frustration at his lack of policy influence and access to the president.[150] On occasion, cabinet members are regarded with deep suspicion because they have succumbed to the tendency of cabinet secretaries to promote departmental interests over the president's agenda, particularly after they have been in office for some time. Cabinet secretaries who "go native" find their access cut off and advice ignored, even when it could prove valuable.

Members of Congress of either political party may be keenly attuned to the political feasibility of new proposals but, as elected officials in their own right, they usually have their own agendas to promote. And, given their distinct electoral and governing roles, their perspectives may differ dramatically from the president's. Carter, for one, deeply distrusted members of Congress; he felt they were too parochial. Indeed, to his dismay he witnessed firsthand the tenacity of local interests in Congress once his proposals went to Capitol Hill. All presidents find this out eventually, and most realize that members of Congress must be heard, if only so that they can warn of the obstacles that may lie ahead.

Career federal bureaucrats know what is feasible technically and economically, but they may have their own policy and institutional goals to consider. Loyalty to their agencies, programs, or own policy ideals may supersede any loyalty to a particular president. In 2006 the Bush administration asked James Hansen, a longtime NASA scientist and specialist on climate change, to clear all public statements with his White House–appointed superiors first. Hansen then publicly accused the Bush administration of trying to prevent him from discussing the causes of global warming.[151] Hansen likely understood that career bureaucrats usually will be in their positions long after any one president has left the White House. They generally can wait out an administration hostile to their views until the political winds change or new leaders come to office.

Outside experts such as academics sometimes offer new ideas and perhaps lend an aura of expertise and legitimacy to controversial issues, but, like many experts, they may not have enough insight into what is feasible politically. Moreover, there is no guarantee that any recommendations made by panels of experts will ever amount to more than reams of paper sitting in a file cabinet. In December 2006, after much anticipation, a commission headed by former secretary of state James Baker and former congressman Lee Hamilton released its congressionally sponsored Iraq Study Group report. Almost immediately, President George W. Bush began distancing himself from the report's most important recommendations, which included negotiating with the governments of Iran and Syria to control the influx of terrorists into Iraq and a reduction in U.S. troop levels there. What experts propose often goes far beyond what politicians are willing to use at a particular time.

In short, many sources for ideas and expertise are available to a president, but only the occupant of the Oval Office can decide which sources will be tapped. Presidents like Franklin Roosevelt, Lyndon Johnson, and Bill Clinton were voracious consumers of advice from a great number of sources. To get a broad spectrum of opinion, Roosevelt surrounded himself with assistants who were known to disagree violently on major issues. Johnson was famous for his midnight

Presidents frequently place a trusted friend or political ally in the position of attorney general. John F. Kennedy appointed his brother Robert.

too immersed in the minutiae of policy to discern or convey to the public the broader goals of public policy or of his office. Reagan, by contrast, apparently viewed himself as chair of the board. He was content to dictate broad goals and directions while allowing his aides to work out specific policy options. His tendency to remain aloof from the particulars of policy often made him appear uninformed in press conferences, but even Reagan's critics admitted that the passion of his ideals provided his subordinates with clear guidelines by which to judge and select policies.

telephone calls to sleepy senators, demanding the latest scoop on a piece of legislation. Both had keen political instincts, and for them information was a resource to be used wisely in political battles. Clinton, an avowed "policy wonk," reveled in seemingly endless discussions on policy matters with virtually anyone who would take part.[152] This style requires, above all, tremendous personal energy and intellect, but it can easily overwhelm a president who does not place some limits on the vast amounts of information headed for the Oval Office daily. Presidents who do not adequately delegate tasks to subordinates risk overload.[153]

Other presidents prefer to let information and policy options "bubble up" through the ranks of advisers and experts, using their closest aides to synthesize advice and present a short list of alternative courses of action. Eisenhower, Reagan, and both Bushes—all Republicans—operated in this manner. Reagan was notably content to let his aides parse out competing choices and to withhold his own views until presented with one or two options. The president's role in this approach is relatively passive, but it can work well when those who actually weigh the alternatives keep the president's values and priorities firmly in mind. Problems arise when a president's aides fail to do so, or when they keep the president in the dark about their activities.

Presidential styles hinge most on personal views and skills, overall goals, and perspectives on the job itself. Carter saw the president's job as one of problem solving, and insisted on being informed of or involved in almost every decision— including, as one story goes, the schedule for the White House tennis courts. His problem, critics charged, was that he was

Lobbying Congress

After legislation is drafted, presidents must persuade Congress to go along with it. Presidential scholar Richard E. Neustadt argues that the primary power of the presidency is the power to persuade others to follow the presidential agenda, but the Constitution is silent on just how presidents are to do so.[154] And that silence is convenient. Presidents seeking little in the way of change can claim that separation of the branches gives them little capacity to influence Congress directly; assertive presidents can use this constitutional silence to justify almost any means of persuasion not expressly forbidden by law or accepted practice. Generally, the way in which presidents organize their lobbying activities and the styles they employ to influence Congress reflect their particular ideology, specific policy goals, knowledge about how government works, and overall personal skills. They also reflect whether—or how much—Congress is willing to be influenced, a state of receptiveness that always is in doubt.

Presidents through the early 1900s were careful to obey the forms of separation of the branches. They had few instruments for influencing legislation, and their activities generally were constrained by prevailing beliefs in congressional supremacy. Party loyalty, favorable newspaper coverage, and politically connected cabinet members were a nineteenth-century president's primary resources, and presidential lobbying tended to be loosely organized and discreet. This picture had changed dramatically by the 1940s because both government and public attitudes about the nature of presidential leadership had undergone a fundamental reordering. But the evolution of presidential lobbying from the indirect and passive styles of earlier presidents to the open and well-organized practices of today took decades.

President George W. Bush meets with Sens. Edward M. Kennedy, D-Mass., Bill Frist, R-Tenn., and James M. Jeffords, I-Vt., in the White House Cabinet Room to answer questions from the press regarding Jeffords's defection from the Republican Party in June 2001. Jeffords cited the increasing conservatism of the president and GOP leadership as the reason for becoming an independent, a decision that caused the first-ever midsession power shift to occur in the Senate. His switch marked the end of the Republicans' Senate reign, which began in 1995, and gave the Democrats a 50–49 majority over the GOP. Sen. Tom Daschle, D-S.Dak., replaced Trent Lott, R-Miss., as majority leader, inheriting that post's power to set the agenda for the Senate.

Theodore Roosevelt may have cut a more dramatic public figure, but Woodrow Wilson stands out among early-twentieth-century presidents for pursuing a strongly personal approach to congressional relations. Although Wilson shied away from open and "direct" lobbying, he vigorously pulled party strings to ensure Democratic support for his agenda and went so far as to sit in on congressional committee deliberations on trade legislation. His chief congressional lobbyist, Postmaster General Albert Burleson, used postal positions as inducements for loyalty to the president's program. Wilson also relied on John Nance Garner, a House Democrat from Texas, to act as his confidential lobbyist within the House. Garner, who sat on the influential Ways and Means Committee, would enter the White House once a week through a side door to consult with Wilson privately on current congressional news and prospects for the president's legislation.

Less than two decades later, Franklin Roosevelt abandoned any pretense of regal noninvolvement and employed an open and direct lobbying strategy. Roosevelt is considered the father of contemporary presidential lobbying styles, beginning with his own sustained and overt role in policy formation. He effectively goaded Congress into action through radio appeals to the public and through a careful cultivation of friendly relations with the press. His personal assistants—James Rowe, Thomas Corcoran, and Benjamin Cohen—wrote bills and lobbied legislators openly. Like Wilson, Roosevelt relied on patronage to reward loyalty and to punish deserters, using Postmaster General James A. Farley, who also served as chair of the national Democratic Party, as his chief enforcer. Inducements included preferential treatment on public works projects and other New Deal spending programs, funds critical to hard-pressed Democrats during election years, and promises for personal campaign appearances by the popular president.[155] At the same time, however, Roosevelt was careful to limit his personal lobbying efforts to his administration's most important initiatives. As he told his cabinet members: "If I make every bill that the government is interested in must legislation, it is going to complicate things. . . .Where I clear legislation with a notation that says 'no objection,' that means you are at perfect liberty to try and get the thing through, but I am not going to send a special message. It is all your trouble, not mine."[156]

Formalizing the Process

Although Roosevelt's overall influence in Congress waxed and waned with changes in the immediate political

President John F. Kennedy appointed longtime political ally Lawrence F. O'Brien to head the Office of Congressional Relations in order to advance his expansive legislative agenda.

conditions, he constructed a more vigorous and more central role for the presidency in the legislative process. Indeed, Roosevelt inaugurated or perfected many of the lobbying techniques employed by contemporary presidents, but he did not make lobbying a formal process. Roosevelt would assign a presidential aide to lobby for a program or bill only if it got into trouble. Legislative liaison—the practice of having aides constantly cultivate a receptive environment in Congress—remained an informal affair, in many ways reflecting Roosevelt's more personal approach to politics and his dislike of rigid organizations.[157]

Dwight Eisenhower, the former general, adopted the antithesis of Roosevelt's highly personal and avowedly disorganized approach. Eisenhower was the first president to formalize the executive lobbying process by creating the Office of Congressional Relations (OCR), a specialized structure reflecting his own hierarchical orientation and general dislike of direct lobbying. Eisenhower, who was less comfortable than Roosevelt in the rambunctious world of politics, also wanted the OCR to act as a buffer between himself and members of Congress, even those from his party.[158] Heading the OCR was Bryce Harlow, a veteran House committee staff member who had no other responsibilities than to cultivate cordial relations with Congress and, especially, to keep House and Senate Republicans happy. But Harlow's office seldom took an active role in legislative development, largely because Eisenhower spent more time opposing congressional Democratic proposals than in pushing his agenda.

John Kennedy, by contrast, planned an aggressive legislative agenda and strengthened the liaison office by appointing longtime political ally Lawrence F. O'Brien as chief lobbyist. O'Brien wanted the congressional liaison staff to "create a general climate in favor and receptivity toward the president and the administration among members of Congress, and . . . use these positive perceptions as a resource when attempting to obtain support for particular pieces of legislation."[159] He organized the OCR along lines that paralleled the political makeup of Congress itself, assigning a staff member to interact with nearly every faction and bloc in the legislature, and constructed cooperative relationships with agency personnel, party leaders, and interest groups—whoever might be useful or necessary to the president's success. Many scholars consider O'Brien to be the architect of modern legislative liaison, and the specific system he established continued through the Carter administration.

Even with O'Brien's efforts, Kennedy generally was unable to push an expansive legislative agenda because conservative Democrats in Congress opposed new social programs and civil rights legislation. Kennedy's narrow victory over Richard Nixon in 1960 did not give him enough personal political clout to pressure even fellow Democrats to go along with his agenda. Although Kennedy's liaison office was credited with a handful of notable victories on trade and tax matters, the political climate in Congress was such that no organized lobbying could readily control it. Later presidents would discover that a good liaison office could not overcome a weak political hand.

Lyndon Johnson fared quite differently. Kennedy's assassination had created in the nation and in Congress a desire to pass some of the slain president's legislation, and Johnson's own decisive 1964 election victory over Barry M. Goldwater gave him the kind of public "mandate" that crafty politicians like Johnson can capitalize on with Congress.[160] The 1964 election also brought into Congress many new liberal Democrats, giving Johnson added congressional support for his domestic policy agenda. Johnson retained the liaison office built by Kennedy to augment his own considerable personal political skills, and he insisted that O'Brien and his liaison staff be consulted closely before initiatives were taken. So closely did Johnson work with Congress that political scientist Charles Jones characterizes Johnson's legislative style as akin to that of a majority leader—which Johnson had been in the Senate before becoming vice president under Kennedy.[161] Johnson, always a creature of Congress, believed that legislators should be consulted regularly on policy initiatives. He knew how to include members of Congress in decision making, he was careful not to overload the system, and he was sensitive to the importance of making loyal supporters look good. Above all, Johnson sought out compromise behind the scenes, going directly to the American public only as a last resort, and his liaison staff worked hard to develop and maintain cooperative relationships all over Capitol Hill.[162]

Richard Nixon's legislative style was not particularly conducive to pushing a legislative program, but in many ways it was well suited to forcing a hostile Congress to accede to his demands or risk a veto, particularly when the politically astute president knew he had public support. Nixon's early successes attest to the degree to which presidents can confront Congress and get their way when they enjoy a high degree of popularity. The opposite also was true: as Nixon's public support fell, so did his capacity to stop Congress from overriding his opposition to major pieces of legislation, such as the 1973 War Powers Resolution.

Gerald Ford in many ways operated more like the Democrat Lyndon Johnson than like fellow Republican Nixon, probably because Ford and Johnson shared longer careers in Congress and believed in the institution more than did Nixon. Like Johnson, Ford committed himself to working with all members of Congress and deployed his legislative liaison team to cultivate friendly relations with both parties. Unlike Johnson, Ford was a minority president, with Democrats in control of both houses of Congress. He, like Nixon, had to rely on the veto as a central part of his overall legislative strategy, using his liaison staff to build coalitions to support his vetoes. In this sense, at least, Ford was effective.

Jimmy Carter was an outsider who had less interest in the process of consensus building than in the substance of policy, and he had a dim view of traditional Washington politics. "Legislative liaison for Carter," Eric Davis suggests, "simply was a matter of convincing members of Congress of the correctness of his positions on the issues."[163] His liaison team as a result was organized initially along issue lines, as opposed to the geographical and voting bloc patterns employed since O'Brien. No single staff assistant could discuss a wide array of issues—or make deals across issues—with any single member of Congress. Also, the Carter White House initially turned its back on the O'Brien method of continually courting members and doling out favors to loyalists and party leaders. Carter's aides so disdained the norms of Washington that even House Speaker Thomas P. "Tip" O'Neill, whose help Carter would need to push through his legislative agenda, could not get good seats for his guests at the inaugural gala—a slight that an old-school politician like O'Neill would never entirely forget or forgive.[164]

Carter's legislative strategy in many ways reflected his arguably accurate reading of the new political realities of the post-Watergate, post-Vietnam era. Johnson's style looked tawdry to a public increasingly wary of "smoke-filled rooms" and insistent that presidents speak directly to them on major issues. Public faith in government and a willingness to follow political leaders were at a nadir after Watergate

and Vietnam, and Congress itself had changed dramatically in the interim. Johnson was able to rely heavily on congressional leaders to carry his banner, because the congressional hierarchy was still strong enough to keep party members in line. But that hierarchy had all but dissolved by the time Carter was elected in 1976, and, to succeed, he had to construct temporary coalitions among as many members as possible. Carter thus tended to present his case to the public first, believing that his primary task was to persuade citizens to adopt his view of an issue and thereby create a political climate favorable to congressional action.

But Carter may have erred too much on the side of first gaining the public's support. Congressional leaders often were not consulted in advance of Carter's statements, and legislative liaison tended toward the exchange of information rather than the still-critical building of legislative coalitions of support.[165] But so fluid had American politics become by the late 1970s that one political scientist likened it to building coalitions out of sand—hard to work with and never quite permanent.[166] Given these realities, Carter's strategy of going directly to the public on important issues is understandable.

Ronald Reagan used Carter's general strategy to better effect, although a great deal of credit also went to an experienced and well-organized legislative liaison staff laden with former Nixon and Ford officials. House Speaker O'Neill called Reagan's victory on the 1981 budget package "the greatest selling job I've ever seen." Reagan's success came about through a mixture of dramatic public appeals by the president, the work of administration officials sent to generate support in key Democratic constituencies, and a good deal of old-fashioned bargaining.[167] Jones has likened Reagan's lobbying style to that of Franklin Roosevelt, with emphasis placed on communicating views and ideals to the public and generating pressure on Congress to go along.[168]

Even for Reagan, however, the strategy had its limits. Appeals to the public can work only so often and only on particularly dramatic issues. Going public tends to have diminishing returns the longer and more frequently a president relies on that strategy, which Reagan discovered during his second term in office. Reagan's immediate successors, regardless of political party, were to discover the difficulty of relying on the public route without having Reagan's unique persona. Neither George Bush nor Bill Clinton—very different personalities facing different legislative terrain—could translate their personal appeals into significant legislative victories. For Bush, the stalemate with a Democrat-controlled Congress was both partisan and ideological, and even his high public approval rating after the Persian Gulf War did not produce action from Congress.[169] For Clinton, the legislative victories of his first two years in office depended almost entirely on remarkably strong party support, with the occasional coalition with Republicans on crime and trade matters. But such an "inside" strategy failed Clinton miserably on health care, largely because his party was fragmented badly on the issue and because Republicans were united in their opposition to Clinton's agenda. After the 1994 midterm election Clinton's legislative posture shifted toward a more centrist strategy, in which he portrayed himself as a moderate bulwark against right-wing Republican extremism. He co-opted a number of Republican positions—supporting welfare reform, balancing the federal budget—but cast them as consistent with "new" Democratic Party principles. Clinton's ability to capture the rhetorical high ground in his political skirmishes with congressional Republicans would serve as the foundation of his legislative strategy for the remainder of his presidency, but his was a defensive posture in an atmosphere marked by tremendous partisan and even personal rancor.

The increased party polarization in Congress also influenced George W. Bush's legislative effectiveness to a far greater degree than did his particular lobbying strategy. For the most part, prior to the 9/11 terrorist attacks Bush's congressional relations can best be characterized as what Charles O. Jones calls "competitive partisanship," in which leaders of both parties moved aggressively to unite their followers in support of their party objectives.[170] For Bush this meant focusing his legislative agenda on a few key issues, including tax cuts, education standards, Social Security and Medicare reform, and federal support for faith-based charities. His lobbying strategy generally involved using campaign-style techniques that focused on mobilizing public support for his agenda. This included emphasizing policy-related symbols in public comments rather than policy details, using public meetings with hand-picked groups to generate favorable publicity, and making sure that all administrative spokespersons stayed "on message." But Bush generally avoided taking a personal role in negotiating legislative details with members of Congress until it became necessary to close a deal.[171] This strategy proved highly successful in pushing a ten-year, $1.35 trillion tax cut through Congress, but less effective on more controversial issues lacking widespread congressional support, such as Medicare reform or aid to faith-based charities. On other issues, such as education reform and agricultural subsidies, Bush was forced to work with leading Democrats to enact his policies.[172]

After 9/11 Bush's congressional orientation changed, and he moved aggressively to capitalize on his commander-in-chief status to dominate the legislative agenda. For their part, congressional Democrats were more willing to work with Bush and congressional Republicans in bipartisan negotiations on terrorist-related policies, including airport security, creation of the Homeland Security Department, and bioterrorist defense. But on other matters, competitive partisanship based on unified parties continued to rule the day. Bush attempted to pressure Democrats by publicly

linking as many of his objectives as possible to the war on terror, including his energy policy, trade promotion authority, and economic stimulus proposals, but with only partial success. After his reelection in 2004, Bush failed to enact immigration and Social Security reform, even as his party maintained a majority over the next two years and Bush declared that the election showed his "political capital."[173] Indeed, some critics argue that Bush's strategy further divided the two parties.[174] True or not, within a year of the terrorist attacks, the bipartisan consensus on Bush's foreign policy began eroding, as reflected in the divided party vote on the October 2002 resolution authorizing Bush to go to war in Iraq.[175] Although he successfully positioned himself to win reelection in 2004, and the election results slightly strengthened the Republicans' margin of control in both congressional chambers, they did not appreciably increase Bush's bargaining leverage in the highly polarized environment.[176] He continued to find his greatest congressional support on war-related measures, such as renewal of the USA PATRIOT Act in 2005. But Democratic opposition stymied progress on most of his domestic priorities, such as Social Security and Medicare reform. After the Democratic takeover of Congress in the 2006 elections, Bush hinted that he would return to a more bipartisan legislative approach for the remaining two years of his presidency. At the same time, however, he appeared unwilling to reverse course in Iraq, setting up a potential showdown with the Democrat-controlled Congress.[177]

Styles of Presidential Lobbying

There is no single best way for presidents to lobby Congress, but certain means—such as favors, consultation, and personal phone calls—are always useful. Each president's particular style and way of organizing lobbying activities reflect personal skills, interests, and views about the relationship among the branches of government. Presidents who see themselves as partners with Congress, such as Lyndon Johnson, operate far differently than those like Nixon, who see the presidency as independent of and generally in competition with the legislature.[178] Each style has its strengths, but neither guarantees success. After all, pushing a legislative agenda also means having to deal with a Congress that sees itself as the energetic center of U.S. government.

Still, even "failed" presidents enjoy a modicum of success in Congress, if success is measured by the percentage of bills supported by the president that Congress passes into law.[179] By some measures, Carter, despite his apparent weaknesses, enjoyed overall success in Congress, while Reagan, for all his mass popularity and rhetorical skills, on average fared much worse. Clinton's generally low public support during his first two years in office also masked a highly productive legislative record. The reason for this disparity may simply be that Carter and Clinton each enjoyed generally supportive Democratic majorities in Congress, while Reagan encountered at least one house dominated by his political foes. Reagan's successes came not on the quantity of bills supported in Congress, but on their scope and importance.

Also noteworthy is the inverse relationship over time between the improvement in any administration's lobbying and organizational skills and congressional support for that same administration. In other words, virtually all presidents have found it more difficult to gain congressional approval for major proposals late in their terms in office, even after years of experience, than when they were new on the job. It is tempting to explain this paradox by comparing presidential success in Congress with the president's popularity. Both scores drop over time, suggesting that broad presidential popularity affects legislative success. Members of Congress, George Edwards points out, "respond to the president's current popularity among their supporters," and thus are reluctant to oppose a popular president.[180] However, they are less reluctant to vote against a president whose public support has weakened, particularly if the president is from the opposing party and the president's term in office is nearing its end. However, efforts to tie presidents' legislative success to their approval ratings have found a marginal relationship at best.[181] It may be that a president's legislative success decreases through time because most of the major issues on which there is broad political support are passed early in the president's term; as time goes on, the legislative agenda is increasingly populated by more controversial issues that are inherently more difficult to pass. If so, it reinforces the fact that systemic factors, rather than the behavior of individual presidents, largely determine their legislative effectiveness.

Despite the tendency of the mass media to focus on personalities, whether a president succeeds or fails probably has less to do with personal attributes or styles than with the political conditions at the time. Presidents certainly can influence political conditions, but they cannot control them. Presidents must play the political cards dealt them by the broader political system and by the world at large. Successful presidents may be those who had strengths or values that meshed well with the tenor of the times or with current congressional majorities. Or they may simply have been lucky.

Public Appeals

As suggested earlier, every president has had on occasion to go directly to the people to exert pressure on a recalcitrant Congress. Be it through speeches to the nation on television, leaks of information to favored journalists, or orchestrated public demonstrations of support, presidents find some way to recruit public opinion in their fights with Congress when they believe conditions and issues warrant it. *(See Table 4-6, p. 192.)*

Going directly to the people has become easier, and thus more desirable, because modern telecommunications technology, particularly television, has enabled presidents to speak their minds with less worry that intermediaries will garble their messages. The rise of television as the primary means by which most Americans receive their news was a primary factor in the emergence of the contemporary presidency and its power to influence the national agenda. Nonetheless, going directly to the people has its risks, for success hinges largely on the issue in question, a president's own rhetorical skills, the ability of the president's opponents to use the same communication tools, and the mood of the public at the moment. None of these factors is predictable.

Early Use of Public Appeals

Presidents before the twentieth century neither had the technologies to speak directly to the people nor did they generally conceive of their roles in exactly the same manner as do their contemporary counterparts. The Founders' fear of demagogues, which fed their efforts to insulate the selection of the president from the mass public, influenced the earliest presidents profoundly. Congress, not the president, was meant to represent the people, and Congress generally considered it illegitimate and intrusive for a president to try to pressure its members on legislation.

From the earliest days of the presidency, however, some presidents did attempt to influence public opinion through indirect, often subtle means. Thomas Jefferson relied heavily on his popular dinner parties to influence key legislators, newspaper reporters, and other important political figures. But it was Andrew Jackson among earlier presidents who began the practice of appealing to the common people for support. Jackson, after all, had entered the office as an outsider—he was the first president not to come from one of the original thirteen colonies—and was a foe of the established ways of doing business. He presaged the contemporary presidency by artfully arranging for official documents to be leaked to supportive newspapers, used friendly journalists to convey his views and desires, and relied on his party organization to stir up public support and put pressure on Congress. "King Andrew," as his enemies came to call him, reaped a great deal of criticism for his unorthodox practices, and most pre–Civil War presidents did not follow his pattern. None had Jackson's popularity or his activist philosophy about the role of the presidency.

Abraham Lincoln was usually on the defensive with Congress over his war policies, but he overcame its opposition by winning public support through the newspapers. Lincoln wrote numerous letters and opinion columns, which received favorable coverage from friendly publishers such as Horace Greeley. Lincoln generated other supportive stories through leaks to reporters. It also was said that Lincoln grew his beard after a supporter remarked that his

TABLE 4-6 **Television Addresses by Presidents, 1961–2011**

President	Year	Topic
Kennedy	1961	Urgent national needs; Berlin Wall
	1962	Racial unrest; quarantine of Cuba
	1963	Civil rights bill; test ban treaty
L. Johnson	1963	Kennedy assassination
	1965	Voting rights bill
	1968	Bombing halt/withdrawal from election
Nixon	1969	National unity in Vietnam; Vietnam peace proposals; Vietnam troop reductions
	1970	Vietnam; Cambodia incursion (2); peace in Indochina
	1971	Withdrawal of troops; economic policy
	1972	Report of trip to People's Republic of China
	1973	Watergate; national energy policy
	1974	White House tapes; resignation
Ford	1974	Post–Nixon resignation speech; inflation
	1975	State of the world
Carter	1977	Energy crisis; energy policy
	1979	Energy crisis; national morale; Soviet troops in Cuba; military spending
	1980	Failure of Iran rescue mission; anti-inflation
	1981	Farewell speech
Reagan	1981	Economic policies and proposals (4)
	1982	Federal budget; Middle East; Lebanon; arms control
	1983	Strategic Defense Initiative and Central America; Grenada; Lebanon
	1985	Tax reform; U.S.-Soviet summit (Geneva)
	1986	Military spending; aid to contras (2); U.S.-Soviet summit (Iceland); Iran arms sales
	1987	Iran arms sales; economic summit; Iran-contra affair; Bork nomination; U.S.-Soviet summit (Washington)
	1988	Contra aid
	1989	Farewell address
G.H.W. Bush	1989	Drug war; invasion of Panama
	1990	Deployment of forces to Persian Gulf; budget agreement
	1991	Commencement of attack on Iraq; cease-fire announcement
	1992	Deployment of relief forces to Somalia
Clinton	1993	Economic plan; air raid on Iraq
	1994	Situation in Somalia; "middle class bill of rights"
	1995	U.S. peacekeeping mission in Bosnia
	1998	Sexual affair with White House intern
	2001	Farewell address
G.W. Bush	2001	Stem cell research; September 11 attacks; response to terrorism; start of Afghan military campaign; homeland security
	2002	proposed Department of Homeland Security; anniversary of terrorist attacks; Iraq update
	2003	Loss of space shuttle; Iraq update; start of Iraq war; end of combat operations; progress in war on terror; Hussein captured
	2004	Health care costs
	2005	Iraq elections; war on terror; Justice Roberts nomination; Hurricane Katrina recovery
	2007	Update on Iraq, war on terror
	2008	Finance industry crisis and economic downturn
Obama[a]	2009	Update on Afghanistan (troop increase)
	2010	Oil spill in Gulf of Mexico; end of Iraq combat operations
	2011	Military operation in Libya; Osama bin Laden killed; update on Afghanistan (troop drawdown); federal budget and debt ceiling impasse

SOURCE: *Congressional Quarterly Almanac*, various issues; *CQ Weekly*, various issues; John Woolley and Gerhard Peters, The American Presidency Project, www. presidency.ucsb .edu.

NOTES: Table does not include State of the Union and inaugural addresses, which also are televised; it only includes those addresses that are not part of a ceremonial occasion. a. Through December 2011.

bare face (and lack of chin) did not look "presidential" enough, and inexpensive lithographs (a new technology) of the newly bearded commander in chief soon graced many a Union household.

Theodore Roosevelt thrived on publicity and made himself easily available to favorite reporters. His love of the press was reciprocated, for the flamboyant and erudite Roosevelt made for good copy.[182] Roosevelt is credited with creating the official White House press release, which he often issued on Sundays—traditionally the slowest news day—to give newspapers something to print the next day. He also devised off-the-record "background" press briefings, which he frequently used to float "trial balloons" as one way to assess public and congressional opinion on issues.

Woodrow Wilson outdid Roosevelt in going directly to the public by resuming the practice of delivering the State of the Union address personally and by instituting regular and formal press conferences. He was most effective, however, in making direct appeals to the public usually through the newspapers or speeches before Congress. The notable exception was his grueling nationwide tour in 1919 to generate support for the Treaty of Versailles, an effort that ultimately ruined his health. Wilson's efforts to go to the people went for naught, for the Senate failed to ratify the treaty.

Franklin Roosevelt and Radio

Although Theodore Roosevelt and Wilson were masters at generating favorable public opinion through the press, they lacked easy access to technology that could enable them to go directly into every citizen's home. But Franklin Roosevelt entered the White House just as radio entered its heyday, and the ebullient New Yorker made superb use of the medium. His public speeches, twenty-seven "fireside" radio chats, hundreds of formal press conferences, countless informal background sessions with selected reporters, and shrewd use of the newsreels, all constructed a public persona that millions of Americans would recall fondly for decades. The response to Roosevelt's first inaugural address, in which he averred that "the only thing we have to fear is fear itself," was so great that humorist Will Rogers wrote: "If he burned down the Capitol, we would cheer and say, 'Well, we at least got a fire started somehow.'"[183]

Roosevelt used radio directly to educate and persuade, and there was no greater example than his first "fireside chat" to the nation, which centered on the banking crisis that had worsened on the eve of his inauguration. Roosevelt explained how the banking system worked and why it was important that people take their money out of their mattresses and put it back into their savings accounts. They did, and Roosevelt was credited with ending the crisis. As Arthur M. Schlesinger Jr. wrote, the fireside chats "conveyed

Roosevelt's conception of himself as a man at ease in his own house talking frankly and intimately to neighbors as they sat in their living rooms."[184]

But the radio speeches and chats were intended for more than soothing the public: they were meant to move Congress into action on Roosevelt's agenda. According to political scientist Wilfred E. Binkley, Roosevelt "had only to glance toward a microphone or suggest that he might go on the air again and a whole congressional delegation would surrender. They had no relish for the flood of mail and telegrams they knew would swamp them after another fireside chat to the nation."[185] Roosevelt, particularly after the first year, did not always win when he went to the airwaves, but those in opposition never took for granted his power to move the public.

The Television Presidency

Roosevelt proved successful with radio in no small part because the medium forces listeners to use their imaginations to visualize both the speaker and the topic under discussion. He had a powerful voice, which offered to the listener an image of strength and determination. The radio image of Roosevelt belied the physical reality: stricken with polio at the age of thirty-nine, Roosevelt could not walk. Americans may have known of Roosevelt's disability in the abstract—it certainly was no secret—but they were not reminded of it continually because, thanks to a tacit agreement with the press, he rarely was photographed head to toe. But if Roosevelt had run for the presidency in the age of television—a visual medium—he would not have been able to control his public image so masterfully. Whether he could have been elected in the first place, since so many people equate physical strength with strong "leadership"—much less rally a nation through a depression and a war—is one of the tantalizing "what ifs" of history.

The contemporary presidency in many ways lives and sometimes dies by television. Eisenhower was the first president to permit press conferences to be filmed for television, but it was Kennedy, arguably the first president of the television age, who allowed *live* telecasts of his press conferences. The public for the first time watched the press question a president live, with no chance for the White House to edit the president's comments. Kennedy's ease with television, his intellect, and his humor made television a potent tool for communicating with the American people. His persuasive television appearance was not enough, however, to ensure congressional approval of his legislative programs.

Lyndon Johnson, superb as he was in the art of personal lobbying, proved uneasy with television, although his live address urging the passage of the 1965 Voting Rights Act did move the nation and Congress. Johnson was probably the first president to discover television's double-edged sword as Americans absorbed televised images of urban riots and antiwar demonstrations, and for the first time witnessed the horrors of war by watching the evening news. Frequently, these televised images appeared to contradict Johnson's assertions about the pace of social progress at home and the success of the war in Indochina, contradictions that shook the nation's confidence in its government. Johnson was particularly wounded by public reaction to the massive North Vietnamese Tet offensive in early 1968, a coordinated assault on South Vietnamese cities that undercut his declarations that the war was winding down. For the North Vietnamese the attack, although a military disaster, was a psychological victory. Johnson's public support plummeted, and he decided not to run for reelection. Johnson's experience was but an early example of how television-magnified events can influence a president's agenda and popularity.

Richard Nixon, who felt that the official press had been hostile to his candidacy in 1960 and who saw how Johnson had fared with the media, used television directly and extensively to re-tailor his image with the public. Distrustful of the Washington press corps, which often proved unwilling to rally around the administration's Vietnam policy, the president spoke directly to the American people far more often than had his predecessors. In his November 1969 address to the nation on Vietnam, for example, Nixon asserted that a "silent majority" of citizens supported his actions despite what members of the press wrote.[186] Nixon also held few Washington press conferences, which he felt only offered opportunities for his critics to attack him, and instead began to hold press conferences in parts of the country where journalists might be more deferential to his office.

Nixon used Vice President Spiro Agnew to make vigorous attacks on the news media, a tactic that produced one of the most memorable phrases in American political lore. In a September 1970 speech in San Diego, Agnew railed that the Washington press corps was filled with "nattering nabobs of negativism. They have formed their own 4-H Club—the 'hopeless, hysterical hypochondriacs of history.'"[187] The tactic was clear: discredit the news media and connect the president more directly to the American people.

Nixon also used television successfully to pressure Congress in selected instances, such as his televised veto of a 1970 appropriations bill. Thousands of supportive telegrams subsequently poured into both the White House and Capitol Hill, giving the impression of massive popular support for Nixon's position. Whether this reaction was spontaneous or orchestrated by Nixon's supporters was irrelevant to many members of the House, which upheld the veto.

As with Johnson, however, television played a major part in Nixon's downfall. The nation watched in fascination as the daily drama of the 1973 Senate Watergate hearings played out on television. Nixon's own performances during televised press conferences, and even in speeches to the

To reverse the mutual distrust between the White House and the media built up during the Nixon administration, Ford worked to convey a simpler image to the press. Here he allows photographers to take pictures as he makes his breakfast.

which he called "the moral equivalent of war," evoked no widespread support and even spawned jokes that the acronym for "moral equivalent of war" was MEOW.

But Carter had some successes as well, most notably the televised signing of the 1979 Camp David peace accords, a moment of high drama when Egyptian president Anwar Sadat signed a peace treaty with Israeli prime minister Menachem Begin. Carter, who had been personally instrumental in bringing these longtime adversaries together, used the signing to rally congressional support for significant American aid to both Israel and Egypt. Generally, however, Carter proved more a victim than a manipulator of television, particularly after Iranian revolutionaries seized and held fifty-three American hostages for more than a year. Each night Americans witnessed on their television sets the humiliation of the hostage situation—a long "crisis" that actually spawned the popular daily ABC news show *Nightline*. Carter's inability to free the hostages contributed to his electoral loss to Ronald Reagan in 1980.

Reagan, who had been a movie and television actor before becoming governor of California, quickly proved a powerful contrast to Carter in his ability to use the media to his political advantage. As radio had been to Franklin Roosevelt, television was to Reagan, and the president relied heavily on his rhetorical talents to whip up support for his dramatic budget and tax policy victories in 1981. Of particular potency was Reagan's May 1981 appeal to a joint session of Congress for support on his budget package, his first public appearance after he was badly wounded in a March 1981 assassination attempt. So powerful was the moment, and so massive the outpouring of public support for the president, that the Democrat-dominated House passed a resolution supporting the outlines of Reagan's budget package a few days later. Reagan also used television to establish intimacy with the American people. Few could resist the emotional pull of his 1984 speech on the cliffs overlooking France's Omaha Beach on the fortieth anniversary of the Normandy invasion, or of his eulogy for the astronauts who died in the 1986 space shuttle *Challenger* disaster.[188]

Reagan's extensive use of mass media to appeal directly to the public even revived the use of a more traditional vehicle—radio. His administration, as if to hearken back to Franklin Roosevelt's fireside chats, began the practice of recording weekly five-minute presidential radio addresses, to be aired each Saturday morning. Democrats subsequently invoked federal rules on political use of the airwaves and got

nation, seemed to many viewers to be the picture of a president trying to deceive the public. After evidence pointing to Nixon's complicity in the Watergate cover-up emerged, the president resigned in disgrace on August 9, 1974.

His successor, Gerald Ford, worked to diminish the distrust between the White House and the media that had built up during the Nixon years. Where Nixon basked in the formal trappings of the office, Ford worked to convey a more down-to-earth image; for example, he allowed himself to be photographed making his own breakfast. Where Nixon rarely held press conferences, Ford held many—and earned high praise from the media for his openness and honesty. Ford did not escape unscathed, however: his every stumble and slip were grist for the humor mill—an irony, no doubt, for a former college football star. In trying to humanize the office, Ford risked being seen as "unpresidential," an image that all presidents try to avoid.

Jimmy Carter, acting on his populist background and belief that Americans had tired of the "imperial presidency," early on cultivated an image as an outsider by holding televised "town meetings" to which citizens called in questions. Carter also tried his own televised version of Roosevelt's fireside chats; wearing a cardigan sweater, he spoke to the public as he sat before a fire. But what had worked for Roosevelt in the days of the depression and radio did not work for Carter on television in the post-Watergate era. Too many Americans regarded Carter's approach as superficial symbolism, and his efforts to use television to stir the public generally failed. His talk to the nation on the energy crisis, the right to air their own five-minute radio segments. This pattern of weekly presidential radio addresses and opposition "rebuttals" has endured to this day. Relatively few Americans may actually hear the addresses on the radio, but their contents are usually covered in evening television news reports, so the addresses remain part of an overall presidential communications strategy.

But even for Reagan mass media appeals had a double-edged effect. Public responsiveness to media appeals almost inevitably wanes the more frequently a president relies on them, as Reagan discovered during his second term. Startling revelations about secret arms sales to the Iranian government and their possibly illegal use to fund the supply of arms to American-backed rebels fighting the government of Nicaragua eroded public confidence in Reagan's leadership. Televised congressional hearings on the affair raised broad public concern about the president's overall command of his office. By 1988, when the three major networks refused to carry another appeal for aid for the Nicaraguan rebels because it "was not news," it was apparent that the skills so integral to Reagan's early successes no longer were potent enough to prevail.

Even with Reagan's later woes, his immediate successors would discover painfully that Reagan had a rare gift for using the mass media to connect to the public. They also discovered, as Reagan did, that popular approval does not always translate into better prospects for legislative success. As Charles O. Jones argues, popularity is "sometimes a recognition or reward for an action deemed successful or an acknowledgment that things are going well."[189] Even though George H. W. Bush enjoyed a stunningly high level of popularity at the end of the Persian Gulf War, he nonetheless was a one-term president. Bush's inability to capitalize on his popularity in part grew out of his apparent discomfort with the demands of the media presidency, an institution that favors high visibility, adeptness at verbal communication, and a nuanced understanding of the symbolic power of the office. The national economic recession and broad public perception that the nation was heading in the wrong direction also contributed to his defeat in the 1992 election, but his presidential style certainly played a role.

But recent presidents' ineffectiveness at "going public" as a means of pressuring Congress to support their legislative priorities reflects more than simply a deficient media style or lack of rhetorical skills; it points to the limits of the strategy itself, particularly in the post-Reagan era. Despite a full-fledged media campaign spearheaded by his own formidable communications skills, Bill Clinton could not translate diffuse public support for health care reform into solid congressional support of his health security legislative proposal. Similarly, George W. Bush failed to mobilize enough public support to pressure Congress into backing his plan to reform Social Security. These cases reveal that presidents'

"communications wars" often fail because they stimulate opposing groups to engage in their own media strategies designed to block the presidents' initiatives. Because of the mainstream press' desire for "balanced" coverage, and its tendency to focus on disagreement and controversy, the concerns raised by these opposition groups get extensive media coverage, often leading to a drop in popular support for presidential initiatives.[190] In addition, the Internet provides a medium for the president's opponents to air their views.

This is not to say that the president's voice is indistinguishable from that of any other political actor. George W. Bush's public speeches in the days and weeks after 9/11 demonstrate that, under certain conditions, the president of the United States still has an unparalleled capacity to dominate the national airwaves. Beginning with his nationwide address on the evening of the attacks through his widely publicized tour of the World Trade Center ruins—during which he memorably proclaimed to the gathered first responders who complained they couldn't hear, "I can hear you. The rest of the world hears you. And the people who knocked these buildings down will hear all of us soon"—to his address to a joint session of Congress on September 20, Bush dominated the nation's airwaves. His approval rating during this period shot to 90 percent, the highest ever recorded. Bush capitalized on this support to push several initiatives through Congress, including an open-ended declaration of war on terror and a $40 billion emergency spending bill to fund that war. In the next several weeks Congress passed a $7 billion airline bailout bill and the controversial USA PATRIOT Act that gave law enforcement agencies more power to prevent further attacks.

Even though congressional support for Bush's policies, particularly those not directly related to national security issues, began to erode soon afterward, in October 2002 he was still able to use public backing for the war on terror to pressure Congress to pass a resolution authorizing him to invade Iraq. Terrorism also played a significant role in the Republican takeover of Congress in the 2002 midterm elections, and in Bush's reelection in 2004. But these electoral campaigns, although ending successfully for Bush and the Republicans, also revealed the hardening of the partisan fissures in Congress, particularly as 9/11 receded in the public's memory.[191]

As Bush's approval ratings underwent a seemingly inexorable decline during the five years after the terrorist attacks, so too did his ability to monopolize the public airwaves. Indeed, the growing criticisms of Bush's policies vividly demonstrated the increasingly fragmented and partisan sources of information and political coverage in the Internet age, in which a growing number of people receive their news from a computer terminal. While John Kennedy could command almost universal public attention because there were few alternatives to the three major television networks, contemporary presidents no longer have access to a media outlet commanding that type of viewership. Instead, they must compete for attention not just on the hundreds of cable and satellite television channels and talk radio shows, but within the Internet-based "blogosphere" as well. Even the "mainstream" media has fractured into smaller outlets, each tailored to attract a particular segment of its audience. At its worst, this produces an echo-chamber effect where people tune into the media service that produces the message they find most compatible with their own ideological views. For many citizens, the president's voice is heard only through this increasingly partisan-driven and controversy-oriented filter.

Barring a widely perceived crisis, then, the increasingly fragmented media environment means that no one person, not even the president, may be able to "monopolize" the public space—indeed, it is no longer clear that there is a single space to monopolize. Instead, presidents seeking to build political coalitions and mobilize support for their legislative initiatives are forced to work even harder to individually tailor their appeals to smaller segments of the polity—and to make those appeals heard in an increasingly cacophonous and partisan atmosphere. President George W. Bush was not considered particularly articulate, nor comfortable making major speeches and public appeals, but with strategic savvy and a solid partisan majority in Congress for the middle four years of his presidency, he capitalized on political momentum and policy crisis to reshape tax policy, foreign affairs, intelligence gathering, industrial regulations, and a landmark bailout of Wall Street in his last months in office. By contrast, President Barack Obama, widely praised for his oratory skills and with several major legislative accomplishments under his belt in his first two years in office, maintained a more ambivalent public presence in the legislative process, preferring to set the agenda and then step back so members of Congress could hammer out the details, while keeping a close eye on proceedings through his Vice President Joseph Biden and other liaison staff. This strategy may undermine the projection of presidential strength all occupants seek, but it also serves to spread policy ownership and accountability to members, as well as treating Congress as a co-equal branch.

While the Framers of the Constitution may have anticipated, and even desired, national presidential leadership to balance narrower congressional passions, the document itself created a legislative obstacle course. The president has few unilateral powers and usually must receive explicit support from Congress to do almost anything in domestic and even foreign policy. In December 2000 President-elect George W. Bush described a meeting with congressional leadership teams and said "[i]f this were a dictatorship, it'd be a heck of a lot easier, just so long as I'm the dictator."[192] While this remark was delivered and perceived as a joke, it is still the case that over the past century, the American public seems to side with the president often on legislative battles, and congressional approval is usually below that of the president. Members of Congress have also gotten used to presidential leadership to such an extent that top Republicans in 2011 chided Obama repeatedly for not leading the budget, deficit, and debt ceiling battles of the year.[193] Why would Obama take such additional risks, though, when voters had just shown support for increasing a balance to his ambitious agenda, as seen in the outcome of the 2010 elections? The Constitution allowed many opportunities for presidential power to expand and be reduced. Instead of a dictatorship, the Framers desired peaceful conflicts over the national interest from a variety of positions. Even in an era of vast policy agendas and the permanent assumption of "modern" presidential power, year-to-year legislative leadership is still deeply complex, as it was intended to be.

NOTES

1 Richard E. Neustadt, *Presidential Power and the Modern Presidents* (New York: Free Press, 1990), 29.

2 See Charles O. Jones, *The Presidency in a Separated System*, 2d ed. (Washington, D.C.: Brookings, 2005); David Mayhew, *Divided We Govern: Party Control, Lawmaking, and Investigations, 1946–1990* (New Haven: Yale University Press, 1991); and Sarah Binder, *Stalemate: Causes and Consequences of Legislative Gridlock* (Washington, D.C.: Brookings, 2003).

3 Louis Fisher, *The President and Congress* (New York: Free Press, 1972), 18–21. See also A. E. Howard, ed., *The United States Constitution: Roots, Rights, and Responsibilities* (Washington, D.C.: Smithsonian Institution Press, 1992).

4 Thomas Jefferson, "Notes on Virginia," in *The Life and Selected Writings of Thomas Jefferson*, ed. Adrienne Koch and William Peden (New York: Random House, Modern Library, 1944), 237.

5 James Madison, *The Federalist* No. 48: These Departments Should Not Be So Far Separated as to Have No Constitutional Control over the Other, February 1, 1788, www.constitution.org/fed/federa48.htm; and *The Federalist* No. 51: The Structure of the Government Must Furnish the Proper Checks and Balances between Different Departments, February 6, 1788, www.constitution.org/fed/federa51.htm.

6 *Guide to Congress*, 4th ed. (Washington, D.C.: Congressional Quarterly, 1991), 552.

7 John Adams, "The State Constitutions as Analogy and Precedent," in *The United States Constitution: Roots, Rights, and Responsibilities*, ed. A. E. Howard (Washington, D.C.: Smithsonian Institution Press, 1992), 3–22.

8 Ibid., 30–31.

9 The exemption of constitutional amendments from the veto was established by the Supreme Court in *Hollingsworth v. Virginia*, 3 Dall. 378 (1798).

10 Alexander Hamilton, James Madison, and John Jay, *The Federalist Papers*, ed. Clinton Rossiter (New York: New American Library, 1961), 443.

11 Ibid., 444.

12 The Constitution gives presidents the authority to approve or veto legislation within ten days after a bill is *presented* to the White House, as opposed to after it is *passed* by Congress. Bills passed by Congress cannot be presented to the president until they have been signed by the Speaker of the House and the president of the Senate (that is, the vice president, although this function is performed normally by the president pro tempore). Thus an indefinite gap can occur between passage and presentation. At times, Congress has delayed presentation of bills because the president has been out of the country. Presidents also have maneuvered to delay presentation of bills to create opportunities for pocket vetoes. In 1970 Richard Nixon had Vice President Spiro Agnew exercise his authority to sign legislation, which Agnew then delayed doing so that several bills would not be presented to Nixon until just a few days before adjournment. On this, see Eric Redman, *The Dance of Legislation* (New York: Touchstone Books, 1973).

13 As upheld by the Supreme Court in *Missouri Pacific Railway Co. v. United States*, 248 U.S. 277 (1919).

14 For example, in 1995 and 1997, Democrat Bill Clinton vetoed similar Republican-sponsored bills outlawing a controversial type of pregnancy termination often referred to by opponents as "partial birth abortion"; both congressional override attempts failed. A similar bill passed the Republican majority in 2003 and was signed into law by a Republican President, George W. Bush.

15 But in those early days, as is the case now, this label is slippery enough to accommodate many kinds of unwanted legislation. Unless Congress is trying to change an enumerated provision by legislation, a veto by the president is an act of constitutional interpretation, whether or not couched in that language explicitly.

16 Clinton Rossiter, *The American Presidency*, 2d ed. (New York: Harcourt, Brace, 1960), 91.

17 For the full message, see http://avalon.law.yale.edu/19th_century/ajveto01.asp,.

18 See James Bryce, *The American Commonwealth*, vol. 1, 2d ed. (New York: Macmillan, 1911), 64. The Supreme Court in 1926 ruled that the power to remove political appointees resided with the president alone. See *Myers v. United States*, 272 U.S. 52 (1926); for more on Johnson's unconventional rhetoric and actions surrounding legislative initiatives and disagreements with Congress, see also Jeffrey K. Tulis, *The Rhetorical Presidency* (Princeton: Princeton University Press, 1987), chap. 3.

19 Louis Fisher, *Presidential Spending Power* (Princeton: Princeton University Press, 1975), 25.

20 Neustadt, *Presidential Power*, 71.

21 Jones, *Presidency in a Separated System*, 270–271.

22 See Neil MacNeil, *Forge of Democracy: The House of Representatives* (New York: David McKay, 1963), 244–245.

23 Jimmy Carter, *Keeping Faith: The Memoirs of a President* (New York: Bantam Books, 1982), 101.

24 *Guide to Congress*, 554.

25 Robert Pear, "Court Is Asked to Define Power of the Pocket Veto," *New York Times*, November 9, 1986, E1.

26 See www.senate.gov/reference/Legislation/Vetoes/BushGW.htm.

27 David Stout, "In First Bush Veto Override, Senate Enacts Water Bill," *New York Times*, November 8, 2007, A1.

28 See www.senate.gov/reference/Legislation/Vetoes/ObamaBH.htm.

29 Bryce, *American Commonwealth*, 59.

30 Charles M. Cameron, *Veto Bargaining Presidents and the Politics of Negative Power* (New York: Cambridge University Press, 2000), 8–9. For additional scholarship on the history of political bargaining and the veto, see the work of Nolan McCarty.

31 George C. Edwards III, *Presidential Influence in Congress* (San Francisco: Freeman, 1980), 24.

32 *CQ Almanac, 1992* (Washington, D.C.: Congressional Quarterly, 1993), 6.

33 Tom Raum, "Bush's Dusty Veto Pen May Soon Get Busy," *Washington Post*, January 6, 2007, www.washingtonpost.com/wp-dyn/content/article/2007/01/06/AR2007010600507.html.

34 Cameron, *Veto Bargaining Presidents*, 152–177.

35 Victoria Alldred, "Versatility with the Veto," *CQ Weekly*, January 20, 2001, 175.

36 Ibid., 175. See also Elizabeth Drew, *Showdown: The Struggle between the Gingrich Congress and the Clinton White House* (New York: Simon and Schuster, 1996).

37 Press Release, U.S. Senate Committee on Appropriations, February 1, 2011, http://appropriations.senate.gov/news.cfm?method=news.view&id=188dc791-4b0d-459e-b8d9-4ede5ca299e7.

38 See www.whitehouse.gov/sites/default/files/omb/legislative/sap/112/saphr2560r_20110718.pdf.

39 See www.whitehouse.gov/sites/default/files/omb/legislative/sap/112/saps627r_20110726.pdf

40 See, for example, Redman, *Dance of Legislation*, 243.

41 Mitchel A. Sollenberger, "The Presidential Veto and Congressional Procedure," CRS Report for Congress, February 27, 2004, www.rules.house.gov/archives/RS21750.pdf.

42 *Pocket Veto Case*, 279 U.S. 644 (1929).

43 Arthur M. Schlesinger Jr., *The Imperial Presidency* (New York: Popular Library, 1974), 237.

44 *Wright v. United States*, 302 U.S. 583 (1938).

45 See Redman, *Dance of Legislation*, 275–277.

46 *Kennedy v. Sampson*, 511 F. 2d 430 (D.C. Cir. 1974).

47 *Kennedy v. Jones*, Civil Action no. 74–194 (D.D.C.).

48 Pear, "Power of the Pocket Veto," 4.

49 *Barnes v. Carmen*, 582 F. Supp. 163 (D.D.C. 1984); *Barnes v. Kline*, 759 F. 2d 21 (D.C. Cir. 1985). The lone dissenter was Judge Robert Bork, who argued that members of Congress had no right to sue the president in the first place and that the court had no jurisdiction over such issues. Lawyers for Congress argued that the courts have every right to adjudicate disputes between Congress and the executive.

50 *Burke v. Barnes*, 479 U.S. 361 (1987).

51 *CQ Almanac, 1990* (Washington, D.C.: Congressional Quarterly, 1991), 21–22.

52 *CQ Almanac, 1991* (Washington, D.C.: Congressional Quarterly, 1992), 235.

53 See Jasmine Farrier, *Passing the Buck: Congress, the Budget, and Deficits* (Lexington: University Press of Kentucky, 2004), 165–214; and Jasmine Farrier, "Presidential Budget Power, Constitutional Conflicts and the National Interest," in *The Constitutional Presidency*, ed. Jeffrey K. Tulis and Joseph Bessette (Baltimore: Johns Hopkins University Press, 2009), 173–202.

54 James Sundquist, *Constitutional Reform and Effective Government* (Washington, D.C.: Brookings, 1986), 209–215.

55 See Louis Fisher, *Politics of Shared Power*, 3d ed. (Washington, D.C.: CQ Press, 1993), 198–202.

56 Ibid., 199.

57 Ibid., 198.

58 Andrew Taylor, "Congress Hands President a Budgetary Scalpel," *Congressional Quarterly Weekly Report,* March 30, 1996, 864–867.

59 Allred, "Versatility with the Veto," 177.

60 George Will, "Power to the President," *Newsweek,* October 12, 1981, 120.

61 Edwards, *Presidential Influence in Congress,* 20. For a full history of impoundment authority, see also Fisher, *Presidential Spending Power.*

62 Stuart Taylor Jr., "Court Rebuffs Reagan on Deferral of Spending Ordered by Congress," *New York Times,* January 21, 1987, A1.

63 Edwards, *Presidential Influence in Congress,* 21.

64 Fisher, *Politics of Shared Power,* 21.

65 *CQ Almanac, 1990,* 16.

66 James P. Pfiffner, "Presidential Signing Statements and Their Implications for Public Administration," *Public Administration Review* 69 (2009): 249–255.

67 Charles Savage, "Bush Challenges Hundreds of Laws," *Boston Globe,* April 30, 2006, www.boston.com/news/nation/articles/2006/ 04/30/bush_challenges_hundreds_of_laws/.

68 See Christopher S. Kelley and Bryan W. Marshall, "The Last Word: Presidential Power and the Role of Signing Statements," *Presidential Studies Quarterly* 38 (spring 2008): 248–267.

69 Charlie Savage, "Administration to Bypass Reporting Law," *New York Times,* October 24, 2008, A16.

70 Charlie Savage, "Obama Looks to Limit Impact of Tactic Bush Used to Sidestep New Laws," *New York Times,* March 9, 2009, A12.

71 Charlie Savaage, "Obama's Embrace of a Bush Tactic Riles Congress," *New York Times,* August 8, 2009, A16.

72 On problem definition and agenda setting, see Frank R. Baumgartner and Bryan D. Jones, *Agendas and Instability in American Politics* (Chicago: University of Chicago Press, 1993); David A. Rochefort and Roger W. Cobb, eds., *The Politics of Problem Definition: Shaping the Policy Agenda* (Lawrence: University Press of Kansas, 1994); and John W. Kingdon, *Agendas, Alternatives, and Public Policies,* 2d ed. (Upper Saddle River, N.J.: Addison-Wesley, 1995).

73 E. E. Schattschneider, *The Semi-Sovereign People: A Realist's View of Democracy in America* (Hinsdale, Ill.: Dryden, 1960), 66.

74 See Arthur M. Schlesinger Jr., *The Age of Roosevelt: The Coming of the New Deal* (Boston: Houghton Mifflin, 1959).

75 Gerald F. Seib, "In Crisis, Opportunity for Obama," *Wall Street Journal,* November 21, 2008, A2. See the full video of Emanuel's comments at "Rahm Emanuel on the Opportunities of Crisis," November 18, 2008, http://online.wsj.com/video-center.

76 Bruce Miroff, "Monopolizing the Public Space: The President as a Problem for Democratic Space," in *Rethinking the Presidency,* ed. Thomas E. Cronin (Boston: Little, Brown, 1982), 218–252.

77 Sidney M. Milkis and Michael Nelson, *The American Presidency: Origins and Development,* 1776–201, 6th ed. (Washington, D.C.: CQ Press, 2011).

78 For a cogent discussion of the constants of American governance and their effects on presidential leadership, see Bert A. Rockman, *The Leadership Question: The Presidency and the American System* (New York: Praeger, 1984), chap. 3. For a variety of academic approaches to contemporary inter-branch dynamics, see James A. Thurber, ed., *Rivals for Power: Presidential-Congressional Relations,* 4th ed. (Lanham, Md.: Rowman and Littlefield, 2009)

79 Thomas P. O'Neill Jr., with William Novak, *Man of the House: The Life and Political Memoirs of Speaker Tip O'Neill* (New York: Random House, 1987).

80 For detailed analysis of the national and local repercussions of the 2010 elections, as well as the prominence of the "Tea Party" movement's opposition to President Barack Obama's first two years in office, see Larry J. Sabato, ed., *Pendulum Swing* (Upper Saddle River, N.J.: Longman, 2011).

81 Sarah A. Binder, "The Disappearing Political Center: Congress and the Incredible Shrinking Middle," Brookings, fall 1996, www.brookings.edu/articles/1996/fall_governance_binder .aspx.

82 Stories of battles for the president's ear are legion. See Hugh Heclo, *A Government of Strangers: Executive Politics in Washington* (Washington, D.C.: Brookings, 1977).

83 Steven S. Smith, *Party Influence in Congress* (New York: Cambridge University Press, 2007).

84 Craig Gordon, "His Social Aims," April 29, 2005, Newsday .com, www.newsday.com/news/nationworld/nation/ny-usbush 294237838apr29,0,3535649.story.

85 Dan Balz, "Shutdown Threat Tests Obama Leadership Style," *Washington Post,* April 7, 2011, A17.

86 Neustadt, *Presidential Power,* 33; for a critique of the American system, see Sundquist, *Constitutional Reform and Effective Government.* For a comparative perspective see also R. Kent Weaver and Bert A. Rockman, eds., *Do Institutions Matter? Government Capabilities in the United States and Abroad* (Washington, D.C.: Brookings, 1993).

87 Ryan Teague Beckwith, "Congress Backed Obama in '09: President Broke 44 Year Old Record for Congressional Support, According to Study," http://origin-www.congress.org/news/2010/01/10/congress_backed_obama_in_09.

88 For a history of the health care legislation and subsequent legislative and judicial developments, see http://topics.nytimes.com/top/news/health/diseasesconditionsandhealthtopics/health_insurance_and_managed_care/health_care_reform/index.html.

89 Rossiter, *American Presidency,* 140.

90 Quoted in Andrew Rudalevige, "The Executive Branch and the Legislative Process," in *The Executive Branch,* ed. Joel D. Aberach and Mark A. Peterson (New York: Oxford University Press, 2005), 420.

91 U.S. White House, President's Budget Message, Office of Management and Budget, February 26, 2009, 1.

92 Bertram Gross, *The Legislative Struggle: A Study of Social Combat* (New York: McGraw-Hill, 1953), 101.

93 See James Sundquist, *The Decline and Resurgence of Congress* (Washington, D.C.: Brookings, 1981).

94 Hamilton, Madison, and Jay, *Federalist Papers,* 423.

95 See George M. Haynes, *The Senate of the United States: Its History and Practice,* Vol. 1 (Boston: Houghton Mifflin, 1938), 62–63.

96 Quoted in George B. Galloway, *History of the House of Representatives* (New York: Thomas Crowell, 1969), 12.

97 Milkis and Nelson, *The American Presidency,* 100–125.

98 Edward S. Corwin, *The President: Office and Powers, 1789–1957,* 4th ed. (New York: New York University Press, 1957), 21.

99 Ibid., 23.

100 Quoted in Galloway, *History of the House,* 245–246.

101 Corwin, *President: Office and Powers,* 28.

102 Theodore Roosevelt, *Theodore Roosevelt: An Autobiography* (New York: Macmillan, 1913), 282.

103 Sundquist, *Decline and Resurgence of Congress,* 130.

104 William Howard Taft. *Our Chief Magistrate and His Powers* (New York: Columbia University Press, 1916), 139–140.

105 Tulis, *Rhetorical Presidency.*

106 Corwin, *President: Office and Powers,* 269.

107 Special address to a joint session of Congress, June 23, 1913; cited in Corwin, *President: Office and Powers,* 269.

108 Rossiter, *American Presidency,* 140.

109 Schlesinger, *Age of Roosevelt,* 1.

110 Neustadt, *Presidential Power,* 6.

111 See, for example, Rockman, *Leadership Question.*

112 *Guide to Congress,* 3d ed. (Washington, D.C.: Congressional Quarterly, 1982), 761. For an examination of the give-and-take dynamics of congressional deference to presidential power, see Farrier, *Congressional Ambivalence* and Andrew Rudalevige, *The New Imperial Presidency: Renewing Presidential Power after Watergate* (Ann Arbor: University of Michigan Press, 2005).

113 Quoted in Rowland Evans and Robert Novak, *Lyndon B. Johnson: The Exercise of Power* (New York: New American Library, 1966), 490.

114 See Stephen Skowronek, *The Politics Presidents Make: Leadership from John Adams to Bill Clinton, Revised Edition* (Cambridge, Mass.: Harvard University Press, 1997); and Skowronek, *Presidential Leadership in Political Time: Reprise and Reappraisal,* 2d ed. (Lawrence: University Press of Kansas, 2011).

115 See Gary Jacobson, "Party Polarization in National Politics: The Electoral Connection," in *Polarized Politics,* ed. Jon Bond and Richard Fleisher (Washington, DC: CQ Press, 2000), 13, 27; and Roger H. Davidson and Walter J. Oleszek, *Congress and Its Members,* 13th ed. (Washington, D.C.: CQ Press, 2012), 253–312.

116 Louis Koenig, *The Chief Executive,* 5th ed. (New York: Harcourt Brace Jovanovich, 1986), 145–146.

117 Jennifer Dlouhy and Keith Perine, "Deal Clears Way for Final Passage of Anti-Terrorism Legislation," *CQ Weekly,* October 20, 2001, 2475–2476.

118 See Paul E. Peterson, ed., *The President, Congress, and the Making of Foreign Policy* (Norman: University of Oklahoma Press, 1994).

119 For different views on Congress's use of foreign policy power, see William Howell and Jon Pevehouse, *While Dangers Gather: Congressional Checks on Presidential War Powers* (Princeton: Princeton University Press, 2007); and Louis Fisher, *Congressional Abdication on War and Spending* (College Station: Texas A&M University Press, 2000).

120 Siobhan Hughes, "House Challenges Obama on Libya," *Wall Street Journal,* June 4, 2011, http://online.wsj.com/article/SB10001424052702304563104576363463784559654.html; and Kathleen Hennessey, "House Rebukes Obama on Libya, But Won't Cut Funds," *Los Angeles Times,* June 24, 2011, http://articles.latimes.com/2011/jun/24/nation/la-na-congress-libya-20110625. For a broader analysis of both branches' views of war powers and criticism of the constitutional stance of President Obama on Libya, see Louis Fisher's testimony before the Senate Committee on Foreign Relations, "Libya and War Powers," June 28, 2011, www.constitutionproject.org/pdf/62811_loufisher_testimonysenforrelationscommittee_libyawarpowers.pdf.

121 Skowronek, *The Politics Presidents Make.*

122 "Annual Messages of the Presidents: Major Themes of American History," in *The State of the Union Messages of the Presidents, 1790–1966,* ed. Fred L. Israel (New York: Chelsea House, 1966), xiv.

123 *Public Papers of Woodrow Wilson,* 1:32; cited in Corwin, *President: Office and Powers,* 269.

124 Fisher, *Shared Power,* 18; see also H. Wayne Morgan, *From Hayes to McKinley* (Syracuse: Syracuse University Press, 1969), 274–319.

125 Charles O. Jones, "Presidential Negotiation with Congress," in *Both Ends of the Avenue: The Presidency, the Executive Branch, and Congress in the 1980s,* ed. Anthony King (Washington, D.C.: American Enterprise Institute, 1983), 99.

126 Ibid., 102.

127 Rudalevige, *Managing the President's Program,* 65.

128 See www.whitehouse.gov/state-of-the-union-2011.

129 Ibid., 71.

130 Fisher, *President and Congress,* 52–53.

131 Cronin, *State of the Presidency,* 118.

132 James S. Young, *The Washington Community* (New York: Columbia University Press, 1966), 167.

133 On the evolution of "central clearance," see Fisher, *Presidential Spending Power.*

134 See Shelley Lynne Tomkin, *Inside OMB: Politics and Process in the President's Budget Office* (Armonk, N.Y.: M.E. Sharpe, 1998); and Allen Schick, *The Federal Budget: Politics, Policy, Process,* 3d ed. (Washington, D.C.: Brookings, 2007).

135 Alexander Mooney, "Controversy Surrounds Obama's Faith Office," CNN, February 5, 2009, http://edition.cnn.com/2009/POLITICS/02/05/obama.faith.based/.

136 See Stephen Hess, *Organizing the Presidency,* 3d ed. (Washington, D.C.: Brookings, 2002); and James P. Pfiffner, ed., *The Managerial Presidency,* 2d ed. (College Station: Texas A&M University Press, 1999).

137 Richard E. Neustadt, "The Presidency and Legislation: Planning the President's Program," *American Political Science Review* 49 (December 1955): 1015; see also Stephen J. Wayne, *The Legislative Presidency* (New York: Harper and Row, 1978), 19.

138 Paul C. Light, "Presidents as Domestic Policymakers," in *Rethinking the Presidency,* ed. Thomas E. Cronin (Boston: Little, Brown, 1982), 360. See also Paul C. Light, *The President's Agenda: Domestic Policy Choice from Kennedy to Clinton* (Baltimore: Johns Hopkins University Press, 1999); and Mark A. Peterson, *Legislating Together: The White House and Capitol Hill from Eisenhower to Reagan* (Cambridge: Harvard University Press, 1990).

139 Steven Waldman, *The Bill: How the Adventures of Clinton's National Service Bill Reveal What Is Corrupt, Comic, Cynical—and Noble—about Washington* (New York: Viking, 1995), 3.

140 On the intellectual genesis of the 1986 tax reform act, see Jeffrey Birnbaum and Alan Murray, *Showdown at Gucci Gulch: Lawmakers, Lobbyists, and the Unlikely Triumph of Tax Reform* (New York: Random House, 1987).

141 See *History of America, 1932–1972* (Boston: Little, Brown, 1974), 95.

142 Julia Eilperin, "White House Outlines Global Warming Fight," *Washington Post,* September 21, 2006, www.washingtonpost.com/wp-dyn/content/article/2006/09/20/ AR2006092001697_pf.html.

143 See Christopher J. Bosso, "Setting the Public Agenda: Mass Media and the Ethiopian Famine," in *Manipulating Public Opinion: Essays on Public Opinion as a Dependent Variable,* ed. Michael Margolis and Gary Mauser (Monterey, Calif.: Brooks-Cole, 1989), 153–174. On the interconnectedness of "foreign" and "domestic" issues, see James Rosenau, *Turbulence in World Politics: A Theory of Change and Continuity* (Princeton: Princeton University Press, 1990).

144 Rudalevige, *Managing the President's Program,* 81.

145 See Joel D. Aberbach and Bert A. Rockman, "Clashing Beliefs within the Executive Branch: The Nixon Administration

Bureaucracy," *American Political Science Review* 70 (June 1975): 456–468.

146   Rudalevige, *Managing the President's Program,* 81.

147   On the relative merits and pitfalls of incremental versus comprehensive policy change, see Charles O. Jones, *Introduction to the Study of Public Policy,* 3d ed. (Monterey, Calif.: Brooks-Cole, 1984), especially chaps. 2, 6.

148   See, for example, Haynes Johnson and David S. Broder, *The System: The American Way of Politics at the Breaking Point* (Boston: Little, Brown, 1996).

149   For details on the history of health care reform and the specific strategies and outcomes of the Clinton administration's efforts, see Theda Skocpol, *Boomerang: Health Care Reform and the Turn Against Government* (New York: Norton, 1996).

150   Robert Reich, *Locked in the Cabinet* (New York: Knopf, 1997).

151   CBS News, "Rewriting the Science," July 30, 2006, www .cbsnews.com/stories/2006/03/17/60minutes/main1415985.shtml.

152   See Woodward, *Agenda.*

153   For a comparison of recent presidents' organizational styles, see Paul J. Quirk, "Presidential Competence," in *The Presidency and the Political System,* 9th, ed., ed. Michael Nelson (Washington, D.C.: CQ Press, 2009), 108–141.

154   Neustadt, *Presidential Power.*

155   The election of Lyndon Johnson to the House of Representatives in 1937 offers a good case in point about Roosevelt's potency as a campaign resource. See Robert Caro, *The Years of Lyndon Johnson: The Path to Power* (New York: Random House, 1981).

156   Matthew J. Dickinson, *Bitter Harvest: FDR, Presidential Power, and the Growth of the Presidential Branch* (New York: Cambridge University Press, 1997), 221.

157   Eric L. Davis, "Congressional Liaison: The People and the Institutions," in *Both Ends of the Avenue: The Presidency, the Executive Branch, and Congress in the 1980s,* ed. Anthony King (Washington, D.C.: American Enterprise Institute, 1983), 60.

158   Ibid., 61.

159   Ibid., 62.

160   On this notion of electoral "mandates," see Patricia H. Conley, *Presidential Mandates: How Elections Shape the National Agenda* (Chicago: University of Chicago Press, 2001).

161   Jones, "Presidential Negotiation with Congress," 106.

162   See Davis, "Congressional Liaison," 78–79.

163   Ibid., 65.

164   O'Neill, *Man of the House,* 310–311.

165   Davis, "Congressional Liaison," 65.

166   Anthony King, "The American Polity in the Late 1970s: Building Coalitions in the Sand," in *The New American Political System,* ed. Anthony King (Washington, D.C.: American Enterprise Institute, 1979), 371–395.

167   Davidson and Oleszek, *Congress and Its Members,* 13th ed., 285. For an insider's view of the 1981 tax and budget battles, see David Stockman, *The Triumph of Politics: The Inside Story of the Reagan Revolution* (New York: Harper and Row, 1986).

168   Jones, "Presidential Negotiation," 126.

169   See Richard Rose, *The Postmodern President: George H. W. Bush Meets the World,* 2d ed. (Chatham, N.J.: Chatham House, 1991).

170   Jones, *The Presidency in a Separated Party System,* 27.

171   George C. Edwards, *Governing by Campaigning* (New York: Pearson Longman, 2007), 155–166.

172   See Matthew J. Dickinson, "The President and Congress," in *The Presidency and the Political System,* ed. Nelson, 401–434.

173   ABC News, "Bush Presidency Floundering," May 9, 2006, http://abcnews.go.com/GMA/story?id=1940034&page=1.

174   See, for example, Gary C. Jacobson, *A Divider, Not a Uniter: George W. Bush and the American People* (New York: Pearson Education, 2007).

175   Joint Resolution 114 passed the Senate by a vote of 77–23, with 22 Democrats and 1 independent voting no, and the House of Representatives by a vote of 296–133, with 126 Democrats and 1 independent voting no.

176   The Republicans gained 4 seats in the Senate, for a 55–44 advantage, and 3 in the House, for a 232–202 margin.

177   See James P. Pfiffner, *Power Play: The Bush Presidency and the Constitution* (Washington, D.C.: Brookings, 2009).

178   Jones, "Presidential Negotiation," 123–125.

179   See Mayhew, *Divided We Govern;* and Jones, *Presidency in a Separated System.*

180   Edwards, *Presidential Influence in Congress,* 110.

181   Jones, *The Presidency in a Separated System,* 134.

182   See Edmund Morris, *The Rise of Theodore Roosevelt* (New York: Ballantine, 1979).

183   Quoted in William Manchester, *The Glory and the Dream: A Narrative History of America, 1932–1972* (Boston: Little, Brown, 1974), 91.

184   Schlesinger, *Age of Roosevelt,* 559.

185   Wilfred E. Binkley, *President and Congress* (New York: Vintage, 1962), 305.

186   Cited in William Safire, *Safire's Political Dictionary* (New York: Ballantine, 1978), 649.

187   Ibid., 444. The phrase "nattering nabobs" was penned by speechwriter William Safire, who later became a popular newspaper columnist and, alternately, a writer on the English language. The term *nabob* is Hindi in origin and has come to mean in English a self-important person.

188   On Reagan's use of television, see, among others, Mark Hertsgaard, *On Bended Knee: The Press and the Reagan Presidency* (New York: Farrar, Straus, Giroux, 1988); and Sam Donaldson, *Hold on, Mr. President!* (New York: Random House, 1987).

189   Jones, *Presidency in a Separated System,* 133.

190   See, for example, Lawrence R. Jacobs and Robert Y. Shapiro, *Politicians Don't Pander: Political Manipulation and the Loss of Democratic Responsiveness* (Chicago: University of Chicago Press, 2000).

191   See Marc Landy and Sidney M. Milkis, "The Presidency in the Eye of the Storm," in *The Presidency and the Political System,* ed. Nelson, 68–107.

192   Transcript, "Transition to Power: President-Elect Bush Meets with Congressional Leaders on Capitol Hill," CNN, December 18, 2000, http://transcripts.cnn.com/TRANSCRIPTS/0012/18/nd.01.html.

193   See Jasmine Farrier, "Barack Obama and Deficits: Signs of a Neo-Whig Presidency?", *Presidential Studies Quarterly* 41 (September 2011): 618–634.

SELECTED BIBLIOGRAPHY

Corwin, Edward S. *The President: Office and Powers, 1787–1984.* 5th rev. ed. New York: New York University Press, 1984.

Cronin, Thomas E., ed. *Rethinking the Presidency.* Boston: Little, Brown, 1982.

Dodd, Lawrence C., and Bruce I. Oppenheimer, eds. *Congress Reconsidered.* 9th ed. Washington, D.C.: CQ Press, 2008

Edwards, George C., III. *At the Margins: Presidential Leadership of Congress.* New Haven: Yale University Press, 1989.

Farrier, Jasmine. *Passing the Buck: Congress, the Budget, and Deficits.* Lexington: University Press of Kentucky, 2004.

———. *Congressional Ambivalence: The Political Burdens of Constitutional Authority.* Lexington: University Press of Kentucky, 2010.

Fenno, Richard F. *The President's Cabinet.* Cambridge: Harvard University Press, 1963.

Fisher, Louis. *Presidential Spending Power.* Princeton: Princeton University Press, 1975.

Greenstein, Fred. *Leadership in the Modern Presidency.* Cambridge: Harvard University Press, 1988.

Hargrove, Erwin C., and Michael Nelson. *Presidents, Politics, and Policy.* Baltimore: Johns Hopkins University Press, 1984.

Hart, John. *The Presidential Branch: From Washington to Clinton.* 2d ed. Chatham, N.J.: Chatham House, 1995.

Heclo, Hugh. *A Government of Strangers: Executive Politics in Washington.* Washington, D.C.: Brookings, 1977.

Hess, Stephen. *Organizing the Presidency.* Rev. ed. Washington, D.C.: Brookings, 1988.

Jones, Charles O. *The Presidency in a Separated System.* 2d ed. Washington, D.C.: Brookings, 2005.

King, Anthony, ed. *Both Ends of the Avenue: The Presidency, the Executive Branch, and Congress in the 1980s.* Washington, D.C.: American Enterprise Institute, 1983.

Mansfield, Harvey C., Sr., ed. *Congress against the President.* New York: Academy of Political Science, 1975.

Mayhew, David. *Divided We Govern: Party Control, Lawmaking, and Investigations, 1946–1990.* New Haven: Yale University Press, 1991.

Nelson, Michael, ed. *The Presidency and the Political System.* 9th ed. Washington, D.C.: CQ Press, 2009.

Neustadt, Richard E. *Presidential Power: The Politics of Leadership from FDR to Carter.* New York: Wiley, 1980.

Peterson, Mark A. *Legislating Together: The White House and Capitol Hill from Eisenhower to Reagan.* Cambridge: Harvard University Press, 1990.

Pfiffner, James P. *Power Play: The Bush Presidency and the Constitution.* Washington, D.C.: Brookings Institution, 2009.

Polsby, Nelson W. *Congress and the Presidency.* 4th ed. Englewood Cliffs, N.J.: Prentice Hall, 1986.

Rockman, Bert A. *The Leadership Question: The Presidency and the American System.* New York: Praeger, 1984.

Rose, Richard. *The Postmodern President: The White House Meets the World.* Chatham, N.J.: Chatham House, 1988.

Rossiter, Clinton. *The American Presidency.* 2d ed. New York: Harcourt, Brace, 1960.

Rudalevige, Andrew. *The New Imperial Presidency: Renewing Presidential Power after Watergate.* Ann Arbor: University of Michigan Press, 2005.

Skowronek, Stephen. *Thse Politics Presidents Make: Leadership from John Adams to George Bush.* Cambridge: Harvard University Press, 1994.

Sundquist, James. *Constitutional Reform and Effective Government.* Rev. ed. Washington, D.C.: Brookings, 1992.

Thurber, James A., ed. *Rivals for Power: Presidential-Congressional Relations.* 4th ed. Lanham, Md.: Rowman and Littlefield, 2009.

Wayne, Stephen J. *The Legislative Presidency.* New York: Harper and Row, 1978.

Weaver, R. Kent, and Bert A. Rockman, eds. *Do Institutions Matter? Government Capabilities in the United States and Abroad.* Washington, D.C.: Brookings, 1993.

chapter 5

Chief Diplomat

by Meena Bose

In the nineteenth century, when U.S. foreign interests were limited primarily to trade and western expansion, presidents were able to concentrate largely on domestic policy. Today, the wide array of U.S. economic, political, and military commitments abroad ensures that presidents will spend at least half of their time on foreign affairs. But, in fact, as economic life becomes more globalized, the distinction between domestic and foreign policy is blurring.

The Constitution makes the president the formal head of state. As the "sole representative with foreign nations," the president speaks for the nation as a whole and is often the focus of national hopes and fears, pride, and shame.[1] In the role of chief negotiator and national spokesperson, the president has great leverage in any competition with Congress for control of the nation's foreign policies, and important decisions on foreign affairs often have been made by the president after consultations with only a few trusted advisers. The desire of political friends and foes alike to present a united front has frequently produced initial support for and general deference to the president's lead.

Circumstances such as wars or threats of armed conflict enhance this advantage and have allowed presidents to dominate the formulation and implementation of foreign policy. During such times, John F. Kennedy noted, "The big difference [between domestic and foreign policy] is that between a bill being defeated and the country [being] wiped out."[2] Even during periods of relative international calm, foreign affairs issues usually have offered presidents the greatest freedom to exercise their power and the best opportunity to affect policy personally. In contrast, domestic policy decisions commonly involve many officials and interest groups, require less secrecy, and entail the full participation of Congress and its committees. Consequently, presidents may choose to retreat to the refuge of foreign affairs where they can exercise their powers most freely as leader of the nation.

Indeed, foreign affairs often afford the president the opportunity to gain an enduring place in history. Steadfast wartime leadership, the prevention or resolution of dangerous crises, bold policy and diplomatic initiatives, and historic summit meetings with important foreign leaders can create presidential legends: Jefferson's Louisiana Purchase, the Monroe Doctrine, Theodore Roosevelt's Panama Canal, Harry S. Truman's Marshall Plan, Kennedy's peaceful resolution of the Cuban missile crisis, Richard Nixon's trip to China. Following the lead of Theodore Roosevelt, whose successful management of negotiations to end the Russo-Japanese War earned him a Nobel Peace Prize, presidents have used their stature and skills to resolve conflicts less directly related to U.S. interests. Jimmy Carter's Camp David summit led to a peace agreement between Egypt and Israel, and Bill Clinton's participation in the Dayton (Ohio) negotiations helped to move the Bosnia conflict toward a resolution. On the other hand, Clinton's repeated efforts to resolve the conflicts in Northern Ireland and between Israel and the Palestinians were, at best, partial and temporary successes.

The foreign policy records of few administrations are completely triumphant. Although George Washington's administration was honored for a balanced policy of neutrality, the Jay Treaty with Great Britain provoked virulent partisan attacks. Thomas Jefferson's purchase of the Louisiana territory must be paired with the miserable failure of his embargo against Great Britain. Woodrow Wilson, the victorious war leader, was humiliated by the defeat of the Treaty of Versailles and his internationalist foreign policy. Carter's triumph in facilitating an Israeli-Egyptian peace accord at Camp David was followed by his inability to resolve the hostage crisis with Iran. While Ronald Reagan's hard-line anticommunist policies combined with his second-term summit meetings with Soviet leader Mikhail Gorbachev played an important role in ending the cold war, his

---

Previous contributors to this chapter include Daniel C. Diller and Stephen H. Wirls.

administration also was mired in the Iran-contra scandal.

Recent presidents who entered office possessing greater expertise and interest in domestic policy have been distracted, seduced, or overwhelmed by foreign affairs. Lyndon B. Johnson's plans for a "Great Society" were undercut by the resource demands of the Vietnam War and the divisions the war created in the American public. Carter, a former governor with little foreign policy experience, became personally absorbed with foreign policy issues such as recognition of the People's Republic of China, arms control, and the Camp David peace process between Egypt and Israel. Events in Somalia, North Korea, Haiti, and Bosnia taught Clinton that even in the post–cold war era no president can avoid the often perilous complications of foreign affairs. Similarly, the terrorist attacks on New York City and Washington, D.C., in September 2001 immediately turned George W. Bush's agenda from domestic policy to engaging in diplomacy and waging war. Upon taking office, Barack Obama made clear that combating terrorism would be his primary foreign-policy goal, and subsequent presidents likely will do the same for the foreseeable future.

While the Constitution makes presidents the sole head of state, it does not give them sufficient authority to make foreign policy simply on their own. The branches of the federal government share foreign policy powers, and Congress has many means of influence over the substance and execution of general and specific policies. In addition, policy must be coordinated within a complex of often competing advisers, departments, and agencies. Even under the most favorable conditions, presidents frequently struggle to maintain control of policy formulation and implementation. In the current era, which lacks the ideological clarity of the cold war and the unifying fears of nuclear confrontation between two superpowers, achieving presidential leadership and control of foreign policy has become more difficult and complicated.

DISTRIBUTION OF FOREIGN POLICY POWER

On balance, the Constitution gives the president fewer powers related to the making of foreign policy than Congress, and the powers of the presidency are checked in ways that seem designed to prevent the president from making unilateral commitments abroad. The only unshared power in this area is the president's responsibility to "receive Ambassadors

He shall have Power, by and with the Advice and Consent of the Senate, to make Treaties, provided two thirds of the Senators present concur; and he shall nominate and, by and with the Advice and Consent of the Senate, shall appoint Ambassadors, other public Ministers and Consuls.... He ... shall receive Ambassadors and other public Ministers.

—from Article II, Sections 2, 3

and other Public ministers." Presidents may appoint ambassadors only with the "Advice and Consent of the Senate," and the Senate was meant to be involved throughout all treaty negotiations. The executive power is limited by the laws the president is to execute "faithfully." The president's authority as commander in chief is constrained, as a policy-making power, by Congress's constitutional control over both declarations of war and the raising and support of all armed forces.

Besides its influence over the use of force and the powers it shares with the president, Congress has broad foreign policy powers that are checked only by the president's veto. As spelled out in Article I of the Constitution, Congress controls the legal context of international affairs through its powers "to define and punish Piracies and Felonies committed on the high Seas and Offences against the Law of Nations; . . . and make Rules concerning Captures on Land and Water." Most significant is Congress's authority to "regulate Commerce with foreign Nations." These powers are broadened by the so-called elastic power to "make all Laws which shall be necessary and proper for carrying into Execution the foregoing Powers."

Altogether, Congress's formal constitutional authority in foreign affairs is broader and less qualified than the president's. In addition, the legislative branch's general power to make laws, control appropriations, and "provide for the common Defence and general Welfare of the United States" gives it broad authority to become involved in any foreign policy decision or action not specifically reserved for the president by the Constitution.[3] Congress and, especially, the Senate were, it seems, to control general policy and any long-term foreign commitments.

Obviously, this strict reading of the Constitution does not fully or accurately describe the actual distribution of foreign policy responsibilities and influence. A more complete account of the Framers' design must acknowledge that they anticipated and encouraged a presidential ambition that would clash with the other branches. The Framers also expected that this officer, "seated on the summit of his country's honors," would not be content as a mere executive and congressional agent. Rather, the design of the office encourages the president to "undertake extensive and arduous enterprises for the public benefit, requiring considerable time to mature and perfect."[4] This anticipation of a presidential inclination toward grand policy initiation justifies presidential scholar Edward S. Corwin's description of the

Constitution as "an invitation to struggle for the privilege of directing American foreign policy."[5]

The affirmative grants of power in the Constitution do not begin to answer all the questions about how foreign policy decisions should be made and implemented, and the actual distribution of shared foreign policy powers between the president and Congress could be established only by events. The particular struggles have produced periods of interbranch stalemate and partnership, presidential subordination and domination.

PRESIDENTIAL DOMINANCE OF FOREIGN POLICY

In 1948, addressing members of the Jewish War Veterans, President Truman stated: "I make foreign policy."[6] Most historians and political scientists would agree that Truman's assessment of presidential power exaggerates only slightly the influence of modern presidents over foreign policy. At least until the end of the cold war with the Soviet Union, Congress retained an important role in foreign affairs; on many occasions it was able to frustrate, delay, modify, or negate presidential foreign policy. The president, however, dominated the formulation and initiation of foreign policy, and Congress's actions were usually responses to presidential policies. Certainly, the American public and foreign governments expect the president to make decisions and to implement them. Particularly in times of crisis, the public looks to the president for leadership, and presidential approval typically records a "rally-around-the-flag" effect, at least for the short term.[7] It is even common for members of Congress from both parties to criticize a president for failing to provide foreign policy leadership. During the cold war, political scientist Aaron Wildavsky concluded that the United States had "two presidencies," one for foreign policy, in which Congress, public opinion, and the courts deferred to executive leadership, and one for domestic policy, in which these constituencies were far more likely to engage in conflict with the president.[8]

Because the constitutional division of power between the executive and legislative branches is relatively ambiguous in the area of foreign affairs, one cannot attribute the establishment of presidential control over foreign relations simply to the affirmative grants of power in the Constitution. The ambiguity of the document ensured that skills, circumstances, public opinion, customs, and precedents would order and reorder the distribution of influence over foreign

President Obama has continued the tradition of maintaining special relationships with the leaders of Germany and Great Britain. Here he jokes with German chancellor Angela Merkel and British prime minister David Cameron.

affairs. The branch most capable of asserting its interests and demonstrating its ability to make effective foreign policy would likely emerge as the more powerful. This branch has proved to be the executive. Yet, at least initially, the principle of "presidential control" seemed to be an inaccurate characterization of foreign policymaking in the era that began with the disintegration of the Soviet Union and the Warsaw Pact. Conflicts between President Clinton and Congress over foreign aid, U.S. participation in UN missions, and many other foreign policy issues suggested a return to a sharper struggle for control of foreign policy.

On the other hand, President George W. Bush's control of the diplomatic and military policies in response to the September 11, 2001, terrorist attacks indicates that the presidency retains its advantage in these policy arenas. Indeed, the Bush administration propounded a "unitary executive" theory of presidential power, holding that the president may ignore legal restrictions on action if national security so requires.[9] The administration used this reasoning to justify interrogation procedures for suspected terrorists that did not always comply with the post–World War II Geneva Conventions on human rights, as well as domestic electronic surveillance of suspected terrorists. In the absence of legal restrictions, the Bush administration held an expansive view of presidential power in foreign affairs—as John Yoo, who served as a deputy assistant attorney general in the Justice Department's Office of Legal Counsel, writes, "If we assume that the foreign affairs power is an executive one, Article II [of the Constitution] effectively grants to the president any unenumerated foreign affairs powers not given elsewhere to the other branches."[10] During the 2008 presidential campaign, Barack Obama was critical of Bush's expansive use of presidential power in foreign affairs and promised to make changes, such as ending military commissions for suspected terrorists, closing their detention center in Guantanamo Bay, Cuba, which was established under Bush, and holding civilian trials in the United States. But congressional resistance as well as a thwarted terrorist bombing of a U.S. airplane resulted in the Obama administration announcing in spring 2010 that it would keep Guantanamo Bay open and resume military commissions there, with judicial protections such as *habeas corpus* for detainees.

Presidential Advantages

The history of foreign policymaking and the eventual rise of presidential responsibility for leadership and control have been shaped by a mix of more or less mutable influences: presidential skills, public opinion, precedents, constitutional principles, and circumstances. The presidents' enduring advantages are their status as chief of state and the various constitutional powers that establish them as the principal communicator, the "sole organ of the nation in its external relations, and its sole representative with foreign nations."[11] Although presidents do not have the full authority to commit the nation and Congress to a foreign policy, their powers, at the very least, allow them to speak first in defining a policy and course of action for the nation. When coupled with the status as the only nationally elected officer (along with the vice president), these powers give an enterprising and determined president considerable leverage over policy. Insofar as any contradiction to their lead may reflect on the nation, presidents can saddle the congressional opposition with responsibility for embarrassing the nation and harming the general credibility of the presidency in future negotiations.

These advantages are enhanced by the president's other positions. As commander in chief of the armed forces, head of the diplomatic corps, and head of the intelligence agencies, presidents should be in the best position to judge the capacity of the U.S. government to carry out a given foreign policy. Congress has regularly recognized the inherent advantages of the presidency's focused responsibility. Unlike Congress, with its many voices and centers of power, presidents are able to work with speed and secrecy, two capabilities that are indispensable in many diplomatic situations, and especially in crises that threaten the security of the nation. As the most identifiable leaders and visible symbols of the nation, presidents are the most capable of rallying national support in a crisis.

Turning these advantages into enduring presidential dominance depends on other factors. Presidents must establish plausible constitutional principles that support their policymaking ambitions, principles that place within their control the ambiguities and voids in the Constitution, such as the responsibility for policy proclamations, international agreements other than treaties, flexible employment of armed forces, and military actions short of war. A significant constitutional resource is the executive power. Because it is difficult to define precisely where policymaking stops and execution begins, even a narrow understanding of the executive power affords presidents some policy influence. Moreover, presidents have claimed that the general executive power authorizes them to fill the constitutional voids and to dominate areas of ambiguity.

Congress retains nonetheless a substantial arsenal of constitutional counterclaims and can at any time reassert itself. The persuasiveness of presidential assertions of authority depends in part on precedent: claims of authority that have received the approbation or acquiescence of Congress, the courts, and public opinion. Successful assertions, and especially those backed by actions with favorable results, tend to strengthen the president's constitutional position and reaffirm the practical advantages of presidential control over policy. Precedents can, however, cut the other way. The war in Vietnam was prosecuted under an expansive interpretation of presidential authority built up through many cold war precedents. However, the immediate effects of the war were a weakened practical argument for presidential control of foreign policy, Congress's reassertion of its constitutional powers, and greater skepticism about the president's claims of broad constitutional authority.

Reaping the full potential of constitutional and practical precedents requires the cooperation of circumstances. Any crisis in foreign affairs that directly or indirectly threatens the security and well-being of U.S. citizens, the nation, or close allies will focus attention on the president as the chief of state and as the officer most able to respond flexibly and decisively in diplomatic and military matters. Congress regularly recognizes its clumsy inability to compete with these presidential qualities. As the French political observer Alexis de Tocqueville noted more than 150 years ago: "If the Union's existence were constantly menaced, and if its great interests were continually interwoven with those of other powerful nations, one would see the prestige of the executive growing, because of what was expected from it and what it did."[12] When Tocqueville wrote this, and for some time after, the United States was following a policy of relative isolation. The enduring elements of foreign policy were westward expansion and commerce. The latter especially was dominated by Congress through its full authority over tariffs and trade. After World War II, the expansive global commitments and permanent national security crises met Tocqueville's conditions and led to a full and enduring realization of the president's constitutional and practical potential in foreign policy leadership and control. In the post–cold war era, the frequent conflicts between Congress and President Clinton over issues such as participation in peacekeeping missions suggest that securing consistent presidential leadership in the future will be much more difficult. On the other hand, Iraq's invasion of Kuwait in 1990 and the September 11, 2001, terrorist attacks on New York City and Washington, D.C., suggest that circumstances can still favor presidential authority and leadership.

Judicial Enhancement of Presidential Power

The president's practical and constitutional advantages in competing with Congress for control of foreign policy are greatly enhanced by the fact that the judicial branch has generally either affirmed presidential assertions or refused to settle conflicts between the president and Congress, especially in this area. *(See box, Supreme Court Cases Related to the President's Foreign Policy Powers, p. 208.)*

The courts have avoided resolving constitutional conflicts in the area of foreign policy through the "political questions" doctrine. Justice Robert Jackson argued that

> the very nature of executive decisions as to foreign policy is political, not judicial. Such decisions are wholly confided by our Constitution to the political departments of the government. . . . They are decisions of a kind for which the Judiciary has neither aptitude, facilities nor responsibility and which has long been held to belong in the domain of political power not subject to judicial intrusion or inquiry.[13]

The Supreme Court has also affirmed broad, inherent national powers in foreign affairs and war, though without settling the exact boundaries between the president and Congress. The most comprehensive of these rulings came in *United States v. Curtiss-Wright,* delivered in 1936.

In 1934 Congress passed a joint resolution granting the president full discretion in determining the government's policy toward private arms shipments to warring nations in South America. After President Franklin D. Roosevelt used this authority to impose an embargo on Bolivia, the Curtiss-Wright Export Corporation conspired to send arms to Bolivia. In court, lawyers for Curtiss-Wright argued that the law was an unconstitutional delegation to the executive of Congress's legislative power.

The Court's reasoning is rather difficult to follow. It clearly argued for a fundamental distinction between domestic and foreign affairs powers; although the national government's domestic powers are strictly limited by the Constitution, its foreign affairs authority comprises all the powers of a sovereign nation. In other words, the Constitution's specific grants do not define the scope of the government's "inherent" powers, and the government generally has access to an unspecified and undefined range of powers in war and foreign affairs.

The Court argued, moreover, that the president's specific powers establish the office as the "sole organ of the federal government in the field of international relations." However, this seems to be limited to the exclusive authority to "speak or listen as a representative of the nation" and does not imply that the president has full policymaking authority. As Justice George Sutherland indicates in his summary, the president is not independent of Congress in broader questions of policy:

> It is important to bear in mind that we are here dealing not alone with an authority vested in the President by an exertion of legislative power, but with such an authority plus the very delicate, plenary, and exclusive power of the President as the sole organ of the federal government in the field of international relations—a power which does not require as a basis for its exercise an act of Congress, but which, of course, like every other governmental power, must be exercised in subordination to the applicable provisions of the Constitution. It is quite apparent that if, in the maintenance of our international relations, embarrassment—perhaps serious embarrassment—is to be avoided and success for our aims achieved, congressional legislation which is to be made effective through negotiation and inquiry in the international field must often accord to the President a degree of discretion and freedom from statutory restriction which would not be admissible were domestic affairs alone involved.[14]

United States v. Curtiss-Wright was a landmark decision. Although the ruling does not seem to support historian Arthur M. Schlesinger Jr.'s conclusion that the Court "affirmed the existence of an inherent, independent and superior presidential power, not derived from the Constitution and not requiring legislation as the basis for its exercise," the ruling did ground past practices in constitutional doctrine, and it provided the president and Congress with a wealth of possible claims to authority.[15]

Conflicts and Precedents during the Washington Administration

Although George Washington exercised his foreign affairs power with great restraint by today's standards, he and his closest adviser, Secretary of the Treasury Alexander Hamilton, believed the president had the constitutional authority and the practical duty to take the initiative in foreign policy. As a result, Washington set several precedents that enlarged the foreign affairs powers of the young presidency beyond a literal reading of the enumerated powers in the Constitution. He established the president's authority to recognize foreign governments, to demand that foreign

SUPREME COURT CASES RELATED TO THE PRESIDENT'S FOREIGN POLICY POWERS

Ware v. Hylton, 3 Dall. 199 (1796). The Court ruled 4–0 that treaties made by the United States overrode any conflicting state laws. The 1783 Treaty of Paris with Britain, which ended the American Revolution, provided that neither Britain nor the United States would block the efforts of the other nation's citizens to secure repayment of debts in the other country. This provision rendered invalid a Virginia law allowing debts owed by Virginians to British creditors to be "paid off" through payments to the state.

Foster v. Neilson, 2 Pet. 253 (1829). By a 5–0 vote, the Court refused to rule on a boundary dispute involving territory east of the Mississippi River claimed by both the United States and Spain. Chief Justice John Marshall described the matter as a "political question" that was not the business of the judiciary to resolve.

Holmes v. Jennison, 14 Pet. 540 (1840). A fugitive from Canada, detained in Vermont, sought release through a petition for a writ of *habeas corpus*. After the state supreme court denied his petition, he asked the Supreme Court to review that action. The Court dismissed the case for lack of jurisdiction, but Chief Justice Roger B. Taney declared in his opinion that states were forbidden by the Constitution to take any independent role in foreign affairs, and thus state governors could not surrender a fugitive within their jurisdiction to a foreign country that sought the fugitive's return.

The Prize Cases, 2 Black 635 (1863). These cases involved the capture of four ships seized while trying to run the Union blockade of Confederate ports, which President Abraham Lincoln instituted in April 1861 and Congress sanctioned in July. By a 5–4 vote, the Court sustained the president's power to proclaim the blockade without a congressional declaration of war. A state of war already existed, the majority said, and the president was obligated "to meet it in the shape it presented itself, without waiting for Congress to baptize it with a name."

Geofroy v. Riggs, 133 U.S. 258 (1890). The Court ruled 9–0 that it is within the scope of the treaty power of the United States to regulate the inheritance by aliens of land and other property in the United States. The Court declared that the treaty power was unlimited except by the Constitution.

Missouri v. Holland, 252 U.S. 416 (1920). After lower courts ruled an act of Congress protecting migratory birds to be an unconstitutional invasion of powers reserved to the states, the U.S. government negotiated a treaty with Canada for the protection of the birds. After the Senate approved it, Congress again enacted protective legislation to fulfill the terms of the treaty. The Court sustained this second act by a 7–2 vote. It ruled that to implement a treaty Congress may enact legislation that without a treaty might be an unconstitutional invasion of state sovereignty.

United States v. Curtiss-Wright Export Corp., 299 U.S. 304 (1936). Although ambiguous, this is the leading case on the general foreign affairs powers. By a 7–1 vote, the Court upheld an act of Congress authorizing the president, at his discretion, to embargo arms shipments to foreign belligerents in a South American war. The Court asserted that the national government has undefined, "inherent" powers in foreign affairs. Justice George Sutherland also argued that the president was "the sole organ of the federal government in . . . international relations." His powers as the "sole organ" were "plenary and exclusive."

United States v. Belmont, 310 U.S. 324 (1937). In the executive agreements that established diplomatic relations between the Soviet Union and the United States in 1933, the two nations had agreed that Soviet assets in the United States would be used to pay the claims of U.S. citizens for property seized in the Soviet Union at the time of the Russian Revolution. When U.S. government officials tried to recover funds from the accounts of Russian nationals in New York banks, the state maintained that its laws prohibited the action. The Supreme Court, however, ruled that the executive agreements on which the action was based constituted an international compact that, like a treaty, superseded conflicting state laws.

Goldwater v. Carter, 444 U.S. 996 (1980). In December 1978 President Jimmy Carter announced that the United States would terminate the 1945 Mutual Defense Treaty with the Republic of China (Taiwan) as part of the process of establishing diplomatic relations with the People's Republic of China. Sen. Barry Goldwater, R-Ariz., brought a suit to stop the action, maintaining that treaty termination, like treaty ratification, required the prior approval of the Senate. The Court tacitly sided with the president by dismissing the case as a political question outside the realm of judicial review.

Hamdi v. Rumsfeld, 542 U.S. 507 (2004). After the terrorist strikes against New York City and Washington, D.C., on September 11, 2001, Congress passed a resolution authorizing the president to use force against nations, individuals, or organizations connected with the attacks. In 2001 Yaser Esam Hamdi, an American citizen, was arrested in Afghanistan for collaborating with the Taliban regime, which was affiliated with the al Qaeda terrorist network behind the U.S. attacks. Hamdi was classified as an "enemy combatant" and detained in the United States. His father filed a *habeas corpus* petition, asserting that the U.S. government was violating Hamdi's constitutional rights by holding him indefinitely without criminal charges. The Court ruled that a U.S. citizen must be accorded due process to challenge detention by the government.

Rumsfeld v. Padilla, 542 U.S. 426 (2004). In 2002 José Padilla, a U.S. citizen, was arrested in Chicago for allegedly working with al Qaeda in Pakistan and plotting to set off a radiological, or "dirty," bomb in the United States. He was declared an "enemy combatant" and held without charge in a military prison. Padilla filed a *habeas corpus* petition, and in 2004 the Court, sidestepping the substantive issue, ruled only that his case needed to be tried in a different jurisdiction. In 2005 the George W. Bush administration moved Padilla to a civilian prison and charged him with conspiring to commit terrorist attacks and supporting al Qaeda. With Padilla's transfer to a civilian prison, the Court in 2006 declined to hear his petition for *habeas corpus*, declaring it moot.

Hamdan v. Rumsfeld, 126 S.Ct. 2749 (2006). In 2001 Salim Ahmed Hamdan, a Yemeni national who had worked as a chauffeur for al Qaeda leader Osama bin Laden, was arrested in Afghanistan and detained by the U.S. military in Guantanamo Bay, Cuba. Hamdan challenged his detention in court, but the Bush administration declared that it would employ special military tribunals for "enemy combatants," and that those tribunals would not be subject to requirements that applied to traditional prisoners of war. The Court ruled that military commissions were obligated to comply with U.S. law and the laws of war, including the Geneva Convention adopted after World War II.

Boumedine v. Bush, 553 U.S. 723 (2008). In January 2002 U.S. forces took Bosnian citizen Lakhdar Boumedine into military custody and detained him in Guantanamo Bay, Cuba, for alleged involvement with al Qaeda terrorists. Writs of *habeas corpus* were submitted to U.S. courts on behalf of numerous detainees, including Boumedine, challenging their detention. The Supreme Court ruled in favor of the detainees' right to *habeas corpus* and overturned the section of the 2006 Military Commissions Act of 2006 that had suspended that right.

ambassadors be recalled, to negotiate treaties without the direction of the Senate, and to withhold from the House documents pertinent to treaty negotiations. Most important, Washington demonstrated that in foreign affairs the president could use the office's inherent executive power to take actions that were authorized neither by Congress nor by a specific presidential foreign policy power in the Constitution. In doing so, his administration initiated a debate that produced history's most complete and enduring constitutional arguments for and against broad presidential authority in foreign affairs.

Neutrality Proclamation of 1793

Washington set the precedent for unilateral presidential policymaking by proclaiming the neutrality of the United States in the war between France and Great Britain in 1793. Although the treaty of alliance with France signed in 1778 was still in effect, and many Americans favored the French, Washington was anxious to avoid involving the United States in the conflict, fearing that it would disrupt the strengthening of the American economy and political institutions.

On April 22, 1793, Washington issued a proclamation that declared that the United States would be "friendly and impartial" toward the belligerents. Although the proclamation was unpopular with many Americans, Congress followed Washington's lead by passing the Neutrality Act of 1794, which endorsed the policy of neutrality already in effect. Washington had shown that the president's executive power could be used to make foreign policy rather than just execute congressional directives.

Hamilton-Madison Debate

Secretary of State Thomas Jefferson was not convinced that the president, without an explicit constitutional grant of power, had the authority to act. Moreover, Jefferson inferred from Congress's exclusive authority to declare war that the president lacked the authority to decide unilaterally that the nation would *not* fight a war. However, his objections to Washington's policy were minor when compared with the horror induced by Hamilton's "Pacificus" essays. Hamilton's defense of the proclamation evolved into a more general argument for broad, inherent presidential powers in war and foreign affairs.

Hamilton's argument took two tacks. First, he argued that Washington was acting within his ordinary authority as chief executive in interpreting the legal obligations of existing treaties and in informing the government and the citizens of their responsibilities under the law. The expansiveness of the other tack was breathtaking. Through a careful, and sometimes clever, analysis of the constitutional text, Hamilton argued that constellations of specific presidential powers implied that the treaty power and the general war power were

executive in nature. Therefore, he concluded, Congress's powers in those areas ought to be interpreted narrowly, as strictly construed exceptions to executive power. The crucial argument was that the Constitution grants the president broad and undefined *inherent* powers through the vesting clause of Article II; whereas Congress is given the "legislative Powers *herein granted*," the executive power is "vested in a President" without a similar limitation. This broad power would not only authorize proclamations but also fill every relevant void in the Constitution. Hamilton acknowledged that the president's use of this power interfered with the free exercise of Congress's power to declare war, but this was an unavoidable consequence, he argued, of the president and Congress having "concurrent powers" in this area.[16]

As a member of Washington's cabinet, Jefferson felt that it would be improper for him to attack Hamilton's argument in public. He urged Madison to respond: "Nobody answers him and his doctrines are taken for confessed. For God's sake, my dear Sir, take up your pen, select the most striking heresies and cut him to pieces in face of the public."[17]

Under the pseudonym Helvidius, Madison's argument rested less on the constitutional text than on a general principle of legislative sovereignty and strict rule of law: "The natural province of the executive magistrate is to execute laws, as that of the legislature is to make laws. All his acts, therefore, properly executive, must presuppose the existence of the laws to be executed."[18] This restrictive interpretation of the executive power then guided his very restrictive reading of all presidential powers in foreign affairs and war. Thus, according to Madison, the president's role in foreign affairs was confined to executing the laws, treaties, and declarations of war made by Congress and performing those duties, strictly construed, that are specifically enumerated in the Constitution. Congress was, according to Madison, the branch of government properly entrusted to formulate foreign policy, including declarations of neutrality.

Although Hamilton's generous reading of the president's constitutional authority has never been fully accepted by the other branches, it has provided presidents with a coherent constitutional foundation for their more adventurous assertions of authority. Indeed, many presidents have spoken and behaved as if they had a general, comprehensive power to conduct foreign affairs, while Congress could only participate if it found an opportunity to use one of its specific powers.

CONGRESSIONAL COOPERATION AND CONFLICT

In spite of their constitutional and practical advantages in the conduct of foreign policy, presidents have regularly struggled, and periodically failed, to control U.S. foreign policy. Congress has significant authority that can be used to thwart and redirect presidential initiatives. At times, Congress has refused to follow the president's leadership and has attempted to legislate its own policy course. Even in eras of presidential domination, Congress has demonstrated that no foreign policy program can be sustained for long without its support. Foreign policy has, therefore, often been shaped through cooperation and accommodation between the two branches.

Early Cooperation and Conflict

Congressional majorities often were willing to cooperate with early presidents on foreign affairs matters. For example, Congress passed the Neutrality Act of 1794 a year after President Washington had declared American neutrality in the war between Britain and France, even though many members of Congress had opposed the original proclamation. In 1803 the Senate followed Jefferson's lead by ratifying the treaty with France that transferred the Louisiana Territory into U.S. control. The full record of these two administrations is, however, more mixed. Although the Senate approved it in 1795, Washington's Jay Treaty with Great Britain ignited a partisan explosion that led to demands from the House for papers related to the negotiations. Against the strong wishes of Jefferson, Congress repealed his embargo policy against Great Britain just before the end of his term.

In 1816 a report by the Senate Foreign Relations Committee reflected Congress's recognition of the practical advantages of presidential leadership in foreign affairs and of the limited practical scope of the Senate's power of advice and consent:

> The President is the Constitutional representative of the United States with regard to foreign nations. He manages our concern with foreign nations and must necessarily be most competent to determine when, how, and upon what subject negotiations may be urged with the greatest prospect of success. For his conduct he is responsible to the Constitution. The committee considers this responsibility the surest pledge for the faithful discharge of his duties. They think the interference of the Senate in the direction of foreign negotiations [is] calculated to diminish that responsibility and thereby to impair the best security for the national safety. The nature of transactions with foreign nations, moreover, requires caution and unity of design, and their success frequently depends on secrecy and dispatch.[19]

Nineteenth Century

Presidents during much of the last two-thirds of the nineteenth century exerted less foreign policy leadership than had earlier presidents. The resolution of the slavery question, the development of the American West, and the Reconstruction of the South following the Civil War were the most important political issues of the period. The primary foreign relations issues—foreign trade and the acquisition of territory from foreign governments—were two matters in which Congress had a large role. Nonetheless, Presidents Chester A. Arthur, Benjamin Harrison, and William McKinley had significant influence over trade policy.

In the years after the Civil War, congressional power was at its peak. The executive branch suffered some serious setbacks, including the impeachment and near removal of President Andrew Johnson from office and the passage of the Tenure of Office Act in 1867, which allowed the Senate to prevent a president from removing an appointee from office.[20] In general, the Senate controlled the executive branch. Indeed, from 1871 to 1895 no major treaty succeeded in gaining the Senate's consent.[21]

The Spanish-American War in 1898 marked a major turning point in foreign policy, because the nation dropped its traditional policy of nonintervention. Although President McKinley originally sought a peaceful resolution of the conflict with Spain over its rule in Cuba, Congress and public opinion favored intervention. The nation went to war and emerged victorious with overseas territories as distant as the western Pacific. With the goal of fostering trade, McKinley extended the nation's international interests and engagements. In particular, the annexation of the Philippines involved the nation in a wide range of Far Eastern affairs, especially those affecting trade. This imperial policy helped to merge the president's foreign affairs and war powers, giving the president greater leverage over Congress in making and implementing foreign policy.

Theodore Roosevelt's Administration

After the Spanish-American War, presidents expanded their control over foreign affairs. In 1901 McKinley was assassinated, and his vice president, Theodore Roosevelt, succeeded to the presidency. For the next seven and a half years, Roosevelt frequently ignored or circumvented Congress while boldly asserting a broad executive prerogative to pursue his perception of U.S. interests abroad. In 1903 he used U.S. naval power to back a small Panamanian revolt against Colombian rule; recognized the state of Panama, which emerged from the revolution; and quickly negotiated a treaty with the new Panamanian government giving the United States the right to dig the Panama Canal. In 1905, after the Senate refused to ratify a treaty giving the United States control of the Dominican Republic's customs houses, Roosevelt implemented his policy through an executive agreement. The same year, Roosevelt personally directed mediation efforts between Russia and Japan without consulting Congress. His efforts led to the Portsmouth Conference in New Hampshire, which ended the Russo-Japanese War and won him the Nobel Peace Prize. In 1907 Roosevelt decided to send the U.S. fleet on a world cruise, primarily to impress the Japanese with U.S. naval strength. Congress threatened to deny funding for the mission, but relented when Roosevelt declared he had sufficient funds to send the navy to the Pacific—and Congress would be left to decide whether it wanted the ships back.[22]

President Roosevelt freely admitted that he had avoided involving Congress in major foreign policy actions. In 1909, while still in office, he wrote: "The biggest matters, such as the Portsmouth peace, the acquisition of Panama, and sending the fleet around the world, I managed without consultation with anyone; for when a matter is of capital importance, it is well to have it handled by one man only."[23]

Versailles to World War II

Presidential disregard for Congress's role in foreign policy reached new heights in 1919. Woodrow Wilson traveled to Versailles, France, to participate personally in the negotiation of a peace treaty to end World War I. Under strong pressure from Wilson, the conference agreed to include provisions in the treaty establishing a League of Nations. The president brought the treaty back to the United States and began a vigorous national campaign for Senate approval. During the war, Congress had cooperated with Wilson by granting him unprecedented war powers, but once the threat had passed, the Senate was ready to reassert legislative influence over foreign policy. Wilson, however, ignored the growing opposition within the Senate and refused to involve senators in the Versailles negotiations or even to inform them of U.S. negotiating positions. In 1919 and 1920 the Senate refused to approve the treaty, thus keeping the country out of the League of Nations.

The demise of the Versailles treaty signaled a new period of congressional activism in promoting a foreign policy of isolation. During the next two decades, Congress limited U.S. involvement overseas, with little resistance from the executive branch. When war threatened in Asia and Europe in the late 1930s, Congress, reflecting the isolationism of the public, tried to legislate neutrality through an embargo on arms shipments and strict controls on the president.[24] But when war finally began, Franklin Roosevelt, like presidents before him in times of crisis, acquired enormous powers through his assertiveness and Congress's

To end the Russo-Japanese War, President Theodore Roosevelt facilitated peace negotiations between Russia and Japan in September 1905. This postcard was meant to celebrate the eventual signing of the peace treaty at the Portsmouth Naval Shipyard in Kittery, Maine.

grants of authority, which were motivated by the need for national unity.

Postwar Presidential Power

After World War II ended, presidential authority in foreign affairs continued to grow. The period brought many new responsibilities and dangers that required a chief executive capable of quick, decisive action and enhanced presidential stature as an international leader. The United States had emerged from the war as the most powerful nation on earth and the leader of the noncommunist world. The threat of communist expansion brought the whole globe into the sphere of U.S. interest. The United States had swung from isolationism in the late 1930s to unprecedented international involvement in the late 1940s, aligning itself with virtually any willing country and sending billions of dollars in economic and military aid overseas.

More immediate dangers to the security of the United States grew along with its commitments. Advances in missile technology and Soviet development of the atomic bomb in 1949 and the hydrogen bomb in 1953 made a devastating attack on the American homeland a possibility. The fall of China to communist forces in 1949 reinforced the belief of many Americans that the United States had to be ready to use troops if necessary to stop communist expansion.

The continual conjunction of military threats and foreign policy in this complex and hostile international environment contributed to a consensus for strong presidential leadership in foreign policy. Congress recognized that only the executive branch had the means to collect and analyze the huge amount of information on foreign policy issues and to act with the speed and flexibility that seemed necessary to manage U.S. global commitments. In addition, the presidential role of guardian of the nuclear switch magnified the commander in chief's stature as guardian of the free world, thereby enhancing presidential authority in other areas of defense and foreign policy.

Although some major initiatives, such as the Marshall Plan, were developed in close cooperation with congressional leaders, Congress did repeatedly pass resolutions supporting presidential policy discretion and authorizing the president to use force if necessary to deal with particular international problems. In 1955 Congress authorized the president to use force to defend Formosa (Nationalist China) and the neighboring islands if they were attacked by Communist China. An even broader resolution was passed in 1957 that supported the "Eisenhower Doctrine," which announced the intention of the United States to defend Middle Eastern countries "against aggression from any country controlled by international communism." Several years later, in 1962, the House and Senate passed resolutions declaring their support for any presidential action, including the use of force, needed to defend the rights of the United States in the divided city of Berlin. The same year, Congress adopted similar resolutions pertaining to the Cuban missile crisis.

In August 1964 Congress passed the sweeping Tonkin Gulf resolution with only two senators out of the 535 members of Congress in opposition. *(See box, Tonkin Gulf Resolution, p. 263, in Chapter 6.)* The resolution had been proposed by the administration of Lyndon Johnson in response to murky evidence that North Vietnamese torpedo boats had attacked U.S. vessels off the coast of Vietnam.[25] The resolution acknowledged and supported the president's full authority to take "all necessary measures to repel any armed attacks against the forces of the United States and to prevent further aggression." At least two months before the incident, Johnson's National Security Council staff had prepared a draft of a similar resolution supporting presidential freedom to act in Vietnam.[26] Because Johnson never asked Congress for a declaration of war, he used the Tonkin Gulf resolution in subsequent years as evidence of congressional support for his expansion of U.S. involvement in the conflict in Vietnam.

Congressional Rebellion and Reassertion

Congress was partly responsible for the expansion of executive power between 1945 and 1969. For the sake of national unity in the fight against communism, the legislature had consented to and even encouraged presidential autonomy in foreign and defense matters. Congress had tended to follow whatever policy direction the president chose and, implicitly or explicitly, accept the enlarged presidential interpretations of executive power.[27] In the late 1960s, however, Congress began to rebel against the growing capacity of presidents to exclude Congress from participation in foreign and defense policy decisions. After passage of the Tonkin Gulf resolution, for example, President Johnson sought the appropriations needed to escalate military involvement in Southeast Asia and never sought congressional approval for any policy or strategy decision about the war. Members of Congress also were unhappy with the increasing number of international commitments made by executive agreement without congressional approval, especially those that expanded the scope of the war.

In June 1969, by a 70–16 vote, the Senate adopted a "national commitments" resolution, which declared the sense of the Senate that a national commitment by the United States results "only from affirmative action taken by the executive and legislative branches of the United States government by means of a treaty, statute, or concurrent resolution of both houses of Congress specifically providing for such a commitment." In 1969 and 1970 some members of Congress repeatedly attempted to terminate funds for U.S. military activities in Indochina. During that period, Congress also used its investigative powers to probe the extent of U.S. commitments abroad.

In the early 1970s, the revelations of a secret Defense Department study of the decision-making process surrounding the Vietnam War (known as the *Pentagon Papers*), the unwillingness of Presidents Johnson and Nixon to include Congress in foreign policy decisions, and the Watergate scandal spurred Congress to seek to recapture the foreign affairs powers it had lost to the executive branch. In 1972 Congress passed the Case Act, which established more rigorous requirements for the reporting of international agreements to Congress by the executive branch. It was followed by passage of the War Powers Resolution of 1973 over President Nixon's veto. The measure set a sixty-day limit on any unauthorized presidential introduction of U.S. troops into hostilities abroad.

In 1974 Congress passed a major trade reform bill, but only after approving the Jackson-Vanik Amendment, which linked trade concessions for communist countries to their easing restrictions on the emigration of Jews. The same year

Congress imposed a ban on military aid and arms shipments to Turkey. In 1978 the Senate conducted a long and contentious debate on the Panama Canal treaties and approved them only after adding numerous amendments. During this period, Congress also conducted investigations of the intelligence community and began to take a more active interest in the specifics of the Defense Department's budget.

Congressional activism in foreign affairs appears to have become a permanent feature of U.S. foreign policy. Congress was routinely submitting alternative plans for weapons acquisition, arms control, and policies on regional problems. In addition, it was passing nonbinding resolutions stating its concerns on a variety of foreign policy issues. Although Congress often supported President Reagan's actions, many of his foreign policies, such as arms sales to moderate Arab nations, were accompanied by tough and sometimes unsuccessful battles for congressional approval. Military assistance to the Nicaraguan rebels, as part of Reagan's general anticommunist foreign policy, met stiff resistance in Congress, and the administration's attempts to circumvent congressional restrictions led to extensive congressional investigations and general damage to the Reagan administration. President George H. W. Bush began his administration in 1989 by forging a bipartisan accord with Congress to defuse the issue. In 1990, faced with mounting congressional criticism, Bush sought congressional approval for his decision to drive the Iraqi army out of Kuwait. In 1991, in the wake of the 1989 Tiananmen Square massacre of prodemocracy demonstrators by the Chinese government, only the failure to override Bush's veto prevented Congress from imposing a human rights condition on the extension of most-favored-nation status to China.[28]

Congress has significant foreign policy powers. It shares with the president the "plenary power" of the national government in foreign affairs and has "vast powers to define the bounds within which a president may be left to work out a foreign policy."[29] Although Congress has not asserted these powers fully even during periods of presidential weakness such as the second Nixon administration, the potential is there. Congress can dominate any policy involving trade, and contrary to the wishes of presidents, it has imposed trade sanctions, for example, on the former Soviet Union, Uganda, and South Africa. It has used its power over trade to force the president to negotiate, or retaliate, over the trade practices of other countries.

Control over spending is Congress's most powerful and comprehensive power, and it has used this power to control foreign aid and, particularly, arms sales.[30] Congress has blocked and mandated spending contrary to the president's wishes. For example, it forbade Nixon to spend for military operations in Laos and Cambodia (1973) and blocked all military assistance to Angola (1975). In 1986 and 1987 Congress used its control over weapons procurement to prevent the Reagan administration from implementing its controversial interpretations of the ABM and SALT II treaties. President Clinton faced numerous attempts by Congress to dictate policy through its spending power. In 1995, faced with congressional opposition, Clinton had to withdraw his request for emergency funds to support Mexico's collapsing economy. Instead, he used existing executive branch funds to implement the policy. Congress then attempted to require congressional approval for the use of those funds.

In general, Congress can be a potent forum for investigations and public criticism of presidential policy. The effectiveness of this capacity depends on congressional willingness to criticize the president and the willingness of the media and the public to listen. The dramatic changes in international circumstances in the 1990s suggested that Congress would use these resources to greater effect. After the collapse of the Soviet Union, the Warsaw Pact, and European communism in general, both Bush and Clinton lacked the great leverage gained from an ongoing global military and political emergency. The growing independence of the European Union and the ebbing U.S. influence in the North Atlantic Treaty Organization (NATO) lowered the president's stature as a world leader and weakened any argument that deference to presidential preferences was essential to the security of the nation and its allies. As issues such as international trade came to the fore, and as the conjunction of military might and foreign policy became more intermittent, the president became more likely to face a more influential and assertive Congress.

The Clinton presidency confirmed this expectation. President Clinton struggled, like his predecessor, President Bush, to formulate general principles of foreign policy outside of the area of trade. Even in that area, President Clinton's successes with the North American Free Trade Agreement (1993) and the General Agreement on Tariffs and Trade (1994) were notable for the weak support he received from his party. Commitments of U.S. forces in Somalia, Haiti, Bosnia, and Kosovo raised extensive congressional protests as well as proposals and resolutions to limit the president's authority to commit forces. In 1995 Congress passed over Clinton's protests a bill requiring that the U.S. embassy in Israel be relocated to Jerusalem; Clinton claimed such a move would interfere with peace negotiations. He allowed it to become law without his signature and invoked the bill's provisions for delaying the move.

During this period, participation of the United States in multilateral peacekeeping operations was of particular concern to Congress. Initially, the Clinton administration operated under the general principle that international engagements were best undertaken through the United Nations and other multilateral arrangements. But strong

FACES OF FOREIGN POLICY: POST–COLD WAR ERA TO THE POST-9/11 WORLD ALLIANCE COMMITMENTS AND PEACEKEEPING IN THE BALKANS

President Bill Clinton's struggle to shape U.S. and alliance policy toward the civil war in the former Yugoslavia illustrates some of the complexities of foreign policy in the post–cold war era. Clinton encountered criticism and resistance for basing foreign policy more on alliance commitments than on clear national interests.

After the end of communist rule, the former Yugoslavia descended into a terrible civil war between Serbs, Croats, and Bosnian Muslims. In 1993 Clinton announced that U.S. involvement in the conflict would be limited strictly to multilateral operations, and the United States began participating in a UN and North Atlantic Treaty Organization (NATO) mission to provide humanitarian relief.[1] In this mission, U.S. air power was used to restrict attacks by Serbs and protect relief operations.

Congressional attitudes toward U.S. involvement were mixed. In 1992 Congress passed a nonbinding resolution calling on the president and the United Nations to act, even with force, to stop the fighting. Yet at the same time, some in Congress were trying to restrict generally the president's authority to commit forces to multilateral operations in Somalia and Haiti as well as the former Yugoslavia. In 1993 Congress passed a nonbinding resolution requiring congressional authorization before ground forces could be sent to the region.

In 1994 President Clinton took a tougher stand, calling for air strikes against the Bosnian Serbs for violating cease-fire agreements, interfering with the relief operation, and besieging various cities that had been designated as protected Muslim "safe areas." After intermittent U.S.-led air strikes failed to halt Serbian aggression, Clinton was unable to lead NATO toward a more consistently forceful response.

President Clinton's policy seemed to be shaped as much by a desire to maintain alliance cohesion as by the situation in Bosnia per se, and in 1994 Congress again attempted to dictate policy. In an extraordinary move, it voted to cut off funds for U.S. enforcement of the UN arms embargo, leading the United States, for the first time, to withdraw from a NATO-approved operation. The Clinton administration tried to repair relations with NATO by shifting its position toward NATO's softer line of seeking a negotiated settlement. On the other side, prominent members of Congress, especially Sen. Robert J. Dole, R-Kans., the majority leader, criticized the "helpless, hopeless," and "maybe irrelevant" NATO for failing to punish and stop Serbian aggression.[2] In summer 1995 Congress passed the Bosnia and Herzegovina Self-Defense Act, which directed the president, under specific conditions, to terminate the U.S. arms embargo against Bosnia and to press for the termination of the UN arms embargo. Clinton vetoed the bill.

The president's general concerns about supporting alliances led to a commitment of additional U.S. forces, including ground troops, to aid in the redeployment or withdrawal of the UN forces being threatened by Serbian forces. Clinton and Congress sparred over any commitment of ground troops for either combat or peacekeeping missions. Then, in a deft move, Clinton deepened his commitments and increased his leverage over Congress by having the United States host the UN-sponsored peace talks, in which Clinton was directly involved. Once the peace accord was signed in Paris in December 1995, Clinton began sending troops on his own authority and without effective congressional resistance. Even former critics such as Senator Dole argued that contradicting the president's commitments would harm the credibility of the United States as an ally and international leader. As for the House, it passed resolutions contradicting the president's authority to send troops, opposing the mission, and yet supporting the troops deployed. Congress and Clinton continued to argue over a deadline for a conclusion to the mission.

These disputes arose again, in 1999, over the U.S. reaction to the brutal Serbian assaults on ethnic Albanians in Kosovo. General support in Congress for NATO air strikes was coupled with a muddled response to the possibility of U.S. ground forces being deployed for either combat or peacekeeping. Congress refused to authorize the sending of combat troops but failed to mount any strong resistance to Clinton sending ground forces for peacekeeping.

Such operations remain a major issue, in part because they divert forces away from national defense and consume defense dollars that could serve other needs and policies, such as weapons modernization, officer retention, and general military readiness. By one estimate, the cost of U.S. peacekeeping commitments was five times higher in 1996 than in 1989.[3]

COALITION LEADERSHIP IN THE WAR ON TERRORISM

September 11, 2001, abruptly exposed another face of post–cold war foreign policy and a new set of challenges to presidential leadership. More than three thousand people were murdered by terrorists flying hijacked airliners into the two towers of the World Trade Center in New York City, the Pentagon near Washington, D.C., and a field in southeastern Pennsylvania. These were not the first Americans killed by foreign terrorists. In 1983, 241 U.S. Marines were killed by a car bomb in Beirut, Lebanon, and many American lives were lost in the suicide bombings of the Khobar Towers in Saudi Arabia in 1996, of the U.S. embassies in Kenya and Tanzania in 1998, and of the USS *Cole* in Yemen in 2000. The 2001 attack, however, was distinguished from these by a combination of features: it occurred within the U.S. borders; unlike the Oklahoma City bombing, it was planned and executed by foreign terrorists; and the attack's high degree of planning, coordination, boldness, and savagery set it far apart from the 1993 car bombing of the World Trade Center.

The reaction of the U.S. government to this attack also was unprecedented. The government had responded to earlier incidents by retreating, imposing trade sanctions, or retaliating with brief, small-scale military actions. There was an implicit and explicit assumption and policy that international terrorism was, for one reason or another, a problem with which Americans had to live.[4] The potential for a major attack on U.S. soil had been foreseen by many, but the remedies tended to be defensive and remedial: sharpening intelligence capabilities to thwart such plots and enhancing preparedness, from missile defense to emergency logistics to stockpiling medications.[5] Few had argued for a vigorous and international counterterrorism policy.[6] President George W. Bush, however, defined the September 11 attack as an act of war and committed his administration to a war not only against the perpetrators and abettors of these killings but also against international terrorism itself.

On the one hand, the early stages of this campaign bore the earmarks of a bygone era. President Bush could creditably frame the U.S. commitment in terms of both a clear national interest in self-defense and a moral purpose of defending liberty and toleration against their determined enemies. The president's declarations received broad support from the general public and immediate authorization from Congress for the use of force. (See box, *Congressional Authorization for a War on Terrorism, p. 272, in Chapter 6.*) All but absent were the familiar reservations about duration, the use of ground troops in combat, and the loss of American lives. Congress also acted quickly on several otherwise controversial measures: an emergency appropriation of $40 billion for military, intelligence, and security measures, half of which was left to the president's discretion; an airline bailout package; and a broad counterterrorism bill that loosened restrictions on domestic surveillance and detention of suspected terrorists. The U.S.-led military and intelligence campaign received immediate backing from NATO and various levels of support and cooperation from a wide range of nations, including Britain, Germany, Switzerland, and even Russia. The Bush administration also secured the crucial participation of Pakistan and the limited cooperation of some Arab states.

On the other hand, the conflict posed some peculiar domestic and diplomatic problems. To begin with, a war on terrorism seeks not to defeat a state or an alliance of states but rather to disable or destroy a large number of often small and shadowy organizations and networks. How and when would the military objectives of a general antiterrorism operation be met, and what would the obligations of the partners be in the meantime? Concerns over a potentially broad and amorphous conflict led Congress, NATO, and other allies to frame their initial statements of support for military action more narrowly, focusing on the perpetrators of the September 11 attack rather than on international terrorism writ large. Yet even the first battle of the larger war foreshadowed difficulties in managing a broad counterterrorism coalition. Defeating Osama bin Laden and his al Qaeda terrorist network required an assault on the Taliban regime in Afghanistan that was harboring and supporting them.[7] A war on an Islamic state, and particularly one involving civilian casualties, risked the loss of cooperation or acquiescence from other Islamic states.

During the campaign in Afghanistan, the Bush administration was able to maintain the acquiescence of many Islamic countries and the active cooperation of Pakistan. Yet some of those countries, in particular Iran and Saudi Arabia, harbored and financed terrorist groups such as Hezbollah, Hamas, and Islamic Jihad, whose stated aims include the destruction of Israel. Saudi Arabia warned the United States against extending its counterterrorism efforts to these organizations. The Bush administration, at first omitting these groups from its list of terrorist organizations whose assets were to be frozen, later added them as their attacks on Israel grew more violent.[8] In his 2002 State of the Union address, President Bush also named Iran and Iraq as parts of an "axis of evil," which was "arming to threaten the peace of the world." His inclusion of the policies and regimes of these large Islamic states as targets of the war on terrorism was met by criticism and warnings from various allies. Moreover, always hanging over any controversy in the Middle East is the desire to maintain stable and cooperative relations with the regional oil states, which have a large impact on the economic well-being of Europe and the United States.

DEFINING A NATIONAL SECURITY STRATEGY FOR THE WAR ON TERRORISM

In September 2002 the Bush administration presented a comprehensive strategy for how the United States would wage the war on terrorism in the coming years. The thirty-one-page document, first distributed on the White House website, neatly summarized the administration's conceptualization of the long-term and multifaceted struggle against terrorism. Historian John Lewis Gaddis described it as "the new grand strategy of transformation."[9]

In many respects, the 2002 National Security Strategy (NSS) consolidated the ideas that President Bush had communicated already in several significant addresses, notably his January 29, 2002, State of the Union message (popularly known as the "axis of evil" speech) and his June 1, 2002, commencement address at the U.S. Military Academy at West Point. In his State of the Union message, Bush had famously identified Iraq, Iran, and North Korea as "an axis of evil, arming to threaten the peace of the world." He went on to declare that "I will not wait on events, while dangers gather. I will not stand by, as peril draws closer and closer."[10] Four months later, Bush announced at West Point that "If we wait for threats to fully materialize, we will have waited too long. . . . [Americans must] be ready for preemptive action when necessary to defend our liberty and to defend our lives."[11] Clearly the cold war strategies of containment and deterrence would no longer be sufficient to protect U.S. interests in the twenty-first century.

The NSS developed these positions further and placed them in the context of broader U.S. goals. The strategy began with a quotation from Bush's West Point speech, declaring that "We will defend the peace. . . . We will preserve the peace. . . . We will extend the peace."[12] After a brief overview, the document went on to discuss

aspirations for human dignity, the importance of strengthening alliances to battle global terrorism, and the need to work with other nations to control regional conflicts. The concept of preemption did not emerge explicitly until nearly halfway through the document, which insisted that "the United States has long maintained the option of preemptive actions to counter a sufficient threat to our national security."[13]

Yet preemption marked the most significant change in American national security strategy since the establishment of the containment doctrine after World War II. By declaring that the United States might need to use force to prevent a conflict before it began, and that "traditional concepts of deterrence will not work against a terrorist enemy," the Bush administration was charting a new direction in international affairs. While international law has long held that states may act in self-defense if an aggressor is about to strike, the key question for preemptive warfare is timing: how imminent is the threat? In stating that "we must adapt the concept of imminent threat to the capabilities and objectives of today's adversaries," the NSS seemed to suggest that what traditionally had been defined as preventive war—a strategy that is much more controversial because of the challenge of identifying the likelihood of an attack—would not be viewed as preemptive war.

The implementation of the NSS with the 2003 war in Iraq raised many questions about the need, cost (both domestically and internationally in terms of allied support), ethics, and precedent of preemptive warfare. When the United States did not find the expected stores of weapons of mass destruction (WMD) in Iraq, critics of preemption reinforced their arguments that the strategy would ensnare the United States in conflicts without sustained international support. Nevertheless, the Bush administration continued to endorse the strategy, declaring in 2006 that "the place of preemption in our national security strategy remains the same."[14] The 2006 strategy focused explicitly on the problems that Iran and North Korea presented for nuclear proliferation, but it did not link the possibility of preemptive warfare to a particular case. The strategy also condemned genocide, and it included a new section on globalization, which addressed nontraditional challenges in national security, such as public health and the environment. Thus, although preemption remained part of the administration's strategy, it no longer seemed to be the driving force, as it was in 2002 with the planning for war in Iraq. The Obama administration's national security strategy did not discuss preemption, and emphasized the importance of preserving national security through promoting domestic prosperity.[15]

1. Louis Fisher, *Presidential War Power* (Lawrence: University Press of Kansas, 1995), 158.

2. "Republicans Lay Siege to Clinton's Policy," *Congressional Quarterly Weekly Report*, December 3, 1994, 3452–3453.

3. *National Journal*, March 16, 1996, 482.

4. See Jeffrey D. Simon, "Misunderstanding Terrorism," *Foreign Policy* (summer 1987); Charles William Maynes, "Bottom-Up Foreign Policy," *Foreign Policy* (fall 1996).

5. See, for example, Richard K. Betts, "The New Threat of Mass Destruction," *Foreign Affairs* (January/February 1998).

6. See Reuel Marc Gerecht, "A Cowering Superpower," *Weekly Standard*, July 30, 2001.

7. See Ahmed Rashid, "The Taliban: Exporting Extremism," *Foreign Affairs* (November/December 1999).

8. Robert Satloff, "The Other Twin Towers," *Weekly Standard*, October 8, 2001.

9. John Lewis Gaddis, "A Grand Strategy of Transformation," *Foreign Policy* (October/November 2002): 50–57.

10. George W. Bush, "State of the Union Address," January 29, 2002.

11. George W. Bush, "Graduation Speech at West Point," June 1, 2002.

12. George W. Bush, "The National Security Strategy of the United States of America," September 2002.

13. Ibid.

14. George W. Bush, "The National Security Strategy of the United States of America," March 2006.

15. Barack Obama, "National Security Strategy," May 2010.

congressional reactions led to modifications in specific cases and to a more general retreat from this policy. For example, after the multilateral mission in Somalia was redefined from one of famine relief to a more aggressive policy of subduing the warring factions—a change that resulted in the death of some U.S. soldiers—Congress forced Clinton to negotiate a deadline for withdrawing U.S. forces.

From the start, in 1993, Clinton's policy toward the bloody conflicts among Bosnian Serbs, Croats, and Muslims in the former Yugoslavia generated a stream of congressional criticism and numerous proposals to limit or change the nature of U.S. involvement in the joint UN/NATO relief and mediation efforts. One of the most important of these was the 1994 amendment forcing Clinton to end U.S. enforcement of the arms embargo of Bosnia. This was the first time the United States had withdrawn from a NATO-sponsored operation. Clinton later vetoed a bill that would have lifted the embargo. (See box, Faces of Foreign Policy: Post–Cold War Era to the Post-9/11 World, pp. 214-215.)

In an effort to ward off more general congressional intrusions, the Clinton administration in 1994 revised its policy on UN missions, restricting U.S. participation to those operations vital to either national or global security. The Serbian assault on ethnic Albanians in Kosovo in 1999 once again brought the president and Congress into conflict. The House and the Senate, however, could not agree on a policy. In the end, Congress did not act to limit Clinton's authority, and he sent ground troops to participate in a peacekeeping mission.

EXECUTIVE DOMINANCE TO COMBAT TERRORISM

Early in the George W. Bush administration, Congress showed signs of continuing its activist role in foreign policy, especially after the Democratic Party took control of the Senate in June 2001. President Bush's policy toward China, his aggressive promotion of missile defense development, and his withdrawal from a number of UN-sponsored pacts and events, for example, were greeted with legislative resistance and unusually vigorous criticism from Democratic leaders. Bush's missile defense requests were slated to be cut, with restrictions placed on how the appropriated funds could be spent.

The September 11, 2001, terrorist attacks on New York City and Washington, D.C., to which Bush responded with a declaration of "war on terrorism," muted some of the criticism and resistance, particularly to missile defense, and fostered a more cooperative relationship that included quick action on an airline bailout bill, a large supplemental defense appropriation, and a controversial package of counterterrorism measures to broaden the government's powers of surveillance and detention. Congress did kill the president's request for broad authority to waive restrictions on

military assistance and weapons exports to certain countries, and it scuttled a plan to turn administration of certain U.S. seaports to a Middle Eastern company. Yet Congress also passed a joint resolution authorizing the president to respond to the 2001 attacks, and the Bush administration used that resolution to justify executive actions in the war on terror.

Among Bush's controversial decisions were the authorization of military tribunals for war detainees, the indefinite imprisonment of detainees at the U.S. base in Guantanamo Bay, treatment of detainees, and a National Security Agency program that permitted bypassing traditional legal procedures to wiretap telephone conversations involving U.S. citizens that may be connected to terrorist threats.[31] Congress also authorized the president to use military force in Iraq, although several members subsequently criticized the administration's postwar planning. Barack Obama pledged during the 2008 campaign to change Bush's policies, and he has prevailed in some areas, such as withdrawing U.S. forces from Iraq, which he completed in 2011. Obama did not, however, succeed in closing Guantanamo Bay during his first year in office, as he had promised, and he resumed military trials for detainees after Congress resisted administration efforts to hold civilian trials in U.S. courts. Nevertheless, in the post-9/11 world, executive leadership in international affairs has largely prevailed, buoyed by congressional reluctance to hinder the war on terror.

POWER OF COMMUNICATION

The Constitution's separation of powers between independent branches left open the question of which branch had the power to receive communications from foreign countries and to speak for the nation. Under the Articles of Confederation, these responsibilities belonged to Congress. The Constitution assigns to the president the three main communication powers: negotiating treaties, sending ambassadors, and receiving ambassadors. The Framers recognized that communications is a function more suited to an office occupied by a single person than to a large deliberative body. Disputes have arisen over the extent to which communication powers imply policymaking authority.

President Washington was eager to establish the presidency as the only organ of government empowered to communicate officially with foreign governments. He recognized that if both the president and Congress presumed to speak for the nation, diplomacy would be impossible, and foreign governments might try to exploit the confusion. During the first year of his administration, Washington received a letter from King Louis XVI of France notifying "the President and Members of the General Congress of the United States" that Louis' son had died. Washington told

Congress that he had received the letter and that he would send a reply to France. The president informed the king that "by the change which has taken place in the national government of the United States, the honor of receiving and answering your Majesty's letter of the 7th of June to 'the President and Members of Congress' has devolved upon me."[32]

In 1793 Washington's secretary of state, Thomas Jefferson, echoed this assertion when he explained to the French ambassador, Edmond Genêt, that the president "being the only channel of communication between this country and foreign nations, it is from him alone that foreign nations or their agents are to learn what is or has been the will of the nation; and whatever he communicates as such, they have the right, and are bound to consider, as the expression of the nation."[33]

Washington's conception of the president's role as national communicator was accepted without serious challenge. In 1799 John Marshall reaffirmed the president's position as the instrument of communication with foreign governments when as a member of the House of Representatives he declared, "The President is the sole organ of the nation in its external relations, and its sole representative with foreign nations."[34] The same year Congress passed the Logan Act, which prohibited any person other than presidents or their agents from communicating with another country with the intention of affecting its policy concerning an issue of contention with the United States.[35] Presumably the Logan Act could be invoked if a senator or representative attempted to usurp the president's power to communicate officially with foreign nations. Informal discussions with foreign leaders by members of Congress have become accepted practices. Speaker Jim Wright's 1987 attempt, secretly and independent of the Reagan administration, to negotiate a settlement between the Nicaraguan government and the contra rebels was widely criticized across both parties and branches.[36]

More frequently, members of Congress use publicity to affect negotiations. In 1986 the media campaign initiated by Sen. Richard Lugar, R-Ind., helped to persuade President Reagan to withdraw his support for Philippine dictator Ferdinand Marcos in favor of the democratically elected Corazon Aquino. Similarly in 1991, through his use of the press, Sen. Al Gore, D-Tenn., was able to help turn the administration of President George H. W. Bush toward cooperation in negotiating an international treaty on global warming. The initial proposals for a cabinet agency focused on homeland security came from Congress, and the Bush

As part of the ongoing conflict in Afghanistan, a U.S. Marine talks to an Afghan district governor through an interpreter. President George W. Bush declared a "war on terrorism" following the September 11, 2001, attacks. U.S. involvement in Afghanistan followed.

administration adopted the issue after strong public support became evident. In 2005 Sen. John McCain, R-Ariz., successfully pressured the administration to include a prohibition on torture in the Detainee Treatment Act, a position that drew public support in the wake of the Abu Ghraib prison scandals in Iraq.

Foreign Policy Declarations

In practice, the president's exclusive authority to communicate with other nations extends well beyond ceremonial functions as chief of state. Since Washington's day, presidents have found that they can make and influence foreign policy simply by making a statement. Presidents have used their communications power to make commitments, formalize decisions, and establish broad policy goals.

Coming from the chief of state and "the sole representative with foreign nations," presidential declarations are, de facto, national commitments. Consequently, Congress often is left with a choice between supporting a presidential commitment and undermining both the president as the national representative and the confidence of other nations in U.S. policy. Thus how a president expresses U.S. interests and intentions can shape U.S. foreign policy. Kennedy's famous speech at the Berlin Wall in 1963, for example, encouraged the people of Berlin to expect U.S. protection, thereby committing the United States to its defense. Theodore Roosevelt explained the connection between communication and policy:

The president carries on the correspondence through the State Department with all foreign countries. He is bound in such correspondence to discuss the proper construction

In 1963 President John F. Kennedy, fourth from right, stands on a platform facing the Berlin Wall and looks toward the Brandenburg Gate. The gate, barely inside East Berlin, was draped with red flags the day before Kennedy's arrival to prevent him from getting a good view of the communist sector of the city.

of treaties. He must formulate the foreign policies of our government. He must state our attitude upon questions constantly arising. While strictly he may not bind our government as a treaty would bind it, to a definition of its rights, still in future discussions foreign secretaries of other countries are wont to look for support of their contentions to the declarations and admissions of our secretaries of state in other controversies as in a sense binding upon us. There is thus much practical framing of our foreign policies in the executive conduct of our foreign relations.[37]

Presidential Doctrines

Beyond specific international commitments, presidents have also outlined general tenets of foreign policy, which have come to be labeled "doctrines." The most famous and durable policy statement by a president has been the Monroe Doctrine. In 1823 President James Monroe announced during his annual message to Congress that the United States would resist any attempt by a European power to interfere in the affairs of a Western Hemisphere country that was not already a European colony. Monroe did not consult Congress before his announcement, and some of its members believed the president had overstepped his authority. House Speaker Henry Clay proposed a joint resolution supporting the president's policy, but Congress did not act on it. Not until 1899 did the Monroe Doctrine receive a congressional endorsement.[38]

Theodore Roosevelt built on the Monroe Doctrine in 1904 when he announced in his annual message to Congress what became known as the Roosevelt Corollary. Roosevelt claimed for the United States the right to act as the Western Hemisphere's policeman if "chronic wrongdoing or impotence" in a country required U.S. intervention.

Broad foreign policy "doctrines" are associated with the administrations of many contemporary presidents. The Truman Doctrine stated that "it must be the policy of the United States to support free peoples who are resisting attempted subjugation by armed minorities or outside pressures."[39] The Eisenhower Doctrine, which was supported by a joint resolution, claimed for the United States the right to intervene militarily in the Middle East to protect legitimate governments from attacks by communist forces. The Nixon Doctrine (also known as the Guam Doctrine) proposed to continue giving allies military and economic aid while encouraging them to reduce their reliance on U.S. troops. The Carter Doctrine declared the Persian Gulf area to be a vital U.S. interest and warned that the United States would use force to prevent any attempt by an outside power to gain control of it. The Reagan Doctrine declared the Reagan administration's intention to support anticommunist insurgencies around the world to further a policy of rolling back communism and promoting liberal democratic government in Latin America, South Korea, the Philippines, and Taiwan. Only the president's policy declarations have a chance of being accepted as national policy, yet they are not always accepted by Congress and do not always last beyond the administration that announces them.

In the post–cold war era, the challenge of formulating a presidential strategy comparable to containment after World War II is evident. President George H. W. Bush's vague "New World Order" and President Clinton's similarly ill-defined policy of international engagement through multilateral operations illustrate the difficulty of formulating general commitments and principles of action. Actions early in the George W. Bush administration—for example, withdrawals from the Kyoto pact on global warming and from the Antiballistic Missile (ABM) Treaty—signaled a new general policy of unilateral action.[40] Criticism of this policy as "isolationist" was muted by the president's response to the 2001 terrorist attacks, and the administration's 2002 national security doctrine, which incorporated the possibility of "preemption," or using military force against another country in anticipation of an attack on the United States.[41] This strategy provided the conceptual justification for the Iraq War, but in the face of much criticism, it was revised in 2006 to place less emphasis on preemption, and the Obama administration's national security strategy made no mention of the concept. The underlying goal of U.S. foreign policy in the twenty-first century continues to be combating terrorism, but the problem of translating that long-term goal into a clearly defined doctrine for U.S. action remains.

THE TREATY POWER

The authors of the Constitution used only one clause to explain how treaties were to be made. Article II, Section 2, Clause 2, declares that the president "shall have the Power, by and with the Advice and Consent of the Senate, to make Treaties, provided two thirds of the Senators present concur." This concise statement blends responsibilities between the legislative and executive branches. Clearly the president is responsible for conducting the actual treaty negotiations; however, the president cannot conclude a treaty without first obtaining the consent of the Senate. The Constitution, therefore, ensures that no formal treaty can be concluded without a strong interbranch consensus, and that presidential negotiations will tend to be influenced by the disposition of the Senate.

The executive branch has established itself as the more influential branch in treaty making. As the sole organ of communication with foreign countries, commander in chief, and head of the foreign policy bureaucracy, presidents have been equipped with the means necessary to lead in most phases of the treaty-making process. The president dominates decisions concerning whether and when treaty

negotiations will be pursued. The president chooses the negotiators, develops the negotiating strategy, and submits completed draft treaties to the Senate for approval.

Moreover, the president's power to "make" treaties is interpreted as including the final power of ratification. Once the Senate has approved a treaty, it does not become law until the president ratifies it. Thus the president has significant leverage over any attempts by the Senate to amend a treaty. If the president decides to ratify a treaty the Senate has approved, an exchange of ratifications occurs between the signatories. Then the treaty is promulgated—that is, officially proclaimed to be law—by the president. At any time the president may stop the treaty-making process. Thus the president has the power of initiative over a treaty from its conception to its ratification.[42]

Creation of Treaty Power

In the eighteenth century, treaties were considered to be the primary tool of foreign policy, and the authors of the Constitution deliberated extensively on how treaties should be made. Under the Articles of Confederation, the treaty power was completely entrusted to the legislature. It selected negotiators, wrote and revised their orders, and made the final decision on whether a treaty would be accepted or rejected. At the Constitutional Convention, delegates initially assumed that this legislative power would be given to the new Congress and specifically to the Senate, which was designed to be wiser and more stable than the House. Late in the convention's deliberations, and after the executive had been made fully independent of the legislature, the convention divided the treaty-making power between the executive and the Senate.[43]

The Framers recognized that the president, as a single national officer, would be "the most fit agent" for making "preparations and auxiliary measures," for managing delicate and often secret negotiations, and for adapting to often rapidly changing circumstances. John Jay noted other advantages of a single negotiator:

> It seldom happens in the negotiation of treaties, of whatever nature, but that perfect secrecy and immediate dispatch are sometimes requisite. There may be cases where the most useful intelligence may be obtained, if the persons possessing it can be relieved from apprehensions of discovery. . . . and there doubtless are many . . . who would rely on the secrecy of the president, but who would not confide in that of the Senate, and still less in that of a large popular assembly.[44]

Similar considerations favored the exclusion of the House from treaty deliberations. Hamilton and Jay argued in *The Federalist Papers* that the Senate is favored by its smaller size, its wiser membership chosen by the "select assemblies" of the states, and the stability secured by longer and overlapping terms. These features also would encourage the Senate to focus on the long-term interests of the nation as a whole. The extraordinary majority required for treaty approval in the Senate would, it was argued, ensure that no treaty would become law without high levels of scrutiny and approval.[45]

By giving the president the power to "make" treaties "by and with the Advice and Consent of the Senate," the authors of the Constitution bolstered the prestige of the executive. They must have understood that the president's position as chief negotiator would afford him great influence over policy. However, they spoke of the Senate controlling the overall "system" of foreign policy. The Framers seemed to have expected that senatorial "Advice and Consent" would operate throughout the process and that the president would obtain "their sanction in the progressive stages of a treaty."[46]

The Constitution also strengthened the legal status of treaties. One weakness of the national government under the Articles of Confederation was its dependence on the states to implement treaties. Congress could not force the states to recognize treaty provisions as law. As a result, several states had violated certain articles of the Peace Treaty of 1783 with Great Britain. The convention's answer to this problem was Article VI, Clause 2, of the Constitution, which states that "all Treaties made, or which shall be made, under the Authority of the United States, shall be the supreme Law of the Land; and the Judges in every State shall be bound thereby, any Thing in the Constitution or Laws of any State to the Contrary notwithstanding."

Chief Justice John Marshall interpreted this clause in his opinion in *Foster v. Neilson* in 1829. He confirmed that any treaty or portion of a treaty that did not require legislation to fulfill its provisions was binding on the states and had equal force to federal law. Therefore, although Congress may have to enact legislation to carry out acts stipulated by a treaty, any self-executing treaty or part of a treaty automatically attains the status of a law, enforceable by the courts. Provisions of various treaties periodically have been the target of legal challenges, but the Supreme Court has never declared a treaty or provision of a treaty made by the United States to be unconstitutional.[47]

Presidential Primacy in Treaty Negotiations

The Constitution clearly states that both the president and the Senate have a role in treaty making, but the form of the Senate's advice on treaty matters and its influence over negotiations has changed over time.

President Washington's initial interpretation of the treaty-making clause was that "Advice" meant he was to seek Senate opinions in person before his representatives began negotiations. On August 21, 1789, Washington and his secretary of war, Henry Knox, questioned the Senate in its chambers about a treaty to be negotiated with the Creek Indians. After some debate, the Senate decided to postpone its response to Washington's questions until the following week so it could discuss the negotiations further. Washington, who had expected an immediate reply, returned on Monday, August 24, and received answers to his questions, but he was angered by the Senate's indecisiveness and pessimistic that he could rely on that body for timely consultations on treaty matters. He never again attempted to use it as an executive council before treaty negotiations. Nonetheless, during the early years of his presidency Washington conscientiously wrote to the Senate for advice on treaty matters before and during negotiations. He also routinely submitted the negotiators' instructions to the Senate and kept that body informed of the progress of talks.[48]

The Senate's role in treaty negotiations would likely have been enhanced had Washington established a precedent of consulting with that body in person. Subsequent presidents, however, agreed with Washington that the advice and consent of the Senate were best obtained from a distance. Several twentieth-century presidents, including Wilson and Truman, went to the Senate to propose or to lobby for treaties, but no president has ever returned to the Senate chamber to seek direct advice on treaty matters.

Washington's handling of the important Jay Treaty of 1794, which avoided war with Great Britain, demonstrated that he had abandoned his initial interpretation of the Constitution's treaty-making clause. In preparation for the Jay Treaty negotiations, Washington submitted only the appointment of his negotiator, Chief Justice John Jay, to the Senate for approval. He withheld from the Senate Jay's instructions about the sensitive negotiations, and the negotiations were held in London without Senate involvement.

Rather than challenging the president's power to make a treaty independently of the Senate, that body responded by amending the completed Jay Treaty in a manner similar to the method by which it amended legislation. Washington accepted the Senate's authority to do this, and after initial protests, the British ratified the amended treaty. The Jay Treaty established a process of treaty making that subsequent administrations and Senates would emulate. As Corwin observed, "The Senate's function as an executive council was from the very beginning put, and largely by its own election, on the way to absorption into its more usual function as a legislative chamber, and subsequent developments soon placed its decision in this respect beyond all possibility of recall."[49]

The often significant influence the Senate has over treaty negotiations comes more from its power to reject a treaty than from any constitutional provision that the president should consider the Senate's advice when making treaties. The Senate, or a minority thereof, can intrude into negotiations by making the conditions of its final approval quite clear. Presidents have, therefore, often cooperated closely with the Senate in the negotiation of a treaty because they recognize that Senate involvement would increase the chances for approval. Excluding the Senate from the negotiating process has often led to troubles and defeats for presidents.[50]

Moreover, Congress can use its control over other policies to influence a president's treaty negotiations. In 1983 some senators threatened to vote against funding the MX missile, a crucial piece of Ronald Reagan's defense modernization program, unless he modified his negotiating position at the Strategic Arms Reduction Talks (START) in Geneva.[51]

The Treaty-making Process

The first step in making a treaty is negotiating with a foreign power. This stage is controlled by the president and presidential advisers and representatives. During or before this phase, members of Congress may offer advice to the president or express their views on the negotiations individually or collectively. A resolution communicating Congress's disapproval may cause the president to change negotiating strategies or abandon a treaty altogether. A supportive resolution, however, may contribute to the executive branch's enthusiasm for a particular treaty. In 1948, for example, the Senate's Vandenberg Resolution, which preceded the development of NATO and other alliance systems, advised the president to negotiate regional security agreements.[52] Regardless of congressional protests or encouragement, the president and representatives of the president cannot be prevented from initiating and conducting treaty negotiations with another country.

Although the executive branch has the power to negotiate a treaty without Congress, many presidents have found that involving individual senators in the negotiating process can be a useful political tool. Such involvement can take several forms. During most treaty negotiations, influential senators are at least asked for their opinions on the proceedings, but a president also may ask senators to help select the negotiating team, observe the negotiations, follow the progress of the talks through briefings, or even be negotiators.[53] Until the end of Madison's administration in 1817, the names of treaty negotiators were referred to the Senate for confirmation. The Senate repeatedly protested subsequent presidents' neglect of that practice, but the Senate never was able to establish firmly its right to confirm negotiators.

The practice of sending the instructions of treaty negotiators to the Senate for review, which Washington had followed early in his presidency, proved to be even more temporary. After Washington's administration, no president asked the Senate to consider the terms of a treaty not yet agreed upon, until Polk submitted the skeleton of a treaty ending the war with Mexico in 1846. Preliminary drafts of treaties were sent to the Senate in a few instances by four other presidents—James Buchanan, Lincoln, Andrew Johnson, and Ulysses S. Grant. In 1919 the Senate requested a copy of the proposed Treaty of Versailles as presented to the representatives of Germany. The secretary of state replied: "The president feels it would not be in the public interest to communicate to the Senate a text that is provisional and not definite, and finds no precedent for such a procedure."[54]

President Wilson generally excluded the Senate from the Versailles treaty negotiations, and the Senate rejected this important treaty. Most later presidents grasped the obvious lesson. While World War II was still being fought, Franklin Roosevelt established the Joint Advisory Committee on Postwar Foreign Policy to provide a forum where members of Congress and the executive branch could discuss the composition of an international peace organization. This committee, along with the administration's private consultations with Senate leaders, helped create bipartisan support for the United Nations.[55] When the negotiations on the United Nations Treaty began in 1945, Truman included senators from both parties in the U.S. delegation.

The Carter administration also tried to limit Senate objections to the SALT II (Strategic Arms Limitation Talks) treaty it hoped to negotiate with the Soviet Union by encouraging senatorial participation in the process. Selected senators were allowed to observe the negotiations, and the administration consulted closely with Senate leaders while the negotiations were in progress. During these consultations, senators voiced suggestions and concerns that prompted Carter to instruct his negotiators to modify their position on several issues.[56] The Senate observers in those talks also persuaded the Soviet Union to provide crucial information on their nuclear forces by arguing that the Senate would never approve the treaty without it. In 1991 the Senate Intelligence Committee's concerns over verification procedures in the Intermediate Nuclear Forces (INF) Treaty led President George H. W. Bush to renegotiate the relevant sections.[57]

Once U.S. negotiators have agreed on the terms of a treaty with a foreign government, the president must decide whether to submit the draft to the Senate for consideration. If it appears that Senate opposition to a treaty will make approval unlikely, the president may decide to withdraw the treaty to avoid a political defeat. Also, international events may change the president's mind about the desirability of ratifying a treaty. Carter withdrew the SALT II treaty from Senate consideration to protest the Soviet invasion and occupation of Afghanistan.

If the president decides to submit a treaty to the Senate for consideration, the Constitution requires that two-thirds of the Senate vote in favor of the treaty for it to be approved. The Senate is not compelled by the Constitution either to approve or to reject a treaty as it has been negotiated by the executive branch. It may attach amendments to a treaty that require the president to renegotiate its terms with the other signatories before the Senate grants its approval. In 1978 the Senate added conditions and reservations to the treaty that provided for the transfer of the Panama Canal to Panamanian control after the year 2000. The most notable of these amendments was written by Sen. Dennis DeConcini, D-Ariz. It claimed for the United States the right to take whatever steps were necessary, including military force, to open the canal if its operations ceased.[58] The Panamanian government agreed to accept the Senate amendments without renegotiation.

Although such amendments can often make agreement between the United States and its negotiating partner difficult or impossible, presidents have little choice but to accept the Senate's power to force renegotiation of parts of a treaty. In effect, when the Senate gives its consent on condition that its amendments are accepted by the negotiating partner of the United States, it is rejecting the treaty while outlining a revision of the treaty to which it grants its consent in advance.[59] Presidents in turn may decide not to renegotiate if they believe the senatorial amendments make the treaty undesirable.

The Senate also has the power to add nonbinding written reservations to a treaty before approving it. This option can be used when the Senate accepts the basic terms of a treaty but wishes to impose its interpretation on the document and its implementation. In 1991 the Senate attached a reservation to the Treaty on Conventional Forces in Europe that stated that the United States would consider the Soviet Union's failure to fulfill its pledge to eliminate additional weapons as equivalent to a violation of the treaty.[60] In 1992 the disintegration of the Soviet Union complicated the ratification process for the first Strategic Arms Reduction Treaty (START I). President Bush had to negotiate "protocols" with the newly independent states, committing them to abide by the terms of the treaty, and the Senate then attached a reservation to the treaty stating that these protocols and all other related agreements were fully part of the treaty's formal terms.

Foreign governments may disagree with, or take offense at, such resolutions. Ratification of the 1976 Treaty of Friendship and Cooperation with Spain was delayed several months by Spanish objections to nonbinding Senate resolutions attached to the treaty. The issue was resolved by an agreement between Congress, the Ford administration, and the Spanish government to attach the resolutions to the U.S. instrument of ratification, the document outlining the U.S. understanding of the treaty, but to exclude them from the Spanish instrument of ratification and the treaty ratification document exchanged by the two countries.[61]

After the Senate approves and the president ratifies a treaty, the treaty may require legislation, such as the appropriation of funds or the enactment of criminal laws.

Because these tasks can only be accomplished by Congress, such treaties are referred to as "non-self-executing."[62] Consequently, non-self-executing treaties give Congress another chance to pass judgment on them after ratification. Although Congress rarely has chosen to undermine a treaty by refusing to appropriate funds or enact implementing legislation, its right to do so is well established.[63]

Treaty Approval

The Senate has approved without changes about 90 percent of the treaties submitted to it by presidents. This success rate is a less striking testament to presidential leadership than it may appear. Presidents regularly anticipate senatorial objections in negotiating a treaty, and they must, as in other legislative matters, make deals to gain the votes of particular senators.[64] Moreover, to avoid a political defeat, presidents often have withdrawn treaties from consideration that were in jeopardy of Senate rejection. Other treaties were neither approved nor rejected by the Senate, but instead left in political limbo. For example, the Genocide Treaty, which instructed signers to prevent and punish the crime of genocide, was approved by the Senate in 1986, almost thirty-seven years after Truman submitted it to that body. Many more pacts that could have taken the form of treaties were concluded as less formal executive agreements between the president and a foreign government to avoid the possibility of Senate rejection.

The success rate of treaties probably reflects the inclination of senators, and representatives, to follow the president's lead in foreign affairs in the interest of projecting a united front abroad. As noted, members of Congress do not wish to be seen as saboteurs of presidential policy. Moreover, Congress must balance its reservations about a particular treaty against the damage rejection would inflict on international confidence in the United States and its chief of state. Finally, even senators of the president's party who have reservations about a treaty often will side with the president for the sake of the party. If the president's party happens to be in control of the Senate, obtaining approval for a treaty may require the support of fewer than half of the senators from the opposition party.

Although the Senate's approval record has been overwhelmingly positive, there have been significant exceptions. Between 1871 and 1898, no major treaty was approved. The most famous treaty rejected by the Senate was the Treaty of Versailles, which ended World War I and established the League of Nations. In 1999 the Senate defeated the Comprehensive [Nuclear] Test Ban Treaty, which had been negotiated by President Bill Clinton. (See Table 5-1, p. 223)

The method by which Congress approves treaties has been the target of periodic criticism. John Hay, the secretary of state under McKinley and Theodore Roosevelt who fought several losing battles with the Senate over treaty approval, called the power of the Senate to veto treaties the "original mistake of the Constitution."[65] After the Senate refused to approve the Versailles treaty, proposals surfaced in both the executive and legislative branches to reduce the fraction of Senate members needed to approve a treaty from two-thirds to three-fifths or to a simple majority. Other proposals would eliminate the requirement of an extraordinary majority in the Senate and replace it with simple majority approval by both houses of Congress. Several resolutions to this effect were introduced in Congress during the 1920s and 1940s, yet none has come close to being implemented.

Termination of Treaties

Although Article VI, Clause 2, of the Constitution declares that treaties are the "supreme Law of the Land," the federal government is not legally constrained from terminating a treaty through agreement with the other party in response to the other party's violations of the treaty or for any other reason. However, the Constitution provides no guidelines about which branch determines that a treaty should be revoked and what sort of approval is needed from another branch. Consequently, both the president and Congress at various times have successfully exercised the power to terminate treaties.[66]

In 1979 this issue was brought before the Supreme Court when the Carter administration sought to terminate the 1954 Mutual Defense Treaty with the Republic of China (Taiwan) as part of the process of establishing formal relations with the People's Republic of China. The treaty had a clause permitting withdrawal, but President Carter took the action without consulting the Senate beforehand. Sen. Barry M. Goldwater, R-Ariz., and twenty-three other members of Congress brought suit to prevent Carter's unilateral termination of the treaty.

U.S. district court judge Oliver Gasch ruled in October 1979 that Carter's action violated the principle of separation of powers and that both historical precedents and the text of the Constitution indicate that treaty termination requires the consent of two-thirds of the Senate or a majority of both houses of Congress. A U.S. Court of Appeals overturned Gasch's decision. However, the Supreme Court dismissed the complaint, with five justices arguing that either this case or the issue in general was not fit for judicial resolution.[67] In 2001 the George W. Bush administration announced that the United States would withdraw from the Antiballistic Missile Treaty, so it could pursue development of a national missile defense program.

EXECUTIVE AGREEMENTS

An executive agreement is a pact other than a treaty made by the president or representatives of the president with a

TABLE 5-1 **Major Treaties Killed by the Senate, 1789–2011**

Date of vote	President	Country	Yea	Vote nay	Subject
March 9, 1825	J.Q. Adams	Colombia	0	40	Suppression of African slave trade
June 11, 1836	Jackson	Switzerland	14	23	Personal and property rights
June 8, 1844	Polk	Texas	16	35	Annexation
June 15, 1844	Polk	German Zollverein	26	18	Reciprocity
May 31, 1860	Buchanan	Mexico	18	27	Transit and commercial rights
June 27, 1860	Buchanan	Spain	26	17	Cuban Claims Commission
April 13, 1869	Grant	Great Britain	1	54	Arbitration of claims
June 1, 1870	Grant	Hawaii	20	19	Reciprocity
June 30, 1870	Grant	Dominican Republic	28	28	Annexation
January 29, 1885	Cleveland	Nicaragua	32	23	Interoceanic canal
April 20, 1886	Cleveland	Mexico	32	26	Mining claims
August 21, 1888	Cleveland	Great Britain	27	30	Fishing rights
February 1, 1889	B. Harrison	Great Britain	15	38	Extradition
May 5, 1897	McKinley	Great Britain	43	26	Arbitration
March 19, 1920	Wilson	Multilateral	49	35	Treaty of Versailles
January 18, 1927	Coolidge	Turkey	50	34	Commercial rights
March 14, 1934	F. Roosevelt	Canada	46	42	St. Lawrence Seaway
January 29, 1935	F. Roosevelt	Multilateral	52	36	World Court
May 26, 1960	Eisenhower	Multilateral	49	30	Law of the Sea Convention
March 8,1983	Reagan	Multilateral	50	42	Montreal Aviation Protocol
June 11, 1991	G.H.W. Bush	Multilateral	—	—	Annex II, international convention on load lines[a]
June 11, 1991	G.H.W. Bush	Multilateral	—	—	Amendments to Annex II, international convention on load lines[a]
October 13, 1999	Clinton	Multilateral	48	51	Comprehensive nuclear test ban

SOURCE: Lyn Ragsdale, *Vital Statistics on the Presidency*, 3d ed. (Washington, D.C.: Congressional Quarterly, 2009), Table 7-15.

NOTE: a. Not formally rejected by a roll call vote, but instead returned to the president.

foreign leader or government. The executive agreement is a particularly powerful foreign policy tool. Presidents have asserted that their power to execute the laws, command the armed forces, and function as the sole organ of foreign policy gives them the full legal authority to make these pacts without any congressional approval. Unlike treaties, they do not supersede U.S. laws with which they conflict, but in every other respect they are binding.

Although the vast majority of international pacts are executive agreements, most executive agreements either are routine extensions of existing treaties or are based on broad legislative directives.[68] Agreements made by the president to carry out legislation or treaty obligations are often called "congressional-executive international agreements." Other executive agreements have been supported by joint resolutions. Occasionally, presidents seek the approval of a majority of both houses of Congress for executive agreements when they do not have the support of two-thirds of the Senate but they do want, or need, some type of specific congressional consent. This practice has, at times, elicited strong objections from senators, but it is generally supported by partisan majorities and by the House, which is, through this procedure, given a much larger voice in foreign policy.[69] Congressional authorization and joint approval have been used frequently in areas, such as tariffs, where congressional, or House, authority is definitive.

The small percentage of agreements (about 3 percent) that do not fall under these categories are the "pure" executive agreements, which are negotiated and implemented without any congressional approval. The presidents' authority to make such agreements is usually not disputed, especially when presidents are otherwise acting within their sphere of authority and when the practical advantages of a flexible power of agreement are great. For example, the commander in chief must frequently make and alter agreements with allies during the course of a war. However, the proper scope of the president's unilateral authority to commit the nation has often been disputed. As the scope of executive agreements has broadened, these have become the most important and the most controversial pacts.

The use of executive agreements grew dramatically in the twentieth century. From 1789 to 1839, executive agreements made up only 31 percent of all international agreements, whereas more than 95 percent of international pacts made between 1980 and 1990 were executive agreements. As of 1992 the United States had entered into approximately 1,700 treaties and approximately 16,000 executive agreements.[70] Today, executive agreements are used to conduct business once reserved for treaties. Indeed, contemporary presidents can accomplish through an executive agreement almost anything that can be accomplished through a treaty. For example, President George W. Bush negotiated several free-trade agreements with "fast-track authority," which meant they could not be changed by Congress. But this authority expired in 2007, and Congress has not renewed it since.

Constitutional Dilemma

The Constitution does not prohibit executive agreements, and the Court in *United States v. Curtiss-Wright* explicitly affirmed the power of the national government to make international agreements other than treaties. However, the Founders' careful division of the treaty power in the Constitution must be interpreted as an attempt to ensure that Congress has a direct voice in making international commitments. The use of executive agreements by presidents and their representatives to avoid congressional interference has been widely regarded by constitutional scholars and members of Congress as a serious deterioration of constitutional checks and balances in the area of foreign policy.

The development of the United States into a world power with security commitments and economic interests in every corner of the world has made some degree of executive flexibility in making executive agreements desirable. Like Jefferson, who was confronted with the irresistible opportunity to buy the Louisiana Territory, contemporary presidents are sometimes faced with an international situation that calls for making commitments with speed and secrecy. Also, executive agreements often provide a simpler method of transacting the less important international business that would overload the already tight legislative schedule if treaties were used.

The crux of the problem is that some important international agreements should receive some sort of congressional approval, yet there are no concrete guidelines to indicate which pacts need Senate consent, which need approval by both houses, and which can be handled simply by the president. Presidents may, therefore, use their discretion in deciding how to make a particular agreement. Numerous presidents, faced with the prospect of fighting for two-thirds approval in the Senate, have used executive agreements to skirt the treaty requirements imposed by the Constitution rather than abandon a diplomatic initiative. Treaties, therefore, have become an exception to the rule, which is presidential policymaking.

Despite the use of executive agreements to avoid the treaty ratification process, the Supreme Court has repeatedly upheld the president's power to make international agreements without the consent of the Senate. The Court's ruling in *United States v. Belmont* in 1937 was particularly significant. At issue was the president's authority to conclude unilaterally several agreements connected with the 1933 recognition of the Soviet Union. In delivering the Court's opinion, Justice George Sutherland wrote:

> The recognition, establishment of diplomatic relations, the assignment, and agreement with respect thereto, were all parts of one transaction, resulting in an international

compact between the two governments. That the negotiations, acceptance of the assignment and agreements and understandings in respect thereof were within the competence of the president may not be doubted. Governmental power over internal affairs is distributed between the national government and the several states. Governmental power over external affairs is not distributed, but is vested exclusively in the national government. And in respect of what was done here, the Executive had the authority to speak as the sole organ of that government.[71]

Justice Sutherland could have based his opinion that the president had the authority to make these agreements on the president's indisputable power to recognize foreign governments. Although he did mention the relevance of this presidential power, he seemed to find authority for the agreements in the president's broader power as the "sole organ" of foreign policy.[72]

Landmark Executive Agreements

The first major executive agreement concluded between a president and a foreign power was the Rush-Bagot agreement with Great Britain.[73] The pact, which imposed limitations on naval forces on the Great Lakes, was concluded under the supervision of President James Monroe in 1817. A year after the agreement was put into operation, Monroe sent the agreement to the House and Senate and asked if they thought it required the consent of the Senate. The Senate endorsed the "arrangement" with a two-thirds vote but did not consider its action to be an approval of a treaty, and instruments of ratification were never exchanged between the United States and Great Britain.[74]

Although Monroe's executive agreement was significant in establishing a precedent, President John Tyler's annexation of Texas by executive agreement in 1845 was even more important, because it was the first time a president had used an executive agreement to accomplish what would have been defeated in the treaty process.[75] Tyler wished to bring Texas into the Union to keep it out of foreign hands and to serve the southern slave interests, but he was not close to having the necessary two-thirds support in the Senate to conclude a treaty of annexation. With sufficient public support for annexation, he called on Congress for a joint resolution to bring Texas into the nation. The resolution passed the House by a 120–98 vote and the Senate by a spare two-vote margin. With this annexation agreement in hand, Tyler invited Texas to become a state. In 1898 McKinley used the same method to annex Hawaii to the United States as a territory.[76]

Predictably, Theodore Roosevelt was not timid about using executive agreements to accomplish foreign policy objectives that would have been delayed or undermined by

During the eighteenth and nineteenth centuries, no president while in office traveled outside the United States. Theodore Roosevelt broke this precedent when he visited Panama in 1906 to inspect the canal under construction.

the treaty process. When Santo Domingo (now the Dominican Republic) fell into heavy debt to European creditors in 1905, Roosevelt oversaw negotiations of a treaty that extended U.S. protection to Santo Domingo and put the United States in control of collecting the country's customs to satisfy the creditors. Roosevelt hoped the Senate would consent to the draft treaty, but when it did not, he continued the arrangement under an executive agreement.[77]

At the outbreak of World War II, Franklin Roosevelt also used an executive agreement to avoid the treaty process when he provided destroyers to the British in 1940. At the time, the United States was still officially neutral, and a predominantly isolationist Senate would not have approved a treaty that provided Britain with ships to defend against German submarines. Roosevelt therefore used an executive agreement to trade old U.S. destroyers for the right to lease several British naval bases in the Western Hemisphere. Because the deal violated two neutrality statutes and altered the neutral status of the United States, it clearly should have been accompanied by some sort of congressional approval.[78]

A dramatic example of the dangers and limits of executive agreements was President Nixon's written assurance to President Nguyen Van Thieu of South Vietnam in 1973 that the United States would "respond with full force" if North Vietnam violated the Paris Peace Agreement, which ended the U.S. military presence in Vietnam. Thieu had consented to the Paris Agreement based on Nixon's personal promise. But Nixon's agreement was little more than the optimistic personal promise of a president who almost certainly would not have had the means to keep it, even if he had remained in office. Thieu, however, regarded Nixon's pledge as a national commitment, and the United States lost credibility when the promise was not kept after the North Vietnamese invaded South Vietnam in 1975.[79]

Yet Congress regularly authorizes the president to avoid the treaty clause, even for major international agreements. In 1993 and 1994 the North American Free Trade Agreement (NAFTA) and a new General Agreement on Tariffs and Trade (GATT), which comprehensively revised the nation's trade policy, were validated only by authorizing legislation passed in the House and Senate. In 2005 Congress narrowly approved the expansion of NAFTA to include the Central America Free Trade Agreement (CAFTA). It has been standard practice for more than a century for Congress to authorize the president to make tariff adjustments through executive agreements, and the House would have had a well-founded complaint if significant changes in tariff laws had been submitted only to the Senate.[80] GATT, however, went beyond the adjustment of tariffs and committed the nation's trade practices to a regime of oversight and sanction by an international body, the World Trade Organization. Even so, the loudest objections were to the agreement itself and not to the mode of approval.

Attempts to Limit Executive Agreements

Since the end of World War II, Congress has made two major attempts to control the president's power to make international agreements and secret commitments. The more intrusive one was a constitutional amendment proposed by Sen. John W. Bricker, R-Ohio, in 1953 that would have placed restraints on the president's power to make executive agreements and decreased the effect of the agreements on domestic law. The second occurred in the early 1970s and culminated in the Case Act of 1972, which was intended to compel the executive branch merely to report all executive agreements to Congress or to selected congressional committees. Except for a clarification of the Case Act passed in 1977, subsequent efforts by Congress to make the executive branch more accountable for its agreements with other nations have been unsuccessful.

Bricker Amendment

Senator Bricker, a conservative Republican, chaired the Senate Interstate and Foreign Commerce Committee for two years beginning in 1953. In the postwar era, when the United States was expanding its defense commitments and its participation in international organizations, the Brickerites argued that the president's broad power to make international agreements that are supreme over the constitutions and laws of states (see *United States v. Belmont*, 1937) threatened the constitutionally guaranteed rights of the states and the American people.[81] Moreover, many senators were alarmed by the growing tendency of presidents to use executive agreements to implement military alliance pacts and UN programs. In January 1953 Bricker and sixty-three cosponsors introduced an amendment aimed at establishing congressional review of executive agreements and making treaties unenforceable as domestic law without accompanying legislation. Two provisions of the amendment would have radically altered the way the United States enters into agreements with foreign governments. Every treaty and executive agreement would have required implementing legislation to make it enforceable as domestic law, and any executive agreement made by a president would have been subject to regulation by Congress. The ability of presidents to make foreign policy through executive agreements and to negotiate treaties without involving Congress would have been severely curtailed. The amendment did not, however, come to a vote by the time Congress adjourned in August 1953. In 1954 a milder version of the Bricker Amendment came within one vote of passing the Senate with a two-thirds majority. Thereafter, support for the amendment ebbed, in part because President Dwight D. Eisenhower strongly opposed it.

Case Act

In the early 1970s, a more modest movement surfaced in Congress to restrain the indiscriminate use of secret agreements. The impetus for this effort was the discovery by a Senate subcommittee in 1969–1970 that the executive branch had made secret commitments and terms of agreements during the 1960s. The Security Agreements and Commitments Abroad Subcommittee of the Senate Foreign Relations Committee, chaired by Sen. Stuart Symington, D-Mo., uncovered secret agreements with Ethiopia, Laos, Thailand, South Korea, Spain, the Philippines, and other countries. The Nixon administration deepened congressional resentment by concluding important executive agreements with Portugal and Bahrain about military bases. The Senate passed a resolution asserting that the agreements should have been made in the form of treaties, which would have required Senate consent.

Congress responded more generally by passing the Case Act in 1972. The act obligates the executive branch to inform Congress of all executive agreements within sixty days of their conclusion. (It also required the executive branch to inform Congress of all executive agreements in existence at the time the law was signed.) The law also provides that the House and Senate committees with jurisdiction over foreign affairs be informed of any executive agreements that the president determines need to be kept secret to ensure national security. The Senate passed the bill by a unanimous 81–0 vote and the House by voice vote.[82] The years following passage of the Case Act saw the emergence of several bills intended to establish a congressional procedure for disapproving executive agreements. Such a bill, introduced by Sen. Sam J. Ervin Jr., D-N.C., passed the Senate in 1974, but the House did not act on it. Hearings on two similar bills were held in 1975 by the Senate Judiciary Subcommittee on the Separation of Powers, but they did not lead to legislation.

After several years, Congress found that many executive agreements were not being reported under the provisions of the Case Act; executive branch officials had labeled them "understandings" rather than executive agreements. Congress reacted by passing legislation in 1977 that required Congress to be informed of any verbal or informal understanding made by any representative of the U.S. government that might constitute a commitment.

Although the Case Act and the legislation that followed it do not limit the president's power to make executive agreements, legislators are better able to check this executive branch power if they know what sort of agreements the president is making. Congress's ability to conduct investigations, issue resolutions, pass legislation, and control appropriations gives it the tools it needs to challenge and refuse to honor executive agreements it believes are unwise or improper. This is especially true of the many executive agreements that depend on supporting legislation.

THE RECOGNITION POWER

Although the Constitution does not explicitly grant presidents the power to recognize foreign governments, Congress has generally accepted that presidents have this power as a consequence of the authority to appoint (Article II, Section 2) and receive (Article II, Section 3) ambassadors. Because the acts of sending an ambassador to a country and receiving its ambassador imply recognition of the legitimacy of

President George W. Bush sent U.S. secretary of state Colin Powell (left) to meet with Israeli prime minister Ariel Sharon in April 2002 to discuss the possibility of an Israeli-Palestinian cease-fire. Israel had launched extensive military attacks on Palestinian areas following a number of suicide bombings in Israel.

the foreign government involved in the exchange, presidents have successfully claimed the general authority to decide which foreign governments will be recognized by the United States. Also, because presidents decide which nations will be recognized, it follows that they have the power to terminate relations with another nation.

This interpretation of presidential power was not universally accepted at the beginning of the Republic. Madison, writing as Helvidius, argued that the duty to receive ambassadors did not give the president the power to rule on the legitimacy of foreign governments.[83] In *The Federalist Papers,* Hamilton did not acknowledge the connection between the ceremonial power to receive ambassadors and the recognition of nations, and he may have considered recognition a power shared with the Senate. Hamilton described the power to receive ambassadors as "more a matter of dignity than of authority. It is a circumstance which will be without consequence in the administration of the government."[84]

The first use of the president's power of recognition occurred in 1793 when Washington agreed to receive Edmond Genêt, the ambassador of the new French Republic. Because most of the members of Congress who were inclined to resist the growth of executive power into areas not specifically granted in the Constitution were also supporters of the new republican regime in France, this expansion of the president's power to receive ambassadors was not questioned.[85] All subsequent presidents have assumed the right to make recognition decisions.

George Washington's decision to accept Genêt's credentials soon began to cause the president problems. Genêt attempted to exploit the American people's sympathy for revolutionary France by privately enlisting their support against his country's enemies, Great Britain and Spain. His activities undercut Washington's Proclamation of Neutrality and threatened to draw the United States into the European hostilities. Washington, therefore, demanded that the French government recall Genêt. The French ordered their ambassador to return home but retaliated by demanding that Washington recall the U.S. minister to France, Gouverneur Morris, on the grounds that he had supported plots to restore the French monarchy.[86] Washington thus established that the president could expel a foreign representative whose conduct was judged unacceptable.

A president also can recognize the rights or interests of national or political groups that do not hold political power. In 1978 Jimmy Carter announced a qualified recognition of the interests of the Palestinians living in Israeli-occupied territories by saying that any Middle East peace settlement must recognize "the legitimate rights of the Palestinian people" and "enable the Palestinians to participate in the determination of their own future."[87] After the agreement of mutual recognition between Israel and the Palestine Liberation Organization (PLO) in 1993, President Clinton and Congress moved to accept the PLO as the legitimate representative of the Palestinians by removing restrictions on, for example, its ability to establish offices in the United States.

Presidents may choose not to exercise the recognition power unilaterally. In 1836 Andrew Jackson realized that the act of recognizing the Republic of Texas could have the effect of a declaration of war against Mexico, which regarded Texas as a Mexican territory. Although Jackson did not repudiate his authority to recognize Texas or any other nation, he announced his willingness to allow Congress to decide if Texas should be recognized: "It will always be considered consistent with the spirit of the Constitution, and most safe, that it [the recognition power] should be exercised when probably leading to war, with a previous understanding with that body by whom war can alone be declared, and by whom all the provisions for sustaining its perils must be furnished."[88]

Congress has powers that it could use to influence recognition decisions. For example, it could implicitly recognize a nation by appropriating funds for the necessary diplomatic positions—and, conversely, eliminate such funding to force the president to withdraw recognition. Only rarely has Congress used its powers to influence presidential decisions. The resolution authorizing President McKinley to expel Spain from Cuba contained an explicit recognition of Cuba's independence as a nation.[89] In 1995 both houses of Congress considered bills that recognized the government in exile as the legitimate government of Tibet, which is occupied by the People's Republic of China, and mandated the appointment of a special envoy with the "personal rank" of ambassador. Otherwise, Congress has no direct role in the recognition process beyond the Senate's approval of the president's nominee for the ambassadorship, which it can refuse to grant. Yet, as with treaties, Congress can pass nonbinding resolutions concerning particular questions of recognition. After France was conquered by the Nazis in World War II, for example, the House and Senate passed resolutions supporting the Roosevelt administration's agreement with other nations in the Western Hemisphere not to allow the transfer of the sovereignty of any European colony in the Americas to another European power.

Recognition as a Policy Statement

A decision to recognize or not to recognize a nation can be a major policy statement that expresses the attitudes and intentions of the United States toward an ideology, toward the character or behavior of a nation's government, and sometimes toward an entire region. Such policy statements can have profound consequences.

For example, in 1913 President Wilson refused to recognize the Mexican regime of Victoriano Huerta on the grounds that it was immoral and did not represent the will of its people.[90] Since Wilson made this decision, the ideology and morality of a foreign regime have become accepted factors in determining whether a government should be recognized. Successive presidents refused to recognize the revolutionary communist regimes in Russia from 1917 to 1933 and in China from 1949 to 1979. President Clinton's 1995 decision to recognize the communist regime in Vietnam was controversial, and the House passed a measure barring the use of funds for an embassy in Hanoi. Closer to home, Clinton continued the policy, begun in 1959, of withholding recognition from Cuba. A president also may deny recognition of a government's legal authority over a part or all of the territory claimed by that government. For example, the United States refused to recognize the legitimacy of the Soviet Union's annexation of Latvia, Lithuania, and Estonia in 1940.

Theodore Roosevelt's recognition of Panama in 1903 after its U.S.-backed revolt from Colombia paved the way to a treaty that gave the United States the right to dig the Panama Canal. It also led to a treaty in 1921 between Colombia and the United States that provided for the United States to pay Colombia $25 million in reparations for the loss of its Panamanian territory.

Harry S. Truman's recognition of Israel on May 15, 1948, was a controversial change of policy. A few minutes after Jews in Palestine proclaimed the state of Israel, Truman rejected the advice of his State Department and made the

United States the first nation to recognize the new country. The recognition indicated U.S. support for Israel and effectively blocked a UN plan to keep Palestine under a temporary trusteeship.[91]

The president's power to sever diplomatic relations has been used as an ultimate sanction to protest another country's behavior. Severance of relations is usually reserved for situations in which the differences between the two nations are so great that there is no hope they may be resolved through normal diplomatic procedures. It is customary to break diplomatic ties with a country before declaring war against it, but many events short of war have prompted presidents to terminate relations. In 1979 President Carter ended diplomatic relations with Iran in response to the hostage crisis.

Even when relations have been broken with a particular country, communication usually continues. "Interests sections" may be established in each country's capital in the embassies of a third country. Foreign nations that lack diplomatic relations with the United States also have used their representatives to the United Nations to communicate with U.S. officials. Nevertheless, such measures do not accommodate communication between the two countries with the same efficiency as normal diplomatic exchanges. A less drastic method employed by presidents to communicate their displeasure with another nation is to temporarily recall the U.S. ambassador in that country for "consultations." President Carter used this tactic after the Soviet invasion of Afghanistan.

U.S. LEGAL RELATIONSHIP WITH TAIWAN

The repercussions for U.S. relations with Taiwan from President Jimmy Carter's recognition of the People's Republic of China (PRC) illustrated the effect a recognition decision can have on U.S. laws and relations with other nations. Successive presidents had refused to recognize the PRC since it was established in 1949. Instead, the United States recognized the Republic of China, the nationalist Chinese government that had fled to Taiwan after its defeat by the Communist Chinese armies. Growing cooperation and friendship between the United States and the PRC in the 1970s, however, made the establishment of diplomatic relations with Beijing a matter of practical importance. In December 1978 the Carter administration announced that on January 1, 1979, it intended to recognize the PRC as the "sole legal government of China."

This recognition could be accomplished only by withdrawing U.S. recognition of the Republic of China as China's legal government. Because many laws and agreements involving commercial, cultural, and security relations with other countries depend on a nation's diplomatic status, the legal framework of the U.S. relationship with Taiwan had to be rebuilt. Without new legislation establishing a special relationship with the Republic of China, the United States could not deal with Taiwan as another nation.

Consequently, Congress passed the Taiwan Relations Act in March 1979. The act was intended to ensure that normal relations would continue between Taiwan and the United States, even though the United States no longer recognized the Republic of China regime that governed the island. The legislation established the American Institute in Taiwan through which the United States would conduct relations with Taiwan. The institute was created as a private, nonprofit corporation that was authorized to enter into, execute, and enforce agreements and other transactions with Taiwan and perform consular functions for U.S. citizens. The act also authorized U.S. government employees, especially foreign service officers, to take temporary leaves of absence from their posts to work for the institute. While in Taiwan, they would not be considered U.S. government employees, but they would retain their seniority, pensions, and other benefits when they returned to work for the government. Thus the Taiwan Relations Act created a nonprofit corporation that could do virtually anything done by an embassy.

Besides creating the American Institute in Taiwan, the act recognized the validity of Taiwan domestic law, contracts entered into under Taiwan law, and all U.S. agreements and treaties with Taiwan except the 1954 Mutual Defense Treaty, which was terminated at the end of 1979. It also authorized the president to grant Taiwan's unofficial representatives in the United States diplomatic privileges and treat Taiwan as a nation with an immigration quota equal to that of the PRC. These and dozens of other provisions of the Taiwan Relations Act addressed the legal difficulties created by the withdrawal of U.S. recognition of the Republic of China.

United Nations and U.S. Foreign Policy

U.S. membership in the United Nations, and particularly in the UN Security Council, often has raised concerns about control of the nation's foreign policy. On the one hand, the UN Participation Act of 1945 assigns control over day-to-day participation in UN affairs to the president; the U.S. permanent representative to the United Nations—more commonly known as the ambassador to the United Nations—is subject to Senate approval but serves "at the pleasure of the president." On the other hand, participation in the United Nations has a potentially large effect on national policy and commitments. Unlike NATO, the United Nations, through its charter, covers peace and security around the globe, without regard to specific U.S. interests. During the cold war, the

rivalry between the United States and the Soviet Union effectively halted decision making on matters of international peace and security in the UN Security Council, with such important exceptions as the UN authorization of force in 1950 to repel North Korea's invasion of South Korea (a resolution that passed because the Soviet Union was boycotting the United Nations at the time for its refusal to seat Communist China). In the post–cold war era, however, the potential commitments of the United Nations in its humanitarian and peacekeeping roles multiplied.

The circumstances of the post–cold war era invited an expansion of U.S. participation in multilateral operations. As the United States began losing its cold war status as an essential military and economic ally, its influence even in NATO began to wane. Because fewer conflicts within and between countries had the clear global implications that once supported U.S. intervention and leadership, presidents sought different ways to maintain U.S. influence in international affairs. Yet engagement in global affairs through multilateral efforts was complicated by the inevitable tensions between national interest and alliance policy. On the one hand, a president who limits the nation's participation in UN missions to matters directly affecting U.S. interests would frustrate the global mission of the United Nations. On the other hand, broad participation in that general mission would risk the loss of national control over foreign policy.

From the start, the Clinton administration struggled with this dilemma. President Clinton began his administration with an enthusiastic endorsement of expanded use of UN missions and of broad U.S. participation in them. Given the model of his predecessor, President George H. W. Bush, who had successfully negotiated a UN Security Council resolution (this time with Soviet support) authorizing the use of force to remove Iraqi troops from Kuwait, the prospects for U.S.–UN decision making initially seemed quite promising. Many in Congress, however, criticized the general policy and attempted to limit the president's authority to involve U.S. forces in multilateral missions. Much of the criticism stemmed from the operation in Somalia to relieve the famine, which the United States joined in 1992 with broad congressional and popular support. The operation was transformed in June 1993 after twenty-three UN peacekeepers were killed by one of the warring factions. The United Nations, with President Clinton's approval, then shifted to a more ambitious mission of subduing the armed factions and rebuilding the nation's political order. As a consequence, eighteen U.S. Rangers were killed and eighty were wounded in an assault on one faction's headquarters. The ensuing debates over this operation revolved around the degree to which the United States should involve itself in policing the world in the absence of clear and substantial national security interests.[92] These concerns were reinforced by Clinton's commitments to UN efforts in Haiti and Bosnia.

In late 1993 Congress forced the Clinton administration to set a deadline for the use of funds for the operation and required U.S. forces to remain under U.S. operational command.[93] In response to these and other criticisms and proposals, the Clinton administration announced more restrictive policy guidelines for U.S. participation in UN missions and especially those that may involve combat. Specifically, such missions must involve national interests or "a real threat to international peace and security." Nonetheless, the Clinton administration defended UN missions as effective and as an important part "of our national security policy" and argued that congressional proposals would be an imprudent and unconstitutional intrusion on the president's foreign policy and war powers.[94] Yet after the Somalia debacle, the United States steered clear of enmeshing itself in UN commitments, as was evident with its

refusal to support a resolution authorizing force to halt the genocide in Rwanda in 1994. Much of Clinton's second term was devoted to persuading Congress to stop withholding U.S. dues owed to the United Nations. Critics in Congress were angry over the misuse of UN funds, the expanding UN peacekeeping role in violent conflicts, and the removal of the United States from the UN Human Rights Commission.

In 2001 the UN support for a united campaign against international terrorism initially helped to sway opinions in Congress, which acted on bills authorizing payments of dues that had been held up for years. But the George W. Bush administration came into conflict with the United Nations in 2002–2003, when it again sought Security Council endorsement of military force against Iraq, this time because of Iraqi leader Saddam Hussein's failure to comply with arms inspections. Although the Security Council passed a resolution calling for "serious consequences" if Hussein did not comply, it could not reach agreement on a second resolution that explicitly authorized force. Consequently, the United States went to war against Iraq in 2003 without UN backing, though several UN members expressed their support for and participated in the military action. After this heated and highly divisive dispute with the UN over Iraq, the Bush administration pressed strongly in its second term for UN reform to make the organization more efficient and effective, but to no avail. The Obama administration demonstrated greater willingness to work through the UN to build multilateral support for its policies, as illustrated by its successful negotiation of a Security Council resolution in March 2011 to authorize international air strikes against Libyan military forces to halt their attacks on rebels. Indeed, Obama faced criticism for seeking UN authorization but not congressional approval to take military action against Libya, though the United States soon transferred responsibility for the operation to NATO.

Mutual Security Agreements

Mutual security agreements raise issues similar to those raised by the UN charter. Following World War II, the U.S. policy of containing communist expansion, backed by U.S. military strength, led presidents to offer security commitments and alliance partnerships to countries worried about their ability to defend themselves. Although they have improved relations with many countries, extended U.S. global influence, and strengthened U.S. defenses, these alliances have been politically contentious because such commitments risk drawing the nation into war.

Since World War II, presidents often have entered alliances without formal action by Congress. On August 14, 1941, for example, President Franklin Roosevelt signed the Atlantic Charter, which laid the groundwork for an Anglo-American alliance once the United States had entered World War II. Roosevelt then signed the Declaration by United Nations on January 1, 1942, which pledged the United States and, by the end of the war, forty-five other nations to support the Allied war effort and not make a separate peace with the enemy nations.[95] After the war, Presidents Truman and Eisenhower used executive agreements to expand NATO into a unified defense organization with a standing military structure. Although no formal alliance treaty exists between the United States and Israel, presidents since Truman have maintained the extensive U.S. commitment to Israeli security.

Because alliance disputes may affect the probability and effectiveness of future cooperation, the president is compelled to consider the effect of U.S. foreign and military policy on the cohesion of the nation's alliances and on public opinion within the allied countries. Even when a foreign policy action does not directly involve an alliance, a president must weigh its effect on allied countries. The concerns of Presidents Johnson and Nixon that other U.S. allies would see abandonment of South Vietnam as evidence of U.S. inability to fulfill its commitments contributed to the escalation of U.S. involvement and their refusal to withdraw U.S. troops from Vietnam without attempting to ensure South Vietnamese security.

The United States has been the dominant military power in every alliance it has joined since World War II. As the need for the U.S. deterrent waned with the disintegration of the Soviet Union and the Warsaw Pact, the U.S. influence in alliances weakened. In the absence of an overriding interest in mutual defense, the allies have experienced more conflicts between national interests and alliance cohesion. Although the United States is still the most influential partner, its influence has been further diminished by the development of the European Union.

Insofar as a president can persuade allies to support U.S. foreign policies, alliances can enhance the president's domestic power. However, failure to gain cooperation can be costly, and alliance responsibilities can harm rather than enhance presidential prestige and influence. Congress is less likely to challenge the foreign policy of a president who is perceived as an effective international leader. But a president who has not been able either to deliver allied support for U.S. policies or to ensure that alliance policy serves U.S. interests will face greater congressional criticism and intrusion. President Clinton's policies in Somalia, Haiti, Bosnia, and Kosovo were criticized for serving alliance interests ahead of national interests. President Obama's decision to wage military action in Libya under UN, and then NATO, auspices, faced similar criticism, and the U.S. House of Representatives later rejected a symbolic measure to support the president's action, though it also defeated an effort by some members to cut off funding for the operation.

POWER TO APPOINT DIPLOMATIC PERSONNEL

Article II, Section 2, of the Constitution states that the president shall "nominate and, by and with the Advice and Consent of the Senate, shall appoint Ambassadors, other public Ministers and Consuls." The power to appoint, and the power to remove, those individuals who will communicate directly with foreign leaders is crucial in establishing the president as the sole organ of foreign communications. The success of a president's foreign policy program depends greatly on the personalities and abilities of the people who fill important diplomatic and advisory posts.

Although the president appoints officials, Congress has the constitutional power to create offices. Nevertheless, presidents have used executive orders to create the government bodies that required them to make appointments. Kennedy established the Peace Corps in this manner, and Gerald R. Ford unilaterally created the Committee on Foreign Intelligence and the Intelligence Oversight Board.[96] In 2001 President George W. Bush created the Office of Homeland Security in the Executive Office of the President and appointed its first director. One year later Congress and the president approved the creation of a new cabinet agency, the Department of Homeland Security.

Senate confirmation of presidential nominees for diplomatic posts is usually routine, but there have been exceptions. For example, Eisenhower's appointment of Charles E. Bohlen as ambassador to the Soviet Union barely survived the confirmation vote, even though Eisenhower's party controlled the Senate.[97] In 1985 and 1986 Sen. Jesse Helms, R-N.C., held up the confirmations of some nominees to protest either the nominee or some related matter of policy, and in 1990 Helms's opposition led to the withdrawal or rejection of two of President George H. W. Bush's nominees. In 1989 President Bush faced wider congressional criticism for a slate of nominees that included many who were notable not for diplomatic experience but for having made large contributions to his campaign and the Republican Party.[98] In 1994 a GOP filibuster led by Sen. Robert C. Smith, R-N.H., prevented President Clinton from appointing Sam Brown as U.S. ambassador to the Conference on Security and Cooperation in Europe. In 2005 Senate divisions over the appointment of John R. Bolton as ambassador to the United Nations prompted President George W. Bush to make a recess appointment, and Bolton subsequently resigned in December 2006, as his appointment was about to expire.

Political Appointees versus the Foreign Service

A question that complicates the diplomatic appointments of contemporary presidents is how to divide ambassadorships and important State Department posts between political appointees and the State Department's career foreign service officers. Senior foreign service officers can offer a president valuable diplomatic experience that can prevent foreign policy mistakes. Also, because they serve successive presidents, they can provide continuity in foreign policy between administrations.[99] Yet presidents often have been reluctant either to waste a source of political rewards or to entrust important ambassadorships and assistant secretary posts to foreign service officers. Because their careers do not depend on the president but on a self-run promotion system, and because many regard foreign policy as an endeavor that should not be subject to partisan politics, foreign service officers have a greater reputation for resisting presidential policies than do political appointees, who are more likely to be politically minded and to appreciate how their jobs fit into the president's domestic and foreign policy goals.

Symbolism and Politics of Appointments

Presidents must take into account more than a candidate's abilities and qualifications when making an appointment. Appointments provide the president with an opportunity to indicate to Congress, the American people, and foreign governments the foreign policy goals the new administration intends to pursue. Ronald Reagan's appointment of conservative Jeane Kirkpatrick as ambassador to the United Nations reaffirmed his intention to make anticommunism a foreign policy theme of his administration, just as Jimmy Carter had underscored his commitment to human rights and developing country issues with his appointment of Andrew Young, an African American civil rights activist, to the same post. In 1986 President Reagan indicated his administration's attitude toward South Africa's racial policies by appointing an African American diplomat, Edward Perkins, as U.S. ambassador to that country.

At times, presidents use appointments to broaden their base of support within their party or to create an atmosphere of bipartisanship. Kennedy tried to disarm potential congressional resistance to his policies by appointing Republicans to senior foreign policy posts. In 1997 President Clinton hoped for a similar result from the appointment of a Republican, former senator William S. Cohen, as secretary of defense.[100] While President George W. Bush made diverse appointments from within the Republican Party, he also placed many longtime personal advisers in top cabinet positions in his second term, notably Condoleezza Rice (foreign policy adviser to Bush during the 2000 presidential campaign and national security adviser in his first presidential term) as secretary of state.

Presidential Envoys

Many presidents have used personal emissaries not subject to Senate confirmation to carry out diplomatic missions. The use of personal envoys allows presidents to inject their own ideas and proposals directly into negotiations without having to go through the State Department or other official channels in which policy could be opposed or compromised. The presence of a personal envoy sent by the president sometimes can stimulate stalemated negotiations by lending greater prestige to the talks and demonstrating the president's interest in them. Presidential representatives also can provide the president with an additional source of information that is relatively free of institutional biases.

The use of presidential envoys is not specifically allowed or disallowed in the Constitution; they fall somewhere between ambassadors and treaty negotiators.[101] Their utility was evident early on. In 1791 Gouverneur Morris, who held no public office at the time, carried out important negotiations with the British at President Washington's direction. By using a personal representative, Washington could explore the possibilities for a treaty without having to involve Congress or deal with the formalities of official treaty negotiations.

The first major controversy over the appointment of diplomats not confirmed by the Senate occurred in 1813, when Madison sent a delegation to the negotiations that produced the Treaty of Ghent, which ended the War of 1812 with Great Britain. The president had dispatched the negotiators without submitting their names for confirmation by the Senate, which was in recess. Madison's critics argued that he could not appoint ministers to offices that had not been authorized by Congress and that the appointments were illegal because the Senate did not have the chance to approve them. The president responded by claiming that it was unnecessary for Congress to create a diplomatic post if the president determined that a need had arisen for one, and that the president was free to fill any vacancy that happened to occur during a congressional recess.[102] Since Madison's time, however, Congress has enacted legislation that gives it control over the creation of new ambassadorships.

Many presidents have used special envoys or personal representatives instead of ambassadors for specific diplomatic tasks. In 1831 Jackson sent unconfirmed representatives to Turkey to conclude a trade and navigation treaty, and in 1893 Cleveland gave his own emissary, J. H. Blount, "paramount authority" over the Senate-approved resident minister in Honolulu at talks on the annexation of Hawaii.[103] Two twentieth-century presidents, Wilson and Franklin Roosevelt, established the use of personal representatives as a common diplomatic device of the president. Wilson made extensive use of his close friend Col. Edward M. House to perform diplomatic missions in Europe before and during World War I. Harry L. Hopkins, Franklin Roosevelt's personal aide, helped to negotiate and direct the lend-lease agreements under which the United States supplied war materiel to Great Britain and other countries at war with Germany. Early in his first administration, President Reagan used Philip C. Habib as a special envoy to the Middle East to negotiate settlements of the conflict in Lebanon between Israel, Syria, and the Palestine Liberation Organization.

Former president Carter was a curious variation on the special envoy. Carter had presented himself publicly as a willing mediator who could resolve the diplomatic deadlocks with North Korea about its nuclear weapons program and Haiti about the return of its democratically elected government. In accepting Carter as an envoy, President Clinton seemed unwilling to take responsibility for missing a chance to resolve the disputes and avoid armed conflict, even though Carter had clearly demonstrated a willingness to publicize his criticisms of the president's policies and to negotiate settlements that contradicted those policies. More regularly, such unsolicited offers are ignored or rebuffed.

SUMMIT MEETINGS

Although presidents have always been responsible for the conduct of diplomacy, they rarely met personally with foreign leaders until World War II. The difficulties of travel, the isolated location of the United States, and the traditional belief that presidents should stay close to their administrative and legislative responsibilities in the capital inhibited presidents from acting as their own negotiators. Today, if a president were to avoid meetings with leaders of foreign governments, the press and public alike would criticize the chief of state as being uninterested in international affairs, or even isolationist. Presidents have found that a highly publicized summit tends to raise their public approval rating. *(See "Presidential Popularity," p. 55, in Chapter 2.)*

Winston Churchill is credited with coining the term *summit.* In 1953 he used the word when he called for a conference between the leaders of the Soviet Union and the Western powers. The media picked up the term and used it to describe the Geneva conference between Soviet and Western leaders in 1955. After Geneva, meetings between national leaders increasingly were referred to as *summits.*[104] The term is used to distinguish meetings that are actually attended by the recognized leaders of states from meetings between foreign ministers or lower-level officials.

Presidential Diplomacy

Although presidential travel to foreign nations was impractical before the twentieth century, presidents throughout U.S. history have conducted personal diplomacy with foreign leaders through direct exchanges of letters. Personal letters between leaders were able to accomplish some of the goals of the modern summit meeting. They gave a president the chance to send and receive information, ideas, and proposals without using intermediaries and to establish trust through personal rapport with a foreign leader. Presidential letters were especially important to early presidents, who did not have the benefit of an extensive diplomatic network with representatives in many foreign capitals. President Jefferson, whose years as secretary of state under Washington had provided him with extensive diplomatic experience, had

Hoping to stimulate arms control negotiations, President Ronald Reagan and Soviet leader Mikhail Gorbachev meet for the first time at a summit in Geneva in November 1985. Four years later at a summit in Malta, Gorbachev met with President George H. W. Bush, acknowledging the end of the cold war.

an ongoing correspondence with Czar Alexander I of Russia during the Napoleonic wars.[105]

Early presidents also met with foreign emissaries who traveled to the United States. The first high-ranking official of a foreign government to visit the United States was a personal emissary of the ruler of Tunis who came to America in 1805 to discuss the passage of U.S. commercial ships in the Mediterranean. The marquis de Lafayette, who had led colonial troops against the British in the American Revolution, was the first official guest to be invited to the United States by the U.S. government. President Monroe received him in 1824 after he arrived on an American ship that Congress had dispatched to France.[106] During the rest of the nineteenth century, visits to the United States by foreign dignitaries were common. Visits by the heads of state of other nations, however, remained rare. Up to the end of World War I, presidents had received only about thirty heads of state.[107]

Presidential Travel

During the eighteenth and nineteenth centuries, a precedent developed that presidents would not travel outside the country during their term. Theodore Roosevelt became the first president to break this precedent when he visited

FDR made a series of trips overseas to confer with Allied leaders about military strategy and postwar issues. In February 1945 an ailing Roosevelt meets with Winston Churchill and Joseph Stalin at Yalta in the Crimea.

Panama in 1906 to inspect the canal under construction. Presidential travel abroad remained uncommon until Franklin Roosevelt made a series of trips to Canada and overseas to confer with Allied leaders about military strategy and the composition of the postwar world. Truman followed Roosevelt's example by attending the Potsdam Conference in 1945 with Joseph Stalin and Winston Churchill (and, later, Clement R. Attlee).

President Eisenhower, however, broadened the role of the president as international diplomat with his 22,000-mile "Quest for Peace" tour of eleven nations in 1959. He believed that establishing goodwill toward the United States in foreign nations was an important presidential function. Accordingly, many of his stops in foreign countries were devoted to ceremony and speech making. Since Eisenhower, presidential visits abroad have been an accepted part of the president's job and have been highly coveted by the leaders of foreign nations. President Kennedy met with Premier Nikita Khrushchev in Vienna in 1961 and toured Europe in 1963, at which time he delivered his famous "Ich bin ein Berliner" speech. President Johnson initially declined taking trips abroad because he had no vice president, but after the election in 1964 his trips included visits to Australia, the Philippines, Vietnam, and Latin America. Nixon embarked on a major European tour in 1969 only a month after he became president. In 1972 he became the first U.S. president to visit the People's Republic of China, which was in itself a momentous change in U.S. policy. All of the more recent presidents have met frequently with foreign leaders overseas to discuss arms control, economic policy, environmental issues, and other common concerns. President Obama traveled abroad more in his first six months as president than his five predecessors, visiting countries in Europe and the

Middle East as well as nations closer to home, such as Canada and Mexico.[108] The awarding of the 2009 Nobel Peace Prize to Obama was widely viewed as a sign of international confidence in his diplomatic abilities and potential.

Constitutional Questions

The Constitution clearly establishes the president's right to conduct diplomatic negotiations personally. A more controversial constitutional question about summit meetings was whether a president traveling abroad could properly fulfill the obligations of office.

In 1972 Richard Nixon became the first U.S. president to visit the People's Republic of China. Here he is greeted by Chinese Communist Party chairman Mao Zedong.

No one questioned the constitutionality of Theodore Roosevelt's short trip to Panama in 1906 or of William Howard Taft's meeting with the Mexican president just across the border in 1909. When President Wilson announced in late 1918 that he planned to go to Europe to attend the peace conference in Versailles, however, numerous critics objected that Wilson's safety could not be ensured and that he would lose touch with the everyday business of his office during the lengthy Atlantic crossing.[109]

Resolutions were introduced in both houses of Congress that would have declared the presidency vacant and required the vice president to assume the president's powers if Wilson left the country. Former president Taft, however, argued in an article in the *Washington Post* on December 5, 1918, that the president could properly fulfill the duties of his office while overseas. He wrote: "There is no constitutional inhibition, express or implied, to prevent the president's going abroad to discharge a function clearly given him by the Constitution. That instrument says that he shall make treaties. . . . It is a curious error to assume that the president himself may not attend a conference to which he can send a delegate."[110] Wilson's critics continued to attack the wisdom of his policy, but the congressional resolutions against Wilson's trip never got out of committee.[111]

Today, presidents travel with large staffs and stay in constant touch with administration and congressional officials. They have the means to carry out virtually any presidential function from any place in the world.

Superpower Summitry

The era of nuclear confrontation between the two superpowers, the United States and the Soviet Union, and their allies, made summits an unavoidable, if not always effective, mode of presidential diplomacy. (*See Table 5-2, this page.*) As former president Nixon argued, developing mutual understandings between the superpowers of their respective interests and patterns of behavior was the primary purpose of a superpower summit. These understandings, which he called "rules of engagement," could not resolve differences between the two countries or end their adversarial relationship; rather, they would reduce the possibility that a crisis would lead to war.[112]

Every president from Franklin Roosevelt to George H. W. Bush met with a Soviet leader at least once. Some meetings, such as the summits in Moscow in 1972, Vienna in 1979,

TABLE 5-2 **U.S.-Soviet Summit Meetings, 1945–1991**

Date	Location	Leaders	Topic
July–August 1945	Potsdam, Germany	President Harry S. Truman, Soviet leader Josef Stalin, British prime ministers Winston Churchill and Clement R. Attlee	Partition and control of Germany
July 1955	Geneva	President Dwight D. Eisenhower, Soviet leader Nikolai A. Bulganin, British prime minister Anthony Eden, French premier Edgar Faure	Reunification of Germany, disarmament, European security
September 1959	Camp David, Md.	President Dwight D. Eisenhower, Soviet leader Nikita S. Khrushchev	Berlin problem
May 1960	Paris	President Dwight D. Eisenhower, Soviet leader Nikita S. Khrushchev, French president Charles de Gaulle, British prime minister Harold Macmillan	U-2 incident
June 1961	Vienna	President John F. Kennedy, Soviet leader Nikita S. Khrushchev	Berlin problem
June 1967	Glassboro, N.J.	President Lyndon B. Johnson, Soviet leader Aleksei N. Kosygin	Middle East
May 1972	Moscow	President Richard Nixon, Soviet leader Leonid I. Brezhnev	SALT I, antiballistic missile limitations
June 1973	Washington, D.C.	President Richard Nixon, Soviet leader Leonid I. Brezhnev	Détente
June–July 1974	Moscow and Yalta	President Richard Nixon, Soviet leader Leonid I. Brezhnev	Arms control
November 1974	Vladivostok, Russia	President Gerald R. Ford, Soviet leader Leonid I. Brezhnev	Arms control
June 1979	Vienna	President Jimmy Carter, Soviet leader Leonid I. Brezhnev	SALT II
November 1985	Geneva	President Ronald Reagan, Soviet leader Mikhail Gorbachev	Arms control, U.S.-Soviet relations
October 1986	Reykjavik, Iceland	President Ronald Reagan, Soviet leader Mikhail Gorbachev	Arms control
December 1987	Washington, D.C.	President Ronald Reagan, Soviet leader Mikhail Gorbachev	Intermediate Nuclear Forces (INF) Treaty, Afghanistan
May 1988	Moscow	President Ronald Reagan, Soviet leader Mikhail Gorbachev	Arms control, human rights
December 1988	New York	President Ronald Reagan, Soviet leader Mikhail Gorbachev	U.S.-Soviet relations
December 1989	Malta	President George H. W. Bush, Soviet leader Mikhail Gorbachev	Arms control, eastern Europe
May–June 1990	Washington, D.C.	President George H. W. Bush, Soviet leader Mikhail Gorbachev	Arms control
September 1990	Helsinki	President George H. W. Bush, Soviet leader Mikhail Gorbachev	Middle East crisis
July 1991	Moscow	President George H. W. Bush, Soviet leader Mikhail Gorbachev	Arms control and Soviet economic and political future

Washington in 1987, and Moscow in 1991, were the culmination of the arms control process at which an agreement was signed. At other meetings, such as the 1985 Geneva summit, the 1986 Reykjavik summit, and the 1989 Malta summit, the leaders hoped to stimulate arms control negotiations. The media and public attention that accompanied these meetings was inspired by hopes that they could produce an agreement or understanding that would reduce the chances of nuclear war and lead to a more cooperative coexistence.

The 1989 Malta summit meeting between President George H. W. Bush and Soviet leader Mikhail Gorbachev marked a dramatic change in the nature of U.S.-Soviet relations and summit meetings. Gorbachev had allowed, and even encouraged, the independence movements in Soviet bloc countries, and at this meeting the two leaders acknowledged the end of the cold war. Later summit meetings focused on advancing arms reduction treaties and normalizing relations. The 1994 meeting between President Bill Clinton and Russian president Boris Yeltsin, and the 2001 meeting between President George W. Bush and Russian president Vladimir Putin, were like ordinary bilateral meetings between the president and the head of an allied country.

Evaluating Summit Diplomacy

Although in the current era summit diplomacy is being used less and for less critical matters than during the cold war, presidents may be tempted to continue to use summits, at the very least to focus attention on their world status and foreign policy leadership. Diplomatic historian Elmer Plischke cites some advantages of summit meetings that can enhance conventional diplomacy. By becoming personally acquainted, a president and a foreign leader may reduce tensions, clarify national interests, and establish mutual respect. Diplomatic impasses may be overcome by shifts in policy that only the top leaders are empowered to make. Summits also allow presidents to focus national attention on specific issues and to improve public understanding of them. And, of course, successful summits can enhance the image of the president and of the United States.[113] However, after his 1995 meeting with Russian president Yeltsin, President Clinton was criticized by members of Congress for failing to secure changes in Russian policies that opposed the inclusion of eastern European nations in NATO and favored aiding Iran's nuclear development program.

Indeed, there are some disadvantages and risks in using summit meetings rather than conventional diplomacy. For example, the potential for a summit to produce a quick breakthrough in stalemated negotiations also bears the risk that a summit can lead to a hasty, imprudent agreement or commitment. Moreover, an inexperienced or inadequately prepared president can harm relations with other countries or inadvertently undermine U.S. interests. Frequent summits also may harm the morale of professional diplomats if they perceive that their talents are being ignored in favor of direct presidential negotiations.[114] The media attention given summits may distort their substance or lead to popular disillusionment by raising public expectations of improved relations with another country beyond what is warranted. A summit, therefore, is a special diplomatic environment with opportunities and pitfalls. In recent years the term "summit meeting" typically applies to any meeting between the president and another head of state, or group of heads of state, and the president's staff highlights the important communications between leaders, even if they do not result in immediate substantive policy changes. When conflicts with other nations make direct diplomacy difficult, presidents may sometimes ask former presidents to intercede on their behalf. Former president Carter served as an envoy to Haiti and North Korea in 1994 on behalf of President Clinton.

In the post–cold war era, economic and other nonsecurity summits have become an increasingly common venue for American presidents to meet their international counterparts and seek progress on issues of common concern. The Group of 20 (G-20), an organization of industrialized and developing countries that was established in the late 1990s to address global financial challenges, began hosting regular summit meetings in response to the economic crisis of the late 2000s. (It has superseded the G-7, a group of seven industrialized countries—later eight, when Russia was invited to join after the cold war—that met annually to address common financial and social concerns.) To date, these meetings have not achieved the far-reaching changes of the 1944 Bretton Woods conference, which established the post–World War II international monetary order. A 2009 conference sponsored by the United Nations produced a statement about the challenges of climate change, but it did not impose any binding commitments on states for reducing carbon emissions.

MANAGER OF THE FOREIGN POLICY BUREAUCRACY

The president's management of the foreign policy bureaucracy is less visible than the president's performance as a diplomat, but it is as important to the success of U.S. foreign policy. The "foreign policy bureaucracy" loosely refers to all executive branch personnel whose primary duties pertain to foreign affairs. Almost every department and agency has employees engaged in activities that affect foreign relations, but the State Department, the Defense Department, the Joint Chiefs of Staff, the intelligence agencies, the National Security Council, and the National Security Council staff dominate the foreign policymaking process. Other agencies, such as the Arms Control and Disarmament Agency (ACDA) and the Agency for International Development (AID), deal with specific aspects of foreign policy.

Although the president is responsible for the conduct of foreign affairs, modern foreign policy cannot be made by one person. Policy results from a process of consultation and compromise among the president and the president's top foreign affairs advisers. Moreover, the lower levels of the administration perform functions that are essential to the success of foreign policy. Presidents Kennedy and Nixon preferred to base their decisions on the advice of a small, close-knit group of advisers, but even presidents such as these need an administrative apparatus to collect information and intelligence, research policy problems, plan for long-range contingencies, represent the United States abroad, and implement presidential directives. A president can attend to only a few of the most pressing matters at one time, and so others must oversee the vast array of daily functions.

It is not only the complexity of this administrative and policy network that makes foreign policy management a massive and continuous presidential headache. Different departments, such as State and Defense, have competing concerns and different modes of operation. As well, more permanent civil servants, such as foreign service officers, tend to resist the president's policy initiatives and to ignore his momentary political needs. Faced with a welter of management problems, each new president reorganizes the policy and administrative structure in the often vain hope of achieving tight control and coherence.

Expansion of the Foreign Policy Bureaucracy

During Washington's administration, the foreign policy bureaucracy consisted of the secretary of state, a small group of clerks, and a few carefully chosen ambassadors to key European states. Although U.S. contacts with other nations expanded during the next hundred years, the foreign policy

OVERSIGHT OF INTELLIGENCE ACTIVITIES

Because of the need for secrecy, the National Security Act of 1947 gave the president nearly exclusive responsibility for oversight of covert intelligence activities. Before the mid-1970s, Congress rarely investigated covert operations, and the president and the intelligence agencies did not willingly offer information about them. Congress routinely approved billions of dollars in funds for the intelligence community with only a few members of its appropriations committees knowing how the money was being spent.

In the mid-1970s, numerous instances of unethical, unauthorized, and illegal activities by the Central Intelligence Agency (CIA) and other intelligence units were uncovered by congressional investigations. Among other abuses, the CIA was involved in the bloody overthrow of the Socialist government in Chile. In addition, the Federal Bureau of Investigation (FBI) and other intelligence agencies conducted illegal surveillance operations and engaged in other activities that violated the civil liberties of individual Americans.

In response, Congress passed a series of laws that created House and Senate intelligence committees and strengthened congressional oversight of intelligence activities. The Hughes-Ryan Amendment to the 1974 foreign aid bill and the 1980 Intelligence Oversight Act required that the president report all U.S. covert intelligence operations to designated congressional committees in a timely fashion. To complement Congress's actions, President Gerald R. Ford established the Intelligence Oversight Board, a three-member White House panel to oversee intelligence activities and report any questions of illegality to the president through the attorney general.

The 1990s revealed a different defect. In 1994 Aldrich H. Ames, a high-level CIA officer, was arrested on charges of selling classified information to the Soviet Union and, later, Russia. Over the course of nine years, Ames had passed on thousands of documents, compromising more than one hundred intelligence operations and probably leading to the assassinations of a number of double agents working for the United States. The Ames case exposed the inadequacies in the

CIA's internal security procedures. Ames's evident drinking problem and his lavish lifestyle, funded by the sales of state secrets, were either not noticed or not investigated. When the CIA director, R. James Woolsey, failed to dismiss any of the negligent officers, Congress intervened.

Citing the CIA's "gross negligence," Congress in 1994 began investigating CIA operations with an eye toward remedies for immediate and long-term problems. The White House argued that intelligence matters ought to be handled within the executive branch, and President Bill Clinton issued a directive that incorporated many of the reform proposals being considered by Congress. Nonetheless, Congress passed, and Clinton signed into law, the Counterintelligence and Security Enhancements Act of 1994 which overhauled the process of internal investigations. The law gave government investigators greater access to the financial and travel records of CIA personnel and turned investigations of all security breaches over to the FBI.

This law also established the blue-ribbon Commission on the Roles and Capability of the United States Intelligence Community, but its 1996 report recommended no major reforms. Troubles continued, nonetheless, as FBI agent Robert P. Hanssen was arrested in 2001 for selling highly classified information to Moscow. His criminal activities had gone undetected by either the FBI or the CIA for fifteen years. His revelations undermined major intelligence and national security operations and led to the assassination of at least one double agent.

In the aftermath of the September 11, 2001, terrorist attacks, a special bipartisan commission (popularly known as the 9/11 Commission) proposed the most significant intelligence reform since the creation of the CIA after World War II. The Intelligence Reform and Terrorism Prevention Act of 2004 created an Office of the Director of National Intelligence (DNI) to coordinate intelligence gathering among the various agencies and report directly to the president. The goal was to centralize the information flow to the president while also ensuring congressional accountability for the DNI.

apparatus of the executive branch remained small. In addition, the low salaries of diplomats and the practice of appointing wealthy campaign contributors and party functionaries to diplomatic posts hindered the development of a professional diplomatic corps.[115] At the end of the nineteenth century, the United States began to upgrade the quality and status of its diplomats to correspond with the nation's growing involvement in international trade and politics. Presidents increasingly relied on the State Department for information, analysis, and staff support.

With the advent of World War II and the emergence of the United States as a superpower with broad international responsibilities, presidents needed greater bureaucratic resources to support their foreign policy decision making. The United States was an international leader and the protector of the free world. In the postwar years, it entered into numerous alliances and mutual defense agreements, distributed massive amounts of military and economic aid, hosted the United Nations, and actively participated in most international organizations. The nation's and the president's foreign policy responsibilities proliferated. An expanded bureaucracy was required to administer the growing number of U.S. programs and activities overseas and to provide the president with the information and analysis needed to construct effective foreign policies.

As a result, the State Department increased in size, and other departments and agencies were created or expanded to provide military, economic, scientific, and intelligence-gathering expertise that the State Department was not equipped to provide. The State Department thus became one player among many in the field of foreign policy. Nevertheless, it has remained the president's primary instrument of negotiation with foreign countries and an important source of information, analysis, and advice on foreign relations.

In 1949 Congress created the Defense Department by unifying the individual armed services. Although the United States demobilized rapidly after World War II, North Korea's invasion of South Korea in 1950 and the growing Soviet threat convinced U.S. leaders that, for the first time in American history, the country needed a large standing military.[116] The size of the unified military budget and the number of people in the armed services ensured that the civilian and military leaders of the new Defense Department would have considerable bureaucratic clout. Moreover, foreign policy had become more thoroughly intertwined with defense and national security. Containing Soviet expansionism, forming and maintaining anticommunist alliances, and remaining ahead in the nuclear arms race were among the most important international goals of the United States. Defense officials consequently became important players in foreign policy decision making. *(See "Department of Defense," p. 284, in Chapter 6.)*

Moscow's aggressive use of its intelligence apparatus and the difficulty of extracting information from the closed Soviet society by conventional means seemed to demand a similar intelligence effort by the United States. The National Security Act of 1947 created the Central Intelligence Agency (CIA) to gather and analyze information from every corner of the globe and to provide the president with a covert operations capability. The intelligence community comprises the CIA, the Defense Intelligence Agency, the intelligence offices of the individual armed services, the State Department's Bureau of Intelligence and Research, the Federal Bureau of Investigation, and the massive National Security Agency, which intercepts and analyzes communication signals. The director of central intelligence was given preeminent status in the intelligence community, with primary responsibility for coordinating intelligence activities and advising the president on intelligence matters. *(See box, Oversight of Intelligence Activities, p. 237.)*

In 2004 Congress enacted the most significant intelligence reform since World War II, responding to the report of the 9/11 Commission that had examined intelligence gathering before the September 11, 2001, attacks. Congress created the Office of the Director of National Intelligence to be responsible for coordinating information from the myriad different intelligence agencies within the federal government, including the CIA, and advising the president accordingly. The Director of National Intelligence (DNI) is the president's principal adviser for intelligence and oversees the president's daily briefings. Through collecting, reviewing, and coordinating data from individual agencies, the DNI is supposed to assist diplomacy by ensuring that the president has all available information about current security and counterterrorism concerns.

National Security Council

The 1947 National Security Act also established the National Security Council (NSC) as a means of coordinating the increasingly elaborate array of agencies involved in national security policy. The NSC's responsibility is "to advise the President with respect to the integration of domestic, foreign, and military policies relating to the national security so as to enable the military services and other departments and agencies of the government to cooperate more effectively in matters involving the national security." The statutory members of the NSC are the president, vice president, and secretaries of defense and state. The director of central intelligence and the chair of the Joint Chiefs of Staff are statutory advisers to the council. Ideally, the NSC is a smaller and more focused forum than the cabinet.

Congress, however, created the NSC not exactly to assist presidents but to force upon them a more collegial decision-making process.[117] In Congress's eyes, decisions in national security matters had become excessively centralized in the White House. Yet presidents cannot be obliged to convene meetings of the NSC or to treat its meetings and deliberations as anything more than advisory. Indeed, many presidents have chosen to de-emphasize NSC meetings, preferring to rely on small groups of trusted advisers to make decisions, using the council only to approve them. Others have used the NSC as the formal centerpiece of an extensive web of committees and interagency groups considering foreign policy. Occasionally, the NSC has been used as a decision-making forum during crises, including the North Korean invasion of South Korea in 1950, the Soviet invasion of Czechoslovakia in 1968, and the *Mayaguez* incident in 1975. At various times, the NSC also has been used for less dramatic functions such as policy planning and budget review.[118]

In addition to creating the National Security Council, the National Security Act established an NSC staff to serve the president and the NSC members. The most important presidential adaptation of the NSC apparatus has been the use of the NSC staff, contrary to Congress's intention, to centralize decision making and implementation in the White House.

Crucial to the staff's influence has been the evolution of the assistant to the president for national security affairs, a post established by Eisenhower and commonly referred to as the "national security adviser." Originally, the national security adviser was to facilitate foreign policy-making by coordinating NSC meetings and overseeing the staff that served the NSC. Under Eisenhower's successors, the national security adviser was often as influential or more so than cabinet members. As a presidential aide, the national security adviser is not confirmed by the Senate and is not burdened by responsibilities for managing an agency or department. The influence of the national security adviser within the administration depends entirely on the president.

Because the national security adviser and most NSC staffers owe their position and status entirely to the president, they have few competing loyalties. Some NSC staffers who were drawn from other departments and agencies may retain institutional loyalty to their parent organization, but during their tenure on the NSC staff they are responsible only to the president. In addition, the NSC staff is beyond the reach of the legislative branch because it has no statutory responsibility to report to Congress. Presidents therefore can use the national security adviser and the NSC staff as a research and advisory arm independent of other agencies and departments. Some national security advisers, such as Henry A. Kissinger and Zbigniew Brzezinski, have served as dominant policy advisers and as negotiators in the most important matters, using the NSC staff to support this work. In the extraordinarily broad and intensive diplomatic efforts of the Nixon administration, Secretary of State William P. Rogers was eclipsed by Kissinger and had no important advisory role.

The accomplishments of Kissinger and Brzezinski built a strong case for the virtues of centralizing foreign policy operations in the White House. On the other hand, investigations of the Iran-contra affair in 1986 and 1987 revealed that the NSC staff could be used to implement not only covert operations but also operations that circumvented the law and were, otherwise, of questionable wisdom. This scandal led to calls for a more collegial decision-making structure, whether oriented around the secretary of state or a reorganized NSC.[119]

President George H. W. Bush made the position of national security adviser stronger than it had been in the Reagan administration. His national security adviser, Brent Scowcroft, played a major role during the Gulf War, and he was generally a voice for more conservative positions on relations with the Soviet Union and Middle East peace prospects. However, foreign policymaking during the Bush administration was dominated by Secretary of State James A. Baker III, with whom President Bush had extensive professional and personal ties. Baker shaped policy in the various arms reduction talks with the Soviet Union and was directly involved in all phases of the transition to post–cold war relations with the Soviet Union. His close relationship with Soviet foreign minister Eduard Shevardnadze facilitated agreements on arms control, the fall of the Berlin Wall, and the reunification of East and West Germany. He also assembled and helped to maintain the international coalition opposing Iraq's 1990 invasion of Kuwait.[120]

Similarly, Bill Clinton's national security advisers were less prominent in foreign policy decisions and activities than his secretaries of state, Warren M. Christopher and Madeleine K. Albright. Clinton's first national security adviser, W. Anthony Lake, came from an academic background, and his second-term national security adviser, Samuel R. Berger, had stronger political than national security expertise. In George W. Bush's first term, his national security adviser, Condoleezza Rice, was probably the closest foreign policy adviser to the president. Bush also consulted regularly with Vice President Richard B. Cheney and Secretary of Defense Donald H. Rumsfeld, relegating Secretary of State Colin Powell to a secondary role. In Bush's second term, however, Rice became secretary of state, thus strengthening the power of that position vis-à-vis that of National Security Adviser Stephen J. Hadley (previously Rice's deputy). President Barack Obama selected his chief competitor for the Democratic nomination, Hillary Rodham Clinton, to be secretary of state, and his national security advisers have kept a low profile. In many respects, then, the characteristics of the individual, particularly foreign policy expertise and access to the president, are most significant in determining the importance of the position.

In 1989 the dismantling of the Berlin Wall and the reunification of West and East Germany exemplified collapsing Communist control of Eastern Europe and heralded the end of the cold war. Here border guards look through from East Germany after demonstrators pulled down one segment of the wall at the Brandenburg gate.

Foreign Policymaking Process

Although the National Security Council and the executive departments and agencies that deal with foreign affairs are established by law, it is up to the president to create and maintain a responsive and effective foreign policymaking process. Because numerous executive branch units are working on foreign policy, their work must be coordinated to minimize the duplication of their efforts and institutional conflict and to ensure that each unit has access to the president. Therefore, as managers of the foreign policy bureaucracy, presidents must establish procedures that determine how policy options and information should be presented to them, who should have access to intelligence, how the efforts of various departments and agencies should be coordinated, how the agendas of foreign policy meetings should be set, who should regularly attend these meetings, who should chair these meetings, and who should be responsible for overseeing policy implementation.

Managing the Foreign Policymaking Process

Since World War II, the central problem within the foreign policy establishment has been deciding who should manage the foreign policymaking process. The president must ultimately referee the inevitable bureaucratic struggle within

the administration for influence, resources, and prestige, but the responsibility for determining the substance of policy leaves the president with little time for matters of management. Therefore, some executive branch unit must serve as the facilitator of the foreign policymaking system. The main rivals for this responsibility have been the State Department under the secretary of state and the NSC staff under the national security adviser. From the Kennedy to the Ford administration, presidents tended to look to their national security advisers to manage their foreign policymaking system. Critics of this trend have maintained that the oversight, coordination, and leadership of the foreign policymaking system properly belong to the State Department.[121] They argue that the State Department was intended to be preeminent in foreign affairs and that its foreign policy expertise, accountability to Congress, and network of embassies in foreign capitals make it the best choice to run the president's foreign policymaking system. The presidents from Ford to Clinton have tried various combinations, emphasizing initially the importance of the secretary of state, but often witnessing sharply divisive conflicts between that official and the national security adviser. President George W. Bush initially relied on his national security adviser, Condoleezza Rice, but then made her secretary of state in his second term, thus increasing the importance of that office.

The State Department, however, like the other departments, has institutional interests that inhibit its ability to be an arbiter between competing departments and agencies. Just as the military mission of the Defense Department or the intelligence mission of the CIA disposes those units to approach foreign affairs from a unique perspective, State's diplomatic mission disposes it to prefer its own foreign policy strategies. Even if State Department officials were able to mediate disputes between other bureaucratic units impartially, those units would never regard State as a neutral department.

The perpetual problem in foreign policy management is finding structures and procedures that can accomplish a number of demanding and often incompatible goals: oversight and coordination of the many and varied departments and agencies administering foreign policy, full information and debate in policy formulation, institutional experience and memory, responsiveness to circumstances, and responsiveness to presidential policy decisions and changes of course. Presidents tend to begin their terms with elaborate structures for collegial deliberation and complementary systems of administrative coordination. But over time, they often find these structures to be indecisive, unresponsive, rife with departmental infighting and parochialism, and generally lacking in coherence. Then they tend to turn to a small group or a single adviser, whether the secretary of state, the national security adviser, or the chief of staff.

When decisions are made by a small group, however, wise and successful policy depends on the skills, knowledge, and integrity of the president and his few advisers. Nixon's successes depended on his intense focus on foreign affairs and on the extraordinary qualities and Herculean diplomatic efforts of Henry Kissinger. The same organization but with high turnover among national security advisers and a less focused president helped produce the Iran-contra fiasco. President George W. Bush faced criticism for the insular decision making that led to the 2003 Iraq War.[122] President Barack Obama demonstrated more engagement in foreign policymaking, as indicated by reports about the deliberations leading up to his decision to increase U.S. troops in Afghanistan.[123]

Even when a more intimate circle of advisers functions well in making policy, a gulf may develop between the policymakers centered in the White House and the administrative arms in the departments and agencies. Then departments and agencies can pursue their distinct and permanent interests by frustrating implementation and by seeking support in the congressional committees with which they are associated.

Foreign Policy Decision-making Systems

Harry Truman's well-founded suspicion that Congress had created the NSC to check his authority and his strained relationships with his first two secretaries of defense, James V. Forrestal and Louis Johnson, initially led him to ignore the NSC. He attended only twelve of the first fifty-seven NSC meetings.[124] During the Korean War, the NSC developed a more important policymaking role. Truman attended most meetings, and he used the group to forge presidential foreign policies. Nevertheless, Truman still emphasized its advisory nature and frequently consulted its individual members or ad hoc groups rather than relying on the entire NSC for policy advice.

Dwight Eisenhower's foreign policy decision-making system reflected his military background. He presided over highly structured weekly meetings of the NSC and created NSC subcommittees to consider specific policy issues. He also established the "Planning Board," a staff body charged with foreign policy planning, and the "Operations Coordinating Board," an interagency committee charged with overseeing implementation of executive decisions.[125] Although Eisenhower's system had the advantages of ensuring that all

parties would participate in decision making and that the president would not become bogged down in details better left to subordinates, it often has been criticized as being too rigid and formalistic. Meetings were sometimes held because they were routinely scheduled rather than because they were necessary. Eisenhower also insisted that his top advisers reach a consensus on issues. His demand for unanimity led to policy papers that were too general and vague to provide direction to lower-level personnel charged with implementing policy.

John Kennedy replaced Eisenhower's formal committees with a less structured collegial decision-making system. Kennedy's reliance on the advice of departmental experts who had advocated the disastrous U.S.-supported Bay of Pigs invasion of Cuba by Cuban nationals in April 1961 convinced him that he needed independent sources of national security advice in the White House. As a result, the NSC staff under the direction of the national security adviser, McGeorge Bundy, not only facilitated the decision-making process, it generated and evaluated policy options for the president. Formal NSC meetings were de-emphasized. During the Cuban missile crisis Kennedy relied on an assembly of his closest advisers known as the "Executive Committee." Unlike the NSC, membership in this ad hoc group depended not on statutory requirements, but on the trust and confidence of the president.[126]

Lyndon Johnson made few changes in either Kennedy's national security decision-making system or the personnel who ran it. The number of advisers involved in ad hoc policymaking sessions declined, however, especially when the Vietnam War was the topic. Johnson developed the practice of discussing the war at Tuesday lunch meetings attended by five or six close advisers. The president used NSC meetings primarily to announce and discuss decisions that had already been made. In 1966 Johnson created formal interdepartmental groups to develop and coordinate policy proposals that would flow up to the NSC, but the work of these groups was largely confined to peripheral issues unrelated to the war.[127]

Richard Nixon tried to create a foreign policymaking system that incorporated the best aspects of the Eisenhower and Kennedy-Johnson systems. He created a formal interagency committee structure similar to Eisenhower's to ensure that all departments and agencies would be heard. Unlike Eisenhower's committee system, however, Nixon's was intended to produce several policy options for the president's consideration rather than an interdepartmental consensus. The committees also were designed to make less important decisions, thereby allowing the president and his top advisers to concentrate on the most important issues. Nixon established a strong NSC staff that enabled the president and his national security adviser, Henry Kissinger, to monitor the activities of the committees.

Secretary of State Hillary Rodham Clinton (front left) walks with President Obama after a meeting with Russian president Medvedev at Prague Castle. Secretary Clinton is one of the most well-known figures ever to hold that position in the modern era, having previously been the first lady of the United States as well as a U.S. senator from New York.

that would filter proposals up to his office. To ensure that he would not be insulated from a diversity of opinion, he had department and agency leaders report directly to him rather than through the chief of staff or the national security adviser. Initially, his principal adviser was the secretary of state, Cyrus R. Vance, who took the lead in general policy formulation. Over time Carter leaned more heavily on the NSC staff and his national security adviser, Zbigniew Brzezinski. Carter's system suffered from a lack of coherence and from frequent disagreements between Brzezinski and Vance, who resigned his post in May 1980 after opposing the U.S. attempt to rescue American hostages in Iran.

Ronald Reagan initially announced his intention to give dominant roles in national security policymaking to his secretaries of defense and state. Nevertheless, Reagan rejected a plan submitted by Secretary of State Alexander M. Haig Jr. to designate the State Department as the manager of foreign policy. The president took a whole year before setting up a formal foreign policymaking system that stressed cabinet predominance.[129] From the beginning of the administration, however, the NSC staff was given a smaller role than under Presidents Nixon, Ford, and Carter. Reagan's first national security adviser, Richard V. Allen, did not even have direct access to the president. Although subsequent national security advisers William Clark, Robert C. McFarlane, John M. Poindexter, Frank C. Carlucci, and Colin Powell did have daily access to the president, none dominated the policymaking process as much as their predecessors Henry Kissinger and Zbigniew Brzezinski.

The most distinguishing feature of the Reagan foreign policymaking system was the president's hands-off administration. Reagan allowed his cabinet secretaries and other subordinates vast discretion in responding to the day-to-day issues affecting their area of foreign policy. He limited his participation primarily to the articulation of broad themes. Some observers during Reagan's presidency praised this style of leadership as an example of how presidents should delegate responsibilities to save their energies for the most important decisions and avoid being overwhelmed by the details of foreign policy. However, the Iran-contra scandal, which was uncovered in 1986, demonstrated the dangers of Reagan's detachment from administration. NSC staff member Lt. Col. Oliver L. North, along with National Security Adviser Vice Adm. John Poindexter and other administration officials, arranged secret arms sales to Iran, a terrorist

Although most scholars consider Nixon's NSC system to be a well-conceived blueprint for national security decision making, that blueprint was not always followed. His strong interest in national security affairs and the delicate nature of the negotiations to end the Vietnam War and improve relations with the Soviet Union and the People's Republic of China led to a centralization of decision making in the hands of Nixon, Kissinger, and the NSC staff that excluded other top advisers and departments. Late in Nixon's presidency, the Watergate scandal dominated the president's time, causing him to rely even more on Henry Kissinger and a small circle of trusted advisers.[128]

Nixon's successor, Gerald Ford, was able to restore balance to the foreign policy decision-making system. Ford used the NSC staff and National Security Adviser Brent Scowcroft primarily as coordinators of national security decision making rather than as policy advisers. The president still relied heavily on Kissinger, who had become secretary of state in 1973, but the views of other departments and agencies were integrated more often into national security decisions than they had been during the latter years of Nixon's presidency.

Jimmy Carter simplified the NSC committee system and established a decentralized advisory system of "shops" state, as barter for U.S. hostages. This contradicted the administration's stated policy and the advice of senior administration officials. In addition, North and Poindexter used the profits from the arms sales to circumvent Congress's prohibition of U.S. government military aid to the contras in Nicaragua. The Tower Commission, appointed by the president to review his NSC system in the wake of the affair, commented on Reagan's management style in its 1987 report:

> The President's management style is to put the principal responsibility for policy review and implementation on the shoulders of his advisers. Nevertheless, with such a complex, high-risk operation and so much at stake, the President should have ensured that the NSC system did not fail him. He did not force his policy to undergo the most critical review of which the NSC participants and the process were capable. Never did he insist upon accountability and performance review. Had the President chosen to drive the NSC system, the outcome could well have been different.

The scandal forced the resignation and indictment of several White House officials and led the president to project a more visible role in foreign policymaking.

George H. W. Bush was directly involved in the foreign policy deliberation and decisions of his administration. He worked closely with his secretary of state, James Baker, on major initiatives. Otherwise, two subgroups within the NSC, the Principals Committee and the Deputies Committee, handled most of the policy decisions and implementation. Bush called few formal NSC meetings and was criticized for the informality of his approach to national security decision making.[130]

Bill Clinton's informal leadership style (in foreign and domestic policy) prompted much criticism in his first year in office, leading Colin Powell, chair of the Joint Chiefs of Staff, to conclude that "discussions continued to meander like graduate-student bull sessions."[131] After the botched intervention in Somalia, riots in Haiti that deterred the dispatch of U.S. military trainers, and a failure to reach policy consensus on the civil war in Bosnia, Clinton adopted more structure in his decision-making process.

George W. Bush, in sharp contrast to Clinton, insisted on highly structured and punctual meetings, adhering to the leadership approach of a chief executive officer in the corporate world. But that tightly managed system came under attack for ideological rigidity and failure to consider alternatives in the aftermath of the 2003 Iraq War.[132] Critics also have faulted Bush for failing to consult sufficiently with career professionals, and for relying heavily on a small inner circle of political appointees.[133] In the postwar reconstruction period in Iraq, however, Bush demonstrated more independent judgment. In 2006 Bush appointed a bipartisan panel, the Iraq Study Group, to make recommendations for what the United States should do in Iraq, and the panel

recommended that the United States draw down its forces.[134] Instead, after consulting with military leaders and others, Bush approved an increase in U.S. troops in Iraq, popularly known as the "surge," to halt internal violence and assist Iraqis in establishing stability.[135] The decision was viewed skeptically by some, but one year later, was widely viewed as successful, despite continuing disagreement over the merits of the initial decision to intervene in Iraq.

President Barack Obama has demonstrated great interest in policy debates, and he appeared comfortable hearing his advisers advocate different policy options in his presence. He insisted on extensive deliberations before such major foreign policy decisions as increasing U.S. forces in Afghanistan and releasing information about treatment of detainees in the previous administration. Obama also immersed himself in policy details, in many ways taking on the responsibilities of an "honest broker" that are typically expected of a close aide such as the national security adviser.[136]

The Bureaucracy as a Source of Presidential Power

The foreign policy bureaucracy can be a great asset to presidents in their struggle with Congress for control of foreign policy and their efforts to provide effective foreign policy leadership. The bureaucracy's most obvious benefit is that it enables presidents and their closest advisers to concentrate on the decisions and initiatives they deem most important while the bureaucracy deals with the many small foreign policy matters the executive branch must handle daily. President Nixon and his national security adviser, Henry Kissinger, spent the vast majority of their foreign policy time during Nixon's first term on three problems: ending the Vietnam War, opening up China, and improving relations with the Soviet Union. Most other foreign policy matters were left to the bureaucracy. Although Nixon and Kissinger certainly neglected other important matters as a result, the extraordinary attention they were able to give these principal issues made progress possible.

The bureaucracy's capacity to supply the president with information and advice is another asset. *(See box, Information: A Foreign Policy Commodity, p. 244.)* No institution, including Congress, has information sources on foreign affairs that can compare with the array of channels supplying the president with current intelligence and professional opinions. Most modern presidents have been briefed daily on foreign policy issues by their secretary of state, national security adviser, or other top aides. These officials receive information and proposals that have been distilled and funneled up to them from their respective departments. This information and advice make it possible for a president to address foreign policy issues intelligently without being an expert.

Besides the information available from normal advisory and diplomatic resources, the nation's vast intelligence-gathering capabilities are at the president's service. The director of central intelligence coordinates intelligence activities and relays important intelligence directly to the president. Many foreign policy decisions, particularly those that involve the use of force, cannot be made without access to intelligence information. For example, President Kennedy decided to blockade Cuba during the Cuban missile crisis after he and his advisers had carefully analyzed all intelligence information.[137] The president's access to sensitive intelligence has provided a rationale for presidential autonomy in foreign policy. Congress's recognition of this presidential advantage contributed to its frequent willingness to accept presidential leadership in foreign affairs after World War II. Since the Vietnam War, however, Congress has more actively sought access to intelligence and has been more reluctant to accept presidential evaluations of international issues.

The professional foreign policy bureaucracy also provides continuity in the policies of successive administrations. When a new president takes office, the general policy directives that provide guidance to the bureaucracy change and the political appointees who head the various departments and agencies are new, but the bureaucrats continue to collect intelligence, write reports, make recommendations, and maintain diplomatic relations with other nations. Useful initiatives begun by the previous president have a chance to find a place in the new administration, and foreign governments that are frustrated by the frequent changes in presidential leadership can take comfort in the continuing presence of career officials with whom they have dealt in the past.

The Bureaucracy as an Impediment to Presidential Power

Although presidents have formal authority over the foreign policy bureaucracy, it is too vast to command and does not always serve their purposes. Indeed, since the end of World War II executive branch departments and agencies often have been a greater obstacle to presidential will in foreign affairs than has Congress. Executive branch obstruction occurs, in large part, because the goals and interests of the bureaucracy conflict with those of the president. Political scientist Richard E. Neustadt has explained why presidents have found it difficult to control the bureaucracy:

Everything somehow involves the President. But operating agencies owe their existence least of all to one another— and only in some part to him. Each has a separate statutory base; each has its statutes to administer; each deals

INFORMATION: A FOREIGN POLICY COMMODITY

The administration exerts extensive control over the foreign policy agenda through its control over information held in the federal bureaucracy. The president benefits from the huge operations of the public relations offices of the Pentagon, State Department, and Central Intelligence Agency. Through the power of classification, the president also can control how much information journalists, scholars, and political activists have at their disposal.

Scholars have raised concerns about the effects of the executive's control over information. A constant tension exists between the democratic value of openness and the strategic value of secrecy. Even as the president speaks more and more in public, the president and government also cloak more matters in secrecy. This development may be attributed to the need for different strategies to overcome and control a growing bureaucracy. Political scientist Francis E. Rourke has written:

To be sure, the bureaucracy did not invent secrecy in American government. The Founding Fathers found it expedient to conduct the deliberations of the Constitutional Convention at Philadelphia in 1787 in private [and] presidents have, through the development of "executive privilege," contributed a great deal to the secrecy surrounding executive activities.... But it remains true that the growth of bureaucracy in American government has brought about an enormous expansion in the secretiveness with which policy is made.[1]

The erection of a "national security state," critics have argued, gives the president almost unchallenged power over foreign affairs and even many areas of domestic policy. Presidents always can assert that "national security" requires withholding information.

Presidents clearly enjoy an important advantage in deciding what information they want released and how they want to do it. President Richard Nixon justified both the "secret" bombing of Cambodia in 1970 and his handling of the Watergate affair on the grounds of national security requirements. The Reagan administration's refusal to allow reporters to witness the invasion of Grenada was based on similar claims. But perhaps more important is the routine information that presidents can keep secret.

After the terrorist attacks of September 11, 2001, the administration of George W. Bush interpreted presidential powers expansively to combat terrorism. One of its most controversial actions was the creation of a secret domestic surveillance program to collect information through overseeing phone calls or e-mails on possible terrorist plans, typically without judicial approval or congressional consultation. When the program was uncovered in 2005, critics maintained that the president lacked the constitutional power to create such a program unilaterally, while supporters declared that the war on terror justified executive action.[2]

1. Francis E. Rourke, *Bureaucracy, Politics, and Public Policy* (Boston: Little, Brown, 1984), 155.
2. James Risen, *State of War: The Secret History of the C.I.A. and the Bush Administration* (New York: Free Press, 2006).

with a different set of subcommittees at the Capitol. Each has its own peculiar set of clients, friends, and enemies outside the formal government. Each has a different set of specialized careerists inside its own bailiwick. Our Constitution gives the President the "take-care" clause and the appointive power. Our statutes give him central budgeting and a degree of personnel control. All agency administrators are responsible to him. But they also are responsible to Congress, to their clients, to their staffs, and to themselves. In short, they have five masters.[138]

The president cannot, therefore, expect his commands to move bureaucrats, well down the line, exactly as he desires. As Neustadt said, the president must "convince such men that what the White House wants of them is what they ought to do for their sake and on their authority."[139]

The sheer number of people involved in even minor matters makes this task daunting. Moreover, foreign service officers, military personnel, members of the intelligence community, and other career executive branch employees involved in foreign affairs neither depend on the president for their jobs nor necessarily agree with presidential goals and policies. Career bureaucrats are naturally concerned with the long-term welfare of their particular department or agency. They usually will fight against policies that could diminish their responsibilities or resources, and they often will resent decisions that show an obvious disregard for their institutional point of view. In addition, foreign policy bureaucrats may regard presidents and their political appointees as temporary invaders of the foreign policy realm whose political goals harm the permanent interests of the United States.

Members of the foreign policy bureaucracy have several means by which they can resist presidential will in foreign affairs. They can delay or undermine the execution of presidential directives, provide the president only with information and options that do not conflict with their interpretation of an issue, leak details of a controversial or covert policy to Congress or the media, publicly oppose a policy, or resign in protest. The president may have the constitutional power to order an agency to carry out a particular task, but if that agency drags its feet or otherwise undermines implementation of the order, the president's power can be diluted or even neutralized.

The most important means available to presidents of controlling the bureaucracy and communicating to it their foreign policy vision is the power to appoint the officials who will head the departments and agencies. These officials serve as department managers as well as members of the inner circle of presidential advisers. In choosing these appointees the president must reconcile, on the one hand, the need to find qualified persons with administrative talent who will be respected by the departments they head, with, on the other hand, the president's desire to maintain control over the bureaucracy. Even the most loyal presidential appointee, however, usually will develop a competing loyalty to the department or agency, which may at times conflict with the goals of the president.[140]

NOTES

1   *United States v. Curtiss-Wright Export Corp.*, 299 U.S. 304 (1936).

2   Quoted in Theodore C. Sorensen, *Kennedy* (New York: Bantam, 1966), 573.

3   Louis Henkin, *Foreign Affairs and the Constitution* (New York: Norton, 1972), 76–77.

4   James Madison, *Federalist* No. 51, and Alexander Hamilton, *Federalist* No. 72, in Alexander Hamilton, James Madison, and John Jay, *The Federalist Papers* (New York: New American Library, 1961), 321–322, 437.

5   Edward S. Corwin, *The President: Office and Powers, 1787–1984*, 5th ed. (New York: New York University Press, 1984), 201.

6   Quoted in Clinton Rossiter, *The American Presidency*, 2d ed. (New York: Harcourt Brace, 1960), 15.

7   John E. Mueller, *War, Presidents, and Public Opinion* (New York: Wiley, 1973).

8   Aaron Wildavsky, "The Two Presidencies," Reprinted in *Perspectives on the Presidency*, ed. Aaron Wildavsky (Boston: Little, Brown, 1975), 448–461.

9   Jane Mayer, "The Hidden Power," *New Yorker*, July 3, 2006. Also see John Yoo, *The Powers of War and Peace: The Constitution and Foreign Affairs After 9/11* (Chicago: University of Chicago Press, 2005). For an analysis of how presidents have employed the "unitary executive" concept in areas other than foreign policy, see Stephen G. Calabresi and Christopher S. Yoo, *The Unitary Executive: Presidential Power from Washington to Bush* (New Haven: Yale University Press, 2008). For a critique of the Bush administration's actions in national security, see James Pfiffner, *Power Play: The Bush Presidency and the Constitution* (Washington, D.C.: Brookings, 2008).

10   Yoo, *Powers of War and Peace*, 18.

11   John Marshall, quoted in *United States v. Curtiss-Wright Export Corp.*, 299 U.S. 304 (1936).

12   Alexis de Tocqueville, *Democracy in America*, ed. J.P. Mayer (Garden City, N.Y.: Anchor, 1969), 126.

13   *Chicago & S. Airlines v. Waterman SS. Corp.*, 333 U.S. 103 (1948), 111.

14   Quoted in Christopher H. Pyle and Richard M. Pious, eds., *The President, Congress, and the Constitution* (New York: Free Press, 1984), 238.

15   Arthur M. Schlesinger Jr., *The Imperial Presidency* (Boston: Houghton Mifflin, 1973), 102–103. See also Henkin, *Foreign Affairs and the Constitution*, 27 n. 19.

16   *The Letters of Pacificus and Helvidius* (Delmar, N.Y.: Scholars' Facsimiles and Reprints, 1976), 5–15.

17   Ibid., ix.

18   Ibid., 57.

19   Quoted in Arthur Bernon Tourtellot, *The Presidents on the Presidency* (Garden City, N.Y.: Doubleday, 1964), 272.

20   Pyle and Pious, *President, Congress, and the Constitution*, 204–205.

21   James M. Lindsay, *Congress and the Politics of U.S. Foreign Policy* (Baltimore: Johns Hopkins University Press, 1994), 15.

22   Richard Harmond, "Theodore Roosevelt and the Making of the Modern Presidency," in *Power and the Presidency,* ed. Philip C. Dolce and George H. Skau (New York: Scribner's, 1976), 72–73.

23   Theodore Roosevelt to H. C. Lodge, January 28, 1909, quoted in Schlesinger, *Imperial Presidency,* 89.

24   Richard M. Pious, *The American Presidency: The Politics of Power from FDR to Carter* (New York: Basic Books, 1979), 53.

25   For a discussion of the Tonkin Gulf incident, see Leslie H. Gelb and Richard K. Betts, *The Irony of Vietnam: The System Worked* (Washington, D.C.: Brookings, 1979), 100–104; and Eugene Windchy, *Tonkin Gulf* (New York: Doubleday, 1971).

26   Gelb and Betts, *Irony of Vietnam,* 103–104.

27   Robert E. DiClerico, *The American President,* 4th ed. (Englewood Cliffs, N.J.: Prentice-Hall, 1995), 58.

28   Lindsay, *Congress and the Politics of U.S. Foreign Policy,* 89–90.

29   Corwin, *President,* 222.

30   Lindsay, *Congress and the Politics of U.S. Foreign Policy,* 86.

31   James P. Pfiffner, *Power Play: The Bush Presidency and the Constitution* (Washington, D.C.: Brookings, 2009).

32   Quoted in Tourtellot, *Presidents on the Presidency,* 274.

33   Quoted in Pious, *American Presidency,* 334.

34   Quoted in Corwin, *President,* 207–208.

35   Henkin, *Foreign Affairs and the Constitution,* 301.

36   Lindsay, *Congress and the Politics of U.S. Foreign Policy,* 120–121, 126.

37   Quoted in Tourtellot, *Presidents on the Presidency,* 298.

38   Schlesinger, *Imperial Presidency,* 27.

39   Quoted in Ibid., 128.

40   Charles Krauthammer, "The Bush Doctrine," *Weekly Standard,* June 4, 2001, 21–25.

41   George W. Bush, "The National Security Strategy," September 2002.

42   Cecil V. Crabb Jr. and Pat M. Holt, *Invitation to Struggle: Congress, the President and Foreign Policy,* 4th ed. (Washington, D.C.: CQ Press, 1992), 15.

43   Jack N. Rakove, "Solving a Constitutional Puzzle: The Treaty Making Clause as a Case Study," *Perspectives in American History,* New Series, I:1984, 233–281.

44   John Jay, *Federalist* No. 64, in Alexander Hamilton, James Madison, and John Jay, *The Federalist Papers* (New York: New American Library, 1961), 392–393.

45   George H. Haynes, *The Senate of the United States* (Boston: Houghton Mifflin, 1938), 575.

46   Alexander Hamilton, *Federalist* No. 75, in Alexander Hamilton, James Madison, and John Jay, *The Federalist Papers* (New York: New American Library, 1961), 452–453.

47   Buel W. Patch, "Treaties and Domestic Law," *Editorial Research Reports,* March 28, 1952, 241.

48   Abraham D. Sofaer, *War, Foreign Affairs and Constitutional Power: The Origins* (Cambridge: Ballinger, 1976), 95–96.

49   Corwin, *President,* 240.

50   Louis Fisher, *Constitutional Conflicts between Congress and the President,* 3d rev. ed. (Lawrence: University Press of Kansas, 1991), 219.

51   Lindsay, *Congress and the Politics of U.S. Foreign Policy,* 95.

52   Joseph E. Kallenbach, *The American Chief Executive: The Presidency and the Governorship* (New York: Harper and Row, 1966), 505.

53   Pious, *American Presidency,* 336.

54   F. M. Brewer, "Advice and Consent of the Senate," *Editorial Research Reports,* June 1, 1943, 352.

55   Louis W. Koenig, *The Chief Executive,* 5th ed. (New York: Harcourt Brace and World, 1986), 206.

56   DiClerico, *American President,* 46.

57   Lindsay, *Congress and the Politics of U.S. Foreign Policy,* 65, 123.

58   Theodor Meron, "The Treaty Power: The International Legal Effect of Changes in Obligations Initiated by the Congress," in *The Tethered Presidency: Congressional Restraints on Executive Power,* ed. Thomas M. Franck (New York: New York University Press, 1981), 116–117.

59   Henkin, *Foreign Affairs and the Constitution,* 134.

60   Lindsay, *Congress and the Politics of U.S. Foreign Policy,* 80.

61   Meron, "Treaty Power."

62   Kallenbach, *American Chief Executive,* 507.

63   Corwin, *President,* 205–206.

64   Pious, *American Presidency,* 338–340.

65   Quoted in Henkin, *Foreign Affairs and the Constitution,* 377.

66   Ibid., 168–170.

67   Pyle and Pious, *President, Congress, and the Constitution,* 258–265.

68   Loch K. Johnson, *The Making of International Agreements: Congress Confronts the Executive* (New York: New York University Press, 1984), 12.

69   Lindsay, *Congress and the Politics of U.S. Foreign Policy,* 83.

70   Harold W. Stanley and Richard G. Niemi, *Vital Statistics on American Politics, 2001–2002* (Washington, D.C.: CQ Press, 2001), 334.

71   Quoted in Henkin, *Foreign Affairs and the Constitution,* 177–178. Also see *United States v. Belmont,* 310 U.S. 324 (1937).

72   Henkin, *Foreign Affairs and the Constitution,* 178–179.

73   Schlesinger, *Imperial Presidency,* 86.

74   Ibid., 86–87.

75   Lawrence Margolis, *Executive Agreements and Presidential Power in Foreign Policy* (New York: Praeger, 1986), 7–9.

76   Ibid., 9.

77   Tourtellot, *Presidents on the Presidency,* 277.

78   DiClerico, *American President,* 47–48.

79   Ibid., 48.

80   Corwin, *President,* 245–246.

81   Johnson, *Making of International Agreements,* 86–87.

82   *CQ Almanac, 1972* (Washington, D.C.: Congressional Quarterly, 1972), 619.

83   Corwin, *President,* 212.

84   Alexander Hamilton, *Federalist* No. 69, in Alexander Hamilton, James Madison, and John Jay, *The Federalist Papers* (New York: New American Library, 1961), 420.

85   Schlesinger, *Imperial Presidency,* 14.

86   Kallenbach, *American Chief Executive,* 493.

87   Seth P. Tillman, *The United States in the Middle East* (Bloomington: Indiana University Press, 1982), 221.

88   Quoted in Tourtellot, *Presidents on the Presidency,* 291.

89   Corwin, *President,* 216–219, 486 n. 105.

90   Crabb and Holt, *Invitation to Struggle,* 18.

91   Pious, *American Presidency,* 335.

92   See Richard N. Haass, *The Reluctant Sheriff: The United States after the Cold War* (Washington, D.C.: Council on Foreign Relations Press, 1998).

93   Louis Fisher, *Presidential War Power* (Lawrence: University Press of Kansas, 1995), 153–154.

94   U.S. Department of State Dispatch, vol. 5, no. 20, May 16, 1994; Fisher, *Presidential War Power,* 160–161.

95   R. Gordon Hoxie, *Command Decision and the Presidency* (New York: Reader's Digest Press, 1977), 40.

96   Arthur S. Miller, *Presidential Power in a Nutshell* (St. Paul, Minn.: West, 1977), 37.

97   Koenig, *Chief Executive*, 206–207.

98   *CQ Almanac, 1989* (Washington, D.C.: Congressional Quarterly, 1990), 537–541.

99   Robert E. Hunter, *Presidential Control of Foreign Policy: Management or Mishap* (New York: Praeger, 1982), 79–80.

100   Koenig, *Chief Executive*, 217.

101   Henkin, *Foreign Affairs and the Constitution*, 46.

102   Corwin, *President*, 235.

103   Ibid., 236.

104   Elmer Plischke, *Diplomat in Chief: The President at the Summit* (New York: Praeger, 1986), 13.

105   Kallenbach, *American Chief Executive*, 498–499.

106   Plischke, *Diplomat in Chief*, 121.

107   Kallenbach, *American Chief Executive*, 499.

108   Brendan J. Doherty, "Barack Obama's First Six Months of International and Domestic Political Travel in Historical Context," 2009 White House Transition Project, www.whitehousetransitionproject.org.

109   Dorothy Buckton James, *Contemporary Presidency*, 2d ed. (Indianapolis: Pegasus, 1974), 127–128.

110   Quoted in Plischke, *Diplomat in Chief*, 202.

111   Ibid., 200–202.

112   Richard Nixon, "Superpower Summitry," *Foreign Affairs* 64 (fall 1985): 1.

113   Plischke, *Diplomat in Chief*, 456–460.

114   Ibid., 460–473.

115   Marcus Cunliffe, *American Presidents and the Presidency* (New York: American Heritage, 1972), 286.

116   Amos A. Jordan, William J. Taylor, and Lawrence J. Korb, *American National Security: Policy and Process*, 4th ed. (Baltimore: Johns Hopkins University Press, 1984), 167–168.

117   Pious, *American Presidency*, 362.

118   John E. Endicott, "The National Security Council," in *American Defense Policy*, 5th ed., ed. John F. Reichart and Steven R. Sturm (Baltimore: Johns Hopkins University Press, 1982), 521–522.

119   See, for example, Carnes Lord, *The Presidency and the Management of National Security* (New York: Free Press, 1988), chap. 4.

120   Christopher Madison, "Scrambling Vicar," *National Journal*, April 20, 1991, 924–928.

121   For an outline of a state-centered foreign policymaking system, see I.M. Destler, *Presidents, Bureaucrats, and Foreign Policy* (Princeton: Princeton University Press, 1974), 254–294.

122   Bob Woodward, *Plan of Attack: The Definitive Account of the Decision to Invade Iraq* (New York: Simon & Schuster, 2004).

123   Bob Woodward, *Obama's Wars* (New York: Simon and Schuster, 2010); Barack Obama, "Remarks by the President in Address to the Nation on the Way Forward in Afghanistan and Pakistan," United States Military Academy at West Point, West Point, N.Y, December 1, 2009, American Presidency Project online data base, www.presidency.ucsb.edu/ws/index.php?pid=86948&st=&st1=#axzz1n4mhXDU8.

124   Endicott, "National Security Council," 522.

125   Zbigniew Brzezinski, "The NSC's Midlife Crisis," *Foreign Policy* 69 (winter 1987–1988): 84–85.

126   Jordan, Taylor, and Korb, *American National Security*, 98.

127   Ibid., 91–92.

128   Charles W. Kegley Jr. and Eugene R. Wittkopf, *American Foreign Policy: Pattern and Process* (New York: St. Martin's Press, 1979), 258–259.

129   Brzezinski, "NSC's Midlife Crisis," 90.

130   Jordan, Taylor, and Korb, *American National Security*, 100, 215–216.

131   Colin Powell, with Joseph E. Persico, *My American Journey* (New York: Random House, 1995), 576.

132   George Packer, *The Assassins' Gate: America in Iraq* (New York: Farrar, Straus and Giroux, 2005).

133   James P. Pfiffner, "Decision Making in the Bush White House," *Presidential Studies Quarterly* (June 2009): 363–384.

134   The Iraq Study Group Report: The Way Forward—A New Approach, 2006, www.usip.org/isg/index.html.

135   George W. Bush, "President's Address to the Nation," January 10, 2007, American Presidency Project online dababase, www.presidency.ucsb.edu/ws/index.php?pid=24432&st=&st1=#axzz1n4mhXDU8.

136   James P. Pfiffner, "Decision Making in the Obama White House," *Presidential Studies Quarterly* (June 2011): 244–262. For an evaluation of the national security adviser as an "honest broker," see John P. Burke, *Honest Broker? The National Security Advisor and Presidential Decision Making* (College Station: Texas A&M University Press, 2009).

137   Graham T. Allison, *Essence of Decision* (Boston: Little, Brown, 1971), 46–62.

138   Richard E. Neustadt, *Presidential Power and the Modern Presidents* (New York: Free Press, 1990), 34.

139   Ibid., 30.

140   Hunter, *Presidential Control of Foreign Policy*, 18.

SELECTED BIBLIOGRAPHY

Ambrose, Stephen E., and Douglas G. Brinkley. *Rise to Globalism: American Foreign Policy Since 1938.* 8th rev. ed. New York: Penguin, 1997.

Burke, John P. *Honest Broker? The National Security Advisor and Presidential Decision Making.* College Station: Texas A&M University Press, 2009.

Corwin, Edward S. *The President: Office and Powers, 1787–1984.* 5th ed. New York: New York University Press, 1984.

Crabb, Cecil V., Glenn J. Antizzo, and Leila E. Sarieddine. *Congress and the Foreign Policy Process: Modes of Legislative Behavior.* Baton Rouge: Louisiana State University Press, 2000.

Crabb, Cecil V., Jr., and Pat M. Holt. *Invitation to Struggle: Congress, the President and Foreign Policy.* 4th ed. Washington, D.C.: CQ Press, 1992.

Destler, I. M. *Presidents, Bureaucrats, and Foreign Policy.* Princeton: Princeton University Press, 1974.

Fisher, Louis. *Constitutional Conflicts between Congress and the President.* 3d rev. ed. Lawrence: University Press of Kansas, 1991.

Henkin, Louis. *Foreign Affairs and the Constitution.* New York: Norton, 1975.

Hersman, Rebecca K.C. *How Congress and the President Really Make Foreign Policy.* Washington, D.C.: Brookings, 2000.

Howell, William G. *Power Without Persuasion: The Politics of Direct Presidential Action.* Princeton: Princeton University Press, 2003.

Hunter, Robert E. *Presidential Control of Foreign Policy: Management or Mishap.* New York: Praeger, 1982.

Johnson, Loch. *The Making of International Agreements: Congress Confronts the Executive.* New York: New York University Press, 1984.

Kallenbach, Joseph E. *The American Chief Executive: The Presidency and the Governorship.* New York: Harper and Row, 1966.

Koh, Harold Hongju. *The National Security Constitution: Sharing Power After the Iran-Contra Affair.* New Haven: Yale University Press, 1990.

Lindsay, James M. *Congress and the Politics of U.S. Foreign Policy.* Baltimore: Johns Hopkins University Press, 1994.

Margolis, Lawrence. *Executive Agreements and Presidential Power in Foreign Policy.* New York: Praeger, 1986.

Mayer, Kenneth. *With the Stroke of a Pen: Executive Orders and Presidential Power.* Princeton: Princeton University Press, 2002.

Mueller, John E. *War, Presidents, and Public Opinion.* New York: Wiley, 1973.

Neustadt, Richard E. *Presidential Power and the Modern Presidents.* New York: Free Press, 1990.

Pious, Richard M. *The American Presidency: The Politics of Power from FDR to Carter.* New York: Basic Books, 1979.

Plischke, Elmer. *Diplomat in Chief: The President at the Summit.* New York: Praeger, 1986.

Pyle, Christopher H., and Richard M. Pious, eds. *The President, Congress, and the Constitution.* New York: Free Press, 1984.

Renshon, Stanley A. *National Security in the Obama Administration: Reassessing the Bush Doctrine.* New York: Routledge, 2009.

Rudalevige, Andrew. *The New Imperial Presidency: Renewing Presidential Power After Watergate.* Ann Arbor: University of Michigan Press, 2005.

Schlesinger, Arthur M., Jr. *The Imperial Presidency.* 2d ed. Boston: Houghton Mifflin, 1989.

Wilcox, Francis O. *Congress, the Executive, and Foreign Policy.* New York: Harper and Row, 1971.

Wildavsky, Aaron. "The Two Presidencies." Reprinted in *Perspectives on the Presidency,* ed. Aaron Wildavsky, 448-461. Boston: Little, Brown, 1975.

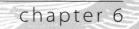

chapter 6

Commander in Chief

by Meena Bose

The Framers of the Constitution distrusted both executive and military power and believed the potential for tyranny was great when the two were combined.

Among the colonial grievances cited in the Declaration of Independence were the charges that the British monarch had "kept among us, in times of peace, Standing Armies without the Consent of our legislatures" and "affected to render the Military independent of and superior to the Civil Power." The document also denounced the quartering of troops in American homes, the impressment of American sailors for British warships, and the unjust war being waged against the colonies. The Framers therefore rejected a proposal to grant the president the authority to declare war, divided the war-making power between the executive and Congress, and placed a strict time limit on military appropriations. On the other hand, many of them could recall as well the feeble military and executive powers of the national government both during and after the revolution. The delegates to the Constitutional Convention were determined to find the balance between effective government and safe government. Their main instruments for accomplishing this constitutional goal were adequate powers regulated by checks and balances.

Although many war powers, including the decision to go to war, could be safely placed in the hands of Congress, command of U.S. forces during a conflict required the unified and flexible leadership that only a single person could provide. As Alexander Hamilton noted: "Of all the cares or concerns of government, the direction of war most peculiarly demands those qualities which distinguish the exercise of power by a single hand."[1] The Framers therefore assigned the commander-in-chief power to the presidency. As political scientist Clinton Rossiter summarized the matter: "We have placed a shocking amount of military power in the President's keeping, but where else, we may ask, could it possibly have been placed?"[2]

Few presidents, however, have been as well suited, in skills and integrity, for the role as the first commander in chief, George Washington. Some presidents have mismanaged military affairs, a few have misused their military power, and there have been many confrontations between the executive and legislative branches over the scope and use of the war powers, with charges of usurpation or abuse of power often being leveled at the president. But contrary to the experiences of many other nations, no president has used the forces at his command to interfere with the ordinary course of electoral accountability or the powers and functions of the other branches.

Because conflicts over the executive's use of the war power typically arise during military engagements, efforts to check the president often falter in the face of ongoing events. During the Civil War, World War I, and World War II, presidents boldly and firmly interpreted the commander-in-chief power broadly, and American success in each case largely stymied any subsequent attempts to limit presidential power. The aftermath of the Vietnam War marked the first time that Congress aimed systematically to constrain the president's ability to send troops into combat. After the terrorist attacks of September 11, 2001, the American public and Congress followed the traditional pattern of "rallying 'round the flag" to support the president's foreign and military policies. But as the global war on terror continued, particularly with difficulties occurring in Iraq, attempts to restrict presidential power in military affairs have developed.

DISTRIBUTION OF WAR-MAKING POWER

The Framers of the Constitution made the highest civilian officer also the commander in chief of the nation's military forces. Article II, Section 2, of the Constitution states: "The President shall be Commander in Chief of the Army and

---

Previous contributors to this chapter include Daniel C. Diller and Stephen H. Wirls.

Navy of the United States, and of the Militia of the several States, when called into the actual Service of the United States." This statement is all the Constitution says about the president's war-making power.

The President shall be Commander in Chief of the Army and Navy of the United States, and of the Militia of the several States, when called into the actual Service of the United States.

—from Article II, Section 2

The Framers did not regard war making as an inherently executive function. Indeed, they originally gave the legislature the comprehensive power to "make war." But fearing that a legislature, cumbersome in itself and frequently out of session, might inhibit action in an emergency, the delegates separated the power to declare war from the power to command or direct the military forces. The latter was given to the president. This division of responsibility left the president free to repel invasions and respond to other acts of war.[3] The Framers were careful, though, to prevent the president from initiating a war on his own authority, and Congress was given the bulk of the war-related powers. The clauses outlining Congress's powers (Article I, Section 8) are detailed and specific:

> To declare War, grant Letters of Marque and Reprisal, and make Rules concerning Captures on Land and Water; To raise and support Armies . . .; To provide and maintain a Navy; To make Rules for the Government and Regulation of the land and naval forces; To provide for calling forth the Militia to execute the Laws of the Union, suppress Insurrections and repel Invasions; To provide for organizing, arming, and disciplining, the Militia, and for governing such Part of them as may be employed in the Service of the United States, reserving to the States respectively, the Appointment of the Officers, and the Authority of training the Militia according to the discipline prescribed by Congress.

As Congress's enumerated war powers indicate, the Framers intended Congress to have full control over the size and character of any national armed forces. A president seeking to become a military dictator would be hindered by Congress's exclusive authority to raise, equip, and organize the armed forces. This includes the authority to eliminate all or any part of the standing forces. Presidents might wish to act, but without Congress's support, they would lack the necessary tools to do so.

The exact authority of the commander in chief was left undefined. Nothing is said directly about the president's authority to initiate military actions short of war in the absence of an invasion or attack. Similarly, the Constitution says nothing directly about the power of Congress to control the scope of conflict once war has been declared. The intentions of many of the Framers to "chain the dog of war" and the clear implications of the Constitution suggest that these questions were settled in favor of congressional control. If the Framers gave the commander-in-chief power to a single federal official to provide for decisive action in emergencies, the balance of constitutional powers still favored Congress.

Textual ambiguities have, nevertheless, allowed presidents to argue that they possess the power or duty traditionally associated with the office of supreme military commander. Consequently, a broad range of actions and powers has been justified under a generous interpretation of the commander-in-chief clause. In addition, foreign policy and chief executive powers give presidents responsibilities in the area of national security that are used in conjunction with the commander-in-chief power to expand the president's war powers.

In practice, controlling the war powers has depended less on precise constitutional provisions and more on the checking capacity of well-balanced institutions.

Power to Declare War

Although Congress's power to raise armies and fund wars and the president's command of the military in times of war are unquestioned, the authority to decide when and where to employ military force has been a source of conflict between the executive and legislative branches. The Framers could have given the president the power to declare war with the "advice and consent of the Senate" as they had with the treaty power. Instead, the Constitution grants Congress the sole authority to take the country from a state of peace into a state of war. By giving Congress the power to declare war, the Framers sought to contain executive ambition and to ensure that these momentous decisions would be made by the deliberative branch and especially by the representatives of the people who would be called on to shoulder the cost in lives and treasure. James Madison wrote:

> Those who are to conduct a war cannot in the nature of things be proper or safe judges whether a war ought to be commenced, continued, or concluded. They are barred from the latter functions by a great principle in free government, analogous to that which separates the sword from the purse, or the power of executing from the power of enacting laws.[4]

The Framers recognized that speed and secrecy, which only a single decision maker could provide, were essential to the safety of the nation. By separating the power to declare war from the power to conduct it, the Framers left the power to repel sudden attacks in the hands of the president. Congress, in short, decides when to go to war unless the hostile actions of another nation thrust the nation in a state of war. In *The Federalist Papers,* Hamilton, one of the foremost advocates of a strong chief executive at the Constitutional Convention, interpreted the commander-in-chief power narrowly:

> The president is to be commander-in-chief of the army and navy of the United States. In this respect his authority would be nominally the same with that of the King of Great Britain, but in substance much inferior to it. It would amount to nothing more than the supreme command and direction of the military and naval forces, as first general and admiral of the Confederacy; while that of the British king extends to the *declaring* of war and to the raising and *regulating* of fleets and armies—all of which, by the Constitution under consideration, would appertain to the legislature.[5]

This straightforward formula is, however, full of ambiguities. How is war to be defined? Does the power to declare war extend to a power to authorize any or all uses of force short of war? Or are there military missions short of war that the president can order without congressional authorization? Can the president try to prevent an attack by attacking first? Can the president order U.S. forces to invade the territory of a neutral nation in pursuit of enemy forces?

The Framers seemed to have agreed that Congress was to control the initiation of all military actions that might involve the nation in a war. The Constitution gives Congress the power to "grant Letters of Marque and Reprisal." This now antiquated instrument allows Congress to authorize, for example, privateers to operate against enemy boats in U.S. waters. The clause suggests that the Constitution gives Congress power over actions, such as retaliations and reprisals, that are hostile in nature but fall short of war.

In *Bas v. Tingy* (1800), the Supreme Court affirmed the authority of the United States to engage in limited or "imperfect" wars, and it affirmed Congress's full authority in all decisions to take the United States from a state of peace into a state of limited hostility or war. Not only could Congress authorize an "imperfect" war by statute, as opposed to a declaration, but it also had full authority to limit the conflict in relation to places, objects, and time. In other words, congressional authority in limited wars extended beyond initiation and deeply into the strategic and tactical questions that are often understood as the prerogative of a commander in chief.[6]

In sum, the consensus of the founding generation was, as President Washington argued, that the Constitution "vests the power of declaring war with Congress; therefore no offensive expedition of importance can be undertaken until they have deliberated upon the subject, and authorized such a measure."[7] Although some ambiguity remains about what an expedition "of importance" would be, the general thrust is clear. The historical record is, however, far more complicated. Congress has declared war only five times— the War of 1812, the Mexican War, the Spanish-American War, World War I, and World War II—and yet the United States has been involved in more than one hundred violent military conflicts. Only some of these have been explicitly authorized by Congress, and some of the unauthorized actions were quite large in scale and arose from radically expansive interpretations of the commander-in-chief power.

This historical record suggests that presidents, having direct command of military forces and being responsible for defending the nation, have been in a better position than Congress to exploit the constitutional ambiguity. When presidents have believed a war or military action to be necessary, they usually have found ways to maneuver the nation into a conflict. Particularly after a direct attack on the United States, such as Pearl Harbor in 1941 or the terrorist attacks of September 11, 2001, presidents have directed military action with full support from Congress and the public. Even if military action extends beyond the immediate response to the attack, as was the case with the Iraq War in 2003, Congress usually defers to presidential leadership and direction in military affairs. Indeed, some scholars argue that the phrase "declare war" grants Congress the power to recognize formally military action by the United States, but that authorizing that action is a power constitutionally reserved to the president.[8] This view is consistent with the "unitary executive" concept of presidential power to which the George W. Bush administration adhered in combating terrorism.

Power to Declare Neutrality and End Declared Wars

Some students of the Constitution have reasoned that Congress's authority to declare war implies that only Congress has the power to declare that the nation will not become involved in a war. Secretary of State Thomas Jefferson made this argument in 1793 when President Washington proclaimed that the United States would remain "friendly and impartial" in the war between the British and the French.[9] Many Americans favored France, their ally in the American Revolution, but Washington believed the treaty of alliance with France did not require U.S. involvement in the conflict with Britain and that any involvement would disrupt the nation's political and economic development. Jefferson supported Washington despite his reservations about the constitutionality of the president declaring neutrality. As a concession to Jefferson, Washington left the word *neutrality* out of his proclamation.

Washington's proclamation of neutrality set off a famous debate in the *Gazette of the United States* between Hamilton, who justified Washington's action, and Madison, who opposed Hamilton's expansive reading of the executive power. Hamilton and Madison were less concerned with neutrality than with the larger issue of whether a president could declare unilaterally what U.S. foreign policy would be. Hamilton conceded that the legislature had the exclusive right to declare war but asserted that until war is declared, the executive has both the responsibility to maintain peace and broad discretion in the choice of means. Madison saw the proclamation of neutrality as a usurpation of Congress's power to declare war. Over time, Hamilton's expansive account of presidential powers has prevailed. *(See "Hamilton-Madison Debate," p. 209, in Chapter 5.)*

When Washington asked Congress to pass judgment on the proclamation, it eventually ratified the president's action by passing the Neutrality Act of 1794.

Later the custom developed that Congress would not declare war without a presidential request. Yet on two occasions Congress demonstrated that it could move a president to accept a war even if the president had reservations about the wisdom of doing so. In 1812 a majority of members of Congress convinced President Madison that war against the British was necessary. In 1898, with public opinion on its side, Congress pressured a reluctant William McKinley to ask for a declaration of war against Spain.

Congress and the president share the authority to end a war. The commander in chief has the power to order the military to stop fighting or to withdraw from an area of conflict. However, if Congress has declared war, the president cannot unilaterally end the legal state of war that exists. Congress must take some action that supersedes its declaration of war. The Framers considered, but rejected, a clause allowing the Senate to conclude a peace treaty on its own authority. As it stands, wars are usually concluded through Senate ratification of a treaty negotiated by the president ending the war and establishing peaceful relations with the enemy nation. The Mexican War, the Spanish-American War, and hostilities in the Pacific theater of World War II were officially terminated in this manner. Congress also may formally end a state of war by repealing its declaration of war. This method was used in 1921 after Congress had refused to ratify the Versailles treaty at the end of World War I and in 1951 formally to end the war with Nazi Germany.[10]

DEVELOPMENT OF PRESIDENTIAL WAR POWERS

The Constitution's assignment of the office of commander in chief to the president created the basis for presidential war powers, but the practical scope of this and related powers in the context of a major conflict or declared war was not defined. Presidential war powers expanded dramatically to meet the general crises of the Civil War and the two world wars. The flexibility, secrecy, speed, and unity of command associated with the president were understood to be crucial to the preservation and defense of the United States. In the circumstances of these wars, presidential power expanded from purely military issues into ancillary questions of the national budget, the domestic economy, and domestic security. According to political scientist Edward S. Corwin, "The principal canons of constitutional interpretation are in wartime set aside so far as concerns both the scope of national power and the capacity of the President to gather unto himself all constitutionally available powers in order the more effectively to focus them upon the task of the hour."[11] Presidential actions that would have raised a great deal of protest in peacetime have been accepted in the name of necessity when the security of the nation has been at stake.

Extensions of presidential power in wartime have established precedents, which future presidents were able to use to justify broad interpretations of their authority. Woodrow Wilson's expansion of presidential war power paved the way for Franklin D. Roosevelt's extraordinary wartime authority, just as Wilson had referred to Lincoln's exercise of power when justifying his own. Until World War II, however, presidents could not continue to wield exceptional power as if an emergency continued beyond the end of armed conflict. After World War II, circumstances changed. President Harry S. Truman retained his emergency powers, many of which were delegated by congressional action, by refusing to declare that the emergency had passed. Moreover, the rise of the cold war with the Soviet Union fostered the development of more permanent and extensive presidential war and emergency powers.

The cold war and especially the development of nuclear weapons created a more or less permanent state of national security emergency. These circumstances fostered and sustained a high level of discretion in the commander in chief's authority to use force, at least until the late 1960s and early 1970s when Congress reacted to executive branch abuses of power by attempting to reassert its role in national security affairs. Although the executive branch still dominates national security policy and has retained the ability to initiate armed conflicts, Congress has scrutinized national security affairs more closely and has been able to restrict presidential policies on a variety of issues.

Until the latter stages of the Vietnam War, the expansion of the president's war powers usually had been accomplished with Congress's approval and often with its active support. Congress validated many of Lincoln's actions, passed legislation delegating sweeping wartime powers to both Woodrow Wilson and Franklin Roosevelt, and acquiesced to the accumulation of power by presidents after World War II. But Congress also had successfully reasserted its authority following each war. The Supreme Court has occasionally ruled against exercises of presidential war power, but it seldom has done so when a war has been in progress and often has let stand presidential actions on the grounds that they are political matters that should be resolved between the executive and legislative branches. A major exception was *Youngstown Sheet & Tube Co. v. Sawyer* (1952), in which the Court ruled against Truman's extension of his emergency and commander-in-chief powers into domestic economic affairs when he ordered a government takeover of a steel mill that was threatened by a labor strike.[12] However, as the Court's approval of the internment of Americans of Japanese descent during World War II demonstrates, the Court has recognized the authority of the president acting in concert with Congress to take virtually any action in response to a grave national emergency.[13]

Early Presidents

Early presidents generally adhered to the principle that Congress was responsible for committing the United States to war. John Adams consulted with Congress in 1798 before allowing U.S. naval forces to attack French vessels that were preying on U.S. commercial shipping. Congress refrained from the drastic step of declaring war, but it passed legislation authorizing the president to order U.S. military forces into battle against the French.[14] This action set the precedent, affirmed by the Supreme Court, that the United States could engage in armed conflicts short of war, but only if "authorized" by Congress. Jefferson and Madison also believed presidents should respect Congress's power to authorize war, yet the events of their administrations demonstrated the desirability of a more flexible commander-in-chief power.

Jefferson and the Barbary Pirates

In 1801 American ships in the Mediterranean were being attacked by pirates from Tripoli and the other Barbary Coast states of Algeria, Morocco, and Tunisia. Jefferson, who wanted to take quick action to resolve the problem, immediately dispatched a squadron of ships to the Mediterranean with instructions to offer the rulers of the Barbary Coast states payments to leave U.S. shipping alone. Jefferson anticipated trouble, however, and informed the commodore of the squadron:

> But if you find on your arrival in Gibraltar that all the Barbary Powers have declared war against the United States, you will then distribute your forces in such a manner, as your judgment shall direct, so as best to protect our commerce and chastise their insolence—by sinking, burning, or destroying their ships and vessels wherever you shall find them.[15]

Jefferson did not disclose these orders to Congress when he went before that body on December 8, 1801, to request approval to take the offensive in the naval war that was already being fought. Rather, he emphasized the constitutional restraints under which the squadron operated:

> I sent a small squadron of frigates into the Mediterranean, with assurance to that power Tripoli of our desire to remain in peace, but with orders to protect our commerce against the threatened attack. . . . One of the Tripolitan cruisers . . . was captured, after a heavy slaughter of her men, without the loss of a single one on our part. . . . Unauthorized by the Constitution, without the sanction of Congress, to go beyond the line of defense, the vessel, being disabled from committing further hostilities, was liberated with its crew.[16]

Congress passed legislation early in 1802 authorizing the naval war that eventually led to a treaty with the Barbary powers. Jefferson had used deception and a *fait accompli* to secure the Mediterranean for U.S. commercial shipping while publicly asserting Congress's authority to determine when military force would be used.[17]

Hamilton, however, found Jefferson's consultations with Congress needless. He asserted that the president did not have to ask Congress's permission to turn loose the navy because "when a foreign nation declares or openly and avowedly makes war upon the United States, they are then by the very fact already at war and any declaration on the part of Congress is nugatory; it is at least unnecessary."[18]

Despite Jefferson's willingness to violate his principles in pursuit of objectives he considered important, he generally abided by the principle of congressional authorization. In 1805, when Spanish subjects in Florida made incursions into the newly acquired Louisiana Territory, Jefferson told Congress: "Considering that Congress alone is constitutionally invested with the power of changing our condition from peace to war, I have thought it my duty to await their authority for using force. . . . The course to be pursued will require the command of means which it belongs to Congress exclusively to yield or to deny." When Congress chose not to grant Jefferson the authority to attack the Spanish in Florida, he accepted its decision.[19]

The War of 1812

The War of 1812 was the first declared war in U.S. history. Sentiment for the war had been aroused by British captures of American commercial ships and their crews, allegations that the British were supplying hostile American Indians on the frontier with arms, and a desire to acquire foreign territory in Canada and Florida. The initial advocates of the war were not President Madison and his close advisers, but members of Congress from the South and the West. These "War Hawks" represented areas that were troubled by Indian attacks and falling agricultural prices. In contrast, the Federalist merchants of the Northeast, who were making large profits on export shipments that avoided capture, were against the war. They feared that war would interfere with their commerce much more than sporadic British seizures of their ships.

Especially because Congress, although bent on war, had not provided for an adequate army and navy, Madison tried sincerely to resolve disputes with the British through

U.S. and Mexican forces clash at the Battle of Buena Vista in 1847. In hopes of securing territory occupied by Mexico but claimed by Texas, President James K. Polk maneuvered the country into a "defensive" war after U.S. soldiers were attacked by Mexican forces.

diplomacy. He was eventually persuaded that the nation must go to war to protect its rights. On June 1, 1812, the president asked Congress for a declaration of war. In his address to lawmakers, Madison called war making a "solemn question which the Constitution wisely confides to the legislative department of the Government."[20] The declaration was passed 79–49 by the House and 19–13 by the Senate. Members of Congress from the South and the West prevailed over their colleagues from the Northeast.

Not only was the nation divided over the war, it was also unprepared to fight. The small U.S. navy was hopelessly overmatched, and despite the war's popularity in the South and West the army had difficulty recruiting volunteers. U.S. forces suffered a string of humiliating defeats, including the capture and burning of Washington, D.C., by the British in August 1814.

After the British forces withdrew from the capital, Congress assembled to consider the war effort. Yet, with the army still at only about half its authorized strength and enlistments falling off, Congress failed to agree on a conscription bill proposed by James Monroe, Madison's secretary of war and state. Fortunately, the British campaign stalled, and peace negotiations revived. The Treaty of Ghent ending the war was signed on December 24, 1814.

Even in this era, presidents found ways to employ force unilaterally to advance their policies. President Monroe's secret and ambivalent orders allowed Gen. Andrew Jackson to pursue the Seminole Indian raiders into Spanish Florida and to attack Spanish forts suspected of sheltering and aiding the raiders. This action, apparently by design, helped convince the Spanish of the vulnerability of the Florida defenses and moved them toward a negotiated sale of the much desired territory.[21]

The Annexation of Texas and the Mexican War

Texas declared its independence from Mexico in 1836 and indicated that it was interested in becoming part of the United States. Although most Americans supported the principle of expansion, the slavery issue made annexation of a new state a tricky political problem for any president. Presidents Andrew Jackson and Martin Van Buren avoided actions on the Texas issue that would anger voters in the North who were opposed to an extension of slavery. However, John Tyler, who succeeded to the presidency after the death of William Henry Harrison in 1841, was a pro-slavery Virginian who wished to strengthen the slave states and limit British influence in Texas.[22] He began secret negotiations on annexation with Texas and initiated a pro-annexation campaign. The Texans, however, were concerned that if they agreed to annexation they would be invaded by Mexico. They informed Tyler that they would be reluctant to agree to annexation without guarantees that he would protect them with U.S. forces. This created a dilemma for Tyler, whose narrow interpretation of the Constitution had led him to reject presidential authority to use military force without congressional approval except in defense of the nation. In early 1844 Tyler showed that he valued the acquisition of Texas more than his strict constructionist principles when he ordered the deployment of U.S. forces in Texas and the Gulf of Mexico while the secret negotiations proceeded. When the needed two-thirds of the Senate refused to approve the annexation treaty produced by the negotiations, Tyler asked Congress to validate the agreement with a majority vote of both Houses. The joint resolution was passed.[23]

Tyler's successor, President James K. Polk, had greater ambitions for expanding the United States, and he used his commander-in-chief power to maneuver the nation into war with Mexico. Polk had decided to ask Congress for a declaration of war, yet he improved the chance of success by provoking an attack. In 1846 he ordered Gen. Zachary Taylor to deploy his army in a strip of territory near the Rio

Grande that was claimed by Texas but occupied exclusively by Mexicans. The Mexican forces attacked Taylor's army, killing American soldiers. Polk told Congress: "Now, after reiterated menaces Mexico has invaded our territory and shed American blood on American soil."[24] On May 13, 1846, Congress recognized "a state of war as existing by act of the Republic of Mexico." Polk's successful maneuvering demonstrated the capacity of the commander in chief to weaken congressional control over the initiation of armed conflict.

Lincoln and the Civil War

President Lincoln's extraordinary exercise of power during the Civil War demonstrated how far the authority of the presidency could be expanded in wartime. Lincoln believed he faced a choice between preserving the Union and adhering to a strict interpretation of the Constitution. He feared that if he carefully observed the law he would sacrifice the flexibility needed to prevent the destruction of the nation. *(See box, Lincoln's Interpretations of the Presidential War Powers, this page.)*

Lincoln's Expanded Powers

The Civil War began on April 12, 1861, when Confederate forces attacked Fort Sumter in Charleston, South Carolina. Recognizing that the strict constructionists in Congress might object to the emergency measures he thought necessary to deal with

---

LINCOLN'S INTERPRETATIONS OF THE PRESIDENTIAL WAR POWERS

To fight a civil war he did not initiate, Abraham Lincoln stretched presidential power until it approached dictatorship. He used the commander-in-chief clause, his oath to protect the Constitution, and his duty "to take Care that the Laws be faithfully executed" to justify these extraordinary powers. As a young member of the House of Representatives, Lincoln had occasion to consider the president's authority to initiate war. He criticized President James K. Polk's use of his peacetime command over troops to provoke a war with Mexico. In a letter to William H. Herndon, his law partner in Illinois, Lincoln explained his view of that power:

Washington, Feb. 15, 1848

Dear William:

. . . Let me first state what I understand to be your position. It is, that if it shall become necessary, to repel invasion, the President may, without violation of the Constitution, cross the line, and invade the territory of another country; and that whether such necessity exists in any given case, the President is to be the sole judge.

. . . Allow the President to invade a neighboring nation, whenever he shall deem it necessary to repel an invasion, and you allow him to do so, whenever he may choose to say he deems it necessary for such purpose—and you allow him to make war at pleasure. Study to see if you can fix any limit to his power in this respect, after you have given him so much as you propose. If, to-day, he should choose to say he thinks it necessary to invade Canada, to prevent the British from invading us, how could you stop him? You may say to him, "I see no probability of the British invading us" but he will say to you "be silent; I see it, if you dont."

The provision of the Constitution giving the war-making power to Congress, was dictated, as I understand it, by the following reasons. Kings had always been involving and impoverishing their people in wars, pretending generally, if not always, that the good of the people was the object. This, our Convention understood to be the most oppressive of all Kingly oppressions; and they resolved to so frame the Constitution that no one man should hold the power of bringing this oppression upon us. But your view destroys the whole matter, and places our President where kings have always stood. Write soon again.

Yours truly,
A. Lincoln[1]

1. *The Collected Works of Abraham Lincoln*, ed. Roy P. Basler (New Brunswick, N.J.: Rutgers University Press, 1953), 451–452.

---

the crisis, Lincoln delayed the convocation of Congress until July 4. He used this three-month period to order a series of executive actions to meet the military emergency.[25]

On May 3, 1861, Lincoln called for the mobilization of 75,000 state militia under a 1795 act that authorized the president to issue such a call. Although this action was considered within the powers of the president, most of Lincoln's actions during the early months of the war, from spending government revenues without congressional authorization to suspending *habeas corpus* (the constitutional guarantee against arbitrary detention and imprisonment), had no explicit constitutional or congressional sanction. In the same proclamation used to mobilize the militia, Lincoln unilaterally increased the size of the regular army by 23,000 troops and the navy by 18,000. In addition, he ordered nineteen vessels added to the navy and directed the secretary of the Treasury to advance $2 million to authorized persons to pay for military requisitions. Lincoln also ordered a blockade of

Southern ports, suspended *habeas corpus* in the vicinity of the routes used by Union forces between Washington, D.C., and Philadelphia, ordered foreign visitors to observe new passport regulations, restricted "treasonable correspondence" from being carried by the Post Office, and directed the military to arrest and detain persons "who were represented to him" as contemplating or participating in "treasonable practices."[26]

When Congress finally convened on July 4, Lincoln asked the members to ratify the actions he had taken in their absence. He maintained that some of his emergency measures, "whether strictly legal or not, were ventured upon under what appeared to be a popular demand and a public necessity, trusting then, as now, Congress would readily ratify them." In justifying his suspension of *habeas corpus*, Lincoln made the constitutional argument that in spite of the placement of the provision on *habeas corpus* suspension in Article I, the Framers must have intended the president to share with

Congress the suspension authority, because emergencies requiring such action would not always occur when Congress was in session. Yet Lincoln defended his action on practical grounds as well, asking Congress, "Are all the laws but one to go unexecuted, and the Government itself go to pieces lest that one be violated?" In asking this question Lincoln implied that an emergency threatening the existence of the nation may empower the president to ignore parts of the Constitution to defend the whole.[27] In April 1864 he explained his reasoning in a letter to Albert Hodges:

> I did understand, however, that my oath to preserve the Constitution to the best of my ability impressed upon me the duty of preserving by every indispensable means, that government—that nation, of which that Constitution was the organic law. Was it possible to lose the nation and yet preserve the Constitution? By general law, life and limb must be protected, yet often a limb must be amputated to save a life; but a life is never wisely given to save a limb. I felt that measures otherwise unconstitutional might become lawful by becoming indispensable to the preservation of the nation. Right or wrong, I assumed this ground and now avow it.[28]

Lincoln did not come to this conclusion lightly. As a member of the House of Representatives, he had questioned the legality and propriety of President Polk's actions that led to the Mexican War. *(See box, Lincoln's Interpretations of the Presidential War Powers, p. 255.)* Lincoln's expansion of his own war-making powers as president, therefore, did not result from a cavalier attitude toward the Constitution but from his recognition of an unprecedented emergency.

During the summer, Congress debated a joint resolution that sanctioned Lincoln's acts. Nagging doubts about the legality of his suspension of *habeas corpus* and blockade of Southern ports prevented a vote on the resolution. Near the end of the session, however, a rider approving Lincoln's actions was attached to a pay bill for army privates that was rushed through Congress. On August 6, 1861, Congress passed the bill and its rider, which declared the president's acts pertaining to the militia, the army, the navy, and the volunteers "in all respects legalized and made valid . . . as if they had been issued and done under the previous express authority and direction of Congress."[29]

Throughout the war, Lincoln continued to extend his commander-in-chief power beyond its constitutional limits. In 1862, when voluntary recruitments were not adequately supplying the army's need for additional troops, Lincoln ordered a draft. The same year he extended his suspension of *habeas corpus* to persons throughout the entire nation who were "guilty of any disloyal practice." He also declared that these persons could be tried by military courts. On January 1, 1863, Lincoln issued the Emancipation Proclamation freeing "all persons held as slaves within any State or designated part of a State, the people whereof shall then be in rebellion against the United States." It was a sweeping confiscation, or destruction, of private property without due process or compensation. Lincoln maintained that his commander-in-chief power gave him the authority to issue the proclamation, which, by liberating the slaves, would reduce the labor force of the South, thereby hindering its ability to carry on the war. It also would provide a new group of army recruits.[30]

The Prize Cases

Although the Supreme Court eventually objected to Lincoln's order that civilians could be tried in military courts, it did sanction his prosecution of a total war against the South. When hostilities began, the president had ordered a blockade of Confederate ports to prevent the South from selling cotton to England and importing supplies. The owners of four vessels seized by the blockade sued for redress on the grounds that the seizures were illegal because Congress had not declared war against the South. Lincoln's duty to suppress the insurrection, they argued, was not equivalent to the power to wage war. Therefore, the president could not legally order an act of war such as a blockade in the absence of a declaration of war.

In 1863 the Supreme Court rejected these arguments in its 5–4 decision on the Prize Cases. Writing for the majority, Justice Robert C. Grier explained:

> It is not necessary to constitute war, that both parties should be acknowledged as independent nations or sovereign states. A war may exist where one of the belligerents claims sovereign rights as against the other. . . . A civil war is never solemnly declared; it becomes such by its accidents—the number, power, and organization of the persons who originate and carry it on. When the party in rebellion occupy and hold in a hostile manner a certain portion of territory; have declared their independence; have cast off their allegiance; have organized armies; have commenced hostilities against their former sovereign, the world acknowledges them as belligerents, and the contest a war.[31]

The decision supported Lincoln's interpretation that the insurrectionist South was without sovereign rights, while the North possessed all rights of a belligerent in wartime. Moreover, the decision gave Lincoln confidence that the Court would not restrict his expansive interpretation of his commander-in-chief powers in the future. Although this case dealt specifically with the president's power to respond to a general insurrection, advocates of a strong presidency have cited it when arguing in favor of a broad interpretation of presidential war power.[32]

The Spanish-American War

The 1895 Cuban rebellion against Spanish rule occurred when the United States was ready to seek a wider role in global affairs. For some Americans, the Cuban crisis offered an opportunity to flex American muscle against a European power and extend U.S. influence. Others, aroused by slanted reports in the press of Spanish atrocities in Cuba, wished to rescue the island's inhabitants from Spanish tyranny. This combination of forces resulted in a popular crusade in the United States to aid Cuban independence.

President Grover Cleveland resisted the temptation to satisfy the nation's appetite for war with Spain during the last two years of his term. In a curious reversal of roles, he even warned members of Congress that, as commander in chief, he would refuse to prosecute any declaration of war.[33] William McKinley entered office in 1897 similarly determined to avoid war. Yet after the mysterious sinking of the U.S. battleship *Maine* in Havana harbor in February 1898, McKinley could no longer stand up to congressional belligerence and public opinion. He asked Congress on April 11, 1898, to approve U.S. armed intervention in Cuba. Spain had already acceded to many American demands for a settlement of the Cuban crisis, but on April 25 Congress passed a declaration of war authorizing the president to use military force to expel Spain from the island. It was adopted by the Senate 42–35 and by the House 310–6.

The brevity of the war, the ease with which victory was achieved, and the popularity of the conflict made McKinley's job as commander in chief easier. Although he had resisted war, McKinley nevertheless extended the conflict from Cuba to Spanish holdings in the Pacific: the Philippines and Guam. The issue of what to do with the Philippines was quite controversial. McKinley decided to take possession of the islands as part of a broader policy of expanding U.S. trade in the Far East.[34]

On December 10, 1898, Spain signed a treaty relinquishing its control over Cuba and ceding the Philippines along with Puerto Rico and Guam to the United States. The Senate approved the treaty after a month of debate by a vote of 57–27, only one vote more than the necessary two-thirds majority, and for the first time a president and Congress acquired territory outside the North American continent through war.

The World Wars

The first involvement of the United States in an overseas war of massive scale provided the occasion for the most dramatic expansion of presidential wartime powers since the Civil War. The basis for Woodrow Wilson's power differed from Lincoln's, however, in that Lincoln had taken emergency actions independently of Congress, whereas Wilson

PRESIDENTIAL CLAIMS TO POLICE ACTION

Periodically, presidents have advanced and acted on doctrines that expand the scope of the president's authority to initiate armed conflict. One such doctrine is derived from the executive power and asserts that the president is responsible for protecting the lives and property of U.S. citizens and may deploy armed forces anywhere to fulfill this duty. For example, in 1900 President William McKinley sent troops into China, ostensibly to protect American lives threatened by a domestic insurrection called the Boxer Rebellion. This doctrine affords the president a pretext for intervening in a wide variety of circumstances and places in pursuit of other aims. This doctrine muddled the well-established constitutional principle—designed to control the executive—that Congress has sole authority to take the nation from a state of peace to a state of war.

Similarly, President Theodore Roosevelt's 1904 "corollary" to the Monroe Doctrine expanded the international police power by asserting that the United States would not only resist foreign intervention in the Western Hemisphere, but it would also "police" the hemisphere by intervening in the domestic affairs of other countries if misbehavior or political turmoil—what Roosevelt termed "chronic wrongdoing"—threatened to invite foreign intervention. Many presidents, from Roosevelt to Barack Obama, have assumed that the president alone has the authority to initiate the use of force in other countries, and they have acted on this basis in Colombia, the Dominican Republic, Nicaragua, Honduras, Cuba, Mexico, and Haiti. Moreover, Roosevelt's assertion of authority suggests that a presidential foreign policy proclamation or doctrine can become the basis for extending the president's power to project armed forces and enter into hostile action, the Constitution notwithstanding.[1] President James K. Polk may have embraced the "manifest destiny" of the nation to expand to the Pacific, but he did not act as if his preferences were sufficient authority for going to war with Mexico. Specifically and generally, Roosevelt's bold assertion altered the basis of presidential claims to a broad commander-in-chief power. *(See also "Police Actions and Rescue Missions," p. 298.)*

1. Louis Fisher, *Presidential War Power*, 2d rev. ed. (Lawrence: University Press of Kansas, 2004), 39–44, 51–61.

was handed most of his expanded war-making authority by statute.[35] Congress gave Wilson not only expanded control of the military and discretion to fight subversion and espionage, but also unprecedented control over industries and the allocation of scarce resources. For example, the Lever Food and Fuel Act of 1917 gave the president "full authority to undertake any steps necessary" for the conservation of food resources. In addition, the 1918 Overman Act gave the president complete authority to reorganize the executive branch. Congress was willing to make these broad delegations of power to Wilson because most members believed that the scope and urgency of the war required unified control and direction of all operations and resources related to the war effort.

In essence, Congress did not just give Wilson broad discretion in implementing its statutes, it abdicated legislative power to him for the duration of the war. Many delegations of authority to the president simply stated their objectives and left Wilson to decide how to achieve them. He commandeered plants and mines, requisitioned supplies, fixed prices, seized and operated the nation's transportation and communications networks, and managed the production and distribution of foodstuffs. The Council of National Defense, an umbrella agency created by Wilson, administered the economy during the war. Wilson created the War

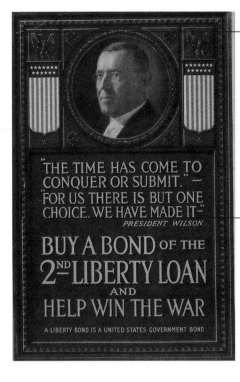

"THE TIME HAS COME TO CONQUER OR SUBMIT." — "FOR US THERE IS BUT ONE CHOICE. WE HAVE MADE IT."
PRESIDENT WILSON.

BUY A BOND OF THE 2ND LIBERTY LOAN AND HELP WIN THE WAR

A LIBERTY BOND IS A UNITED STATES GOVERNMENT BOND

Seen here on this war bonds poster, President Wilson won his second term as president on the platform of having kept America out of war. Shortly after his second inauguration, however, he led America into the First World War in order to further the cause of democracy.

Industries Board using his authority as commander in chief. Wall Street broker Bernard Baruch, who had been appointed by Wilson to head the board, became a dictator of sorts over U.S. industry. The president also established by executive order the Committee of Public Information, under whose direction a system of voluntary news censorship was instituted and various government publicity services were organized. On April 28, 1917, Wilson imposed strict censorship of cable messages, which later was extended to other forms of communication with foreign countries under authority of the Trading with the Enemy Act of October 6, 1917.

Presidential war powers reached their apex during World War II. Constitutional scholar Edward S. Corwin wrote: "The relation . . . of the First World War to the Second as regards constitutional interpretation is that of prologue and rehearsal."[36] Like Wilson during World War I, Franklin Roosevelt was delegated wide powers by Congress to manage the economy and direct the war effort, but Roosevelt went beyond Wilson in asserting his power as commander in chief to take any action he deemed necessary to the war effort.

Overcoming Neutrality

The president's war powers were tightly restrained during the 1930s by the prevailing mood of isolationism in Congress and among the American people. Congress enacted and Roosevelt signed a series of laws designed to keep the United States out of the conflicts brewing in Europe and Asia. These laws included the Neutrality Acts of 1935 and 1937, which prohibited shipments of arms, ammunition, or implements of war to any belligerent nation, including those that had been the

victims of aggression. After Adolph Hitler's invasion of Poland in September 1939, which brought Great Britain and France into the war against Nazi Germany, Roosevelt began maneuvering the country toward active support of Britain and the other allies, whose survival he believed was crucial to U.S. security.

On September 3, 1940, Roosevelt announced he had concluded an agreement with Great Britain under which that country would receive fifty "over-age" destroyers in return for the right to lease certain British territory in the western Atlantic for U.S. naval and air bases. Roosevelt's destroyer deal was accomplished through an executive agreement—a legally binding pact between the president and the British government—rather than a Senate-ratified treaty. The trade violated at least two congressional statutes, but Roosevelt's attorney general, Robert H. Jackson, asserted that the president acted legally under his commander-in-chief authority to "dispose" of the armed forces. It also was argued that the commander in chief was responsible for securing adequate bases for national defense.

On March 11, 1941, Congress passed the Lend-Lease Act, described by Corwin as the most "sweeping delegation of legislative power" ever given to a president.[37] It authorized the president to manufacture any defense article and to "sell, transfer title to, exchange, lease, lend or otherwise dispose of" the defense articles to the "government of any country whose defense the President deems vital to the defense of the United States." The act gave President Roosevelt the power to aid the Allied cause as he saw fit by virtually any means short of using the armed forces.

Yet Roosevelt did use the armed forces to aid the Allied cause despite the absence of any congressional sanction for acts of war. After Germany occupied Denmark in April 1941, Roosevelt ordered U.S. troops to be stationed in Greenland. Three months later, American forces occupied Iceland. Both moves were made without consulting Congress, which had forbidden the deployment of U.S. reserves and draftees outside the Western Hemisphere in the Reserves Act of 1940 and the Selective Service Act of 1941.[38] By the summer of 1941, U.S. naval vessels under presidential orders were escorting Allied convoys across the Atlantic. After the U.S. destroyer *Greer* exchanged shots with a German submarine on September 4, the president declared that henceforth U.S. warships providing protection to supply convoys bound for Britain would be under orders to attack Axis vessels on sight. Three months before Congress declared war, therefore, Roosevelt had already maneuvered the nation into an undeclared naval war in the Atlantic.[39]

Roosevelt's "Dictatorship"

The U.S. entry into World War II was accompanied by the concentration of almost all war powers in the president's hands. Congress delegated vast authority to the president to prosecute the war as it had during World War I, but it also acquiesced to Roosevelt's many unsanctioned appropriations of power and his broad interpretations of congressional statutes. Although Roosevelt saw the wisdom of obtaining Congress's approval for controversial actions, he was far more assertive than Wilson in using his commander-in-chief power to establish complete control over the war effort.

Roosevelt created dozens of executive regulatory agencies that were not based on a specific statute, such as the Office of Emergency Management, Board of Economic Warfare, National War Labor Board, Office of Defense Transportation, and War Production Board. Anything remotely connected to the nation's war effort, including managing national resources and economic activity, was regulated by these war management agencies, which were responsible to the president rather than to existing departments or independent regulatory agencies. Roosevelt justified their creation by citing general delegations of power from Congress, the powers available to him under his emergency proclamations of 1939 and 1941, and his own powers as commander in chief.[40]

On September 7, 1942, the president demonstrated how far he believed his war powers extended. In a speech to Congress, Roosevelt issued an ultimatum to lawmakers to repeal certain provisions contained in the Emergency Price Control Act of 1942:

I ask the Congress to take this action by the first of October. Inaction on your part by that date will leave me with an inescapable responsibility to the people of this country to see to it that the war effort is no longer imperiled by threat of economic chaos.

In the event that the Congress should fail to act, and act adequately, I shall accept the responsibility and I will act.

At the same time farm prices are stabilized, wages can and will be stabilized also. This I will do.

The President has the power, under the Constitution and under Congressional acts, to take measures necessary to avert a disaster which would interfere with the winning of the war. . . .

I have given the most thoughtful consideration to meeting this issue without further reference to the Congress. I have determined, however, on this vital matter to consult with Congress. . . .

The American people can be sure that I will use my powers with a full sense of my responsibility to the Constitution and to the country. The American people can also be sure that I shall not hesitate to use every power

vested in me to accomplish the defeat of our enemies in any part of the world where our own safety demands such defeat.

When the war is won, the powers under which I act automatically revert to the people—to whom they belong.[41]

With this declaration, Roosevelt claimed, according to Corwin, "the right and power to disregard a statutory provision which he does not deny, and indeed could not possibly deny, that Congress had full constitutional authority to enact, and which, therefore, he was under obligation by the Constitution to 'take care' should be 'faithfully executed.'"[42] Roosevelt was threatening to suspend the Constitution in the interest of national security if Congress did not act. Not even Lincoln during the Civil War had claimed the power to repeal a specific congressional statute.

Many members of Congress were shaken by Roosevelt's ultimatum, and a few denounced it. Republican senator Robert A. Taft of Ohio called the speech "revolutionary and dangerous to the American form of government . . . an assertion that the laws of this country can be made by executive order."[43] The American public, however, supported Roosevelt's position, and with the war raging, there was little desire in Congress to engage the president in a constitutional showdown. Congress therefore amended the Emergency Price Control Act to meet Roosevelt's objections.

Postwar Congressional Acquiescence

After World War II, differences between the United States and the Soviet Union brought on the cold war, a state of continuous international tension that contributed to increased presidential control over national security policy. The specter of an aggressive Soviet Union pushing out wherever the West failed to resist made Congress reluctant to impose restrictions on executive action. A consensus developed that because presidents possessed both the capacity to act immediately and the access to the most detailed and reliable information, they alone were suited to direct foreign and military policy. Their status as leaders of the free world and caretakers of the U.S. nuclear arsenal, the most devastating military force ever created, contributed to their unchallenged authority.

The Korean War

When the North Korean army swept into South Korea on June 24, 1950, President Harry Truman believed he had to act to save South Korea and discourage further communist aggression. The next day the United States called an emergency session of the United Nations Security Council, which passed a resolution condemning the invasion and asking UN members to "render every assistance" to South Korea. By coincidence, the Soviets were boycotting the Security

Council to protest the exclusion of the new communist government of China from the UN. Consequently, their representative was not present to veto the resolution. That evening, Truman made up his mind to use air and naval forces to defend South Korea. He authorized Gen. Douglas MacArthur to evacuate Americans from South Korea, transport supplies to the South Koreans, and bomb military targets below the thirty-eighth parallel. After Truman announced his intention to defend South Korea and initiated U.S. involvement, the UN Security Council passed a second resolution explicitly calling on members to give military assistance to South Korea. By June 30, Truman had authorized MacArthur to use U.S. ground forces and to bomb targets in North Korea, thereby completing the U.S. commitment to defend South Korea.[44]

The Korean War involved a massive qualitative change in presidential assertion of war powers. President Truman claimed and exercised an authority to engage the United States in a war without any congressional declaration or authorization. Truman could easily have secured a congressional resolution approving his use of military forces in Korea, but the president wished to avoid an appearance of dependence on Congress. Truman had been advised by Secretary of State Dean G. Acheson and chair of the Senate Foreign Relations Committee Thomas T. Connally, D-Tex., that his commander-in-chief power and the UN Security Council resolution gave him ample authority to use the armed forces. According to Acheson, Truman considered the presidency "a sacred and temporary trust, which he was determined to pass on unimpaired by the slightest loss of power or prestige."[45] Past presidents had ordered U.S. forces to rescue Americans overseas, police the hemisphere, or undertake some other type of limited military mission. The Truman administration cited these precedents in justifying its interpretation of the commander-in-chief power.[46]

The Korean War, however, was quite without precedent in American history. Although by then numerous precedents had established the president's power to use the armed forces for very limited missions, there was no precedent for presidential authority to commit the nation to a large-scale, bloody war of indefinite length involving hundreds of thousands of military personnel. By every definition, the United States was waging war in Korea, regardless of the Truman administration's restrictions on the use of military force against Chinese territory and its assertions throughout the war that U.S. involvement amounted to participation in a UN "police action."[47]

In addition, Truman's use of a UN Security Council resolution as a basis for unilateral presidential action contradicted the language and history of the UN Charter. As constitutional scholar Louis Fisher argues, no treaty can alter the Constitution by delegating the war power to the UN or to the president. Both the Charter and the UN Participation Act specify that any Security Council agreement involving the use of troops is subject to ratification in accordance with each country's "constitutional processes." The congressional debate over the effect of the UN Charter on the war powers revolved around whether the relevant constitutional process was senatorial approval or a two-house resolution. The UN Charter was approved with the understanding that both houses of Congress would have to authorize the use of armed forces in hostilities, and the UN Participation Act clearly affirmed this.[48]

A few Republicans protested Truman's failure to involve Congress in the decision. Influential Republican senator Robert Taft announced on June 28 that although he agreed that U.S. forces should be used in Korea, the president had "no legal authority" to send them without the approval of Congress. In general, though, members of Congress overwhelmingly supported Truman's decision to commit U.S. forces and, initially, did not challenge Truman's sweeping claims of authority. During the fall of 1950, the war remained popular as UN forces were successful in driving the North Koreans up the peninsula. In November General MacArthur's forces had occupied most of North Korea and appeared close to reunifying North and South.[49] In November and December, however, Communist Chinese forces entered the war and drove UN forces back across the thirty-eighth parallel into South Korea.

With Congress already alarmed by reversals in the military campaign, Truman announced on December 19 that he planned to send four more divisions to Europe to bolster Allied defenses under the North Atlantic Treaty Organization (NATO). This time the president's intention to send so many troops abroad without congressional approval triggered a congressional reevaluation of U.S. defense and foreign policy that was known at the time as the "great debate." The debate, which lasted from January to April 1951, was concerned not only with Truman's deployment of troops to Europe, but also with the president's authority to involve the nation in the Korean War. The fear, expressed most fully by Senator Taft, was that the president could use treaties and executive agreements as authority to place U.S. armed forces in situations that would nullify Congress's control over the initiation of war. In the end, the Senate passed two resolutions approving the dispatch of four divisions to Europe. One of the resolutions declared that it was the sense of the Senate that Congress should approve any future deployment of ground troops to Europe.

Truman hailed the resolutions as an endorsement of his policies. They were not. But the Senate and the House failed to pass any binding resolutions that would have put teeth into their assertions of constitutional prerogative in controlling the commitment of the nation's forces. Similar debates leading to similarly weak legislative responses were repeated during the next twenty years.

Truman's actions set the stage for a period of broad presidential control of foreign and national security policy. Truman did suffer a setback in 1952 when the Supreme Court ruled in *Youngstown Sheet and Tube Co. v. Sawyer* that he did not have the authority to take over steel mills to prevent a strike that might damage the Korean War effort.[50] Otherwise, as historian Arthur M. Schlesinger Jr. wrote: "By bringing the nation into war without congressional authorization and by then successfully defending his exercise of independent presidential initiative, Truman enormously expanded assumptions of presidential prerogative."[51]

Joint Resolutions

The period following the Korean War was characterized by the passage of congressional resolutions granting or acknowledging the authority to use such force as presidents deemed necessary to repel armed attacks or threats against designated nations or regions. The purpose behind some of these resolutions was to deter potential aggressors by making it clear that the U.S. government was united in a commitment to respond. Between 1955 and 1962, four joint resolutions of this type were passed. The Formosa Resolution, signed into law on January 29, 1955, authorized presidents to use U.S. forces to protect Formosa and the Pescadores Islands against attack from the People's Republic of China. The Middle East Resolution, signed into law on March 9, 1957, proclaimed U.S. intentions to defend Middle East countries "against any country controlled by international communism." The Cuban Resolution, signed into law on October 3, 1962, authorized presidents to take whatever steps they believed necessary to defend Latin America against Cuban aggression or subversion and to oppose the deployment in Cuba of Soviet weapons capable of threatening U.S. security. The 1962 Berlin Resolution did not have the force of law but expressed the sense of Congress that the United States was determined to defend West Berlin and the access rights of the Western powers to that city.

These resolutions received wide support in Congress, although they did have critics who charged that the resolutions gave too much discretionary power to the president and absolved Congress from any responsibility for national security. Schlesinger describes the extent of congressional abdication during this period:

> In the decade after Korea Congress receded not alone from the effort to control the war-making power but almost from the effort to participate in it, except on occasions when national-security zealots on the Hill condemned the executive branch for inadequate bellicosity. Mesmerized by the supposed need for instant response to constant crisis, overawed by what the Senate Foreign Relations Committee later called "the cult of executive expertise," confused in its own mind as to what wise policy should be, delighted to relinquish responsibility,

Congress readily capitulated to what Corwin at the start of the fifties had called "high-flying" theses of presidential prerogative.[52]

The Vietnam War

No single president was entirely responsible for U.S. participation in the war in Vietnam; rather, a succession of presidents gradually increased U.S. military involvement in Southeast Asia. In 1954 Vietnamese revolutionary forces defeated the French, who had controlled the region as a colonial power. President Dwight D. Eisenhower had continued the Truman administration's policy of sending aid to the French, but Eisenhower refused to intervene militarily to prevent a French defeat. After the French departed, Vietnam was temporarily partitioned, with the communist government of Ho Chi Minh ruling the North and anticommunists in Saigon controlling the South. Eisenhower undercut reunification efforts, which he feared would result in communist control over the entire country, by ignoring the scheduled reunification elections in 1956 and supporting the noncommunist regime in the South. The North Vietnamese and their supporters in the South launched a guerrilla war in an effort to achieve reunification through force. Although Eisenhower stepped up economic and military aid to the Saigon government, which included a small number of U.S. military advisers, he avoided more extensive U.S. military involvement.

President John F. Kennedy, however, fearing the collapse of the Saigon government, responded to South Vietnamese requests for greater assistance by sending additional military advisers and counterinsurgency units to South Vietnam. By November 1963, the Kennedy administration had deployed 16,500 U.S. military personnel to Vietnam.

President Lyndon B. Johnson continued the gradual escalation of U.S. involvement in the widening war. The Gulf of Tonkin incident in August 1964 resulted in a resolution supporting any presidential effort to combat North Vietnamese aggression. *(See box, Tonkin Gulf Resolution, p. 263.)* Armed with this congressional sanction and fearing an imminent communist takeover, Johnson ordered the first regular combat troops to Vietnam in 1965. Their mission was to defend the U.S. airbase at Da Nang, but soon they were conducting patrols and actively engaging the enemy in combat. Although Johnson believed his commander-in-chief powers and the Tonkin Gulf Resolution gave him the authority to send the troops to Vietnam, he nevertheless wanted Congress on record as approving the move. He therefore requested a specific appropriation of $700 million for U.S. military operations in Vietnam. Within two days, both houses had passed the bill with little dissent.[53] By 1968, Johnson had increased U.S. troop strength in Vietnam to

Soldiers of the U.S. 9th Division patrol through an abandoned rice paddy past a flooded shell crater during the Vietnam War. Throughout history presidential ability to wage war has continually expanded, even after Congress passed the War Powers Resolution in 1973. The resolution reasserted congressional authority to approve military activities begun by the president.

more than 500,000. But the communists' Tet offensive early that year, although a military failure, caused Americans, including Johnson, to begin to lose confidence that the war could be won.

President Richard Nixon began slowly withdrawing U.S. forces from Vietnam in 1969. Nixon's goal was to extricate the United States from the Vietnam quagmire while achieving "peace with honor." In January 1973 the United States and North Vietnam signed a peace accord. The North Vietnamese returned U.S. prisoners of war and allowed the regime of South Vietnamese president Nuygen Van Thieu to remain in power. In return, the United States withdrew its forces from Vietnam and allowed North Vietnamese army units already in South Vietnam to remain there. Without U.S. military support, however, South Vietnam was unable to defend itself against a 1975 North Vietnamese offensive that resulted in the fall of Saigon. Although President Nixon had promised Thieu that the United States would intervene if communist forces threatened to conquer the South, Nixon had already resigned from the presidency in 1974, and Congress refused to fund any further military involvement in Southeast Asia.

Although less so than the Korean War, the Vietnam War was a presidential war. The executive branch dominated decision making about goals and strategy in Vietnam with little congressional influence. Indeed, after 1965 neither Johnson nor Nixon sought congressional approval for their prosecution of the war. Nevertheless, the picture of these presidents carrying on military activities in Indochina without congressional consent often was overdrawn by critics of the war. Congress continually voted in favor of military appropriations and the draft, two resources vital to Johnson's and Nixon's prolongation of the war. Once troops and materiel had been committed to battle, most members of Congress believed that denying U.S. forces the money and reinforcements they needed to wage the war would be perceived as unpatriotic.

Resurgence of Congress

In 1969 the growing number of U.S. casualties in Vietnam, the lack of support for the increased commitment necessary to win the war, and failing public support for the effort encouraged Congress to assert its war powers. In that year, the Senate passed the National Commitments Resolution, which stated that a national commitment "results only from affirmative action taken by the legislative and executive branches . . . by means of a treaty, statute, or concurrent resolution of both houses of Congress specifically providing for such commitment." Although the resolution only expressed the sense of the Senate and had no force of law, it represented Congress's growing dissatisfaction with its exclusion from national security and foreign policy decisions. Later in the year, Congress adopted an amendment supported by President Nixon prohibiting the use of U.S. ground forces in Laos and Thailand. For the first time in three decades, Congress had exercised its authority to limit military activities overseas.[54]

In 1970, even as U.S. forces were being withdrawn from Southeast Asia, President Nixon secretly ordered U.S. forces into Cambodia to attack communist sanctuaries. When Nixon announced the operation on April 30, 1970, many college campuses erupted in protest against the expansion of the war, and four student demonstrators at Kent State University in Ohio were killed by National Guard troops. An estimated 100,000 protesters marched on Washington, D.C. After months of debate, a lame-duck Congress passed an amendment in December 1970 barring the use of U.S. ground forces in Cambodia. This amendment had little effect because Nixon had withdrawn U.S. ground troops from Cambodia months before and lawmakers had backed away from prohibiting the use of U.S. aircraft over Cambodia. Later in December, Congress repealed the Tonkin Gulf Resolution.

During the early 1970s, momentum for legislation that would restore Congress's role in the foreign policy process

TONKIN GULF RESOLUTION

Each of the joint resolutions sanctioning presidential use of force passed by Congress between 1955 and 1962 represented a declaration of national policy upon which there was broad agreement. The supporters of these resolutions considered them to be effective means of allowing Congress to create a united front behind presidential action without a formal declaration of war. This was the intention of members of Congress when they voted almost unanimously in favor of the Tonkin Gulf resolution in 1964.

On August 2, 1964, the U.S. destroyer *Maddox*, which the navy contended was on a routine mission in the Tonkin Gulf off the coast of North Vietnam, was attacked by North Vietnamese patrol boats. Two nights later the *Maddox*, which had been joined by another destroyer, the *C. Turner Joy*, reported a second patrol boat attack. Neither ship was damaged. President Lyndon B. Johnson responded to the incidents by ordering U.S. warplanes to bomb North Vietnamese torpedo boat bases.

Johnson informed Congress that U.S. ships had been attacked and asked both houses to pass a resolution empowering him to respond to further North Vietnamese aggression. The administration depicted the incidents as unprovoked acts of belligerence. On August 7, Congress passed the Gulf of Tonkin Resolution by votes of 88–2 and 416–0. The resolution stated that "Congress approves and supports the determination of the President, as Commander-in-Chief, to take all necessary measures to repel any armed attack against the forces of the United States and to prevent further aggression." Within the resolution a broader clause declared that the United States was "prepared, as the President determines, to take all necessary steps, including the use of armed force, to assist any member or protocol state of the Southeast Asia Collective Defense Treaty requesting assistance in defense of its freedom."[1]

By overwhelmingly passing the resolution, Congress was following the practice set during the previous decade of deferring to the president's judgment in national security matters in the name of expediency and unity.

Key members of Congress understood that the Tonkin Gulf Resolution could be interpreted as a "blank check."[2] Members of the Johnson administration and the president himself frequently cited the resolution as evidence of congressional authorization of their policies in Vietnam. Although the resolution in combination with U.S. membership in the Southeast Asia Treaty Organization may not have been the "functional equivalent" of a declaration of war, as Under Secretary of State Nicholas Katzenbach claimed in 1967, it did provide a justification for almost any presidential military decision in Vietnam.

Investigations by the Senate Foreign Relations Committee in 1968 revealed that the *Maddox* was actually gathering sensitive intelligence within the territorial waters claimed by the North Vietnamese and that a South Vietnamese naval attack against North Vietnam was taking place nearby. Furthermore, U.S. intelligence had warned that the North Vietnamese navy was under orders to respond to U.S. vessels in the vicinity of the South Vietnamese operation as if they were part of that operation, and U.S. ships had been moved to reinforce the Maddox before it was attacked.[3]

The 1968 revelations about the Tonkin Gulf incidents and growing congressional discontent with the war led to the repeal of the Tonkin Gulf Resolution on December 31, 1970. The repeal provision was added to a foreign military sales bill, which was signed by President Richard Nixon on January 12, 1971. However, the Nixon administration claimed that the president's commander-in-chief power gave him sufficient authority to carry on the war in Vietnam.

1. Quoted in Christopher H. Pyle and Richard M. Pious, *The President, Congress and the Constitution* (New York: Free Press, 1984), 339–340.
2. Quoted in Leslie H. Gelb with Richard K. Betts, *The Irony of Vietnam: The System Worked* (Washington, D.C.: Brookings, 1979), 103.
3. Richard M. Pious, *The American Presidency* (New York: Basic Books, 1979), 387.

continued to build in Congress. Meanwhile, President Nixon was undertaking a series of controversial military actions without consulting Congress. He provided air support for South Vietnam's 1971 invasion of Laos, ordered North Vietnam's Haiphong harbor mined in May 1972, and launched massive bombing raids against North Vietnam in December 1972. Furthermore, Nixon's "secret" war in Cambodia in 1970, the publication in 1971 of the *Pentagon Papers* (which disclosed the deception of the executive branch during the 1960s), and the revelations about secret national security commitments uncovered by a Senate Foreign Relations subcommittee chaired by Stuart Symington, D-Mo., contributed to the growing perception of lawmakers that executive branch secrecy was out of control. After three years of work and debate, Congress's attempts to construct a bill that would reestablish its war and national security powers culminated in passage of the War Powers Resolution in 1973.

WAR POWERS RESOLUTION

Implicit in the War Powers Resolution (HJ Res. 542, PL 93-148), which was enacted in November 1973 over President Nixon's veto, was an admission by Congress that it had contributed to the debacle in Vietnam by abdicating its war-making responsibilities to the executive branch. The results of the Vietnam War had cast grave doubts on the assumption that the executive branch, with its superior intelligence resources, its unity of command, and its ability to act quickly, should be largely responsible for determining when and how the nation should go to war. With the passage of the War Powers Resolution Congress attempted to reassert its constitutional prerogative to authorize all significant military engagements. The bill's preamble stated that its purpose was

> to fulfill the intent of the framers of the Constitution of the United States and insure that the collective judgment

of both the Congress and the President will apply to the introduction of U.S. armed forces into hostilities, or into situations where imminent involvement in hostilities is clearly indicated by the circumstances, and the continued use of such forces in hostilities or in such situations.

The most important and controversial provisions of the legislation outlined the situations under which presidents could commit troops; permitted Congress at any time by concurrent resolution to order the president to disengage forces involved in an unauthorized military engagement; and required presidents to withdraw armed forces from a conflict within sixty days—ninety if the president certified that more time was necessary to disengage U.S. military personnel safely—unless Congress specifically authorized the continued use of U.S. forces. Other provisions in the act obligated presidents to report to Congress within forty-eight hours on large troop movements abroad and urged them to consult with Congress "in every possible instance" before ordering U.S. forces into hostilities or a situation where hostilities might be imminent.

These provisions are not easily reconciled. On the one hand, the "Purpose and Policy" section seems to confine presidential authority within strict constitutional limits; a president may introduce armed forces into a hostile situation only if Congress has formally authorized the action or if there is a national emergency created by an attack on the United States, its territories, or its armed forces. On the other hand, the procedural sections on reporting, consultation, and time limits seem to suggest otherwise. But they do not actually say that the president has the constitutional authority to engage in hostilities for sixty days. Rather, they acknowledge that the president can and will move troops into hostile or potentially hostile circumstances. The resolution then specifies procedures, including time limits, for congressional scrutiny of such decisions.

To strengthen the resolution's clear purpose that all long-term military engagements must have explicit congressional authorization, Congress included a provision denying that a president could infer congressional authorization for the introduction of troops into hostilities or potentially hostile situations "from any provision of law . . . including any provision contained in any appropriation Act, unless such provision specifically authorizes the introduction of United States Armed Forces into hostilities or into such situations and states that it is intended to constitute specific statutory authorization within the meaning of this resolution." The provision also denied the president the authority to infer congressional authorization for presidential war making from a ratified treaty. Thus Congress attempted to restrict the means through which it could be said to have approved presidential war making to explicit authorizations of military action.

Passage of the War Powers Resolution was heralded by its supporters as a major step in reasserting Congress's war-making powers. Republican senator Jacob K. Javits of New York, a chief architect of the Senate's version of the legislation, declared:

> With the war powers resolution's passage, after 200 years, at least something will have been done about codifying the implementation of the most awesome power in the possession of any sovereignty and giving the broad representation of the people in Congress a voice in it. This is critically important, for we have just learned the hard lesson that wars cannot be successfully fought except with the consent of the people and with their support.[55]

The resolution was opposed by some conservatives in both houses and a small group of liberals who agreed that the measure was unconstitutional, but for different reasons. The leading liberal opponent of the resolution, Democratic senator Thomas F. Eagleton of Missouri, called the act "the most dangerous piece of legislation" he had seen in his five years in the Senate.[56] Eagleton and other liberal critics of the War Powers Resolution charged that although it may force the president to deal with Congress within ninety days after troops are committed, it sanctions practically any use of the military by the president during those ninety days, thereby enhancing rather than restricting presidential war-making power. He warned: "By failing to define the president's powers in legally binding language, the bill provided a legal basis for the president's broad claims of inherent power to initiate a war. Under the formula, Congress would not participate in the war-making decision until *after* forces had been committed to battle."[57] Although the resolution gave Congress the power to withdraw troops from a conflict, Eagleton believed Congress would rarely have the political will to do so, because such action would be seen by many constituents as unpatriotic or lacking in resolve.

In President Nixon's October 24, 1973, veto message of the war powers bill, he stated that the resolution would impose restrictions on the authority of the president that would be "both unconstitutional and dangerous to the best interests of the nation."[58] On November 7, the House overrode the president's veto by a vote of 284–135—only four votes more than the required two-thirds majority. Later in the day, the Senate followed with a 75–8 override vote. The congressional override was made possible, in part, by the Watergate scandal, which had weakened Nixon's support among legislators of his party.

Legal Questions

Many of the War Powers Resolution's critics and even a few of its supporters have expressed doubts that all of its provisions will stand up to judicial review. President Nixon denounced the war powers bill as unconstitutional when he vetoed it in 1973. The major provisions of the bill, he contended, would "purport to take away, by a mere legislative act, authorities which the president has properly exercised under the Constitution for almost 200 years." These provisions were unconstitutional, he asserted, because "the only way in which the constitutional powers of a branch of the government can be altered is by amending the Constitution—and any attempt to make such alterations by legislation alone is clearly without force."[59]

Neither the executive branch nor a majority of members of Congress has appeared eager to let the Supreme Court decide whether the War Powers Resolution is an unconstitutional legislative intrusion into the powers of the president. It may be that both branches have believed they have more to lose than to win from such a confrontation. On the one hand, because presidents have been able to ignore the most potent provisions of the War Powers Resolution, they have had little incentive to seek a decision on the issue in court that might force them to comply more strictly with its provisions. On the other hand, Congress may have been dissuaded from mounting a legal challenge to presidential war making by the Supreme Court's historic tendency to favor the presidency on matters of foreign policy and national security. A Supreme Court ruling striking down the resolution would deprive lawmakers of any leverage provided by their threats to invoke the resolution and would symbolically weaken Congress's claim to a place in the national security decision-making process.

The Chadha Decision

In 1983 the Supreme Court's decision in an unrelated case called into question at least one crucial provision of the War Powers Resolution. The Court ruled 7–2 in *Immigration and Naturalization Service v. Chadha* that legislative vetoes of presidential actions are unconstitutional. Legislative vetoes are provisions of laws that give Congress the power to review and rescind executive actions otherwise authorized by law. They had been used by Congress for more than fifty years, primarily to maintain some control over executive implementation of congressional policies. The Court in *Chadha* ruled that legislative vetoes circumvent the president's constitutionally granted executive and veto powers. Writing for the majority, Chief Justice Warren Burger emphasized, "The hydraulic pressure inherent within each of the separate branches to exceed the outer limits of its power, even to accomplish desirable objectives, must be resisted."[60]

The *Chadha* ruling raised questions about the sections of the War Powers Resolution empowering Congress to compel the president to withdraw U.S. forces engaged in hostilities by passing a concurrent resolution, which does not require presidential approval. Such a concurrent resolution may constitute a legislative veto over executive action.[61] The War Powers Resolution, however, does not delegate any power to the president, and it denies that introducing armed forces into hostilities is within the president's constitutional authority. The resolution may, therefore, fall outside the reach of the *Chadha* decision. As Louis Fisher argues, the Constitution itself gives Congress a veto insofar as it must authorize military action. Giving the president a veto over any resolution restricting military action would require a two-thirds majority in both houses to control the president's war-making power.[62]

Uses of Force under the War Powers Resolution

Every president thereafter has denied the constitutionality of the War Powers Resolution, and each of these presidents has used military force, often on a large scale, without complying with its terms. They have seldom consulted Congress before using the military, they have dissembled about the nature of the hostilities, and they have ignored efforts by Congress to force them to start the sixty-day war powers clock. When presidents have reported to Congress, they have generally claimed full constitutional authority for their actions. The many military operations undertaken since the resolution was passed have underscored the inability to control presidential war making in the absence of Congress's firm determination to assert its authority. Some significant and telling examples follow.

Mayaguez Incident

The first major test of the War Powers Resolution occurred on May 12, 1975, when Cambodian Communist gunboats seized the U.S. merchant ship *Mayaguez* and its crew of thirty-nine off the disputed island of Poulo Wai in the Gulf of Siam. President Gerald R. Ford unilaterally ordered U.S. forces to free the sailors and their ship and to bomb Cambodian targets in retaliation. The rescue attempt succeeded in freeing the *Mayaguez* and its crew but resulted in the deaths of forty-one marines.

In this case, there was general agreement that the president had the authority to commit U.S. troops without receiving congressional authorization. Ford complied with the war powers provision that required him to report to Congress within forty-eight hours, but he consulted only with selected members of Congress and only after the order to attack had been issued.

Ford, however, defended his approach: "When a crisis breaks out, it is impossible to draw the Congress in with the decision-making process in an effective way." Ford also criticized the resolution itself as "a very serious intrusion on the responsibilities of the President as Commander-in-Chief and the person who formulates and ought to execute foreign policy."[63]

Iranian Hostage Rescue Attempt

In April 1980 President Jimmy Carter sent a small contingent of U.S. forces into Iran in an attempt to rescue forty-nine American embassy personnel held hostage in Tehran.

Equipment failure forced the mission to be aborted after eight commandos died in a helicopter crash. Carter justified his decision not to consult with Congress by citing the mission's dependence on secrecy. Many members of Congress agreed with Carter's decision. Sen. John Glenn, D-Ohio, remarked, "If I were on that raid, I wouldn't want it all over Capitol Hill."[64] Carter also maintained that the mission was a "humanitarian" rescue attempt rather than a military action against an enemy nation and therefore fell outside the scope of the War Powers Resolution.[65]

Lebanon

In 1982 President Ronald Reagan sent U.S. troops to Lebanon as part of a multinational peacekeeping force. Marines initially were introduced into that country on August 24, 1982, with the specific mission of observing the evacuation of Palestine Liberation Organization (PLO) forces from Beirut under an agreement mediated by the United States. The marines left Beirut on September 10, after the PLO withdrawal had been completed. Before this operation, the president held constructive consultations with the foreign relations committees of both houses.[66] Reagan had reported to Congress on the deployment of marines the day before it took place. He stated that he was reporting to Congress "consistent" with the resolution rather than "under" it.[67]

After the assassination of President Bashir Gemayel of Lebanon on September 14, 1982, and the massacre of Palestinians at the Sabra and Shatila refugee camps by Lebanese Christian militia on September 16, Reagan ordered twelve hundred U.S. marines to return to Lebanon. The mission of the peacekeeping force, which arrived on September 29, was to join with Italian, French, and British forces in providing a buffer between warring factions, thereby improving stability in Lebanon and the Middle East.

The marines were obviously in a situation in which hostilities were "imminent," but Congress did not demand that the War Powers Resolution's sixty-day clock be started. On August 29, 1983, U.S. forces sustained their first casualties. President Reagan authorized the marines to defend themselves from their positions and ordered warships in the Mediterranean to shell positions in the hills outside Beirut from which the marines had been receiving hostile fire.

Congressional pressure forced the president to negotiate with Congress on terms for keeping the marines there. On October 12, President Reagan signed a joint resolution that started the War Powers Resolution clock but also authorized him to keep the marines in Lebanon for eighteen months. The compromise resolution stated that the marines had been in a situation of imminent hostilities since August 29, 1983, and that this legislation was "the necessary specific statutory authorization under the War Powers Resolution for continued participation by United States Armed Forces

in the Multinational Force in Lebanon." The compromise favored the president and demonstrated Congress's reluctance to apply the War Powers Resolution's strict terms to presidential use of the military.[68] Although the resolution was the basis for the congressional threats that brought the president to the bargaining table, President Reagan denied the constitutionality of the War Powers Resolution and even the legal validity of the joint resolution he was signing:

> I do not and cannot cede any of the authority vested in me under the Constitution as President and as Commander-in-Chief of the United States Armed Forces. Nor should my signing be viewed as any acknowledgment that the President's constitutional authority can be impermissibly infringed by statute, that congressional authorization would be required if and when the period specified in . . . the War Powers Resolution might be deemed to have been triggered and the period had expired, or that the 18-month authorization may be interpreted to revise the President's constitutional authority to deploy United States Armed Forces.[69]

Grenada

On October 25, 1983, two days after the killing of 241 marines in Lebanon, President Reagan ordered nineteen hundred U.S. troops to invade the small Caribbean island of Grenada. The action, which Reagan called a "rescue mission," was undertaken to overthrow Grenada's pro-Cuban, Marxist government, to restore order to the island, and to ensure the safety of approximately one thousand American citizens living there, most of whom were medical students. U.S. forces were joined by troops from six Caribbean nations belonging to the Organization of East Caribbean States, which had officially asked the United States to intervene.

Reagan reported to Congress but claimed that he was acting under his own authority. The House overwhelmingly voted that the sixty-day clock of the War Powers Resolution had begun when U.S. troops invaded Grenada, and the Senate prepared to pass similar legislation. The president declared an end to the fighting on November 2, and he announced plans to withdraw all combat troops by December 23, the end of the sixty-day period.[70]

The invasion, whose objectives were achieved quickly, was viewed favorably by the U.S. public, and Congress generally supported the Grenada action.

Persian Gulf Naval Escorts

In 1987 during the war between Iran and Iraq, Iranian attacks on Kuwaiti neutral ships threatened to slow the flow of Arab oil through the Persian Gulf. In response to Kuwaiti pleas for assistance, President Reagan offered on March 10, 1987, to place tankers owned by Kuwait under the U.S. flag so they could be escorted through the gulf by

In November 1990 President George H. W. Bush and Gen. H. Norman Schwarzkopf review U.S. troops stationed in the Persian Gulf region. Two months later the United States led a coalition of twenty-eight nations to a crushing victory over Iraq in liberating Kuwait.

U.S. warships. The escort of the Kuwaiti tankers was intended to ensure the flow of oil through the gulf and to prevent the Soviet Union, which Kuwait also had asked for help, from increasing its influence among moderate Arab nations and its naval presence in the gulf.[71]

On July 24, two days after the escort missions began, a reflagged Kuwaiti tanker was damaged by an Iranian mine. Critics of the administration's Persian Gulf strategy pointed to the incident as evidence that the naval escorts could involve the United States in the gulf conflict, and many lawmakers called on the president to invoke the War Powers Resolution. The Reagan administration refused, however, to acknowledge that the escort missions placed U.S. forces into hostilities or an area of imminent hostilities even though military personnel were receiving danger pay.[72]

Panama

In December 1989 President George H. W. Bush sent U.S. forces into Panama. "Operation Just Cause" was a major intervention in a sovereign nation at peace with the United States undertaken without congressional authorization. President Bush justified the invasion as necessary to protect American lives and property, to arrest Panamanian leader Manuel Noriega as a drug trafficker, to ensure the integrity of the Panama Canal Treaty, and to restore democracy to Panama. Factually, and as justifications for an invasion, all of these reasons were highly debatable, especially as bases for presidential authority to invade another nation.[73]

In the period leading up to the invasion, President Bush had kept congressional leaders informed about developments in Panama and the canal zone, and he informed them by phone hours before the invasion was launched. After the operation began, his formal notice to Congress was accompanied by an assertion that the War Powers Resolution

was "unconstitutional."[74] Nevertheless, Bush seemed careful to confine the operation to the resolution's sixty- to ninety-day limit.

Persian Gulf War

In August 1990 Iraqi leader Saddam Hussein invaded Kuwait. Citing both the gross violation of national sovereignty and the vital national interest in protecting the flow of critical oil supplies from the Middle East, President Bush responded swiftly with a massive U.S. military buildup in the neighboring nation of Saudi Arabia. These forces were sent without congressional consultation. President Bush notified Congress but denied that the 100,000 troops were in a situation that was likely to evolve into hostilities.[75] Bush also denied any need for congressional authorization even after he sent an additional 150,000 military personnel. Although he claimed that the policy was to establish a defensive "shield," clearly the forces had been increased to offensive capability. Consequently, members of Congress called on Bush to seek authorization for any offensive action.

Instead, President Bush built an international coalition and secured a UN Security Council resolution authorizing UN members to use all necessary means to restore the sovereignty of Kuwait. Bush claimed that this resolution and his constitutional authority as commander in chief gave him sufficient authority to act. Yet, ruling on a suit filed by fifty-four members of Congress seeking an injunction against any offensive action, Judge Harold Greene argued that, although he could not issue an injunction at that time, congressional authorization was required by the Constitution.[76]

In January 1991 Bush asked for congressional support for "Operation Desert Storm," which would drive the Iraqis out of Kuwait. After a lengthy debate in both houses, Congress explicitly "authorized" offensive action under the War Powers Resolution while limiting that action to the terms of the Security Council resolution.[77] Bush, however, denied the validity of the War Powers Resolution and denied that congressional authorization was constitutionally required.

Somalia

Late in his term, and under pressure from Congress, President Bush ordered troops to Somalia, which was suffering from a civil war. The objectives of the mission were limited strictly to assisting in the international effort to relieve the famine-wracked population and to preparing for a more permanent UN force to continue the operation.

The operation was redefined in June 1993 after twenty-three UN peacekeepers were killed by one of the warring factions. U.S. warplanes and ground troops then joined in a retaliatory strike. The United Nations, with President Bill Clinton's approval, shifted to a more ambitious mission of subduing the armed factions and rebuilding the nation's political order. In October eighteen U.S. Rangers were killed and eighty wounded in an assault on one faction's headquarters.

Although U.S. forces were under fire, experiencing casualties, and receiving combat pay for an offensive operation, Clinton did not consult with, or formally report to, Congress on the change in policy. With the death of U.S. soldiers, the operation had become unpopular. Eventually, Congress and the Clinton administration agreed on a deadline for the use of funds for the operation.

Haiti

After the Somalia debacle, congressional criticism of the Clinton policy toward Haiti was less about the War Powers Resolution and more about the president's authority to commit forces in multilateral operations.

In 1991 a military coup overthrew the democratically elected government of Jean-Bertrand Aristide. President Bush declared that the coup "would not stand" and initiated an economic boycott as well as other nonmilitary measures to pressure the military rulers of Haiti. President Clinton continued the Bush policies until the military rulers openly reneged on their July 1993 agreement to cede power and U.S. forces sent to assist the transition were prevented from landing in October 1993. Then Clinton committed his administration to more forceful action to restore the democratically elected government. Congress debated a number of measures to restrict the president's capacity to send armed forces but passed, in May 1994, only a nonbinding resolution that asserted the need for congressional authorization.[78]

In July 1994 the UN Security Council passed a resolution inviting member nations to use "all necessary means" to restore the democratic government. The Senate passed another nonbinding resolution stating that the Security Council action was not sufficient authority, but Clinton denied that he needed congressional authorization.

Bosnia

In 1993 the United States began participating in a joint UN/ NATO effort to relieve the famine caused by the civil war between Serbs, Croats, and Muslims in the former Yugoslavia. U.S. forces were dispatched to help enforce a ban on unauthorized military flights over Bosnia-Herzegovina. President Clinton did not seek congressional authorization either for deployment or for engagement in combat. In 1994 U.S. fighter planes took part in NATO attacks on Bosnian Serb forces. Clinton used his commander-in-chief power as well as the UN and NATO resolutions to claim the full authority to order these missions.

Congress made several attempts to legislate restrictions on the use of additional forces in Bosnia. In 1993 Congress and Clinton agreed on a nonbinding resolution outlining conditions for the placement of U.S. forces under foreign command and stating that funds should not be used to deploy ground forces to oversee a peace agreement.[79] In August 1995 U.S. forces led extensive NATO air strikes against Bosnian Serb positions, and in September President Clinton promised twenty thousand U.S. troops to assist in NATO's oversight of a peace accord. Clinton deepened this commitment by having the United States host the peace talks in Dayton, Ohio. Once the peace accord was signed in Paris on December 14, 1995, Clinton began sending troops on his own authority and with a promise to limit the mission to one year. The House passed resolutions contradicting the president's authority to send troops, opposing the mission, and yet supporting the troops deployed. The Senate passed a resolution supporting the president's commitments while asserting the one-year limit on the mission.

Kosovo

Four years later, the United States again became enmeshed in the Balkans when it led NATO air strikes in Kosovo to halt Serbian leader Slobodan Milosevic's mass attacks in the region. The air strikes followed extensive peace talks that Serbia ultimately rejected.[80] President Clinton conducted the air strikes with divided Senate support, and House opposition, though neither chamber actually tried to stop the military action. The air war concluded successfully in ten weeks, with no ground troops and no U.S. combat casualties. Yet Congress's ability to participate in decision making over the use of military force was questioned once again.

Afghanistan

After the terrorist attacks of September 11, 2001, George W. Bush promised swift retaliation against its perpetrators. As the president said in his address to the nation on September 20, 2001, "Every nation, in every region, now has a decision to make. Either you are with us, or you are with the terrorists."[81] In the speech Bush identified the network of terrorist groups known as al Qaeda as responsible for the attacks, and he identified their close ties with the repressive and misogynistic Taliban regime in Afghanistan. A few weeks later, on October 7, 2001, the United States attacked al Qaeda camps and Taliban military posts in Afghanistan.

Although Congress had not issued a declaration of war against Afghanistan—and, indeed, had not declared war since World War II—congressional, public, and international support for the U.S. attacks was strong. Just three days after September 11, Congress had passed a joint resolution authorizing the president "to use all necessary and appropriate force against those nations, organizations, or persons he determines planned, authorized, committed, or aided the terrorist

President Obama talks with Gen. Stanley McChrystal, right, and U.S. Ambassador Karl Eikenberry, left. General McChrystal was the commander of armed forces in Afghanistan until June 2010 when he made controversial statements about civilian leadership to Rolling Stone *magazine. Afterward, he was brought on board by the Obama administration to lead an initiative that works to support military families.*

attacks of September 11, 2001, or harbored such organizations or persons."[82] Public approval of the president soared to the highest levels ever recorded, surpassing the previous record set by former President George H. W. Bush after the 1991 Gulf War. Countries around the world rallied to support the United States in battling terrorists who posed a global threat to security. Within a few months, coalition forces led by the United States had successfully toppled the repressive Taliban regime, albeit without capturing al Qaeda leader Osama bin Laden, and then began the arduous task of building a new regime in Afghanistan.[83] The United Nations established an International Security Assistance Force (ISAF) to ensure stability, and the North Atlantic Treaty Organization (NATO) later assumed control of the mission, with several nations contributing troops, though the vast majority came from the United States. Over the next several years, security forces battled insurgents and worked with Afghan forces to establish stability, a viable governing structure, and a functioning economy. But the George W. Bush administration's decision to wage war against Iraq fostered criticism that it had diverted attention and resources from the primary U.S. interest of routing terrorist networks in Afghanistan.

Barack Obama pledged during the 2008 presidential campaign that he would reduce U.S. forces in Iraq and focus foremost on establishing a secure and independent political regime in Afghanistan. One year after taking office, following

extensive deliberation with his national security team, President Obama announced in December 2009 that he would substantially increase U.S. military forces in Afghanistan to make progress in battling al Qaeda, halting a resurgence by the Taliban, and establishing a stable governing system.[84] In so doing, Obama both rejected the advice of Vice President Joseph Biden, who had argued for reducing the U.S. presence in Afghanistan, and modified the military's request for a larger commitment of American forces. Over the next several months, the United States sent 30,000 additional troops to Afghanistan (for a total of nearly 100,000 American forces there), similar to the "surge" of U.S. forces in Iraq that President George W. Bush had authorized in 2007. Despite criticism from both supporters and opponents of the military mission, Obama persevered, and the United States scored a major victory in May 2011 when a CIA-led elite military unit of Navy SEALS killed bin Laden in a firefight in Pakistan. The next month, Obama announced that the United States would begin withdrawing troops from Afghanistan, with the goal of transferring full control to Afghan security forces by 2014.

Iraq

Within a few months of the 2001 attacks on Afghanistan, the Bush administration began to hint of forthcoming military action against Iraq as well. In his January 2002 State of the Union address, Bush identified Iraq, Iran, and North Korea as "an axis of evil, arming to threaten the peace of the world."[85] The day after the one-year anniversary of the September 11, 2001, terrorist attacks, Bush addressed the United Nations General Assembly and called for it "to serve the purpose of its founding"[86] by enforcing its many resolutions demanding that Iraq comply with weapons inspections. Although Bush did not explicitly link the September 11, 2001, terrorist attacks with Iraq, he fully iterated the dangers that weapons of mass destruction in this dictatorial regime posed to the world. The next front for the United States in the war on terror was clear.

Following the model that his father had established before the first Gulf War in 1991, Bush sought to secure both congressional and UN approval for the use of military force against Iraq. Congress complied swiftly, passing a joint resolution in October 2002 that authorized the president to use armed force to defend the United States against the threat posed by Iraq and to enforce relevant UN Security Council resolutions. The UN Security Council also seemed initially to support the Bush administration's agenda, unanimously passing a resolution in November 2002 that called for "serious consequences"[87] if Iraq did not comply with arms inspections. Yet the apparent international consensus soon broke down, and ultimately, the United States was unable to secure a second Security Council resolution that explicitly authorized military action against Iraq. The United States waged war against Iraq in 2003 with congressional support but not UN backing, though many member states of the United Nations endorsed U.S. actions.[88]

By early 2007 the American public had grown weary over mounting U.S. causalities and the lack of stability in Iraq. Although Bush had congressional approval for the use of military force, newly empowered Democrats, in control of both houses of Congress for the first time since 1994, began to exert pressure on the president to end the war. In February 2007 the House passed a nonbinding resolution opposing Bush's plan to send additional troops to Iraq, popularly known as the "surge." Soon after, Congress passed a supplemental Iraq spending bill that included a timetable for U.S. troop withdrawal. President Bush vetoed the bill partly because it set an "arbitrary date" for withdrawal. Lacking the votes to override the veto, and not wanting to cut funding to troops already deployed in the field, Congress then passed a spending bill that gave Bush what he wanted without a withdrawal deadline. Yet Democratic leaders vowed immediately to keep up pressure for a change of course in the war, and upon taking office, President Barack Obama pledged to conclude the combat mission within eighteen months. He announced the end of Operation Iraqi Freedom in an Oval Office address on August 31, 2010, after the last brigade of U.S. combat forces had departed, and nearly seven-and-a-half years after the conflict began.[89] Approximately 50,000 U.S. troops remained in Iraq temporarily as advisers to Iraqi security forces, but by the end of 2011, the Obama administration had completed its withdrawal of U.S. forces.

North Africa, the Middle East, and Libya

The winter of 2010–2011 unexpectedly became a transformational period in global politics, when civil unrest in several countries in North Africa and the Middle East successfully overturned longtime repressive governing regimes. In Tunisia, street demonstrations against high unemployment, rising food prices, and corruption led to the president's ouster, in what became known as the "Jasmine Revolution." In Egypt, civil resistance and labor strikes forced the president's resignation. A wave of protests and uprisings across North Africa and the Middle East followed, in such places as Jordan, Yemen, and Syria. As these events unfolded, the United States expressed its support for democratic governance in the region, and employed military force in one case: Libya.

In February 2011 civil unrest in Libya against dictator Muammar Qaddafi swelled quickly to become an uprising seeking his removal from office. The harsh response of Qaddafi's forces to the protestors raised the prospect of becoming a large-scale massacre, prompting international outcry and intervention. In March 2011, after securing a U.N. Security Council resolution authorizing the use of military force to protect civilians in Libya, President Obama approved U.S. air strikes to establish a no-fly zone there.[90] Within days, the United States handed over military command of the no-fly zone to NATO, and by summer's end, Qaddafi had fled from power; he was killed by rebel forces in October 2011. But Obama faced criticism for not seeking a congressional resolution authorizing the use of force in Libya; while the administration claimed that the War Powers Resolution did not apply to this limited engagement, which did not involve ground troops, Congress disagreed, and in June the House rejected a bill to authorize military action in Libya, though it did not approve a measure to halt funding for the operation. Qaddafi's departure eased concerns about the United States becoming entangled in another military conflict, but the constitutional debate about the president's authority to wage such a conflict without congressional approval continued.

Effects of the War Powers Resolution

The War Powers Resolution has, on the one hand, probably influenced some conflict-related decisions. During President Reagan's deployment of marines to Lebanon in 1982 and 1983, the prospect of the invocation of the resolution helped to produce a formal compromise between the legislative and executive branches on the limits of a military operation. Similarly, President Clinton was forced by an assertive Congress to agree to an even stricter time limit on forces in

Somalia. On the other hand, since passage of the resolution in 1973, neither congressional resolutions nor the automatic sixty-day time limit has forced a president to disengage U.S. troops from a conflict. The War Powers Resolution has, then, not been much of a rein on the president's war powers, but mainly because it has never been enforced. Moreover, presidents have appeared undaunted by the resolution's potential to restrict the introduction of American armed forces into hostile situations.

The resolution could be strengthened as law. Currently, it is based on an interpretation of the president's commander-in-chief power, and it has been weakened by the historical precedents that back a president's claims of broad authority to commit armed forces. The resolution could be strengthened by tying the president's authority to commit troops to Congress's clear authority over expenditures.[91] The effectiveness of the resolution depends on the collective will of Congress to challenge presidential actions. If this collective will exists, Congress has ample means to check the president's war-making power and to expand its role in deciding when and how military force should be used. In 1995 Congress considered measures that would repeal the War Powers Resolution, retain the consulting and reporting provisions, and place specific restrictions on U.S. participation in multilateral operations, including UN peacekeeping missions.

MILITARY RESPONSES TO TERRORISM

Periodically, presidents have called on the military to battle not just other nations but also extragovernmental groups that have threatened Americans and their interests. For example, the navy fought pirates in the eighteenth and nineteenth centuries, and in 1916 President Woodrow Wilson sent Gen. John J. "Blackjack" Pershing and six thousand troops into Mexico in pursuit of the Mexican bandit Pancho Villa after he raided Columbus, New Mexico.

Beginning in the 1970s, international terrorist groups have regularly threatened and attacked U.S. citizens, civilian and military alike. The groups committing these acts and the nations that have supported them are generally Arab or Islamic. The motives of these often fanatical groups are largely religious and ideological.

Initially, these attacks were on a relatively small scale. In response, intelligence agencies expanded their efforts to identify terrorists, and the U.S. military stepped up its antiterrorist preparations and formed elite counterterrorist

President George W. Bush addresses a crowd of firemen, rescue workers, and volunteers at Ground Zero—the 16-acre plot where the 110-story World Trade Center towers once stood—three days after two hijacked planes struck the buildings on September 11, 2001. The terrorist attack in New York killed almost 2,900 people in the towers and 147 passengers and crew aboard the two airplanes.

units to provide presidents with a more credible military option should they decide to use force against terrorists. But military operations against terrorists were usually thought to be risky and impractical, and presidents generally refrained from using significant military force against terrorists. The costs of such operations, in lives and diplomatic relations, always appeared to be greater than the possible benefits of what was judged to be unwinnable conflicts.[92] Those directly responsible, moreover, were difficult to identify with precision; they often shielded themselves by locating their operations in densely populated areas. As a result, military operations against terrorists would not only violate sovereign borders, but also risk harming innocent civilians. The more common antiterrorist weapon has been the imposition of economic sanctions on nations such as Syria, Iraq, and Iran that have supported terrorist organizations.

Beginning in the 1980s, terrorists increased the scope and brutality of their attacks. In 1983, 241 marines were killed by a car bomb in Beirut. Many more American lives were lost in other bombings: of a West Berlin discotheque frequented by U.S. military personnel (1986), of the Khobar Towers in Saudi Arabia (1996), of the U.S. embassies in Kenya and Tanzania (1998), and of the *Cole* in Yemen

(2000). The Reagan administration began responding with limited military operations. In October 1985 navy fighters intercepted an Egyptian airliner carrying terrorists who had seized a passenger ship and killed a U.S. citizen in the Mediterranean. In April 1986 U.S. warplanes bombed targets in Libya after U.S. intelligence obtained evidence that Libyan leader Col. Muammar Qaddafi sponsored the West Berlin discotheque bombing. President Clinton also used force in ordering cruise missile attacks on terrorist bases in Afghanistan and a possible chemical weapons operation in the Sudan.

The savage September 11, 2001, attacks on New York City and the Pentagon demonstrated the ineffectiveness of sanctions and of short-term, small-scale military actions. President George W. Bush, responding to the attacks, announced that his administration would prosecute a comprehensive "war on terrorism." Unlike in most recent military operations, the commander in chief received immediate support and cooperation from Congress. The controversies that had been occupying Congress and the White House—tax cuts, spending priorities, missile defense, and Medicare and Social Security reform—were pushed aside. With little debate or controversy, Congress passed a $40 billion emergency appropriation and a resolution authorizing the use of force against terrorist organizations and the nations that support

them; it said little about avoiding the use of ground troops and minimizing American losses. *(See box, Congressional Authorization for a War on Terrorism, this page.)*

Congress also passed a controversial counterterrorism bill that expanded the national government's powers of surveillance and detention. Reports of a sweeping intelligence order, authorizing covert actions by the Central Intelligence Agency (CIA) against Osama bin Laden and the al Qaeda organization, with extraordinary cooperation between CIA and military units, were not greeted with the usual suspicions and congressional investigations.[93] Perhaps most significantly, the president and his advisers propounded a "unitary executive" theory of presidential power, which essentially held that the executive possessed the inherent power to prosecute the war on terrorism without seeking approval from Congress or the courts. The unitary executive concept was used to justify the indefinite detention of terrorist suspects, interrogation methods and military tribunals for those detainees, and domestic wiretapping without judicial review for alleged links to terrorist threats.[94]

As a military campaign, a war on terrorism raised questions about war powers. What exactly was the legal and constitutional status of this sort of conflict? With whom, or what, was the nation at war? As with piracy, the immediate enemy was not another country. But was the nation at war

CONGRESSIONAL AUTHORIZATION FOR A WAR ON TERRORISM

In response to the September 11, 2001, terrorist attacks on New York City and Washington, D.C., President George W. Bush committed the nation to what he called a "war on terrorism." Although the president did not acknowledge any need for congressional approval, Congress formally authorized the "use of force" just days after the attacks.[1]

However, the resolution, passed on September 14, 2001, was marked by ambiguity. The authorization seemed to be narrower than the president's commitment. It authorized the use of force against "nations, organizations, or persons" in any way culpable in "recent attacks," with the purpose of preventing "any future acts of international terrorism by such nations, organizations or persons" (section 2a). While permitting a war on the al Qaeda terrorists responsible for the attacks and their abettors, the resolution was not broad enough to cover the president's general war on international terrorism.

Yet the statement of facts included a more comprehensive statement of purpose: to deter and prevent acts of international terrorism against the United States. This section also seemed to acknowledge that the president had full authority "under the Constitution" to prosecute this broad aim. In other words, the resolution acknowledged that the president's constitutional authority already encompassed the powers that Congress was claiming to authorize.

How expansively the 2001 congressional resolution interpreted presidential power sparked heated debate as the George W. Bush administration

vigorously prosecuted the war on terrorism. The president adhered to a "unitary executive" concept of presidential power, which held that the Constitution granted the president broad authority to take action without first seeking congressional authorization.[2] The Bush administration claimed this authority to justify the indefinite detention of prisoners, authorization of military tribunals for "enemy combatants," domestic surveillance of terrorist suspects, and other controversial actions. The 2001 congressional resolution was further cited as evidence of Congress's support for presidential leadership in combating terrorism. The Supreme Court ruled in 2006 that the president did not possess unchecked power to establish military tribunals without attention to international laws governing treatment of prisoners. In response, Congress passed the Military Commissions Act of 2006, though the Supreme Court ruled in 2009 that a section of the law denying *habeas corpus* review to detainees was unconstitutional. *(See box, Supreme Court Cases Related to the President's Foreign Policy Powers, p. 208, in Chapter 5.)* President Barack Obama initially promised to close Guantanamo Bay and hold civilian trials for detainees in the United States, but in the face of congressional resistance, the Obama administration announced in 2011 that it would continue the practice of holding military tribunals at Guantanamo.

1. *CQ Weekly*, September 15, 2001, 2158.
2. Jeffrey Rosen, "Power of One," *New Republic*, July 24, 2006.

if it was not warring on another sovereign state? Also like piracy, however, the immediate enemy needed the cooperation or acquiescence of nation-states to harbor its operations and, especially in the case of terrorism, to fund its activities. This relationship could lead, as it did in Afghanistan, to hostile actions against governments. But because the principal aim of military operations would be to debilitate or destroy a criminal element, they would not necessarily entail military victory over those states, which is the defining objective of a war. Considered in this way, a campaign against terrorist organizations seemed more akin to international policing than to war, and it invited a reconsideration of Theodore Roosevelt's rationale for an international police power. On the other hand, the U.S. operation in Afghanistan turned almost immediately to the defeat of the Afghan government, which brought it much closer to a formal war.

These considerations led to another set of war powers questions about the scope of the conflict. Congress's authorization of the use of force was ambiguous, but President Bush defined the sides in this conflict sharply: either you are with us or you are with the terrorists. When the Taliban government of Afghanistan refused to arrest the al Qaeda leadership and dismantle the al Qaeda terrorist training camps, it became the target of retaliation and antiterrorist operations. If the same reasoning and response were applied to other countries that harbor and finance terrorist organizations, a long-term military campaign against international terrorism could involve the United States in numerous conflicts that would be, in form and fact, wars.

In his January 2002 State of the Union address, President Bush took a step in this direction; he singled out Iraq, Iran, and North Korea for their development of weapons of mass destruction and support for international terrorism. He declared that the United States would vigorously oppose this "axis of evil." Later that year, the Bush administration published its National Security Strategy, in which it explicitly declared that the United States "will, if necessary, act preemptively" to combat terrorist threats.[95] President Bush followed through on this strategy with the 2003 Iraq war, which Congress endorsed. But what role Congress would play in deciding upon a future preemptive attack remained unclear. The 2006 national security strategy stated that "the place of preemption in our national security strategy remains the same,"[96] but it placed greater emphasis on diplomacy and alliance-building, as well as the need to address the national security challenges and opportunities created by globalization. The 2002 case for preemption appeared to apply primarily to Iraq, but not to set a precedent for future U.S. military action.

The Obama administration recast the U.S. national security strategy in several ways. It identified four underlying national interests: security, prosperity, values, and international order. It declared that the United States would work with other nations through institutions such as the UN and NATO to determine when military intervention abroad was necessary. And it emphasized the close linkage between American security and domestic prosperity.[97] Obama's desire to minimize sending U.S. troops abroad was reflected through his increased use of remotely controlled aircraft, or drones, to target terrorist networks. The Obama administration further distanced itself from its predecessor by rejecting the phrase "global war on terror" (GWOT) for identifying a tactic of extremist groups as the enemy; instead, Obama favored a broader approach to undermining the root causes of extremist threats to the United States.

INTERNATIONAL AGREEMENTS AND THE WAR POWERS

As events beginning with the Korean War demonstrate, efforts to control presidential use of force have been complicated by U.S. participation in the United Nations and numerous mutual security agreements with other nations. Presidents have used the UN Charter, Security Council resolutions, and other multilateral agreements as authority to commit U.S. forces without additional congressional authorization. They have claimed that Congress granted the authority to act by approving these agreements. They also have used these agreements to invoke their broad foreign policy powers as additional authority for the unilateral use of force.

United Nations Peacekeeping

Presidents often have promoted UN peacekeeping missions and, when appropriate, have offered the services of the U.S. military to those missions. UN peacekeeping missions have some advantages over unilateral U.S. action: UN peacekeepers may be less threatening to the nations in which they are deployed, the economic costs to the United States may be lower, and a UN peacekeeping force might promote a spirit of international accountability and cooperation in solving a particular regional problem. Early in his administration, President Clinton was an enthusiastic supporter of an expanded use of UN missions and of broad U.S. participation in them as a way to remain engaged in international affairs in the post–cold war era. Especially after U.S. soldiers were killed in Somalia in 1993, Clinton's policy generated repeated legislative attempts to restrict U.S. participation in UN missions.

The primary responsibility for the peace and security function of the United Nations resides with the Security Council. The council assesses threats to peace and attempts to use peaceful measures to prevent aggression. If nonmilitary actions fail or are inappropriate, the Security Council

A UN armored personnel carrier rumbles through the streets of Pakrac, Croatia, in May 1995. When the Muslim-led government of Bosnia-Herzegovina declared independence from the central Yugoslavian government in February 1992, the Bosnian war began. Following a relentless "ethnic cleansing" campaign by the Bosnian Serbs to rid the Muslim-held territory of Muslims and Croatian Catholics, the United Nations sent a peacekeeping force. It was largely ineffective because there was no international agreement on how to stop the war. After a brief cease-fire in early 1995, the fighting resumed as Croatian forces captured significant chunks of land from the Serbs.

During the late 1980s, the status of UN-sponsored peacekeeping forces grew as UN peacekeepers were awarded the 1988 Nobel Peace Prize and the Soviet Union and United States both advocated the use of UN peacekeeping troops to monitor negotiated settlements of several regional conflicts. The United Nations created new peacekeeping forces to oversee peace accords in Afghanistan, Angola, and Cambodia, and to prevent the war in Bosnia and Serbia from spreading into the former Yugoslav republic of Macedonia. Moreover, in 1992 UN Secretary General Boutros Boutros-Ghali proposed a qualitative change in the type of missions undertaken. He suggested the possibility of a permanent UN force that would not simply oversee peace accords but also intervene forcefully to settle disputes.

This expanded use of UN peacekeepers and the potential for more aggressive use of UN forces led to criticism in Congress and to attempts to restrict U.S. participation in peacekeeping missions. The primary issue was the president's authority, under the UN Charter and Security Council resolutions, to commit armed forces without congressional authorization. Although presidents have argued that their powers in conjunction with UN resolutions provide sufficient authority, such claims are not supported by the text and legislative history of the UN Charter and the United Nations Participation Act.

Any UN Security Council actions calling for member nations to supply armed forces are subject to approval through each member nation's "constitutional processes." The most contentious issue in the 1945 Senate debate on U.S. membership in the United Nations was the nature of those "processes": who had the power to commit U.S. forces to Security Council peacekeeping operations? The Senate did not want to hand the executive exclusive authority to provide the United Nations with troops, and the House refused to allow the Senate and the president to usurp its constitutional role.

The clear understanding that emerged from the debate was that majorities in both houses of Congress would be needed to authorize the commitment of armed forces to UN missions.[99] This understanding was affirmed in the United Nations Participation Act of 1945, which stated in part:

> The President is authorized to negotiate a special agreement or agreements with the Security Council which shall be subject to the approval of the Congress by appropriate Act or joint resolution, providing for the numbers and types of armed forces, their degree of readiness and

may vote to use military force.[98] A Security Council decision to use military force or to create a detachment of military observers cannot be adopted without the unanimous approval of the council's permanent members. The United States, Russia, Great Britain, France, and the People's Republic of China are permanent members of the Security Council. UN peacekeeping forces have been used to separate combatants, monitor cease-fire agreements, and protect civilians.

During the cold war, UN missions were limited by the veto power of the United States and the Soviet Union. For example, the most dramatic use of the UN security function, the Security Council's resolution to resist the North Korean invasion of South Korea in 1950, was possible only because the Soviets were not present to exercise their veto. When the Soviet Union threatened to exercise its Security Council veto to block the creation of any UN peacekeeping force for the Sinai, as part of the 1979 Camp David peace accords between Egypt and Israel, the United States was compelled to organize a multinational force, which included U.S. troops.

general location, and the nature of facilities and assistance, including rights of passage, to be made available to the Security Council on its call for the purpose of maintaining international peace and security.

Thus presidents are expressly prohibited by the Participation Act from unilaterally concluding an agreement with the Security Council under their powers to negotiate treaties, execute the laws, or defend the United States. The president cannot legally aid or commit U.S. forces to UN military missions without an approving congressional resolution.[100] Nonetheless, Presidents Truman (Korea), George H. W. Bush (Kuwait), and Clinton (Haiti) have used UN resolutions as authorization to commit armed forces without congressional approval.

Early in his administration, President Clinton enthusiastically embraced broad U.S. engagement in world affairs through the United Nations and other multilateral organizations. However, in the absence of the global threat of communist expansion, the U.S. interests served by the expenditure of lives and tax dollars in remote parts of the world are more difficult to define and explain. Unlike the Persian Gulf War, in which the United States had a clear interest in protecting the flow of oil from the Persian Gulf states, the United States had only indirect interests, beyond humanitarian concerns, in Somalia, Haiti, Bosnia, and Kosovo. Therefore, the debates over U.S. participation revolved around the degree to which the United States should involve itself in policing the world in the absence of national or global security interests.

U.S. participation in UN missions can be measured in several ways. On the one hand, the United States supplies only a small number of troops to official UN peacekeeping forces. In 1994 only about 800 of 63,000 UN military personnel were Americans. On the other hand, the United States is extensively involved in UN activities and resolutions. For example, the 1994 Haiti operation was under the aegis of a UN resolution, but the U.S. troops sent were not part of a UN command. In early 1995 more than 60,000 U.S. troops were involved in such "contingency" operations with more than half of those stationed in South Korea. Between 1989 and 1996, U.S. spending on peacekeeping increased 500 percent.[101]

In 1993 Congress passed a nonbinding resolution specifying the conditions under which the president could place U.S. forces under foreign command and under which the United States could participate in UN missions.[102] In 1995 both houses of Congress considered similar measures to restrict U.S. participation in UN missions. One provision would have subtracted the cost of unreimbursed spending on "contingency" operations from U.S. payments to the United Nations for peacekeeping missions. Because the unreimbursed expenses exceed U.S. peacekeeping payments to the United Nations by as much as $500 million a year, the measure would have, as intended by its proponents, hindered

UN peacekeeping generally by eliminating all U.S. financial support.

In response to these criticisms and proposals, the Clinton administration announced more restrictive policy guidelines for U.S. participation in UN missions, especially those that may involve combat. Specifically, such missions must involve national interests or "a real threat to international peace and security." These guidelines still asserted that the president had, under the United Nations and other alliances, the full authority to commit armed forces. President Clinton maintained that the congressional proposals would be an imprudent and unconstitutional intrusion on the president's foreign policy and war powers.[103] The fight over UN dues and peacekeeping costs went on for years. Late in the Clinton presidency, Congress, the president, and the United Nations reached an agreement that addressed some of the critics' concerns and committed the United States to paying most of its debt.

Apart from peacekeeping, the president also may seek UN support for military action against aggressor nations. Perhaps the most significant precedent was set in 1990, when President George H. W. Bush, who previously had served as U.S. ambassador to the United Nations, requested a Security Council resolution to authorize the use of force to repel Iraq's invasion of Kuwait. Although the administration maintained that it did not require UN backing, it successfully guided a resolution through the Security Council. In 2002 the administration of President George W. Bush seemed to be following that precedent when it secured a Security Council resolution warning of "serious consequences" if Iraq did not disarm and submit to weapons inspections. But a few months later, the Security Council refused to endorse a second resolution explicitly authorizing force, and the United States ultimately waged war against Iraq without UN support, though many members of the organization supported the United States in what the administration termed a "coalition of the willing."[104] In 2011 President Barack Obama secured the Security Council's support for waging air strikes against the Qaddafi regime in Libya, but he did not seek congressional authorization.

Alliances and Mutual Security Agreements

Until the post–World War II period, the United States shunned alliances. During most of the nineteenth and early twentieth centuries, the military establishments of the great powers of Europe were concerned primarily with defending against threats from their neighbors. Because the security of the United States did not depend on having allies, Americans generally preferred to remain isolationist. Except for the Franco-American Alliance of 1778, which was effectively voided by George Washington's 1793 neutrality proclamation toward Britain and France, the United States did not participate in a formal peacetime alliance until after World War II.[105] Even when the United States entered World War I against Germany in 1917, U.S. leaders demonstrated the national aversion to alliances by claiming to be only an "associated power" of Britain and France.

World War II shattered the isolationist policies of the United States. The nation emerged from the war not just as a member of the international community, but also as a world leader. Alarmed by the growth of Soviet military power and the establishment of Soviet control over Eastern Europe after World War II, many nations sought the security of an alliance or friendly relationship with the United States. Under Presidents Truman and Eisenhower, the United States responded by enthusiastically erecting a global network of multilateral and bilateral alliances intended to contain Soviet expansionism. The Rio Pact, signed in 1947, reaffirmed the long-standing U.S. commitment to defend the Western Hemisphere. The 1949 North Atlantic Treaty created the North Atlantic Treaty Organization, an alliance between the United States, Canada, and most Western European democracies that developed into the cornerstone of the U.S. containment strategy. Then, in 1951, the ANZUS alliance between Australia, New Zealand, and the United States was created. The United States also joined the Southeast Asia Treaty Organization (SEATO) in 1954 and established ties with, although not membership in, a Middle Eastern alliance known as the Central Treaty Organization (CENTO) in 1956. These multilateral alliances were complemented by bilateral alliances with Japan and the Philippines in 1951, Korea in 1953, Taiwan in 1954, and Iran, Pakistan, and Turkey in 1959.[106]

The purpose of and motivation to maintain these alliances have been in a state of flux in the post–cold war era. Many of them, including SEATO and CENTO, no longer exist. Without an overriding single interest in mutual defense or a dependence on U.S. economic, military, and especially nuclear power, there are more potential conflicts between national interests and alliance policy. The movement of European NATO nations toward the more Europe-centered defense structure of the Western European Union (WEU) was encouraged by the withdrawal of the United States from the NATO-sponsored naval blockade of the former Yugoslavia.[107] Indeed, the weakening of U.S. influence in NATO was manifest in the many conflicts between the United States and the other NATO nations over alliance policy and actions in that region. President Clinton was committed to working through NATO and the United Nations, and his policy toward Bosnia was shaped by a desire to avoid ruptures between the United States and its NATO allies. In 1995 Clinton vetoed a bill directing him to depart from UN and NATO policy by terminating the U.S. arms embargo against Bosnia, and he committed the United States to providing 20,000 troops to support NATO oversight of a Bosnian peace accord.

In 2001 NATO invoked its charter and declared that the savage terrorist attacks of September 11 would be considered "an attack against all of the parties." Early in the war on terrorism, NATO followed, at least in principle, the U.S. lead. It supported U.S. military action in Afghanistan, and in 2003, as authorized by the UN Security Council, NATO assumed leadership of the International Security Assistance Force (ISAF), which was responsible for stabilizing and rebuilding Afghanistan's political and economic system. In so doing, NATO took on its first mission outside Europe.[108] In Iraq, NATO trained security forces, but this program was not part of the combat mission led by the United States.[109] In Libya in 2011, NATO soon assumed control of the no-fly zone authorized by the UN, but NATO members were sharply divided over the extent of the organization's responsibilities.

Alliances and the War Powers

U.S. membership in an alliance creates additional presidential responsibilities and claims to war-making authority. The most important of these is the president's obligation, as commander in chief and the person who executes the laws, to fulfill the terms of a treaty. This obligation depends on the terms of the alliance agreement and the declared policy of the United States. The NATO treaty states that "an attack on one or more [of the parties] shall be considered as an attack against all of the parties." Advocates of presidential power could argue that by ratifying a treaty with such language Congress has given presidents the same authority to repel an invasion of a NATO country as they have to repel an attack on the United States.[110] Those on the other side argue that a treaty, involving only the Senate and the president, cannot alter the Constitution, which gives the House of Representatives a controlling voice in the commitment of armed forces. Indeed, Article II of the North Atlantic Treaty specifies that its provisions shall be "carried out by the Parties in accordance with their respective constitutional processes."[111]

Beyond the language of a treaty, the declared policy of the United States has had significant effects on the president's authority and ability to act in defense of an alliance partner. During the cold war, the president would have been expected to direct U.S. troops to repel an attack on NATO. Similarly, presidents would have assumed they had full authorization to respond to attacks on South Korea and Japan, not only because of treaties with those nations, but because many U.S. troops have been based there and numerous acts of Congress have recognized and supported U.S. defense commitments in East Asia. As the dire general threats recede in the post–cold war era, the effects of such commitments on subsequent policy and presidential latitude in use of force will be weaker.

PRESIDENT AS MILITARY COMMANDER

The commander-in-chief clause gives presidents clear authority to command the military as the nation's first general and admiral. They possess all decision-making powers accorded to any supreme military commander under international law. Presidents not only order troops into battle, but they are also expected to approve major strategic decisions and keep a watchful eye on the progress of any military campaign. Most presidents since World War II have even regarded specific tactical decisions related to certain military operations to be among their commander-in-chief responsibilities.

In making the president the commander in chief, the Framers attempted to ensure that civilian authority would always direct the armed forces. Military leaders who might otherwise use their authority over the army and navy to accumulate political power or enhance their personal reputation would be subordinate to a president who is elected by the entire country and is responsible for the welfare and security of all the people. Designating the president as commander in chief also ensured more effective military leadership; a single leader at the top of the military hierarchy would be recognized by all as the legitimate and indisputable supreme military commander.

Military experience has been fairly common among presidents. Although some presidents with no military experience, such as James Madison and Woodrow Wilson, have led the nation during wartime, as of 2000 twenty-seven of forty-two chief executives had served in the military. A significant number of these were high-ranking officers. Twelve served as generals, and six of these twelve—George Washington, Andrew Jackson, William Harrison, Zachary Taylor, Ulysses S. Grant, and Dwight Eisenhower—attained at least the rank of major general.[112]

Dwight D. Eisenhower was one of twelve generals who later served as president. On D-Day—June 6, 1944—he personally encouraged American paratroopers of the 101st Airborne Division before their drop into France as the vanguard of the invasion.

Three presidents—Grant, Eisenhower, and Carter—graduated from a military academy. Franklin Roosevelt, a wartime president who never entered the military, gained defense-related experience as assistant secretary of the navy.

Presidential Direction of Military Operations

The degree to which presidents have become involved in the direction of military operations has varied according to their military expertise and the circumstances of the military situation. Once troops have been committed to battle, presidents have usually delegated authority for battlefield strategy to their generals and admirals. The Constitution, however, does not prohibit a president from taking direct command of troops in the field. Several delegates to the Constitutional Convention suggested that the president should be prohibited from taking personal command of troops, but the convention rejected these proposals.[113]

George Washington was regarded as the nation's greatest general, and neither Congress nor the American public would have thought it wrong for him to have led U.S. troops into battle while he was president. Indeed, in 1794 Washington came close to doing just that when he personally supervised the organization of the militia charged with putting down the Whiskey Rebellion.[114] In 1799, when an undeclared naval war with France threatened to spread to the North American continent, President John Adams delegated his authority as commander in chief to then-retired Washington. Adams, who recognized his own lack of military experience and the advantages of enabling the country to rally around a national legend if war came, asked Washington to accept the post of "Lieutenant General and Commander-in-Chief of all the armies raised or to be raised in the United States." Washington agreed on the condition that he would not have to take command of the army unless "it became indispensable by the urgency of circumstances." The hostile engagements with France remained confined to the high seas, and Washington never had to leave his retirement at Mount Vernon to

During the early stages of the Civil War, Abraham Lincoln became deeply involved in battlefield strategy. He occasionally issued direct orders to his generals regarding their troop movements and frequently conferred with them at the front.

assume active command of U.S. forces.[115]

The poor performance of Union generals during the early stages of the Civil War and the proximity of the fighting to Washington, D.C., compelled President Abraham Lincoln to become deeply involved in battle-field strategy. He occasionally issued direct orders to his generals regarding their troop movements and frequently conferred with them at the front. Although Lincoln's interference in purely military matters has been criticized by some historians and applauded by others, he did allow his generals broad discretion in their implementation of his orders. After Lincoln gave command of the army to General Grant, in whom he had confidence, the president removed himself from tactical decisions.[116]

President Woodrow Wilson, like John Adams, recognized his lack of military experience and delegated responsibility for strategy and tactics to military leaders. Moreover, the distance between the president and the fighting made personal leadership impractical. He confined his commander-in-chief role during World War I to the domestic war effort and broad military decisions, such as his rejection of a French and British proposal in 1918 that the United States open a major front in Russia to prevent the Germans from transferring troops to the West after the Russians had negotiated a separate peace with Germany.[117]

World War II created conditions that necessitated the involvement of the president in strategic decisions. Because the war effort against Germany and Japan depended on the concerted action of the United States, Great Britain, the Soviet Union, and other nations, Allied strategy had to be determined through negotiations among the leaders of these countries. As a result, Presidents Roosevelt and Truman made decisions, such as when to launch the invasion of Europe and where to concentrate U.S. forces, not just because they were the commander in chief, but also because they were the nation's chief diplomat.

Sophisticated communication technologies also have facilitated presidential involvement in military operations. For example, in April 1988 the pilot of a navy aircraft patrolling the Persian Gulf observed Iranian gunboats attacking a set of oil rigs. Because U.S. forces in the Persian Gulf were authorized to respond only to attacks on American aircraft, ships, and facilities, the pilot radioed his aircraft carrier for permission to attack the Iranian vessels. The pilot's request was transmitted up the chain of command from the aircraft carrier commander to the admiral in charge of the naval task force. Then the request was relayed via satellite through the chief of the U.S. Central Command in Florida to the chair of the Joint Chiefs of Staff and the secretary of defense at the Pentagon, who called President Reagan. The president authorized U.S. planes to attack the Iranian gunboats, and the order was relayed back through the chain of command to navy pilots who moved to attack only three minutes after permission had been requested.[118]

In the aftermath of the Vietnam War, in which President Lyndon B. Johnson was criticized for micromanaging operational decisions, presidents typically have made a point of not second-guessing the battlefield choices of military commanders.[119] President George W. Bush insisted that he would not direct the operations of his military leaders. But the question of micromanagement arose for Bush's secretary of defense, Donald H. Rumsfeld, in connection with the Iraq War. Several retired military officers, including leaders who had commanded troops in Iraq, called for Rumsfeld's resignation in the spring of 2006, declaring that the secretary of defense had not planned adequately either for the war or postwar reconstruction. Although President Bush strongly affirmed his commitment to keeping

Rumsfeld at the Pentagon, the public debate raised questions about the administration's management of military operations in Iraq.[120] Throughout the rest of the year public support of the war and President Bush continued to drop, and after Democrats recaptured both houses of Congress in November 2006, Rumsfeld resigned as defense secretary. In 2010 President Barack Obama relieved his military commander in Afghanistan, General Stanley McChrystal, after the publication of a *Rolling Stone* article that contained negative remarks about administration officials by McChrystal and his top aides. Obama replaced McChrystal with General David Petraeus, who had led U.S. forces in Iraq, and had been McChrsytal's superior as head of the U.S. Central Command. (After directing the U.S. mission in Afghanistan, Petraeus became director of the Central Intelligence Agency in 2011.)

Command of Nuclear Weapons

Despite the absurdity of a modern president ever leading U.S. troops into battle, the realities of nuclear warfare, especially during the cold war, have made the president the nation's "first soldier." The decision to use nuclear weapons is entirely the commander-in-chief's, whose claim on this authority is reinforced by the need for speedy and secret decisions. For example, in the event of a submarine-launched nuclear attack, the president would have no more than ten to twelve minutes to receive positive verification of the attack, decide how to respond, and transmit orders to the military commanders in charge of U.S. nuclear forces. Even if the attack was launched from missile silos in Russia, the president would have little more than twenty to thirty minutes before the weapons detonated.[121] A decision that has to be made this quickly must be assigned to a single individual with indisputable authority.

Although presidents alone have the authority to order the use of nuclear weapons, they do not possess perfect control over them. The U.S. nuclear arsenal consists of thousands of nuclear warheads, delivery vehicles for all types of nuclear missions, and a vast network of personnel, computers, communications equipment, and the information and intelligence gathering and processing systems necessary to manage the weapons.[122] Because of the size and complexity of the U.S. nuclear weapons arsenal and the requirements of deterrence, presidents cannot depend on controlling every weapon by simply pushing a button or making a phone call. Their control could be undermined by the failure or destruction of the U.S. early warning and communications systems, of the personnel who manage the nuclear weapons, or of the weapons themselves.

Presidential control of nuclear weapons has been aided by permissive action links (PALs), which are electronic locks that prevent nuclear weapons from being fired without prior presidential authorization. Intercontinental ballistic missiles (ICBMs) based in missile silos and nuclear warheads carried by U.S. strategic bombers are equipped with PALs. The military commanders of certain other types of nuclear weapons, however, have the physical capability, although not the authority, to launch them without receiving a presidential order. Nuclear missiles deployed in submarines, for example, are not equipped with PALs and therefore could be fired by the officers of a submarine who mistakenly believed that the president had issued a launch order. The navy continually seeks to minimize the danger of an unauthorized nuclear launch through intensive psychological screening of submarine personnel and elaborate launch procedures that require the coordination of several officers aboard any one vessel.

Evolution of Presidential Nuclear Decision Making and Strategies

Since Franklin Roosevelt directed U.S. scientists to build the atomic bomb, presidents have dominated nuclear weapons policy and the formulation of nuclear strategy. Nuclear age presidents during the cold war counted nuclear decision making as among their most important and burdensome responsibilities. Dwight Eisenhower once said in a speech:

> When the push of a button may mean obliteration of countless humans, the President of the United States must be forever on guard against any inclination on his part to impetuosity; to arrogance; to headlong action; to expedience; to facile maneuvers; even to the popularity of an action as opposed to the righteousness of an action. . . . He must worry only about the good—the long-term, abiding, permanent good—of all Americans.[123]

U.S. Nuclear Monopoly

In the summer of 1945, after the war against Nazi Germany had been won, President Truman decided to drop newly manufactured atomic bombs on the Japanese cities of Hiroshima and Nagasaki to bring an end to World War II. Truman maintained that using the atomic bombs was the only way to end the war without an invasion of Japan. In a radio address to the American public on August 9, 1945, Truman explained that he had ordered the attacks "to shorten the agony of war, in order to save the lives of thousands and thousands of young Americans."[124]

Historical evidence suggests that other considerations also were involved. Certainly Truman wanted to end the war quickly to prevent the Soviet Union, which was about to enter the war against the Japanese, from having a role in the occupation of Japan. He also may have regarded the bomb as an impressive demonstration of American power that would cause the Soviets to be more conciliatory toward the West.[125]

From the bombing of Hiroshima to the early 1950s, the United States enjoyed a nuclear monopoly. The Soviet Union tested its first atomic bomb in 1949, but it did not

A dark mushroom cloud rises 20,000 feet above Nagasaki, Japan, after the dropping of the atomic bomb on August 9, 1945. President Harry S. Truman ordered the bombing—here and three days earlier on Hiroshima—the only wartime use of nuclear weapons.

have an operational capability for several more years. The U.S. ability to destroy Soviet population centers with atomic weapons served as an effective deterrent against the threat to Western Europe from superior numbers of Soviet conventional forces.[126] Although the U.S. nuclear advantage prevented war with the Soviet Union through the 1940s and 1950s, the Korean War demonstrated the difficulty of using nuclear weapons in limited wars. Truman rejected their use in Korea because of allied opposition and the need to conserve the U.S. nuclear arsenal to defend against a Soviet attack on Western Europe. A moral prohibition against the use of nuclear weapons also had developed, especially against an underdeveloped nation such as North Korea whose citizens were victims of communist expansion.

U.S. Nuclear Superiority

The Soviet nuclear arsenal early in the 1950s was much inferior in number and quality to the U.S. nuclear force. President Dwight Eisenhower attempted to use U.S. nuclear

superiority to deter Soviet aggression. He believed that maintaining a conventional military force capable of countering the Soviets and their clients anywhere in the world would be disastrous for the federal budget and would not be supported by the American public. In addition, a threat to use nuclear weapons against China had helped end the Korean War. The administration therefore declared in 1954 that the United States would use nuclear weapons not only in response to a Soviet attack on Western Europe, but also in response to unspecified lesser provocations.[127]

This strategy, which was known as "massive retaliation," lacked credibility as a response to limited acts of communist aggression such as Soviet-supported guerrilla movements or political subversion. Furthermore, as the Soviet nuclear capability grew during the 1950s, the possibility that the United States could launch a nuclear attack against the Soviet Union without itself and its allies receiving a nuclear counterblow became remote. The successful Soviet launch of the *Sputnik* satellite in 1957 even engendered false speculation that the gap in military technology that Americans assumed to be in their favor actually favored the Soviets.

President Kennedy sought to bring declared nuclear policy in line with current realities. Upon taking office, he announced a new strategy of "flexible response." Kennedy and his advisers saw that improvements in the Soviet nuclear arsenal had diminished the capacity of U.S. nuclear forces to deter anything but a Soviet nuclear attack or massive invasion of Western Europe. Kennedy also recognized that the United States was faced with many forms of communist aggression that called for limited responses. Nuclear deterrence remained the centerpiece of U.S. defense, but conventional and counterinsurgency forces also were built up to be able to wage limited wars.[128]

Soviet placement of medium-range nuclear missiles in Cuba in 1962 precipitated a crisis that pushed the United States to the brink of nuclear war with the Soviet Union. Kennedy refused to accept this alteration of the balance of forces. He ordered a blockade of Cuba to prevent further construction of the Soviet missile sites and demanded that the Soviets withdraw the missiles. After two tense weeks, during which Kennedy estimated the chances of nuclear war at "between one out of three and even," the Soviets agreed to remove their missiles.[129] The Cuban missile crisis highlighted the threat to U.S. security from the growing Soviet nuclear arsenal and stimulated a further modernization of nuclear weaponry.

The Era of Parity

Presidents Nixon and Ford subscribed to the basic nuclear strategy established by Kennedy and Johnson. The concept of strategic defense—building defensive weapons systems capable of destroying attacking enemy missiles and bombers—had been widely debated during Johnson's presidency.

President Nixon, however, concluded a treaty in 1972 with the Soviet Union that placed strict limitations on antiballistic missile systems. This treaty formalized the doctrine of "mutual assured destruction" (MAD) that had characterized the nuclear relationship between the superpowers since the Soviets achieved strategic nuclear parity in the late 1960s. The MAD doctrine asserted that neither superpower could attack the other with nuclear weapons without its rival launching a devastating counterstrike. Each, therefore, would achieve security by holding the population of the other hostage.

During the Carter administration, U.S. nuclear war strategy was reevaluated. Presidential Directive 59 (PD-59), which was signed by President Carter in July 1980, stressed that the United States had to be prepared to fight a protracted nuclear war lasting up to sixty days. The directive ordered nuclear planners to develop a wider range of limited nuclear war options and assigned a higher priority to destroying the Soviets' leadership, military capabilities, and economic base if nuclear war occurred. It also called for an improvement of U.S. command, control, and communications to ensure that the president and other top leaders could direct a protracted nuclear war effectively.[130] Critics of PD-59 charged that U.S. officials had made nuclear war more likely by promoting the perceptions that a nuclear war could be fought like any other war and that nuclear destruction could be limited to an acceptable degree. On the other hand, the Carter administration argued that preparing to fight a nuclear war was the best way to deter one.

Assuming the presidency in 1981, Reagan vowed to rebuild U.S. defenses, including nuclear forces. He contended that during the 1970s while the United States observed the letter and spirit of nuclear arms control agreements, the Soviets had continued to build nuclear weapons that would give them a first-strike advantage in a nuclear war. Reagan argued that this "window of vulnerability" in the U.S. deterrent could be closed either by building new U.S. weapons or by getting the Soviets to reduce and reconfigure their arsenals. This policy led to a new phase in arms control.

Nuclear Arms Control

Since the development of atomic weapons, presidents have tried to enhance U.S. and world security by controlling the development and deployment of nuclear arms. Arms control agreements have been an important measure of a president's diplomatic success, and, until Clinton, every president from Eisenhower on concluded some agreement with the Soviet Union/Russia or the international community that contributed to the control or reduction of nuclear weapons.

As commander in chief and possessor of the treaty negotiation power, presidents have dominated arms control policy. Congress has tried to goad the president into action by, for example, creating the Arms Control and Disarmament Agency in 1961.[131] However, the president has general control over the initiation and oversight of arms control negotiations. During the cold war, arms control agreements were perceived to be among the most important agreements made by the president, and they generally were concluded as treaties. The Senate usually has approved arms control treaties, but its assent has not been automatic. Three nuclear arms control treaties have remained unapproved: the 1974 Threshold Nuclear Test Ban Treaty, the 1976 Peaceful Nuclear Explosions Treaty, and the 1979 Strategic Arms Limitation Talks Treaty (SALT II).

Presidents may choose to avoid the Senate treaty ratification process, however, by concluding arms control accords in the form of executive agreements, as did President Nixon in 1972 when he signed the SALT I Interim Offensive Arms Agreement, which imposed limitations on the strategic nuclear arsenals of both superpowers. Presidents also may choose to abide by an arms control treaty that the Senate has refused to ratify. President Carter announced in 1980 that the United States would not violate the provisions of the unratified SALT II treaty if the Soviet Union also did not violate it. President Reagan continued Carter's policy of observing SALT II until late 1986 when the administration announced that because of Soviet violations the United States would no longer consider itself bound by the treaty. However, Congress continued to abide by its limits through its appropriations control over weapons development and deployment.

A major shift in arms control policy was initiated by the Reagan administration in 1982. Critics of earlier arms control had argued that agreements limiting the growth of arsenals generally had favored the Soviet Union, which was building massive, multiple warhead rockets. These rockets could deliver a devastating first strike. In conjunction with a weapons modernization program, the Reagan administration announced a new negotiating goal of arms *reductions* to eliminate the Soviet advantage. Because the Soviets would resist any such measure, many observers dismissed this as a ploy by Reagan to avoid all arms negotiations while also shifting the responsibility for stalemate onto the Soviets. Arms talks on this principle did stall during Reagan's first term. However, the end result, driven in part by the political revolutions in the Soviet Union and the Warsaw Pact countries, was four treaties, concluded between 1987 and 1993, that reduced nuclear and conventional arms. Each required the Soviet Union, and later Russia, to make disproportionately large arms cuts. *(See Table 6-1, p. 283.)*

The first arms reduction agreement was the Intermediate Nuclear Forces (INF) Treaty, signed in 1987, which mandated the removal and destruction of most medium-range missiles in the European theater. This paved the way for progress on the first Strategic Arms Reduction

Treaty (START I), which covered long-range missiles. Before that treaty was completed, President George H. W. Bush signed the Conventional Forces in Europe Treaty in 1990. This treaty addressed the large Soviet/Warsaw Pact advantage in conventional arms, which had to be reduced before any reductions in the U.S./NATO nuclear deterrent could be settled. START I was signed in 1991, but Senate ratification was delayed by the collapse of the Soviet Union. Protocols of agreement to abide by the treaty's terms had to be negotiated between the United States and the newly independent nuclear nations of the former Soviet Union such as Ukraine.[132] Before START I was ratified, President Bush initiated new force cuts and negotiations toward another reduction treaty (START II), which was signed by Bush and Russian president Boris Yeltsin in January 1993. Both treaties have been ratified.

Arms control efforts continued to concentrate on controlling the development and deployment of nuclear weapons by additional nations and the threat of regional nuclear conflicts. Without great success, Presidents Bush and Clinton worked independently and with the United Nations in trying to enforce the Nuclear Nonproliferation Treaty against Iraq, Iran, North Korea, and Pakistan.

The November 2001 summit meeting between President George W. Bush and Russian president Vladimir Putin signaled an end to the stalemate in U.S.-Russian relations that had marked the Clinton years. The two presidents took steps into a new era of friendly and cooperative relations. Without long and distrustful negotiations over strategic balances, and even without a formal agreement, Bush committed the United States to cutting the number of deployed nuclear warheads by two-thirds during the next decade. Such a step would reduce the U.S. arsenal to less than two thousand warheads (compared with more than ten thousand at the height of the cold war). The Russian president promised to do the same. Putin also reiterated his support for the U.S.-led war on terrorism. Nine years later, U.S. President Barack Obama and Russian President Dmitry Medvedev signed a treaty to reduce further each country's nuclear arsenal, decreasing each country's missile launchers by half and limiting the number of nuclear warheads to approximately 1,550 each. *(See Table 6-1, p. 283.)*

Antiballistic Missile Defense Policy

On March 23, 1983, a proposal by Reagan sparked a significant change in U.S. nuclear strategy. In a nationally televised address he urged the scientific community to develop the technology for a space-based antiballistic missile defense that would some day make nuclear weapons "impotent and obsolete."[133] Implicit in the plan was a rejection of the status quo doctrine of mutual assured destruction. Reagan proposed to achieve security in the future not solely by deterring a Soviet nuclear attack, but also by being able to destroy

most incoming Soviet missiles. The Reagan administration was hoping as well that the cost of trying to match U.S. development of strategic defenses would weaken the Soviets and move them toward arms reductions.

Although Reagan's optimistic vision led to an extensive research and development program (called the Strategic Defense Initiative by its supporters and "Star Wars" by its opponents), many scientists admitted that even if insulating the United States from a Soviet missile attack were possible, it would take decades of research and hundreds of billions of dollars to accomplish. (Indeed, by 2000 more than $60 billion had been appropriated.) By 1987, budget constraints and growing scientific skepticism that Reagan's "Peace Shield" could be built led to a reorientation of the plan toward the more attainable goal of using defensive weapons to enhance deterrence.[134] In 1991, with the success of the arms reduction talks (START) and with the collapse of the Warsaw Pact and the Soviet Union, President George H. W. Bush and Congress again reoriented the development of missile defenses toward defending against a limited nuclear attack or an accidental launching.[135] In 1993 President Clinton pursued this aim with the intention of remaining within the terms of the 1972 Antiballistic Missile (ABM) Treaty, which limits the development and deployment of strategic missile defenses. His "Ballistic Missile Defense" program focused on the development of ground-based systems to be used as "theater" defenses for troops in the field. These systems also would be available to defend the home front. The roles switched after the 1994 midterm elections, with the newly Republican Congress pushing, against Clinton's resistance, for more money and accelerated development of strategic missile defenses.

The advocates of an unrestricted and accelerated program of development and deployment argue that the ABM treaty is outdated. It was designed for a bipolar world of hostile superpowers and a defense strategy of deterring a first strike through an assured and massive retaliation. Moreover, the ABM treaty may be void because one signatory, the Soviet Union, no longer exists. This argument is countered by one that points out that abandoning the treaty will foster another arms race, with Russia and China, and that the treaty ought to be renegotiated, particularly with Russia, before proceeding with the full development and deployment of a missile defense system.

Arguing that the measures would violate the ABM treaty and interfere with progress on arms reductions, Clinton resisted establishing a deadline for deployment. In 1999, however, he signed a bill calling for deployment of a national defense system as soon as possible. Although the bill did not set a specific deadline, it implicitly set aside concerns about the ABM Treaty.

President George W. Bush pushed from the start of his administration for accelerated development, testing, and

TABLE 6-1 **Major Arms Control Agreements, 1963–2010**

President	Year signed	Agreement	Senate action	Provisions	Parties
Kennedy	1963	Partial Nuclear Test Ban Treaty	Ratified	Prohibits nuclear tests underwater, in the atmosphere, and in outer space	Multilateral
Johnson, L.	1967	Outer Space Treaty	Ratified	Prohibits all military activity, including deployment of nuclear weapons, in outer space	Multilateral
Johnson, L.	1968	Nuclear Nonproliferation Treaty	Ratified	Prohibits acquisition of nuclear weapons by nations not already possessing them and establishes international safeguards to prevent the spread of nuclear weapons capability	Multilateral
Nixon	1971	Sea Bed Treaty	Ratified	Prohibits deployment of nuclear weapons on the ocean floor	Multilateral
Nixon	1972	SALT I ABM Treaty	Ratified	Limits size and number (two) of antiballistic missile systems in U.S. and Soviet Union. A 1974 executive agreement reduced number of sites permitted to one	U.S.–Soviet Union
Nixon	1972	SALT I Interim Offensive Arms Agreement	Executive agreement; no action	Established a five-year freeze on number of intercontinental ballistic missiles and submarine-launched ballistic missiles deployed by U.S. and Soviet Union	U.S.–Soviet Union
Nixon	1974	Threshold Nuclear Test Ban Treaty	Unratified	Prohibits underground nuclear test explosions greater than 150 kilotons	U.S.–Soviet Union
Ford	1976	Peaceful Nuclear Explosions Treaty	Unratified	Prohibits nuclear explosions greater than 150 kilotons for excavation and other peaceful purposes	U.S.–Soviet Union
Carter	1979	SALT II Offensive Arms Treaty	Unratified	Limits numbers and types of strategic nuclear weapons	U.S.–Soviet Union
Reagan	1987	Intermediate Nuclear Forces Treaty	Ratified	Mandates the removal and destruction of all land-based nuclear missiles with ranges between 300 and 3,400 miles	U.S.–Soviet Union
Bush, G.H.W.	1990	Conventional Forces in Europe Treaty	Ratified	Reduced conventional weapons and troop strength of NATO and the former Warsaw Pact nations	Multilateral
Bush, G.H.W.	1991	Strategic Arms Reduction Treaty (START I)	Ratified	Mandates a one-third reduction in long-range nuclear warheads and restrictions on delivery systems	U.S.–former Soviet Union nations
Bush, G.H.W.	1993	Strategic Arms Reduction Treaty (START II)	Ratified	Sets a ceiling of 6,500 warheads per nation, requiring a two-thirds reduction in warheads and elimination of multiple warheads (MIRVs)	U.S.–Russia
Clinton	1997	Strategic Arms Reduction Treaty (START III)	Framework proposed, but treaty never negotiated because of failure to implement START II	Proposed destruction of and further reductions in strategic nuclear warheads	U.S.–Russia
Clinton	1996	Comprehensive Nuclear-Test-Ban Treaty	Unratified	Prohibits nuclear weapons test explosions	Multilateral
Bush, G.W.	2002	Strategic Offensive Reductions Treaty (SORT)	Ratified; superseded by New START.	Commits the United States and Russia to reducing their nuclear arsenals to 1,700 to 2,200 warheads	U.S.–Russia
Obama	2010	New Strategic Arms Reduction Treaty (New START)	Ratified	Reduces each country's nuclear missile launchers by half, and limits number of deployed nuclear warheads to 1,550 each.	U.S.–Russia

deployment of a missile defense system. His policy was predicated on the ABM Treaty being outdated and void. While not opposed to pursuing an agreement with Russia on development and deployment of a missile defense system, he declared that he was ready to move ahead in the absence of such an agreement.[136] Democrats, particularly in the Senate, were prepared to cut funding and, in the absence of an agreement with Russia or congressional authorization, prohibit testing that might violate the ABM treaty. After the September 11 terrorist attack, both of these restrictions were dropped from the 2002 appropriations bill. During their summit meeting in November 2001, Bush failed to convince Russian president Putin to accept an interpretation of the ABM Treaty that would permit continued testing and development of missile defense systems, thereby deferring a controversial decision to abandon the treaty until those systems could be deployed. Soon after, the Bush administration unilaterally withdrew the United States from the ABM accord.

PRESIDENT AS DEFENSE MANAGER

Before World War II, the isolation and size of the United States rendered it nearly immune to serious invasions by the armies of Europe. This geographic advantage as well as wary attitudes toward standing armies worked to keep the peacetime defense establishments small. When the United States found itself in a war, it mobilized troops and resources until the war was won, and then promptly demobilized its armed forces, returning the country to a state of peace and nonalignment.

After World War II, a national consensus developed that the United States should adopt an internationalist defense policy designed to contain the expansion of communism and limit the coercive potential of Soviet military strength. In pursuit of these regional objectives presidents signed various regional mutual security treaties, the most important of which was the North Atlantic Treaty, which committed the United States to the defense of Western Europe. The expanded defense commitments of the United States and its adversarial relationship with the Soviet Union required the United States to maintain a large peacetime military establishment for the first time in its history.

Although the Constitution gives Congress the authority to raise and equip an army and navy, much of the task of administering the defense bureaucracy and maintaining the nation's defenses in the post–World War II era has been delegated to or assumed by the president and the executive branch. The growth in the size and activities of the military and the perception that nuclear weapons and the cold war had created a condition of constant emergency combined to legitimize the president's role as defense manager. The president functioned not just as the commander in chief in wartime but also as the manager of the routine operations and preparations of the military in peacetime.

The Defense Establishment

The president is positioned at the top of a large and complex defense establishment. The Defense Department is made up of three military services and numerous agencies, offices, and unified multiservice commands, all under the leadership of the secretary of defense. Between the mid-1980s and the mid-1990s, the number of active duty military personnel was cut by about 25 percent, from 2 million to 1.5 million. The Defense Department employs more than 1 million civilians, about one-third of all federal civilian employees. In addition to the Defense Department, other executive departments and agencies have national security roles. The Central Intelligence Agency and the State Department provide intelligence about foreign governments and groups; the Federal Bureau of Investigation is responsible for combating domestic espionage; the Energy Department develops, tests, and produces nuclear warheads; and the Federal Emergency Management Agency (FEMA) oversees civil defense programs. The Defense Department, however, is the president's principal means of executing national security policy.

Department of Defense

Before 1947, the War and Navy Departments functioned independently of each other. Each had its own cabinet-level secretary, military command structure, and procurement operations. The National Security Act of 1947 created the post of secretary of defense, but its occupant was not given a staff or significant power over the individual services. The defense secretary functioned as the coordinator of the loose confederation of the Departments of the Army (the old War Department) and Navy, and the new Department of the Air Force. A 1949 amendment to the National Security Act created the Defense Department and recognized the primacy of the defense secretary, but in practice the individual services retained authority over their budgets and were administered autonomously by the service secretaries. The three services were not unified into one military organization, because reformers believed such an organization could more easily threaten civilian control of the military.

The Department of Defense Reorganization Act of 1958 placed the secretary of defense at the top of the military command structure, second only to the president. The act gave the secretary the means to centralize authority over defense operations and planning within the Office of the Secretary of Defense (OSD). In 1961 Robert S. McNamara became defense secretary with a mandate from President Kennedy to take control of the Defense Department. Under Kennedy and then Lyndon Johnson, McNamara greatly expanded the role of OSD and demanded unequivocal support from the military for the administration's programs.[137] He established the four major roles of the modern defense secretary: principal adviser to the president on defense issues, deputy commander in chief behind the president, director of the Defense Department and its huge military budget, and representative of the Defense Department before Congress and within the executive branch. This enlargement of the role of the secretary of defense gave presidents greater control over the defense establishment and assisted in the integration of defense and foreign policy.

Joint Chiefs of Staff

The Joint Chiefs of Staff (JCS) is the body of military officers responsible for formulating unified military strategy and providing the president with advice on military matters. The JCS comprises a chair appointed from any of the services, the chiefs of staff of the army and the air force, the chief of naval operations, and the commandant of the Marine Corps.

All five of the chiefs are appointed by the president with the advice and consent of the Senate. Since 1967, the chair has been appointed for a two-year term, which can be renewed once by the president. The four service chiefs serve one nonrenewable four-year term.

A president can appoint several types of officers to the Joint Chiefs of Staff, depending on the president's conception of its advisory role. Most chiefs have been officers nominated by their services and accepted by presidents with little consideration of their political compatibility with the administration. The president may receive the goodwill of the services for endorsing their choices, but the president will have little political control over these nominees. Presidents also have looked beyond the service's candidates and chosen officers whose professional reputation has come to their attention. These appointments may displease the services, but they allow a president to choose an officer with experience and a temperament compatible with the administration. Finally, a few presidents have appointed close associates to the JCS. For example, Kennedy appointed Gen. Maxwell Taylor chair of the JCS in 1962. Earlier, in 1961, Taylor had been offered the post of director of the CIA, but he had chosen instead to become a special military representative to the White House. When the general was appointed chair of the JCS, he quickly became a member of Kennedy's inner circle of advisers. The military usually dislikes such nominees, because their first priority is promoting the policies of the president rather than protecting their service's interests.[138]

In the decades after its creation in 1947, the JCS was criticized by many observers, including influential service chiefs and blue-ribbon panels commissioned to study its organization. These critics identified several problems with the JCS. First, the joint chiefs were given the conflicting tasks of being service chiefs responsible for the welfare of their services and members of the JCS responsible for developing unbiased policy plans and proposals for the president. But the chiefs seldom were able to do both and usually put service interests first. Second, because the entire JCS was considered to be the president's military adviser, the chiefs were compelled to develop consensus positions. As a result, their advice consisted of uncontroversial compromise recommendations of little value to the president. Third, although the JCS was supposed to develop military plans, it was outside the military's chain of command. Consequently, JCS budgetary, procurement, and strategy proposals often were unrelated to the needs of the commanders in chief (CINCs) of the multiservice operational commands in specified geographic areas.[139]

In 1986 President Reagan signed a bill reorganizing the JCS. The legislation was intended to improve interservice coordination and to create an organizational framework that would streamline the chain of command and minimize the influence of service parochialism on the military advice given to the president by the JCS. The reorganization bill sought to accomplish these goals by increasing the authority of the chair of the JCS. By making the chair the president's supreme military adviser, the bill's advocates theorized that the chair would be free to develop advice and options independent of service interests. Among other things, the bill placed the JCS staff under the direct control of the chair to bolster the chair's bureaucratic resources and created the post of vice chair. To ensure that the service chiefs would continue to have an advisory role, the chair was required to forward their dissenting views to the president and secretary of defense upon the chiefs' request. The bill also enhanced the authority of the CINCs, giving them greater control over the training, supply, organization, and operations of their command.[140]

Homeland Security and the War on Terrorism

Rarely in the history of the United States has its own territory been one of the war fronts. The attack on Pearl Harbor, well off the mainland, put the West Coast on alert and led to extraordinary measures such as the internment of Japanese Americans. (See "Korematsu v. United States," p. 296.) During World War II, German submarines regularly cruised U.S. coastal waters, and espionage by communists during the cold war was a continuous concern. But outside of the nuclear stalemate of the cold war, imminent military threats against U.S. territory and civilians have been rare. Even attacks on U.S. citizens by international terrorists had been, in the main, overseas. The deaths of more than three thousand civilians in the terrorist attacks of September 11, 2001, clearly demonstrated the will and capacity of foreign terrorist organizations to carry their war on the United States to the U.S. proper. The fact that the terrorists who hijacked and

Secretary of Defense Donald H. Rumsfeld inspects conditions at "Camp X-ray," a detention facility for the captured al Qaeda and Taliban terrorists suspected of planning the attacks on the World Trade Center and the Pentagon on September 11, 2001. Rumsfeld announced that President George W. Bush's administration would not grant prisoner of war status to the detainees because they did not represent a recognized government and their terrorist acts violated internationally accepted laws of warfare. The U.S. Supreme Court would later rule that detainees did possess the right of habeas corpus.

crashed the four airliners—two into New York City's World Trade Center, one into the Pentagon, and one into a Pennsylvania field—trained for their attack while living in the United States, indicated that the war on terrorism would have a broad domestic front.

The relative safety of the U.S. home front had always allowed a fairly strict separation between the two principal and coercive functions of government, domestic police and national defense. The dangers of blending these executive powers were evident in President Nixon's broad claims of extralegal authority in the name of national security. Partly in response to Nixon's abuses, strict limits, more in line with ordinary police procedures, were placed on domestic surveillance and intelligence activities. Yet the 2001 attacks and threats of covert foreign aggression began to break down the distinction between policing and defending, because domestic law enforcement became an important element in national defense. This change was evident in the reorientation of the Federal Bureau of Investigation (FBI). The bureau had devoted its resources mainly to ordinary crime, leaving large-scale foreign threats to the CIA and the Department of Defense. But soon after the 2001 attacks, the FBI began to distribute some of its ordinary crime responsibilities to other agencies, such as the Drug Enforcement Agency (DEA) and the Bureau of Alcohol, Tobacco, and Firearms (ATF) and focus more of its resources instead on counterterrorism activities.[141]

Also in the aftermath of September 11, President George W. Bush and Attorney General John Ashcroft sought and received significant new powers of investigation. Although controversial, the USA PATRIOT Act (HR 3162) was passed and signed in late October 2001. It modified many laws, including the restrictive Foreign Intelligence Surveillance Act of 1978, and broadened the national government's powers: of surveillance, including wire tap warrants that cover individuals rather than single phones; of preventative detention of noncitizen suspects; of access to e-mail, voice mail, and other forms of electronic communication; and of search without prior notice. The law also facilitated greater sharing of confidential information from grand juries and financial institutions, and it mandated cooperation between the Justice Department and, for example, the CIA and the Department of Defense.

The complexity of a coordinated domestic counterterrorism effort—involving foreign intelligence, domestic police, disaster relief, disease control, medical facilities, and the myriad state and federal agencies—was recognized by President Bush when he created, by executive order (No. 13228), a new Office of Homeland Security and made the directorship of this office a cabinet-level post. The president appointed the former governor of Pennsylvania Thomas J. Ridge to head the new office. According to the president's order, this office would be responsible for developing "a comprehensive national strategy to secure the United States from terrorist threats or attacks" and for coordinating "the executive branch's efforts to detect, prepare for, prevent, protect against, respond to, and recover from terrorist attacks within the United States."

President Bush's order also created a Homeland Security Council. Similar to the National Security Council, it was intended to advise the president on policy and help coordinate the approximately forty agencies working in the area of domestic security and emergencies. The council members included the president and vice president, the attorney general, the secretaries of defense, health and human services, transportation, and Treasury, and the directors of the FBI, the CIA, and the Federal Emergency Management Agency.

In June 2002, in response to congressional initiatives, President Bush proposed the formation of a Department of Homeland Security (DHS). The creation of the department in late 2002 marked the most significant reorganization of government agencies since the National Security Act of 1947. It placed twenty-two previously independent agencies under the jurisdiction of one cabinet department, including the Citizenship and Immigration Services agency (formerly Immigration and Naturalization Service), Coast Guard, FEMA, and Secret Service. Making homeland security part of the cabinet would ensure both executive and legislative oversight, albeit with sometimes competing visions of the department's responsibilities.

One of DHS's first actions was to created a color-coded threat assessment scale for the nation, with a red alert signifying a "severe risk of terrorist attacks," and a green alert signifying a "low risk of terrorist attacks." The system prompted criticism and jokes for not providing practical information for people about terrorist risks, but the department maintains that the alerts give important security guidance for government agencies, as well as for individuals. The agency also has faced criticism for excessive spending and an ineffective response to Hurricane Katrina in 2005. Nearly ten years after its creation, DHS is the third largest cabinet department, with more than 200,000 employees and a budget of almost $100 billion.

Presidential Control of the Military

Despite the enhanced authority of the civilian leadership of the Defense Department since 1947, presidents have not dominated the military. Like any government organization, the military has its own organizational objectives and is capable of resisting policies it believes are against its interests. Military leaders have been particularly successful in cultivating friends in Congress who pressure the administration to accept the military's perspective on given issues.

In addition to the military's political clout, presidential control of the armed forces is limited by the president's dependence on the military for evaluations of the nation's military capabilities. Civilian advisers can offer opinions on many military problems, but their assessments must depend on the factual information supplied by the military. Moreover, estimates of the force requirements and prospects for success of a given combat operation can only be supplied

President Truman pins a medal on Gen. Douglas MacArthur at their October 15, 1950, meeting on Wake Island. Truman called the meeting to discuss MacArthur's strategy in Korea. Six months later, Truman would fire MacArthur for insubordination.

by the military.[142] The president may be confident that a particular military operation is justified on moral and political grounds, but the president rarely will order the operation if the military is pessimistic about its chances for success. Presidents also depend on the military to implement their military orders. Whereas presidential initiatives in areas such as diplomacy can be accomplished through several channels, only the military can carry out a combat operation.

Because of the political leverage of the armed services and their monopoly on military information and resources, the White House is forced to bargain with the services for cooperation in implementing its programs. Presidents, however, are not always willing and able to compromise with the military. For those presidents who want to reduce their dependence on military sources of defense information and to overcome military opposition to their orders and plans, several options are available. They can support defense reorganizations, bring a military officer into the White House as an adviser, rely on the secretary of defense and other civilian advisers for military advice, give the Office of Management and Budget (OMB) greater authority over defense spending, and appoint presidential commissions to study defense problems.[143]

Presidents also can exercise control of the military through their appointments of military officers. Congress establishes the ranks to which officers can be promoted, and the Senate confirms presidential appointees, but the power to assign military officers to posts, including the Joint Chiefs of Staff, gives presidents the opportunity to shape the leadership of the military. Moreover, one of the most important instruments of presidential control is the commander in chief's prerogative in wartime to dismiss members of the military who are incompetent or insubordinate. *(See box, Truman and General MacArthur, this page.)*

Defense Budget

A frustrating and complicated aspect of presidential defense management is the defense budget. Every year the executive branch must submit to Congress a defense budget, which proposes both the general defense spending level and the specific military programs on which funds will be spent.

The general spending level is a highly visible political issue on which many Americans have an opinion—even presidential candidates feel compelled to announce their intentions. The specifics determine force structure and defense strategy, and they are decided through a complicated process of conflict and compromise between the president, Congress, the Defense Department's civilian leadership, and the individual armed services, all under the lobbying pressure of defense contractors and public interest groups.

TRUMAN AND GENERAL MACARTHUR

The most famous clash between a president and a member of the armed forces was Harry S. Truman's dispute with Gen. Douglas MacArthur during the Korean War. The conflict led to Truman's dramatic firing of MacArthur and tested the principle of presidential control of the military.

Few military leaders in the history of the United States were as respected and revered by the American public as General MacArthur was in the early stages of the Korean War. He had been a decorated hero of World War I, the triumphant commander of U.S. forces in the Pacific in World War II, and the successful military governor of Japan, overseeing that nation's transformation into a modern democratic state. When the Korean War broke out, he was made supreme commander of the UN forces in Korea. His landing at Inchon behind North Korean lines in September 1950 reversed the tide of the war and reinforced his reputation as a tactical genius. Many Americans and members of Congress saw MacArthur as indispensable to the success of the Korean War effort. Republican leaders regarded the eloquent and handsome general as a possible candidate in a future presidential election.

The conflict between Truman and MacArthur arose when they disagreed about the goals to be pursued in the Korean War. When Truman sent forces to Korea in June 1950, he intended to drive the North Korean forces out of South Korea and reestablish a secure border at the thirty-eighth parallel. Once the military campaign succeeded, Truman and his advisers ordered MacArthur to cross into North Korea and attempt to unify the nation.[1] Concerned about provoking Communist China, Truman prohibited MacArthur from attacking North Korean bases in China.

MacArthur, however, envisioned a grand Asian strategy in which the United States would seek to overthrow the government of Communist China. At the least, MacArthur wanted the latitude to bomb North Korean sanctuaries and supply lines inside China. During the fall of 1950, he openly criticized Truman's policies and encouraged his supporters in Congress to press the administration to give him discretion to widen the war.

When in November 1950 Communist China entered the war and pushed U.S. forces back across the thirty-eighth parallel, MacArthur blamed his retreat on Truman's constraints. Truman responded with a presidential directive on December 5 that instructed overseas military commanders and diplomats to clear all public statements with Washington. Unable to accept either Truman's strategy or Gen. Matthew Ridgeway's remarkable progress on the battlefield, MacArthur released a press statement that blamed Truman for the "savage slaughter of Americans."[2]

Later, MacArthur tried to undercut Truman's efforts to arrange cease-fire negotiations with the Chinese by issuing a proclamation that insulted the Communist Chinese government and suggested that the United States might "depart from its tolerant efforts to contain the war to the area of Korea." MacArthur failed to explain or apologize for the communiqué. On April 5, House minority leader Joseph Martin, R-Mass., a MacArthur ally, read a letter from the general on the floor of the House. "If we lose the war to Communism in Asia, the fall of Europe is inevitable.... There is no substitute for victory." With that, Truman found he could no longer tolerate MacArthur's insubordination, and it was announced at a news conference at one o'clock in the morning on April 11 that the president was relieving MacArthur of his command.[3]

Truman's public approval ratings, as measured by the Gallup organization, slipped from an abysmal 28 percent in late March to just 24 percent after he fired MacArthur. Sixty-one percent of Americans disapproved of the way the president was doing his job. Impeachment became a frequent topic of conversation as members of Congress accused the president and his top advisers of appeasing communism or even falling under the influence of communist agents.[4] MacArthur's welcome home as a war hero intensified the pressure on the Truman administration. The general delivered an emotional farewell address before Congress on April 19 and received a New York City parade attended by an estimated seven million people.

The Truman administration, however, was able to focus attention on the general's insubordination and the constitutional principle of civilian control of the armed forces. At the joint Senate Foreign Relations and Armed Services Committees' hearings on MacArthur's firing and Korean War strategy, administration officials united behind the president in denouncing MacArthur's actions and endorsing military restraint in Korea. Most important, Truman received the support of the military. Chair of the Joint Chiefs of Staff Gen. Omar Bradley told the committees that MacArthur's Korean strategy "would involve us in the wrong war, at the wrong place, at the wrong time, and with the wrong enemy."[5] Talk of impeachment subsided, and Congress took no action against the president.

1. John Spanier, *American Foreign Policy Since World War II*, 11th ed. (Washington, D.C.: CQ Press, 1988), 76.
2. David M. McCullough, *Truman* (New York: Simon and Schuster, 1992), 834–835.
3. Ibid., 836–843.
4. James A. Nathan and James K. Oliver, *United States Foreign Policy and World Order*, 2d ed. (Boston: Little, Brown, 1981), 149.
5. McCullough, *Truman*, 853–854.

The amount of money devoted to the defense budget and its distribution among services and weapons systems not only determine the defense policy and capabilities of the United States. They also create a backdrop for U.S. international relations. Adversaries and allies alike scrutinize the defense budget for clues about U.S. global intentions. Increases, decreases, and shifts in defense spending, particularly for items such as naval vessels and aircraft, indicate to foreign governments the nation's specific and general capabilities to project force in the world. Particularly in the late 1980s and 1990s, when large budget deficits were common, all parties in the budget process fought over the redistribution of scarce resources and the redefinition of strategic needs.

In recent years, the debate over the defense budget has revolved around two general quandaries. One is the appropriate size of the standing armed forces in the post–cold war world. Some argue that the United States must be prepared to fight two major conflicts simultaneously. Indeed, they point out that given the many areas of potential conflict such as the Korean peninsula, Iraq, Taiwan, and Israel, such a scenario is more than plausible. Moreover, if the country is prepared for only one major conflict, it would resist engaging in any one conflict, because that would leave it unable to respond to another crisis. Those on the other side argue that budget realities, especially in the post–cold war circumstances, require cuts in forces. Both sides have had to contend with how to account for the increasing expenditures on peacekeeping operations. Another debate is over the distribution of available defense dollars. The poor state of military readiness, including the retention of experienced personnel and the maintenance of equipment, was a regular theme in the criticism of Clinton's diversion of forces and funds for peacekeeping. President George W. Bush's secretary of defense, Donald H. Rumsfeld, argued instead for shifting resources, and even cutting active personnel, for the sake of the modernization of weaponry and the development of a new generation of high-tech weapons. After the September 11, 2001, terrorist attacks, however, the United States nearly doubled defense spending (though it remained comparatively low in the post–World War II era as a percentage of gross domestic product [GDP]) to combat terrorism and wage war in Afghanistan and Iraq. As the Obama administration wound down U.S. involvement in those wars, the post–cold war era debates about how much defense spending was needed to protect American national security recurred. In early 2012 the Obama administration announced that it would slow the growth of defense spending over the next decade, in part by adopting a new strategy that would remove the longtime premise of having a military that could wage two major wars simultaneously.

The defense budget has enormous consequences for the U.S. economy. Despite the deep cuts of the 1990s, the current defense budget of nearly $700 billion is the largest part of the discretionary budget—the part of the national budget that can be cut or shifted from year to year. *(See Chapter 7, Chief Economist.)* Defense spending affects the economy in particular ways as well. Although most economists believe the economy is better stimulated by tax cuts than increased military expenditures, boosting defense spending can increase the demand for goods and services, which, in turn, can reduce unemployment and lift the country out of a depression or recession. Defense spending can spur technological development with various commercial applications and is essential to the economies of particular regions.

Defense Budget Process

The annual defense budget, a large and complex document, is prepared with the help of many bureaucratic entities, including the National Security Council, OMB, and various Defense Department agencies. About a year and a half before a fiscal year begins, the defense secretary issues a study assessing military threats and defines departmental goals and spending priorities. Using this outline, the military services develop budget requests. These requests are reviewed and amended by the defense secretary and OMB, who reevaluate them in the context of defense and nondefense spending priorities. The resulting comprehensive defense budget is then submitted to Congress.[144]

Presidential participation in the defense budget process is limited by the size and complexity of the budget. Even if a president has had executive branch experience with the defense budget, the many demands of the presidency would not allow its occupant to become immersed in the details. The president therefore must rely heavily on career military officers and Defense Department bureaucrats familiar with the process.

Nevertheless, presidents, more than any other individual or groups, influence the general outlines of the defense budget, because their assessments of U.S. military capabilities, the threats to U.S. national security, and understandings of military readiness carry great weight in any debate. Presidents cannot be expected to review every item in the defense budget, but they do determine the approximate level of defense spending, and their general defense policy affects which types of programs will be emphasized. Although a president rarely will participate in discussions of how much to pay privates, a presidential policy of improving the quality of recruits will guide those discussions.

Besides establishing a general national security policy, presidents function as the final arbiter of disputes between executive departments and agencies about specific defense budget decisions. OMB and the Defense Department often disagree on budget issues, because OMB's mission of overseeing spending often clashes with Defense's mission of enhancing national security. Early in his term, President Reagan had to choose between the conflicting defense budget recommendations of defense secretary Caspar Weinberger, who had been charged with building up the nation's defenses, and OMB director David Stockman, who had been given the task of reducing federal spending. Reagan sided with Weinberger, thus subordinating budget reduction to the defense buildup.[145]

After World War II, Congress usually gave presidents most of the funds they requested for defense. Yet especially since the end of the cold war, Congress has scrutinized the defense budget more carefully, though always with an eye toward protecting specific projects that directly benefit states and congressional districts. This sort of parochialism leads to frequent and important disputes over force structure as particular weapons systems are defended against the president's larger policy changes. In particular, Congress had made military bases, large sources of local employment and spending, all but immune to budget cuts. Yet in 1988, under the pressure of chronic budget deficits, Congress and the president initiated a complex base closure process that removed both Congress and the president from specific choices. Under the new procedure, an independent commission studies the utility of the various bases and submits a list of recommended closings. Congress is allowed to vote only on the list as a whole, and its decision is subject to a presidential veto. Since this procedure was initiated, Congress has decisively defeated all attempts to reject the commission's recommendations. In 1996, however, President Clinton violated the spirit of the policy and procedure. He picked two bases off the approved closure list and decided instead to privatize their operations. The two bases were located in key electoral states, Texas and California. Many critics claimed that the president had undermined the integrity of this valuable process by putting his reelection interests ahead of the public good. There were in fact no more rounds of base closings during Clinton's second term, and Congress rejected President George W. Bush's request for another round in 2003. In 2005 the commission recommended closing an additional thirty-three bases, which would provide an estimated annual savings of $5 billion, and these recommendations became law, with an implementation deadline of September 2011. Overall, the executive branch has retained the initiative in the defense budget process, but Congress has challenged the president on funding for individual weapons systems and defense programs such as the MX missile. In addition, the creation of the Congressional Budget Office in 1974 and the expansion of congressional committee staffs that deal with the defense budget have enhanced Congress's ability to detect waste and fraud in the spending programs that are approved.[146]

Weapons Development and Procurement

Presidents and their scientific and military advisers must choose from a wide variety of options which weapons systems to develop and build. Many different agencies and offices within the Pentagon engage in weapons research, development, and acquisition. In 1986 Congress, in an attempt to centralize oversight and direction of the huge procurement bureaucracy, enacted laws creating the office of under secretary of defense for acquisition and designating the under secretary as the Pentagon's third-ranking official.

Weapons procurement decisions seldom are based solely on rational calculations of how a particular weapons system might contribute to national security. The individual services press presidents and top defense officials to adopt various procurement strategies. The U.S. nuclear triad—the policy of deploying some nuclear weapons on land-based missiles, others on bombers, and the rest on submarines and surface ships—arose in part from the individual services' demands for a nuclear mission. Even groups within the services will maneuver to protect their share of their service's procurement funds.

Technological advances also drive weapons procurement. Since the end of World War II, the defense establishment has operated under the premise that the quality of weapons is more important than their quantity. Presidents must serve as a mediator between competing factions in the procurement process and attempt to develop a mix of weapons that best meets the needs of national security at an affordable cost.

Presidents seldom become personally involved in minor procurement matters, but they must become involved in decisions with significant effects on defense policy. For example, in the early 1980s Reagan's belief that U.S. strategic nuclear forces were threatened by a window of vulnerability led to the deployment of the MX missile and a revival of the B-1 bomber project, which had been scrapped under Carter.

Weapons systems often take more than a decade to move from conception to deployment and may be conceived under one president, tested under another, and mass-produced under a third. Presidents have been reluctant to cancel weapons systems that have reached the production stage because of the time and money already spent on their development. In addition, the longer a weapons program has been around, the more likely it has developed constituencies in the defense bureaucracy and Congress that will resist its cancellation. President Carter's decision not to build the B-1 bomber in 1977 and Secretary of Defense Richard B. Cheney's 1991 decision to cancel the A-12 attack plane are rare examples of executive branch cuts after a weapon was ready for production.

Ultimately, presidents must secure congressional approval for appropriations to pay for the projects they favor. Not only must they contend with members of Congress who do not share their views of procurement priorities, but they also must deal with lawmakers who defend weapons because they happen to be built in their home states and districts. Canceling a program is even more difficult because lawmakers whose district or state will lose jobs as a result will contend that halting the program poses a threat to national security. Sometimes, though, budgetary concerns can prompt cancellations, if legislators are persuaded that national security will not suffer. In 2011, for example, after five years of petitioning by the George W. Bush and Obama administrations, the U.S. House of Representatives voted to cancel the F-35 Joint Strike Fighter program, at an estimated savings of $3 billion in the coming years, even though some of the program development was based in the home state of the House Speaker John Boehner of Ohio. Outgoing Defense Secretary Robert M. Gates had criticized the program as unnecessary, and his support for cancellation helped the Obama administration to build support on Capitol Hill.[147]

Budget and Procurement Inefficiency

Distrust of special interests, congressional parochialism, and the huge defense bureaucracy have fed general and long-standing suspicions that the defense budget is filled with fraud and waste. Charges of misuse of defense dollars increased during the Reagan administration defense buildup, giving rise to many anecdotes suggesting that there were serious problems with defense procurement and budgeting procedures. For example, it was reported that military services were purchasing a twelve-cent Allen wrench for $9,606 and toilet seats for $640. Many such horror stories are based on a misunderstanding. To simplify accounting, contractors will distribute their total cost of development and production for an entire system equally across every item within that system. Thus the total cost of, for example, a self-contained toilet for a transport plane would be distributed equally across all parts, including the relatively inexpensive toilet seat. So the "price" of the seat only seems to be high.[148] The problems of procurement lie elsewhere.

Although waste occurs in every government department and agency, several characteristics of the Defense Department have made its problem particularly acute. The enormous size of the defense budget not only creates more opportunities for waste, but also makes central control of its details nearly impossible.[149] Each service, moreover, tends to promote its interests at the expense of the others and often avoids consulting with the other services when developing budget and procurement proposals. Neither the president, the secretary of defense, OMB, nor Congress can assess the worthiness of every one, or even most, of the thousands of line items that make up the defense budget.

In addition, the scope and complexity of weapons development and procurement increase the opportunities for outright fraud. In the late 1980s, several major defense contractors were found guilty of price gouging, bribery, and tax fraud. In June 1988 the Justice Department disclosed evidence of a procurement scandal, involving dozens of defense contracts costing tens of billions of dollars, that threatened to dwarf all previous defense budget scandals.

In response to procurement waste and scandals, a study of procurement reform was commissioned in 1990. The 1993 commission report was incorporated into Vice President Al Gore's general study of government efficiency,

HOMOSEXUALITY AND MILITARY SERVICE

Attempting to fulfill a campaign pledge, President Bill Clinton stirred up a political storm in 1993 by announcing his determination to end the ban on homosexuals in the armed services. The military's policy was to discharge anyone who engaged in homosexual activities or even disclosed his or her homosexual orientation. Moreover, the military actively sought to ferret out and investigate homosexuals. During the decade leading up to 1993, the armed services had discharged more than fourteen thousand servicemen and women under this policy.[1]

Clinton had the authority to change this policy. The president, as commander in chief, has the constitutional power to "make Rules for the Government and Regulation of the land and naval Forces" as long as these rules do not conflict with congressional decisions. Nevertheless, the president's decision to end the ban was greeted with strong resistance especially from prominent members of the defense establishment, including the Joint Chiefs of Staff and Georgia senator Sam Nunn, a leading congressional authority on defense and a member of the president's party. The criticism may have been amplified by Clinton's lack of credibility in military matters; it was generally known that he had avoided military service during the Vietnam War.

Under a threat from Congress to override the president by writing a ban on homosexual orientation into law, President Clinton settled on a compromise policy known as "don't ask, don't tell" (DADT). The ban on homosexual conduct was retained, but recruits would no longer be asked about their sexual orientation, and individuals were to keep their orientation to themselves. Investigations would be initiated only by senior officers with reasonable cause to suspect a violation of the ban. Congress then wrote the ban on homosexual conduct into law. These modest changes fell far short of President Clinton's original intentions. In 1995 a federal district court struck down the compromise policy as an unconstitutional infringement of free speech, but the ruling was overturned on appeal. In 2006 the Supreme Court unanimously ruled that the federal government could deny funding to universities that refused to permit military recruiters on campus, which several schools had done in protest of the DADT policy, declaring that it violated their own nondiscrimination policies.[2]

Barack Obama pledged during the 2008 presidential campaign to repeal the law, and he announced in his 2010 State of the Union address that he would work with Congress and the military to do so. With support from the secretary of defense and the chair of the Joint Chiefs of Staff, as well as a November 2010 Pentagon report that stated the ending of DADT would not harm military readiness, Obama persuaded Congress to approve repeal. The repeal became law in December 2010.[3]

1. *CQ Almanac*, 1992 (Washington, D.C.: Congressional Quarterly, 1993), 454.
2. *Rumsfeld v. Forum for Academic and Institutional Rights, Inc.* 547 U.S. 47 (2006).
3. Elisabeth Bumiller, "Obama Ends 'Don't Ask, Don't Tell' Policy," *New York Times*, July 22, 2011, www.nytimes.com/2011/07/23/us/23military.html.

the National Performance Review. The major recommendations for streamlining military procurement were part of legislation passed in 1994. Among other changes, the legislation reduced the regulatory requirements for smaller contracts and allowed many contracts with specific providers to be replaced by off-the-shelf purchases from the best available sources.

A crucial problem is how the Defense Department makes and tracks payments. To begin with, the flow of money is staggering. The Defense Department pays out more than $35 million an hour in payroll alone. Added to that are the hundreds of billions of dollars that flow each year through the department and out to private contractors. In 1995 investigations by the General Accounting Office and the Defense Department's comptroller, John J. Hamre, revealed that the department's antiquated accounting systems could not keep track of who had paid whom and for what. At least $15 billion spent during the preceding decade could not be accounted for. One official estimated that each year the department overpays contractors by at least $500 million. Although an overhaul of the system was begun in 1995, the procurement system cannot be shut down for repairs. The department's comptroller compared any attempt at reform to "changing a tire on a car while driving 60 miles an hour."[150]

Military Personnel Policy

Although the Constitution charges Congress with the responsibility to "make rules for the government and regulation" of the army and navy, the executive branch has substantial authority in military personnel policy. Much of this authority has been delegated to the executive branch by Congress, but authority also has been claimed by presidents under the commander-in-chief power to make regulations that do not conflict with congressional statutes. As a result, the laws passed by Congress governing the armed forces have been supplemented by a body of executive rules and regulations.[151]

Presidents usually take the initiative in proposing changes in the size of the armed forces, the methods by which the ranks are filled, and where U.S. forces will be stationed. Ultimate authority for raising an army resides in Congress, but legislators often accept presidential actions and recommendations on these issues. In 2010, for example, in response to pressure from the Obama administration, Congress decided to repeal the "Don't Ask, Don't Tell" policy that had prohibited homosexuals in the military from publicly revealing their sexual orientation. (See box, *Homosexuality and Military Service, p. 291.*)

Recruitment and the Draft

Conscription was not used in the United States until the Civil War. The 1863 Enrollment Act set up a draft system run by the War Department and administered by military officers. During World War I, Congress again authorized conscription to fulfill troop goals. The 1917 Selective Service Act was challenged in the courts, but the Supreme Court upheld Congress's authority to draft Americans in the *Selective Draft Law Cases.* The Court held that military service was one of a citizen's duties in a "just government."

Not until 1940, however, did Congress pass a draft bill while the nation was at peace. Although the United States had not yet become involved in World War II, President Franklin Roosevelt urged Congress to adopt the measure. In summer 1941, with the threat of war looming larger, Roosevelt had a difficult fight before winning enactment of amendments that widened the draft. The measure was passed in the House by just one vote. Although earlier drafts had been administered by the War Department, the Selective Training and Service Act of 1940 established an independent Selective Service System, headed by a presidential appointee, to oversee the draft.

In 1947 Congress followed President Truman's recommendation to allow the 1940 draft act to expire. A year later when enlistments failed to meet troop needs, Truman proposed a renewal of the draft and universal military training. Truman's plan would have required all physically and mentally able men to receive one year of military training and serve six months in the reserves. Congress rejected universal military training but passed the Selective Service Act of 1948, which renewed the peacetime draft.

After the 1973 signing of the Paris peace accords, ending U.S. involvement in the Vietnam War, Congress followed the recommendation of President Nixon and finally allowed the draft to expire. This was the first step toward an all-volunteer armed forces, an idea that had been under study since 1969. Military pay was raised dramatically to attract volunteers. Since 1973, the armed services have succeeded in meeting their personnel requirements.

In 1980, amid the international tension created in late 1979 by the takeover of the U.S. embassy in Tehran and the invasion of Afghanistan by the Soviet Union, Jimmy Carter asked Congress to reinstitute draft registration, a step intended to reduce the time required to bring draftees into the armed services after a mobilization. The measure that Congress approved provided only for registration and required further authorization from Congress before anyone could be called up for service.[152] Although Reagan opposed draft registration during the 1980 presidential campaign, he ordered its continuation in January 1982. Since then, the few attempts to eliminate funding for registration have failed. Controversy over the Iraq war prompted some calls for reinstituting a draft in the first decade of the twenty-first century, as supporters hoped a draft would spark greater public engagement in policy decisions about the use of U.S. military force. But the proposal did not gain momentum, and as of 2011, the armed services declared they were setting record recruitment goals, due in part to the weak U.S. economy.[153]

The rise of the all-volunteer force has changed civil-military relations in one highly significant way: the political leaders who make decisions about the use of U.S. military force abroad are much less likely to have served in the military than in the past. As of 2011, about 22 percent of Congress had served in the armed forces, whereas in 1969, veterans comprised nearly 75 percent of Congress.[154] In the post–cold war era, decisions about sending troops abroad sparked tensions between elected officials and military leaders over how to define, and achieve, American national interests.[155] Nevertheless, in the United States, civilian control of the military is a bedrock principle of governance that underlies the military profession.[156] But efforts to limit U.S. military commitments abroad mean that postconflict operations receive insufficient attention, as was evident in both Afghanistan and Iraq, and that private contractors increasingly assume responsibilities previously undertaken by the military, often logistical assignments, but sometimes security tasks as well.[157]

Peacetime Military Deployments

Presidents have used the commander-in-chief power to justify unilateral decisions on relocating armed forces, but they have generally respected the laws limiting their freedom to redeploy armed forces in peacetime.[158] In 1940 Congress attached a proviso to the Selective Training and Service Act that prohibited troops drafted under the act from being used outside the Western Hemisphere. Franklin Roosevelt accepted this limitation, although he maintained that Iceland was part of the Western Hemisphere and sent troops there in 1941.

A more recent example of a congressional limit on troop deployments occurred in 1982. In that year, Congress attached to a defense appropriations bill an amendment limiting the number of active-duty U.S. military personnel stationed in Europe to 315,000. The Reagan administration opposed the limit, arguing that increases in U.S. troop strength in Europe might be required by changes in the military balance between NATO and the Soviet Union and its allies. Despite the administration's objections, defense secretary Caspar Weinberger assured Congress that the troop ceiling would be observed. The amendment included a provision that allowed the president to waive the troop limit if the president certified that "overriding national security requirements" made such action necessary. By including this provision, Congress was recognizing that the purpose of peacetime military deployments is to deter war and that the president as commander in chief should have wide authority to redeploy troops for that purpose.

If a president does refuse to observe limitations that Congress has placed on peacetime troop deployments, Congress could cut off funds for the base where the troops

In the middle of a wave of democratic uprisings in the Middle East and North Africa, which became known as the Arab Spring, President Obama decided to intervene militarily in Libya on behalf of the rebels. In a joint effort with other NATO forces, the U.S. was the first to use air strikes to establish a no-fly zone over Libya. Until this turn of events in 2011, the U.S. had only rhetorically supported the surge of democratic movements in the region.

were stationed or for the supplies needed to sustain the troops. During the Clinton presidency, Congress considered a number of proposals to limit the president's capacity to deploy U.S. forces in, for example, Bosnia, Haiti, and any UN peacekeeping mission without specific congressional authorization. In 2011 President Obama approved air strikes in Libya following authorization by the UN Security Council, but he did not seek congressional support. The House subsequently refused to grant approval for the mission, but an effort to deny funding failed.[159]

PRESIDENTIAL WARTIME EMERGENCY POWERS

In 1810, after Thomas Jefferson had left the presidency, he wrote:

A strict observation of the written laws is doubtless *one* of the high duties of a good citizen, but it is not the *highest.* The laws of necessity, of self-preservation, of saving our country when in danger, are of higher obligation. To lose our country by a scrupulous adherence to written law would be to lose the law itself, with life, liberty, property . . . thus absurdly sacrificing the end to the means.[160]

Governing Conquered Territory

On many occasions U.S. military forces have occupied enemy territory during hostilities. Presidential authority to administer a recently occupied territory through the armed forces is nearly absolute; neither the U.S. Constitution nor the former laws of a conquered nation constrain the president. Moreover, several hundred Supreme Court cases have upheld the president's authority to function as a dictator over occupied territory subject only to the "laws of war."[1] Presidents and their appointed military representatives may set up new government institutions, make laws by decree, establish a court system, collect taxes, or do anything else they believe necessary to administer the conquered area. Presidential rule over occupied territory lasts until it is annexed to the United States or a treaty is concluded that transfers power back to a local government. The president may not, however, unilaterally annex acquired territory. Article IV of the Constitution grants Congress the power to "dispose of and make all needful Rules and Regulations respecting the Territory or other Property belonging to the United States." Therefore, Congress must approve a treaty of cession or pass legislation annexing the territory before it can become part of the United States.[2]

1. Clinton Rossiter, *The Supreme Court and the Commander in Chief* (Ithaca: Cornell University Press, 1976), 122–123.
2. Joseph E. Kallenbach, *The American Chief Executive: The Presidency and the Governorship* (New York: Harper and Row, 1966), 541.

Jefferson maintained that such acts of self-preservation, although justified, were strictly illegal and in no way authorized by the Constitution. Later presidents have derived their emergency powers from a broad reading of constitutional authority and have claimed the authority to violate parts of the Constitution to ensure the security of the nation.

When it is evident that conditions of national peril exist, Congress and the American public turn to the president for leadership. Under such conditions Lincoln and Franklin Roosevelt stretched, reinterpreted, and in some cases brazenly violated the Constitution in the name of national security. Their claims to an inherent executive power to safeguard the nation were accepted because the American people generally agreed with their assessment of the gravity of the emergency at hand.[161] Presidential assertions of an inherent executive power based on a doubtful claim of national emergency, however, will likely fail the test of public and judicial scrutiny. President Nixon was not able to convince the American people or the courts that his administration's use of wiretaps and break-ins was justified by dire threats to national security.

Nowhere does the Constitution mention presidential emergency powers, but the courts often have been sympathetic to exercises of emergency power by presidents in wartime, especially when action is taken with the cooperation of Congress. Yet this approval has not been automatic, especially when the rights and property of U.S. citizens are involved. Total war in any age requires sacrifices from civilians and security measures at home, but a wartime emergency does not give the president unrestrained freedom to violate the rights of Americans.

Martial Law and Civil Rights

The most extreme wartime emergency measure a president may take is a declaration of martial law. Under such a declaration, ordinary law and judicial process are temporarily replaced by military rule. Substitution of military for civilian authority may be general or confined to a region. In addition, it may be absolute, or it may apply only to a specific civil function by the military. Even cases of limited martial law, however, entail some curbing of individual rights.

The Constitution does not provide for a power to declare martial law, although it does mention the suspension of *habeas corpus* under Article I, which outlines Congress's powers. The declaration of martial law, however, is usually presumed to be a presidential function flowing from the president's powers to command the armed forces and execute the laws. Because there is no specific constitutional basis for martial law, presidents must justify their decision to proclaim it on the grounds that protecting the welfare and security of the nation requires them to govern through military force rather than ordinary civil institutions and laws.

No president has ever declared a condition of absolute martial law that applied to the entire country. Moreover, not since President Lincoln placed several areas of the nation under martial law during the Civil War has any president directly proclaimed martial law on behalf of the national government. Martial law has been declared, however, by presidential agents or military officers, often with the explicit or implied approval of the president. For example, Gen. Andrew Jackson declared martial law in New Orleans before his battle with the British there in 1814; the commander of federal troops sent to Idaho in 1899 to quell labor unrest declared martial law with President McKinley's approval; and after the Japanese attack on Pearl Harbor on December 7, 1941, the territorial governor of Hawaii declared martial law on the islands with the support of Franklin Roosevelt.[162]

Although the courts may reject the president's assessment of the necessity of martial law, historically they have done so only after the emergency has passed. In 1866 the Supreme Court ruled in *Ex parte Milligan* that Lincoln's suspension of the civil court system in Indiana during the Civil War was illegal.[163] Similarly, in 1946 the Court declared in *Duncan v. Kahanamoku* that the establishment of martial law during World War II in

Hawaii by the governor with President Roosevelt's approval had been unlawful.[164] Yet neither decision had any effect on either president's ability to abrogate civil liberties during the wars.

Suspension of Habeas Corpus

The only emergency power mentioned in the Constitution is the crucial provision for the suspension of the writ of *habeas corpus*—the right of prisoners to have the legality of their detention reviewed by the courts and to be released upon the court's orders. The Constitution states: "The Privilege of the Writ of Habeas Corpus shall not be suspended, unless when in Cases of Rebellion or Invasion the public Safety may require it." The Framers did not, however, specify which branch had this authority, although their placement of it in Article I has led many legal scholars, judges, and legislators to argue that it was intended as a congressional power.

The issue of presidential suspension of *habeas corpus* arose most dramatically during the Civil War. In response to sabotage by Confederate sympathizers, President Lincoln ordered in the spring of 1861 that *habeas corpus* be suspended along the route between Washington and Philadelphia. Lincoln believed this and other emergency measures were essential to the survival of the Union. On May 25, John Merryman, a prominent Maryland citizen who had been involved in secessionist activities in that state, was arrested and detained by military authorities. Merryman immediately appealed to Chief Justice Roger Taney for a writ of *habeas corpus*. Taney reviewed the case and ordered the army to release Merryman, but Lincoln defiantly refused to permit his release. Taney denounced Lincoln's action and wrote an opinion asserting that the Constitution had conferred authority to suspend the writ on Congress, not the president. Lincoln maintained that since the suspension of *habeas corpus* was an emergency measure and emergencies could occur when Congress was out of session—as it had been in this case—presidents must have authority to suspend the writ unilaterally.

The conflict between the president and the chief justice showed that a president willing to defy legal procedures during a genuine crisis that was widely recognized as such could suspend *habeas corpus* regardless of whether the president has the constitutional authority to do so. Presidential scholar Clinton Rossiter remarked,

> The one great precedent is what Lincoln did, not what Taney said. Future Presidents will know where to look for historical support. So long as public opinion sustains the President, as a sufficient amount of it sustained Lincoln in his shadowy tilt with Taney and throughout the rest of the war, he has nothing to fear from the displeasure of the courts. . . . The law of the Constitution, as it actually exists, must be considered to read that in a condition of martial necessity the President has the power to suspend the privilege of the writ of habeas corpus.[165]

Trial of Civilians by Military Courts

In addition to suspending *habeas corpus,* President Lincoln also declared that for some crimes civilians could be tried by military courts. On September 24, 1862, he announced that as long as the Civil War continued

> all rebels and insurgents, their aiders and abettors, within the United States, and all persons discouraging volunteer enlistments, resisting militia drafts, or guilty of any disloyal practice affording aid and comfort to rebels against the authority of the United States, shall be subject to martial law and liable to trial and punishment of courts-martial or military commissions.

Lincoln went on to suspend *habeas corpus* for such persons and declared that they could be imprisoned in military facilities. Although Congress had passed legislation approving many of Lincoln's emergency measures, it never approved his subjection of civilians to military courts.[166]

Lambdin P. Milligan, a citizen of Indiana, was arrested in 1864 by military authorities who charged him with aiding a Confederate raid into Indiana from across the Ohio River. On May 9, 1865, Milligan was found guilty and sentenced to death. Milligan's case eventually came before the Supreme Court.

The Court held 9–0 in *Ex parte Milligan* that the president did not have the authority to subject civilians to military tribunals in an area where civilian courts were functioning.[167] The Court also ruled 5–4 that even the president and Congress together lacked power to authorize trials of civilians by military courts outside of a war zone. The majority opinion, written by Justice David Davis, admitted that in regions "where war actually prevails" and makes it "impossible to administer criminal justice according to the law," military government is justified. However, the Court rejected the idea that such conditions existed in Indiana—hundreds of miles from the war front—where civilian courts were functioning normally.

Beyond their verdict, the justices used this case to defend the inviolability of the Constitution. Davis wrote:

> The Constitution of the United States is a law for rulers and people, equally in war and in peace, and covers with the shield of its protection all classes of men, at all times, and under all circumstances. No doctrine involving more pernicious consequences was ever invented by the wit of man than that any of its provisions can be suspended during any of the great exigencies of government.

Milligan is regarded as significant by legal scholars for asserting that constitutional limits to presidential power are not suspended even during the most dire military emergency. However, the logic in Lincoln's defense of his policy is also compelling:

To state the question more directly, are all the laws, *but one,* to go unexecuted, and the government itself go to pieces, lest that one [law] be violated? Even in such a case, would not the official oath to faithfully execute the laws be broken, if the government should be overthrown, when it is believed that disregarding the single law, would tend to preserve it?[168]

When the Supreme Court ruled on *Milligan* in 1866, the war was over and Lincoln was dead. Consequently, the Court was able to strike down a presidential emergency action without confronting an incumbent president during a wartime crisis.

Military Tribunals and Terrorism

In November 2001 President George W. Bush authorized the use of military tribunals for trying foreigners accused of terrorist acts against the United States. The president claimed that emergency powers under the commander-in-chief clause gave him the latitude to institute these extraordinary procedures. The Bush administration cited in particular Franklin Roosevelt's use of a military tribunal to prosecute eight Nazi saboteurs caught in the United States with explosives. All eight were convicted, and six were executed.

Under this order, the president would decide, case by case, which defendants would be tried in a military tribunal. The selection of judges and all the rules of procedure for evidence and witnesses would be left to the secretary of defense. The decision was announced just as the four defendants being tried for the 1986 terrorist bombing of a Berlin discotheque were convicted in an ordinary criminal proceeding, and critics viewed the decision as an unnecessary violation of accepted principles of fairness and the rule of law. The Bush administration defended this decision on several grounds. For one thing, it claimed that the high barriers of evidence and strict standards of fairness in ordinary criminal proceedings, which are designed to prevent an innocent person from being convicted, are not appropriate when the consequences of allowing a guilty party to go free may be so terrible. Ordinary criminal procedures also can result in long trials—the prosecution of the Berlin terrorists took four years—and long trials would make the judges, the jury, and the country in general more inviting targets for intimidation and retaliation. Finally, the secrecy of a military tribunal would help to protect the valuable intelligence sources and methods that are needed in the ongoing struggle against terrorism.

Military tribunals were intended for the several hundred prisoners that the United States had detained at Guantanamo Bay, Cuba, mostly from the 2001 war in Afghanistan. But the White House, Congress, and the Supreme Court have disagreed sharply on how these tribunals should operate. The Supreme Court ruled in *Hamdi v. Rumsfeld* (2004) that the government could not detain U.S. citizens who were suspected terrorists without due process. In 2006 the Court declared in *Hamdan v. Rumsfeld* that the

United States would have to comply with the rule of law in creating military tribunals, including international law such as the post–World War II Geneva Convention, which prescribed rules for treatment of prisoners of war.[169] The Court stated that the president could seek congressional approval for creating special military commissions, but that he could not establish them independently. The Court further held, contrary to the administration's position, that federal courts may adjudicate appeals from detainees held overseas by the United States.

Congress then passed the Military Commissions Act in 2006 to authorize the use of military tribunals, but two years later, the Supreme Court ruled in *Boumediene v. Bush* (2008) that the section of the law that suspended the writ of *habeas corpus* for detainees was unconstitutional. Upon taking office in 2009, President Obama pledged to close Guantanamo Bay in one year and to replace military tribunals with civilian trials. But Congress refused to appropriate funds to close the facility and transfer detainees to the United States for oversight by federal civilian courts, and in March 2011 the Obama administration announced that Guantanamo Bay would remain open and that military trials would continue. Civil liberties advocates criticized the administration's decision, saying that indefinite detention of suspected terrorists violated the Geneva Conventions on human rights.[170] *(See box, Supreme Court Cases Related to the President's Foreign Policy Powers, p. 208, in Chapter 5.)*

Korematsu v. United States

Three-quarters of a century after *Milligan,* a case involving the violation of individual rights by an exercise of wartime emergency power came before the Court while the emergency still existed.

After the Japanese attack on Pearl Harbor on December 7, 1941, President Roosevelt ordered several controversial measures to enhance security on the West Coast. These included the imposition of a curfew on persons of Japanese descent and the relocation of 120,000 Japanese Americans to internment camps in the U.S. interior. Both the curfew and the relocation applied to persons of Japanese ancestry regardless of their citizenship or loyalty. Congress subsequently passed legislation validating the president's directives.

This wholesale suspension of the rights of American citizens led to several Supreme Court cases. In 1943 the Court ruled unanimously in *Hirabayashi v. United States* that together the president and Congress had the power to impose the curfew and that the extreme emergency created by Japan's threat to the Pacific Coast made the curfew justifiable.[171] The Court did not reach a consensus, however, on the more severe violation of rights involved in the relocation of Japanese Americans. In *Korematsu v. United States,* it ruled 6–3 that the threat to national security justified the joint action of Congress and the president.[172] Writing for the majority, Justice Hugo Black explained: "Compulsory exclusion of large groups of citizens from their homes, except under circumstances of direct emergency and peril, is inconsistent with our basic governmental institutions. But when under conditions of modern warfare our shores are threatened by hostile forces, the power to protect must be commensurable with the threatened danger." In a bitter dissenting opinion, Justice Francis Murphy rejected the premise of the Court's decision that the emergency on the West Coast warranted the exclusion from the West Coast of all persons of Japanese ancestry. "Such exclusion," he wrote, "goes over 'the very brink of Constitutional power' and falls into the abyss of racism."

Justice Robert Jackson's dissenting opinion got closer to the heart of the dilemma. On the one hand, he admitted that there are military emergencies that warrant extraordinary measures. But he also argued that judges are not qualified to assess the circumstances, and the Court ought not to corrupt the law by ruling that momentarily necessary violations of civil rights are also constitutionally permissible.

> But if we cannot confine military expedients by the Constitution, neither would I distort the Constitution to approve all that the military may deem expedient. That is what the Court appears to be doing. . . . [A] judicial construction of the due process clause that will sustain this order is a far more subtle blow to liberty than the promulgation of the order itself. . . . The principle then lies about like a loaded weapon ready for the hand of any authority that can bring forward a plausible claim of an urgent need. . . . I should hold that a civil court cannot be made to enforce an order which violates constitutional limitations even if it is a reasonable exercise of military authority.[173]

Seizure of Property

During wartime, it is sometimes necessary for a government to seize private property that is vital to the war effort. Congress has traditionally passed legislation governing the seizure of property belonging to U.S. citizens. Before and during World War I, Congress empowered the president to seize transportation and communications systems if such actions became necessary. President Wilson used these statutes to take over railroad, telephone, and telegraph operations, which were returned to civilian control after the war. Similarly, Franklin Roosevelt was authorized by the War Labor Disputes Act of 1943 to seize control of industries important to the war effort that were in danger of being shut down by labor disputes.[174]

But presidents have not always waited for congressional approval before seizing property. Lincoln personally authorized military units to take possession of telegraph lines during the Civil War, and in 1914 Wilson ordered the seizure of a wireless station that refused to comply with naval censorship rules. Several decades later, Franklin Roosevelt took control of several strike-threatened industries before the War Labor Disputes Act of 1943 authorized such action. Yet unilateral

seizures of property by presidents have been exceptions to accepted practice, and the courts generally have rejected the proposition that presidents possess inherent emergency powers that authorize them to seize private property.

The most famous court case on this question was *Youngstown Sheet and Tube Co. v. Sawyer,* also known as the *Steel Seizure Case,* in which the Supreme Court ruled on President Truman's authority to seize steel mills during the Korean War. Truman believed that a steelworkers strike, scheduled for April 9, 1952, would damage the Korean War effort, and on April 8, he directed Secretary of Commerce Charles Sawyer to seize and operate the steel mills. He justified his seizure of the mills solely on the basis of his power as commander in chief and his responsibility to execute the laws. Truman conceded in his report to Congress that it had the authority to countermand his directive, but Congress failed to approve or reject the president's action.

The steel companies brought suit against the government, seeking an injunction to stop the president's action. The case quickly reached the Supreme Court, where, by a vote of 6–3, Truman's action was held unconstitutional. The Court claimed that the president had usurped Congress's law-making power. It cited several acts in which Congress had provided procedures for responding to strikes that Truman had ignored. In the debate on one of these laws, the Taft-Hartley Act of 1947, Congress had considered empowering the government to seize an industry to prevent strikes but had refused to include such a provision in the law. Truman, therefore, had not just taken action without congressional authorization; he had taken an action that Congress had rejected.[175]

Although it is unclear whether the Court would have ruled differently had the emergency been more grave or had Congress not rejected the inclusion of property seizure provisions in the Taft-Hartley Act, the decision was generally read as a rejection of inherent emergency powers. In a concurring opinion, Justice William O. Douglas explained:

> There can be no doubt that the emergency which caused the president to seize these steel plants was one that bore heavily on the country. But the emergency did not create power; it merely marked an occasion when power should be exercised. And the fact that it was necessary that measures be taken to keep steel in production does not mean that the President, rather than the Congress, had the constitutional authority to act.[176]

In an era of rapidly expanding presidential power, the *Steel Seizure Case,* as Clinton Rossiter observed, "revived, for the moment, the notion that Presidents were subject to congressional limitations in foreign affairs."[177]

ARMED FORCES IN PRESIDENTIAL DIPLOMACY AND FOREIGN POLICY

From the time the Constitution was ratified until the present, presidents have used the military to accomplish limited missions in peacetime—to intimidate potential aggressors, impress trading partners, reassure friends, strengthen alliances, and mediate international disputes. The Constitution does not specifically sanction these peacetime military operations, but presidents have justified them under their power to command the military, defend the United States and its citizens, enforce the laws, and conduct foreign policy. Beyond the use or threat of force in a specific international hot spot, the strength of U.S. armed forces since World War II has allowed presidents to improve relations with other countries by offering them security guarantees and memberships in multinational alliances—although such inducements may prove less potent in the absence of a hostile superpower.

Police Actions and Rescue Missions

Some of the most consequential peacetime military operations have been police actions and rescue missions to protect U.S. citizens and interests abroad. The vast majority of these operations have been minor incidents, and many of them were so brief that Congress had no time even to consider an authorizing resolution. In any case, presidents have argued that these limited missions require no congressional authorization because they have limited goals that otherwise fall under the executive responsibility to protect the lives and property of U.S. citizens. *(See box, Presidential Claims to Police Action, p. 257.)* As long as military operations have not involved the United States in a wider war and casualties have remained low, presidential popularity usually has been bolstered by limited uses of force.

Congress and the courts generally have refrained from challenging the president's authority to protect U.S. citizens and property overseas, even when military actions taken under presidential orders have been unjust. For example, in 1854 a naval commander acting on the vague but belligerent orders of President Franklin Pierce completely destroyed the Nicaraguan city of Greytown when it refused to pay inflated damage claims filed by a U.S. company. Congress investigated the incident but did not condemn the Greytown bombardment or make Pierce account for his actions. A U.S. district court dismissed a suit filed by a Greytown property owner against the naval commander on the grounds that the bombardment was a political matter.[178]

Pierce's successor, James Buchanan, claimed that without the consent of Congress he could not "fire a hostile gun in any case except to repel the attacks of an enemy."[179] Yet most twentieth-century presidents have interpreted the commander-in-chief power to meet the needs and goals of the moment.

No president did more, in principle and in practice, to expand presidential authority to order limited military missions than Theodore Roosevelt. In what became known as the Roosevelt Corollary to the Monroe Doctrine, he asserted the president's right to exercise an "international police power" in Latin America to protect U.S. and hemispheric interests and peace. He argued that if Latin American governments were unable to rule justly, maintain civil order, or meet their international obligations, then they were jeopardizing the security of the hemisphere.

After Roosevelt, presidents exercised the "police power" in the Western Hemisphere with little hesitation or consultation with Congress. William Taft, Woodrow Wilson, Calvin Coolidge, John Kennedy, Lyndon Johnson, Ronald Reagan, George H. W. Bush, and Bill Clinton all used U.S. forces—or foreign troops trained and supplied by the United States—to intervene in the affairs of Latin American nations.[180] Most recently in 1994, President Clinton threatened an invasion of Haiti to restore the democratic government to power. A negotiated settlement with Haiti's military rulers made the invasion unnecessary but still involved U.S. troops in overseeing the transition to democracy.

Even if the president's power to order limited military missions is conceded, there is still the problem of defining which missions fall under the president's police and rescue powers and which should be authorized by a congressional sanction if not a declaration of war. Like the power to repel invasions, the police and rescue powers can be manipulated by presidents to justify military actions that Congress might not sanction. For example, President Reagan ordered nineteen hundred troops to the tiny Caribbean island of Grenada in 1983 on what he called a "rescue mission." The administration maintained that the pro-Cuban military coup had placed U.S. citizens on the island in danger and threatened to turn Grenada into a Cuban-supported communist military base. U.S. troops evacuated about one thousand Americans from the island and proceeded to depose Grenada's new leadership.[181]

The invasion of Grenada was clearly more than a rescue mission. The president used armed force to accomplish geopolitical goals without the consent of Congress. Nevertheless, the historical precedent supporting the authority of presidents to order military missions and the perceived urgency of the situation at hand have influenced presidents and the U.S. public more often than strict interpretations of the Constitution and of international law.

Military Exercises and Shows of Force

Throughout U.S. history presidents have ordered conspicuous deployments of U.S. military power to dissuade potential aggressors, support allies, and reinforce U.S. diplomatic bargaining positions. Demonstrations of force before World War II almost always involved the navy.

In 1853 Millard Fillmore successfully changed Japanese foreign policy by sending a squadron of ships under Commodore Matthew Perry to Japan. The Japanese had excluded Westerners from their ports and had abused U.S. seamen shipwrecked off their shores. This show of U.S. naval power helped to produce the Treaty of Kanagawa, which declared friendship between the United States and Japan, opened several Japanese ports to U.S. commercial vessels, and established provisions for the treatment of U.S. citizens shipwrecked off Japan.

Perhaps the most famous show of force by a president was Theodore Roosevelt's dispatch of the U.S. fleet in 1907 on a cruise around the world. The cruise was primarily intended to impress Japan with U.S. naval power and demonstrate Roosevelt's resolve to oppose any act of aggression by the Japanese. He believed the "Great White Fleet's" cruise also would be a valuable exercise and would promote respect and goodwill for the United States throughout the world. The trip went smoothly, with the navy observing protocol at each port of call. Roosevelt later asserted, "The most important service that I rendered to peace was the voyage of the battle fleet around the world."[182]

In October 1994 President Clinton rushed U.S. forces to Kuwait in response to Iraqi troop movements toward the Kuwaiti border. Clinton's aim was to demonstrate to the Iraqis that the United States was again prepared and willing to resist any aggression in that region.

Shows of force may also be used to reassure a friendly government. On March 17, 1988, President Reagan sent 3,150 additional U.S. troops to Honduras in response to the incursion there of Nicaraguan government troops. The Nicaraguan forces reportedly crossed the Honduran border to destroy a supply depot of the antigovernment Nicaraguan contra rebels, who were supported by the Reagan administration. Secretary of State George P. Shultz said of the troops: "They're not near where the fighting is taking place, but they're designed to say to the Government of Honduras that, 'we are your friend and we stand with you, and if you are invaded you can count on the United States.'"[183] The contingent of troops conducted maneuvers in Honduras and withdrew from the country after ten days without engaging in combat.

Training and Advising Foreign Troops

During the cold war, military advisers became an established part of the superpowers' struggle for influence. Both the United States and the communist bloc sent military personnel into developing countries to instruct the local armed forces in organization, tactics, and the use of weapons. Often these military advisers were sent specifically to teach local troops how to use military equipment that the superpower had given or sold to that nation.

Because U.S. military advisers usually are instructed not to participate in combat, their deployment traditionally has not required congressional approval. Sending military advisers to a foreign country, however, can be controversial. This was certainly true of the U.S. experience in Vietnam, which began with the deployment of fewer than one thousand military advisers in that country by Dwight Eisenhower. During the Kennedy administration, although U.S. forces were still called "advisers," they had active combat roles. By the end of 1963, more than 16,000 advisers were in Vietnam. A year later this number had swelled to 23,210.[184]

When President Reagan introduced military advisers into El Salvador in 1981, critics of Reagan's policy charged that the U.S. military involvement in Central America could escalate as it had in Vietnam. Reagan promised to limit the number of U.S. military advisers in El Salvador to fifty-five, but the House Foreign Affairs Committee was concerned enough to outline in a report what it considered to be unacceptable activities for U.S. military advisers in all countries. These included accompanying local units into combat, arming or fueling combat aircraft, and delivering weapons and supplies to local troops in combat areas. These guidelines did not have the force of law.

By the end of 2011, the Obama administration completed its withdrawal of U.S. forces from Iraq. It did not keep a small contingent of active duty soldiers there as military advisers, as originally planned, because Iraq would not grant U.S. soldiers immunity from its laws. In Afghanistan, the phased withdrawal of U.S. troops that Obama announced in the summer of 2011 continued, with plans to end the combat mission by December 2014. Some political and military leaders suggested that by 2014 delaying full withdrawal of combat troops, or maintaining a contingent of military advisers, might be needed to ensure security there, but such decisions would depend on the political and military situation at the time.

⭐

NOTES

1 Alexander Hamilton, "No. 74," in Alexander Hamilton, James Madison, and John Jay, *The Federalist Papers* (New York: New American Library, 1961), 447.

2 Clinton Rossiter, *The American Presidency,* 2d ed. (New York: Time, 1960), 13.

3 Max Farrand, *The Records of the Federal Convention of 1787* (New Haven: Yale University Press, 1966), 1:318–319.

4 James Madison, *The Gazette of the United States,* August 24, 1793, quoted in *The Power of the Presidency,* ed. Robert S. Hirschenfield (New York: Atheton, 1968), 59.

5 Alexander Hamilton, "No. 69," in Alexander Hamilton, James Madison, and John Jay, *The Federalist Papers* (New York: New American Library, 1961), 417–418.

6 *Bas v. Tingy,* 4 U.S. 37 (1800); Louis Fisher, *Presidential War Power* (Lawrence: University Press of Kansas, 1995), 2–3, 18–19, 23–24.

7 Quoted in Fisher, *Presidential War Power,* 15.

8 John Yoo, *The Powers of War and Peace: The Constitution and Foreign Affairs after 9/11* (Chicago: University of Chicago Press, 2005), 144–155.

9 Michael P. Riccards, *A Republic, If You Can Keep It: The Foundation of the American Presidency, 1700–1800* (New York: Greenwood Press, 1987), 152–153.

10 Joseph E. Kallenbach, *The American Chief Executive: The Presidency and the Governorship* (New York: Harper and Row, 1966), 535–536.

11 Edward S. Corwin, *The President: Office and Powers, 1787–1984,* 5th rev. ed. (New York: New York University Press, 1984), 297.

12 *Youngstown Sheet and Tube Co. v. Sawyer,* 343 U.S. 579 (1952).

13 Clinton Rossiter, *The Supreme Court and the Commander in Chief* (Ithaca: Cornell University Press, 1976), 48–52.

14 Robert E. DiClerico, *The American President,* 4th ed. (Englewood Cliffs, N.J.: Prentice Hall, 1995), 31.

15 Quoted in Richard M. Pious, *The American Presidency* (New York: Basic Books, 1979), 392.

16 James D. Richardson, *A Compilation of the Messages and Papers of the Presidents, 1789–1910* (New York: Bureau of National Literature, 1917), 1:314–315.

17 Pious, *American Presidency,* 392.

18 Quoted in Corwin, *President,* 229.

19 Quoted in Arthur M. Schlesinger Jr., *The Imperial Presidency* (Boston: Houghton Mifflin, 1989), 23.

20 Quoted in Thomas Eagleton, *War and Presidential Power* (New York: Liveright, 1974), 23.

21 Christopher H. Pyle and Richard M. Pious, eds., *The President, Congress, and the Constitution* (New York: Free Press, 1984), 293–295.

22 Lawrence Margolis, *Executive Agreements and Presidential Power in Foreign Policy* (New York: Praeger, 1986), 9.

23 Schlesinger, *Imperial Presidency,* 39–41.

24 Quoted in Wilfred E. Binkley, *The Man in the White House* (Baltimore: Johns Hopkins University Press, 1964), 192.

25 Schlesinger, *Imperial Presidency,* 58.

26 Corwin, *President,* 264.

27 Ibid., 265.

28 John Nicolay and John Hay, eds., *The Complete Works of Abraham Lincoln* (New York: Francis Tandy, 1891), 10:66.

29 Phillip Shaw Paludan, *The Presidency of Abraham Lincoln* (Lawrence: University Press of Kansas, 1994), 81–82.

30 Binkley, *Man in the White House,* 194.

31 *Prize Cases,* 67 U.S. (2 Black) 635 (1863).

32 Rossiter, *Supreme Court,* 71–75.

33 Fisher, *Presidential War Power,* 42.

34 Louis L. Gould, *The Presidency of William McKinley* (Lawrence: University Press of Kansas, 1980), 96–98.

35 Corwin, *President,* 271–272.

36 Ibid., 272.

37 Ibid.

38 Eagleton, *War and Presidential Power,* 64.

39 Jacob K. Javits, *Who Makes War: The President Versus Congress* (New York: Morrow, 1973), 225–226.

40 Schlesinger, *Imperial Presidency,* 115.

41 Quoted in Corwin, *President,* 285–286.

42 Edward S. Corwin, *Presidential Power and the Constitution* (Ithaca: Cornell University Press, 1976), 114.

43 Quoted in Javits, *Who Makes War,* 230.

44 Cecil V. Crabb Jr. and Pat M. Holt, *Invitation to Struggle: Congress, the President and Foreign Policy,* 4th ed. (Washington, D.C.: CQ Press, 1992), 134–136.

45 Dean Acheson, *Present at the Creation: My Years in the State Department* (New York: Norton, 1969), 415.

46 Schlesinger, *Imperial Presidency,* 133.

47 James L. Sundquist, *Decline and Resurgence of Congress* (Washington, D.C.: Brookings, 1981), 109.

48 Fisher, *Presidential War Power,* 70, 77–81.

49 R. Gordon Hoxie, *Command Decision and the Presidency* (New York: Reader's Digest Press, 1977), 178.

50 *Youngstown Sheet and Tube Co. v. Sawyer,* 343 U.S. 579 (1952).

51 Schlesinger, *Imperial Presidency,* 141.

52 Ibid., 169.

53 Sundquist, *Decline and Resurgence of Congress,* 124–125.

54 Ibid., 249.

55 Quoted in *CQ Almanac, 1973* (Washington, D.C.: Congressional Quarterly, 1974), 906.

56 Ibid., 906–907.

57 Eagleton, *War and Presidential Power,* 203.

58 Quoted in *CQ Almanac, 1973,* 907.

59 Ibid., 907.

60 *Immigration and Naturalization Service v. Chadha,* 462 U.S. 919 (1983).

61 *CQ Almanac, 1983* (Washington, D.C.: Congressional Quarterly, 1984), 568–569.

62 Fisher, *Presidential War Power,* 194–197.

63 Quoted in Larry Berman, *The New American Presidency* (Boston: Little, Brown, 1987), 75.

64 Ibid., 76.

65 DiClerico, *American President,* 41.

66 Jacob Javits, "War Powers Reconsidered," *Foreign Affairs* (fall 1985): 135.

67 Robert J. Spitzer, *President and Congress* (New York: McGraw-Hill, 1993), 176.

68 Javits, "War Powers Reconsidered," 136.

69 Quoted in Crabb and Holt, *Invitation to Struggle,* 148.

70 Fisher, *Presidential War Power,* 141–142.

71 Mary H. Cooper, "Persian Gulf Oil," *Editorial Research Reports,* October 30, 1987, 567.

72 Pat Towell, "New Gulf Incident Rekindles an Old Debate," *Congressional Quarterly Weekly Report,* April 23, 1988, 1051–1058.

73 Fisher, *Presidential War Power,* 145–148.

74 Spitzer, *President and Congress,* 180.

75 Ibid., 182.

76 *Dellums v. Bush,* 752 F. Supp. 1141 (D.D.C. 1990).

77 Fisher, *Presidential War Power,* 150–151.

78 Ibid., 155–156.

79 Ibid., 157–161.

80 David Fromkin, *Kosovo Crossing: The Reality of American Intervention in the Balkans* (New York: Touchstone, 1999).

81 George W. Bush, "Address to a Joint Session of Congress and the American People," 20 September 2001.

82 Joint Resolution Authorizing Use of United States Armed Forces Against Those Responsible for Recent Attacks on the United States, 14 September 2001, www.thomas.loc.gov.

83 For a discussion of presidential decision making after September 11, 2001, and the war in Afghanistan, see Bob Woodward, *Bush at War* (New York: Simon and Schuster, 2002).

84 Barack Obama, "Remarks by the President in Address to the Nation on the Way Forward in Afghanistan and Pakistan," United States Military Academy at West Point, West Point, N.Y, December 1, 2009, American Presidency Project online dababase, www.presidency.ucsb.edu/ws/index.php?pid=86948&st=&st1=#axzz1n4mhXDU8. For an analysis of how Obama decided to increase U.S. troops in Afghanistan, see Bob Woodward, *Obama's Wars* (New York: Simon and Schuster, 2010).

85 George W. Bush, "State of the Union Address," January 29, 2002.

86 George W. Bush, "Remarks at the United Nations General Assembly," 12 September 2002.

87 United Nations Security Council Resolution 1441, 8 November 2002, www.un.org.

88 The decision-making process leading up to the 2003 Iraq War is discussed in Bob Woodward, *Plan of Attack* (New York: Simon and Schuster, 2004).

89 Barack Obama, "Remarks by President in Address to the Nation on the End of Combat Operations in Iraq," Oval Office, August 31, 2010, American Presidency Project online dababase, www.presidency.ucsb.edu/ws/index.php?pid=88362&st=&st1=#axzz1nE4xKnd8.

90 Barack Obama, Speech on Libya, National Defense University, Washington, D.C., March 28, 2011, American Presidency Project online dababase, www.presidency.ucsb.edu/ws/index.php?pid=90195&st=&st1=#axzz1nE4xKnd8.

91 Fisher, *Presidential War Power,* 192.

92 See Jeffrey D. Simon, "Misunderstanding Terrorism," *Foreign Policy* (summer 1987); Charles William Maynes, "Bottom-Up Foreign Policy," *Foreign Policy* (fall 1996).

93 Bob Woodward, "CIA Told to Do 'Whatever Necessary' to Kill bin Laden," *Washington Post,* October 21, 2001, A1.

94 Jeffrey Rosen, "Power of One," *New Republic,* 24 July 2006. Also see Yoo, *The Powers of War and Peace.*

95 George W. Bush, "The National Security Strategy of the United States of America," September 2002, whitehouse.gov.

96 George W. Bush, "The National Security Strategy of the United States of America," March 2006, whitehouse.gov.

97 Barack Obama, "The National Security Strategy of the United States of America," May 2010, whitehouse.gov.

98 Corwin, *President,* 249.

99 Sundquist, *Decline and Resurgence of Congress,* 105–106; Fisher, *Presidential War Power,* 77–79.

100 Corwin, *President,* 251; Fisher, *Presidential War Power,* 80–81.

101 Dick Kirschten, "A Contract's Out on U.N. Policing," *National Journal,* January 1, 1995, 231–232; James Kitfield, "Fit to Fight," *National Journal,* March 16, 1996, 5825–5886.

102 107 Stat. 1478–80, sec. 9001 (1993).

103 U.S. Department of State Dispatch, vol. 5, no. 20 (May 16, 1994); Fisher, *Presidential War Power,* 160–161.

104 Steve Schiffres, "U.S. Names 'Coalition of the Willing,'" *BBC News Online in Washington,* March 18, 2003.

105 Hoxie, *Command Decision and the Presidency,* 130.

106 Amos A. Jordan and William J. Taylor Jr., *American National Security: Policy and Process* (Baltimore: Johns Hopkins University Press, 1984), 473.

107 "Wooing the WEU," *Economist,* March 4, 1995, 56–57.

108 Congressional Research Service, "NATO in Afghanistan: A Test of the Transatlantic Alliance," December 3, 2009.

109 Rick Rozoff, "Iraq: NATO Assists in Building New Middle East Proxy Army," *Global Research* (Quebec, Canada: Centre for Research on Globalisation, August 2010), http://globalresearch.ca/index.php?context=va&aid=20610.

110 Pious, *American Presidency,* 395–396.

111 Fisher, *Presidential War Power,* 93–97.

112 Kallenbach, *American Chief Executive,* 531.

113 Charles A. Beard, *The Republic* (New York: Viking, 1944), 101.

114 Riccards, *A Republic, If You Can Keep It,* 164–166.

115 Jacob E. Cook, "George Washington," in *The Presidents: A Reference History,* ed. Henry F. Graff (New York: Scribner's, 1984), 24.

116 Corwin, *President,* 294.

117 Kallenbach, *American Chief Executive,* 530.

118 Molly Moore, "Stricken Frigate's Crew Stitched Ship Together," *Washington Post,* April 22, 1988, A1.

119 For a discussion of Johnson's conflicts with the military over the Vietnam War, see H. R. McMaster, *Dereliction of Duty: Johnson, McNamara, the Joint Chiefs of Staff, and the Lies that Led to Vietnam* (New York: HarperCollins, 1997).

120 The retired generals' public call for Rumsfeld's dismissal is discussed in James Kitfield, "Stakes High in Battle between Rumsfeld Generals," *Government Executive,* May 5, 2006.

121 Jordan and Taylor, *American National Security,* 231.

122 For a detailed description of the U.S. nuclear infrastructure, see William Arkin and Richard W. Fieldhouse, *Nuclear Battlefields* (Cambridge: Ballinger, 1984).

123 *Public Papers of the Presidents of the United States, Dwight D. Eisenhower, 1960–1961* (Washington, D.C.: Government Printing Office, 1963), 851.

124 *Public Papers of the Presidents of the United States, Harry S. Truman, 1945* (Washington, D.C.: Government Printing Office, 1961), 212.

125 James A. Nathan and James K. Oliver, *United States Foreign Policy and World Order,* 2d ed. (Boston: Little, Brown, 1981), 41–42.

126 Hoxie, *Command Decision and the Presidency,* 13–14.

127 Miroslav Nincic, *United States Foreign Policy: Choices and Tradeoffs* (Washington, D.C.: CQ Press, 1988), 292.

128 Arthur M. Schlesinger Jr., *A Thousand Days* (Greenwich, Conn.: Fawcett, 1965), 778–783.

129 Theodore Sorensen, *Kennedy* (New York: Harper and Row, 1965), 705.

130 Arkin and Fieldhouse, *Nuclear Battlefields,* 87.

131 James M. Lindsay, *Congress and the Politics of Foreign Policy* (Baltimore: Johns Hopkins University Press, 1994), 102.

132 *CQ Almanac, 1992* (Washington, D.C.: Congressional Quarterly, 1993), 513–514.

133 For text of speech and further commentary, see *Historic Documents of 1983* (Washington, D.C.: Congressional Quarterly, 1984), 305–316.

134 R. Jeffrey Smith, "Pentagon Scales Back SDI Goals," *Washington Post,* March 27, 1988, A1.

135 *CQ Almanac, 1991* (Washington, D.C.: Congressional Quarterly, 1992), 407–408.

136 *CQ Weekly,* July 14, 2001, 1716.

137 Lawrence J. Korb, "The Evolving Relationship between the White House and the Department of Defense in the Post-Imperial Presidency," in *The Post-Imperial Presidency,* ed. Vincent Davis (New Brunswick, N.J.: Transaction, 1980), 103.

138 Richard K. Betts, *Soldiers, Statesmen, and Cold War Crises* (Cambridge: Harvard University Press, 1977), 52–68.

139 For discussions of the problems that led to the reform of the JCS, see James Buck, "The Establishment: An Overview," in *Presidential Leadership and National Security: Style, Institutions, and Politics,* ed. Sam C. Sarkesian (Boulder: Westview Press, 1984), 59–64; and John G. Kestor, "The Role of the Joint Chiefs of Staff," in *American Defense Policy,* ed. John F. Reichart and Steven R. Sturm (Baltimore: Johns Hopkins University Press, 1982), 527–545.

140 Pat Towell, "Major Pentagon Reorganization Bill Is Cleared," *Congressional Quarterly Weekly Report,* September 20, 1986, 2207–2208.

141 Philip Shenon and David Johnston, "Focus of FBI Is Seen Shifting to Terrorism," *New York Times,* October 21, 2001.

142 Morton Halperin, "The President and the Military," in *The Presidency in Contemporary Context,* ed. Norman C. Thomas (New York: Dodd, Mead, 1975), 277.

143 Ibid., 280–284.

144 Alice Maroni, "The Defense Budget," in *Presidential Leadership and National Security: Style, Institutions, and Politics,* ed. Sam C. Sarkesian (Boulder: Westview Press, 1984), 194–196.

145 Ibid., 196.

146 Richard Haass, "The Role of the Congress in American Security Policy," in *American Defense Policy*, ed. John F. Reichart and Steven R. Sturm (Baltimore: Johns Hopkins University Press, 1982), 558–560.

147 Christopher Drew, "House Votes to End Alternate Jet Engine Program," *New York Times*, 16 February 2011.

148 James Fairhall, "The Case for the $435 Hammer," *Washington Monthly*, January 1987, 47–52.

149 George F. Brown Jr. and Lawrence Korb, "The Economic and Political Restraints on Force Planning," in *American Defense Policy*, ed. John F. Reichart and Steven R. Sturm (Baltimore: Johns Hopkins University Press, 1982), 583.

150 Quoted in Dana Priest, "Billions Gone AWOL," *Washington Post Weekly Edition*, May 22–28, 1995, 6–7.

151 Kallenbach, *American Chief Executive*, 543.

152 Marc Leepson, "Draft Registration," *Editorial Research Reports*, June 13, 1980, 427–430.

153 Tamara Keith, "A Weak Economy Is Good for Military Recruiting," *National Public Radio*, July 29, 2011.

154 Jennifer E. Manning, "Membership of the 112th Congress: A Profile," Washington, D.C.: Congressional Research Service, March 1, 2011.

155 Peter D. Feaver and Richard H. Kohn, eds. *Soldiers and Civilians: The Civil-Military Gap and American National Security* (Boston: MIT Press, 2001); Bruce E. Fleming, *Bridging the Military-Civilian Divide: What Each Side Must Know About the Other—and About Itself* (Dulles, Va.: Potomac Books, 2010).

156 Eliot A. Cohen, *Supreme Command: Soldiers, Statesmen, and Leadership in Wartime* (New York: Anchor Books, 2003); Suzanne C. Nielsen and Don M. Snider, eds., *American Civil-Military Relations: The Soldier and the State in a New Era* (Baltimore: Johns Hopkins University Press, 2009).

157 Mackubin Thomas Owens, *U.S. Civil-Military Relations After 9/11: Renegotiating the Civil-Military Bargain* (New York: Continuum, 2011); P.W. Singer, *Corporate Warriors: The Rise of the Privatized Military Industry*, updated ed. (Ithaca: Cornell University Press, 2007).

158 Kallenbach, *American Chief Executive*, 537.

159 Associated Press, "House Vote to Defund Libya Mission Fails," MSNBC.com, June 24, 2011.

160 Quoted in Pyle and Pious, *President, Congress, and the Constitution*, 62 (emphasis in original).

161 Robert S. Hirschfield, "The Scope and Limits of Presidential Power," in *Power and the Presidency*, ed. Philip C. Dolce and George H. Skau (New York: Scribner's, 1976), 301–302.

162 Kallenbach, *American Chief Executive*, 553–554.

163 *Ex parte Milligan*, 4 Wallace 2 (1866).

164 *Duncan v. Kahanamoku*, 327 U.S. 304 (1946).

165 Rossiter, *Supreme Court*, 25.

166 Ibid., 27.

167 *Ex parte Milligan*, 4 Wallace 2 (1866).

168 Quoted in Pyle and Pious, *President, Congress, and the Constitution*, 67 (emphasis in original).

169 *Hamdi v. Rumsfeld*, 542 U.S. 507 (2004).

170 Richard A. Serrano, "Obama to Resume Military Trials for Guantanamo Detainees," *Los Angeles Times*, March 8, 2011, http://articles.latimes.com/2011/mar/08/nation/la-na-obama-guantanamo-20110308. Also see James P. Pfiffner, "Decision Making in the Obama White House," *Presidential Studies Quarterly* 41 (June 2011): 249–252.

171 *Hirabayashi v. United States*, 320 U.S. 81 (1943).

172 *Korematsu v. United States*, 323 U.S. 214 (1944).

173 Quoted in Pyle and Pious, *President, Congress, and the Constitution*, 118–119.

174 Kallenbach, *American Chief Executive*, 557.

175 Corwin, *Presidential Power and the Constitution*, 124–125.

176 *Youngstown Sheet and Tube Co. v. Sawyer*, 343 U.S. 579 (1952).

177 Rossiter, *Supreme Court*, xxi.

178 Javits, *Who Makes War*, 104–115.

179 Quoted in Arthur Bernon Tourtellot, *The Presidents on the Presidency* (Garden City, N.Y.: Doubleday, 1964), 326.

180 Donald L. Robinson, *To the Best of My Ability* (New York: Norton, 1987), 224; and Fisher, *Presidential War Power*, 145–148, 154–157.

181 Nincic, *United States Foreign Policy*, 231–233.

182 Theodore Roosevelt, *An Autobiography* (New York: Scribner's, 1920), 548.

183 Quoted in Steven V. Roberts, "3,000 G.I.'s and Questions," *New York Times*, March 18, 1988, A1.

184 Timothy J. Lomperis, *The War Everyone Lost and Won* (Washington, D.C.: CQ Press, 1984), 60.

SELECTED BIBLIOGRAPHY

Corwin, Edward S. *The President: Office and Powers, 1787–1984.* 5th rev. ed. New York: New York University Press, 1984.

Crabb, Cecil V., Jr., and Pat M. Holt. *Invitation to Struggle: Congress, the President and Foreign Policy.* 4th ed. Washington, D.C.: CQ Press, 1992.

Ely, John Hart. *War and Responsibility: Constitutional Lessons of Vietnam and Its Aftermath.* Princeton: Princeton University Press, 1993.

Fisher, Louis. *Presidential War Power.* 2d rev. ed. Lawrence: University Press of Kansas, 2004.

Goldsmith, Jack. *The Terror Presidency: Law and Judgment Inside the Bush Administration.* New York: Norton, 2007.

Haass, Richard. *War of Necessity, War of Choice: A Memoir of Two Iraq Wars.* New York: Simon and Schuster, 2009.

Herspring, Dale R. *The Pentagon and the Presidency: Civil-Military Relations from FDR to George W. Bush.* Lawrence: University Press of Kansas, 2005.

Javits, Jacob K. *Who Makes War: The President versus Congress.* New York: Morrow, 1973.

Jordan, Amos A., William J. Taylor Jr., Michael J. Meese, and Suzanne C. Nielson. *American National Security: Policy and Process.* 6th ed. Baltimore: Johns Hopkins University Press, 2009.

Kallenbach, Joseph E. *The American Chief Executive: The Presidency and the Governorship.* New York: Harper and Row, 1966.

Kelley, Christopher S. *Executing the Constitution: Putting the President Back in the Constitution.* New York: State University of New York Press, 2006.

Koh, Harold Hongju. *The National Security Constitution: Sharing Power after the Iran-Contra Affair.* New Haven: Yale University Press, 1990.

Mayer, Jane. *The Dark Side: The Inside Story of How the War on Terror Turned into a War on American Ideals.* New York: Doubleday, 2008.

Nincic, Miroslav. *United States Foreign Policy: Choices and Tradeoffs.* Washington, D.C.: CQ Press, 1988.

Pious, Richard M. *The American Presidency.* New York: Basic Books, 1979.

Rossiter, Clinton. *The Supreme Court and the Commander in Chief.* Ithaca: Cornell University Press, 1976.

Sarkesian, Sam C., ed. *Presidential Leadership and National Security: Style, Institutions, and Politics.* Boulder: Westview Press, 1984.

Schlesinger, Arthur M., Jr. *The Imperial Presidency.* Boston: Houghton Mifflin, 1989.

Wilson, George C. *This War Really Matters: Inside the Fight for Defense Dollars.* Washington, D.C.: CQ Press, 2000.

Yoo, John. *The Powers of War and Peace: The Constitution and Foreign Affairs after 9/11.* Chicago: University of Chicago Press, 2006.

chapter 7

Chief Economist

by Bruce Nesmith

The American people have come to expect presidents to produce economic prosperity for the United States just as presidents are expected to enforce its laws and ensure its security. The presidency is, after all, the nation's most powerful and identifiable political office, with the performance of the federal government reflecting most directly on the current president. As political scientist Clinton Rossiter observed near the end of the Eisenhower administration:

> The people of this country are no longer content to let disaster fall upon them unopposed. They now expect their government, under the direct leadership of the President, to prevent a depression or panic and not simply wait until one has developed before putting it to rout. Thus the President has a new function which is still taking shape, that of Manager of Prosperity.[1]

From today's perspective, it is surprising to recall that the authors of the Constitution clearly intended Congress, not the executive, to be the branch of government most concerned with the economic affairs of the nation. Article I, Section 8, of the Constitution grants Congress numerous economic powers, including the authority to

> lay and collect taxes, duties, imposts and excises, to pay the debts and provide for the common defense and general welfare of the United States. . . ; borrow money on the credit of the United States. . . ; regulate commerce with foreign nations, and among the several states. . . ; and coin money, regulate the value thereof, and of foreign coin.

In contrast, the Constitution grants the president no specific economic powers. Nevertheless, the Framers expected presidents to have significant influence over the economy. They would, after all, oversee the implementation of Congress's spending and taxing decisions, suggest economic legislation in their State of the Union address and other communications to Congress, negotiate commercial treaties with foreign nations, and have the power to veto legislation on economic matters.

Every president has been concerned with the U.S. economy, but close presidential supervision of its performance is a relatively recent historical development. Before the Great Depression of the 1930s, Americans generally believed that extensive government intervention in the economy was counterproductive. The human suffering of the Depression, however, convinced the American public and its leaders that the government should intervene to relieve and prevent periods of economic trauma. By the time World War II ended, a national consensus had developed that the government, and especially the president, should use every means available to produce the best economic conditions possible even if the economy was not in trouble. The president had become not just a guardian against economic disaster but an economic manager whose popularity usually depended on a strong and stable economy.

Presidential economic power today, then, has far surpassed the expectations of the Framers. Presidents have effectively used their visibility and their prerogatives in the execution of policy to promote their economic programs. In addition, as management of the economy grew more complex during the twentieth century, Congress gave presidents greater economic power through statutes.

PRESIDENTIAL POWER OVER THE ECONOMY
Assets and Opportunities

Presidents have a number of advantages in shaping economic policy. Probably the most important is the visibility of the office, which has been accentuated in the past 100 years by developments in electronic news media. From the time of Franklin D. Roosevelt's "fireside chats," presidents have had access to the public's attention that no member of Congress can rival. Even when the president is not addressing the public directly, news reporting on politics and government emphasizes the White House far more than any other part of government. The public looks to the president

Previous contributors to this chapter include Jim Granato, Daniel C. Diller, and Dean J. Peterson.

for economic policy leadership, and the president is uniquely positioned to impact public opinion.[2]

The association between the president and the state of the economy may work to a president's political advantage. Presidents are quick to take credit for economic growth, price stability, and low unemployment. Presidential candidate Ronald Reagan, who had capitalized on poor economic conditions in 1980 to defeat incumbent Jimmy Carter, benefited four years later, when the economy was in the midst of a strong expansion. He repeated the same question to voters in 1984 that he had asked in 1980: "Are you better off now than you were four years ago?" The American people reelected him in a landslide.

Secondly, the president's constitutional functions touch on the economy in a number of ways. As chief executive the president oversees the government's economic and regulatory functions, and appoints cabinet and Federal Reserve Board members who make many economic decisions; as chief legislator the president proposes federal spending, taxation, and other economy-related legislation, and can use the veto—or the threat of the veto—to influence legislation before Congress; as commander in chief the president oversees the multibillion-dollar purchases of the Defense Department; as chief diplomat the president negotiates with foreign governments about trade and currency issues; and as chief of state the president affects the morale, attitudes, and expectations of the American people.

Thirdly, the president has historically had better access to economic information than Congress, though that gap has been closed in recent years. Each president devotes a considerable amount of attention to advising structures—coordinating data from the Treasury Department, the Office of Management and Budget, and other executive branch agencies—that can present him with digestible information and recommendations. President Bill Clinton created the National Economic Council to broker policy proposals; President Barack Obama added an Economic Recovery Advisory Board to address economic stabilization. Presidents today receive "considerable and generally continual" expert policy influence.[3] (See "Economic Advisers to the President," p. 322.)

Finally, the president is the sole leader of the executive branch, which means the president can shift policy quickly, and in some cases can take unilateral action. President George W. Bush reallocated funds during the 2008 recession to provide financial help to the automobile industry after his legislative proposal was blocked by the Senate. Unlike a policy entrepreneur in Congress, the president does not have to persuade a majority of his colleagues to go along with him.[4]

Limitations

Despite the expectations of the American people and the president's pivotal role in economic policymaking, the president's ability to influence economic conditions does not measure up to presidential responsibility for them. All presidents would like to be able to adjust the economy from a central switch in the White House, but no absolutely reliable controls exist.

The federal government is only one actor, albeit a powerful and influential one, in an economy that is predominantly private. Presidential control over the economy is limited by forces outside the reach of the federal government. The economic stimulus policies during the recession that officially began in December 2007 were substantial and expensive by government standards, but were small in relation to a $14.5 trillion economy. Private enterprise does not always respond to policy change in ways that government intended, as when financial institutions chose to keep much of the stimulus money they received in 2008 and 2009 rather than using it to increase lending. State and local government policies may undercut those of the federal government; international events such as wars, oil price increases, or recessions in foreign countries may exacerbate U.S. economic problems; bad weather may limit agricultural production; public expectations may make certain economic options such as large cuts in Social Security politically impossible; and corporations may make business decisions that aggravate unemployment, inflation, the trade deficit, and other economic problems. The 2001 collapse of a giant energy company, Enron, and the ensuing controversy about the accuracy and quality of corporate accounting and independent auditing practices contributed to investor wariness about business fundamentals and the stock market, which already had plunged markedly since 2000. Since then the American economy has suffered the impact of the September 11, 2001, terrorist attacks, Hurricane Katrina in 2005, floods in the Midwest, a series of killer tornadoes, a currency crisis in Europe, and political instability in the oil-rich Middle East. While the effects of such developments wear off in time, their immediate impact can offset the best of intentions and policies from government.

Institutional factors also limit presidential control over the U.S. economy. The chief executive must share power with other individuals and governmental bodies. As the enumeration of congressional economic powers shows, Congress has the constitutional authority to frustrate virtually any presidential economic initiative. Most important, the president cannot levy taxes or appropriate money without the approval of Congress. In 2011 President Obama's desire for further economic stimulus was blocked by congressional opposition, particularly in the Republican-controlled House of Representatives. "The President wanted to lower unemployment but didn't see a way to get more money out of Congress," one adviser told the New York Times.[5]

Executive branch organizations also cut into presidential economic power. The independent Federal Reserve Board, which sets monetary policy, is not legally obliged to cooperate with the president. Spending and taxing policies adopted by presidents to achieve one economic result may be undercut by monetary policies of the Federal Reserve Board that are designed to achieve a conflicting result. *(See "Monetary Policy," p. 312.)* The president's economic advisers also can check presidential power by implementing the chief executive's directives unenthusiastically or by refusing to join a policy consensus. Their missions often conflict, making agreement on policy goals difficult and creating rivalries within an administration.

A third factor limiting presidential control of the economy is the highly complex and theoretical nature of economics itself. Presidents with little formal training in economics may feel overwhelmed, as did Warren G. Harding, who once confided to an associate:

> I don't know what to do or where to turn on this taxation matter. Somewhere there must be a book that tells all about it, where I could go to straighten it out in my mind. But I don't know where the book is, and maybe I couldn't read it if I found it. There must be a man in the country somewhere who could weigh both sides and know the truth. Probably he is in some college or other. But I don't know where to find him, I don't know who he is and I don't know how to get him.[6]

The imprecision of economic information limits presidential power as well. When presidents attempt to adjust the economy, they assume that they have accurate and timely information about the economy's performance. But economic statistics provide, at best, a rough approximation of economic reality. The size and complexity of an evolving economy of 300 million people necessitates that economic statistics be developed from "a slag heap of samples, surveys, estimates, interpolations, seasonal adjustments, and plain guesses."[7]

In addition, economic statistics and indicators do not measure the immediate conditions of the economy but rather the conditions that prevailed between one and four months earlier, depending on the particular economic measure. Consequently, presidents who take action on the basis of the latest economic information may be reacting to a problem that no longer exists or that is much worse than believed. For example, incomplete economic information induced President Jimmy Carter to take measures in 1980 that exacerbated the economy's troubles. Carter imposed credit controls designed to lower inflation, which had skyrocketed to 18 percent. Later in the year, economic statistics showed that a widely predicted recession was already under way when Carter acted, so that his tight credit policy had contributed significantly to the sharpest decline in gross national product (GNP) in a single three-month period since World War II.[8]

Finally, political realities often intrude on presidential policymaking. Oftentimes the public objects to the impact on some groups of presidential policies—promoting free trade, for example—that are intended to affect economic activity in the nation as a whole. Opponents of free trade

British economist Adam Smith promoted a laissez-faire approach to government economic activity. American presidents generally adhered to his theories until the 1930s, when the Great Depression led to a more activist presidential role in managing the economy.

argue that import restrictions will save jobs, which may be true in the industries that are affected, such as steel manufacturing. Economists argue that, in the entire economy, import restrictions are not likely to save jobs outside of the affected industries. This is because more efficient businesses are not allowed to beat out less efficient businesses, which results in a loss of jobs in the economy as a whole as well as fewer innovative products becoming available to the public.[9] A good example occurred in early 2002 when President George W. Bush departed from his characteristic support of free trade to impose tariffs on steel and lumber imports. Observers noted that certain states, such as Pennsylvania and West Virginia, which were expected to be important to Bush if he sought reelection in 2004, had troubled steel industries, including companies that faced bankruptcy. The lumber industry was also important to influential members of Congress, including Senate Minority Leader Trent Lott of Mississippi, who were in a position to help the Bush administration win free trade agreements in coming months.[10]

Public opinion also complicates budgeting. The American people consistently indicate in surveys that they believe government spending should be reduced. Yet this desire for less government spending is accompanied by a reluctance to sacrifice funding for specific programs that have developed constituencies. The public traditionally has believed the government spends too much in only a few policy areas such as foreign aid, welfare, and space exploration.[11] Thus the budget is one of the most persistent political dilemmas facing presidents. They must try to reduce overall spending while funding the programs that Americans have come to expect. President Obama's public approval dropped to 40 percent in August 2011 when he was unable to both achieve the deficit reduction the public said they wanted and provide economic stimulus that would help to create jobs.[12]

More generally, the advances of technology—the use of the Internet and blogging—have the potential to contribute to rapid transmission of (mis)information on vital political and economic matters.[13] This is particularly true when leaders and politically active citizens in society are more ideologically polarized than the general public.[14] Political scientist Lawrence R. Jacobs described how George W. Bush's attempt to sell his 2005 Social Security proposals—similar to Bill Clinton's attempt to sell health care reform in 1993–1994—was overwhelmed by communications from opponents of the effort. Jacobs presciently anticipated that Obama's sophisticated communications strategy for economic policies would be similarly drowned out.[15]

TYPES OF ECONOMIC POLICY

Presidents since the Great Depression have attempted to create the best economic conditions possible through their stabilization policies. The U.S. economy, as with all capitalist economies, experiences cyclical patterns of expansion and contraction in which the levels of inflation, unemployment, and economic growth vary. *(See Table 7-1, this page.)*

During periods of economic contraction, businesses lose sales, investment decreases, unemployment grows, and prices tend to increase at a slow rate or even fall. During expansionary periods consumers spend more, investment increases, unemployment declines, and prices tend to increase at a faster rate. The objective of stabilization policy is to smooth out the natural swings in the economy, so unemployment does not become too severe during contractionary periods and inflation does not get out of control during expansionary periods. Ideally, an administration should achieve these goals while maintaining a steady rate of economic growth and balancing the federal budget, or at least running manageable deficits that can be corrected during periods of prosperity.

The main tools presidents use to stabilize the economy are *fiscal policy* and *monetary policy*. Fiscal policy refers to the government's taxing and spending decisions. Presidents make fiscal policy in cooperation with Congress, which passes spending and tax bills. The government can choose to combat unemployment and stagnant economic growth by stimulating the economy through tax cuts or increased spending, or both. Congress and the president can choose to fight inflation by contracting the economy through tax increases or reduced spending. Monetary policy refers to decisions about the supply of money. Although presidents do not have legal control over monetary policy, which is determined by the independent

TABLE 7-1 **Inflation and Unemployment, 1929–2011 (percent)**

Year	Inflation, all items[a]	Unemployment	Year	Inflation, all items[a]	Unemployment	Year	Inflation, all items[a]	Unemployment
1929	0.0%	3.2%	1962	1.0	5.5	1987	3.6	6.2
1933	−5.1	24.9	1963	1.3	5.7	1988	4.1	5.5
1939	−1.4	17.2	1964	1.3	5.2	1989	4.8	5.3
1940	0.7	14.6	1965	1.6	4.5	1990	5.4	5.6
1941	5.0	9.9	1966	2.9	3.8	1991	4.2	6.8
1942	10.9	4.7	1967	3.1	3.8	1992	3.0	7.5
1943	6.1	1.9	1968	4.2	3.6	1993	3.0	6.9
1944	1.7	1.2	1969	5.5	3.5	1994	2.6	6.1
1945	2.3	1.9	1970	5.7	4.9	1995	2.8	5.6
1946	8.3	3.9	1971	4.4	5.9	1996	3.0	5.4
1947	14.4	3.9	1972	3.2	5.6	1997	2.3	4.9
1948	8.1	3.8	1973	6.2	4.9	1998	1.6	4.5
1949	−1.2	5.9	1974	11.0	5.6	1999	2.2	4.2
1950	1.3	5.3	1975	9.1	8.5	2000	3.4	4.0
1951	7.9	3.3	1976	5.8	7.7	2001	2.8	4.7
1952	1.9	3.0	1977	6.5	7.1	2002	1.6	5.8
1953	0.8	2.9	1978	7.6	6.1	2003	2.3	6.0
1954	0.7	5.5	1979	11.3	5.8	2004	2.7	5.5
1955	−0.4	4.4	1980	13.5	7.1	2005	3.4	5.1
1956	1.5	4.1	1981	10.3	7.6	2006	3.2	4.6
1957	3.3	4.3	1982	6.2	9.7	2007	2.8	4.6
1958	2.8	6.8	1983	3.2	9.6	2008	3.8	5.8
1959	0.7	5.5	1984	4.3	7.5	2009	−0.4	9.3
1960	1.7	5.5	1985	3.6	7.2	2010	1.6	9.6
1961	1.0	6.7	1986	1.9	7.0	2011	3.2	8.9

SOURCE: The inflation data can be found in the Department of Labor, Bureau of Labor Statistics, "Consumer Price Index," ftp://ftp.bls.gov/pub/special.requests/cpi/cpiai.txt. The unemployment data can be found in the Department of Labor, Bureau of Labor Statistics, "Employment Status of the Civilian Noninstitutional Population, 1940 to Date," www.bls.gov/cps/cpsaat1.pdf.

NOTE: a. Average percentage change in consumer price index year to year.

Federal Reserve Board, they do exercise much informal influence over it.

Fiscal Policy

Fiscal policy evolved significantly in the last seventy years of the twentieth century. Before the Great Depression most economists believed that the president could best contribute to the health of the economy by working for a balanced federal budget and not overregulating business activity. Deficit spending by the federal government was regarded as an imprudent and irresponsible practice that eroded business confidence in the monetary system and produced inflation.

The U.S. economy did not always run smoothly, however. As the country became increasingly industrialized in the late nineteenth and early twentieth centuries, fluctuations in employment became more frequent and severe. The growth of industry also created new demands on the nation's financial system and forced the government to protect consumers and workers from the power of monopolies. This economic orthodoxy handcuffed President Herbert Hoover when the stock market crashed and the Depression began in 1929. All of Hoover's efforts to turn the economy around proved ineffectual, and by 1933 unemployment had reached a staggering 25 percent of the workforce—one in every four workers was out of a job. Americans came to believe that government should work to prevent crises and create a stable and fair business environment. The public increasingly looked to the president, the symbol of government and the leader of the ruling party, for economic innovation and direction. By the time the Depression struck, laissez-faire attitudes toward the executive's economic role had already begun to give way to more activist conceptions of governmental and presidential power.

Budget and Accounting Act of 1921

The more activist presidents who followed Hoover made use of an important fiscal policymaking tool: the authority to prepare the federal budget. During the eighteenth and nineteenth centuries, presidents had no formal responsibility to submit a budget to Congress or even conduct a comprehensive review of executive branch spending proposals. Executive departments and agencies submitted budget requests directly to Congress in a "Book of Estimates." A number of presidents, such as John Quincy Adams, Martin Van Buren, John Tyler, James K. Polk, James Buchanan, Ulysses S. Grant, and Grover Cleveland, did insist on revising budget estimates, but the budgeting process continued to be dominated by Congress and individual executive departments and agencies.[16]

During the budget process, Congress had no means to balance expenditures with revenues or evaluate alternative spending programs. As a result, the overlapping or extravagant spending proposals submitted by executive departments and agencies could not be weeded out of the budget. Moreover, the lack of central coordination made the use of the budget as an instrument of fiscal policy impossible.[17]

Before and during World War I, the nation had incurred a series of budget deficits that created a debt problem and led Congress to seek to reform the financial machinery of the executive branch. With the 1921 Budget and Accounting Act, Congress set up new procedures and organizations to provide more central coordination of the budget process.[18] The act established two important offices—the Bureau of the Budget (which became the Office of Management and Budget in 1970) and the General Accounting Office (which became the Government Accountability Office in 2004). The former was created to centralize fiscal management of the executive branch under the president; the latter was designed to enable Congress to oversee how the executive spent the money legislators appropriated.

The act also ended the practice of allowing executive departments and agencies to address their annual budget proposals directly to Congress. The Budget Bureau, originally a subdivision of the Treasury Department but later placed under the direct control of the president, became a central clearinghouse for all budget requests. The Budget Bureau evaluated these requests, adjusted them to fit the president's goals, and consolidated them into a single executive branch budget for Congress's consideration. Consequently, the Budget Act of 1921 transformed budget making from a random and fragmented process over which presidents had little control into a tool with which presidents could advance their social, economic, and defense priorities.

Keynesian Approaches to Fiscal Policy

While the United States and the world struggled through the Depression, the theories of the British economist John Maynard Keynes became widely known. Keynes outlined his ideas in *The General Theory of Employment, Interest, and Money,* published in 1936. He argued that recessions occurred when industrial, consumer, or government demand for goods and services fell. This caused unsold inventories to mount, industries to scale back their operations, and unemployment to rise.

Keynes posited that the government could counteract a recession by cutting taxes or increasing its expenditures. Lower taxes would put more money into the hands of consumers, thereby stimulating demand for goods and services. Tax cuts given to industry would create new jobs by boosting businesses' investment in their productive facilities. Greater government expenditures would create jobs and prime the economy through a "multiplier effect." According

FISCAL POLICY AND THE ELECTION CYCLE

The performance of the economy during a president's term affects the incumbent's chances for reelection as much as any other issue. In times of peace many Americans will "vote their pocketbooks," basing their votes on whether the American economy has given them the opportunity to meet their economic expectations. Moreover, an economy that improves during the year before an election can erase voters' memories of a longer period of economic stagnation or inflation.

Even second-term or newly elected presidents who are not immediately concerned with their reelection chances understand that economic conditions will affect the outcome of midterm elections, which will determine the strength of their party in Congress. Because the entire House and one-third of the Senate face an election every other year, significant turnover in congressional membership is possible. If an administration loses too many congressional allies, its programs may be threatened and the president's reelection chances in two years may be weakened. Fiscal policy, therefore, is never completely free from the influence of electoral politics and in an election year may be dominated by it.

The connection between economic conditions and the political success of presidents is a powerful incentive for an incumbent administration to try to create short-term improvements in the economy before an election. Economist Edward R. Tufte identified several economic trends that correspond to the U.S. election cycle. His studies of the economy from 1948 to 1976 showed that the unemployment rate on presidential election days tends to be significantly lower than twelve to eighteen months before and after an election.[1]

The elections that occurred during Dwight D. Eisenhower's presidency were notable exceptions to this trend. Eisenhower believed that Americans were more concerned with achieving a balanced budget and low inflation than with low unemployment and economic growth. He therefore opposed short-term stimulations of the economy for political purposes. The Republican losses in Congress in 1954 and 1958 and John F. Kennedy's victory over Richard Nixon in 1960, all of which occurred during economic slumps, provide evidence that Eisenhower may have been wrong.[2] After his 1960 defeat, Nixon wrote:

> The bottom of the 1960 dip did come in October and the economy started to move up in November—after it was too late to affect the election returns. In October, usually a month of rising employment, the jobless rolls increased by 452,000. All the speeches, television broadcasts, and precinct work in the world could not counteract that one hard fact.[3]

Tufte also found that increases in Social Security payments—the most direct way to put more money into the hands of voters—usually were enacted with the president's approval in even-numbered years during the ten months preceding an election. Because the increases in payroll taxes required to pay for the higher Social Security payments start at the beginning of a year for administrative

reasons, the price of Social Security increases was not felt by taxpayers until after the election.[4] In 1975, however, Social Security benefits were indexed so that recipients automatically receive annual cost-of-living increases to offset inflation, thereby weakening the justification for politically motivated benefit increases.

In addition to stimulative fiscal policies and increased transfer payments, other presidential economic policies have been affected by electoral politics. Lyndon B. Johnson did not press Congress for a tax hike in 1966 partly because he did not wish to focus attention on the growing costs of the Vietnam War before the midterm congressional elections.[5] Despite Nixon's personal distaste for severe government economic intervention, he imposed wage and price controls on the nation in August 1971 because the deteriorating economic situation threatened his upcoming 1972 reelection bid.[6]

Presidential efforts to manipulate the economy for political purposes are seldom in the best interests of the nation's long-term economic health. Although some politicians may argue that election-year economic stimulations are attentive political responses to the desires of voters, the public pays a price for these short-term boosts. Presidents and Congresses do not always have the political will to take away preelection benefits and tax cuts after the election. Consequently, electoral pressures on economic policy contribute to budget deficits and inflation. Even when the president and lawmakers agree on measures to offset their election-year generosity, there is evidence that short-term decreases in unemployment brought about by election-year tax cuts and spending hikes may be more transitory than the increases in inflation that usually accompany them.[7]

Beyond the inflationary and budgetary costs of pandering to voters' short-term economic desires, this practice makes coherent economic policymaking difficult. Tufte concluded: "The electoral-economic cycle breeds a lurching, stop-and-go economy the world over. Governments fool around with transfer payments, making an election-year prank out of the Social Security system and the payroll tax. There is a bias toward policies with immediate, highly visible benefits and deferred, hidden costs—myopic policies for myopic voters."[8]

1. Edward R. Tufte, *Political Control of the Economy* (Princeton: Princeton University Press, 1978), 19–21.

2. Ibid., 7–9.

3. Richard M. Nixon, *Six Crises* (New York: Doubleday, 1962), 310–311.

4. Tufte, *Political Control of the Economy*, 29–33.

5. Norman C. Thomas and Joseph A. Pika, *The Politics of the Presidency*, 4th ed. (Washington, D.C.: CQ Press, 1996), 371.

6. Dorothy Buckton James, *The Contemporary Presidency*, 2d ed. (Indianapolis: Bobbs-Merrill, 1974), 106.

7. William R. Keech, "Elections and Macroeconomic Policy Optimization," *American Journal of Political Science* 24 (1980): 345–367.

8. Tufte, *Political Control of the Economy*, 143.

to Keynes, each dollar spent by the government could stimulate more than a dollar's worth of private economic transactions.

One major feature of Keynesian fine-tuning was to focus policy on reducing unemployment. The scientific basis for this emphasis centered on the work of A. W. Phillips. In

1958 Phillips showed there was an inverse relationship between wages and unemployment: higher unemployment was associated with lower wages, while higher wages were associated with lower unemployment. This relation was extended to incorporate a trade-off between inflation and unemployment. In the late 1950s and up to the late 1960s most economists assumed that there was a stable trade-off between unemployment and inflation. In fact, this stable relationship could be graphically demonstrated, on what is now called the Phillips curve. This assumption of a stable relationship had powerful appeal to presidents and policymakers. One could simply pick a mix of inflation and unemployment on the Phillips curve and conduct monetary (and fiscal) policy in accordance with those goals in mind.

Keynesian fiscal policy gained credibility with economists and policymakers when it appeared to produce favorable results. When Roosevelt returned to the orthodox approach by cutting spending in 1936–1937, at the same time the Federal Reserve was tightening the money supply, a recession resulted; the deficit spending that followed, particularly on the massive scale that occurred during World War II, was seen as finally breaking the back of the Depression.[19]

By Roosevelt's last term in office, which began in early 1945, Keynesianism had become the dominant economic theory in both policymaking and academic circles. Many members of Congress believed that because Keynesian theory had provided the federal government with a tool with which it seemingly could hold down the level of joblessness, the government should be obliged to use that tool to promote full employment. The Employment Act of 1946 stated that the government should work for "maximum employment, production and purchasing power." Democratic supporters had to pull some of their Keynesian punches to get the bill passed, deleting references to "full" employment and using budget deficits as a tool to achieve high employment. A statement also was added that measures taken to implement the act must be consistent with the free enterprise system. Economist Herbert Stein wrote of the revision of the bill:

> Given the experience of the 1930s, it was inconceivable that the government would fail to commit itself to maintaining high employment. . . . But the form that commitment took in the United States, as embodied in the Employment Act of 1946, could hardly have been more satisfactory to conservatives. That is, after a major national discussion the Congress rejected an overly ambitious, inflationary definition of the goal, rejected exclusive reliance on deficit financing as the means, and reaffirmed its devotion to the free enterprise system.[20]

The Employment Act of 1946 nevertheless reflected a new national consensus that government should be involved deeply in the management of the economy. Beyond stating

A common sight during the Great Depression was a line of unemployed workers, such as here in 1939, waiting for daily jobs.

the government's responsibility to work for low unemployment, the act reinforced the president's role as the public official primarily responsible for managing the economy. Although the legislation did not provide presidents with new economic powers, it did require them to report annually to Congress on the state of the economy, which contributed to presidential agenda-setting power; more importantly, it created the Council of Economic Advisers, which gave presidents an economic advisory body answerable only to them.[21] These measures encouraged Congress, the business community, and the American public to continue to look to presidents for economic leadership as they had done during the depression.

In the two decades that followed, Keynesian policies particularly as pursued by Democratic presidents, seemed to contribute to American economic prosperity.[22] Until the late 1960s the emphasis on fine-tuning was widely accepted. Economists and public policy planners needed only to construct statistical models to accurately determine the effects of monetary and fiscal initiatives on unemployment and output. Walter Heller, who served as chair of the Council of Economic Advisers under Kennedy, declared in 1966 that "[e]conomics has come of age in the 1960s."[23] Heller and many of his colleagues believed that the combination of Keynesian economic theory, computer technology, and enlightened leaders had made it possible for the government to successfully promote prosperity through stabilization policy. The low unemployment and inflation of the mid-1960s seemed to bear out Heller's optimism.

And then, suddenly, they no longer did. No sooner had Republican president Richard Nixon famously stated that "I am now a Keynesian in economics" than the consensus around Keynesian economics collapsed. The decade of the 1970s featured several harrowing runs of "stagflation," where high unemployment coincided with high inflation, that appeared to defy Keynesian solution. Without a dominant organizing paradigm, policymakers faced a crucial information challenge—a mountain of undifferentiated data—while economists argued as to how best to sort them out and respond to them.[24]

By the late 1970s, economists were skeptical of the ability of the elected branches of government to guide the economy, believing them to be too slow and too constrained by political pressures. One problem in applying Keynesian theory to the management of the economy was that the political process made the Keynesian solution to inflation—cutting spending and raising taxes—difficult to enact. Politicians were predictably unwilling to adopt measures to control inflation because high taxes and cuts in government programs were unpopular with their constituents. Even if an administration were willing to propose a tax increase to combat inflation, it would seldom be able to persuade Congress to risk a recession, especially in election years.[25] Keynesian theory, therefore, offered presidents a politically practicable fiscal response only to recession. As a consequence, countercyclical policy emphasized stabilizing unemployment at the expense of ensuring price stability.

An alternative theory to which many national leaders turned was monetarism. The monetarists, led by economist Milton Friedman, argued that inflation occurs when the money supply is allowed to grow faster than the economy, because a greater number of dollars is available to chase the goods and services produced. The best way to control inflation, the monetarists believed, was to reduce the amount of money in circulation. For elected officials, economists now recommended a hands-off approach, relying on the Federal Reserve Board's monetary policy to provide stability and steady growth.[26]

The president and Congress were further constrained by seemingly chronic budget shortfalls. Since the late 1970s, economic policymaking has been largely a struggle to limit budget deficits despite erratic economic growth and dramatic increases in spending for entitlements, social programs, and defense. (See Table 7-2, p. 313.) The wave of antitax sentiment that hit the United States during the late 1970s and 1980s complicated deficit reduction. Presidential candidates during this period who advocated a tax increase, such as 1984 Democratic nominee Walter Mondale and 1988 Democratic contender Bruce Babbitt, were praised by many observers for their realism but fared poorly with voters. Mondale won only thirteen electoral votes in his election battle with Reagan, and Babbitt bowed out of the race

for the 1988 Democratic nomination after receiving meager support in the early primaries.

Supply-Side Experiment

During the late 1970s, a new approach to fiscal policy—supply-side economics—gained influential supporters, including Ronald Reagan, who became president in 1981. Supply-side theorists advocated using tax policy to encourage individuals and businesses to invest more and be more productive, which would result in economic growth and low unemployment. The supply-siders asserted that income tax rates (marginal tax rates) affect people's choice between work and leisure and between saving and consumption. The higher the tax rate, the less incentive they have to work and save. Similarly, the more businesses are taxed, the less money they have to invest in new plants and equipment that can raise their productivity. By cutting marginal tax rates, the theorists believed, the government could increase personal and corporate productivity and investment, thereby increasing the amount of goods and services produced, without creating inflation.

Many supply-side advocates also predicted that the expansion of the economy brought on by a supply-side strategy would generate enough revenue to decrease deficits even though tax rates were lower. This principle was illustrated by the Laffer curve, developed by Arthur B. Laffer of the University of Southern California. Laffer posited that government revenues rise with tax rates until they reach a point at which the increases in revenue brought by higher rates are less than the loss of revenue caused by the public's reduced incentive to work. Laffer and his adherents challenged the assumptions of most professional economists by arguing that the tax rates in force under the Carter administration, 1977–1981, were above this optimal level. Therefore, they believed, tax revenues could be increased not by raising rates, which would intensify the disincentives to produce, but by lowering the rates so that they would be closer to the optimal rate of taxation.[27]

In the end, arguments on both sides were made regarding the effectiveness of tax rate cuts, but most economists remained skeptical, questioning the thoroughness of the data on which the Laffer curve predictions were based.[28] Economic indicators following the Reagan administration's implementation of supply-side tax cuts were mixed: sustained economic growth (though average by long-term standards), low inflation, and stock market gains, but also dramatically higher budget and trade deficits.[29]

Monetary Policy

Monetary policy, like fiscal policy, is a tool with which the government attempts to stabilize the economy. It is based on the relationship of the supply of money in circulation to the performance of the economy. Because changes in the rate of

TABLE 7-2 **U.S. Federal Debt and Budget Deficits, 1940–2011 (billions of dollars)**

Fiscal year	Total federal debt	Federal debt as percentage of GDP	Budget deficit (surplus)	Deficit (surplus) as percentage of GDP
1940	$50.7	52.4%	–$2.9	–3.0%
1950	256.9	94.1	–3.1	–1.1
1960	290.5	56.0	0.3	0.1
1970	380.9	37.6	–2.8	–0.3
1975	541.9	34.7	–53.2	–3.4
1976	629.0	36.2	–73.7	–4.2
1977	706.4	35.8	–53.7	–2.7
1978	776.6	35.0	–59.2	–2.7
1979	829.5	33.2	–40.7	–1.6
1980	909.1	33.4	–73.8	–2.7
1981	994.8	32.5	–79.0	–2.6
1982	1,137.3	35.3	–128.0	–4.0
1983	1,371.7	39.9	–207.8	–6.0
1984	1,564.7	40.7	–185.4	–4.8
1985	1,817.5	43.8	–212.3	–5.1
1986	2,120.6	48.2	–221.2	–5.0
1987	2,346.1	50.4	–149.8	–3.2
1988	2,601.3	51.9	–155.2	–3.1
1989	2,868.0	53.1	–152.5	–2.8
1990	3,206.6	55.9	–221.2	–3.9
1991	3,598.5	60.7	–269.4	–4.5
1992	4,002.1	64.1	–290.4	–4.7
1993	4,351.4	66.1	–255.1	–3.9
1994	4,643.7	66.6	–203.3	–2.9
1995	4,921.0	67.0	–164.0	–2.2
1996	5,181.9	67.1	–107.5	–1.4
1997	5,369.7	65.4	–22.0	–0.3
1998	5,478.7	63.2	69.0	0.8
1999	5,606.1	60.9	125.5	1.4
2000	5,629.0	57.3	236.4	2.4
2001	5,770.3	56.4	128.2	1.3
2002	6,198.40	58.8	–157.8	–1.5
2003	6,760.00	61.6	–377.6	–3.5
2004	7,354.70	63.0	–412.7	–3.6
2005	7,905.30	63.6	–318.3	–2.6
2006	8,451.35	64.0	–248.2	–1.9
2007	8,950.74	64.6	–160.7	–1.2
2008	9,986.08	69.7	–458.6	–3.2
2009	11,875.85	85.2	–1,412.7	–10.0
2010	13,528.81	94.2	–1,293.5	–8.9
2011	14,764.22	98.7	–1,299.6	–8.7

SOURCE: The total federal debt data and budget deficit data can be found in Office of Management and Budget, "Federal Debt at the End of Year: 1940–2016;" "Summary of Receipts, Outlays, and Surpluses or Deficits in Current Dollars, Constant (FY 2005) Dollars, and as Percentages of GDP: 1940–2016," www .whitehouse.gov/omb/budget/Historicals/.

NOTE: GDP = gross domestic product.

growth of the money supply profoundly affect unemployment, inflation, and interest rates, the government can regulate economic activity by controlling the supply of money. Increasing the rate of growth of the money supply will stimulate the economy; decreasing it will contract the economy and combat inflation.

In contrast to fiscal policy, which is made through a slow public process of conflict and compromise among the president, Congress, and executive departments, monetary policy is determined within the Federal Reserve System, known as the "Fed." The Fed consists of twelve regional banks, several advisory bodies, and a Board of Governors.

The members of the Board of Governors, who are appointed by the president, are responsible for setting monetary policy and overseeing the operations of the Fed. The chair of the Fed dominates its policymaking and has often been described as the second most powerful person in Washington, after the president.[30]

After 1836, when the charter of the Second Bank of the United States was allowed to expire, the United States did not have a central bank for the rest of the century. In 1907, however, a severe banking crisis prompted policymakers to reexamine the American banking system. In 1912 a commission appointed by Congress recommended that the country

Economic Terms

Classical economic theory: a body of theory developed during the late eighteenth and early nineteenth centuries maintaining that economies naturally tend to achieve full employment and that government intervention in economic matters should be limited.

Contractionary policy: restrictive fiscal or monetary policy designed to decrease demand, thereby reducing inflation.

Deficit: The amount by which government expenditures exceed government receipts during a fiscal year.

Expansionary policy: stimulative fiscal or monetary policy designed to increase demand, thereby decreasing unemployment and promoting economic growth.

Federal Reserve System: the central bank of the United States; oversees the nation's banking system and controls monetary policy.

Fiscal policy: the manipulation of government spending and tax rates for the purpose of altering the levels of unemployment, inflation, and economic growth.

Gross national product: the value of goods and services produced by an economy in a given year; the principal measure of economic growth.

Inflation: a sustained increase in prices.

Keynesian theory: the body of economic theory developed by British economist John Maynard Keynes that advocates government intervention in the economy to stimulate or dampen demand as a way to deal with high unemployment or inflation.

Laissez faire: an approach to economic policy that advocates a limited government role in the economy in favor of a reliance on free-market forces.

Monetarism: an approach to economic policymaking that emphasizes the role of the money supply in determining inflation, unemployment, and economic growth.

Monetary policy: the manipulation of the money supply for the purpose of altering the levels of unemployment, inflation, and economic growth.

National debt: The amount of money owed by the federal government to all its foreign and domestic creditors at any given time.

Price stability: the absence of inflation.

Protectionism: an attempt by a government to protect the domestic markets of its industries from foreign competition by erecting trade barriers.

Recession: a prolonged downturn in the economy during which investment, incomes, and employment all decline.

Stabilization policy: monetary and fiscal policies designed to smooth undesirable fluctuations in inflation, unemployment, and the rate of economic growth.

Stagflation: simultaneous high inflation and unemployment.

Supply-side theory: an economic theory that focuses on the role played by incentives in achieving economic growth; supply-siders generally favor lower tax rates and government efforts to stimulate investments.

Tariff: a tax on imports or exports.

Trade barriers: protectionist devices such as tariffs or import quotas that make it more difficult for foreign companies to sell their goods and services in a given country.

Trade deficit: condition when a nation's imports exceed its exports.

---

establish a central bank to regulate credit conditions and provide stability to the U.S. banking system. With these goals in mind, Congress in 1913 passed with President Woodrow Wilson's support the Federal Reserve Act, which created the Fed.

Congress gave the Fed a permanent charter to avoid the type of political fight that prevented the First and Second Banks of the United States from being rechartered. The Federal Reserve Act does not mention a stabilization policy role for the Fed. This role evolved gradually after the Great Depression, until stabilization of the economy through monetary policy became one of the Fed's primary functions.[31]

The Fed studies the economy and constructs economic forecasts that it uses to determine its monetary policy. As with fiscal policy, the goals of monetary policy include low inflation, low unemployment, and strong economic growth. Fighting inflation, however, has traditionally been the Fed's first priority. This usually means more restrictive monetary policies when the Fed perceives inflation to be a threat.[32] Higher interest rates, higher unemployment, and lower output—for a short period of time—result.

Monetary policy was an attractive policy tool because it is less constrained by politics than is fiscal policy, which is produced through an unwieldy process of negotiation and compromise between the legislative and executive branches. Because the monetary policymaking structure created by Congress was intended to be nonpolitical, politicians usually have tried to avoid the appearance of interfering in the Fed's business. In addition, the complexity of monetary policy discourages many potential critics from looking over the Fed's shoulder.[33] Nonetheless, numerous conservative Republicans attacked the Fed's November 2010 decision to purchase government debt in order to stimulate the economy. Rep Mike Pence (R-Ind.) introduced legislation to limit the Fed's authority to achieving a low, stable rate of inflation.[34]

Even though the maintenance of price stability is an important national goal, the political and economic costs can be formidable. Transitions to price stability are not cheap politically or economically. Although economists disagree about the long-term effects of restrictive monetary policies, there is much agreement that, in the short term, monetary actions favor some individuals in society while harming others in direct and palpable ways. Restrictive measures to counter inflation often come at the expense of groups, such as builders, labor, and export-dependent industries that suffer disproportionately from high interest rates, a strong dollar, and high unemployment. Overall,

PRESIDENTIAL INFLUENCE OVER MONETARY POLICY

The Federal Reserve Board (Fed) manages the Federal Reserve System and is relatively free of formal congressional or executive control. Although there are other independent agencies, none serves such an important and politically sensitive function as formulating monetary policy.

The Fed ultimately is answerable to Congress, but the only formal powers Congress has over the Fed are Senate confirmation of appointees to the board and the passage of legislation restricting or revising the Fed's powers. Congress can neither pass judgment on nor veto Fed policies. Because the Fed is self-financing (it is funded by the interest it receives from government securities and the fees it charges to banks), Congress also cannot gain leverage by threatening to withhold appropriations. The Fed's independent control of monetary policy is a potent restriction on presidential control of the economy. Except for their power to appoint Fed officials, presidents have no formal means through which they can influence monetary policy. Yet presidents will receive most of the blame or the praise for changes in the economy brought about by monetary policy. Given this situation, presidents naturally try to exert as much informal influence over Fed decisions as possible.

Often this influence is exercised through public statements by presidents or their subordinates suggesting changes in Fed policy. These statements usually are crafted to avoid overt criticisms of the Fed or threats to its independence. For example, on June 1, 1992, with President George H. W. Bush's reelection chances jeopardized by a weak economy, Treasury Secretary Nicholas F. Brady commented: "I think it is clear that if the Fed pulls down the lever of money supply in 1992, as was the case in 1991 when the first appearance of growth started in midsummer, then we are taking a chance with this economic recovery that I don't think is wise for this country."[1] Such statements mark presidential monetary policy positions and distance the president from ensuing Fed policies that conflict with those positions.

Board members recognize a practical need to coordinate fiscal and monetary policy and, despite some prominent exceptions, have usually cooperated with presidential efforts to do so. The Fed also has been mindful that the president is the elected representative of the people who, theoretically, embodies the policy directions preferred by the American electorate.

Although the independence of the Fed is a restraint on presidential control of the economy, it does enable presidents to rely on the Board of Governors to make politically unpopular economic decisions, thus taking some public pressure off the White House. For example, in 1965 President Lyndon B. Johnson's advisers urged him to propose a tax increase to cool down the economy, which was beginning to produce inflation. Johnson, however, refused to propose higher taxes, thus forcing the Fed to bear the responsibility for fighting inflation. When the Fed raised the discount rate, Johnson told reporters, "The Federal Reserve Board is an independent agency. Its decision was an independent action. I regret, as do most Americans, any action that raises the cost of credit, particularly for homes, schools, hospitals, and factories." As political scientist Richard Pious has noted, "Had Johnson fought for the politically unpopular but necessary tax increase, there would have been no need to blame the board for its action."[2]

1. Clyde H. Farnsworth, "Brady Warns That Fed Could Delay Recovery," *New York Times*, June 2, 1992.
2. Richard Pious, *The American Presidency* (New York: Basic Books, 1979), 315.

---

however, as former Fed chair Paul Volcker noted, price stability facilitates activities that lead to greater prosperity:

> In the end there is only one excuse for pursuing such strongly restrictive monetary policies. That is the simple conviction that over time the economy will work better, more efficiently, and more fairly, with better prospects and more saving, in an environment of reasonable price stability.[35]

Widespread agreement has developed that the social cost of a persistent inflation exceeds the social cost of a once-and-for-all return to a stable price level. The experiences of the late 1960s and 1970s show that persistent inflation does not proceed in an orderly way but rather is an erratic process with major uncertainties producing large variations in real growth and high unemployment.

Tax Policy

Traditionally, presidents have exerted less influence over tax policy than over spending matters. Whereas presidents are required to submit an executive budget to Congress outlining their spending proposals each year, tax laws do not require the executive to make major annual revisions. In addition, legislators, especially members of the powerful House Ways and Means and Senate Finance Committees, have historically regarded tax policy as a special province of Congress.

Establishment of the Income Tax

During the eighteenth and nineteenth centuries the federal government had financed its activities through excise taxes, sales of the vast national lands that stretched to the Pacific, and, most important, tariffs. Tariffs were simple to administer but were not always an adequate source of income. In wartime, when the government required increased revenue, tariff receipts would fall as trade with other countries was disrupted.[36]

During the Civil War, Congress levied a tax on incomes to help make up the gap between peacetime revenues and wartime expenses. The tax expired in 1872, and no attempt was made to revive it until 1894 when Congress levied a 2 percent tax on personal incomes greater than $3,000. In 1895, however, the Supreme Court declared the income tax unconstitutional in *Pollock v. Farmers' Loan & Trust Co.* The Court held that an income tax was a direct tax that violated Article I, Section 9, Clause 4, of the Constitution, which prohibited direct taxes unless each state paid a share in proportion to its population.

With the support of President William Howard Taft, this obstacle was overcome on February 23, 1913, when the Sixteenth Amendment was ratified. It stated: "The Congress shall have power to lay and collect taxes on incomes from whatever source derived, without apportionment among the several states, and without regard to any census or enumeration." Congress passed a 1 percent income tax in 1913 with President Wilson's backing. But the power of the income tax as a source of revenue was not demonstrated until World War I, when an expanded income tax generated the revenues necessary for U.S. participation in the war.

Thereafter income taxes grew in importance. In 1915 customs duties and excise taxes provided 85 percent of federal revenues. By 1930 income taxes were providing more than half of the funds coming into the Treasury, while the share from customs and excises had fallen below 30 percent.[37]

The Sixteenth Amendment greatly expanded presidential power by providing a source of revenue that could finance presidential foreign policy and domestic initiatives. As political scientist Emmet J. Hughes noted, the income tax was "ready for lavish use by future Presidents to meet future needs or crises. And without such a reservoir of funds, there hardly could have followed any grand dreams of Presidential programs in the realms of welfare, education, health, housing, and transport."[38] The tax also enhanced the president's ability to make fiscal policy. Increasing and decreasing income taxes would become one of the methods most commonly used by presidents and Congress to combat inflation and recession.

Presidential influence over tax policy has grown since World War II.[39] As Congress and the nation have become accustomed to looking to the president for economic initiatives, the chief executive has taken over much of the burden of proposing and campaigning for changes in the tax code.

In addition to proposing tax legislation, presidents influence tax policy by standing ready to veto tax bills passed by Congress that they believe are unfair, excessive, or harmful to the economy. Until a multiyear conflict between President Clinton and a Republican Congress in the late 1990s, presidents after World War II rarely had to veto tax bills because the threat to veto them usually has been enough to stop congressional tax initiatives opposed by the president. President Reagan's success at preventing tax increases during his second term, despite huge budget deficits, demonstrates the president's power over tax policy. Presidents may not be able to get their tax measures passed by Congress, but they will usually be able to stop or at least force the modification of any tax bill they do not like. This was true of the Clinton–Congress standoff, particularly in the 106th Congress of 1999 and 2000. Republicans, in control of both chambers, moved aggressively both to fulfill tax-cutting pledges and to define their party's agenda in contrast to Democrats in preparation for the 2000 presidential elections in which no incumbent

was running. The Republicans sent Clinton large tax cut bills and small tax cut bills, the latter often just pieces of the larger one broken into sizable bites to attract enough Democratic support for passage. But in almost all cases Clinton vetoed the measures and the Republicans did not come close to overriding his vetoes.[40] Congress, however, has similar power to negate the president's tax proposals. Political scientist John F. Witte has written:

> Although the earlier notion that presidents should set only general revenue targets has been replaced by more detailed, almost annual tax proposals, the majority of the tax agenda is still set by Congress. Furthermore, there is no doubt that when presidential requests run counter to legislative momentum or the short run mood of Congress, they can and are summarily dismissed by congressional actions.[41]

The strategy of using tax policy as a tool of fiscal policy is complicated by the government's need for revenue. Tax cuts meant to stimulate the economy may succeed, but policymakers risk higher budget deficits. Although some tax cuts have generated greater revenues, most notably the 1964 tax rate cut that had been proposed the year before by President John F. Kennedy, tax cuts usually result in less revenue and higher deficits than would have ensued had they not been enacted. Conversely, raising taxes may increase revenues in the short run but also contract the economy, resulting in higher unemployment. Moreover, the unpopularity of tax increases, however, has made them difficult to enact with the speed that is necessary if they are to be an effective fiscal policy tool. Godfrey Hodgson has written of President Lyndon B. Johnson's experience with this problem:

> Even a timely shift in the direction of tax policy for macroeconomic reasons is generally beyond the capacity of . . . congressional procedures. Johnson found this to his cost in 1965–1968, when he tried to raise tax revenues to pay for the Vietnam War. His inability to do so may have cost him the presidency. Certainly it spelled the end for his great society programs and gave a sharp new impetus to the inflation combined with economic stagnation that has troubled the economy ever since.[42]

Tax Reform

Presidents have led efforts to simplify the tax code since the 1960s. A particular goal has been elimination of *tax expenditures,* provisions that allow specified groups to pay lower taxes than others at the same level of income.[43] The most successful such effort was the Tax Reform Act of 1986, a sweeping attempt to simplify the tax code and eliminate loopholes without increasing or decreasing tax revenues. The measure originated in separate efforts in Congress by Sen. Bill Bradley (D-N.J.) and Rep. Jack F. Kemp (R-N.Y.), and gained impetus in January 1984 when President Reagan directed the Treasury Department to develop a tax reform plan.[44]

The bill that resulted reduced the number of tax brackets from fourteen to just two. It cut the top individual tax rate from 50 to 28 percent and taxed 85 percent of taxpayers at the bottom rate of 15 percent. President Reagan hailed the law as "the best anti-poverty bill, the best pro-family measure, and the best job-creation program ever to come out of the Congress of the United States."[45]

Few Americans, however, believed that the bill had made paying their federal income taxes much easier. By 1993 the number of income tax rates had grown from two back up to five. The income tax's complexity and the intrusiveness of the Internal Revenue Service (IRS) audits stirred a populist movement aimed at finding alternatives to the income tax system. Critics pointed out that the IRS estimated that it failed to collect about $127 billion per year in income taxes. Simultaneously, many economists and policymakers wanted to restructure the tax system so that it would target consumption, thereby raising the low U.S. savings rate that was weakening productivity gains and causing wages to stagnate.[46]

International Monetary Policy

Presidents are responsible for maintaining the stability of the dollar in international currency markets, as well as representing American interests in negotiations over the international monetary system. The president's international economic powers have become increasingly important as nations have become more economically interdependent as high volumes of trade, integrated financial markets, and multinational corporations bind the world's economies. Because of this shared economic destiny among industrial nations, presidents must function not just as national economic managers but also as international economic coordinators. They dispatch the U.S. trade representative to international negotiations aimed at reducing trade barriers, oversee the Treasury Department's negotiations with other finance ministries about the value of major currencies, and announce U.S. economic policies to the international community.

The effort by developed nations to promote trade by establishing stable exchange rates grew out of the chaos of the Great Depression. The United States sought to build a predictable international currency system that would prevent both destabilizing fluctuations in exchange rates and deliberate currency devaluations that could threaten free trade. Forty-four nations signed an agreement at Bretton Woods, New Hampshire, in 1944 that made gold the standard by which currencies were valued. The Bretton Woods agreement established the International Monetary Fund (IMF) to oversee adjustments in exchange rates and the World Bank to provide loans for postwar reconstruction.

At first, nations used the dollar as an international trading currency and as a reserve of wealth just like gold. In effect, the United States functioned as banker to the world, because the United States held most of the world's gold reserves and the U.S. dollar's value was backed by the government's pledge to convert dollars into gold. Each member of the IMF was required to declare a par value for its currency in relation to the U.S. dollar, which was pegged to gold at $35 per troy ounce. Official exchange rates of the world's currencies were not allowed to fluctuate more than 1 percent from their par value.[47]

The Bretton Woods arrangement worked well during the 1940s, 1950s, and early 1960s. The stability it produced brought an enormous increase in world trade and the resurgence of economies devastated by World War II. By the mid-1960s, however, the dollar's role as an international reserve currency was causing the United States economic problems. Because other nations wanted to hold dollars to trade and back up their own currencies, dollars flowed overseas but failed to return. The result was a growing U.S. balance-of-payments deficit that weakened international confidence in the dollar and led many foreign investors to exchange their dollars for gold. U.S. gold reserves fell from more than $23 billion in 1949 to just $10 billion in 1971.

In response to this problem, on August 15, 1971, President Nixon stunned the world by announcing that the U.S. Treasury would no longer convert dollars into gold. The dollar's value would be allowed to float to a level determined by international currency markets. Because other currencies depended on the dollar, they, too, would have to float. The dollar, which had been overvalued, declined against other currencies, making U.S. goods cheaper overseas.[48] Nixon's decision ushered in a new era of international monetary relations that required a higher degree of coordination among governments. Although several countries proposed plans to salvage the Bretton Woods system, by 1973 all major currencies adopted some form of a floating exchange rate regime.

Managing the Value of the Dollar Today

Under the post–Bretton Woods system of floating exchange rates, governments have—for political reasons—often attempted to adjust the value of their currency through intervention in the currency markets. The United States and other governments intervene in currency markets through their central banks. If U.S. policymakers decide that the value of the dollar is too high, they can lower its value by selling dollars on the open market. Conversely, a weak dollar can be strengthened if the central bank shrinks the supply by buying dollars on the open market.

Intervention in currency markets is primarily the responsibility of the secretary of the Treasury, but the Federal Reserve Board also plays a major role. Decisions to intervene are usually made jointly by representatives of the Treasury Department and the Fed. For major interventions, the Treasury secretary and the Fed chair will usually consult.

PRESIDENTIAL APPOINTMENT OF BOARD MEMBERS

The most obvious source of influence presidents have over monetary policy is their power to appoint the members of the Federal Reserve System's Board of Governors. The Fed's Board of Governors consists of a chair appointed by the president to a four-year term with the approval of the Senate and six members appointed to fourteen-year terms, also subject to Senate confirmation. The members' terms are staggered so that one of their terms expires at the end of January in each even-numbered year. Barring deaths or resignations by board members, a president will appoint two members and a chair during each four-year term. In practice, however, presidents often make additional appointments to the Board of Governors. Perhaps because salaries paid to board members are generally far below what they can earn in the private sector, board members frequently resign before completing a full fourteen-year term.[1]

The chair's term, which is renewable, does not coincide with the president's term. Consequently, during the first part of their time in office first-term presidents must work with a chair appointed by their predecessor.

Given the influence of Fed chairs and their potential effect on a president's reelection chances, one would expect presidents to choose Fed chairs from among their closest economic allies. Yet the expectations of the financial and scholarly communities that presidents will appoint board members with high academic credentials and relatively nonpartisan backgrounds serve as a check against overly political appointments. Presidents are mindful that an appointment that appears to conflict with the Fed's traditional goals may cause financial markets to react in a way that hurts the economy (and therefore their own reelection chances). In addition, a president who nominates a close ally to be chair will be unable to disavow Fed policies that are perceived to be damaging to the economy.

Consequently, presidents often have reappointed Fed chairs who originally were appointed by their predecessors. In several cases, presidents have even reappointed a chair who was appointed by a president of a different party. William McChesney Martin was appointed Fed chair by President Harry S. Truman in 1951. He was reappointed by Dwight D. Eisenhower, John F. Kennedy, and Richard Nixon, serving continuously until he retired in 1970. Paul Volcker, a Jimmy Carter appointee, was reappointed by President Ronald Reagan. Alan Greenspan, a Reagan appointee, was reappointed by presidents George H. W. Bush, Bill Clinton, and George W. Bush. Greenspan retired in January 2006 whereupon President George W. Bush nominated Ben Bernanke to succeed him; he was reappointed by President Barack Obama.

The chances that the Fed will cooperate with the president, however, are increased greatly if the Fed chair is appointed by the incumbent president and shares the president's basic economic philosophy. In 1977 President Carter's expansionary fiscal policy was countered by the anti-inflationary monetary policy of Fed chair Arthur Burns, the conservative appointee of Nixon. When Burns's term expired in 1978, Carter replaced him with G. William Miller, a Carter associate who worked closely with the president's economic team.[2]

1. Frederic S. Mishkin, *The Economics of Money, Banking, and Financial Markets*, 3d ed. (New York: HarperCollins, 1992), 398.
2. Michael Bradley, *Economics* (Glenview, Ill.: Scott, Foresman, 1980), 576–577.

Treasury and the Fed independently control distinct accounts that can be used for the purpose of currency intervention. The actual transactions from both accounts are conducted by the Federal Reserve Bank of New York. The Fed, therefore, has the means to intervene in currency markets on its own initiative. But in practice, it will not do so if Treasury has an objection.[49]

The importance of currency intervention was illustrated dramatically in the early 1980s. The strong dollar had encouraged American consumers to buy foreign goods and made American goods too expensive overseas to compete with comparable foreign products, thus contributing to the growing U.S. trade deficit. Early in his first term President Reagan maintained that the exchange markets were inherently stable. His administration largely ignored the dollar's value in the belief that any market fluctuations that occurred were prompted by uncertainty about government intentions. Therefore a policy that consistently avoided intervention would yield the most stable exchange rates.[50] But when the current account deficit jumped from $44.5 billion in 1983 to $99.7 billion in 1984, the Reagan administration for largely political reasons (that is, pressure from export dependent industries) concluded that it had to act to bring down the value of the dollar. It announced in January 1985, shortly after James A. Baker III had taken over as Treasury secretary, that the United States would intervene in the currency markets to bring down the value of the dollar. U.S. intervention, sometimes with the cooperation of other central banks, was probably the reason the value of the dollar temporarily fell from its peak reached in February 1985.

Currency interventions do not technically require presidential approval. But the central role of the Treasury secretary, who serves at the pleasure of the president, ensures that the chief executive can exercise decisive influence over the process. In addition, even with their sizable reserves, it is difficult for Treasury and the Fed to alter the value of the dollar without cooperation from the central banks of the other industrialized powers. Consequently, coordination of exchange rate policies among the major industrialized countries is usually necessary to affect currency values. The president, as chief economic manager and the official charged with negotiating with foreign countries, must oversee this coordination.

Since 1975 presidents also have attended annual economic summits where the leaders of the major industrial nations have met to confer on broad issues of economic policy. These meetings, which are attended by the leaders of the United States, Japan, Germany, France, Great Britain, Italy, Canada and Russia (known collectively as the Group of Eight or G-8), have greatly increased international economic coordination.

These economic summits have focused attention on the international component of economic policy, forced politicians to develop a better understanding of international economic issues, created a justification for frequent meetings between finance ministers and other economic officials, and provided a forum where economic matters can be discussed in the broader context of allied relations. Because the annual meetings compel the leaders of the world's top industrial powers to face one another, they have had a positive influence on free trade. The leader of a country that has erected protectionist trade barriers or taken other measures contrary to the interests of the group must justify those measures to the other leaders and face their collective pressure to reverse the action.

Negotiations between governments often have resulted in informal agreements to take concerted action to adjust exchange rates. In January 1989, for example, the Fed and the other central banks of the major industrial nations agreed to slow the rise of the dollar, which was being pushed up near a previously agreed-upon secret limit by rising interest rates in the United States that were attracting foreign capital. At the same time, West Germany wanted its currency to be held up because of fears in that country that a weaker mark would lead to inflation by increasing the costs of imports. The world's major central banks responded by buying German marks with dollars, thereby holding down the dollar's rise and propping up the mark.[51]

Recent U.S. administrations have not intervened this directly in currency markets to influence the dollar's value. The United States has, however, repeatedly tried to convince China to allow the value of its currency to rise, which would reduce America's huge trade deficit with the Chinese and possibly help growth in exporting industries. China did allow the renminbi (its currency) to gain 5 percent in value in 2010, but this rise is considered too small to have any impact on either the dollar or the U.S. trade deficit. Speaking at the meeting of the Group of Twenty (G-20) industrial nations in Seoul, South Korea, President Obama asserted the renminbi "is undervalued. And China spends enormous amounts of money to keep it undervalued." Neither the G-20 nor the United States took any direct action, however. At the same time, the Fed's actions to increase the American money supply were seen by other countries—including Brazil, China, and Germany—as intentionally weakening the dollar's value.[52]

Trade Policy

Because the Constitution gives Congress the power "to regulate Commerce with foreign Nations," the rules governing foreign trade are set by legislation. Since the Great Depression, however, trade legislation has contained broad grants of power to the president to implement the laws through international negotiations and through tariffs and other trade barriers designed to force other countries to open up their markets to American products.

Congress has granted the executive broad trade powers because only the president has the authority to negotiate with foreign governments. Therefore, when Congress adopted the strategy of pursuing mutual reductions in tariffs through international negotiations in 1934, it had to turn to the president to carry out those negotiations. In addition, Congress wanted to isolate U.S. trade policy from pressures for protectionism from specific industries. Because individual members of Congress have to be concerned with the economic conditions in their states and districts, protectionist sentiments have tended to be stronger in Congress than in the executive branch. If a single industry such as agriculture or steel predominates in a congressional district, then that district's representative often will be disposed to support protectionist measures for that industry. According to political scientist Erwin C. Hargrove, by delegating power to the president Congress is able to respond to the local interests of its constituents without undermining the free trade position of the nation:

> Congress would rather not have responsibility for setting specific tariff levels because the flood of demands for individual industrial areas would be far too intense. Therefore, it has allowed the Executive to set such levels within parameters set by Congress. This permits members of Congress to make their requests in behalf of constituency interests and still permit the President to do what is needed for a national position on international trade.[53]

Promoting Free Trade

Reducing barriers to international trade has been the policy of presidents of both parties since President Franklin Roosevelt acted in 1933 to reverse the onerous Smoot-Hawley tariff that economists later were to conclude contributed significantly to the Great Depression. With the enthusiastic support of Secretary of State Cordell Hull, Roosevelt asked the Democratic-controlled Congress to delegate to him the authority to reduce U.S. tariffs up to 50 percent in return for equal tariff concessions by other nations. Despite nearly unanimous Republican opposition, Congress passed the Trade Agreements Act of 1934, which delegated this power to the president. Armed with new authority, the Roosevelt administration negotiated bilateral agreements with many nations that cut tariffs and increased the flow of trade. The increased access to foreign markets that resulted helped stimulate the U.S. economy. After the initial success of Roosevelt's negotiations, congressional grants of power to the president to negotiate mutual tariff reductions became a regular feature of U.S. trade policy.

After World War II, President Truman sought to establish more sweeping arrangements to reduce international protectionism. At the urging of the United States, twenty-three nations signed the General Agreement on Tariffs and Trade (GATT) in 1947. Since then most nations have signed

The leaders of the Group of Eight gather in Birmingham, England, for their annual summit, May 1998. Pictured, from left to right, are Jean Chrétien of Canada, Helmut Kohl of Germany, Boris Yeltsin of Russia, Tony Blair of Great Britain, Jacques Chirac of France, Romano Prodi of Italy, Ryutaro Hashimoto of Japan, President Bill Clinton, and Jacques Santer of the European Commission. The group includes seven nations that account for about two-thirds of the world's output plus Russia, which joined the group in 1997.

the agreement. Under GATT, multilateral negotiations aimed at reducing trade barriers were to be held at regular intervals. The signatories also agreed to the most-favored-nation principle, which committed each nation to apply tariff rates equally to all the other GATT participants. In addition, the agreement prohibited certain restrictive trade practices, such as import quotas, and set up procedures to mediate trade disputes and implement sanctions against violators of the agreement.

Since 1947, GATT signatories have held eight multinational trade negotiation rounds. The first five rounds produced small but significant tariff reductions. The sixth (Kennedy) round of GATT resulted in tariffs on industrial products being cut by an average of more than 35 percent. In addition, for the first time the GATT participants discussed nontariff barriers to trade.

An even more dramatic breakthrough came in 1994, with the completion of the eighth (Uruguay) round of GATT. More than one hundred nations agreed to reduce tariffs on most manufactured items by an average of one-third. The round was the first to reduce barriers on agricultural products, protect intellectual property rights, and establish rules covering trade in services.

The most controversial aspect of the far-reaching agreement, however, was the establishment of the World Trade Organization (WTO), which would replace GATT's existing institutional structure. Some critics charged that it would damage U.S. sovereignty because its dispute resolution procedures could not be vetoed by the United States. If the United States were judged to be at fault in a trade dispute, it would have to accept the WTO's ruling or open itself up to sanctions. But supporters of the agreement argued

successfully that such a mechanism was precisely what was needed to protect American commercial interests. Because of the relatively open trading posture of the United States, Americans were far more often the injured party in trade disputes. Therefore, they contended, reforms that put teeth into GATT enforcement procedures would be a great advantage to American exporters.

Recent presidents have faced increasing protectionist pressures in Congress, as sectors of the economy that have been negatively affected by trade liberalization and foreign competition have made their presence felt.[54] After the Kennedy Round, dozens of bills with protectionist provisions were introduced in Congress. Few were passed, but the drive for trade barrier reduction had temporarily peaked. Congress did not renew the president's authority to participate in multilateral trade negotiations, which had expired in 1967, until it passed the Trade Act of 1974 after the next GATT round was already under way. Although this act extended the president's authority to negotiate reductions of trade barriers, it placed more restrictions on the president's power.

Protectionist pressure further increased in the 1980s, when the U.S. trade surplus began to decline rapidly as exports failed to keep pace with imports. The large current account deficit cost the U.S. economy good jobs because Americans were buying so many products manufactured overseas. In addition, because the United States had to borrow to finance the trade imbalance, the current account deficit was increasing the U.S. dependence on foreign credit and adding to the debts of the nation. Many Americans viewed the trade deficit as a sign of American economic decline relative to its major industrial allies.[55] Congress

TRADE POLICY: PROTECTIONISM VERSUS FREE TRADE

The primary question that trade policy must decide is whether to pursue free trade or whether to erect barriers that protect U.S. industries but ultimately risk reducing the overall flow of trade. Few economists or politicians would argue against the proposition that the ideal trade environment for enhancing international prosperity is one in which nations can trade goods and services without trade barriers such as tariffs, import quotas, embargoes, and strict licensing procedures for importing goods. Yet even the most ardent free trade advocates recognize that the threat of protectionism is the most effective negotiating tool the government has to convince other nations to end their unfair trading practices. Appeals for protection from specific industries often have diverted national policy from the ideal of free trade. Nevertheless, since 1934, even when Congress has enacted bills to protect specific industries or to pry open foreign markets, policymakers in the executive branch have maintained the posture that the U.S. economy will benefit from free trade.

Throughout U.S. history, tariffs have been a contentious political issue. The nation's first Treasury secretary, Alexander Hamilton, supported high tariffs, which he hoped would nurture the infant industries of the Northeast. Although the tariffs enacted during the Federalist era were not swept away when Thomas Jefferson took power in 1801, the pro-agrarian Democratic-Republicans favored trade policies that enhanced the ability of farmers to sell their products overseas.

During most of the nineteenth century, the industrial and commercial interests of the North contended with the agricultural interests of the South over national tariff policy. Because the South depended on foreign markets for its agricultural products, it opposed tariffs that could trigger a retaliatory response from its foreign customers. In addition, tariffs raised the price of many goods the South needed to buy from foreign countries. The intersectional tensions over trade policy led to the nullification crisis in South Carolina in 1832. After Congress passed a high-tariff bill in 1832, the South Carolina state legislature passed an ordinance declaring the tariff void in that state. President Andrew Jackson, determined to assert federal authority, threatened to enforce the law in South Carolina with federal troops. Hostilities were averted when Jackson and South Carolina leaders accepted a compromise tariff. Tensions caused by the tariff issue remained, however, and eventually contributed to the secession of southern states in 1861 that brought on the Civil War.

For the rest of the nineteenth century, tariffs remained high as American industries desirous of protection grew in influence and the protariff Republican Party dominated national politics. Average U.S. tariff rates generally ranged from 35 to 50 percent of the cost of imports subject to tariffs. With the election of President Woodrow Wilson in 1913, tariff policy was reversed. That year, with President Wilson's strong support, Congress enacted the Underwood-Simmons Tariff Act, which cut tariffs sharply. Wilson saw tariff reduction as a way to help American consumers, limit the influence of powerful probusiness lobbyists, and stimulate competition.

America's participation in World War I rekindled the "America first" sentiments in the United States that led to a return of high tariffs. The Tariff Act of 1921 and the Fordney-McCumber Act of 1922, both supported by Republican president Warren G. Harding, returned tariffs roughly to their pre-1913 levels.

When the Depression struck in 1929, the governments of the major industrialized nations reacted by erecting trade barriers to protect their domestic industries. In 1930 Congress passed the Smoot-Hawley Act, which established the highest tariffs the United States had ever erected. The trade war of the early 1930s strangled trade among nations until it was a small fraction of what it had been. Protectionist measures left the world to dig out of the Great Depression without the benefits of international trade.

The counterproductive results of Smoot-Hawley created a consensus among several generations of executive branch policymakers that a U.S. free trade posture was essential to American prosperity and international security. Political scientist I. M. Destler described the role of Smoot-Hawley in solidifying free trade as a goal:

> In this consensus, the Smoot-Hawley Act of 1930 played the same role for economic affairs that Munich played for military. Just as British Prime Minister Neville Chamberlain's sincere search for "peace in our time" had only strengthened those who made war, so too had congressional use of trade barriers to aid Depression-hit American producers backfired, postwar leaders believed. Other nations had retaliated, exports had plummeted even more than imports, and the world economic catastrophe helped to spawn both Adolf Hitler's Nazi regime in Germany and aggressive militarism in Japan. Only by building a more open world could we prevent the sort of mutually destructive, beggar-thy-neighbor competition that had produced national economic disaster and international bloodshed. This meant reducing barriers to trade, and to cross-border economic transactions in general.[1]

Partly because of the president's role as chief negotiator and partly because the presidency's national constituency reduced the pressure that could be brought to bear by labor unions and specific industries seeking protection, presidents, both Democratic and Republican, became the primary force for advancing the free trade agenda. The parochial nature of the legislative branch ensured that Congress would always contain a sizable number of protectionists. But presidents were generally successful in securing congressional support for initiatives to liberalize trade.

1. I. M. Destler, *American Trade Politics*, 2d ed. (Washington, D.C.: Institute for International Economics, 1992), 6.

passed the Omnibus Trade and Competitiveness Act in 1988, which mandated retaliatory responses to unfair foreign trade practices. President Reagan's firm support of free trade prevented Congress from enacting a more protectionist trade bill.

Protectionist pressures made Congress occasionally unwilling to extend fast-track trade authority to the president. First appearing in the Trade Act of 1974, *fast-track authority* meant a president could negotiate a trade agreement, and then submit for Congress's approval comprehensive, nonamendable legislation to implement the agreement. Congress had to consider that legislation within a set time period under expedited rules. Because Congress could not amend trade agreements negotiated under fast-track authority, the president had broad power over the details of negotiation. Particularly, the president had latitude to negotiate complex trade agreements without having to prevail on multiple votes in Congress designed to chip away pieces of the agreement. From 1974 until 1991, fast-track authority was extended as part of broader trade legislation, with increasingly contentious debate and close votes in Congress. After another brief extension in 1993, it was suspended from 1994–2002. President George W. Bush won extensions in 2002 and 2005, but it expired again in 2007.[56] Leaders of the newly elected Democratic-led House said at the time, "Our legislative priorities do not include the renewal of fast track authority. Before that debate can even begin, we must expand the benefits of globalization to all Americans."[57]

Presidents have continued to achieve trade agreements despite these widespread public concerns. President George H. W. Bush concluded negotiations on the North American Free Trade Agreement (NAFTA) with Canada and Mexico before leaving office in January 1993; President Clinton demonstrated the centrality of the presidency to the maintenance of the free trade position by mounting a bipartisan campaign for NAFTA's passage in Congress. Despite advice from some advisers in August 1993 that securing approval of NAFTA was a lost cause, Clinton skillfully rallied a bipartisan coalition containing more Republicans than Democrats to pass the agreement.[58] In 1994 President Clinton lobbied heavily for GATT, and implementing legislation was passed by decisive votes in the House and Senate. President George W. Bush achieved the Central American Free Trade Agreement (CAFTA), including Costa Rica, the Dominican Republic, El Salvador, Guatemala, Honduras, and Nicaragua, which was approved by narrow votes in both houses of Congress in 2005. President Barack Obama achieved congressional approval of trade agreements with Colombia, Panama, and South Korea.[59]

ECONOMIC POLICYMAKING INSTITUTIONS

Economic Advisers to the President

As presidential economic responsibilities increased during the twentieth century, the fulfillment of those responsibilities became increasingly institutionalized. Congress created new organizations, and presidents expanded existing organizations to increase the executive branch's capacity to analyze, coordinate, and manage the American economy and economic relations with other countries. Although White House political advisers and virtually all cabinet secretaries have some influence on economic policy, three executive branch units dominate presidential economic policymaking: the Treasury Department, the Council of Economic Advisers (CEA), and the Office of Management and Budget (OMB). The leaders of these three units function as the president's chief economic advisers and meet frequently with one another to coordinate economic policy. Recent presidents also have established working groups beneath the three leaders with representatives from various departments to develop and analyze economic policies.

Treasury Department

The Treasury Department, one of the original cabinet departments created in 1789 by an act of Congress, was the first executive branch unit to be responsible for advising the president on economic policy and has remained an important participant in economic policymaking throughout U.S. history. The department has a variety of economic responsibilities, including collecting taxes and customs, managing the nation's currency and debt, developing tax legislation, and working with foreign governments and the Federal Reserve to adjust the value of the dollar relative to other currencies. Because the Treasury oversees the financing of the debt, the department traditionally has advocated taxes that will bring balanced budgets and monetary policies that yield low interest rates.

The Treasury secretary's position as head of a large cabinet department lends status to the post relative to other top presidential economic advisers. The Treasury secretary's influence on presidential economic decision making, however, may be constrained in some administrations by the amount of time the secretary spends overseeing the many operational responsibilities of the department. As the world's economies have become more interdependent, the Treasury secretary's international economic policy activities have become increasingly important. James A. Baker III, Treasury secretary during Ronald Reagan's second term, spent much of his time formulating exchange rate policies and developing a plan to reschedule Latin American debt payments to the United States. In early 1995, immediately on assuming the post of Treasury secretary, Robert E. Rubin orchestrated the commitment to Mexico of $20 billion in U.S. loans and loan guarantees and an additional $30 billion in international loans to avert severe international repercussions from Mexico's currency crisis.

Within the executive branch, the Treasury Department has primary responsibility for tax policy. Its Office of the Tax Legislative Counsel drafts tax legislation and reviews tax regulations. The Office of Tax Analysis estimates the effect tax changes will have on revenues. In addition, the Treasury Department's Internal Revenue Service is responsible for collecting taxes and enforcing the tax laws passed by Congress. Other officials in the administration, particularly the OMB director, also are involved in formulating tax strategies.

Council of Economic Advisers

The Council of Economic Advisers (CEA) is a three-member body appointed by the president and subject to Senate confirmation. It is headed by a chair who oversees the operations of the council's small staff, reports to the president, and represents the CEA before the rest of the executive branch and Congress.

The primary function of the CEA is to provide the president with expert economic advice and analysis. The

Employment Act of 1946, which established the CEA as a unit in the Executive Office of the President, states that each member of the council "shall be a person who, as a result of his training, experience and attainments is exceptionally qualified to analyze and interpret economic developments, to appraise programs and activities of the government . . . and to formulate and recommend national economic policy." Because the council does not represent a large bureaucratic body and has no responsibilities in operating the government other than preparing the president's annual economic report, Congress hoped that the CEA would have the time and independence to provide presidents with long-term, nonpartisan advice on economic policy and professional analysis of economic conditions. Traditionally, the CEA was primarily concerned with promoting growth and managing the trade-off between inflation and unemployment. In recent years, however, it has addressed a wider range of economic issues, including trade, productivity, pollution, and health care.

The CEA's influence depends almost entirely on the president. If the president values its advice and involves it in decision making, the CEA can have considerable power because its three members and small staff of professional economists usually possess the greatest amount of economic expertise within an administration. Walter Heller, Kennedy's CEA chair, sold the president on Keynesian theory and convinced him to propose a stimulative tax cut in 1963.[60] Because of this expertise, however, CEA members can be vulnerable to charges from other economic advisers that they approach the realities of economic policymaking from a perspective that is too theoretical. The nadir of CEA influence came during the Reagan administration, when Treasury Secretary Donald Regan suggested publicly that the sections of the *Economic Report of the President* authored by CEA chair Martin Feldstein could be thrown away. After Feldstein resigned in frustration in 1984, Reagan allowed the post to remain vacant for over a year.[61] CEA members must, therefore, be careful to pay adequate attention to the president's political needs if they wish to retain their influence.

Office of Management and Budget

In 1921 Congress created the Bureau of the Budget to coordinate and modify the budget estimates of the executive departments. It was originally located within the Treasury Department but was placed under the newly created Executive Office of the President in 1939. In 1970 Richard Nixon expanded its staff and duties and renamed it the Office of Management and Budget (OMB).

OMB's primary function is to formulate an executive branch budget for the president that considers how much revenue the government is likely to raise through taxes and how much each federal agency and program should receive. OMB, therefore, continually analyzes the merits of budget requests and makes recommendations to the president on what funding should be cut, maintained, or expanded. The office is also responsible for budget forecasts that estimate the size of the budget deficit or surplus. The institutional bias of OMB has been to limit spending. Because department and agency heads tend to request as much funding as is politically possible for their units, OMB has become the central budgetary control within the administration to pare down the budget requests.

The post of budget director has become highly politicized since the Nixon administration. Budget directors frequently testify before Congress and are involved in shaping and promoting the president's social agenda through their budget recommendations. David A. Stockman, budget director under Ronald Reagan from 1981 to 1985, epitomized the budget director's new role. President Reagan gave him a broad mandate to cut items from the budget in pursuit of smaller budget deficits. In the first six months of the Reagan administration, Stockman became not only the dominant presidential adviser on the budget, but also a symbol of Reagan's domestic budget cuts and social agenda, which emphasized a more limited role for the federal government.

The forecasting role of OMB also has pushed it into the political spotlight. Because budgets depend on long-term forecasts of economic growth, tax receipts, and entitlement spending, the assumptions of OMB and its legislative branch counterpart, the Congressional Budget Office (CBO), are critical to plans aimed at reducing the deficit. In 1995 Congress insisted that President Bill Clinton agree to base efforts to balance the budget on forecasts from the traditionally independent CBO. Most observers agree that direct presidential control of OMB has led to the politicization of its budget forecasts under recent presidents.[62] Clinton agreed in November 1995 to use CBO budget estimates that were developed after consultations with OMB.

Rivals to Power

The president, as previously discussed, shares authority over the economy with other parts of government, mainly Congress and the Federal Reserve Board.

Congress

Congress, while usually happy to delegate day-to-day responsibility for the economy to the president, reserves for itself authority to approve the administration's economic and budget initiatives, appropriate money to specific governmental functions, and legislate changes to the authority of the president and Federal Reserve. This is particularly true during periods of divided government: Republicans repeatedly challenged Barack Obama's antirecession proposals, resisting additional deficit spending as well as any measures to increase government revenue. Similarly, in another recession twenty years earlier, Democrats thwarted George H. W. Bush's attempts to reduce the capital gains tax rate.

Budgeting

Prior to 1974, congressional attention to spending was fragmented and incremental—one reason Congress delegated budget authority to the president in 1921. Authority over appropriations was assigned in the 1860s to standing Appropriations Committees in each house, but they tended to reflect the recommendations of the other committees who oversaw specific parts of the bureaucracy. Revenue was and is the province of the House Ways and Means Committee and the Senate Finance Committee.

Three developments challenged this long-standing informality: the establishment and growth of entitlement programs, so that by the 1970s much of the budget was beyond the reach of year-to-year appropriations decisions; the end in about 1973 of long-term postwar economic growth, and the concomitant collapse of the Keynesian policy consensus; and the trend toward divided government that began with the election of Richard Nixon in 1968.[63] Congress now found their rivalry with the presidency to be more pronounced, and felt themselves at a disadvantage both in information and in process.

The Budget and Impoundment Control Act of 1974 grew out of congressional Democrats' frustration with their inability to compete with President Nixon in making economic policy.[64] It created the CBO as a source of economic information and advice independent of the executive branch, as well as Budget Committees in the House and Senate that would be responsible for drafting annual continuing resolutions that detailed overall revenue and spending plans. Congressional action on appropriations and revenues would then need to be reconciled with this budget.

Finally, the 1974 Budget Act attempted to assert congressional authority over presidential spending decisions. More precisely, Congress wished to review presidential decisions not to spend money appropriated by law. The Constitution does not spell out whether presidents are required to promptly spend funds Congress appropriates or whether they can make independent judgments about the timing and even the necessity of putting appropriated funds to use. Many presidents have taken advantage of this constitutional ambiguity to impound appropriated funds they believed unnecessary or wasteful. Presidents Harry S. Truman, Dwight D. Eisenhower, and Kennedy all clashed with Congress over their withholding of appropriations for defense projects. In 1966 President Lyndon B. Johnson impounded $5.3 billion in domestic appropriations to slow inflationary trends brought on by the Vietnam War.

Presidential impoundments reached their zenith after Nixon became president in 1969. Nixon impounded billions of dollars of appropriations during the first five years of his presidency. He argued that he was withholding funds only as a financial management technique designed to slow inflation. Democratic leaders in Congress, however, charged that Nixon used impoundments to overturn Congress's spending decisions and further his own social goals. For example, after Congress overrode a presidential veto to pass the 1972 Clean Water Act, Nixon impounded $9 billion that was intended to implement the act.

The 1974 Budget Act created new procedures designed to prevent a president from impounding appropriations against the will of Congress. Under the act presidents could only impound (rescind) or defer appropriations subject to the approval of Congress. And they did—Congress approved $20 billion worth of rescission requests in the first two years of the Reagan administration.[65] But the growth of the budget deficit in the 1980s led many members of Congress to conclude that the 1974 restrictions on presidential impoundment authority had been a mistake. They made various proposals to control congressional spending, including a balanced budget constitutional amendment, mandatory deficit-reduction targets (as in the Gramm-Rudman-Hollings acts of 1985 and 1987), biennial budgeting, and a strengthened presidential impoundment power.[66]

Line-item Veto (1996–1997)

The *line-item veto* or *item veto* refers generically to a number of proposals intended to strengthen the president's authority to rescind specific spending items within an appropriations bill. The two most prominent forms of the line-item veto are enhanced and expedited rescission. *(See "Line-item Veto," p. 160, in Chapter 4.)*

Expedited rescission authority involves a modest expansion of presidential power under the 1974 Budget and Impoundment Control Act. Under this procedure presidents would propose reducing or eliminating items in appropriations bills. These rescissions would not go into effect unless both houses of Congress approved them within a set time period. Thus, Congress could not overrule the president's rescission proposal merely through inaction.

Enhanced rescission authority would allow presidents to propose reductions in appropriations bills that would go into effect automatically, unless both chambers of Congress voted to reject them. The president could then veto the legislation disapproving of the rescissions, forcing both houses to muster a two-thirds vote to override the veto. Enhanced rescission would mean a vast expansion of the presidential impoundment power because the president's rescission choices would prevail unless Congress could muster enough votes to clear the high hurdle of a veto override.

This is the approach the Congress took when it passed the Line Item Veto Act in 1996, with warm support from President Clinton. However, the law—which went into effect in early 1997—was a short-lived experiment. Clinton used it sparingly but on items dear to the heart of congressional members. He vetoed several parts of military construction appropriations bills, which traditionally have been vehicles to bring federal spending to members' districts and states, thereby helping them with voters. Congress promptly rejected the vetoes, Clinton vetoed the rejection, and Congress overrode Clinton's vetoes.

But the death of the idea came at the hands of the Supreme Court in 1998 when it declared the 1996 law unconstitutional on a 6–3 vote. The Court ruled that the line-item veto violated provisions of the Constitution that established the procedure for the enactment of laws. Writing for the 6–3 majority, Justice John Paul Stevens said:

> If the Line-Item Veto Act were valid, it would authorize the president to create a different law—one whose text was not voted on by either House of Congress or presented to the president. If there is to be a new procedure in which the president will play a different role in determining the final text of what may 'become a law,' such change must come not by legislation but through . . . [constitutional] amendment.[67]

Federal Reserve Board

The Federal Reserve Board is the descendant of the Bank of the United States, created in 1791 at the initiative of Treasury Secretary Alexander Hamilton. He asked Congress to charter a national bank to assist in the financial operations of the United States. It was to be run primarily by private directors and funded by private capital. Of the bank's original $10 million capitalization, only $2 million was to come from the Treasury, while the rest would be provided by individual investors. In persuading President George Washington to sign the bill, Hamilton stressed the necessity of a broad interpretation of the government's economic powers.[68]

The First Bank of the United States functioned well for twenty years, but Congress refused by one vote to recharter it in 1811. The strong political opposition to the bank, combined with the lobbying efforts of commercial banks that competed for business with the national bank, led to its demise.[69] Congress chartered the Second Bank of the United States in 1816, but the bank existed for only twenty years until forced out of existence by its arch opponent, President Andrew Jackson.

From 1836 to 1913 the United States had no formally constituted monetary authority. During this period monetary policy was governed by the combination of the gold standard and powers vested in the Treasury Department. However, a variety of bank panics and subsequent depressions paved the way for reform. A banking panic and recession in 1907 led to reforms that would create a lender of last resort. In 1908 Congress created the National Monetary Commission that drew up recommendations that culminated in the creation of the Federal Reserve Act of 1913, which created the Federal Reserve Board (Fed). While the Fed was created to provide financial stability, sufficient vagueness existed in the law that allowed the Fed to evolve into the policymaking body it is today. In particular, the law gave the Fed flexibility to respond to seasonal fluctuations in the demand for money.

Coordination of Fiscal and Monetary Policy

Until 1951 the Treasury Department was the most influential in affecting monetary policy. One consequence of this arrangement was that the Fed had to conduct policy consistent with supporting the prices of government securities and keeping interest rates low. During World War II this was particularly important to keep the cost of financing down.

With the Accord of 1951, the Fed was given the freedom not only to support government securities but also to minimize monetization of the debt. The effect of this agreement between Congress, the Treasury, and the Fed was to provide the Fed with considerable freedom in conducting monetary policy. In effect, countercyclical policy—such as the use of monetary policy to offset inflationary or deflationary pressures—was instituted with this agreement. Modern monetary policy in the United States is in large part a function of the Accord of 1951.

Although the organization of the Fed is designed to insulate it from outside influence, monetary policy is most effective when it is coordinated with the administration's fiscal policy. Coordination is accomplished through informal meetings between the Fed chair and the president's top economic advisers. The Fed chair, the Treasury secretary, the budget director, and the chair of the CEA—a group known as the "quadriad"—usually meets at least once a month to discuss coordination of fiscal and monetary policy. Any agreements forged out of these discussions, however, are nonbinding, and the Fed may pursue a monetary policy at odds with the administration's goals.

The intent of both fiscal and monetary policy is to promote economic stability and prosperity, but the effects of one may cancel, blunt, or distort the intended effects of the other if the president and the Fed do not cooperate. For example, the president may ask Congress to stimulate the economy by spending more than the government receives in revenues. This requires the government to borrow funds, which increases competition for loans, thereby driving up interest rates. The higher interest rates, however, may offset the stimulative effects of the government's spending increases unless the Fed accommodates the president's fiscal policy by increasing the money supply.

The Fed has sometimes "leaned against the wind" to counter administration policies it considered wrong. In

1957 the Fed kept a tight rein on the money supply while the Eisenhower administration was pursuing a moderately expansionary fiscal policy. Similarly, the Fed fought inflation during the late 1960s, while spending on the Vietnam War and Johnson's Great Society social programs stimulated the economy.

The Fed may even use public pressure to attempt to change administration policies. In 1977 Fed chair Arthur Burns testified against Carter's tax cut proposals, raising the possibility that if the tax cuts were passed, the Fed would use monetary policy to offset their stimulative effect. Fed chair Alan Greenspan warned the incoming Bush administration through testimony before Congress on January 24, 1989, that the Fed would not tolerate an acceleration of inflation. George H. W. Bush and his economic advisers had placed a high priority on continued strong economic growth, but Greenspan indicated the Fed might slow growth in the near future to combat inflation, saying, "The Federal Reserve policy at this juncture might be well advised to err more on the side of restrictiveness than stimulus."[70]

Presidents, therefore, generally try to coordinate their fiscal policies with the Fed to produce the best economic results and limit political friction between economic policymakers. In 1993 President Clinton went out of his way to establish a good relationship with Greenspan, who had been appointed chair of the Fed in 1987 by President Reagan and reappointed in 1992 by George H. W. Bush. In a show of their mutual desire for bipartisan coordination of economic policy, Greenspan sat with First Lady Hillary Rodham Clinton at the 1993 State of the Union address. Later that year Clinton wrote to House Banking Committee chair Henry Gonzalez defending Fed policies. Gonzalez had introduced legislation aimed at restricting the Fed's independence. Clinton expressed his opposition to Gonzalez's efforts, saying the monetary system "is functioning well and does not need an overhaul just now."[71]

Yet even as Clinton and Greenspan sought to establish a good working relationship, both demonstrated their independence. Clinton nominated Alan Blinder and Janet Yellen to fill two Federal Reserve Board seats that came open in 1994. The appointment of these economists, who were considered to be more tolerant of inflation than Greenspan, was perceived as signaling Clinton's desire for the Fed to be more growth-oriented. For his part, Greenspan backed up the efforts of congressional Republicans to balance the budget by testifying in February 1995 that if their planned budget cuts deflated the economy, he would lower interest rates. Later that year, Greenspan also began lobbying Congress and the president to consider a reduction in the consumer price index (CPI) as a means of limiting the budget's growth.

Fed chair Ben Bernanke cooperated with Presidents George W. Bush and Barack Obama on efforts to stimulate the economy during the recession that began in 2008. Between 2008 and 2010, the Fed cut interest rates effectively to zero; directly intervened to increase the money supply through a number of actions known collectively as "quantitative easing"; and pumped about $7.8 trillion into the economy through emergency loans and asset purchases. In August 2011, with stock markets reacting wildly to the government's lengthy stalemate and deadline deal over raising the debt limit, Bernanke announced the Fed's intention to keep interest rates near zero for another two years, and expressed the possibility of another round of quantitative easing. Five months later, the Fed's published forecast predicted it would not increase interest rates until late in 2014. While a significant minority of Fed members continued to caution against the dangers of inflation, Bernanke and the Fed majority clearly saw the stagnant economy as the most pressing economic problem. This put them at odds with congressional Republicans who blocked President Obama's fiscal stimulus efforts and pushed spending reductions. The Fed acted when the elected branches could not. Texas Governor Rick Perry, a candidate for the Republican presidential nomination in 2012, called Bernanke's stimulus efforts "treasonous."[72]

HISTORICAL DEVELOPMENT OF ECONOMIC POLICY

From the beginning of the Republic presidents understood that promoting the nation's prosperity was as much a part of their job as ensuring its security and enforcing its laws. Presidents did not, however, attempt to affect the performance of the economy through spending and taxing decisions until the Great Depression of the 1930s. Before then, the classical theory of economics, associated with the writings of Adam Smith, the eighteenth-century British economist, generally prevailed. This theory held that a laissez-faire approach to economic activity—one that allowed farmers, merchants, and manufacturers to operate unencumbered by government intervention and regulation—would result in the most prosperous economic conditions. Consequently, if the economy were running smoothly, the president's economic responsibilities were limited primarily to executing the spending and revenue measures passed by Congress, promoting a balanced budget, and working with business leaders and foreign governments to expand industrial development and trade.

Economic Policy before the Great Depression

George Washington ensured that economic affairs would have a central place in his administration when he appointed Alexander Hamilton as secretary of the Treasury. Hamilton often worked independently of Washington, who seldom intervened in his Treasury secretary's projects. Hamilton recognized that the international reputation of the United States and its ability to command respect among its citizens—many of whom felt stronger loyalties to their home state than to the new federal government—depended on the government's financial stability and the vibrancy of the American economy. Hamilton, therefore, aggressively promoted the interests of merchants and manufacturers and tried to create an atmosphere of confidence through measures that included the assumption of state debts by the national government and the establishment of a national bank.

Both the federal government and the states had gone heavily into debt to finance the Revolutionary War. Congress and the states had borrowed money from virtually anyone who would lend it. The United States owed money to the French government, Dutch bankers, state treasuries, and individual holders of bonds and promissory notes. A comprehensive plan was needed that would allow the government to pay back the debts without imposing burdensome taxes on its citizens, establish good international credit, and reconcile the competing interests of its domestic creditors.

Ten days after Hamilton assumed the office of secretary of the Treasury, the House of Representatives asked him to draft a plan for the "adequate support of the public credit." Hamilton used this simple mandate to construct an ambitious plan to resolve the debt situation and bring fiscal stability to the federal government.[73]

The scope and intricacy of Hamilton's plan surprised Congress when he presented it to that body on January 14, 1790. It called for federal assumption of the $25 million in debts incurred by the states during the Revolutionary War and refunding of the national debt through various bonds and securities. Existing tariffs, which Congress eventually continued at Hamilton's urging, would provide the primary source of revenues to retire the debt gradually.

The most politically divisive aspect of the debt question was how and to what degree the federal government would assume the debts of states. Predictably, the states that had paid their wartime debts, including Georgia, Maryland, North Carolina, and Virginia, were against having the federal government take over the financial burdens of the states with large debts, while the latter, including Connecticut, Massachusetts, and South Carolina, pressed for full assumption.

Division over the assumption question initially led to rejection of Hamilton's plan by a slim margin in both houses of Congress. With Secretary of State Thomas Jefferson's help, however, a compromise was reached whereby the debt assumption bill was linked to a measure moving the capital from New York to Philadelphia for ten years and then to what would become Washington, D.C. This act placated a few southern members of Congress, who changed their votes. The bill was passed, and President Washington signed it on August 4, 1790.[74]

The election of Jefferson as president in 1800 ushered in an economic era in the United States that was dominated by agrarian interests. Jefferson and his successors, most notably Andrew Jackson, rejected the Federalist presidents' policy of concentrating the federal government's economic activities on the promotion and protection of industry and business.[75] Most economic regulatory activity and most responsibility for internal improvements that benefited commerce, such as the construction of roads, bridges, and railroads, were left to the states. Even central banking came to be considered outside the government's proper domain. Although it had refused to recharter the national bank in 1811, Congress chartered the Second Bank of the United States in 1816 after experiencing difficulties with national finance during the War of 1812. In 1832, however, Jackson vetoed the bill that would have rechartered the Second Bank of the United States. Its charter later expired in 1836. The United States went without a central bank until 1914, when the Federal Reserve System was established.

Nevertheless, the federal government did not entirely abandon business promotion. It maintained tariffs to protect industries from foreign competition, provided systems of money and patents, and in 1817 gave U.S. ships a monopoly on East Coast trade. Yet until the Civil War, the United States remained essentially an agrarian society with the proponents of agriculture dominating national politics.[76]

The Civil War brought both greater industrialization and the political division of northern and southern agrarian interests. The Republican presidents of the second half of the nineteenth century were generally conservatives who favored federal promotion of business affairs, but not federal regulation. These presidents, in cooperation with Congress, aided manufacturing and commercial interests by raising protective tariffs to new highs, giving land to railroads, and continuing to rely on regressive taxes.[77]

As the American business community grew, however, the need for regulation became more apparent. By the 1880s the power of major corporations had begun to alarm many members of the public. State governments no longer were adequate to control companies that operated in many states and functioned as monopolies. The federal government gradually responded to growing demands for regulation. In 1887 Congress passed the landmark Interstate Commerce Act, which created the first independent regulatory agency, the Interstate Commerce Commission, to regulate the nation's railroads.

In the 1890s Congress passed the Sherman Antitrust Act and other laws that gave the president and the executive branch the power to break up monopolies and otherwise regulate business activity. Presidents Theodore Roosevelt and William Howard Taft increased government prosecutions of antitrust cases and expanded other regulatory activities, setting the stage for further economic reforms under President Woodrow Wilson that would widen presidential authority over the economy.

During his first term, Wilson saw Congress enact legislation establishing the Federal Reserve System, the Federal Trade Commission, and federal aid for agriculture. Wilson also expanded the government's antitrust powers and labor regulations. When the United States entered World War I during his second term, Wilson responded with highly interventionist economic policies, such as the Lever Act of 1917, which included government management of the production, supply, and price of many commodities and government takeovers of the railroad, telephone, and telegraph industries. Although these policies ended shortly after the war, they set a precedent for government intrusion in the economy during times of crisis.[78]

Like presidents before him, Herbert Hoover believed in the conventional wisdom that public debt could undermine the economic health of the nation just as private debt could undermine a person's financial well-being. He therefore was suspicious of deficit spending programs that would have reduced the severity of the Depression. Nevertheless, in his search for an answer to the country's economic troubles Hoover did try a variety of measures, including a tax reduction, intended to put more money into the hands of the public. He quickly gave up on this approach, however, when it appeared not to be working and returned to a conservative strategy of cutting expenditures in an effort to balance the budget.[79] This policy, combined with the Federal Reserve Board's failure to expand the money supply, deepened the Depression.[80] In fact, many modern economists believe the Depression would have been limited to a severe recession had the president and the Federal Reserve Board not exacerbated the problem.

While campaigning for the presidency in 1932, Franklin D. Roosevelt did not advocate revolutionary fiscal policies. Like Hoover before him, he promised to cut expenditures and balance the budget. During the campaign Roosevelt attacked Hoover for failing to achieve a balanced budget.

Roosevelt, however, was a pragmatic leader who believed that the government should take emergency measures to fight the Depression. Once in office he initiated "New Deal" policies, government construction and relief programs that threw the federal budget into deficit. The deficit spending, however, was not a fiscal strategy designed to stimulate the economy but a byproduct of the president's decision to spend the money necessary to reduce the suffering of the poor, the elderly, and the unemployed and to begin putting Americans back to work. Indeed some federal workers were terminated within a few years. Other programs, however, including Social Security, federal credit assistance to home buyers, small businesses, and farmers, and unemployment insurance became permanent government commitments.

In May 1937, after the U.S. economy had achieved a partial recovery, a new recession confronted Roosevelt. This recession was caused in part by the Federal Reserve Board, which had again contracted the money supply in its concern about preventing inflation.[81] The president initially ignored the advice of newly converted Keynesians in his administration and attempted to cut spending in an effort to balance the budget. Roosevelt's strategy deepened the recession and solidified a consensus among his advisers in favor of government spending designed to stimulate demand. By April 1938 the president himself was convinced that greater government expenditures were needed to combat the Depression. Roosevelt continued to pay lip service to a balanced budget, but he worked to increase expenditures and accepted growing budget deficits as a necessary evil in a difficult economic period.[82] Unemployment gradually declined from its 1933 high of 25 percent to less than 15 percent in 1940.

World War II ultimately brought massive government expenditures financed by borrowing that woke the U.S. economy from the nightmare of the 1930s. Annual federal expenditures grew from just $8.8 billion in 1939 to $92.7 billion in 1945. In 1944 unemployment stood at just 1.2 percent. Most economists saw the economic results of New Deal and wartime expenditures as a validation of Keynesian theory.

Truman Administration

When Harry S. Truman succeeded to the presidency following President Roosevelt's death in April 1945, the U.S. economy was booming, and unemployment was virtually nonexistent. Many Americans feared that the economic sluggishness of the 1930s would return when the war ended, but the years following the war saw continued expansion and a relatively smooth transition from a wartime to a peacetime footing. Many women and elderly workers who took jobs during the war because labor was in short supply retired when the war ended, thus making room in the workforce for returning soldiers. The influx of GIs also created greater demand for housing and consumer goods that partially offset the decrease in demand caused by reduced government spending for defense.

Inflation was a more serious problem. Although Truman had enthusiastically supported the original version of the Employment Act, which mandated measures to achieve full employment, as president he followed a pragmatic course that often made fighting inflation the highest economic priority. After the war, inflation was fueled by consumers who demanded goods that had been in short supply during the conflict. Moreover, wartime controls had held the prices of many goods below their true value. As these price controls were lifted in 1946 and 1947, prices rose dramatically to correct the artificial imbalance. Inflation, which had been just 2.3 percent in 1945, rose to 8.3 percent in 1946 and 14.4 percent in 1947. Truman, who had vetoed one price control removal bill but reluctantly signed a second in July 1946, urged labor groups to resist price and wage hikes and sent an anti-inflation program to Congress in October 1947 that included consumer credit controls, rent controls, price ceilings on selected products, and controls over the allocation of some scarce commodities. The Republican Congress put off most of the program until the following year and then enacted only part of it.[83] Inflation fell anyway, however, declining to 8.1 percent in 1948 and then disappearing entirely in 1949 when the economy endured a recession.

In 1947 and 1948 Congress tried to force a tax cut on the president, which, it maintained, would reverse the tax-and-spend policies of Truman and of Roosevelt before him. Truman vetoed three such bills on the grounds that they would lead to budget deficits and greater inflation. Congress, however, overrode the last of Truman's vetoes in April 1948. The tax cut was timely, because the economy fell into a mild recession later in the year. The extra money in the hands of consumers stimulated demand, thereby reducing the recession's severity.

The Korean War, which began on June 24, 1950, rekindled inflationary pressures. Growing military expenditures on the war effort stimulated industrial activity. Demand for consumer goods also increased as consumers bought many items in anticipation of wartime shortages. In 1951 inflation shot back up to 7.9 percent. Congress reluctantly granted part of Truman's tax increase request and agreed to wage, price, and credit controls, which succeeded in reducing inflation to 1.9 percent in 1952 and holding it below 1 percent in 1953.

One other significant development during the Truman administration was the Accord of 1951. This agreement between the administration and the Fed allowed for greater independence in monetary policy from administration or congressional preferences. In particular, the accord furthered the Fed's autonomy to conduct restrictive monetary policies.

Eisenhower Administration

In spite of the prominence of Keynesian thought among economists, President Dwight D. Eisenhower entered office skeptical of its utility. He emphasized the traditional conservative economic priorities of balancing the federal budget, limiting government interference in the economy, and, most important, fighting inflation.[84] During Eisenhower's eight years in office, 1953–1961, he produced three budget surpluses.

Throughout his presidency, Eisenhower was willing to accept higher rates of unemployment than his Keynesian critics thought necessary. In response to a recession in 1953 and early 1954, the administration accepted some minor tax decreases and sped up government expenditures. Although the administration took credit for helping the recovery with "speedy and massive actions," the modest antirecession measures of 1954 were an exception to Eisenhower's rule of nonintervention.[85]

During his second term Eisenhower pursued an antiinflationary strategy in defiance not only of his critics but also of several of his advisers, who urged him to support a tax cut. Unemployment averaged a post-Depression high of 6.8 percent during the 1958 recession, but Eisenhower remained true to his noninterventionist principles. Moreover, he vetoed a number of spending bills during his last two years in office in pursuit of a balanced budget and low inflation.[86]

When signs of a recession appeared in the spring of 1960, Eisenhower's vice president, Richard Nixon, who was running for president that year, advocated following CEA chair Arthur Burns's advice to increase defense expenditures and loosen credit. Eisenhower, however, sided with other administration economic advisers who rejected the proposal because they did not believe the recession, if there was one, would be of sufficient magnitude to warrant government intervention.[87] Nixon undoubtedly lost votes because of the economic slump.

Although Eisenhower's stiff resistance to antirecession measures appears old-fashioned, he was successful in holding down consumer prices, which never climbed more than 4 percent in any year of his presidency.

Kennedy Administration

With the election of John F. Kennedy to the presidency in 1960, Democrats believed they could change the economic goals of the nation. Kennedy and his advisers were determined to achieve full employment and sustained economic expansion through fiscal stimulation. They hoped to be able to correct the swings of the business cycle as well as to stimulate the economy to greater growth and productivity. They were motivated by their desire to alleviate poverty and to improve medical care, education, and other social services and by their concern over the apparent rapid growth of the Soviet economy and its military expenditures.

Kennedy believed the economy never would create jobs for everyone without government stimulation. He and his advisers were confident they could direct the economy to greater prosperity. For the first time the Keynesian views of professional economists were fully applied to the political situation.[88]

In the opening months of Kennedy's term, the economy was pulling itself out of the recession that had begun in 1960. Because the budget was in deficit and inflation was a concern, Kennedy hoped that he would not have to use fiscal stimulation to achieve his employment and expansion goals. By early 1962, however, the economy had begun to slow.

Kennedy agreed with his advisers that the economy should be stimulated through increased government spending. They believed such a policy would help low-income people and be less controversial than a tax cut at a time when budget deficits persisted. When Congress resisted Kennedy's spending plans, the president responded in late 1962 by proposing a tax cut.

The president and his economic advisers attempted to sell the tax cut by promoting the concept of the "full employment budget." The administration argued that, although the government was currently running budget deficits, the greater tax revenues produced by an economy operating at full employment would result in budget surpluses. Therefore, if a tax cut could produce full employment and sustained economic expansion, it would increase government revenues, not decrease, them.[89] Kennedy lobbied Congress to pass the tax cut in 1963 but was assassinated before he could persuade lawmakers to pass the legislation.

The monetary policy of the Kennedy administration was committed to maintaining price stability. Kennedy himself, for all his considerable progrowth beliefs and comments, was wedded to the belief that "a nation was only as strong as the value of its currency."[90] Some of his advisers, in fact, felt Kennedy was too concerned about inflation.[91] Still, his advisers were not prone to support policies that would ignite a new inflation.

Throughout the administration's first year, Walter Heller and other advisers publicly pressured the Fed to lower interest rates. But this abruptly ended in early 1962. Concern about a deteriorating U.S. trade balance prompted the Kennedy administration to emphasize a tighter monetary policy (and an aggressive inflation stance) and a more expansive fiscal policy. The logic behind this was to attract foreign investment from abroad through the higher interest rates and ensure that the higher interest rates did not reduce aggregate demand.

Johnson Administration

Following Kennedy's death in November 1963, President Lyndon B. Johnson delivered an emotional speech to Congress. In that address, on November 27, 1963, he asked lawmakers to honor Kennedy by passing his civil rights bill and added: "No act of ours could more fittingly continue the work of President Kennedy than the early passage of the tax bill for which he fought all this long year." Johnson also used his legendary lobbying skills and Congress's feelings for the slain president to push the tax cut through Congress quickly. Johnson signed the Revenue Act of 1964 on February 26. It was the largest tax cut in U.S. history up to that time. The act reduced personal income taxes for 1964 and 1965 by about 20 percent and corporate taxes by 4 percent.[92]

The 1964 tax cut was a milestone in the history of U.S. stabilization policy. It was the first time the president and Congress had intentionally stimulated the economy through a tax cut while the economy was expanding. Unemployment fell from 5.7 percent in 1963 to 4.5 percent in 1965. The impressive results of the tax cut generated enthusiasm and confidence among President Johnson's economic advisers. They believed they could fine-tune the economy through Keynesian stabilization policies.

The Vietnam War, however, forced Johnson to reconsider his economic priorities. By 1966 expenditures on the war and social programs Johnson was pushing under his domestic Great Society initiative had produced a growing budget deficit and rising inflation. Johnson's advisers urged him to correct the overstimulation of the economy caused by the deficit spending through an excise tax or an increase in income taxes. Congress, however, showed no enthusiasm for a tax hike, and Johnson feared that higher taxes would erode public support for the Great Society.[93] Consequently, Johnson did not push for an income tax increase until 1967, and the task of fighting inflation was left to the Federal Reserve Board's monetary policy.

The anti-inflation monetary policy during Johnson's administration was largely determined by the fiscal policies that followed from the Kennedy-proposed tax cut, spending on Great Society programs, and military expenditures for the Vietnam War. These ambitious undertakings swelled the federal budget deficit from $1.5 billion in 1965 to $25 billion by the end of fiscal year 1968.

As a result the Fed could either provide sufficient credit to make sure that the fiscal stimulus was not choked off by higher interest rates or pursue a restrictive policy that held inflationary pressures in check. Throughout the remainder of his time in office Johnson left no doubt that he favored unrestrictive monetary policy. To achieve this goal, the administration resorted to public pressure on the Fed as well as private negotiations. In both informal and formal meetings, coordination between monetary and fiscal policy was a central topic for the rest of his term. By 1966 a tentative deal was worked out between the administration and the Fed. In exchange for a tax increase to close the deficit, the Fed would agree to keep interest rates down.

By the third quarter of 1966 the Fed again eased credit conditions. Johnson reciprocated by agreeing to reduce federal spending. The central bank continued its policy of monetary ease throughout 1967 and 1968 in the face of a rapidly expanding economy.

By 1967 Johnson recognized that he had to slow inflation and reduce the deficit. He proposed new taxes, but Congress did not pass Johnson's 1967 tax hike plan until the summer of 1968, due to congressional leaders' demands for corresponding spending reductions.[94] By that year inflation had risen to 4.2 percent from just 1.6 percent in 1965, and the deficit had expanded to $25.2 billion from only $1.6 billion in 1965. This deficit disappeared in 1969, when Johnson's 10 percent tax increase, combined with the efforts of Johnson's successor, Nixon, to cut government spending, led to the first budget surplus since 1960. This belated fiscal restraint failed, however, to eliminate the long-run inflationary pressures that had been built into the economy or the rising unemployment that was left for Nixon to combat.

Nixon Administration

Richard Nixon entered office intending to fight inflation through small spending cuts coordinated with a tight monetary policy. He hoped his incremental strategy would reduce inflation while holding unemployment near 4 percent.[95] But when he came into the White House in 1969 monetary policy issues were already framed by the onset of combined inflation and low economic growth in the late 1960s. Nixon initially encouraged the Fed to tighten monetary policy to arrest inflation but was not consistent in this course, and he was known to believe that the Fed's tight monetary policy during the 1960 presidential campaign exacerbated already weak economic conditions and contributed to his defeat by Kennedy. This ambivalence diminished prospects for a steady and consistent price stabilization policy. The ensuing upward pressure on interest rates produced dramatic losses in some parts of the economy in 1969 and 1970. In the end Nixon encouraged a shift in monetary policy emphasis that placed more weight on avoiding a major recession than on reducing inflation.

Nixon submitted a budget to Congress for fiscal 1970 that projected a small budget surplus. Congress, controlled by Democrats, trimmed some spending but refused to go along with Nixon's cuts, many of which targeted social programs. The relationship between Nixon and his many intensely partisan Democratic critics in Congress became increasingly confrontational as the president vetoed a number of appropriations bills and resorted to impounding appropriated funds.[96]

By 1970 inflation had reached 5.7 percent. Moreover, the increase in inflation was not accompanied by a corresponding decrease in unemployment, which had risen from 3.6 percent in 1968 to 4.9 percent in 1970. The worsening unemployment situation was exacerbated by the de-escalation of the Vietnam War, which brought thousands of troops back into the civilian workforce.

Congress responded to the bleak economic conditions by passing the Economic Stabilization Act of 1970. Under this act, Congress gave the president the authority to combat inflation through wage and price controls. Nixon signed the act but renounced the use of such controls, saying on June 17, 1970: "I will not take this nation down the road of wage and price controls, however politically expedient they may seem." Nixon objected to wage and price controls because he believed they were an incursion on the rights of Americans and would only postpone a burst of inflation.

In 1971, with his reelection bid less than two years away, Nixon was unwilling to fight inflation by allowing a recession as Eisenhower might have done. Early that year he

had abandoned his attempts to achieve a balanced budget and had initiated stimulative fiscal policies to combat rising unemployment, which averaged 5.9 percent for the year. Nixon, like Kennedy, justified deficit spending by arguing that the budget would be balanced if the economy were operating at full employment and output. Nixon admitted to an interviewer in January 1971, "Now I am Keynesian."[97]

Inflation, however, was the more troubling economic problem. The president was being pressured by Congress, the public, and even prominent leaders of his party to take dramatic action against inflation. On August 15, 1971, President Nixon announced that, owing to the economic crisis, he was using the authority granted to him by Congress the previous year to impose a wage and price control policy.

His "New Economic Policy" had several phases. Phase I froze wages, prices, and rents for ninety days. Phase II created a pay board and price commission that acted to limit inflation to 3 percent and wage increases to 5.5 percent per year. In January 1973 Phase III relaxed the controls, and in July of that year Phase IV replaced controls with commitments from businesses to limit price increases for a year. In April 1974 all wage and price control activity ended when Congress refused to extend President Nixon's wage and price control authority.

Initially the controls were successful and popular. Consumer prices rose 4.4 percent in 1971 but just 3.2 percent in 1972. Unemployment fell from 5.9 percent in 1971 to 5.6 percent in 1972 and 4.9 percent in 1973. The brightening economic picture helped Nixon easily win a second term as president in the November 1972 elections.

As Nixon had feared, however, the problems with wage and price controls began to surface during his second term. Shortages of some goods occurred when many manufacturers began exporting a greater share of their products overseas, where prices were higher. In addition, the numerous exemptions from the controls program that had been granted to various industries caused economic distortions. For example, grain prices had been exempted from controls while meat prices remained fixed. Consequently, high feed costs forced many meat producers to slaughter their stock, causing meat shortages and meat price increases later in the decade.

A good deal of blame can be put on Nixon's policy choices. The wage and price controls proved to be only a temporary remedy for inflation—as economic theory predicts. In addition there were numerous problems with policy implementation. For example, in 1972 the growing number of price and wage exemptions weakened the controls, and in the second half of the year the consumer price index began rising again because of the administration's overexpansive monetary policy the preceding year.

By October 1973, the economy received a severe shock when the Arab oil-producing states imposed an embargo on

During the OPEC oil crisis of 1973, President Nixon asked Americans to ration their gas consumption, especially at the pumps where often consumers were limited to only ten gallon sales for the duration of the oil embargo.

the United States in retaliation for its support of Israel during the Yom Kippur War of 1973. The price of a barrel of oil rose from less than $3 in early 1973 to between $10 and $14 in 1974. Rising oil prices, a poor 1973 harvest, and the phasing out of price controls—begun in 1973 and completed in 1974—led to a dramatic jump in inflation. Prices increased 6.2 percent in 1973 and a painful 11.0 percent in 1974. That year the Nixon administration attempted to fight inflation with more restrictive fiscal and monetary policies, but the Watergate scandal made cooperation with Congress difficult. In August Nixon resigned to avoid impeachment for his part in the Watergate affair.

Ford Administration

Like Nixon, Gerald R. Ford—Nixon's second vice president, who moved into the presidency on Nixon's resignation—assumed the office intending to fight inflation through moderate fiscal restraint supported by a tight monetary policy. The inflationary effects of the 1973 Arab oil embargo and the removal of the wage and price freeze remained strong after Ford took office. He asked Congress for a 5 percent tax surcharge on corporations and the upper class and for selected spending cuts and deferrals.[98]

A minor part of Ford's economic program, however, received the most attention. He encouraged Americans to fight inflation voluntarily by saving more, conserving energy, increasing charitable contributions, and resisting price and wage increases. The voluntary measures were to be symbolized

by "WIN" buttons, which stood for "Whip Inflation Now." The buttons were ridiculed as a symbol of the ineffectuality of the administration's policies.[99]

Ford was forced to abandon his anti-inflationary strategy in early 1975. Data showed that the economy had fallen into a deep recession in 1974 before he took office, partly as a result of the sharp rise in oil prices, which forced businesses to cut back their operations. Unemployment reached 9 percent late in the year.

Ford responded in December 1974 by signing bills to extend unemployment benefits and provide public service jobs.[100] In January 1975 he asked Congress for a temporary $16 billion tax cut and new investment tax credits for business. Congress passed a $23 billion tax cut bill in March that favored lower-income Americans; Ford agreed to the larger cut but promised to resist additional spending.[101] The tax cut, however, was enacted in March 1975 when the recession began to ease. Consequently, by the time the benefits of the cut reached Americans, the economy was already growing.[102]

During the rest of 1975 and early 1976 Ford battled Congress over economic policy, repeatedly vetoing spending measures he considered inflationary, including increases in farm-price supports, housing subsidies, and public service jobs.[103] Nevertheless, Ford signed a tax cut in December 1975 even though it did not contain the spending cuts he had demanded; this along with large unemployment compensation and welfare payments caused by the recession, increased the federal deficit to new highs of $53 billion in 1975 and $74 billion in 1976.

In early 1976 inflation leveled off, and the economy appeared to be improving just in time for Ford's reelection bid. Inflation had fallen from 11 percent in 1974 to 9 percent in 1975 and just 5.8 percent in 1976. Meanwhile, unemployment averaged 7.7 percent in 1976, which was an encouraging improvement after 8.5 percent in 1975. But it did not prove enough for Ford to win reelection in his own right. The country narrowly voted to put Carter in the White House because the incumbent was unable to overcome the recent hard times and, as well, still carried some of the burden of the disgraced Nixon administration.

Carter Administration

Jimmy Carter took over an economy that had improved slightly during the last year of the Ford administration. The Fed's tight monetary policies had brought inflation down to

5.8 percent for 1976, and Carter entered office intending to lower unemployment.

Despite these hopes, the era would be dominated by forces outside Carter's control. During the late 1960s and 1970s, several factors had combined to produce an increasingly difficult economic environment in which astute stabilization policy could not be relied on to produce prosperity. The inflationary pressures built up during the Vietnam War had not yet dissipated. In addition, the Organization of Petroleum Exporting Countries (OPEC) engineered the second major oil price hike of the decade in 1979. Oil prices increased from less than $15 a barrel in 1979 to almost $40 a barrel in 1981. Also, the growth of federal regulation during the 1970s in areas such as environmental protection, job safety, and consumer protection increased the cost of producing goods and contributed to inflation. Simultaneous with these inflationary pressures, the economy was declining in productivity relative to foreign competitors—a trend that had begun in the 1960s. Finally, the growth of federal benefit programs, especially Social Security and Medicare, had decreased the controllable portion of the budget that could be cut from year to year, nearly ensuring budget deficits in the absence of a tax increase or substantial spending cuts.[104] Although Carter was not responsible for the underlying economic conditions he faced as president, his policies did little to help the situation.

At the beginning of his presidency Carter proposed a stimulative program that included a $50 tax rebate per person. He withdrew the rebate proposal when economic statistics showed that unexpectedly strong economic growth threatened to spark a renewed surge of inflation, but much of the rest of his plan, including increased spending for jobs programs and public works, was enacted. Carter also encouraged the Fed to pursue a stimulative monetary policy that brought the biggest expansion of the money supply of any three-year period since World War II.[105] As a result, the economy continued the expansion that had begun in late 1975.

During this period, however, the public became increasingly concerned about inflation. Consumer prices had risen 7.6 percent in 1978, up from 5.8 percent in 1976. The OPEC price hike of 1979 triggered a further jump in inflation, which rose to 11.3 percent for the year. By late 1978, Carter recognized that inflation had become the nation's foremost economic problem. In November of that year, Congress approved his request to reduce and delay the tax cuts, and to adopt a program of voluntary wage and price controls.[106]

One of Carter's key economic decisions was the appointment of Paul Volcker as chair of the Federal Reserve Board in 1979. On October 6, 1979, Volcker indicated that he would use monetary policy vigorously to fight inflation. Although in the long run Volcker's contractions of the money supply were effective in bringing down inflation, the

consumer price index did not respond to the tight monetary policy in 1979 and 1980. Consequently, interest rates soared without an accompanying drop in inflation. In 1980 inflation rose to 13.5 percent, real per capita income declined 0.7 percent, and the prime lending rate of banks stood at a whopping 15.25 percent. Carter complemented Volcker's tough stand with fiscal restraint designed to combat inflation and lower the budget deficit. Just as the demands of economic management had induced a conservative Nixon to adopt the liberal tool of wage and price controls, so they led Carter to abandon his liberal goal of achieving low levels of unemployment and to adopt the traditionally conservative strategy of fighting inflation with monetary and fiscal policies while pursuing smaller budget deficits.[107] He actually proposed a balanced budget in fiscal 1981, though the projected balance was quickly undone by the deteriorating economy.[108]

However, inflation expectations were not falling as fast as hoped. For the first time since presidents began submitting an annual economic report thirty years before, Carter's 1980 report forecasted a recession. In the second quarter of that year the recession came as predicted, while double-digit inflation remained. In response to lack of downward movement in inflation and inflation expectations, the Carter administration instituted a far more draconian measure—credit controls—which had an immediate and severe effect on borrowing. As one observer, journalist William Greider, noted, this policy caused economic activity not only to slow down but also come to a crashing halt:

> The recession, long predicted by forecasters, finally began in earnest. But it was not the gradual contraction that many expected. The loss of economic activity was swift and alarmingly steep. Within three months the Gross National Product would shrink by 10 percent—the sharpest recession in thirty-five years. For a time it looked like a free-fall descent.[109]

The sharp downturn in 1980 solidified the popular perception that Carter's policies had undermined the economy.[110] Republican presidential nominee Reagan attacked Carter for producing a "misery index" (the sum of the inflation and unemployment rates) of greater than twenty. In August 1980 a CBS News/*New York Times* poll found that only 19 percent of those polled approved of Carter's handling of the economy. Although the economy's performance during the first three years of the Carter administration had not been as dismal as the public perceived, with voters convinced of the president's inability to manage economic affairs, Reagan defeated Carter in a landslide in the 1980 presidential elections.

Reagan Administration

With the nomination in 1980 of Reagan as the Republican presidential candidate, supply-side theory was thrust into the political limelight. Reagan had become a believer in supply-side theory during the late 1970s as he prepared to run for the Republican presidential nomination. Reagan had been defeated for the nomination in 1976 by incumbent Ford in part because Reagan had advocated stringent budget cuts with tax relief only possible if spending cuts succeeded in reducing the deficit.[111] Supply-side theory gave Reagan a justification for moving away from painful economic prescriptions in the 1980 campaign without abandoning his conservative philosophies about balancing the budget.

Reagan's plan held out the promise of prosperity without increased budget deficits and inflation. During Reagan's campaign for the 1980 nomination, his Republican opponent and eventual vice president, George H. W. Bush, reflected the skepticism of many economists and politicians when he labeled Reagan's supply-side strategy "voodoo economics." The American public, however, chose Reagan handily over the incumbent Carter.

Reagan entered office facing the most severe peacetime economic situation since the Great Depression. Inflation, unemployment, government spending, and average tax burdens had all risen during the 1970s.[112] To deal with this situation he had some specific policy priorities. One priority was passing the largest spending and tax cuts in U.S. history. His landslide victory enabled him to claim a mandate for his plan to cut personal income taxes by 30 percent, introduce new tax incentives for businesses, and cut nondefense expenditures sharply.

Some Democrats in Congress attacked the plan as a disguised attempt to lighten the tax burden of the wealthy while cutting back on government aid to the poor. Reagan and his advisers acknowledged that their tax cut would benefit upper-income individuals but argued that these were precisely the people who would be best able to invest their tax break in new jobs and productive capacity, thus fueling the economic expansion for everyone. Reagan's critics called this reasoning a return to a predepression Republican "trickle down" strategy in which benefits for the rich were justified on the grounds that the poor would eventually benefit from a stronger economy.

Although many Americans perceived Reagan's taxing and spending strategy as inequitable, a considerable majority of Americans supported it,[113] and his congressional allies were able to push most of the plan through Congress despite the solid Democratic majority in the House. The president signed the Economic Recovery Tax Act of 1981 in August. It reduced individual tax rates 25 percent—5 percentage points less than Reagan had wanted—over thirty-three months. In addition, the bill indexed the tax system for the first time ever to keep inflation from forcing taxpayers into higher brackets as their incomes kept pace with prices. Reagan also was successful in 1982 in pushing $35 billion in nondefense spending cuts through Congress, along with $26.5 billion in defense spending increases.

Reagan had hoped that his tax cut would create an economic boom that would bring increases in tax revenues. These increased revenues along with lower domestic spending would reduce the federal budget deficit until the budget was balanced. In 1980, while running for the presidency, Reagan had attacked Carter and the Democratic-controlled Congress for their deficit spending and promised to balance the budget by 1983. By late 1981, however, economic statistics showed that the country was entering a recession. This recession, the deepest since the Great Depression, lasted through 1982. It nearly doubled the budget deficit because reduced tax revenues were further depressed by declining industrial output and personal income, while government spending on unemployment insurance and welfare increased. Many of the spending cuts that were going to lead to a balanced budget had been left unspecified in the president's 1981 proposal, and ultimately did not materialize.

In November 1981, after less than a year in office, Reagan conceded that he probably could not balance the budget in one term. In 1982, despite his position against taxes, Reagan agreed to a tax increase initiated by the Republican-controlled Senate Finance Committee that reduced the 1981 tax cut by about a quarter, with most of the restored revenue coming out of corporate taxes.[114] Another, smaller tax increase followed in 1984.

A second priority was eliminating inflation. Reagan did not obstruct the Fed's price stabilizing policy, which had a dramatic impact on the economy. Unemployment rose from 7.4 percent in the first quarter of 1981 to nearly 11 percent by the end of the fourth quarter in 1982. But inflation was cut drastically, falling from about 13 percent in 1980 to 3.8 percent by December 1982.

By the middle of 1982, Reagan's popularity had plummeted, and the GOP faced a daunting challenge in that year's congressional elections. Republicans managed to hold their majority in the Senate but lost twenty-six seats in the House, effectively denying Reagan the working majority of Republicans and conservative Democrats that he enjoyed in his first two years in office.

Beginning in 1983 the economy began a sustained period of economic growth. Inflation stabilized and remained between 3 percent and 4 percent, and interest rates began to fall. The economic expansion would last through the decade. By 1988, the last year of Reagan's term, unemployment had dropped to just 5.5 percent.

Another priority of the Reagan administration was a balanced federal budget. On this score Reagan failed. Against the recommendation of several advisers, including budget director David A. Stockman and Chief of Staff James A. Baker, Reagan refused to consider appointing a deficit reduction commission. While he acceded to tax increases in 1982 and 1984, he helped to block a major deficit-reduction effort initiated by the Republican leadership of the Senate

Budget Committee in 1985. His "Oak Tree Agreement" with Democratic House Speaker Tip O'Neill contained no tax increases while preserving Social Security spending.[115] A 1987 budget summit with congressional leaders proposed a small amount of deficit reduction, arguably more gimmick than substance.[116] Reagan maintained through the remainder of his presidency that higher taxes would threaten economic growth and would not substantially reduce the budget deficit because Congress would find a way to spend most of the additional revenue.[117]

In addition, the president fought against cuts in defense spending. Reagan had charged that Carter had allowed the nation's defenses to deteriorate while the Soviet Union continued to pursue a massive military buildup. According to Reagan, the growing Soviet advantage in military capability threatened the security of the United States and its allies. During the early 1980s public support for a military buildup and tensions between the United States and the Soviet Union led Congress to accept many of Reagan's defense spending proposals. Military expenditures rose from 5.0 percent of gross national product (GNP) in 1980 to 6.2 percent in 1987.

George H. W. Bush Administration

George H. W. Bush's political dilemma in handling the economy was more acute than that of most new presidents because he could not repudiate the policies of his predecessor. Republican President Reagan, for example, could explain the 1982 recession by blaming conditions that he had inherited from Carter, a Democrat. But Bush had served as Reagan's vice president and had promised to extend the Reagan peacetime economic expansion.

This would not be an easy task. The Reagan expansion had begun in 1983 and had been fueled in part by large tax cuts and defense expenditures. After such a long period of sustained expansion, the business cycle could be expected soon to produce a recession. Moreover, persistently high budget deficits and the collapse of the Soviet Union would create pressure to cut government spending, especially for defense. If recession did come, Bush would have little room to combat it with an expansionary fiscal policy.

Bush complicated his political position by pledging not to raise taxes. At the 1988 Republican convention he threw out a memorable challenge to Congress that was repeatedly quoted back to him during his presidency: "Read my lips: No new taxes." The pledge made Bush appear decisive, and it sharply distinguished his economic platform from that of his Democratic opponent, Michael S. Dukakis. But with Congress firmly in the control of the Democrats and the budget deficit projected to grow, Bush's pledge reduced his capacity to govern. Only by compromising with Congress could President Bush hope to achieve a significant reduction in the deficit. But the Democratic Congress's budget priorities were targeted to benefit its constituencies, which were different from Bush's. Moreover, Democratic leaders were aware that they could wound the president politically either by forcing him to break his "no new taxes" pledge or by allowing the deficit to rise. Congress would never let Bush off the hook by approving a deficit-reduction package without a tax increase, especially when the "no new taxes" pledge had been used as a cudgel against Democrats in the 1988 election.[118]

In 1989 the Bush administration deferred serious budget discussions by releasing highly optimistic estimates of the size of near-term budget deficits. But by May 1990 it was clear to the Bush administration that the deficit would accelerate rapidly in the absence of a significant deficit reduction package. Bush indicated that month that he might accept a tax increase as part of a larger deficit-reduction package. This set in motion highly partisan budget negotiations between the president and Congress.

On June 26 Bush agreed to include tax increases in a deficit-reduction package. Negotiations made little progress, however, until September. By then Congress had the upper hand. The final budget deal passed Congress on October 28 and was signed by Bush on November 5. The five-year package was projected to reduce the budget deficit by nearly $500 billion, with a roughly two-to-one ratio of spending cuts to tax increases. Even more importantly, the deal imposed a "pay-as-you-go" procedure on Congress, requiring all spending increases to be offset by cuts elsewhere.[119]

Bush attempted to bring the public around to the budget deal by praising the deficit reduction it contained. He remarked, "I think the spending cuts, when you look at them, are good. The entitlement reform is good. The tough enforcement provisions are tougher than I ever thought we could ever get in any way out of this Congress." The Bush administration attempted to pin responsibility for the higher taxes on congressional Democrats, saying that it had been forced to pay a "ransom" of tax increases to secure congressional approval for spending cuts. But the president paid an enormous political price. Political scientist Stephen Skowronek wrote:

> Bush had made the tax pledge the linchpin of his and his party's credibility, and when he pulled it out, the reaction was swift and predictable. The reversal put Republicans in far more difficult straits than Democrats, and Bush's fellow partisans rose up in revolt, charging their leader with the "big lie."[120]

Bush could not even, in the short term, point to deficit reduction to defend his 1990 budget deal. The cost of the Persian Gulf War, the ongoing government bailout of failed savings and loan institutions, inflation in government health care programs, and increased entitlement costs arising from the recession pushed the deficit from $221.2 billion in 1990 to an all-time high of $290.4 billion in 1992. To the public, Bush's tax increases had yielded nothing.[121] The public fallout over Bush's broken pledge was less acute than it would have been had not the United States been engaged in the crisis arising from the Iraqi invasion of Kuwait. From August 2, 1990, when Iraq invaded, until February 1991, when the American-led coalition won a speedy victory, public attention was focused on the Middle East. The overwhelming success of the military operation sent President Bush's approval ratings as high as 89 percent. However, Bush could not translate this positive public sentiment into sustained support for his domestic policies.

After the war, Bush's close attention to foreign policy was perceived to come at the expense of economic policy. These perceptions, combined with a shallow but persistent recession that had begun in the summer of 1990, steadily eroded Bush's high level of support. In June 1992, fifteen months after the decisive victory in the Gulf War, a CBS News/New York Times poll showed that only 34 percent of the respondents approved of Bush's performance. Only 16 percent approved of his handling of the economy, lower than President Carter's worst rating.[122]

During late 1991 and 1992, the decline of the economy focused voters' minds on Bush's incremental style of leadership.[123] Real economic growth averaged only about 1 percent per year, and real per capita income fell. Even after the recession officially ended in mid-1991, recovery was painfully slow, with weak retail sales and low consumer confidence.[124] Unemployment peaked at 7.8 percent in June 1992, an eight-year high.

Bush was criticized in the media for doing nothing to pull the country out of recession. Given the budget problem, however, there was not much that he could do. In the 1990 budget negotiations, he had campaigned for a cut in the capital gains tax as a tool to stimulate economic growth; Democrats in Congress opposed it as a tax cut for the rich, and proposed an alternative package of middle-class tax cuts, expanded unemployment benefits, and funds for highway construction. Economists cautioned against stimulus, arguing that the economy would recover on its own, and that excessive stimulus would aggravate the budget deficit.[125]

During the last two years of Bush's presidency, Congress criticized or ignored his economic initiatives.

Presidential Power in International Economics: 1995 Mexican Financial Crisis

The extent of presidential power in the area of international economics was demonstrated in early 1995 by President Bill Clinton's response to the Mexican financial crisis. On December 20, 1994, Mexico unexpectedly devalued the peso. Concerns in the international currency markets about political instability in Mexico, and about that country's debt level and trade deficit, created strong downward pressure on the peso. The next day, the Mexican government decided to let its currency float freely. The value of the peso plummeted 40 percent within a few days.

The peso's collapse sent the American financial community into a panic. Banks that had made large loans to Mexico feared that they would take huge losses. The value of mutual funds and retirement funds that had invested in Mexico dropped sharply. Businesses in the United States that had expanded to take advantage of the prospect of increased exports to Mexico faced the possibility that Mexicans would no longer be able to afford their products and services. The Clinton administration estimated that 700,000 jobs in the United States depended on reestablishing financial stability in Mexico.

Initially, the president planned to present a financial rescue plan to Congress for its authorization. The plan would have provided $40 billion in American loans and loan guarantees to Mexico in exchange for promises of further Mexican economic reforms. Although congressional leaders of both parties voiced support for such a package, congressional vote-counters doubted that the plan had enough support to pass. Many rank-and-file House members saw a Mexican financial relief plan as an unnecessary taxpayer bailout of a corrupt government and of Wall Street brokers who had made bad investments.

Facing defeat in Congress on the plan, Clinton decided to act without congressional approval. On January 31, 1995, he announced that despite Congress's reluctance to go along with a Mexican rescue plan, the United States would provide $20 billion to Mexico in short-term loans and longer-term loan guarantees. The president also announced that he and Treasury Secretary Robert E. Rubin had secured from the International Monetary Fund and other international lending sources an additional $30 billion in loans to Mexico.

The White House also issued a joint statement by Clinton and congressional leaders saying that the president "has full authority to provide this assistance." Some critics in Congress blasted the president for bypassing Congress, but most members were relieved that they would not have to cast a politically difficult vote on the issue.

The $20 billion in loans came from the Exchange Stabilization Fund (ESF), which has about $25 billion in reserves. The primary role of the fund, which was established in 1934 by the Gold Reserve Act, has been to provide a means by which the Treasury secretary, acting with the approval of the president, could stabilize the dollar on foreign exchange markets. During the Ronald Reagan and George H. W. Bush administrations, the ESF had been used to provide small short-term loans to Latin American nations experiencing financial problems. For example, President Ronald Reagan had authorized an $825 million short-term loan to Mexico from the ESF in response to a 1982 peso crisis. But the Clinton rescue plan far exceeded previous uses of the ESF for bailouts of foreign currencies.

By early 1996 the rescue plan was generally viewed as a qualified success. Mexico had begun to repay the loans, and investment capital was returning to that country. Clinton's use of the ESF undoubtedly established a precedent that future presidents could use to address foreign financial crises of similar magnitude. The action also reaffirmed presidential primacy and flexibility in international economic policymaking.

Economic data would later reveal that the nation had pulled out of recession and had begun a strong comeback in the fourth quarter of 1992. But by that time, the voting public had made up its mind. Bush was defeated by Democrat Bill Clinton, who had promised to focus "like a laser beam" on the economy.

Clinton Administration

Bill Clinton was president during almost the entire ten-year run of the longest economic expansion in American history. The president's detractors in the Republican Party instead gave the credit to the American public and business community, as well as to the monetary policies of the Federal Reserve Board, headed by Republican Greenspan. Clinton argued that luck was only part of the equation and that his government's budgetary and economic policies provided a solid basis for the expansion.

The voters apparently sided with Clinton instead of the Republicans in 1996, returning him to office for a second term, making him the first Democrat to serve two full terms in his own right since Franklin Roosevelt more than half a century earlier.

Clinton entered office in January 1993 soon after the federal government reported a budget deficit of $290.4 billion for the 1992 fiscal year that ended just four months earlier and a national debt exceeding $4 trillion. Clinton's economic program, similar to President Bush's immediately before him, would be constrained by the necessity to address the debt problem. But, unlike Reagan's entrance into office in 1981, Clinton was the beneficiary of nearly a decade of price stability and low inflation expectations, and relatively low interest rates.

During the 1992 campaign and immediately after his election, Clinton capitalized on the public perceptions of Bush as detached from economic policy by emphasizing that he would devote himself fully to economic matters. On December 15, 1992, at the conclusion of a two-day economic policy conference in Little Rock, Arkansas, President-elect Clinton described his commitment to make economic policy his priority:

> I'm not going to stop working and our team is not going to stop working until the economic challenges have been faced and tackled, until we have given it our best shot and our best response. As long as people are out of work and children are left behind, as long as families struggle, as long as the potential of this country is not being fulfilled, we will not rest. We will explore every idea and challenge every prejudice; we won't stop looking or pushing or trying until our job is done.[126]

Clinton's claim to economic leadership was not based on economic theory or ideology; it was based on a promise to put economic management at the core of his agenda and transcend the conflicting economic goals pushed by the left and right. Clinton attempted to distance himself from both the traditional image of a Democratic Party rooted in taxing and spending and preference of conservatives to grant business and wealthy individuals lower taxes that they claimed would generate investment and jobs.[127]

Because Clinton was governing in an era of price stability, he did nothing overt to pressure the Fed for a stimulative economic package. In fact, the Fed was already moving in that direction by early 1993. More important, for the whole of his eight-year term, Clinton was to support a monetary policy that reflected in many ways the attitudes of the administrations of Kennedy in the 1960s and Reagan in the 1980s.

During Clinton's tenure in the White House, economic growth averaged 4.0 percent per year, compared with an average growth of 2.8 percent during the expansion of the 1980s. The high point was in 1997 and 1998, when the economy expanded by 4.4 percent (as measured by the real, or inflation-adjusted, gross domestic product), but the growth slowed considerably in 2000, to just 3.4 percent. Most of the slowdown occurred in the second half of 2000, when business investment (especially in high-technology equipment and software) declined sharply.

In terms of fiscal policy initiatives, Clinton's first budget proposal in early 1993 contained three major economic priorities: reducing the deficit, shifting some of the tax burden from poor Americans to wealthy Americans, and expanding public investment—especially in infrastructure, education, environmental protection, and scientific research. He had postponed a campaign promise for a middle-class tax cut out of concern for the deficit.[128]

But even with his party in control of both houses of Congress, Clinton found enactment of his budget priorities difficult. In spite of substantial changes aimed at appeasing conservative Democrats, not a single Republican in either house voted for Clinton's budget. The public investment measures were blocked by a Republican filibuster in the Senate. He was able to pass the budget by a 218–216 vote in the House and with Vice President Al Gore breaking a 50–50 tie in the Senate.[129] Clinton signed the Omnibus Budget Reconciliation Act of 1993 into law on August 10, 1993.

The budget contained little new investment, but it did shift some tax burden from the poor to the wealthiest taxpayers. It repudiated policies of the Reagan era, though with its spending cuts and attention to the deficit, it was not a traditionally liberal economic plan. It was instead a pragmatic, deficit-driven compromise for which there was little enthusiasm, even within the Democratic Party. Like the 1990 budget bill that so harmed President Bush, Clinton's budget demonstrated the constraints on presidential authority in budget matters and the central role of accommodation with Congress.[130]

Even as the economy improved, voters continued to feel anxiety. Real wages remained stagnant in spite of declining unemployment. Some of this anxiety was reflected in growing protectionist sentiments. Clinton had achieved some of his most notable legislative successes in free trade, as he led successful bipartisan campaigns to push the North American Free Trade Agreement and the General Agreement on Tariffs and Trade through Congress. Yet large segments of the public, especially labor unions and the followers of billionaire presidential candidate H. Ross Perot, distrusted these agreements. (See "Trade Policy," p. 319.)

This undercurrent of economic anxiety contributed to the stunning Republican landslide in the 1994 congressional elections. The Republican victory, in which the GOP won control of both houses in Congress for the first time since 1953 when Eisenhower became president, defied the conventional wisdom that incumbent parties do well when the economy is growing. At the beginning of 1995 the Clinton administration faced what no Democratic administration had faced since Truman: a Republican-controlled Congress. Republicans, led by Speaker Newt Gingrich of Georgia, proposed revolutionary changes, including the achievement of a balanced budget in seven years, the enactment of a significant tax cut, and the passage of a balanced budget amendment and the line-item veto. Most of it came to naught, as Clinton demonstrated once again the power of the presidency to control the public debate and issue agenda even while compromising with adversaries.

During the summer of 1995, Clinton surprised many of his Democratic allies by repudiating the budget he had submitted to Congress earlier that year and embracing a plan to balance the budget in ten years. Although Clinton voiced his opposition to GOP priorities and the pace of the budget cuts, his endorsement of a balanced budget validated the goal of reaching balance within a prescribed time. By the fall, Clinton had indicated he might accept a seven-year balanced budget bill. He rejected, however, the Republicans' choice of spending cuts and the inclusion of tax cuts in the budget.

These differences led to one of the severest budget standoffs in American history. On November 20, 1995, Congress passed the fiscal 1996 budget reconciliation bill that was estimated to balance the budget in seven years. It would have cut $894 billion over that period by slowing the growth of entitlements and mandating cuts in future appropriations for discretionary programs. It also included a $245 billion tax cut. As expected, President Clinton vetoed this bill on December 6, claiming that it cut programs for the needy too deeply; made unsound programmatic reforms in Medicare, Medicaid, welfare, farm subsidies, and environmental programs; and contained an overly generous tax cut. This theme was to be repeated frequently in budget and tax battles between Clinton and the Republican Congress in the president's second term.

In January 1996 House Speaker Gingrich and Senate Majority Leader Bob Dole, R-Kans., began leading their party away from the shutdown strategy. By the end of April—seven months into the fiscal year—President Clinton and Congress finally agreed to a compromise on the final 1996 appropriations bill, essentially ending the crisis.[131]

Thus the stage was set for the fully unexpected accommodations the two parties made early in Clinton's second term that produced the structure for long-range budget savings. Although the outcome—an end to budget deficits—was pushed along by the unprecedented prosperity of the 1990s that saw tax revenues soar, the acceptance by both parties of achieving budget discipline proved to be a primary legacy of the odd combination of a Democrat in the White House and a Republican majority on Capitol Hill. The end of fiscal year 1997 showed a budget deficit at a level (as a percent of the gross domestic product) not seen since 1970. The $22 billion deficit was less than one-tenth of the deficits run at the beginning of the Clinton administration.[132] The last three years of the Clinton administration saw three consecutive surpluses. The achievement demonstrated the malleability of the American political process and the unexpected dexterity of Clinton and his GOP counterparts on the Hill.

But it was a peace of the moment between the parties that faded in Clinton's final years, which were characterized by deadlock with Congress and repeated vetoes that each party seemed to welcome to define its approach to economic policy. The budget surpluses, as welcome as they were, spawned more fundamental controversy between Democrats and Republicans about how to spend the surplus. Clinton's suggested priorities were "saving" the financially troubled Social Security system and paying off the national debt, which stood close to $6 trillion. Congressional Republicans pressed instead for tax cuts for individuals and businesses. Public opinion polls showed that the voters generally sided with Clinton, and Congress eventually set aside much of the early surpluses to pay off the debt. During fiscal years 1998–2000, the government bought back $363 billion in debt, saving tens of billions of dollars in long-term interest.

George W. Bush Administration

Texas governor George W. Bush, the son of President George H. W. Bush, who held office from 1989 to 1993, inherited a vastly improved economic situation. Not since the Kennedy administration in the early 1960s did an incoming president have price stability, relatively low unemployment, and a total federal spending level at about 18 percent of the gross domestic product. However, there was evidence that the U.S. economy was slowing down.

In monetary policy, the Fed was easing back to create lower interest costs. This policy pattern continued throughout all of 2001. On the fiscal side, President Bush had campaigned in 2000 largely on a tax cut. His argument during the campaign, which expressed standard Republican thinking,

After terrorists hijacked four commercial airliners, crashing two into the World Trade Center in New York City, one into a field in rural Pennsylvania, and one into the Pentagon outside Washington, D.C., on September 11, 2001, the demand for air travel immediately declined. Congress and the Bush administration provided federal aid to the airline industry and other industries, such as tourism, that were affected by the attacks. One week later, the Continental Airlines ticket counter at the Orlando International Airport in Orlando, Florida, the largest tourist destination in the world, was practically empty.

was that a tax cut was a way to give the predicted generous federal budget surpluses back to the taxpayers.[133] But by early 2001 the Bush administration was also making the traditional supply-side and Keynesian arguments on the utility of the tax cut.[134]

With Congress under narrow but firm Republican control following the 2000 elections, and a Republican in the White House, a major tax-reduction package was all but guaranteed. Over vigorous Democratic opposition, Congress passed a huge tax-reduction plan that would cost $1.35 trillion dollars over a ten-year period. The lowest tax rate was cut to 10 percent from 15 percent and the top rate to 35 percent from 39.6 percent. Democrats argued that the size of the reduction in federal revenues would deprive the government of needed funds for programs for years to come. The final package was similar to the bills the previous Congress had sent to President Clinton, who vetoed almost all of them.[135]

Economists noted that the legislation would not provide an immediate stimulus because many provisions would take effect only later in the decade. For example, the high-profile tax rate reductions were scheduled to phase in gradually in 2001, 2004, and 2006.[136] The bill did provide an immediate tax rebate to approximately 96 million taxpayers that for married couples generally totaled $600, with lesser amounts to single persons and heads of households. There were additional concerns about the distributional effects of the tax cuts, which were heavily slanted toward upper-income brackets.[137]

On September 11, 2001, the entire calculus of government policy, including the role of president as chief economist, changed with the terrorist attacks on the United States. In successfully hijacking four commercial airliners, and flying three of them into major U.S. buildings—two into New York

City's World Trade Center towers and the third into the Pentagon outside Washington, D.C. (a fourth crashed in rural Pennsylvania)—the terrorists set the Bush administration and the government on a war footing.

The response to the attacks of September 11 displayed a mix of fiscal and monetary policy to ensure economic stability. The Bush administration's reactions were a classic response to both the immediate challenges following the attacks and the longer-term problems resulting from the mild recession that had set in after the long economic boom of the 1990s. In either case, the government's actions were focused on an expansionary fiscal and monetary policy.

In the aftermath of the attack, the airline industry all but collapsed for a time, spreading economic trouble to industries that depended either directly or indirectly on air travel such as tourism. Within a week after the attack an estimated 100,000 jobs in the airline industry alone were eliminated. But many other segments of the economy slowed as uncertainty about the future spread.

Congress and the administration quickly considered a variety of legislation to help industries, particularly airlines, and workers most hurt by the economic effect of the terrorist attacks. The total figure for all assistance, including the airline aid, was nearly $40 billion, which was to be dispensed by no fewer than seventeen federal agencies or departments. The vigorous U.S. military response that got under way within months promised substantial additional defense spending down the road.

The expansionary fiscal policy reflected in these new government expenditures was bolstered by an expansionary monetary policy. From January to September 2001 the Fed cut interest rates eight times, dropping the level from 6.5 percent to 3.0 percent. Subsequent reductions in interest rates

On May 16, 2011, the U.S. hit its debt ceiling. President Obama made repeated calls for both Republicans and Democrats to work together to solve America's budgetary and economic problems. Setting an example, President Obama, along with Vice President Biden, meets with Republican Congressional leaders, Speaker of the House John Boehner (left), and House Majority Leader Eric Cantor (right).

lowered the federal funds rate to 1.0 percent by May 2004. The moves by the Fed, which were under way in response to slowing economic activity even before the attacks, were the most expansionary since the recession of 1991.

Bush's expansionary policies led to large budget deficits for the period 2001–2006, which helped to cushion the economic slowdown. The recession of 2000–2001 was one of the mildest on record. By the election year of 2004, GDP was growing at an average rate of 4.4 percent. The unemployment rate, which had peaked at 6.3 percent in June of 2003, was at 5.4 percent in November of 2004. This downward trend would continue after Bush's 2004 reelection. The unemployment rate dropped to 4.7 percent by the summer of 2006.[138] In the longer run, however, the deficits and lost revenue left the government in a vulnerable position when a severe recession arrived in 2008.[139]

Two events occurred in late August and September 2005 that had immediate economic consequences. Hurricanes Katrina and Rita devastated the Gulf of Mexico coast. The hardship was palpable. Nearly 800,000 workers were separated from their jobs, unemployment among evacuees was nearly 12 percent by year's end, and the value of the homes destroyed was estimated to be more than $60 billion.[140] Besides the human cost, there was also immediate harm done to energy production in the Gulf: the fourth quarter of 2005 saw total U.S. natural gas production fall by 10 percent because of the devastation in the area. Oil extraction in the United States fell by 1.08 million barrels a day in the third quarter and by 0.7 million barrels in the fourth quarter of 2005.

Another economic challenge—with longer term ramifications—that the Bush administration was forced to

wrestle with was the rising cost of energy on world markets. The rapid expansion of China and India meant that the world demand for oil was going to continue its upward trend. The effects of the Hurricanes Katrina and Rita merely reinforced the effect on supply. But the trends were clear. In 2004 consumer energy prices went up 18 percent and in 2005 by an additional 21 percent. Spending on energy goods and services jumped from 4.2 percent of personal disposable income in 2002 to 6.0 percent in 2005. This meant an additional $700 of the average household's budget was being diverted to energy expenditures.

The effect of the higher energy prices also put the Federal Reserve in a bind. On the one hand, the higher energy prices could reduce demand in the economy. On the other hand, it could also lead the Fed to pursue overly stimulative policies to help counteract the slowdown. This was the policy error made in the 1970s, and it was unlikely the Fed would make the same mistake twice. While inflation had tripled from 2001 to 2006 to nearly 4 percent (on an annual rate), the Fed had responded since 2004 by raising the federal funds rate from 1.0 percent to 5.25 percent by the fall of 2006. The Fed was erring on the side of price and inflation stability.

The Great Recession and the Obama Administration

The shape of the American economic policy debate drastically changed in 2008 with the onset of the most severe slowdown since the 1930s. Prior to that, as discussed above, there was widespread preference for neoclassical theories that discouraged government intervention. The consensus was that whatever economic stabilization might be needed could be supplied more effectively by the deft monetary touch of the Federal Reserve Board than by the fiscal approaches of the elected branches.[141] Liberal and conservative disagreement over tax rates, income inequality, and the intensity of business regulation occurred within that broader consensus; the Bush administration tended to take conservative positions, guided by free market philosophy as well as political ties to affected firms.[142]

The 2008 recession, however, necessitated a different approach, as it breached the capacities of both market and monetary mechanisms. The crisis began in the housing market, where prices began to collapse in mid-2007 after rising rapidly earlier in the decade. By early 2008 investors became aware that many loans had been imprudently made to homeowners with no hope of repaying them. Investment in mortgage-backed securities put financial institutions at risk, leading to the collapse or restructuring of five major financial firms.[143] On September 15, 2008, the money market firm Lehman Brothers declared bankruptcy after the Treasury Department and Federal Reserve announced the government would not provide them financial assistance as they had to Bear Stearns in March; this led to a collapse in investor confidence and a sharp decline in stock prices, which by year's end had lost one-third of their January 1 value.[144] The already wobbly economy melted down, with gross domestic product dropping 6.8 percent in the fourth quarter of 2008, and all other economic indicators sharply negative.[145] The monetary toolbox was quickly exhausted: the Federal Reserve lowered the federal funds rate throughout 2008, until it was effectively zero in December.[146]

The Bush administration responded by steadily shifting toward more aggressive countercyclical policies. Early in 2008, the president and Congress agreed on a substantial package of fiscal stimulus including individual income tax credits and rebates; tax incentives for business equipment purchases; and regulatory change allowing federal housing agencies to take on larger mortgages.[147] As the economy continued to worsen, Bush's policies became more aggressive. He asked for, and Congress approved, authority to pump money into Fannie Mae and Freddie Mac, the government-sponsored home lending agencies. Treasury Secretary Henry Paulson proposed the Troubled Asset Relief Program (TARP), a $700 billion fund to assist financial institutions in danger of failing. After an initial defeat in the House of Representatives, the program was passed by Congress in October. Tactics shifted as the crisis continued to worsen. Initially intending to purchase troubled assets from banks, the Treasury Department decided instead to buy shares of bank stock and encourage buyouts of weak banks. Later, when Bush sought to provide financial help to auto manufacturers to help them avoid bankruptcy, the measure was blocked by a Senate filibuster, so he used money from TARP to accomplish the same purpose.[148]

When Barack Obama took office in January 2009, there was no question that his administration would take exceptionally strong action to deal with the teetering economy. There was broad consensus among politicians as well as economists that dramatic action was needed, though they disagreed over whether government spending or tax reduction was the preferred method. Obama's strategic approach was pragmatic; like Franklin Roosevelt in the Great Depression, Obama was willing to try anything that would work. Christina Romer, chair of the Council of Economic Advisers, called him "A moderate, middle-of-the-road guy. . . . He worked to fix what we have, not throw it out and start over. To the extent that he had to take emergency action, it was born of circumstances."[149] In contrast to his predecessor, Obama appointed centrist experts to top economic policy posts; these included, besides Romer, Timothy Geithner of the Federal Reserve Board as Treasury secretary, former Treasury secretary Lawrence H. Summers as director of the National Economic Council, and Peter Orszag as director of the Office of Management and Budget. While their qualifications were unquestionable, they did not always work together well, and in time Obama largely relied on Geithner and Summers.[150]

Obama's fiscal approach was even more aggressive and more improvised than Bush's had been. During the transition, he charged his economic team with designing a substantial plan to create jobs and prevent "a deflationary spiral."[151] He presented the broad outlines of his proposal in meetings with congressional leaders of both parties before his inauguration: a mixture of spending programs and tax cuts, including $500 for low- and middle-income taxpayers, business cuts, spending on public works projects such as transportation and energy efficiency, and substantial transfer payments to state governments.[152] The overall package was smaller than many economists recommended, and Senate leaders had to scale back spending further in order to win enough moderate Republican votes to overcome a filibuster. Still, the final version of the American Recovery and Reinvestment Act, signed by Obama February 17, 2009, carried a hefty estimated total cost of $787 billion.[153] In March Geithner announced an additional, complicated program of financial aid to banks and homeowners along with stress tests for banks seeking to leave TARP supervision. Obama had approved it, while rejecting calls from economists outside the administration for even more aggressive action such as seizing control of the most troubled banks.[154] The administration also used its financial leverage over General Motors and Chrysler to require the companies to restructure.

With his policies enacted, but their benefits as yet largely imperceptible to the public, Obama soon found himself on the defensive about the economy. This exemplifies the risks presidents run when they aggressively intervene. Economists largely credited the stimulus with averting economic catastrophe and positively assessed its impact on jobs. The economy began to grow in the third quarter of

2009 and grew by 2.6 percent in 2010. The financial industry was stabilized, with most of the "bailout" money repaid.[155] But if the economy was less awful than it would otherwise have been, it was little consolation to an anxious public. Joblessness remained high: the official unemployment rate topped 10 percent in October 2009, remained above 9 percent well into 2011, and surely understated the true extent of the problem. Consumer confidence surveys showed persistently low results, and vast majorities of survey respondents believed the country was on the "wrong track."

Moreover, the massive stimulus had contributed to huge budget deficits that were an obvious point of vulnerability for the president. Most of the deficits resulted from revenue losses from the sour economy, as well as policies undertaken before Obama had become president—large supply-side tax cuts in 2001 and 2003, a prescription drug benefit added to Medicare in 2003, and lengthy military involvements in Iraq and Afghanistan.[156] However, the public saw the $1.4 trillion deficit in fiscal 2009, nearly three times larger in current dollars than any previous deficit, as inextricably linked with Obama's aggressive fiscal stimulus. They were less likely to perceive any personal benefit from the stimulus: Obama's tactic of hiding the 2009 tax cuts through reduced withholding instead of rebate checks so that people would be more likely to spend them proved too clever by half, as only 10 percent of the public in September 2010 was aware of the tax cuts.[157]

Obama's Republican opponents seized control of the policy dialogue. Republican political candidates, along with a burgeoning tax protest movement calling itself the Tea Party, pointed repeatedly to the deficit and unemployment numbers as evidence that Obama's management was making the economy worse. Further fiscal stimulus was thwarted by deficit consciousness. The Senate blocked three stimulus measures in 2010 that contained individual and business tax cuts as well as unemployment benefit extensions and some public works spending.[158]

Obama made several major policy concessions to Republicans as his political position weakened. He agreed in December 2010 to extend the expiring tax cuts from the Bush years, because that was the price of extending unemployment benefits, and any other form of stimulus was out of the question. "The president wanted to lower unemployment but didn't see a way to get more money out of Congress," one adviser admitted. "He grew frustrated because the economic team didn't have that magic combination."[159] He shifted his rhetorical emphasis from job creation to deficit reduction, as early as his 2010 State of the Union address, when he proclaimed, contrary to any economic theory, "families across the nation are tightening their belts and making tough decisions. The federal government should do the same."[160] In February 2010 he appointed a presidential advisory Commission on Fiscal Responsibility and Reform, chaired by former Republican senator Alan Simpson and

former Democratic presidential adviser Erskine Bowles; its "Co-Chairs' Proposal" received a great deal of positive attention, although it did not immediately result in legislation or presidential proposals.[161] In early 2011 Obama agreed to a series of spending cuts in negotiations with congressional Republicans—newly in control of the House after enormous gains in the midterm elections—over appropriations bills, in hopes of defusing the deficit issue. A White House statement after passage admitted that "the administration would not have agreed to many of these cuts under better fiscal circumstances, [but] the bill reflects a compromise that will help the federal government live within its means while protecting those investments that will help America compete for new jobs."[162] Obama remained on the defensive through 2011, as a lengthy struggle with congressional Republicans over a bill to raise the debt limit resulted in an August deal calling for substantial spending cuts with no revenue increases. Congress and the president did achieve agreement on extending a payroll tax cut through 2012, as well as a partial extension of unemployment benefits. Meanwhile, the economy showed signs of improvement, with unemployment falling to just above 8 percent in mid-2012, giving rise to cautious optimism among administration officials, economists, and investors. Even so, most estimates assumed it would be a matter of years before economic health returned to prerecession levels.[163]

FUTURE CHALLENGES

Controlling Entitlement Spending

Presidents hoping to limit government spending must face the fiscal difficulties brought by the expenditures that are required from year to year by existing law. These are known as *entitlements* or uncontrollable budgetary items. Although the term "uncontrollable" is somewhat misleading because these programs can be changed by an act of Congress, it does accurately describe the lack of power presidents have over these items in any given year. Entitlements pose a special problem for presidents because the payments are not based on a yearly congressional appropriation or the government's ability to pay for them. They continue from year to year unless a law is passed that supersedes or alters the measure that created them. Moreover, in 1974 Congress established cost-of-living increases for Social Security payments, thereby ensuring that these benefits would not be reduced by the eroding effects of inflation.[164]

Before the Great Depression, most of the federal budget was devoted to the costs of running the government and, in times of war, the costs of the military. With the establishment of Social Security in the 1930s, however, the government began making large-scale payments directly to people who qualified for them. These entitlements now include Medicare, Medicaid, welfare, job training assistance, student loan guarantees, food stamps, school lunches, farm subsidies, unemployment compensation, and federal retirement benefits. They are intended to alleviate suffering and poverty, promote the health and advancement of individuals, and provide a safety net for those members of society who cannot provide for themselves because of economic recession, poverty, old age, or physical infirmity. Some of these entitlement programs, such as welfare and unemployment insurance, also act as automatic economic stabilizers because they increase the amount of money in the hands of the public when the economy goes into recession.[165]

The ability of presidents to propose significant cuts in the budget from year to year has been reduced as federal entitlements have claimed a greater portion of the budget. In 1963 entitlement spending accounted for 22.6 percent of the budget. By fiscal year 1983 it had risen to 45.2 percent of the budget. This upward trend continues as entitlement spending is now more than 50 percent of the budget.

Predictably, presidents and Congress have been hesitant to assume the political risk of significantly reducing entitlement programs as the capacity of the government to pay for them has fallen. The growth of entitlements has been accompanied by an increase in the activities of interest groups that attempt to protect these payments from cutbacks. Lobbyist organizations representing senior citizens, veterans, farmers, and other groups can pressure the president or members of Congress to protect benefits for their constituents by offering or withholding campaign contributions, threatening them with negative publicity, and mobilizing blocs of voters that can make or break their candidacies. The activities of these lobbyists and the negative public reaction to cuts in entitlements received by tens of millions of Americans have made large sections of the budget politically dangerous to touch.[166]

Presidents seeking to reduce government spending in a particular year, therefore, can search for cuts in only a fraction of the budget. According to political scientists Kim Quaile Hill and John Patrick Plumlee, this trend has diminished presidential budgetary power: "Presidential budgetary discretion has been significantly eroded. . . . The President in fact must propose and defend a budget much of which is determined elsewhere and in prior years."[167]

Health Care

Rapidly rising costs of health care represent a major economic challenge. Since 1980, health care costs rose several times faster than the overall rate of inflation, increasing from 9.2 percent of GDP to 17.6 percent in 2009.[168] Both the rate of growth and the amount of spending are vastly higher in the United States than in other industrialized countries. These costs have been borne by governments at all levels, where they consume an enormous proportion of annual budgets; by businesses that provide health insurance to their workers; and by individuals who pay an increasing percentage

of their income for health care, or may be shut out of the health care market altogether. (About 22 percent of Americans aged eighteen to sixty-five lacked access to health insurance in 2009.[169]) In 2010 Congress and President Obama achieved passage of the Patient Protection and Affordable Care Act, which was designed to provide access to insurance for 30 million Americans through a variety of subsidies and mandates. The new law drew intense opposition from conservatives—no Republicans supported it on the House or Senate floors—and may not survive constitutional challenges or repeal efforts in the next Republican presidential administration. Still, whoever is president cannot ignore this problem.

Health care inflation has a number of causes, as well as an unusually wide variety of affected interests. This complexity has made finding solutions especially difficult. The leading factors contributing to rising health care costs are:[170]

- Rapidly developing medical technology allows for a higher number of medical procedures, and hospitals have overinvested in technology as they compete for patients;
- People are living longer and encountering more health problems as a matter of course;
- The cost of procedures has increased, as has compensation for health care providers;
- *First-dollar insurance* has made patients with coverage less cost-sensitive than they might otherwise be; and
- The costs of malpractice litigation, at least in some states, have arguably led to overtreatment as doctors seek to protect themselves from future lawsuits.

The two most common strategies for overcoming these challenges are government regulation of health care provisions, such as allocating resources within a centralized health care budget; or increasing competition, as with the Affordable Care Act's creation of insurance-purchasing exchanges.[171]

Any changes to the health care system must address the interests of businesses that provide employee health care benefits, businesses that do not provide such benefits, physicians, hospitals, pharmaceutical companies, insurance companies, and possibly organized labor.[172] Theodore R. Marmor and his coauthors note that any policy attempt to control health care inflation "would cost providers . . . much more than it would benefit patients."[173] This certainly complicates the policy process, as witness the often-unpalatable negotiations over the 2010 health reform.[174] It would complicate any future reform efforts as well.

Employment

Future presidents and Congresses will need to address changes in employment. The recession of 2008–2009 highlighted several uncertainties that hang over the employment market in the new economy.[175] Traditional blue-collar jobs have for decades been disappearing, replaced by technology or exported to foreign countries where labor costs are considerably cheaper. There has been a growth in low-skill service sector jobs that, on the whole, pay less well and offer fewer if any benefits. The nature of even white-collar employment is changing: few college-educated workers can expect to work in the same field for their entire working lives, much less for the same employer. This puts a premium on self-marketing, as well as meaning longer spells of unemployment for many workers. Economic recoveries have been increasingly slow and flat, leading to common use of the phrase "jobless recovery." At the same time, disparities in income and wealth have increased dramatically since the 1970s, creating an economic divide between haves and have-nots.[176] U.S. Census Bureau data reported in September 2011 showed median household income had fallen, and poverty risen, throughout the previous decade, even during a six-year period (2001–2007) of economic growth. Economist Lawrence Katz called it "truly a lost decade."[177]

Whatever the future direction of the economy, many Americans are likely to experience employment insecurity, particularly later in their working lives. Presidents frequently will face high levels of unemployment and underemployment in America as a whole, as well as among those in formerly industrial regions, nonwhites, the poor, the less-well-educated, and the youngest and oldest workers. Responding to these developments will test the policy creativity of elected officials. Hacker and Pierson suggest stronger unions among other ideas,[178] but political support for such a policy seems a distant prospect. Education is often touted as the vehicle for equality of opportunity, but educational outcomes tend to reflect inequalities among individuals instead of reducing them.[179] Employment programs have had some success with retraining workers, but their broad record has been mixed.[180] Protectionist trade policies and anticompetitive regulations, by adding inefficiencies to the economy, probably do more harm than good.[181] Economic policymaking is never easy for very long, but the twenty-first century promises to be especially challenging.

★

NOTES

1 Clinton Rossiter, *The American Presidency*, 2d ed. (New York: Harcourt Brace, 1960), 21.

2 Samuel J. Kernell, *Going Public: New Strategies for Presidential Leadership*, 4th ed. (Washington, D.C.: CQ Press, 2007).

3 Robert C. Wood, *Whatever Possessed the President?: Academic Experts and Presidential Policy, 1960–1988* (Amherst: University of Massachusetts Press, 1993), 21.

4 Rossiter, *The American Presidency*, chap. 1; Richard E. Neustadt, *Presidential Power and the Modern Presidents: The Politics of Leadership from Roosevelt to Reagan* (New York: Free Press, 1990), chap. 1.

5 Peter Baker, "The White House Looks for Work," *New York Times Magazine*, January 19, 2011, www.nytimes.com/2011/01/23/magazine/23-Economy-t.html.

6 Quoted in Francis Russell, *The Shadow of Blooming Grove* (New York: McGraw-Hill, 1968), 559.

7 Charles Morris, "It's Not the Economy, Stupid," *Atlantic Monthly*, July 1993, 50.

8 Hugh S. Norton, *The Quest for Economic Stability: Roosevelt to Reagan* (Columbia: University of South Carolina Press, 1985), 199–207.

9 Susan M. Collins, "Economic Integration and the American Worker: An Overview," in *Imports, Exports, and the American Worker*, ed. Susan M. Collins (Washington, D.C.: Brookings, 1998), 36–37.

10 Graham Wilson, "Bush II and the World," in *The George W. Bush Presidency: Appraisals and Prospects*, ed. Colin Campbell and Bert A. Rockman (Washington, D.C.: CQ Press, 2004), 309–310.

11 James P. Pfiffner, "The Crisis of Confidence in U.S. Economic Policy," in *The President and Economic Policy*, ed. James P. Pfiffner (Philadelphia: Institute for the Study of Human Issues, 1986), 2.

12 John Harwood, "Voters Want a Change Politicians Can't Deliver," *New York Times*, August 8, 2011, A10.

13 David M. Anderson and Michael Cornfield, eds., *The Civic Web: Online Politics and Democratic Values* (Lanham, Md.: Rowman and Littlefield, 2003).

14 Morris P. Fiorina, Samuel J. Abrams, and Jeremy C. Pope, *Culture War? The Myth of Polarized America* (New York: Pearson-Longman, 2006).

15 Lawrence R. Jacobs, "The Presidency and the Press: The Paradox of the White House Communications War," in *The Presidency and the Political System*, 9th ed., ed. Michael Nelson (Washington, D.C.: CQ Press, 2010), 236–263.

16 Louis Fisher, *The Politics of Shared Power: Congress and the Executive*, 3d ed. (Washington, D.C.: CQ Press, 1993), 177–178.

17 James E. Anderson, *Politics and the Economy* (Boston: Little, Brown, 1966), 123.

18 Aaron Wildavsky, *The New Politics of the Budgetary Process*, 2d ed. (Berkeley: University of California Press, 1992), 64–66.

19 Norton, *Quest for Economic Stability*, 72–78; Herbert Stein, *Presidential Economics: The Making of Economic Policy from Roosevelt to Clinton*, 3d rev. ed. (Washington, D.C.: American Enterprise Institute, 1994), chap. 3.

20 Stein, *Presidential Economics*, 77; Anthony S. Campagna, *U.S. National Economic Policy, 1917–1985* (New York: Praeger, 1987), 196.

21 Norton, *Quest for Economic Stability*, 78–84.

22 Charles E. Jacob, "Macroeconomic Policy Choices of Postwar Presidents," in *The President and Economic Policy*, ed. James P. Pfiffner (Philadelphia: Institute for the Study of Human Issues, 1986), 69.

23 Walter W. Heller, *New Dimensions of Political Economy* (Cambridge, Mass.: Harvard University Press, 1966), 1.

24 Stein, *Presidential Economics*, 322, refers to a "vacuum in economic policy." For an economic diagnosis of the failure of Keynesianism, see G. Calvin Mackenzie and Saranna Thornton, *Bucking the Deficit: Economic Policymaking in America* (Boulder: Westview, 1996), 31–32.

25 William R. Keech, *Economic Politics: The Costs of Democracy* (Cambridge: Cambridge University Press, 1995), 28–29.

26 Keech, *Economic Politics,* 33–41; Thomas J. Sargent and Neal Wallace, "Rational Expectations, the Optimal Monetary Instrument, and the Optimal Money Supply Rule," *Journal of Political Economy* 83 (April 1975): 241–254.

27 Campagna, *U.S. National Economic Policy,* 485–488.

28 See, for example, Paul Krugman, *Peddling Prosperity* (New York: Norton, 1994); Stein, *Presidential Economics,* chap. 7; Campagna, *U.S. National Economic Policy,* 487–491. For a more positive assessment, see Lawrence Lindsey, *The Growth Experiment: How the New Tax Policy is Transforming the U.S. Economy* (New York: Basic Books, 1990).

29 John W. Sloan, *The Reagan Effect: Economics and Presidential Leadership* (Lawrence: University Press of Kansas, 1999), esp. 228–231; see also Joseph J. Hogan, "Reaganomics and Economic Policy," in *The Reagan Presidency: An Incomplete Revolution?,* ed. Dilys M. Hill, Raymond A. Moore, and Phil Williams (New York: St. Martin's, 1990), 150–156, on the budget and trade deficits.

30 For more on the Fed, see Irwin L. Morris, *Congress, the President and the Federal Reserve: The Politics of American Monetary Policy-Making* (Ann Arbor: University of Michigan Press, 2000); David M. Jones, *Unlocking the Secrets of the Fed: How Monetary Policy Affects the Economy and Your Wealth-Creation Potential* (New York: Wiley, 2002); Martin Mayer, *Fed: The Inside Story of How the World's Most Powerful Financial Institution Drives the Markets* (New York: Penguin, 2002); and John T. Wooley, *Monetary Politics: The Federal Reserve and the Politics of Monetary Policy* (Cambridge: Cambridge University Press, 1984).

31 Michael D. Reagan, "The Political Structure of the Federal Reserve System," *American Political Science Review* 55 (1961): 64–76.

32 The "Taylor Principle" recommends increasing interest rates by a higher percentage than the rise in inflation. See Michael Woodford, "The Taylor Rule and Optimal Monetary Policy," *American Economic Policy* 91:2 (2001), 232–237; Richard Clarida, Jordi Gali, and Mark Gertler, "Monetary Policy Rules and Macroeconomic Stability: Evidence and Some Theory," *Quarterly Journal of Economics* 115:1 (2000), 147–180.

33 Paul Peretz, "The Politics of Fiscal and Monetary Policy," in *The Politics of American Economic Policy Making,* ed. Paul Peretz (Armonk, N.Y.: Sharpe, 1987), 149.

34 Steven Sloan, "Doubts Surface about the Fed's Dual Mandate," *CQ Weekly,* November 22, 2010, 2702; Annie Lowrey, "End the Fed?: Actually, Maybe Not," *Slate,* February 9, 2011 www.slate.com/id/2284503/.

35 Paul Volcker and Toyoo Gyohten, *Changing Fortunes* (New York: Times Books, 1992), 176.

36 Arthur M. Johnson, *The American Economy* (New York: Free Press, 1974), 52.

37 John F. Witte, "The President vs. Congress on Tax Policy," in *The President and Economic Policy,* ed. James P. Pfiffner (Philadelphia: Institute for the Study of Human Issues, 1986), 166.

38 Emmet J. Hughes, *The Living Presidency* (Baltimore: Penguin, 1974), 216–217.

39 Witte, "President vs. Congress," 180.

40 "GOP Offers Party-Defining Tax Cut Proposal; Clinton Responds with Veto," *Congressional Quarterly Almanac* 55 (1999), XXI, 7–23.

41 Witte, "President vs. Congress," 180.

42 Godfrey Hodgson, *All Things to All Men* (New York: Simon and Schuster, 1980), 227.

43 For economic criticisms of tax expenditures, see John F. Witte, *The Politics and Development of the Federal Income Tax* (Madison: University of Wisconsin Press, 1985); Susan B. Hansen,

The Politics of Taxation: Revenue without Representation (New York: Praeger, 1983); and Christopher Howard, *The Hidden Welfare State: Tax Expenditures and Social Policy in the United States* (Princeton: Princeton University Press, 1997).

44 Jeffrey H. Birnbaum and Alan S. Murray, *Showdown at Gucci Gulch: Lawmakers, Lobbyists and the Unlikely Triumph of Tax Reform* (New York: Random House, 1987), 27–41; Timothy J. Conlan, Margaret T. Wrightson, and David R. Beam, *Taxing Choices: The Politics of Tax Reform* (Washington, D.C.: Congressional Quarterly, 1990), 45–48.

45 Ronald Reagan, "Remarks on Signing the Tax Reform Act of 1986," *Public Papers of the President,* 22 October 1986, www.presidency.ucsb.edu/ws/index.php?pid=36629&st=&st1=#axzz1S62QLy39.

46 Charles E. McLure, *The Value-Added Tax: Key to Deficit Reduction?* (Washington, D.C.: American Enterprise Institute, 1987).

47 Miroslav Nincic, *United States Foreign Policy, Choices, and Trade-offs* (Washington, D.C.: CQ Press, 1988), 337–338.

48 Stein, *Presidential Economics,* chap. 5.

49 Owen F. Humpage, "Institutional Aspects of U.S. Intervention," *Economic Review* 30 (first quarter, 1994): 2–6.

50 Humpage, "Institutional Aspects of U.S. Intervention," 6.

51 Walter S. Mossberg, "Dollar Selling Aimed at Curbing Its Rise," *Wall Street Journal,* January 12, 1989, A2, A7.

52 Sewell Chan, "Obama Ends G-20 Summit with Criticism of China," *New York Times,* November 12, 2010, www.nytimes.com/2010/11/13/business/global/13group.html.

53 Erwin C. Hargrove, *The Power of the Modern Presidency* (Philadelphia: Temple University Press, 1974), 159.

54 See I. M. Destler, *American Trade Politics,* 4th ed. (Washington, D.C.: Institute for International Economics, 2005); Martha L. Gibson, *Conflict amid Consensus in American Trade Policy* (Washington, D.C.: Georgetown University Press, 2000); James Shoch, *Trading Blows: Party Competition and U.S. Trade Policy in a Globalizing Era* (Chapel Hill: University of North Carolina Press, 2001).

55 Stein, *Presidential Economics,* 416.

56 Destler, *American Trade Politics,* 98–100; Jasmine Farrier, *Congressional Ambivalence: The Political Burdens of Constitutional Authority* (Lexington: University Press of Kentucky, 2010), chap. 3.

57 House Committee on Ways and Means, Press Release, "Pelosi, Hoyer, Rangel, and Levin Statement on Trade," July 2, 2007, quoted at Farrier, *Congressional Ambivalence,* 113.

58 R. W. Apple, "A High-Stakes Gamble That Paid Off," *New York Times,* November 18, 1993, A1.

59 Binyamin Applebaum and Jennifer Steinhauer, "Congress Ends 5-Year Standoff on Trade Deals in Rare Accord," *New York Times,* October 12, 2011, www.nytimes.com/2011/10/13/business/trade-bills-near-final-chapter.html.

60 Edward S. Flash, "Conversion of Kennedy from Economic Conservative to Economic Liberal," in *J.F. Kennedy and Presidential Power,* ed. Earl Latham (Lexington, Mass.: Heath, 1972), 76–81.

61 Norton, *Quest for Economic Stability,* 234; Bert A. Rockman, "The Style and Organization of the Reagan Presidency," in *The Reagan Legacy: Promise and Performance,* ed. Charles O. Jones (Chatham, N.J.: Chatham House, 1988), 21–22.

62 Erik J. Engstrom and Samuel Kernell, "Serving Competing Principals: The Budget Estimates of OMB and CBO in an Era of Divided Government," *Presidential Studies Quarterly* 29 (December 1999): 820–829.

63 Eric Patashnik, "Budgets and Fiscal Policy," in *The Legislative Branch,* ed. Paul J. Quirk and Sarah A. Binder (Oxford: Oxford University Press, 2005), 383–387.

64 Jasmine Farrier, *Passing the Buck: Congress, the Budget, and Deficits* (Lexington: University Press of Kentucky, 2004), chap. 3.

65 Farrier, *Passing the Buck,* 167.

66 Ibid., 36–46.

67 *Clinton v. City of New York,* 97-1374 (1998), Part VI, 31.

68 Michael P. Riccards, *A Republic, If You Can Keep It: The Foundation of the American Presidency, 1700–1800* (New York: Greenwood Press, 1987), 101.

69 Jonathan Hughes and Louis P. Cain, *American Economic History,* 4th ed. (New York: HarperCollins, 1994), 200.

70 John M. Berry and Kathleen Day, "Worker Pay, Benefits Up 4.9% in '88," *Washington Post,* January 25, 1989, F1.

71 Steven Greenhouse, "Showdown: The Populist vs. the Fed," *New York Times,* October 12, 1993, www.nytimes.com/1993/10/12/business/showdown-the-populist-vs-the-fed.html.

72 "Federal Reserve (The Fed)," *Times Topics,* http://topics.nytimes.com/top/reference/timestopics/organizations/f/federal_reserve_system/index.html; Binyamin Applebaum, "Its Forecast Dim, Fed Vows to Keep Rates Near Zero," *New York Times,* August 9, 2011, www.nytimes.com/2011/08/10/business/economy/fed-to-hold-rates-exceptionally-low-through-mid-2013.html; Jeff Zeleny and Jackie Calmes, "Perry Links Federal Reserve Policies and Treason," *New York Times,* August 16, 2011, www.nytimes.com/2011/08/17/us/politics/17perry.html?_r=2; Bob Ivry, Bradley Keoun, and Phil Kuntz, "Secret Fed Loans Gave Banks $13 Billion Undisclosed to Congress," *Bloomberg,* November 27, 2011, www.bloomberg.com/news/2011-11-28/secret-fed-loans-undisclosed-to-congress-gave-banks-13-billion-in-income.html.

73 Riccards, *Republic,* 90.

74 Ibid., 91–97.

75 Anderson, *Politics and the Economy,* 9.

76 Ibid., 9–10.

77 Ibid., 11–12.

78 John Milton Cooper Jr., "The Great Debate," *Constitution* 6 (spring 1994): 42–43.

79 Stein, *Presidential Economics,* 32–33.

80 Campagna, *U.S. National Economic Policy,* 101.

81 Ibid., 131.

82 Ibid., 141.

83 Ibid., 210–211.

84 Jacob, "Macroeconomic Policy Choices," 65.

85 Campagna, *U.S. National Economic Policy,* 238–243.

86 Jacob, "Macroeconomic Policy Choices," 67.

87 Richard Nixon, *Six Crises* (New York: Doubleday, 1962), 309–310.

88 Jacob, "Macroeconomic Policy Choices," 67.

89 Stein, *Presidential Economics,* 106–107.

90 Arthur M. Schlesinger Jr., *A Thousand Days: John F. Kennedy in the White House* (Boston: Houghton Mifflin, 1965), 654.

91 Donald F. Kettl, *Leadership at the Fed* (New Haven: Yale University Press, 1986), 96.

92 Campagna, *U.S. National Economic Policy,* 306–307.

93 Hobart Rowen, *Self-Inflicted Wounds: From LBJ's Guns and Butter to Reagan's Voodoo Economics* (New York: Times Books, 1994), 3–19.

94 "Congress Votes Surtax with Expenditure Controls," *CQ Almanac* 24 (1968), 265–278.

95 Campagna, *U.S. National Economic Policy,* 351.

96 John B. Gilmour, *Reconcilable Differences: Congress, the Budget Process and the Deficit.* (Berkeley: University of California, 1990), 46–49.

97 Stein, *Presidential Economics,* 173.

98 John Robert Greene, *The Presidency of Gerald R. Ford* (Lawrence: University of Kansas Press, 1995), 71.

99 Stein, *Presidential Economics,* 214.

100 Yanek Mieczkowski, *Gerald Ford and the Challenges of the 1970s* (Lexington: University of Kentucky Press, 2005), 131.

101 Greene, *Presidency of Gerald R. Ford,* 75–76; Mieczkowski, *Gerald Ford,* 167–172.

102 Campagna, *U.S. National Economic Policy,* 401–402.

103 Greene, *Presidency of Gerald R. Ford,* 77; Mieczkowski, *Gerald Ford,* 190–191.

104 Jacob, "Macroeconomic Policy Choices," 75.

105 Stein, *Presidential Economics,* 218.

106 Campagna, *U.S. National Economic Policy,* 422–430.

107 Stein, *Presidential Economics,* 228–232.

108 Allan Schick, *The Capacity to Budget* (Washington, D.C.: Urban Institute Press, 1990), 64.

109 William Greider, *Secrets of the Temple* (New York: Simon and Schuster, 1987), 185.

110 Jacob, "Macroeconomic Policy Choices," 74; Ann Mari May, "Fiscal Policy, Monetary Policy, and the Carter Presidency," *Presidential Studies Quarterly* 23 (fall 1993): 700–701.

111 Stein, *Presidential Economics,* 255–256.

112 Hugh Heclo and Rudolph G. Penner, "Fiscal and Political Strategy in the Reagan Administration," in *The Reagan Presidency: An Early Assessment,* ed. Fred I. Greenstein (Baltimore: Johns Hopkins University Press, 1983), 22–24.

113 Richard Auxier, "Reagan's Recession," *Pew Research Center Publications,* December 14, 2010, http://pewresearch.org/pubs/1818/reagan-recession-public-opinion-very-negative.

114 Heclo and Penner, "Fiscal and Political Strategy," 34–36; W. Elliott Brownlee and C. Eugene Steurle, "Taxation," in *The Reagan Presidency: Pragmatic Conservatism and Its Legacies,* ed. W. Elliott Brownlee and Hugh Davis Graham (Lawrence: University Press of Kansas, 2003), 163.

115 Darrell M. West, *Congress and Economic Policymaking* (Pittsburgh: University of Pittsburgh Press, 1987), 122.

116 Schick, *Capacity to Budget,* 114.

117 Brownlee and Steurle, "Taxation," 166–168.

118 Stein, *Presidential Economics,* 420–421.

119 John Robert Greene, *The Presidency of George Bush* (Lawrence: University Press of Kansas, 2000), 86; Daniel P. Franklin, *Making Ends Meet: Congressional Budgeting in the Age of Deficits* (Washington, D.C.: CQ Press, 1993), 98–99.

120 Stephen Skowronek, *The Politics Presidents Make: Leadership from John Adams to George Bush* (Cambridge: Harvard University Press, 1993), 438.

121 For an argument that George H. W. Bush was to blame for inadequately explaining the deal to the public, see David Mervin, *George Bush and the Guardianship Presidency* (New York: St. Martin's, 1996), 151–153.

122 David E. Rosenbaum, "On the Economy, Bush Followed Reagan's Lead, Not His Success," *New York Times,* June 29, 1992.

123 Ryan J. Barilleaux and Mark J. Rozell, *Power and Prudence: The Presidency of George H. W. Bush* (College Station: Texas A&M University Press, 2004), chap. 1.

124 John R. Cranford, "Hill's Response to Recession Defies Economists' Advice," *CQ Weekly Report,* January 25, 1992, 160–163.

125 Peter Passell, "Spurning Fine-Tuning," *New York Times,* December 11, 1991, A1, C4.

126 Robert Solow, James Tobin, and William Jefferson Clinton, *President Clinton's New Beginning, The Complete Text, with Illustrations, of the Historic Economic Conference Conducted by*

President Bill Clinton & Vice President Al Gore in Little Rock, Arkansas, December 14–15, 1992 (New York: Dutton Adult, 1993).

127 Paul J. Quirk and Joseph Hinchliffe, "Domestic Policy: The Trials of a Centrist Democrat," in *The Clinton Presidency: First Appraisals,* eds. Colin Campbell and Bert A. Rockman (Chatham, N.J.: Chatham House, 1996), 262–289.

128 Christopher J. Bailey, "Clintonomics," in *The Clinton Presidency: The First Term, 1992–1996,* eds. Paul S. Herrnson and Dilys M. Hill (New York: St. Martin's, 1999), 86–88; William C. Berman, *From the Center to the Edge: The Politics and Policies of the Clinton Presidency* (Lanham, Md.: Rowman and Littlefield, 2001), 20–21.

129 George Hager and David S. Cloud, "Democrats Tie Their Fate to Clinton's Budget Bill," *Congressional Quarterly Weekly Report,* August 7, 1993, 2122–2129.

130 Quirk and Hinchliffe, "Domestic Policy," 272–274.

131 George Hager, "Congress, Clinton Yield Enough to Close the Book on Fiscal '96," *Congressional Quarterly Weekly Report,* April 27, 1996, 1155–1157.

132 "Pact Aims to Erase Deficit by 2002," *CQ Almanac* 53 (1997), II, 22; Peter Passell, "Economic Scene," *New York Times,* May 8, 1997, C2.

133 "The 2000 Campaign: Exchanges between the Candidates in the Third Presidential Debate," *New York Times,* October 18, 2000, A26.

134 Frank Bruni, "Bush Says Rebate Isn't a Substitute for His Tax Plan," *New York Times,* March 28, 2001, A1; David E. Rosenbaum, "House Passes Bill for 2 More Pieces of Bush's Tax Cut," *New York Times,* March 29, 2001, A1.

135 "Congress Cuts Deal on Taxes," *CQ Almanac* 57 (2001), XVIII, 3–14.

136 Jeff Madrick, "Plans to Cut Taxes May Be Clever Politics, but They're Not Wise Fiscal Policy," *New York Times,* February 15, 2001, A12; Daniel Altman, "Bush's Stimulus Plan and Its Two Big Ifs," *New York Times,* February 18, 2003, C1–C2.

137 Jeff Madrick, "Economic Scene," *New York Times,* June 7, 2001, C2; Edmund L. Andrews, "Report Finds Tax Cuts Heavily Favor the Wealthy," *New York Times,* August 13, 2004, A16.

138 Barry Bosworth, "The Budget Crisis: Is It All Déjà Vu?" *Issues in Economic Policy* 2 (February 2006): 13.

139 Lori Montgomery, "Running in the Red: How the U.S., On the Road to Surplus, Detoured to Massive Debt," *Washington Post,* April 30, 2011, www.washingtonpost.com/business/economy/running-in-the-red-how-the-us-on-the-road-to-surplus-detoured-to-massive-debt/2011/04/28/AFFU7rNF_story.html; Annie Lowrey, "Happy 10th Birthday, Bush Tax Cuts!" *Slate,* June 8, 2011, www.slate.com/articles/business/moneybox/2011/06/happy_10th_birthday_bush_tax_cuts.html. For Bush's impact on the huge budget deficits of the Obama years, see "Policy Changes Under Two Presidents," *New York Times,* July 24, 2011, www.nytimes.com/imagepages/2011/07/24/opinion/sunday/24editorial_graph2.html.

140 See Douglas Brinkley, *The Great Deluge: Hurricane Katrina, New Orleans, and the Mississippi Gulf Coast* (New York: Morrow, 2006).

141 Keech, Economic Politics, 33–41; Mackenzie and Thornton, Bucking the Deficit, chap. 1; Sargent and Wallace, "Rational Expectations," 241–254.

142 John D. Graham, *Bush on the Home Front: Domestic Policy Triumphs and Setbacks* (Bloomington: Indiana University Press, 2010), chap. 2; Lawrence Jacobs and Desmond King, "America's Political Crisis: The Unsustainable State in a Time of Unraveling," *PS* 42 (April 2009), 277–285.

143 Robert J. Shiller, *The Subprime Solution: How Today's Global Financial Crisis Happened, and What to Do about It* (Princeton: Princeton University Press, 2008); Russell Cooper and Jonathan L. Willis, "Coordination of Expectations in the Recent Crisis: Private Actions and Policy Responses," *Economic Review* 95:1 (2010), 5–39; Michael Comiskey and Pawan Madhogarhia, "Unraveling the Financial Crisis of 2008," *PS* 42 (April 2009), 271–275.

144 Stephen Labaton, "Wall Street in Worst Loss Since '01 Despite Reassurances by Bush," *New York Times,* September 16, 2008, A1.

145 Kelly Evans, "Economy Dives as Goods Pile Up," *Wall Street Journal,* January 31, 2009, 1.

146 Neil Irwin, "Fed Cuts Key Rate to Record Low," *Washington Post,* December 17, 2008, A1.

147 Mark Zandi, *Financial Shock: Global Panic and Government Bailouts—How We Got Here and What Must Be Done to Fix It* (Upper Saddle River, N.J.: Pearson Education, 2009), chap. 11; Benton Ives, "Mortgage Relief on the Horizon," *CQ Weekly Report,* July 28, 2008, 2056–2058.

148 Graham, *Bush on the Home Front,* chap. 11; Krishna Guha, "Paulson Rues Shortage of Firepower as Battle Raged," *Financial Times,* 31 December 2008, www.ft.com. For congressional "ambivalence" about delegating broad antirecession authority to President Bush, see Farrier, *Congressional Ambivalence,* 9–16.

149 Baker, "White House Looks for Work."

150 Jonathan Alter, *The Promise: President Obama, Year One* (New York: Simon and Schuster, 2010), chap. 12; Baker, "White House Looks for Work."

151 "Off to Work They Go: Barack Obama's Economic Team," *Economist,* 29 November 2008, 31–32.

152 David Clarke and Joseph J. Schatz, "The Devil's in the Stimulus Plan Details," *CQ Weekly Report,* January 12, 2009, 77.

153 Farhana Hossain, Amanda Cox, John McGrath and Stephen Weitberg, "The Stimulus Plan: How to Spend $787 Billion," http://projects.nytimes.com/44th_president/stimulus.

154 John Cassidy, "No Credit: Timothy Geithner's Financial Plan is Working—and Making Him Very Unpopular," *New Yorker* 86 (March 15, 2010), 26; Alter, *The Promise,* 199–208.

155 Allen Sloan with Doris Burke, "Surprise! The Big Bad Bailout Is Paying Off," *CNN Money,* July 8, 2011, http://finance.fortune.cnn.com/2011/07/08/surprise-the-big-bad-bailout-is-paying-off/. The Congressional Budget Office estimated the stimulus act resulted in a net gain of 1.9 to 4.7 million jobs. See Baker, "White House Looks for Work."

156 David Leonhardt, "America's Sea of Red Ink Was Years in the Making," *New York Times,* June 9, 2009, www.nytimes.com/2009/06/10/business/economy/10leonhardt.html; David Wessel, "The Deficit: Just as Bad under McCain?" *Real Time Economics,* August 25, 2009, http://blogs.wsj.com/economics/2009/08/25/the-deficit-just-as-bad-under-mccain/.

157 Michael Cooper, "From Obama, The Tax Cut That Nobody Heard Of," *New York Times,* October 18, 2010.

158 "Economic Stimulus (Jobs Bills)," *Times Topics,* topics.nytimes.com.

159 Baker, "White House Looks for Work."

160 Barack Obama, "Remarks by the President in State of the Union Address," January 27, 2010, www.whitehouse.gov/the-press-office/remarks-president-state-union-address.

161 "Co-Chairs' Proposal," November 11, 2010, www.fiscalcommission.gov/sites/fiscalcommission.gov/files/documents/CoChair_Draft.pdf; Josh Barro, "Why We Should Be Thankful for

the Fiscal Commission," *Real Clear Markets*, November 24, 2010, www .realclearmarkets.com.

162   Kerry Young and Sam Goldfarb, "Funding Clears Despite Grumbles," *CQ Weekly Report*, April 18, 2011, 862.

163   Robert Pear and Jennifer Steinhauer, "Tax Cut Extension Passes; Everyone Claims a Win," *New York Times*, February 17, 2012, www.nytimes.com/2012/02/18/us/politics/congress-acts-to-extend-payroll-tax-cut-and-aid-to-jobless.html; Jackie Calmes, "Obama Advisers Offer Rosier Jobs Outlook," *New York Times*, February 8, 2012, www.nytimes.com/2012/02/09/business/economy/obama-advisers-offer-rosier-jobs-outlook.html.

164   R. Kent Weaver, "Controlling Entitlements," in *The New Direction in American Politics,* ed. John E. Chubb and Paul E. Peterson (Washington, D.C.: Brookings, 1985), 312; Dennis S. Ippolito, *Uncertain Legacies: Federal Budget Policy from Roosevelt through Reagan* (Charlottesville: University of Virginia Press, 1990), 48–49.

165   Anderson, *Politics and the Economy,* 113.

166   MacKenzie and Thornton, *Bucking the Deficit,* 140–142; Weaver, "Controlling Entitlements," 310–311.

167   Kim Quaile Hill and John Patrick Plumlee, "Presidential Success in Budgetary Policymaking: A Longitudinal Analysis," *Presidential Studies Quarterly* 12 (spring 1982): 179.

168   Data from the U.S. Department of Health and Human Services, Centers for Medicare and Medicaid Services, www.cms .gov/NationalHealthExpendData/02_NationalHealthAccounts Historical.asp#TopOfPage.

169   Kaiser Family Foundation, http://statehealthfacts.org.

170   Henry J. Aaron, *Serious and Unstable Condition: Financing America's Health Care* (Washington, D.C.: Brookings, 1991), 39–48.

171   Kant Patel and Mark E. Rushefsky, *Health Care Politics and Policies in America* (Armonk, NY: M.E. Sharpe, 1995), 131–137; David F. Drake, *Reforming the Health Care Market: An Interpretive Economic History* (Washington, D.C.: Georgetown University Press, 1994), 128, 148.

172   Aaron, *Serious and Unstable Condition,* 2–4.

173   Theodore R. Marmor, Donald A. Wittman, and Thomas C. Heagy, "The Politics of Medical Inflation," in *Political Analysis and American Medical Care: Essays,* ed. Theodore R. Marmor (Cambridge: Cambridge University Press, 1983), 66.

174   Jacob S. Hacker, "The Road to Somewhere: Why Health Reform Happened, or Why Political Scientists Who Write about Public Policy Shouldn't Assume They Know How to Shape It," *Perspectives on Politics* 8:3 (September 2010), 867–870.

175   For a concise review of economic change, see Jeffrey E. Cohen, *Politics and Economic Policy in the United States* (Boston: Houghton Mifflin, 2d ed., 2000), 31–40; see also Laura Pappano, "The Master's as the New Bachelor's," *New York Times*, July 22, 2011, www.nytimes.com/2011/07/24/education/edlife/edl-24masters-t .html.

176   Adam Davidson, "Making It in America," *The Atlantic* (January/February 2012), www.theatlantic.com/magazine/archive/2012/01/making-it-in-america/8844/; Kevin Phillips, *The Politics of Rich and Poor: Wealth and the American Electorate in the Reagan Aftermath* (New York: Random House, 1990); Jacob S. Hacker and Paul Pierson, *Winner-Take-All Politics: How Washington Made the Rich Richer—and Turned Its Back on the Middle Class* (New York: Simon & Schuster, 2010); Barry Bluestone, "The Inequality Express," *American Prospect* 20 (winter 1995), 81–93.

177   Sabrina Tavernise, "Poverty Reaches a 52-Year Peak, Government Says," *New York Times*, September 14, 2011, A1, A19.

178   Hacker and Pierson, *Winner-Take-All Politics*, 305.

179   See Jennifer Hochschild and Nathan Scovronick, *The American Dream and the Public Schools* (New York: Oxford University Press, 2003), 21–25, though the authors are hopeful the connection between poverty and low educational outcomes can be overcome; Maris A. Vinovskis, *From A Nation at Risk to No Child Left Behind: National Education Goals and the Creation of Federal Education Policy* (New York: Teachers College Press, 2009), 210–212.

180   Alan B. Krueger, "New (and Sometimes Conflicting) Data on the Value to Society of the Job Corps," *New York Times*, January 5, 2006, C3; Gary Mucciaroni, *The Political Failure of Employment Policy, 1945–1982* (Pittsburgh: University of Pittsburgh Press, 1990).

181   Susan M. Collins, "Economic Integration and the American Worker: An Overview," in *Imports, Exports and the American Worker,* ed. Susan M. Collins (Washington, D.C.: Brookings, 1998) 3–45; Richard H. K. Vietor, *Contrived Competition: Regulation and Deregulation in America* (Cambridge, Mass.: Belknap/Harvard, 1994), chap. 1.

SELECTED BIBLIOGRAPHY

Anderson, James E. *Politics and the Economy.* Boston: Little, Brown, 1966.

Bartels, Larry. *Unequal Democracy: The Political Economy of the New Gilded Age.* Princeton: Princeton University Press, 2008.

Campagna, Anthony S. The Economy in the Reagan Years: The Economic Consequences of the Reagan Administrations. New York: Greenwood, 1994.

_____ . *U.S. National Economic Policy, 1917–1985.* New York: Greenwood, 1994.

Conlan, Timothy J., Margaret T. Wrightson, and David R. Beam. *Taxing Choices: The Politics of Tax Reform.* Washington, D.C.: CQ Press, 1990.

Destler, I. M. *American Trade Politics.* 4th ed. Washington, D.C.: Institute for International Economics, 2005.

Dolan, Chris J., John Frendreis, and Raymond Tatalovich. *The Presidency and Economic Policy.* Lanham, Md.: Rowman and Littlefield, 2008.

Farrier, Jasmine. *Passing the Buck: Congress, the Budget, and Deficits.* Lexington: University of Kentucky Press, 2004.

Frankel, Jeffrey, and Peter Orszag, eds. *American Economic Policy in the 1990s.* Cambridge, Mass.: MIT Press, 2002.

Gilmour, John B. *Reconcilable Differences: Congress, the Budget Process and the Deficit.* Berkeley: University of California, 1990.

Greider, William. *Secrets of the Temple.* New York: Simon and Schuster, 1987.

Hacker, Jacob S., and Paul Pierson. *Winner-Take-All Politics: How Washington Made the Rich Richer—And Turned Its Back on the Middle Class.* New York: Simon and Schuster, 2010.

Kettl, Donald F. *Leadership at the Fed.* New Haven: Yale University Press, 1986.

Kotlikoff, Laurence J. *Generational Accounting.* New York: Free Press, 1993.

Mackenzie, G. Calvin, and Saranna Thornton. *Bucking the Deficit: Economic Policymaking in America.* Boulder: Westview, 1996.

Morris, Irwin L. *Congress, the President and the Federal Reserve: The Politics of American Monetary Policy-Making.* Ann Arbor: University of Michigan Press, 2000.

Peretz, Paul, ed. *The Politics of American Economic Policy Making.* Armonk, N.Y.: Sharpe, 1987.

Pfiffner, James P., ed. *The President and Economic Policy.* Philadelphia: Institute for the Study of Human Issues, 1986.

Schick, Allen. *The Federal Budget: Politics, Policy, Process.* 3d ed. Washington, D.C.: Brookings, 2007.

Schier, Steven E. *A Decade of Deficits: Congressional Thought and Fiscal Action.* Albany: State University of New York, 1992.

Schlesinger, Arthur M., Jr. *A Thousand Days: John F. Kennedy in the White House.* Boston: Houghton Mifflin, 1965.

Stein, Herbert. *Presidential Economics: The Making of Economic Policy from Roosevelt to Clinton.* 3d rev. ed. Washington, D.C.: AEI Press, 1997.

Tatalovich, Raymond, Chris J. Dolan, and John Frendreis. *The Presidency and Economic Policy.* Lanham, Md.: Rowman and Littlefield, 2008.

Witte, John F. *The Politics and Development of the Federal Income Tax.* Madison: University of Wisconsin Press, 1985.

★ ILLUSTRATION CREDITS AND ACKNOWLEDGMENTS

★ INDEX

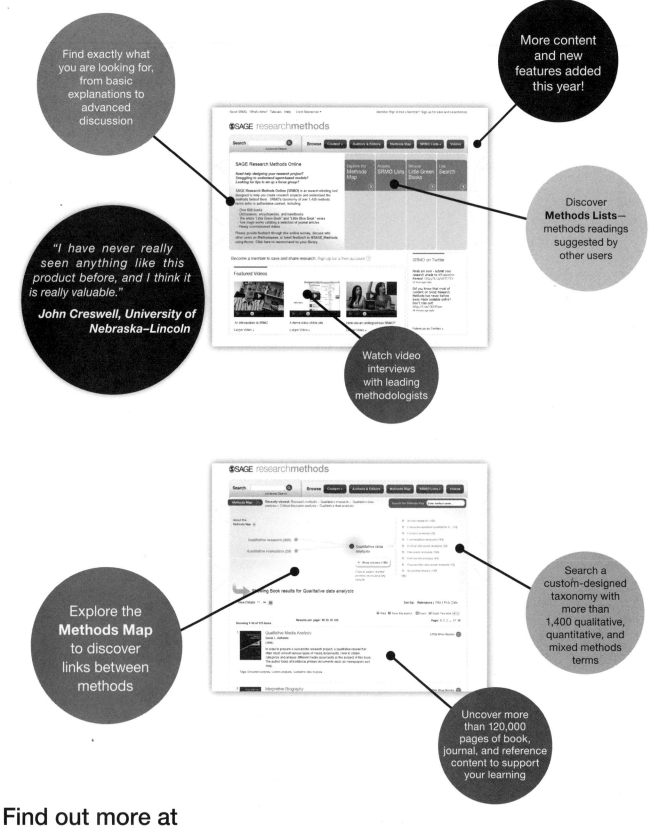

SAGE researchmethods

The essential online tool for researchers from the world's leading methods publisher

Find exactly what you are looking for, from basic explanations to advanced discussion

More content and new features added this year!

"I have never really seen anything like this product before, and I think it is really valuable."

John Creswell, University of Nebraska–Lincoln

Discover **Methods Lists**— methods readings suggested by other users

Watch video interviews with leading methodologists

Explore the **Methods Map** to discover links between methods

Search a custom-designed taxonomy with more than 1,400 qualitative, quantitative, and mixed methods terms

Uncover more than 120,000 pages of book, journal, and reference content to support your learning

Find out more at
www.sageresearchmethods.com